CINEMA SEWER

THE ADULTS ONLY GUIDE TO HISTORY'S SICKEST AND SEXIEST MOVIES

EDITED BY
ROBIN BOUGIE

VOLUME

A
FAB
PRESS
PUBLICATION

CINEMA SEWER VOL. 6

THIS SECOND PRESSING PUBLISHED BY FAB PRESS, FEBRUARY 2021
FIRST EDITION PUBLISHED BY FAB PRESS, AUGUST 2017

FAB PRESS LTD
2 FARLEIGH
RAMSDEN ROAD
GODALMING
SURREY
GU7 1QE
ENGLAND.UK

www.FABPRESS.com

A CIP CATALOGUE RECORD FOR THIS BOOK IS AVAILABLE FROM THE BRITISH LIBRARY.

ISBN 9781903254912

COVER ART BY THE ALWAYS AMAZING VINCE RUARUS. VISIT HIM AT:
WWW.VENIVIDIVINCE.COM

THIS BOOK IS DEDICATED TO:

CLASSIC PORN STAR JODY MAXWELL. MY FRIEND JODY (WHO WAS INTERVIEWED ON PAGE 98 OF CINEMA SEWER BOOK 3) PASSED AWAY ON FEBRUARY 12TH, 2017, JUST AS THIS VOLUME WAS NEARING COMPLETION. SHE WAS ONE OF THE NICEST PEOPLE -- ALWAYS <u>SO</u> KIND AND SWEET. I'VE NEVER HEARD ANYONE SAY A BAD WORD ABOUT JODY. SHE WAS BORN IN 1945, AND WORKED IN THE ADULT INDUSTRY IN THE 1970S NOT ONLY AS A MODEL FOR MAGAZINES AND ADULT MOVIES, BUT AS A WRITER, AND A REPORTER, AND ALSO AS A PHONE SEX GIRL WHEN THAT BECAME A THING IN THE 1980S. WORKING AS A PUBLIC SCHOOL TEACHER IN HER LATER YEARS, SHE WAS INCREDIBLY INTELLIGENT AND FUNNY, AND I LOVED TO LIVE CHAT ONLINE WITH HER WHILE WATCHING ONE OF HER OLD PORN FILMS. WE WOULD KID AROUND AND SHE WOULD TELL ME ALL KINDS OF FUNNY BEHIND-THE-SCENES STORIES ABOUT WHAT WAS GOING ON, AND IT WAS LIKE HAVING YOUR OWN PRIVATE AUDIO COMMENTARY. SHE LOVED HER FANS SO MUCH, AND WE WERE ALL HER FRIENDS BECAUSE SHE MADE YOU FEEL THAT WAY. SHE WAS A BEAUTIFUL SOUL, AND I STILL CAN'T BELIEVE SHE'S GONE. <u>FUCK CANCER.</u>

VISIT:
CINEMASEWER.STORENVY.COM
AND MY DAILY ART BLOG:
BOUGIEMAN.LIVEJOURNAL.COM

HERE WE GO AGAIN!

WELCOME TO VOLUME 6 OF THE CINEMA SEWER TREASURY. THESE BOOKS COLLECT THE BEST OF THE MAGAZINE SERIES, CINEMA SEWER, AND INCLUDE A FAT 75 TO 85 BRAND NEW NEVER-BEFORE-SEEN PAGES PER BOOK. THIS PARTICULAR TOME COLLECTS THE VERY BEST OF ISSUES #27, #28, AND #29, AND SHOULD BE THE LAST COLLECTED BOOK FOR AT LEAST A HANDFUL OF YEARS, SINCE ISSUE 30 OF THE MAGAZINE JUST SAW PRINT, AND I ONLY RELEASE THE ISSUES ANNUALLY-- EVERY FEBRUARY. CINEMA SEWER CAN BE ORDERED BOTH FROM FABPRESS.COM IF YOU'RE IN THE UK OR EUROPE, OR IF YOU'RE IN NORTH AMERICA, FROM MY WEBSITE CINEMASEWER.STORENVY.COM

YOU DON'T NEED TO READ CS BOOKS IN ANY KIND OF ORDER, SO STARTING WITH BOOK 6 IS TOTALLY FINE FOR NEW READERS, AND IF THAT'S YOU, AN INTRODUCTION IS IN ORDER! I'M A GENERALLY HAPPY CANADIAN GUY WHO LIVES WITH HIS ANIMATOR WIFE, REBECCA DART, AND HIS TWO TWIN CATS (HERBIE AND MARVIN) NEAR THE DOWNTOWN CORE OF VANCOUVER, BRITISH COLUMBIA, CANADA. I'VE BEEN A COMIC BOOK CREATOR SINCE I WAS IN JUNIOR HIGH, AND I'VE BEEN PUBLISHING THIS MOVIE MAGAZINE FOR 20 OF MY 43 YEARS. I'VE ALSO BEEN WORKING IN CONJUNCTION WITH FAB PRESS ON THESE BOOKS SINCE OCTOBER OF 2007, AND HAVE ALSO DONE THE ACCLAIMED 'GRAPHIC THRILLS' SERIES OF BOOKS WITH THIS PUBLISHER AS WELL.

THE CINEMA SEWER WRITING STYLE IS A MIXTURE OF INFORMATION, HUMOUR, AND PERSONALITY. I FIRMLY BELIEVE THAT READERS WANT TO HEAR AN INDIVIDUAL'S VOICE, NOT THE VOICE OF A FACELESS CORPORATE CONGLOMERATE WHEN THEY READ ABOUT SOMETHING AS ARTISTIC AND CREATIVE AS A MOVIE -- EVEN A LOWLY PORNO OR A GRINDHOUSE EXPLOITATION FEATURE. THAT MEANS: NO, I DON'T JUST WRITE A SYNOPSIS AND THEN GIVE IT A THUMBS UP OR DOWN, THAT MIGHT BE GOOD ENOUGH FOR 80% OF THE BLOGGERS OUT THERE, BUT IT'S NOT GOOD ENOUGH FOR THE SEWER.

I STRIVE FOR ALL THE RESEARCH OF AN ACADEMIC PAPER, AND ALL THE RELAXED "ANYTHING GOES" ATTITUDE AS FOUND IN PERSONAL CORRESPONDENCE, AND ONE OF THE THINGS I DO WHEN I FINISH SOMETHING IS DO TWO EDITS -- ONE RIGHT AWAY, AND ANOTHER AT A LATER TIME AFTER I'VE HAD A NICE LONG BREAK TO THINK ABOUT OTHER THINGS. I HACK THE BULLSHIT OFF, BECAUSE I THINK WE AS WRITERS TEND TO LOVE OUR OWN WORDS A LITTLE TOO MUCH, AND THAT DOESN'T OFTEN SERVE THE READER. TO PARAPHRASE WINSTON CHURCHILL, I FIGURE THE LENGTH OF AN ARTICLE FOR CINEMA SEWER SHOULD BE LIKE A WOMAN'S SKIRT: LONG ENOUGH TO COVER THE SUBJECT, BUT SHORT ENOUGH TO KEEP IT INTERESTING.

CS IS REALLY DIRTY. IF YOU'RE A KID: GET THE HECK OUTTA HERE, YOU LITTLE TURD! IF I CATCH YOU WITH THIS BOOK AGAIN, I'LL TELL YOUR MOM! ARE THEY GONE? PROBABLY NOT. I USUALLY THREATEN THEM WITH TORTURE WHEN THEY PICK UP THE BOOKS OFF MY TABLE AT CONVENTIONS. LAST YEAR A 10-YEAR-OLD GOT INTO A DEBATE WITH ME AS TO WHY HE COULDN'T LOOK. I SWEAR, HE VERY NEARLY BEAT ME IN THAT GAME OF WITS, BUT I MANAGED TO HOLD MY OWN BY DISTRACTING HIM WITH INFO ON WHERE TO FIND A POKEMON ON THE OTHER SIDE OF THE CONVENTION HALL. PHEW, THAT WAS A <u>CLOSE ONE</u>.

WELL, IT'S TIME TO TURN THE PAGE AND ENTER THE CINEMA SEWER! THANKS SO MUCH TO ALL THE CONTRIBUTORS WHO HELPED WITH WRITING AND ART. THEY'VE BEEN CREDITED AT THE BEGINNING OR END OF EACH ARTICLE THEY WORKED ON, AND IF YOU DON'T SEE ANYTHING CREDITING THEM, YOU CAN ASSUME IT WAS WRITTEN AND DRAWN BY MOI. THANKS FOR TAKING A CHANCE ON THIS PUBLICATION, I HOPE TO MAKE IT WORTH YOUR WHILE!

-ROBIN BOUGIE XXX OOO ♡ '17

enter my dark passage
the seventies occultist porn film

BY Robin Bougie · 2016 · CINEMA SEWER.COM

YES, THE DARK CABAL OF MYSTIC SECRETS **OWNS** YOU.

PRAISE THE GRAND LORD OF SHADOWS!

MAY WE ALL BECOME IMMORTAL THROUGH BLACK MAGICK!

THE TERM "OCCULT" IS GENERALLY ASSOCIATED WITH DARK AND MYSTERIOUS SECRET KNOWLEDGE AND PRACTICES DEALING WITH THE SUPERNATURAL, USUALLY AS A MEANS TO OBTAIN PERSONAL POWER VIA SUMMONING SPIRITS OR DEMONS. PRACTICES REVOLVING AROUND THIS CONCEPT OFTEN EMPLOY MAGIC, ALCHEMY, ASTROLOGY, CONSCIOUSNESS ALTERING DRUGS, CONJURING OR OTHER SECRET AND MYSTERIOUS SUPERNATURAL POWERS.

OF COURSE, HOW MUCH VALIDITY ANY OF THAT HAS GENERALLY DEPENDS ON YOUR SUSPENSION OF DISBELIEF AND INTEREST IN SATANISM, AND AS I'VE ALWAYS BEEN FOND OF TELLING REBELLIOUS TEENAGE METAL-HEADS: "SATAN IS A CHRISTIAN CONCEPT. IF YOU IDENTIFY AS BELIEVING IN SATAN, YOU'RE ALSO IDENTIFYING AS CHRISTIAN. SAME FABLE, DIFFERENT LEAD CHARACTER."

BUT WITH THAT SAID, IT'S VERY IMPORTANT TO NOTE THAT DESPITE THE COMMON VIEW OF THE OCCULT AND ITS SYMBOLISM (THE PENTAGRAM FOR INSTANCE) BEING THOUGHT OF AS INHERENTLY SATANIC, THIS IS NOT ACTUALLY THE CASE AT ALL. SATANIC RITES ARE SIMPLY ONE EXAMPLE OF MANY FROM THIS ARCANE, MYSTERIOUS WORLD.

THE LATE 1960s AND EARLY 1970s SAW A RAPID AND UNEXPECTED INCREASE OF PUBLIC INTEREST IN THE OCCULT, PAGANISM AND WITCHCRAFT IN NORTH AMERICA, AND WHILE IT HAS BEEN WIDELY REPORTED ON HOW THIS WAS REFLECTED IN THE HORROR MOVIES THAT WERE PRODUCED, MUCH LESS HAS BEEN SAID ABOUT HOW IT PROLIFERATED THE PORNOGRAPHY THAT SOCIETY CONSUMED AS WELL. MUCH OF THIS GROUNDSWELL OF INTEREST HAD TO DO WITH A SINGLE DIRTY OLD MAN: ANTON SZANDER LAVEY WHO, IN 1966, HAD INAUGURATED THE 'CHURCH OF SATAN' IN SAN FRANCISCO. WITHIN A FEW SHORT YEARS HE WAS MAKING APPEARANCES IN ALL FORMS OF MEDIA ACROSS THE LAND, AND THAT INCLUDES NUDIE MAGAZINES AND SLEAZY TABLOIDS. SIN IS SEXY AND THE MEDIA WAS TITILLATED AND FASCINATED IN EQUAL AMOUNTS BY ANTON'S BALD HEAD AND STRIKING ICY GLARE.

4

YESSSS, I HAVE NOW AWOKEN FROM MY LOW SLUMBER IN TIME FOR THE WITCHING HOUR!!

AND NOW I DEMAND TO DINE ON **HOT JUICY CUNT!**

SHE MEANS IT, FOLKS! HIDE YOUR **GODDAMN** DAUGHTERS!

ON THE NEWS STAND AND IN THE SMUT SHOPS BOTH LAVEY AND HIS INFLUENCE APPEARED IN THE FORM OF SKIN-SOAKED STROKE MAGAZINES SUCH AS WITCHCRAFT, SEXUAL WITCHCRAFT, PAGAN, SATAN'S SCRAPBOOK, SEXTROLOGY, AND WITCHES AND BITCHES. LEATHER FETISHISM, BONDAGE, AND SADOMASOCHISM WERE USUALLY HOW OCCULTISM WAS SERVED UP TO ERECT READERS, BUT NOT ALWAYS. SOMETIMES IT WAS JUST THE SINFULLY RESOLUTE AESTHETICS OF SATANISM AND THE OCCULT THAT WERE TRANSPLANTED WHOLESALE INTO OTHERWISE FAIRLY INNOCUOUS PHOTO-SPREADS.

ONE SUCH MAGAZINE THAT RAN FOR 3 NOTEWORTHY ISSUES IN 1972 AND 1973 WAS THE GLOSSY GOTHIC ODDITY KNOWN AS BITCHCRAFT. "IT TYPIFIED THE GENRE OF SOFTCORE S&M WITCHCRAFT SATAN PORN" WROTE AUTHOR TOM BRINKMANN IN HIS EXCELLENT 2009 HEADPRESS SOFTCOVER ODE TO TAWDRY VINTAGE PUBLICATIONS ENTITLED BAD MAGS 2. "BITCHCRAFT MORE LIKELY THAN NOT, TOOK ITS TITLE FROM THE CHAPTER OF THE SAME NAME IN ANTON LAVEY'S BOOK 'THE COMPLETE WITCH; OR WHAT TO DO WHEN VIRTUE FAILS' (1971), AND THAT'S NOT ALL THAT WAS BORROWED FROM LAVEY'S BOOK. ALL OF THE ISSUES OF BITCHCRAFT USE THE MAGICAL ALPHABET KNOWN AS 'THEBAN' AS A BORDER AROUND THE COVER PHOTO."

IN ADDITION, ALL THREE ISSUES OF THE MAGAZINE OPEN WITH AN EDITOR'S STATEMENT WHICH I FIND VERY TELLING. IT ENDS WITH THE FOLLOWING PARAGRAPH: "INTRIGUING AND POSSIBLY FRIGHTENING, BITCHCRAFT IS A JOURNEY THROUGH THE VEILED, UNKNOWN REGIONS OF THE UNIVERSE WHERE THE FETISHIST REIGNS SUPREME, WHERE MEN AND WOMEN DERIVE PLEASURE THROUGH PAIN, PERFORM RITUAL INTERCOURSE WITH OCCULTISTS AND EVEN THE DEVIL HIMSELF AND WORSHIP OTHER UNGODLY FORCES."

BUT IT WASN'T JUST WANK MAGS WHERE THE RITUALISTIC PRACTITIONERS OF THE DARK MACABRE ARTS WERE SEEN MIXING SEX INTO THEIR MYSTICAL SOUP. NO, PORNOGRAPHERS MAKING FILMS WERE JUST AS ENTICED BY THE IDEA OF HOODED CULT MEMBERS WITH BIG HOODED MEMBERS. THROUGHOUT THE 1970s THERE WERE OVER 60 EXAMPLES OF OCCULTISM IN HARDCORE THEATRICALLY-SCREENED MOVIES. HERE ARE JUST A FEW OF MY FAVORITES IN ORDER OF THEIR RELEASE:

The Last Step Down (aka Even Devils Pray. 1970) Directed by Lawrence Ramport

THE OPENING SCENE IN ONE OF THE FIRST ADULT FILMS TO DEAL WITH THE OCCULT IN THE 1970s FEATURED ROBED, CHANTING PHALLUS-DEVOTEES FILING INTO A CHURCH WHERE THEY ANOINT TWO FEMALE INITIATES (MALTA, AKA NEOLA GRAF, AND USCHI DIGARD), WHO TAKE IT UPON THEMSELVES TO CARNALLY WRITHE BEFORE BEING BROUGHT TO ORGASM ON AN ALTAR OF PAGAN IDOLATRY. THE TWO CULT MEMBERS DUNK A DILDO IN A CHALICE BEFORE THEY RUB IT ALL OVER THE LADIES, BUT WHAT SIGNIFICANCE THAT HAS, I HAVE NO CLUE, AND I'M QUITE SURE THE DIRECTOR DIDN'T EITHER. ANYWAY, IT TURNS OUT THESE TWO SATANIK "NUNS" WITH BIG OL' TITTIES ARE ALSO PROSTITUTES, AND ARE CURRENTLY IN THE MARKET FOR A NEW GIRL TO BRING INTO THEIR BIZ -- AND INTO THE CULT AS WELL.

"HOW DO WE BREAK HER IN?" LEGENDARY LARGE-BREASTED SEXPLOITATION STAR USCHI SAYS

5

THROUGH HER THICK EUROPEAN ACCENT. TERRY JOHNSON, ANOTHER FUCK-FILM STARLET FROM THE ERA IN QUESTION, PLAYS THE FRESH-FACED NOOB HOOKER, AND SHE'S INDOCTRINATED INTO HER NEW LIFESTYLE OF SUCKING OFF SATANISTS FOR FUN AND BLOWING EVERYONE ELSE FOR BUSINESS. IT'S A VERY CHEAP AND CHINTZY LITTLE BACKROOM PRODUCTION, BUT IT DOES HAVE ITS QUIRKY CHARMS AND A SMALL PLACE IN MY HEART. EVEN THOUGH THE MOVIE IS TECHNICALLY SOFTCORE (OR 'SEMICORE' AS I LIKE TO CALL THE SUBGENRE THAT SNUGLY FITS RIGHT BETWEEN SOFT AND HARDCORE) THERE IS ENOUGH FULL FRONTAL NUDITY AND SLIGHTLY OBSCURED ONSCREEN INSERTIONS TO GRANT IT A SPOT ON THE LIST.

Madam Satan (1970) Directed by Tom Gordon

YOU WON'T GET TURNED ON, BUT YOU WILL HAVE A BALL FREAKING OUT WITH THIS GROOVY (YET POORLY SHOT) 1970S SEMICORE RELEASE. IT IS ENTERTAINING ENOUGH TO WARRANT INCLUSION HERE DESPITE MOST OF THE SEXUAL GOING-ONS BEING SIMULATED, AND SOME FAIRLY PATHETIC FILMMAKING SKILLS BEING PUT ON DISPLAY. THE PLOT INTRODUCES US TO A STRANGE SATANIC CULT WHO GET TOGETHER FOR GROUP SEX SESSIONS. THIS IS AN ENCLAVE HEADED UP BY THE SADISTIC MADAME COBRA (THE BUSTY LINDA VROOM CHEWS THE SCENERY IN BLACK LINGERIE, STILETTO-HEELED BOOTS, AND A FUCKING CAPE) WHO IS VERY FOND OF WHIPPING DUDES WHEN THEY CAN'T GET BONERS, AND INSERTING VIBRATORS INTO PEOPLE. ANOTHER LEADER OF THE GROUP IS THE BURLY JAMES MATHERS, WHO SPORTS A POT-BELLY, A MOUSTACHE, AND BIG BUSHY SIDEBURNS. HE'S A HIGH PRIEST WHO CACKLES MANIACALLY AT EVERY GODDAMN THING.

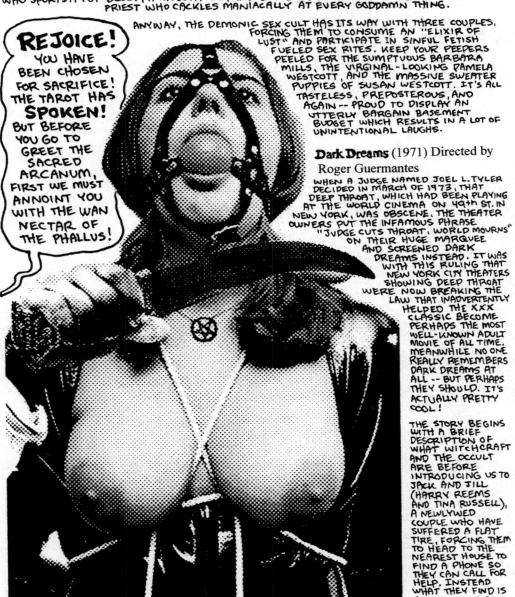

REJOICE! YOU HAVE BEEN CHOSEN FOR SACRIFICE! THE TAROT HAS **SPOKEN!** BUT BEFORE YOU GO TO GREET THE SACRED ARCANUM, FIRST WE MUST ANNOINT YOU WITH THE WAN NECTAR OF THE PHALLUS!

ANYWAY, THE DEMONIC SEX CULT HAS ITS WAY WITH THREE COUPLES, FORCING THEM TO CONSUME AN "ELIXIR OF LUST" AND PARTICIPATE IN SINFUL FETISH FUELED SEX RITES. KEEP YOUR PEEPERS PEELED FOR THE SUMPTUOUS BARBARA MILLS, THE VIRGINAL-LOOKING PAMELA WESTCOTT, AND THE MASSIVE SWEATER PUPPIES OF SUSAN WESTCOTT. IT'S ALL TASTELESS, PREPOSTEROUS, AND AGAIN -- PROUD TO DISPLAY AN UTTERLY BARGAIN BASEMENT BUDGET WHICH RESULTS IN A LOT OF UNINTENTIONAL LAUGHS.

Dark Dreams (1971) Directed by Roger Guermantes

WHEN A JUDGE NAMED JOEL L. TYLER DECIDED IN MARCH OF 1973 THAT DEEP THROAT, WHICH HAD BEEN PLAYING AT THE WORLD CINEMA ON 49th ST. IN NEW YORK, WAS OBSCENE, THE THEATER OWNERS PUT THE INFAMOUS PHRASE "JUDGE CUTS THROAT, WORLD MOURNS" ON THEIR HUGE MARQUEE AND SCREENED DARK DREAMS INSTEAD. IT WAS WITH THIS RULING THAT NEW YORK CITY THEATERS SHOWING DEEP THROAT WERE NOW BREAKING THE LAW THAT INADVERTENTLY HELPED THE XXX CLASSIC BECOME PERHAPS THE MOST WELL-KNOWN ADULT MOVIE OF ALL TIME. MEANWHILE NO ONE REALLY REMEMBERS DARK DREAMS AT ALL -- BUT PERHAPS THEY SHOULD. IT'S ACTUALLY PRETTY COOL!

THE STORY BEGINS WITH A BRIEF DESCRIPTION OF WHAT WITCHCRAFT AND THE OCCULT ARE BEFORE INTRODUCING US TO JACK AND JILL (HARRY REEMS AND TINA RUSSELL), A NEWLYWED COUPLE WHO HAVE SUFFERED A FLAT TIRE, FORCING THEM TO HEAD TO THE NEAREST HOUSE TO FIND A PHONE SO THEY CAN CALL FOR HELP. INSTEAD WHAT THEY FIND IS A WICKED OLD

6

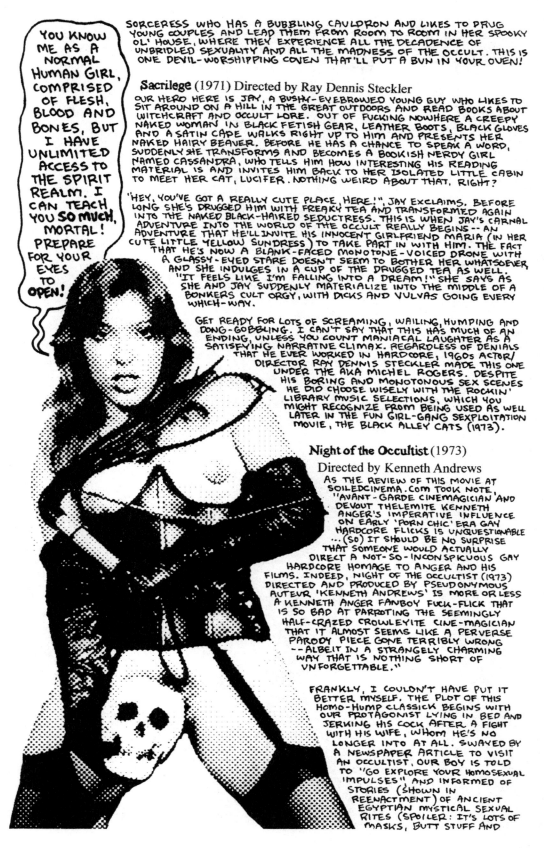

SORCERESS WHO HAS A BUBBLING CAULDRON AND LIKES TO DRUG YOUNG COUPLES AND LEAD THEM FROM ROOM TO ROOM IN HER SPOOKY OL' HOUSE, WHERE THEY EXPERIENCE ALL THE DECADENCE OF UNBRIDLED SEXUALITY AND ALL THE MADNESS OF THE OCCULT. THIS IS ONE DEVIL-WORSHIPPING COVEN THAT'LL PUT A BUN IN YOUR OVEN!

Sacrilege (1971) Directed by Ray Dennis Steckler

OUR HERO HERE IS JAY, A BUSHY-EYEBROWED YOUNG GUY WHO LIKES TO SIT AROUND ON A HILL IN THE GREAT OUTDOORS AND READ BOOKS ABOUT WITCHCRAFT AND OCCULT LORE. OUT OF FUCKING NOWHERE A CREEPY NAKED WOMAN IN BLACK FETISH GEAR, LEATHER BOOTS, BLACK GLOVES AND A SATIN CAPE WALKS RIGHT UP TO HIM AND PRESENTS HER NAKED HAIRY BEAVER. BEFORE HE HAS A CHANCE TO SPEAK A WORD, SUDDENLY SHE TRANSFORMS AND BECOMES A BOOKISH NERDY GIRL NAMED CASSANDRA, WHO TELLS HIM HOW INTERESTING HIS READING MATERIAL IS AND INVITES HIM BACK TO HER ISOLATED LITTLE CABIN TO MEET HER CAT, LUCIFER. NOTHING WEIRD ABOUT THAT, RIGHT?

"HEY, YOU'VE GOT A REALLY CUTE PLACE HERE!", JAY EXCLAIMS. BEFORE LONG SHE'S DRUGGED HIM WITH FREAKY TEA AND TRANSFORMED AGAIN INTO THE NAKED BLACK-HAIRED SEDUCTRESS. THIS IS WHEN JAY'S CARNAL ADVENTURE INTO THE WORLD OF THE OCCULT REALLY BEGINS -- AN ADVENTURE THAT HE'LL INVITE HIS INNOCENT GIRLFRIEND MARIA (IN HER CUTE LITTLE YELLOW SUNDRESS) TO TAKE PART IN WITH HIM. THE FACT THAT HE'S NOW A BLANK-FACED MONOTONE-VOICED DRONE WITH A GLASSY-EYED STARE DOESN'T SEEM TO BOTHER HER WHATSOEVER, AND SHE INDULGES IN A CUP OF THE DRUGGED TEA AS WELL. "IT FEELS LIKE I'M FALLING INTO A DREAM!" SHE SAYS AS SHE AND JAY SUDDENLY MATERIALIZE INTO THE MIDDLE OF A BONKERS CULT ORGY, WITH DICKS AND VULVAS GOING EVERY WHICH-WAY.

GET READY FOR LOTS OF SCREAMING, WAILING, HUMPING AND DONG-GOBBLING. I CAN'T SAY THAT THIS HAS MUCH OF AN ENDING, UNLESS YOU COUNT MANIACAL LAUGHTER AS A SATISFYING NARRATIVE CLIMAX. REGARDLESS OF DENIALS THAT HE EVER WORKED IN HARDCORE, 1960s ACTOR/ DIRECTOR RAY DENNIS STECKLER MADE THIS ONE UNDER THE AKA MICHEL ROGERS. DESPITE HIS BORING AND MONOTONOUS SEX SCENES HE DID CHOOSE WISELY WITH THE ROCKIN' LIBRARY MUSIC SELECTIONS, WHICH YOU MIGHT RECOGNIZE FROM BEING USED AS WELL LATER IN THE FUN GIRL-GANG SEXPLOITATION MOVIE, THE BLACK ALLEY CATS (1973).

Night of the Occultist (1973)

Directed by Kenneth Andrews

AS THE REVIEW OF THIS MOVIE AT SOILEDCINEMA.COM TOOK NOTE, "AVANT-GARDE CINEMAGICIAN AND DEVOUT THELEMITE KENNETH ANGER'S IMPERATIVE INFLUENCE ON EARLY 'PORN CHIC' ERA GAY HARDCORE FLICKS IS UNQUESTIONABLE ...(SO) IT SHOULD BE NO SURPRISE THAT SOMEONE WOULD ACTUALLY DIRECT A NOT-SO-INCONSPICUOUS GAY HARDCORE HOMAGE TO ANGER AND HIS FILMS. INDEED, NIGHT OF THE OCCULTIST (1973) DIRECTED AND PRODUCED BY PSEUDONYMOUS AUTEUR 'KENNETH ANDREWS' IS MORE OR LESS A KENNETH ANGER FANBOY FUCK-FLICK THAT IS SO BAD AT PARROTING THE SEEMINGLY HALF-CRAZED CROWLEYITE CINE-MAGICIAN THAT IT ALMOST SEEMS LIKE A PERVERSE PARODY PIECE GONE TERRIBLY WRONG --ALBEIT IN A STRANGELY CHARMING WAY THAT IS NOTHING SHORT OF UNFORGETTABLE."

FRANKLY, I COULDN'T HAVE PUT IT BETTER MYSELF. THE PLOT OF THIS HOMO-HUMP CLASSICK BEGINS WITH OUR PROTAGONIST LYING IN BED AND JERKING HIS COCK AFTER A FIGHT WITH HIS WIFE, WHOM HE'S NO LONGER INTO AT ALL. SWAYED BY A NEWSPAPER ARTICLE TO VISIT AN OCCULTIST, OUR BOY IS TOLD TO "GO EXPLORE YOUR HOMOSEXUAL IMPULSES" AND INFORMED OF STORIES (SHOWN IN REENACTMENT) OF ANCIENT EGYPTIAN MYSTICAL SEXUAL RITES (SPOILER: IT'S LOTS OF MASKS, BUTT STUFF AND

YOU KNOW ME AS A NORMAL HUMAN GIRL, COMPRISED OF FLESH, BLOOD AND BONES, BUT I HAVE UNLIMITED ACCESS TO THE SPIRIT REALM. I CAN TEACH YOU **SO MUCH**, MORTAL! PREPARE FOR YOUR EYES TO OPEN!

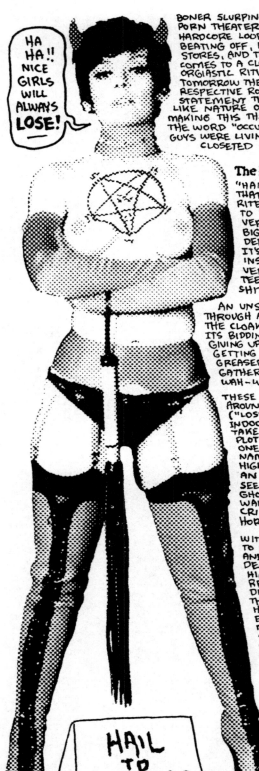

HA HA!! NICE GIRLS WILL ALWAYS LOSE!

HAIL TO URANUS

BONER SLURPING). AFTER THAT IT'S A VISIT TO A SKEEZY GAY PORN THEATER TO WATCH SOME OLD BLACK AND WHITE HARDCORE LOOPS BEFORE DRIVING AROUND TOWN WHILE BEATING OFF, FUCKING GUYS HE MEETS IN HARDWARE STORES, AND TAKING PART IN AN S+M ORGY. AS THE FILM COMES TO A CLOSE, THE NARRATOR INTONES: "AND SO THIS ORGIASTIC RITUAL CONTINUES INTO THE NIGHT, AND TOMORROW THE PARTICIPANTS SHALL RESUME THEIR RESPECTIVE ROLES IN CONVENTIONAL SOCIETY", A STATEMENT THAT PERFECTLY SUMMARIZES THE OCCULT LIKE NATURE OF WHAT IT WAS TO BE GAY IN THE 1970s, MAKING THIS THE MOST TRUE-TO-LIFE MOVIE ON THIS LIST. THE WORD "OCCULT" LITERALLY MEANS "HIDDEN", AND THESE GUYS WERE LIVING IN AN UNDERGROUND SECRET SOCIETY: A CLOSETED CULT OF SEXUAL SECRETS.

The Rites of Uranus (1975) Director: unknown

"HAIL TO URANUS, ENTER MY DARK PASSAGE." THAT'S THE MESSAGE THAT THE OCCULTISTS IN THE RITES OF URANUS CHANT, AND YOU'RE GOING TO HEAR IT QUITE A FEW TIMES. ONE OF THE VERY FIRST SHOTS IN THIS GRUNGY FILM IS A BIG SPIRALLY RIBBED CANDLE BEING PUSHED DEEP INTO A WOMAN'S TIGHT ASSHOLE IN CLOSEUP. IT'S A DARK, SCUM-WAD OF WEIRD OCCULT ANAL INSANITY, THIS PICTURE, AND IT'S ONE OF THE VERY FIRST ADULT FILMS I SAW AS A TEENAGER. (NO WONDER I'M INTO ALL THIS ODD SHIT...)

AN UNSEEN VOICE THAT SPEAKS TO EVERYONE THROUGH A WEIRD HORN STUCK TO THE WALL DIRECTS THE CLOAKED FOLLOWERS OF THE URANUS CULT TO DO ITS BIDDING -- THE LARGE MAJORITY OF WHICH INVOLVES GIVING UP ALL OF THEIR WORLDLY POSSESSIONS AND GETTING TOGETHER TO SODOMIZE BEAUTIFUL, GREASED-UP "NOVICE" WOMEN DURING BLACK MASS GATHERINGS. ALL OF THIS TRANSPIRING WHILE FUNKY WAH-WAH GUITAR RIFFS BLEAT OUT.

THESE HOODED ACOLYTES OF THE ASSHOLE WANDER AROUND LOS ANGELES HANDING OUT FLYERS ("LOST? FIND YOURSELF IN URANUS!") HOPING TO INDOCTRINATE NEW "URANUSITES" THEY CAN TAKE BACK TO THEIR FETID DEN OF INIQUITY. THE PLOT TAKES A TWIST INTO THE MACABRE WHEN ONE OF THE LOVELY RED-HAIRED NOVICES NAMED SARAH ACCIDENTALLY SMOTHERS THE HIGH PRIEST BY SITTING ON HIS FACE DURING AN ORGY. NONE OF THE OTHER FOLLOWERS SEEM THE LEAST BIT SURPRISED BY THIS GHOULISH TURN OF EVENTS, BUT THE HORN IN THE WALL COMMANDS THAT SHE BE JAILED FOR HER CRIME, AND YOU SAY "HOW HIGH?" WHEN THE HORN SAYS JUMP.

WITH THAT, THE HIGH PRIESTESS CHANTS "PRAISE BE TO THE MIGHTY COCK! ENTER MY DARK PASSAGE", AND PROCEEDS TO SUCK THE DINGUS OF THE DEAD (YET ERECT?!) MAN. EVERYONE SEEMS HIGH AS SHIT IN THIS WEIRD UNDERGROUND XXX RELEASE, AND DELIVER THEIR SCATTERBRAINED DIALOG AS IF THEY WERE THINKING IT UP RIGHT ON THE SPOT. OFTEN THAT CAN BE ANNOYING, BUT HERE IT ACTUALLY GIVES THE FILM AN ENTERTAINING DOCUMENTARY FEEL THAT MELDS COMFORTABLY WITH THE CONCEPT. THIS SHIT IS FUCKING GREAT. A TOTALLY UNHINGED WAD OF FILTH, MOSTLY DEVOID OF ANY SOCIALLY REDEEMING VALUES.

Baby Rosemary (1976)

Directed by John Hayes

THIS IS MY PERSONAL FAVORITE FILM ON THIS LIST. IT'S VERY UNDERRATED, EVEN AMONGST CLASSIC PORN FANS, AND REALLY DESERVES TO BE MENTIONED AMONGST THE GREAT AMERICAN HARDCORE MOVIES. THE FILM WAS DIRECTED BY JOHN HAYES, A DIRECTOR WHO WAS RIGHTLY FAWNED OVER BY AUTHOR STEPHEN THROWER IN HIS SEMINAL 'NIGHTMARE USA'.

SHARON THORPE IS THE TITULAR CHARACTER, A SEXUALLY REPRESSED YOUNG WOMAN WHOSE COP BOYFRIEND (JOHN LESLIE) IS SO TOTALLY

FRUSTRATED BY HER NOT PUTTING OUT, THAT AFTER THEIR DATES HE GETS A HOOKER (LESLLIE BOVEE) TO CALL HERSELF "ROSEMARY" SO HE CAN PORK HER TIGHT BUTTHOLE AND JIZZ ON HER FACE. AS WE JUMP THREE YEARS INTO THE FUTURE, WE FIND THAT IN THE WAKE OF HER FATHER DYING, ROSEMARY HAS ENDED UP SINKING INTO A DEEP DEPRESSION AS SHE FINDS HERSELF IMMERSED IN A MELODRAMATIC NIGHTMARE JOURNEY OF SEX AND DESTRUCTION.

GET READY PERVERTS. BECAUSE THIS ONE HAS INSANE DADDY ISSUES, DEGRADED WOMEN, VIOLENCE, MELANCHOLIC SEX, TWO (COUNT 'EM), TWO FUNERAL HOME ORGIES, AND CHANTING PAGAN SEX OCCULTISTS IN WHITE ROBES. THIS IS TRANSGRESSIVE FILMMAKING LIKE WE ONLY SAW IN THE 1970s.

FASCINATING LEAD ACTRESS SHARON THORPE WASN'T 'SUPER MODEL' BEAUTIFUL, BUT SHE HAD A LIKABLE DOWN TO EARTH VIBE AND IS ONE OF THE REAL SCENE STEALERS IN TERMS OF EROTIC ENERGY IN THE HISTORY OF ADULT CINEMA IN AMERICA. SHE'S AN ACTRESS THAT XXX FILMMAKER BOB CHINN REMEMBERS AS "A SWEET GIRL FROM MISSOURI WHO WAS FIERCELY INDEPENDENT AND EXTREMELY INTELLIGENT. I LOVED WORKING WITH HER. SHE COULD GO FROM PLAYING A STONE COLD KILLER LIKE IN LOVE SLAVES TO DOING COMEDY, WHICH SHE DID PLAYING 'SARGE' IN CANDY STRIPERS."

Teenage Twins (1976) Directed by Carter Stevens

IF I HAD TO PICK A SECOND FAVORITE ON THIS LIST, I'D HAVE TO SADDLE UP TO GOOD OL' TEENAGE TWINS. HISTORICALLY SIGNIFICANT, THIS WAS SHOT IN THREE DAYS BY THE LEGENDARY CARTER STEVENS, AND WAS THE VERY FIRST ADULT XXX FEATURE FILM TO STAR REAL LIFE TWIN SISTERS (BROOKE AND TAYLOR YOUNG). SOMEHOW THEIR COLLEGE PROFESSOR STEPFATHER (PLAYED BY LEO LOVEMORE) HAS COME TO FIND THE NECRONOMICON IN HIS POSSESSION, WHICH HE NEEDS FOR HIS WITCHCRAFT CLASS. RIGHT. THAT'S THE THING TO DO WITH THE MOST POWERFUL AND VALUABLE BOOK OF DARK MAGIC ON EARTH... PLAY SHOW-AND-TELL WITH SOME 20-YEAR-OLD TURDBRAINS IN COMMUNITY COLLEGE. INVITING A HORNY FRIEND (ERIC EDWARDS) TO HELP HIM WITH TRANSLATING THE ANCIENT TOME, THE TWO MEN DECIDE TO GIVE THE NECRONOMICON A TEST DRIVE AND PERFORM A RITUAL THAT'S SUPPOSED TO GIVE ETERNAL LIFE -- WHICH OF COURSE GOES ALL WRONG.

ON TOP OF ALL THE WEIRD LOVECRAFTIAN INCANTATIONS AND THE AWESOME IDENTICAL (AND I DO MEAN IDENTICAL) LESBIAN SIBLING CARPET MUNCHING, THERE IS ALSO A FEMALE MASTURBATION SCENE USING THE BIBLE AS A SEX TOY. CARTER WAS REALLY DOING EVERYTHING HE COULD DO TO TRY AND OFFEND DELICATE GOD-FEARING SENSIBILITIES HERE, AND ULTIMATELY THAT MEANS THAT THIS LOW BUDGET SHIT-SCAB OF A MOVIE STILL ENTERTAINS, EVEN TODAY.

"THEY LIKED QUAALUDES" CARTER STEVENS TOLD ME OF BROOKE AND TAYLOR YOUNG IN 2012. "IN FACT, WE ALL CALLED THEM THE QUAALUDE TWINS. SEXUALLY, THEY WERE RATHER UNSCHOOLED. THEY DID NOT FOOL AROUND WITH ONE ANOTHER OFF SCREEN. IT WAS STRICTLY MY IDEA TO PAIR THEM UP. I HAD NEVER HEARD OF IT DONE IN ANY MOVIE BEFORE THAT. I DO REMEMBER ERIC EDWARDS COMING UP TO ME DURING SHOOTING AND TELLING ME THAT HE HAD A REAL PROBLEM. HE HAD ASKED ONE OF THEM TO GO OUT WITH HIM AFTER THE SHOOT AND ONLY AFTER SHE HAD SAID 'YES' DID HE REALIZE THAT HE HAD ASKED OUT THE WRONG TWIN."

NOTE: A COUPLE OF OTHER MOVIES THAT DESERVE TO BE ON THIS LIST, BUT WERE OMITTED BECAUSE I WROTE ABOUT THEM AT LENGTH IN PREVIOUS BOOKS, ARE DEVIL'S DUE FROM 1973 (IN CINEMA SEWER VOLUME 4) AND ALL THE DEVIL'S ANGELS FROM 1978 (IN VOLUME 2).

ROBIN HAS A THOUGHT ABOUT MOVIE-WATCHING:

IT'S KINDA ODD HOW HUNG UP PEOPLE GET ON THE "THEY DON'T REALLY GO ANYWHERE, SO IT SUCKS" THING WHEN CRITICIZING MAD MAX: FURY ROAD.

DO THEY NOT GET THAT THERE HAVE BEEN MANY FANTASTIC MOVIES THAT TAKE PLACE IN A SINGLE HOUSE OR ROOM?

THIS TYPE OF CRIT MAKES ME THINK THERE ARE TWO TYPES OF FILMGOERS. THOSE WHO HAVE AN IDEA OF HOW A STORY SHOULD BE, AND WANT THAT ADHERED TO.

AND THOSE WHO HAVE AN IDEA OF HOW A STORY SHOULD BE, AND WANT THAT EXCEEDED AND EXPANDED UPON.

WAIT, DID THAT SOUND LIKE I WAS BEING A CONDESCENDING ASS HOLE?

I CAN'T EVEN TELL ANY MORE.

THE TWIG AND MUD ENCRUSTED WORLD OF
WOODS PORN

BY ROBIN BOUGIE · 2016

"YOU KNOW, IT USED TO BE REALLY HARD TO COME BY A MAGAZINE LIKE THAT WHEN I WAS A KID. I'D HAVE TO GO DIGGING UNDER THE BUSHES BY THE FREEWAY, AND SNEAK INTO MY DAD'S STASH. BEFORE THE INTERNET, EVERY GIRL WAS A LOT MORE SPECIAL." -- SWISS ARMY MAN (2016)

BACK IN 1980, I HAD MY FIRST RUN-IN WITH PORNOGRAPHY. THESE WERE DAMP MAGAZINES COVERED IN DIRT THAT I FOUND IN A WOODED AREA NEAR A SUBURB IN GRADE 2. I WAS WITH THREE LITTLE GIRLS WHO WERE MY PLAYMATES IN RED DEER ALBERTA, AND WE THOUGHT PORNOGRAPHY WAS UTTERLY FASCINATING. ONE OF THESE GIRLS GREW UP TO BE A NEWSCASTER ON AMERICAN NETWORK TELEVISION, BUT BACK THEN SHE WAS JUST THE DAUGHTER OF ONE OF MY MOM'S BEST FRIENDS. I REMEMBER CLEARLY ALL THE PUBES GOING ON IN THOSE PAGES, AND DID NOT KNOW WHAT THE HELL TO MAKE OF THAT. WE SPREAD THE SOGGY MAGAZINES OUT ON A TREE STUMP TO PONDER OVER THEM, AND ENDED UP LEAVING THEM THERE, WHERE I CAN ONLY ASSUME THEY WERE FOUND BY OTHER CHILDREN AS WELL.

I REMEMBER SEEING A GLISTENING PINK VULVA FROM THE FRONT IN ONE PHOTO, AND THINKING "OH, THAT'S WHAT THAT LOOKS LIKE", AND THEN TURNING THE PAGE. AND THERE WAS A ANOTHER WOMAN DOING A DOGGY STYLE POSE FROM THE BACK, AND THE PUSSY LOOKED TOTALLY DIFFERENT FROM THAT ANGLE, AND I WAS JUST UTTERLY CONFUSED. I REMEMBER THINKING "SO IT'S DIFFERENT ON EACH GIRL? NO TWO ARE THE SAME?!"

IN 1999 JOHN WOZNIAK OF THE BAND MARCY PLAYGROUND COINED THE PHRASE "I AM A CHILD OF THE FREE TO BE YOU AND ME GENERATION" IN THE SONG "OUR GENERATION". 'FREE TO BE YOU AND ME' WAS A TV SPECIAL, ALBUM, AND BOOK THAT MANY KIDS WHO GREW UP IN THE 1970S AND EARLY 1980S EXPERIENCED, AND ITS OVERRIDING CONCEPT WAS TO FOSTER GENDER NEUTRALITY, INDIVIDUALITY, TOLERANCE, AND COMFORT WITH YOURSELF AND OTHERS. YOU KNOW, HIPPY-DIPPY POST-1960S SHIT, BUT REALLY PROGRESSIVE AND FORWARD THINKING AT THE TIME WHEN OUR MEDIA WAS CONSERVATIVE, WHITE-WASHED, AND HOMOPHOBIC. HOW UNLIKELY IT WOULD BE TODAY, TO SEE 8, 9 AND 10-YEAR-OLDS WANDERING AROUND IN THE WOODS ON THEIR OWN? WE WEREN'T RAISED PERFECT OR ANYTHING, BUT MAN, OUR GENERATION WAS AMAZING FOR STUFF LIKE THAT. JUST PURE FREEDOM TO DISCOVER THE WORLD AS A CHILD. WE WERE <u>FREE TO BE YOU AND ME</u>. THERE WAS A 'HANDS OFF APPROACH' TO PARENTING THAT IS TOTALLY IN DIRECT OPPOSITION WITH WHAT WE UNDERSTAND TO BE CHILD-REARING TODAY, WITH ALL ITS SUPERVISED PLAY-DATES AND WHATNOT.

WHERE DID THIS PORN COME FROM? MY THEORY IS THAT IT WAS STOLEN BY OTHER CHILDREN FROM THEIR PARENTS' SECRET STASHES, OR SHOPLIFTED. THE TOTS COULDN'T KEEP IT AT HOME BECAUSE IT WOULD BE FOUND BY MEDDLING ADULTS, SO THEY TOOK IT TO THE ONE PLACE A KID HAD PRIVACY: THE WOODS. THEN THESE PULPY ODES TO SWEATY COPULATION AND THE CLOTHING-FREE HUMAN FORM WOULD BE FOUND BY OTHER KIDS, AND THE CYCLE WOULD CONTINUE.

ANOTHER POSSIBLE SOURCE: HOMELESS GUYS. PEOPLE FORGET THAT THEY NEED TO JERK OFF TOO. MORE THAN MOST OF US, EVEN, SEEING AS THEIR BODY ODOUR AND LACK OF FINANCIAL STABILITY TENDS TO KEEP PROSPECTIVE SEX PARTNERS AT A DISTANCE.

THE GENERATION AFTER US (NOW IN THEIR THIRTIES), THE FIRST TO GROW UP WITH THE INTERNET, DIDN'T DISCOVER PORN THE SAME WAY WE DID. ALL THE ONES I'VE TALKED TO ABOUT IT FOUND THEIRS ONLINE -- USUALLY WITH HENTAI ANIME BEING THEIR SMUTTY GATEWAY DRUG. POKEMON AND SAILOR MOON WERE BOTH MASSIVELY POPULAR, AND ONCE YOU'RE INNOCENTLY GOOGLING FOR THAT STUFF, XXX HENTAI IS ONLY A CLICK OR TWO AWAY. AFTER THAT, THE FLOODGATES OF PUBERTY OPEN, AND THE NATURAL NEED TO JACK (OR JILL) OFF PROMPTS A SWEET-TOOTH FOR LURID CONTENT.

FROM THE REPORTS THAT I'M GETTING, THE FILTHY STROKE MAGAZINES ARE STILL OUT THERE IN THE WOODS, BUT JUST NOT IN THE SAME GREAT NUMBERS THAT THEY USED TO BE. WE HUNTED THE BUFFALO TO NEAR EXTINCTION, AND WHEN WE INVENTED THE INTERNET, WE NEARLY

"LIFE WAS NEVER THE SAME"

ERADICATED 'WOODS PORN' TOO. BUT AS I MENTIONED BEFORE, STREET DUDES NEED TO UNLOAD TOO. I THINK THEY'RE THE ONES STILL DITCHING THE GOODS OUT THERE IN THE URBAN WILDERNESS. IF THE YOUNGLINGS NEED 'WOODS PORN', IT MIGHT STILL BE THERE FOR THEM IF THEY'RE LUCKY. BUT LET'S FACE IT, KIDS DON'T OFTEN GO OUTSIDE ANYMORE. NOT WITH ALL THOSE AWESOME VIDEOGAMES TO PLAY AND PORN TO WATCH ON THEIR PHONES. WHO WOULD?

NOW THAT MY OWN THOUGHTS ON THE SUBJECT ARE OUT OF THE WAY, I WANT TO NOTE THAT I FIRST BECAME AWARE THAT THIS PHENOMENON WAS A COMMON AND SHARED EXPERIENCE AFTER TALKING TO SO MANY MALE AND FEMALE PEERS FROM MY AGE RANGE, AND IN NOVEMBER 2016, I ASKED FACEBOOK FRIENDS TO SHARE THEIR EXPERIENCES ON THIS TOPIC AS A BONDING EXERCISE. HERE ARE A FEW OF MY FAVOURITES FROM THE NEARLY 200 RESPONSES THAT CAME IN.

"I DIDN'T KNOW THAT "WOODS PORN" WAS A THING THAT EVERYONE EXPERIENCED UNTIL THE INTERNET CAME ALONG AND I SAW OTHER PEOPLE TALKING ABOUT IT. YEAH, I FOUND SOME PORN IN THE WOODS WITH MY BEST FRIEND BACK IN 1983 IN LOUISVILLE, KY, AND WE TOOK IT HOME AND SHARED IT (HE WOULD GET A FEW MAGS FOR A WEEK, I'D GET THE REST, THEN WE'D SWAP). THE MAGAZINES WE FOUND WERE GALLERY, OUI, HARVEY, AND A COUPLE OF HUSTLERS. I REMEMBER ONE OF THE HUSTLERS WAS THE ONE WITH THE ANTON LAVEY ARTICLE IN IT. I'VE OFTEN WONDERED SINCE IF THERE WAS SOME KIND OF JOHNNY APPLESEED OF PORN DISTRIBUTING TO EVERY WOODED AREA IN AMERICA." – CHRISTOPHER BICKLE

"DID ALL THIS 'WOODS PORN' END UP THERE BECAUSE SOMEONE WAS FORCED OR COMPELLED TO RID THEMSELVES OF IT BY AN HYSTERICAL PARENT OR WIFE? A WOODLAND AREA A FEW STREETS AWAY FROM ME WOULD REGURGITATE AMAZING HARDCORE AND SOFTCORE MAGS FROM TITLES LIKE COLOR CLIMAX, NEW CUNTS, BAWDY (AN AUSSIE HARDCORE RAG), PENTHOUSE, SWANK, CLUB INTERNATIONAL, PARK LANE, AND THE NEW BACHELOR. USUALLY THE MAGS HAD COMPACTED, SOGGY PAGES, BUT THAT WAS FIXED BY LYING THEM OUT IN THE SUN. OF COURSE, SOME PAGES WOULD THEN STICK, AND THEY'D TEAR WHEN YOU OPENED THEM. I ONCE FOUND A PRETTY GROTESQUE MAG CALLED 'SADIO', AND THAT SHOCKED THE TEN-YEAR-OLD ME QUITE A BIT. THAT WOODED AREA IS STILL THERE, AND WHEN I WALK THROUGH THERE WHILE VISITING MELBOURNE, I LOOK FOR ANY LEFTOVERS. HAVEN'T FOUND ANY LATELY." – MARK SAVAGE

"I FOUND PORN IN A STORM DRAIN, ONCE. I WAS MAYBE 15. IT WAS DVDS STRUNG ON FISHING LINE AND DANGLED DOWN INTO THE DRAIN. THERE WAS A PENCIL USED TO HOLD IT IN PLACE ABOVE THE GRATE AND KEEP IT FROM FALLING IN. ONE WAS CALLED "THE PRETTIEST ASIAN I EVER CAME ACROSS". I FOUND WOODS PORN TOO. IN A COOLER." – JESSICA OLIVER

"THE BRIT VERSION OF THIS IS "HEDGE PORN". PORN MAGS SHOVED INTO HEDGES AND LARGE BUSHES. THIS WAS PLACED THERE BY 'HEDGE TIPPERS', SEXUALLY PENT UP MIDDLE AGED FAMILY MEN WHO LIKE TO "RELAX IN A GENTLEMAN'S FASHION" TO STUFF LIKE BARELY LEGAL PORN THAT LOOKS LIKE THEIR DAUGHTERS' FRIENDS OR STRAPPING SCALLY LADS. THEIR

GUILT OVER THEIR ONANISM AND WANK CHOICES LEADS THEM TO CONCEAL THE PORN ON THEIR PERSON, TAKE THE DOG FOR A WALK AND THEN SHOVE IT IN A COUNCIL HEDGE. THEY WANT TO TRASH THE PORN, BUT IT WAS EXPENSIVE AND THEY ONLY USED IT FOR A 3 MINUTE WANK SO THEY CAN'T MAKE THEMSELVES TOSS IT IN THE TRASH -- SO INTO THE HEDGE IT GOES, WHERE THEY MAY BE BACK, OR FIND ANOTHER MAN'S GUILTY GOLD." — PAT THEILGES

"(FOUND IT) IN RAILWAY EMBANKMENTS, AND AMONGST TREES BEHIND THE PUB I GREW UP NEXT DOOR TO. THE TWO THAT STICK IN MY MIND THE MOST ARE THE STACK OF PORN WE FOUND IN A RUSTED ABANDONED TRACTOR, AND THE MA-HOO-SIVE TRASHBAG FULL THAT WE FOUND IN THE WOODS -- AND WHEN WE SHOOK IT OUT TO SIFT THROUGH IT, A HUGE SHIT AND BLOOD-ENCRUSTED DILDO FELL OUT TOO." — PAUL ROBERTSON

"I FOUND STACKS AND STACKS OF PLAYBOYS AND PENTHOUSE MAGS WITH A BUNCH OF NEIGHBOURHOOD KIDS AT THIS DUMPSTER NEXT TO THESE CONDOS WHEN I WAS ABOUT SIX. IT WAS AMAZING. THEN I FOUND MORE IN MY DAD'S ROOM. I USED TO PRAY TO GOD EVERY NIGHT TO GIVE ME BOOBS LIKE THE GIRLS IN THE MAGAZINES." — VALERIE WEST

"IN THE 5TH GRADE, WE FOUND A FEW MAGS IN THE WOODS IN WINTER BEFORE THE SNOW ARRIVED. MY FAMILY WAS HEADING NORTH FOR A CHRISTMAS TRIP TO SEE MY GRANDPARENTS AND I PACKED THE MAGS IN MY LUGGAGE FOR SOME REASON. I MUST HAVE BEEN ACTING REALLY WEIRD BECAUSE MY PARENTS FOUND THE MAGS, CONFISCATED THEM AND I GOT GROUNDED." — TIM HULSIZER

"PENTICTON BC, 1982-ISH. I WAS 11 OR SO. MY FRIENDS AND I WERE OUT ON AN ADVENTURE AND WE CAME UPON A DUMP OF WEATHERED AND WATER DAMAGED PLAYBOYS. WE SPLIT THEM UP EVENLY AND MADE OFF FOR OUR RESPECTIVE HOMES. I TUCKED THE MAGS UP UNDER MY SHIRT AND WALKED IN MY HOUSE. I MUST HAVE HAD A CRAZY GUILTY LOOK ON MY FACE BECAUSE MY STEP MOM WAS ASKING ME "WHAT'S GOING ON?!" I RAN DOWNSTAIRS AND SHOVED THE MAGS UNDER THE WASHING MACHINE AND RAN TO THE COUCH TRYING TO PLAY IT COOL. SHE LOOKED AT ME FOR 30 SECONDS BUT IF FELT LIKE FOREVER. SHE ASKED ME WHAT I DID AND I TOLD HER ME AND MY FRIENDS WERE 'JUST HANGING OUT'. SHE KNEW SOMETHING WAS UP, AND GETTING THOSE MAGS OUT FROM UNDER THE WASHING MACHINE WAS LIKE A MISSION IMPOSSIBLE MOVIE." — KEN MACKENZIE

"WE FOUND IT IN A SUITCASE UNDER A BUSH. I WAS ABOUT 9 AND MY BROTHER WAS 12. IT WAS A PILE OF ISSUES OF CHERI, OUI, AND SOME HARDER STUFF --BONDAGE MAGS WITH NAKED ANGUISHED WOMEN TIED UP AND DOMINATRIXES FORCING SIMPERING MEN TO LICK THEIR BOOTS. WE WERE SO ENTHUSIASTIC ABOUT OUR SCORE THAT WE MADE THE MISTAKE OF TELLING MY OLDER TEENAGE SISTER, AND SHE ANGRILY THREW IT ALL IN A TRASH BIN AND TOLD US WE WERE DAMN LUCKY SHE DIDN'T RAT US OUT TO OUR PARENTS. A DECADE LATER OVER BEERS SHE ADMITTED TO ME THAT SHE WENT BACK LATER AND GRABBED THE RAUNCHIEST MAGS FOR HERSELF!" — JENNIFER SMITH

"I WAS PROBABLY THE LAST FOUND-PORN GENERATION. BY THE TIME I WAS 15 WE WERE JERKIN' OFF WITH COMPUTERS, BUT AT 10 YEARS OLD ME AND A FRIEND FOUND A MAGAZINE IN A DITCH AND HID IN A BIG DRAIN PIPE TO LOOK THROUGH IT. I ACTUALLY ENJOYED READING IT. SOME OF THE MOVIE REVIEWS WERE REALLY FUNNY, BUT EVEN THEN I KNEW THE 'TRUE STORY' LETTERS WERE HILARIOUSLY IMPLAUSIBLE." — GILBERT R. SMITH

"WE FOUND IT IN A SUITCASE"

"MY GIRLFRIEND IS SO YOUNG THAT ALL SHE'S EVER KNOWN IS INTERNET PORN. I HAD TO TELL HER ABOUT THE GOOD OLD DAYS OF JUST FINDING MAGAZINES OUTSIDE IN THE WOODS, OR IN BROKEN DOWN CABINS, SHEDS OR HOUSES. I GUESS IT WAS A THING EVERYWHERE. I REMEMBER FINDING A PLAYBOY WITH BARBI BENTON IN IT AND HAVING A SLIGHT FASCINATION WITH HER." — JOHNNY RIGGS

"I REMEMBER STUMBLING ACROSS A PORN MAG WHILST ON A FAMILY WALK IN THE MENDIPS (HILLS IN THE UK). I KEPT QUIET ABOUT IT AND THEN AFTER THE WALK GOT MY SISTER TO COVER FOR ME AND I RAN BACK UP THE HILL, NABBED IT AND KEPT IT IN THE INSIDE OF MY TROUSER LEG FOR THE WHOLE TWO HOUR CAR JOURNEY HOME. HAHA! PLAYGROUND LEGEND FOR ABOUT 5 MINUTES AFTER THAT ONE!" — RICHARD SAMPSON

"ONLY FOUND IT ONCE. I WAS AT UTAH'S TABBY MOUNTAIN ATTENDING A WILDERNESS PROGRAM FOR TROUBLED TEENS ONE WINTER. IT WAS CRUMPLED AND TORN IN THE FREEZING SNOW, MUCH LIKE HOW I VIEWED MYSELF IN THOSE BRUTAL MOUNTAINS. IT EVENTUALLY GOT INTO THE HANDS OF MY FRIEND WITH A CHRONIC MASTURBATION PROBLEM WHO I UNFORTUNATELY SHARED A DAMN TENT WITH." — MOJO MALAES

"THERE WAS A PLACE IN MY NORTHEAST COLA NEIGHBOURHOOD CALLED 'THE PIT'. IT WAS A WOODED AREA THAT DROPPED INTO THIS GIANT HOLE THAT HAD GROWN TREES AND UNDERGROWTH. NO HOUSES COULD BE BUILT THERE, AND IT CONNECTED INTO THE BACK OF CLEMSON RESEARCH FACILITY. THERE WERE ALWAYS RUMOURS OF MAN-EATING ALLIGATORS BACK THERE, BUT NEIGHBOURHOOD KIDS AND I WOULD BRAVE THE PIT ANYWAYS. ONE DAY WE WERE THUSLY REWARD WITH WEATHER WORN, TORN OUT PICTURES FROM HUSTLERS AND PLAYBOYS. LIFE WAS NEVER THE SAME." — TRAVIS BLAND

"I FOUND PORN THAT HAD BEEN CHOPPED INTO LITTLE BITS BY A LAWNMOWER. IT WAS THE FIRST TIME I'D SEEN A GUY GOING DOWN ON A WOMAN. MY CHILD BRAIN THOUGHT IT MUST HAVE BEEN A GUY WITH TITS GETTING HIS DICK SUCKED COS GIRLS DON'T HAVE ANYTHING DOWN THERE YOU CAN SUCK." — GREBO SMITH

"I REMEMBER FINDING AN ABSOLUTE TREASURE TROVE OF A MASSIVE ENVELOPE FULL OF PORN IN AN ABANDONED HOUSE ON A STREET THAT WAS MARKED FOR DEMOLITION, THAT ME AND SOME FRIENDS WERE PLAYING IN. SOME OF IT WAS SOGGY AND SOME CHOPPED UP, BUT I KEPT EVERYTHING I COULD CARRY AND HID IT UNDER MY BUNK BED. IT WAS MOSTLY RAZZLE LEVEL GROT BUT SOME HARDCORE STUFF TOO. I STUDIED EVERY SINGLE IMAGE INTENTLY AND PIECED TOGETHER ALL THE CHOPPED UP BITS." — JAMES FULK

"THERE WAS A WOODED AREA BEHIND THE APARTMENTS WHERE I GREW UP. WE USED TO BUILD FORTS THERE ALL THE TIME. MY FIRST PORN SCORE (THERE WERE MANY) WAS A RAGGEDY SUITCASE FULL OF NOT ONLY MAGS BUT POLAROIDS. (IT) WAS PRETTY WEATHER BEATEN. WE PUT THEM UP IN OUR FORT. I BELIEVE IT WAS MOSTLY TOPLESS/LINGERIE POSES. MOST LIKELY ESCORTS. THE BUILDING I GREW UP IN WAS RIGHT DOWN THE STREET FROM A BIG FACTORY. A LOT OF THE MALE WORKERS LIVED IN THE BUILDING, SO WE WERE ALWAYS FINDING CRAZY SHIT." — DARRELL MARSH

"FROM ABOUT 8-16, WE HAD A BIT OF A CLANDESTINE PORN CO-OP. ABOUT SIX OF US. PEOPLE WOULD SCAVENGE PORN WHEREVER THEY DID. MAGAZINES AND VHS'S. I NEVER KNEW IF ANYONE WAS REALLY IN CHARGE OF THE PORN LIBRARY, BUT IT WOULD JUST MATERIALIZE AT SLEEPOVERS, AND PEOPLE WOULD RETURN THINGS AND SWAP. WE NEVER GOT CAUGHT, EITHER. NOT ONE OF US, NOT ONCE. THERE WERE SOME GOOD ONES IN THERE, TOO! SMOOTH AS SILK, SEX FIFTH AVENUE, AND SUMMER CAMP GIRLS! I THINK THE SECRET TO OUR SUCCESS WAS THE REALIZATION THAT SUBURBAN WHITE PARENTS WOULD NEVER THINK TO BREACH DECORUM BY SEARCHING ANOTHER KID'S SLEEPING BAG FOR NO REASON." — JINX STRANGE

"ME AND A MATE FOUND A PILE OF HARDCORE MAGS IN SOME BUSHES DOWN BY A NEARBY RIVER WHEN WE WERE IN OUR

".. AN ABSOLUTE TREASURE TROVE.."

MID-TEENS. HE SHOWED ME A COUPLE OF PAGES AND I THREW UP EVERYWHERE. I'D NEVER SEEN ANYTHING LIKE THAT BEFORE. I WAS COOL WITH STUFF LIKE PLAYBOY AS A KID BUT THE HARDCORE STUFF FREAKED ME OUT. I'VE SINCE RECOVERED." — SEAN PATRICK BRADY

"I FOUND MINE RIPPED UP IN A LOCAL GLEN AND STREWN ACROSS SOME BUSHES AND A DITCH. LATER HAD SEX IN THE SAME DITCH. LOL." — JILL NAUS

"THERE WAS A MASSIVE FOREST/WOODSY AREA WHERE I GREW UP. TRAILS, OVERGROWN TREES AND BUSH. SOMETIMES YOU COULDN'T SEE THE LIGHT FROM THE SKY. I WAS CHUMMING WITH THE AGARAND BROTHERS, AND WE DECIDED TO BUILD A FORT IN OUR OWN SECTION. THERE WERE A TON OF OTHER FORTS, AND PEOPLE WOULD RAID EACH OTHER'S FORTS, AND SOME GROUPS WOULD BAND TOGETHER AND HAVE A TRADE SYSTEM. THE AGARAND BROTHERS AND I WERE BANDITS AND FOLLOWED OUR OWN CODE. ONE DAY WE RAIDED ANOTHER FORT, AND THERE DIDN'T SEEM TO BE ANYTHING FOR US TO TAKE UNTIL ONE OF US NOTICED A SUITCASE. INSIDE WERE A TON OF "DIRTY MAGAZINES". TALK ABOUT HITTING THE JACKPOT! OUR 10-YEAR-OLD BRAINS WERE A BUZZIN' FOR A WEEK. ALL WAS WELL UNTIL THE AGARAND BROTHERS TOLD THEIR PARENTS, WHO MADE THEM BRING THE SUITCASE BACK TO THEIR HOUSE, AND WE WEREN'T ALLOWED TO HANG OUT TOGETHER ANYMORE." — NATHAN HILL

"WHEN I WAS ABOUT SEVEN, I LIVED NEXT TO A MENTALLY CHALLENGED GUY IN HIS 30S WHO LIVED WITH HIS MOTHER. EVERY MONTH, HE WOULD BUY A HUSTLER, READ IT QUICK, AND TOSS IT IN THE WOODS NEAR A CREEK. I WOULD FIND THE MOST RECENT ISSUE AROUND THE SAME TIME EACH MONTH, USUALLY IN PRETTY GOOD CONDITION. APPARENTLY, HE COULDN'T RISK HIS MOM FINDING THEM. ANYWAY, I WOULD SNATCH THEM UP, GO TO SCHOOL, AND SELL PAGES FOR LUNCH MONEY. ABOUT $2 A POP." — LUCAS GUTMAN

"WHEN I FINALLY LEFT HOME (A BIT EMBARRASSINGLY AT 28 YEARS OLD) I HAD QUITE A LARGE COLLECTION OF PORN MAGS. I WASN'T ABOUT TO BRING THEM WITH ME SO A FRIEND OF MINE MENTIONED THE STEREOTYPE OF FINDING PORN MAGS IN THE WOODS. THIS STARTED A CONVERSATION ABOUT JUST HOW THEY GET THERE. SO WE DECIDED TO DO THE YOUTH A SERVICE AND WENT TO OUR LOCAL WOODS WITH MY LARGE COLLECTION AND DISTRIBUTED THEM ABOUT THE PLACE. WE PUT THEM UP TREES, UNDER THINGS AND EVEN THREW SOME IN SOME QUITE PERILOUS PLACES TO MAKE THE KIDS WORK FOR IT. WE FELT LIKE WE WERE MAKING SOMEONE'S DAY. WE WENT BACK A WEEK OR SO LATER AND COULDN'T FIND A SINGLE TRACE OF ANY OF THEM. NOT ALL HEROES WEAR CAPES." — GAVIN RYE

— END —

RED, HOT AND BLUE MOVIES:
Remembering the Savoy, the Squamish 5 and the Vancouver anti-porn movement

SAVOY THEATER OWNER / OPERATOR SEAN DALY

ON PAGE 33 OF CINEMA SEWER BOOK 3, I DID AN ARTICLE ABOUT THE FOX THEATER HERE IN VANCOUVER, WHICH RESIDES AT THE CORNER OF MAIN STREET AND KINGSWAY. THAT LITTLE 311 SEAT PORN THEATER HAS AN INTERESTING HISTORY, AND WAS MY CHERISHED LOCAL GRINDHOUSE FOR A GOOD LONG WHILE. WITH THAT IN MIND, LET ME REVEAL THAT THERE IS SOME BACK STORY TO BE TOLD. BEFORE IT BECAME THE FOX IN THE MID 1980S, IT WAS VANCOUVER'S PRIME DESTINATION FOR FILM-BUFFS, AND IT WAS CALLED THE SAVOY.

OPENING IN MAY 1980, THE SAVOY WAS OWNED AND OPERATED BY SEAN DALY, WHO NAMED IT AFTER THE FIRST THEATER TO EXIST IN THE CITY (OPENING IN 1901 AT THE CORNER OF CAMBIE AND CORDOVA). AND TO MATCH ITS TINY SIZE, SEAN RAN THE PLACE WITH A LOT OF INDY LOVE, SELLING HOMEMADE OATMEAL COOKIES AND EARL GREY TEA FROM THE LOBBY'S TINY CONCESSION STAND, WHICH IS SO SMALL, YOU CAN BARELY TURN AROUND IN IT. THE MINIATURE THEATER SIZE ALSO MEANT THAT DALY COULD TAKE CHANCES WITH ODD AND UNUSUAL FILMS THAT PROBABLY WOULDN'T DRAW MANY PEOPLE, BECAUSE IT WAS FAR EASIER TO FILL THE HOUSE.

MARIANNE FAITHFUL IS

NAKED UNDER LEATHER

APRIL 4, 1981

SOME OF THOSE RISKS THAT PAID OFF DURING THE 4-YEAR EXISTENCE OF THE THEATER FROM 1980 TO 1984 WERE A WEEK-LONG FESTIVAL OF "THE WORLD'S WORST MOVIES" (YEARS BEFORE BEING INTO "BAD" MOVIES WAS A HIP THING), AN ANNUAL THREE STOOGES FILM FESTIVAL (HOSTED BY POPULAR LOCAL RADIO DJ DOC HARRIS), A LOT OF HORROR MOVIE SCREENINGS (SUCH AS CREEPSHOW, SUSPIRIA, MOTEL HELL, HALLOWEEN, AND PHANTOM OF THE PARADISE), STRANGE ART-HOUSE OFFERINGS, MORE CULT MIDNIGHT MOVIES THAN YOU COULD SHAKE A STICK AT, AND A REVIVAL OF 3D -- A FORMAT THAT HAD FALLEN OUT OF FAVOUR WITH FILMGOERS UP UNTIL THAT TIME.

"SEAN DALY WAS THE PROJECTIONIST AT THE RIDGE THEATER, WHICH IS WHEN I FIRST MET HIM BACK IN 1978", FORMER SAVOY EMPLOYEE IAN FREEMAN TOLD ME VIA TELEPHONE. "HE WAS THERE AT THE RIDGE FOR A COUPLE YEARS, AND HE JUST DIDN'T SEEM TO GET ALONG WITH THE MANAGER, LEONARD SCHEIN, WHO ENDED UP BEING THE ONE WHO FOUND THE LOCATION FOR THE SAVOY FOR HIM."

"MY SISTER GLORIA WORKED THERE AFTER I DID", FREEMAN CONTINUED. "ALTHOUGH SHE LEFT ON BAD TERMS WITH HIM OWING HER TWO PAYCHEQUES WORTH OF MONEY. BUT I GOT ALONG GREAT WITH SEAN. I DID ALL KINDS OF JOBS, JANITORIAL WORK, WORKING THE BOX OFFICE AND THE CONCESSION, PUTTING UP POSTERS, AND UNLOADING THE TRUCKS WHEN THEY WOULD DROP OFF THE SUPPLIES. I LIKED IT, BUT IT WAS A SMALL OPERATION, AND HE DIDN'T HAVE MUCH MONEY FOR ADVERTISING. I MEAN, EVEN IF THAT PLACE WAS FULL, IT WASN'T THAT MANY TICKETS SOLD."

A SUGGESTION BOX WAS PROVIDED, AND MOST OF THE FILMS THAT PLAYED WERE CULLED FROM THE REQUESTS OF REGULAR CUSTOMERS, A HIGHLY UNUSUAL PRACTICE THAT TOTALLY FLEW IN THE FACE OF WHAT THE REST OF THE FIRST-RUN THEATERS IN THE CITY WERE DOING AT THE TIME. IT MEANT THAT THE SAVOY QUICKLY CAME TO BE A SOCIAL HUB WHERE THE LOCAL COMMUNITY AND OBSESSIVE MOVIE FANS FELT A REAL CONNECTION TO THE PLACE.

"I REMEMBER SEEING WARHOLS FRANKENSTIEN AND DRACULA IN 3D ALL IN ONE VERY COOL NIGHT", SAID JOHNNY ROMAN. "WHEN I WAS IN HIGH SCHOOL WE PROBABLY HIT THE SAVOY EVERY OTHER WEEK. WE USED TO WALK UP TO THE 7-11 ON 14TH TO AVOID THE EXPENSIVE THEATRE FOUNTAIN DRINKS. WHAT WAS COOL ABOUT THAT THEATRE, IS THAT THEY WOULD SNIFF OUR DRINKS TO MAKE SURE THERE WAS NO BOOZE, AND THEN THEY WOULD LET US IN WITH OUR DISCOUNTED 7-11 BIG GULPS."

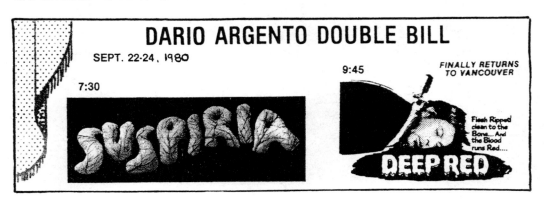

DARIO ARGENTO DOUBLE BILL
SEPT. 22-24, 1980

7:30

SUSPIRIA

9:45

FINALLY RETURNS TO VANCOUVER

Flesh Ripped clean to the Bone... And the Blood runs Red....

DEEP RED

ALEXANDRO JODOROWSKY DOUBLE BILL

SEPT. 29-OCT. 1, 1980

7:30

9:45

"THE SAVOY NEVER SEEMED TO HAVE A LOT OF PEOPLE AT VIEWINGS", LONGTIME VANCOUVER RESIDENT JUDITH BEEMAN TOLD ME. "WHICH, FROM MY PERSPECTIVE, WAS QUITE PLEASANT. BEING UNCROWDED WHILE MOVIE WATCHING IS PERFECTION. THE MOST PACKED SCREENING I SAW WAS CALIGULA, MAYBE IN 1983. IT WAS THE SECOND TIME IT HAD BEEN SHOWN IN VANCOUVER. THE FIRST WAS WHEN IT WAS PICKETED BY SIMMA HOLT AT ANOTHER LONG GONE REPERTORY DOWNTOWN ON GRANVILLE AT SMITHE. BACK IN THE DAY SEEING OUT-THERE SHOWS LIKE CALIGULA, AND LATER BLUE VELVET, REALLY ADDED TO THE 'WE'RE BEING BAD' PART OF THE EXPERIENCE."

"I WAS AT A MIDNIGHT SCREENING OF THE HARDER THEY COME, STARRING JIMMY CLIFF", ARTIST NICOLE STEEN MENTIONED TO ME. "I BARELY REMEMBER ANYTHING ABOUT IT, EXCEPT THAT THE THEATER WAS SO FULL OF POT SMOKE YOU COULD HARDLY SEE THE MOVIE ON THE SCREEN. AH, THE GOOD OLD DAYS."

EVEN BEFORE THE SAVOY BECAME THE INFAMOUS FOX PORN THEATER, THE BUILDING HAD A CONNECTION TO PORN, AS EVIDENCED BY A CURIOUS INCIDENT IN 1983 THAT WAS REPORTED IN THE LOCAL PAPER. "SAVOY STOMPS ON PORN" BLEATED A HEADLINE ON A CLIPPING FROM THE AUGUST 28TH ISSUE OF THE PROVINCE NEWSPAPER THAT MY FRIEND AND FELLOW PORN HISTORIAN DIMITRIOS OTIS MAILED TO ME. HE KNEW I WAS RESEARCHING THE HISTORY OF THE SAVOY, AND HE WISELY ASSUMED THAT THIS PORN ANGLE TO THE STORY WOULD BE ONE I WOULD GOBBLE UP.

THE CLIPPING REVEALED THAT, EMBOLDENED BY THE PREVIOUS SCREENING OF A HEAVILY EDITED ADULT MOVIE, DALY HAD PLANNED TO RUN EROTIC SOFT-CORE CLASSICS THE STORY OF O (1975) AND EMMANUELLE (1974) BUT CAME UP AGAINST A WALL IN THE FORM OF LOCAL WOMEN'S GROUPS. THESE WERE NOT A HANDFUL OF FROWNING HOUSEWIVES, BUT AN ORGANIZED COLLECTIVE WHO THREATENED THAT THERE WOULD BE SERIOUS CONSEQUENCES IF THE SAVOY WENT AHEAD WITH THE SCHEDULED SCREENINGS. DALY RELENTED, AND BENT OVER BACKWARDS TO PLEASE THE GROUPS, BUT IN ORDER TO PROPERLY CLARIFY WHY ANYONE WOULD WANT TO KOWTOW TO SUCH DEMANDS IN A FREE COUNTRY, I'LL HAVE TO PROVIDE SOME IMPORTANT CONTEXT.

OUT-OF-TOWNERS AND NEWER RESIDENTS CAN'T POSSIBLY COMPREHEND THE ATMOSPHERE AND STIGMA AGAINST PORN IN THE CITY IN THE EARLY 1980S. EVEN TODAY THE BRANDING OF "NO FUN CITY" STICKS, BUT IT FOUND SOME

JOHN CARPENTER DOUBLE BILL

APRIL 23 - APRIL 26, 1981   7:30   9:15

Savoy
CINEMA
2321 MAIN AT 7TH

BOX OFFICE OPENS 7PM

Adults	3.00
Children 12 & under	
Handicapped	1.00
Golden Age	
Midnite shows	4.00
Stereovision 3D	5.00

OF ITS ORIGINATION IN THE DILIGENT WORK DONE BY PLENTIFUL AND POWERFUL LOBBYISTS AND COLLECTIVES THAT WERE DETERMINED TO STAMP THEIR NARROW WORLD VIEWS ON THE COMMUNITY AT LARGE. VANCOUVER WAS ALSO A HAVEN FOR EXTREME LEFTISTS AT THE TIME, GIVING BIRTH TO GREENPEACE AND MANY OTHER FAMOUS GRANOLA POLITICAL GROUPS, NOT TO MENTION THE SQUAMISH FIVE.

OH MAN, THE SQUAMISH FIVE. WHERE TO BEGIN? ANN HANSEN, BRENT TAYLOR, JULIET BELMAS, DOUG STEWART AND GERRY HANNAH (GUITARIST FOR THE CANADIAN PUNK BAND "SUBHUMANS") MADE UP THIS ANARCHIST COLLECTIVE, AND THEY UNLEASHED A CAMPAIGN OF BOMBINGS IN 1982 THAT INCLUDED A HYDRO POWER SUBSTATION ($5 MILLION IN DAMAGES), THE HEADQUARTERS OF CRUISE MISSILE GUIDANCE SYSTEM MANUFACTURER (10 INJURIES — INCLUDING TWO PASSING MOTORISTS WHO WERE BADLY HURT), AND THREE LOCATIONS OF A VANCOUVER PORN RETAIL CHAIN "RED HOT

16

The Montreal Gazette - 23 Nov 1982

Vancouver pornography shops firebombed

VANCOUVER (CP) — The manager of a videotape store that was firebombed by an anti-pornography group said yesterday he is scared but won't be forced out of business.

"I'm frightened all right, but there's no way I'm going to quit

claimed responsibility.

In letters to Vancouver news offices, the group said Red Hot Video "sells tapes that show wimmin (sic) and children being tortured, raped and humiliated. We are not the property of men to be used and abused."

VIDEO", WHO LOCAL ANTI-PORN GROUPS IGNORANTLY CLAIMED WERE OPENLY SELLING "SNUFF MOVIES".

"WE DECIDED TO EXAMINE WHAT WAS IN THESE VIDEOS" SAID LEE LAKEMAN, A CHAIRMAN FOR ONE OF SAID WOMEN'S GROUPS. "AND IT WAS AS BAD AS WE FEARED. CAUSE THEY WERE VIDEOS THAT HAD NAMES LIKE "VIRGIN SLUTS" AND "BLACK WHORES". YOU KNOW, OVERTLY RACIST, SEXIST, MISERABLE, VIOLENT, DEGRADING CRAP... WE NEEDED TO FIGURE OUT STRATEGIES OURSELVES TO CREATE DIRECT ACTIONS AND PUBLIC EDUCATION PRACTICES THAT WOULD INTERFERE WITH PORNOGRAPHY... AND COST THESE BUSINESSES SOME MONEY."

RED HOT STORES WERE PICKETED, WINDOWS WERE BROKEN, AND WALLS WERE SPRAY PAINTED. THEN THE SQUAMISH FIVE STEPPED IN AND FUCKED SHIT UP REAL GOOD. AMAZINGLY, NO ONE WAS KILLED IN THE BOMBINGS. "WE ARE LEFT NO VIABLE ALTERNATIVE BUT TO CHANGE THIS SITUATION OURSELVES THROUGH ILLEGAL MEANS", THE GROUP (CALLING THEMSELVES "THE WIMMIN'S FIRE BRIGADE") SAID IN A LETTER TO THE MEDIA. THE THREE RED HOT TORCHINGS MADE FOR GOOD COPY, AND THE STORY BLEW UP NATIONWIDE.

THE INSTIGATOR AND MAIN PERPETRATOR IN THE RED HOT VIDEO ATTACKS WAS JULIET BELMAS, A YOUNG AND ATTRACTIVE COMMERCIAL DRIVE PUNK WHO WAS AN EXTRA IN THE 1982 POST-PUNK MUSIC MOVIE 'LADIES AND GENTLEMEN, THE FABULOUS STAINS' (ONE OF THE BEST MOVIES EVER SHOT IN VANCOUVER), AND GREW UP NEXT DOOR TO PROSTITUTE SERIAL KILLER ROBERT PICKTON WHO AT ONE POINT STOLE HER DOG. SHE WAS IN THE BAND NO EXIT, AND PENNED "NOTHING NEW," WHICH SHE HUMBLY CALLS "ONE OF THE BEST PUNK ANTHEMS THAT CAME OUT OF THE VANCOUVER PUNK SCENE."

JULIET BELMAS

"THE GOAL WAS NOT TO ANGER PEOPLE BUT TO SCARE THEM", BELMAS SAID IN A 2012 INTERVIEW WITH EARTH FIRST JOURNAL. "PICKETING SEEMED LIKE A WASTE OF TIME; NOTHING EVER CHANGES. I TARGETED RED HOT VIDEO BECAUSE IT WAS DOING BUSINESS NEAR MY FAMILY HOME IN PORT COQUITLAM, AND I WAS VERY DISTURBED BY IT. ALL I WANTED TO DO WAS DESTROY IT — SMASH IT UP AND BURN IT DOWN! ACTUALLY, I WANTED TO BLOW IT TO SMITHEREENS WITH THE DYNAMITE WE STOLE, BUT THE OTHERS WOULDN'T GO ALONG WITH THAT. RED HOT VIDEO WAS THE ONLY ACTION I CHOSE AND THE ONLY ACTION I NEVER REGRETTED. NOT ONE BIT!"

"(I) BELIEVED THAT VIDEO PORN SHOULD BE PROHIBITED BECAUSE IT WAS DANGEROUSLY DESENSITIZING TO THE VIEWER AND CORRELATED WITH INCREASED LEVELS OF VIOLENCE AGAINST WOMEN AND CHILDREN... I WOULD REMAIN SUBJUGATED FOR THE REST OF MY LIFE IF I REMAINED COMPLACENT AND LET FUCKED UP PEOPLE TELL ME WHAT TO DO, AND ON AND ON IT WOULD GO. I WANTED TO SEIZE THE TIME AND EXPRESS MY FEMININITY IN A WAY THAT SMASHED OTHER PEOPLE'S IDEAS OF HOW I SHOULD BEHAVE."

DECLARING ADULT FILMS "SEXUAL TERRORISM", THE B.C. FEDERATION OF WOMEN (AN UMBRELLA ORGANIZATION OF 36 WOMEN'S LIBERATION GROUPS STATIONED AT 77 EAST 20TH AVENUE) CONSISTENTLY BULLIED THIRTEEN SMALL BUSINESS OWNERS IN THE COMMUNITY WITH IMPUNITY AND FORCED SEVERAL STORES OUT OF BUSINESS WITH THEIR PROLONGED PICKETING AND PROPERTY DAMAGE. TO THE BEST OF MY KNOWLEDGE, THEY WERE NEVER CRITICIZED FOR THESE ACTIONS BY THE MEDIA. "WE'RE GOING TO MAKE IT SO UNCOMFORTABLE FOR THEM THAT THEY'LL MOVE AWAY",

SAID NORMA JEAN MCLAREN, A KEY REPRESENTATIVE OF THE GROUP WHO WAS INTERVIEWED BY THE OTTAWA CITIZEN ON DEC. 16TH, 1982.

IN THE HOPES OF CALLING A TRUCE ON THE ASSAULT ON THEIR BUSINESS, ONE SHOP WAS EVEN BROWBEAT INTO SURRENDERING THEIR ENTIRE STOCK OF XXX VHS TAPES TO THE GROUP, WHO TOLD THE MEDIA THEY PLANNED TO BURN THEM IN A PUBLIC BONFIRE. LIKE SO MANY CENSORSHIP-BASED ASSOCIATIONS, HOWEVER, THEY INSTEAD ENDED UP WATCHING THEM OVER AND OVER AGAIN, YOU KNOW, TO REALLY GET AS DEEPLY FAMILIAR AS THEY COULD WITH THAT FILTHY SEX AND PERVERSION. "WE KEPT THOSE FOR YEARS -- TO HAVE A RECORD OF HOW HIDEOUS THEY WERE", LAKEMAN SAID IN A 2012 INTERVIEW.

"I'M FRIGHTENED ALL RIGHT," RED HOT VIDEO OWNER TED EMERY TOLD THE MONTREAL GAZETTE ON NOVEMBER 23RD. "BUT THERE'S NO WAY I'M GOING TO QUIT BECAUSE OF THE ACTIONS OF SOME RADICAL GROUP".

REACTIONARIES PROMOTING CENSORSHIP, SCAPEGOATING, AND ENFORCED UNIFORMITY OF THOUGHT? MANY OF THESE RADICAL GROUPS VANCOUVER FOSTERED IN THE 1980S WOULD BE BETTER DESCRIBED AS FASCISTS. FASCIST IDEOLOGY IS SPECIFIC IN THAT IT ASSERTS TO ITS MEMBERS THAT THEY ARE BOTH OPPRESSED AND SUPERIOR. THESE GROUPS, IN THEIR ATTEMPTS TO PROTECT AND EMPOWER, REDUCED WOMEN TO NOTHING BUT HELPLESS, CRINGING MARTYRS TO MALE COERCION. PROFOUNDLY INSULTING WOMEN CONTINGENT TO THE WORST OF THE PATRIARCHAL IDEOLOGIES THEY RALLIED AGAINST, THESE ABSOLUTISTS WERE THEIR OWN WORST ENEMIES.

ONE OF THEIR MAIN ARGUMENTS WAS THAT PORNOGRAPHY TRIVIALIZES RAPE, WHEN THE TRUE TRIVIALIZATION OF A HORRENDOUS CRIME IS TO NOT ADDRESS IT DIRECTLY, SUPPOSING INSTEAD THAT IMAGES DETERMINE AND CAUSE THE PROBLEMS IN OUR CULTURE, RATHER THAN SIMPLY PORTRAYING OR REFLECTING THEM. AND WHILE SO MANY WOULD ARGUE IN HINDSIGHT THAT THEY WERE NEVER AGAINST SEX, ONLY SEXISM, IT'S WORTH NOTING THAT ONLY HUSTLER AND ITS ILK WERE EVER THE OUTSPOKEN TARGET -- NEVER RESOLUTELY SEXIST NON-PORNOGRAPHIC NEWSSTAND FARE SUCH AS COSMOPOLITAN.

USING PORNOGRAPHY AS A SCAPEGOAT FOR THE CAUSE OF SEXUALIZED VIOLENCE HAD BEEN EXECUTED QUITE SUCCESSFULLY IN CANADA ONLY A FEW YEARS EARLIER IN TORONTO, WHICH SURELY GAVE ANTI-PORN GROUPS CONFIDENCE THAT THEY COULD ENTIRELY STAMP OUT PORNOGRAPHY IN CANADA WITH A PROPERLY PLACED BLOW. THAT WAS WHEN A NEON AND GRIME COATED STREET THAT USED TO BE CALLED "THE SIN STRIP OF NORTH AMERICA", YONGE STREET IN TORONTO, WAS NEARLY TOTALLY WHITEWASHED SIMPLY AS A REACTION TO THE RAPE AND MURDER OF A 12-YEAR-OLD PORTUGUESE SHOESHINE BOY NAMED EMANUELE JACQUES.

ON JULY 28, 1977, JACQUES WAS LURED AWAY FROM HIS CURBSIDE SHINE BOX AND INTO A FLOPHOUSE ABOVE THE CHARLIE'S ANGELS MASSAGE PARLOUR AT 245 YONGE STREET, WHERE HE WAS REPEATEDLY SODOMIZED AND TORTURED FOR TWELVE HOURS BEFORE BEING DROWNED IN A KITCHEN SINK. HIS BODY WAS THEN WRAPPED IN A GREEN GARBAGE BAG AND DISCARDED ON THE ROOF OF THE BUILDING BY THE THREE THUGS WHO ATTACKED HIM, VILE MONSTERS WHO TURNED OUT TO BE EMPLOYED AS BOUNCERS AND DOORMEN AT THE LURID DOWNSTAIRS ESTABLISHMENT.

A MEDIA FRENZY WHIPPED UP PEOPLE INTO

AN AD THAT THE OWNERS OF RED HOT RAN IN NEWSPAPERS ACROSS THE COUNTRY.

A LEAFLET HANDED OUT IN EARLY 1983

PROTESTS AND DEMONSTRATIONS IN THE STREETS, WHERE THE MASSES FOUND PORN, THE SEX TRADE, AND HOMOSEXUALITY TO BE THE MOST SENSATIONAL, AND THEREFORE CLEAR ROOT CAUSES OF THE CRIME. IF A CHILD HAD BEEN RAPED AND MURDERED BY THREE WINOS ABOVE A LIQUOR STORE, SOCIETY WOULD NEVER DREAM OF PUSHING TO BAN THE SALE OF ALCOHOL, BUT WITHIN A PERIOD OF ONLY A SINGLE MONTH, ALMOST ALL THE YONGE STREET PORN SHOPS, MASSAGE PARLOURS, AND SEX-TOY BOUTIGUES WERE RAIDED AND CLOSED. WHAT HAD BEEN OVER 80 PROFITABLE AND TOTALLY LEGAL BUSINESSES HAD BECOME TEN, AND THE SHOPS THAT WERE LEFT HAD THEIR RENTS JACKED UP, AND WERE SOON PUSHED OUT. OTHER MAJOR CANADIAN CITIES FOLLOWED TORONTO'S LEAD. WINNIPEG, CALGARY, EDMONTON, AND VANCOUVER ALL SAW MULTIPLE POLICE CRACKDOWNS AND CLOSURES ON PORN STORES IN THE WAKE OF THE NATIONAL PUBLIC OUTCRY OVER THE JACQUES MURDER.

"WHEN SOMETHING WORRIES CANADIANS", WROTE JUNE CALLWOOD IN HER 1985 ESSAY ENTITLED FEMINIST DEBATES AND CIVIL LIBERTIES, "THE SOLUTION THEY EMBRACE IS HAVING THE

18

GOVERNMENT MOVE IN TO SUPPRESS IT. BECAUSE OF THIS LEGACY, CANADA HAS NEVER BEEN A FERTILE GROUND FOR CIVIL LIBERTIES."

AN INFAMOUS 1982 ESSAY ("WHOSE BODY? WHOSE SELF?") BY ACCLAIMED AWARD-WINNING CANADIAN AUTHOR MYRNA KOSTASH SUMS UP THE HARDLINE STANCE ON PORN BY MOST CANADIAN FEMINISTS OF THE EARLY 1980s. "THE 'RIGHT' TO PRODUCE AND CONSUME PORNOGRAPHY MUST BE CURTAILED IF OUR WOMEN'S RIGHT TO FREEDOM FROM SLANDER AND INJURY IS TO BE RESPECTED", WROTE KOSTASH. "PORNOGRAPHY IS ABOUT WOMEN BEING AFRAID. WHILE THERE IS PORNOGRAPHY, WE ARE NOT SAFE. IT IS NOT A QUESTION OF LEARNING TO 'LIVE WITH IT'; WE ARE DYING WITH IT."

CANADIAN ANTI-SMUT ICON, SUSAN G. COLE

"THE VIOLENCE IS REAL IN PORNOGRAPHY", WROTE CANADIAN AUTHOR SUSAN G. COLE IN A PIECE ENTITLED 'PORNOGRAPHY AND THE SEX CRISIS.' "THE PERVASIVENESS OF PORNOGRAPHY TENDS TO MAKE WOMEN INVISIBLE AS HUMAN BEINGS, VISIBLE ONLY AS THINGS OR OBJECTS. THE WOMEN ARE CONSIDERED NOT HUMAN ENOUGH TO WORRY ABOUT... FOR ALTHOUGH VIOLENCE IS CLEARLY THERE ON THE SCREEN OR IN THE PICTURE, VIEWERS HAVE DIFFICULTY SEEING IT AS VIOLENCE. PORNOGRAPHY DISTORTS THEIR PERCEPTIONS."

"A GOOD WAY TO UNDERSTAND HOW PORNOGRAPHY IS CONSTRUCTED, IS TO EXAMINE CHILD PORNOGRAPHY", COLE EDUCATES US VIA HER SEXIST THEORY THAT FINDS ADULT WOMEN AND CHILDREN INTERCHANGEABLE. "WHEN AN ADULT HAS SEX WITH A CHILD, HE IS EXERCISING SEXUAL POWER OVER SOMEONE WHO IS POWERLESS, THEN HE TAKES HER PICTURE, AND A RECORD OF SEXUAL ABUSE IS SHARED, SO AS TO VALIDATE THE SEXUAL ABUSE THAT HAS OCCURRED."

IT IS THIS OVERWROUGHT ALARMIST RHETORIC THAT LED TO A DEMONSTRATION BY A GROUP CALLED "WOMEN AGAINST VIOLENCE AGAINST WOMEN" TO STORM THE CINEMA 2000 ON YONGE STREET IN TORONTO, WHICH WAS PLAYING A FEATURE FILM CALLED SNUFF. INFORMED BY GROUP LEADERS — AUTHOR SUSAN G. COLE AMONG THEM - THAT THE MOVIE FEATURED THE ACTUAL KILLING OF A WOMAN, TWENTY OF THEM BOLTED THROUGH THE FRONT DOORS, RUSHED THE PROJECTOR BOOTH, SMASHED THE PROJECTOR, AND STAGED A SIT-IN THAT DIDN'T END UNTIL 5 OF THEIR MEMBERS WERE ARRESTED.

COLE WOULD, YEARS LATER, CALL THE INCIDENT "A LAUNCHING POINT FOR A NEW FEMINIST AWARENESS IN CANADA ABOUT WHAT WAS HAPPENING IN THE PORNOGRAPHY INDUSTRY". BOLD AND SELF-CONGRATULATORY WORDS, BUT ALSO WORDS SEEPED IN IGNORANCE. COLE HAD NOT EVEN SEEN THE MOVIE SHE AND HER FRIENDS PROTESTED, AND DIDN'T KNOW THAT SNUFF WAS NOT A PORN MOVIE AT ALL, BUT AN UNINTENTIONALLY HILARIOUS HORROR MOVIE.

THE CINEMA 2000 IN TORONTO --CIRCA 1974

WITH SAID RADICALS HARASSING LAW-ABIDING CITIZENS AND THEN TURNING TO FOCUS THEIR GAZE UPON THE LITTLE SAVOY THEATER ON MAIN STREET, IT'S NO WONDER OWNER SEAN DALY DID WHAT HE COULD TO SAVE HIS BUSINESS. HE GAVE THE MOB EXACTLY WHAT THEY DEMANDED IN PLACE OF A SHOWING OF THE STORY OF O: A SCREENING OF THE NFB ANTI-PORN PROPAGANDA FILM NOT A LOVE STORY (1981) -- THE MOST POPULAR AND COMMERCIALLY SUCCESSFUL THEATRICAL FILM THE NATIONAL FILM BOARD EVER MADE.

VANCOUVER ANTI-PORN FEMINIST BONNIE SHERR KLEIN DIRECTED THIS ONE-SIDED POLEMIC, AND USED IT TO SHOWCASE INDIVIDUALS SUCH AS ANDREA DWORKIN -- A WOMAN WHO EQUATED SEXUAL IMAGERY WITH CULTURAL WARFARE. THE MOVIE STARRED LOVELY BURLESQUE DANCER LINDALEE TRACEY, AS WE BORE WITNESS TO HER UNUSUAL TRANSFORMATION. LINDA STARTS OUT DEPICTED IN THE DOCUMENTARY AS ENTHUSIASTIC ABOUT HER JOB, AND THEN -- THROUGH THE USE OF CREATIVE EDITING (TO MAKE IT APPEAR AS IF SHE WAS SHOWN THE ERROR OF STRIPPING FOR A LIVING) IS TRANSFORMED INTO A SOBBING "VICTIM". TRACEY WOULD IN 1997 WRITE A BOOK REVEALING THAT SHE WAS "EXPLOITED" BY THE FILMMAKERS. SHE WAS NEVER AGAINST ALL FORMS OF SEX-WORK THE WAY THE MOVIE LEADS THE VIEWER TO BELIEVE SHE IS WHEN THE CREDITS ROLL.

DALY LIKELY DIDN'T WANT TO FUCK AROUND AND RISK THE DESTRUCTION OF HIS PROPERTY, WHICH INCLUDED AN EXPENSIVE STEREOVISION PROJECTOR AND SILVER SCREEN HE'D BROUGHT IN TO BECOME, WHAT HE CALLED, "VANCOUVER'S ONLY ALL ENCOMPASSING 3-D THEATRE". DALY DID VERY WELL WITH HITCHCOCK'S 1954 CLASSIC DIAL M FOR MURDER (WHICH HAD BEEN SHOT WITH THE PROCESS DURING THE SHORT-LIVED 3D TREND OF THE 1950S, AND THEN RELEASED WITHOUT THE EFFECTS WHEN THE FAD FADED AWAY), THE 1981 SPAGHETTI WESTERN COMIN AT YA!, AND 1982'S PARASITE, STARRING A YOUNG DEMI MOORE. EVEN PARAMOUNT PICTURES TOOK NOTICE OF HIS REPORTED SUCCESS WITH THEIR 1953 PICTURE, HOUSE OF

WAX, AND THEN ISSUED A 3D RE-RELEASE FOR THE REST OF CANADA.

ANOTHER ONE OF THE MANY 3D FILMS THAT PLAYED TO A FULL HOUSE AT THE SAVOY WAS THE INCREDIBLE BOBBY MING KUNG-FU EPIC, DYNASTY. MOSTLY FORGOTTEN TODAY BECAUSE IT NEVER GOT A DVD RELEASE, DYNASTY (AKA SUPER DRAGON), FEATURES INCREDIBLE FLYING GUILLOTINE ACTION, BIG NINJA THROWING STARS, A VILLAIN WHO HAS FREDDY KRUEGER-LIKE CLAWS, A PAPER UMBRELLA THAT CAN DEFLECT ANY MANNER OF METAL BLADE, A GUY THAT CONTINUES TO FIGHT EVEN AFTER HIS HANDS GET CUT OFF, AND ENOUGH BEHEADINGS TO CHOKE A GOAT. THE ENDING REALLY POPS TOO, BECAUSE THE BIG BOSS TAKES OFF HIS CHAIN-MAIL OVERCOAT, TRANSFORMS IT INTO A GIANT SHARPENED CROSS, AND STARTS WHIPPING IT AROUND LIKE A BOOMERANG! NOT A SINGLE MINUTE GOES BY IN

DYNASTY WHERE SOMETHING ISN'T BEING SHOVED IN THE AUDIENCE'S FACE, AND THAT INCLUDES THE LIMBS OF ITS STAR, BOBBY MING, AKA TAN "FLASHLEGS" TAO-LIANG.

THE LAST FILM THE SAVOY WOULD SHOW IN APRIL OF 1984, WOULD BE THE SAME MOVIE IT BEGAN WITH, ALFRED HITCHCOCK'S PSYCHO. IT WAS THEN CONVERTED TO AN "EROTIC" THEATRE IN A BID TO BE ABLE TO PAY THE RENT EASIER. WEARY OF THE ANTI-PORN MOVEMENT DALY WAS CAREFUL TO POINT OUT TO THE LOCAL MEDIA THAT ALL OF HIS PRINTS HAD ALL THE EJACULATION AND PENETRATION SCENES REMOVED, AND WERE THEREFORE EROTICA, AND NOT PORN. "WOMEN'S GROUPS DO NOT OBJECT TO EROTICA", HE SAID TO A GEORGIA STRAIGHT REPORTER, WITH A HOPEFUL TONE IN HIS VOICE.

"BOTH MY SISTER GLORIA AND I COULDN'T FIGURE OUT HIS THINKING", FORMER EMPLOYEE IAN FREEMAN SAID OF THE CHANGE OVER TO SMUT. "I GUESS HE FIGURED THAT IF EVERYONE IS WATCHING REGULAR FILMS AT HOME ON VIDEO, THEN HE COULD MAKE MONEY SHOWING PORNO FILMS. BUT TO BOTH OF US, IT SEEMED LIKE THOSE WOULD BE THE FIRST TYPE OF FILMS THAT PEOPLE WOULD WATCH AT HOME ON VIDEO. I MEAN C'MON — ARE YOU GOING TO WATCH THIS ADULT MOVIE AT HOME WHERE NO ONE WILL KNOW, OR ARE YOU GOING TO GO LINE UP WITH EVERYONE AT THE SAVOY? IT DIDN'T MAKE ANY SENSE."

IT ALSO DIDN'T MAKE ANY SENSE TO THE WOMEN THAT PICKETED OUTSIDE THE SAVOY AFTER THE ANNOUNCEMENT WAS MADE. "I WAS DOWNTOWN NURSING A HANGOVER AT THE EXCELLENT LITTLE JAPANESE BREAKFAST PLACE THAT USED TO BE ON THURLOW — THEY SERVED HUGE GLASSES OF ICED TOMATO JUICE — WHEN I RAN INTO A FRIEND WHO TOLD ME ABOUT THE PROTEST AT THE SAVOY", VANCOUVER RESIDENT JULIET O'KEEFE SAID TO ME IN NOVEMBER 2013. "SHE WAS ANGRY, AND WAS RALLYING THE TROOPS. I STOPPED BY THE THEATRE LATER THAT AFTERNOON TO FIND A GROUP OF WOMEN HOLDING SIGNS AND, IN MY MEMORY, CHANTING. THERE WERE PERHAPS 15 OR 20 PROTESTORS; IT WASN'T LARGE, BUT IT WAS SERIOUS. IT MADE THE EVENING NEWS, ALBEIT BRIEFLY."

"I DIDN'T STAY TOO LONG, AS TO BE COMPLETELY HONEST, I WAS EASILY BORED IN THOSE DAYS. I WAS ANGRY ABOUT LOSING THE SAVOY, BUT WASN'T OPTIMISTIC THAT THE PROTEST WOULD CHANGE ANYTHING. THE OTHER WOMEN THERE WERE PERHAPS LESS CYNICAL THAN I."

OBVIOUSLY THE PROTESTERS DIDN'T GIVE A DAMN IF DALY LABELED HIS NEW THEATRICAL SCHEDULE AS EROTICA OR PORN –– EITHER WAY IT WAS BY THEIR ESTIMATION THE EXPLOITATION OF VICTIMIZED WOMEN AND THE LOSS OF WHAT O'KEEFE CALLED "A GATHERING PLACE" FOR HERSELF AND HER FRIENDS. THE NEW SCREENINGS WOULD BE WAY TOO DIRTY FOR THEM, AND NOT NEARLY DIRTY ENOUGH FOR THE GENERAL PUBLIC. WHO WANTS TO SEE CENSORED SMUT WITHOUT ANY ACTUAL FUCKING IN IT? THE VENUE CLOSED FOUR SHORT MONTHS LATER ON JULY 12TH OF 1984.

DALY RECALLED IN A NEWSPAPER ARTICLE PUBLISHED IN AUGUST OF THAT YEAR, THAT THE WRITING-ON-THE-WALL REALIZATION THAT HE'D HAVE TO SHUT HIS BUSINESS DOWN HIT HIM ONE NIGHT IN JANUARY 1983 WHEN, IRONICALLY, THE SAVOY WAS DOING FANTASTIC BUSINESS DURING A DOUBLE BILL OF THE ROAD WARRIOR (1981) AND BLADE RUNNER (1982).

"SOMEONE TOLD ME, 'YOU KNOW, THESE ARE THE ONLY FILMS ON YOUR PROGRAM THAT AREN'T OUT ON VIDEO'," DALY CONFIDED TO REPORTER MARKE ANDREWS.

Women make headway in anti-porn campaign

By Ben Tierney
Southam News

VANCOUVER — The headlines that resulted from last month's fire-bombing of video tape stores here have vanished, but British Columbia's porn war goes on.

And the women are winning.

In the three weeks since an underground organization calling itself the Wimmin's Fire Brigade bombed

On Nov. 26, four days after the firebombing, they staged a rally in Vancouver's downtown Robson Square in which they denounced the sales of hard-porn tapes as "sexual terrorism."

Last weekend they took to picketing Red Hot Video stores, chanting "Pornography is the theory, rape is the practice."

It slowed Saturday's normally

continue his general investigation into the overall distribution and sale of tapes in the province.

Provincial Attorney General Allan Williams, meanwhile, has not budged from his position that action against the most offensive of the tapes — in the form of legislation to create a screening and censoring board — will be taken when the provincial legislature resumes sit-

nouncing "the Canadian legal system" for its "unwillingness to protect women and children from pornography."

"Women," said the press release, "will no longer be silent while the state's inaction condones the abuse of women's bodies for profit."

The women are also sticking to their vow that, by one means or another, they'll shut down all Red Hot

IT WAS A GOOD POINT. THE VIDEOSTORE I WORK AT EVEN TODAY, VIDEOMATICA, HAD OPENED UP IN THE SPRING OF 1983 AND IT AND A HANDFUL OF OTHER VANCOUVER VIDEO STORES WERE OFFERING BLADE RUNNER, THE ROAD WARRIOR, AND ALL THE REST OF THE STUFF THE SAVOY WAS SCREENING, BUT FOR LOWER PRICES, AND VIEWABLE IN THE COMFORT AND CONVENIENCE OF YOUR OWN HOME. THE <u>VIDEO AGE</u> HAD ARRIVED.

AS MENTIONED AT THE BEGINNING OF THIS PIECE, THE SAVOY EVENTUALLY BECAME THE FOX ON AUGUST 17TH, 1984. THE FOX SHOWED ITS OWN COLLECTION OF A HUNDRED OR SO 35MM XXX PRINTS FOR DECADES, AND IS NOTEWORTHY FROM A HISTORICAL POINT OF VIEW, SINCE IT WAS -- UNTIL JULY 2003 -- THE LAST PORN THEATER IN NORTH AMERICA STILL SHOWING FILM PRINTS IN REGULAR ROTATION. FOR THE LAST 10 YEARS HOWEVER, IT HAS SIMPLY BEEN SCREENING GENERIC MODERN DVD-PROJECTED XXX, AND IN OCTOBER 2013 IT ENDED ITS TIME AS A CINEMA. UNDER NEW OWNERSHIP IT BECAME A LIVE MUSIC AND BURLESQUE VENUE. THE FOX NAME WAS RETAINED.

THE FOX'S COLLECTION OF OVER A HUNDRED ADULT PRINTS WERE UNCEREMONIOUSLY (AND ILLEGALLY) DUMPED IN GARBAGE CANS IN THE ALLEYWAYS BEHIND MAIN AND CAMBIE OVER A SERIES OF NIGHTS IN THE SUMMER OF 2013 BY AN IGNORANT FUCKFACE THAT SHALL GO UNNAMED. A HANDFUL OF THE PRINTS WERE PULLED FROM THE TRASH AND SOLD FOR HUNDREDS OF DOLLARS, BUT MANY OF THE RARE 35MM CANISTERS WERE HAULED AWAY BY THE TRASHMAN, NEVER TO BE SEEN AGAIN.

THE SQUAMISH FIVE WERE CAPTURED BY CANADIAN POLICE IN 1983. THEY PLED GUILTY, AND WERE GIVEN SENTENCES RANGING FROM 6 YEARS TO LIFE IMPRISONMENT. ALL FIVE, HOWEVER, WERE FREE WITHIN A DECADE, AND EVEN TODAY ARE CELEBRATED AS ICONS IN THE LOCAL POST-PUNK MUSIC COMMUNITY.

THE PLENTIFUL FEMINIST GROUPS IN VANCOUVER ALTERED AS THE VICTIMIZED-YET-MILITANT SECOND WAVE OF FEMINISM GAVE WAY TO THE PROGRESSIVE, PRO-SEX THIRD WAVE. AFTER THE GAY AND LESBIAN VANCOUVER BOOK STORE, LITTLE SISTERS, WAS RAIDED AND HARASSED TIME AND TIME AGAIN BY HOMOPHOBIC CANADIAN GOVERNMENT AGENCIES, IT BECAME ABUNDANTLY CLEAR THAT THERE WAS NOTHING EVEN CLOSE TO A UNANIMOUS OPINION ABOUT PORN WITHIN THE ENCLAVE OF FEMINISM. THE "PROTECTION" FROM GRAPHIC IMAGERY WOMEN HAD DEMANDED WAS INSTANTLY USED AS A WEAPON AGAINST THEM. THE VERY FIRST SEIZURE OF BANNED MATERIAL UNDER THE NEW CATHARINE MACKINNON SUGGESTED DEFINITION OF OBSCENITY IN CANADA (TO ONE BASED ON "HARM" TO WOMEN) WAS THE LESBIAN SEX ZINE "BAD ATTITUDE", WHICH WAS TAKEN FROM GLAD DAY, A GAY AND LESBIAN BOOK STORE IN TORONTO.

"(IS IT) DESIRABLE IN ANY SHAPE OR FORM TO HAVE STATES AND GOVERNMENTS IN ANY WAY INTERVENE?" ASKED AUTHOR CAROLE VANCE. "IF FEMINISTS THEMSELVES CAN'T AGREE ABOUT THIS, IT'S A LITTLE FOOLISH TO BE HANDING THIS (POWER) OVER TO A STATE, WHICH IS USUALLY NOT FEMINIST-CONTROLLED."

IT BECAME MORE PREVALENT AMONGST THIRD WAVE FEMINISTS TO SEE THE PARALLELS BETWEEN PORN AND FEMINISM. INSTEAD OF INSISTING THAT IMAGES OF SEX ARE SYNONYMOUS WITH ABUSE AND THEN TRYING TO BAN THE TYPES OF IMAGERY THEY DIDN'T LIKE, THEY MADE AND CELEBRATED THE KINDS THEY DID PREFER. INSTEAD OF THRASHING BLINDLY UNDER A BLANKET OF MORALISTIC VICTIMHOOD, THEY REPOSSESSED THEIR SEXUALITY, BECOMING ASSERTIVE IN SEEKING SOMETHING FOR THEMSELVES IN A MALE-DOMINATED SEX CULTURE.

RED HOT VIDEO FLOURISHED FOR DECADES BUT WAS UNCEREMONIOUSLY KILLED OFF IN THE MID 2000S — DUE NOT TO PROTESTS AND BOMBS, BUT TO THE PROLIFERATION OF FREE XXX ON THE INTERNET. COINCIDENTALLY, THIS WAS THE FIRST METHOD OF PORN CONSUMPTION IDEAL FOR WOMEN, ALLOWING THEM TO BYPASS AWKWARD AND EMBARRASSING PUBLIC VISITS TO SHOPS LIKE RED HOT AND THEATERS LIKE THE FOX TO SATISFY THEIR FILTH-TOOTH.

☆ —ROBIN BOUGIE NOV. 2013.

APRIL 20 APRIL 27 1984 • GEORGIA STRAIGHT

SAVOY CINEMA FALLS PREY TO VIDEO BOOM

The Savoy Theatre has become the second Vancouver independent film house to fall victim to the boom in Pay-TV and video cassettes.

However, unlike the Lux Theatre, which closed its doors several months ago, the Savoy will just be changing its policy. Beginning with today's (Friday) noon show-

ing of *Inside Annie Sprinkle*, the theatre will be showing erotic films in place of the moveover and second run pictures with which it has been identified since its

Dear Robin...
I'm curious: Let's say a major Hollywood studio approached you with major Hollywood studio $$$ and said *Through puffs of cigar smoke* "Robin, we want you to make any picture you want, here's a shit ton of money!", what would you make? It could be anything. When I read Cinema Sewer I often think "Seriously what picture would he make?!". I'm curious what would come outta the Bougie brain.
-- Zak Pearson (via facebook)

I'M NOT SURE EXACTLY WHAT THE PLOT WOULD BE BUT I CAN TELL YOU THIS: IT WOULD STAR PUPPETS, AND IT WOULD BE FOR ADULTS. NOT MARIONETTES LIKE TEAM AMERICA BUT MUPPET-STYLE PUPPETS. IT WOULDN'T BE A COMEDY LIKE MEET THE FEEBLES, BUT IT WOULD HAVE SEX SCENES, AND WEIRDNESS, AND ACTION SCENES WITH GORE, AND COOL ANIMATRONIC GADGETS AND REMOTE CONTROL VEHICLES. IT WOULD BE SHOT IN EXOTIC LOCATIONS WITH AN INCREDIBLE SCORE, AND BE TOTALLY FUCKING AMAZING. CAN YOU IMAGINE THAT KIND OF THING WITH A DECENT BUDGET BEHIND IT? I THINK THERE IS A LOT OF ROOM -- THERE ARE A LOT OF THINGS THAT HAVE NOT BEEN DONE WITH PUPPETS FOR AN ADULT AUDIENCE.

If you find where this wonderful completely crazy version of Hollywood exists, please let me know.
— Troy Nixey

I'LL KEEP MY EYES PEELED, TROY! I'M SURE IT'S JUST OVER THIS HILL.

CINEMA SEWER'S 50 FAVE FILMS MADE BY WOMEN

YOU CAN READ ABOUT HOW GREAT JANE CAMPION, NORA EPHRON, CLAIR DENIS, MIRA NAIR, AND OTHER RESPECTED DIRECTORS OF PAINFULLY DRY AND TEDIOUS DRAMAS ARE IN RESPECTABLE FILM JOURNALS. HERE AT CINEMA SEWER WE INSTEAD APPRECIATE THE SALACIOUS, THE ACTION-PACKED, THE ZANY, THE STRANGE, THE VIOLENT, THE SEXY, THE EXPLOITIVE, AND THE AWESOME. HERE IS YOUR GUIDE AND CHECKLIST TO THE MOST ENTERTAINING GENRE FILMS IN HISTORY (AS OF 2013) TO BE HELMED BY WOMB-OWNERS! PLEASE CHECK THESE 50 MOVIES OUT, AND DON'T PAY A LICK OF ATTENTION WHEN THE IGNORANT MORONS SAY THAT WOMEN CAN'T SUPPLY THE CINEMATIC GENRE FILM RADNESS. HERE'S TO THE LADIES!! WOOOOOOO !!

1. **Near Dark** (1987. Dir: Kathryn Bigelow)
2. **Ravenous** (1999. Dir: Antonia Bird)
3. **Streetwalkin'** (1985. Dir: Joan Freeman)
4. **Hookers on Davie** (1984. Janis Cole and Holly Dale)
5. **Vanishing Waves** (2012. Dir: Kristina Buozyte)
6. **Deep Inside Annie Sprinkle** (1981. Dir: Annie Sprinkle and Joe Sarno)
7. **Not a Love Story** (1981. Dir: Bonnie Sherr Klein)
8. **You Can't Stop the Music** (1980. Dir: Nancy Walker)
9. **I'm from Hollywood** (1989. Dir: Lynne Margulies and Joe Orr)
10. **The Decline of Western Civilization** (1981. Dir: Penelope Spheeris)
11. **Lost in Translation** (2003. Dir: Sofia Coppola)
12. **Blue Steel** (1990. Dir: Kathryn Bigelow)
13. **The Central Park Five** (2012. Dir: Sarah Burns and Ken Burns)
14. **Exhausted** (1981. Dir: Julia St. Vincent)
15. **American Psycho** (2000. Dir: Mary Harron)
16. **Viva** (2007. Dir: Anna Biller)
17. **Wendy and Lucy** (2008. Dir: Kelly Reichardt)
18. **Wanda** (1970. Dir: Barbara Loden)
19. **The Decline of Western Civilization Part II** (1988. Dir: Penelope Spheeris)
20. **Terminal Island** (1973. Dir: Stephanie Rothman)
21. **Iron Angels 2** (1988. Dir: Raymond Leung)
22. **The Hitch-Hiker** (1953. Dir: Ida Lupino)
23. **Trouble the Water** (2008. Dir: Tia Lessin and Carl Deal)
24. **The Tiffany Minx** (1981. Dir: Roberta Findlay)
25. **Fat Girl** (2001. Dir: Catherine Breillat)
26. **Streets** (1990. Dir: Katt Shea)
27. **Iron Angels 3** (1989. Dir: Teresa Woo and Stanley Tong)
28. **Deliver Us from Evil** (2006. Dir: Amy Berg)
29. **Point Break** (1991. Dir: Kathryn Bigelow)
30. **A Woman's Torment** (1977. Dir: Roberta Findlay)
31. **Mystique** (1979. Dir: Roberta Findlay)
32. **Water Lilies** (2007. Dir: Céline Sciamma)
33. **Fast Times at Ridgemont High** (1982. Dir: Amy Heckerling)
34. **Harlan County U.S.A.** (1976. Dir: Barbara Kopple)
35. **Suburbia** (1983. Dir: Penelope Spheeris)
36. **F** (1980. Dir: Svetlana)
37. **Swept Away** (1974. Dir: Lina Wertmuller)
38. **Punisher: War Zone** (2008. Dir: Lexi Alexander)
39. **The Boys Next Door** (1985. Dir: Penelope Spheeris)
40. **Suspicious River** (2000. Dir: Lynne Stopkewich)
41. **The Night Porter** (1974. Dir: Liliana Cavani)
42. **Big** (1988. Dir: Penny Marshall)
43. **The Playgirl** (1982. Dir: Roberta Findlay)
44. **The Runaways** (2010. Dir: Floria Sigismondi)
45. **Strange Days** (1995. Dir: Kathryn Bigelow)
46. **The Cool World** (1963. Dir: Shirley Clarke)
47. **The Student Nurses** (1970. Dir: Stephanie Rothman)
48. **Jesus Camp** (2006. Dir: Heidi Ewing and Rachel Grady)
49. **Pet Sematary** (1989. Dir: Mary Lambert)
50. **Hollywood Vice Squad** (1986. Dir: Penelope Spheeris)

NOTE: AUTHOR, JOURNALIST AND NPR HOST PETER SAGAL (WHO WAS HIRED TO GHOSTWRITE AN UNPUBLISHED AUTOBIOGRAPHY) CLAIMS THE FOCUS OF THE BOOK, GAIL PALMER, DID NOT ACTUALLY DIRECT THE MOVIES IN HER FILMOGRAPHY, AND WAS A FRONT FOR THE PRODUCTION COMPANY WHO WOULD OFTEN HIRE BOB CHINN TO DIRECT HER RELEASES. FOR THAT REASON, I'VE LEFT OUT 3 OF HER MOVIES, WHICH WOULD HAVE MADE THE LIST OTHERWISE. ALSO, MESSIAH OF EVIL (1973) WOULD HAVE MADE MY TOP 10, BUT DESPITE GLORIA KATZ BEING LISTED AS A CO-DIRECTOR BY MOST REVIEWERS, IT SEEMS SHE WAS ACTUALLY A SCREENWRITER FOR THE FILM AND HER HUSBAND DID THE DIRECTING CHORES.

THE 10 MOST FUCKABLE MOMS IN TV SITCOM HISTORY

AH LOVES THEM MILFS!

ARTICLE BY ROBIN BOUGIE. 2015

AN INFORMAL SOCIAL MEDIA POLL OF CINEMA SEWER READERS IN 2014 RETRIEVED SOME INTERESTING RESULTS -- SPECIFICALLY WHEN THE C.S. ARMY WAS ASKED ABOUT SEXY SITCOM MOMS. I LIKED WHAT THE PEOPLE CAME UP WITH SO MUCH, I DECIDED TO EXPAND UPON THE EXCELLENT SUGGESTIONS AND ALSO WRITE UP SOME STUFF ABOUT THE PICKS. OK-- LET'S DO THIS, THEN! KA-POW!

10. Patricia Richardson as "Jill Taylor" on Home Improvement (1991 to 1999)

ANY POOR SOUL THAT HAS TO SMASH GENITALS WITH ANY CHARACTER PLAYED BY THE DOOFBULB KNOWN AS TIM ALLEN DESERVES, AT THE VERY LEAST, A SYMPATHY SPOT ON THIS LIST. THANKFULLY PATRICIA IS MORE THAN WORTHY ALL ON HER OWN, I DARE SAY. IN FACT, JILL WAS QUITE THE DOMINEERING WIFE, WASN'T SHE? AHH, WHAT WE WOULDN'T GIVE TO HAVE HAD HER GET INTO HER RED AND BLACK LEATHER FETISH GEAR AND LEAD US DOWN TO THAT TOOL-FILLED BASEMENT ON A LEASH. SHE WOULD BE OH-SO CRUEL, BUT ALSO KIND WHEN IT COUNTED -- BECAUSE THAT'S HOW MOMS ARE. JILL WAS THE TYPE THAT KNEW HOW TO SHOW YOU WHO'S THE BOSS. THAT'S RIGHT, I SAID WHO'S THE BOSS, AND NO, JUDITH LIGHT (AS ANGELA BOWER) IS CERTAINLY **NOT** GOING TO MAKE THIS LIST, SO DROP THAT IDEA RIGHT NOW, BUCKOS. ALYSSA MILANO ON A LIST OF 'HOTTEST SITCOM DAUGHTERS' ON THE OTHER HAND... NOW **THAT** WOULD BE SOMETHING.

HOW MAY I SERVE YOU?

9. Barbara Billingsley as "June Cleaver" on Leave It to Beaver (1957 to 1963)

BARBARA BILLINGSLEY AS "JUNE CLEAVER"

JUNE WAS LADYLIKE AND ALWAYS DRESSED SEMI FORMAL AS A PARTY HOSTESS EVEN WHILE DOING HOUSEWORK AND MAKING DINNER. THE IDEAL SUBMISSIVE HOUSEWIFE, SHE WAS NEVER PRESENTED WITHOUT PERFECTLY COIFFED HAIR AND PERFECTLY APPLIED MAKEUP, WHICH OF COURSE MAKES ANY SELF RESPECTING DOMINANT WANT TO MESS UP THAT HAIR AND GET THAT MASCARA RUNNING DURING SOME FILTHY SEX-PLAY. SHE AND HER HUSBAND WARD AND THEIR TWO SONS WALLY AND BEAVER WERE THE ARCHETYPAL 1950s WHITE SUBURBAN FAMILY, AND MOST EVERYTHING THEY SAID AND DID WAS PERFECT, ALTHOUGH THERE WERE A FEW LINES OF DIALOG, WHICH, PLACED IN A MODERN CONTEXT, SEEM WAY MORE RISQUE THAN THEY ACTUALLY WERE. CASE IN POINT: MRS CLEAVER ASKING WALLY "WHERE ARE YOUR RUBBERS?", AND ALSO REPRIMANDING HER HUSBAND FOR BEING "TOO HARD ON THE BEAVER LAST NIGHT". JUNE ALWAYS HAD ON HER TRADEMARK PEARLS, EVEN WHEN GARDENING. INSERT A JOKE RIGHT HERE ABOUT GIVING HER A PEARL NECKLACE. ALSO ADD A JOKE CONCERNING THE AFOREMENTIONED USE OF THE WORD "INSERT". GIGGITY.

8. Meredith Baxter as "Elyse Keaton" on Family Ties (1982 to 1989)

ELYSE KEATON HAD THAT WHOLE EX-1970s HIPPIE THING GOING ON THAT MADE HER RATHER UNIQUE IN THE SITCOM LEXICON. THIS MADE IT VERY EASY TO FANTASIZE ABOUT HER TOPLESS AND HIGH AT A C.C.R. CONCERT, GLEEFULLY EXPOSING HER HAIRY BLONDE PUSSY WHILE SKINNY DIPPING, AND EAGERLY SPREADING THOSE CREAMY

THIGHS FOR BOTH MEN AND WOMEN -- BECAUSE THAT WAS JUST HOW YOU GOT GROOVY AND STUCK IT TO THE SYSTEM BACK THEN, MAN. JUSTINE BATEMAN AS "MALLORY KEATON" GOT ALL THE FAMILY TIES MEDIA BONERS AT THE TIME WITH HER VERY SHORT-LIVED MOVIE CAREER, BUT IT WAS THE MORE MATURE ELYSE WHO REALLY DESERVED THEM. WHY? BECAUSE IT'S ELYSE WHO WOULD BE FREAKY IN THE SACK AND THEN AFTERWARDS WOULD SMOKE A BIG DOOBIE WITH YOU, NAKED, AND OFFER ALL OF THE WIT AND WARMTH OF YOUR BEST PAL CROSSED WITH YOUR FAVORITE AUTHOR. JUST LOOK AT HER EYES AND TELL ME I'M WRONG. SURE, SHE'S A GRANOLA-MUNCHING LEFTY IDEALIST, BUT SHE'S SEEN SHIT SHE CAN'T UNSEE. THAT'S **HOT**.

SILLY BOUG

LOOK! I'M ALL DECKED OUT IN MY MILF BOOB HAT!

I AM PROTECTED FROM THE ELEMENTS!

7. Lori Loughlin as "Rebecca Donaldson" on Full House (1988 to 1995)

MOST PEOPLE SEEM TO REMEMBER 3 DADS RAISING ALL THOSE GIRLS ALONE ON THIS LATE EIGHTIES SITCOM THAT MADE STARS OUT OF THE FUCKTARDED OLSEN TWINS, BUT LET'S REMEMBER THAT IN THE SECOND SEASON JESSE (JOHN STAMOS) BECAME THE HOST OF A TV MORNING SHOW, AND HIS CO-HOST WAS THE REBECCA DONALDSON CHARACTER. SHE IMMEDIATELY (AND RIGHTFULLY) CATCHES HIS EYE, AND BY SEASON 4 BECOMES HIS WIFE AND A MOM FIGURE IN THE HOUSE WHICH IS CLEARLY FULL. SO YEAH, THIS ONE IS A BIT OF A CHEAT SINCE SHE'S JUST A STEP-MOM, BUT I MUST FORGO DISQUALIFYING HER BECAUSE REBECCA IS JUST SO INSANELY, INTENSELY FUCKABLE. THAT JESSE, THE OTHER TWO GENTLEMEN, AND THE FAMILY DOG, COMET, SOMEHOW MANAGED TO KEEP FROM SHOOTING THEIR DICKS AT HER LIKE PLASTIC LAWN DARTS EVERY TIME SHE WALKED IN THE ROOM IS NOTHING SHORT OF ONE OF THE GREATEST UNSOLVED MYSTERIES IN SITCOM HISTORY.

6. Diahann Carroll as "Julia Baker" on Julia (1968 to 1971)

I'VE HEARD PEOPLE (GRANTED, NOT MANY) SAY THAT PHYLICIA RASHAD AS MRS CLAIR HUXTABLE ON THE COSBY SHOW IS THE HOTTEST BLACK MOM IN SITCOM HISTORY, BUT I BEG TO DIFFER. THAT HONOUR MUST GO TO THIS FAR LESSER KNOWN MAIN CHARACTER FROM THE GROUND-BREAKING SITCOM, JULIA. THIS WAS THE VERY FIRST ONE TO EVER DEPICT AN AFRICAN AMERICAN WOMAN AS A LEAD CHARACTER IN A ROLE OTHER THAN A SERVANT TO A WHITE FAMILY. JULIA BAKER WAS A NURSE, A NO-NONSENSE SINGLE MOM, AND A WHOLE LOT OF ULTRA-FINE CHOCOLATE LOVE! DIAHANN WAS DEFINITELY ALL THAT, AND GOT TO WEAR ALL KINDS OF FOXY 1960s MOD DRESSES WITH GROOVY GEOMETRIC PATTERNS -- THAT IS WHEN SHE WASN'T DRIVING VIEWERS CRAZY IN THAT NURSE'S UNIFORM OF HERS. THIS SHOW WAS AMONG THE VERY FEW FROM THIS GENRE IN THE SIXTIES THAT DID NOT USE A LAUGH TRACK, ALTHOUGH 20TH CENTURY FOX DID END UP ADDING ONE IN THE LATE 1980s WHEN JULIA WAS REISSUED FOR SYNDICATION.

5. Betty Rubble on "The Flintstones" (1960 to 1966)

THIS ONE REALLY DOESN'T NEED MUCH EXPLANATION OR CONTEXT, AS FAR AS I'M CONCERNED. WHO AMONGST US OVER THE AGE OF THIRTY HASN'T SEEN THE FLINTSTONES? AND OF THAT GROUP WHO HASN'T HAD AT LEAST A LITTLE CRUSH ON BETTY? SHIT, I'VE EVEN MET GAY DUDES WHO SHYLY ADMIT TO HAVING A LITTLE SOMETHING FOR BARNEY RUBBLE'S WIFE. SHE'S TIMELESS AND DOESN'T EVEN NEED TO EXIST AS AN ACTUAL HUMAN BEING TO BE ONE OF THE TOP 5. NOW **THAT** IS IMPRESSIVE. YOU ROCK, BETTY. OH, AND THIS PICK MIGHT SEEM LIKE A STRETCH AT FIRST GLANCE, BUT REMEMBER THAT THIS CARTOON AIRED DURING PRIME TIME, AND WAS MODELED AFTER THE CLASSIC SITCOM, THE HONEYMOONERS. THAT MAKES IT A TRUE SITCOM.

4. Carolyn Jones as Morticia Addams on The Addams Family (1964 to 1966)

YET ANOTHER SOLID INDICATOR THAT THE MID 1960s WAS AN ABSOLUTELY AMAZING TIME FOR BLISTERINGLY HAWT MOMS ON TV. A FULL 6 OUT OF 10 OF THE WOMEN ON THIS LIST WERE DOING THEIR THING IN THAT DECADE. I WASN'T EVEN BORN YET, SO DON'T CLUCK YOUR TONGUE AND THINK THAT ANY OF THIS IS NOSTALGIA TALKING ON MY BEHALF. LIKE I SAID EARLIER, THIS ARTICLE WAS DIRECTLY INSPIRED BY THE CRUSHES OPENLY DISPLAYED BY CINEMA

BETTY RUBBLE: THE 5th HOTTEST SITCOM MOM OF ALL TIME

SEWER READERS JUST LIKE YOU! BORN IN AMARILLO TEXAS IN APRIL OF 1930, CAROLYN JONES SUFFERED FROM SEVERE ASTHMA AS A CHILD, AND WAS OFTEN TOO SICK TO TAKE PART IN HER FAVORITE PASTIME -- GOING TO THE MOVIES. MARRYING TELEVISION PRODUCER AARON SPELLING HELPED HER CAREER, AS DID MULTIPLE HORROR MOVIE ROLES IN HOUSE OF WAX (1953), INVASION OF THE BODY SNATCHERS (1956), AND THEN FOLLOWING THAT WITH AN IMPRESSIVE PERFORMANCE IN KING CREOLE (1958) -- WHICH IS GENERALLY CONSIDERED TO BE ELVIS PRESLEY'S STANDOUT PICTURE. DIVORCING AARON SPELLING (CAROLYN ASKED FOR NO ALIMONY) JUST BEFORE GETTING THE ROLE ON THE ADDAMS FAMILY AS "MORTICIA", JONES FOUND HERSELF TOTALLY TYPECAST BY THE POPULARITY OF THE CHARACTER, AND HAD TROUBLE EVER GETTING HER CAREER BACK ON TRACK. A SOAP OPERA ACTRESS IN HER LATER YEARS, SHE WAS DIAGNOSED WITH COLON CANCER IN 1981, AND DIED IN 1983. HER EPITAPH READS: "SHE GAVE JOY TO THE WORLD", AND AIN'T THAT THE TRUTH? SURELY ONE OF THE HOTTEST SITCOM MOMS OF ALL TIME.

3. Mary Tyler Moore as "Laura Petrie" on The Dick Van Dyke Show (1961 to 1966)

RITCHIE PETRIE'S MOM ON THE DICK VAN DYKE SHOW WAS LAURA, AS PLAYED BY THE MAGNIFICENTLY FUNNY MARY TYLER MOORE. BETTER KNOW TODAY FOR HER LATER SUCCESS ON THE SITCOM, MARY TYLER MOORE (WHICH RAN FROM 1970 TO 1977), THIS EARLIER SERIES IS REALLY WHERE MARY GOT HER FEET WET AND WAS AT HER HOTTEST AND DOWNRIGHT MILF-IEST. FOXY AS HELL IN THOSE TIGHT LITTLE PENCIL SKIRTS AND WITH THAT LITTLE SWOOP ON HER CUTE 1960s HAIRCUT, MARY SHOWED HOW A YOUNG MOTHER AND HOMEMAKER COULD RUN THINGS ALL DAY AND STILL BE THE MOST ADORABLE THING GOING. SURE, SHE HAD THAT WHINEY NASAL VOICE, BUT HER DELIVERY WAS SO FUNNY IT WAS IMPOSSIBLE TO BE ANNOYED BY IT. HER DISHY SONG AND DANCE NUMBER (CALYPSO STYLE) FROM THE EPISODE "SOMEBODY HAS TO PLAY CLEOPATRA" (SEASON 2) IS THE STUFF OF TV LEGEND. FUNNY WOMEN GIVE ME SUCH A WARM LUMP IN MY UNDEROOS. (WAIT.. THAT SOUNDS LIKE I'M TALKING ABOUT POOP, DOESN'T IT?! UGH...) AND I'M NOT THE ONLY ONE. AS RICHARD METZGER UNCOVERED, THERE WAS EVEN A "SOCIETY" IN THE 1970s AND 1980s DEDICATED TO "JACKING OFF" TO PHOTOGRAPHS OF THE BELOVED ACTRESS AND COMEDIENNE. THEY HAD A NEWSLETTER AND EVERYTHING! THE "MARY TYLER MOORE MASTURBATION SOCIETY" WAS FOUNDED BY JAMES J. KAGEL OF CLEAVELAND, OHIO, AND HAD A DIRECT FOCUS ON MARY'S "SUCCULENT GAMS", AND I DO WONDER HOW MANY PEOPLE ACTUALLY SUBSCRIBED TO HIS BIZARRE MONTHLY NEWSLETTER.

2. Elizabeth Montgomery as "Samantha" on Bewitched (1964 to 1972)

I AM HONESTLY NOT SURE IF A CUTER NOSE EVER TWITCHED ON AMERICAN TV. PLAYING A SUBURBAN WITCH WITH SUPERNATURAL POWERS NAMED SAMANTHA, ADORABLE ELIZABETH MONTGOMERY CAPTURED THE WORLD'S HEART IN THE LATER HALF OF THE 1960s. MARRIED TO A MORTAL PLAYED BY DICK YORK (AND LATER BY DICK SARGENT), SHE HAS TWO MAGICAL CHILDREN BY HIM, AND GENERALLY TRIES NOT TO USE HER POWERS -- HOPING TO FIT IN AMONGST A NORMAL, SORCERY-FREE MAINSTREAM SOCIETY. HER MYSTIC FAMILY FULL OF WARLOCKS AND WITCHES DON'T MUCH APPROVE OF HER MIXED WITCH/MORTAL MARRIAGE, WHICH GAVE THE SHOW AN INTERESTING AND SNEAKY WAY TO COMMENT ON AND DEAL WITH THE TOPIC OF RACISM AND MIXED MARRIAGES.

MONTGOMERY RECEIVED FIVE EMMY AND FOUR GOLDEN GLOBE NOMINATIONS FOR HER ROLE IN THIS SERIES, AND IF HER SUCCESS ON THE SHOW WAS IN DOUBT WHATSOEVER, TAKE INTO ACCOUNT THAT PRIOR TO THIS THE NAME "SAMANTHA" WAS RELATIVELY RARE. SINCE 1964, THOUGH? SINCE THEN, THE NAME HAS REMAINED CONSISTENTLY POPULAR AMONGST YOUNG PARENTS. YOU FIGURE IT OUT.

1. Katey Sagal as Peg Bundy on Married with Children (1987 to 1997)

UNDISPUTABLE NUMBER ONE PICK. AS THE ONLY MOM ON TV THAT DRESSED LIKE AN OVER-SEXED ITALIAN PROSTITUTE (OH MY -- THOSE BIG BOUNCY BANGS ON THAT GIANT TEASED RED BOUFFANT -- GLORIOUS) PEG BUNDY WAS PURE UNFILTERED WANK-INSPIRATION FOR AN ENTIRE GENERATION OF HORNY BOYS GROWING UP IN THE LATE 1980s. HELL, HER CHARACTER'S MAIDEN NAME WAS EVEN "WANKER", FER GAWDS SAKE! IT WAS ALL JUST TOO MUCH: THE INSANELY ALLURING CIGARETTE PANTS, LEATHER SKIRTS, ANIMAL PRINT TOPS, AND SKINNY JEANS THAT HUGGED HER ASS SO TIGHT, IT SEEMED LIKE HER PERFECT POSTERIOR WAS GOING TO EXPLODE RIGHT OUT OF THEM. ON TOP OF ALL THAT, MULTIPLE REFERENCES WERE MADE TO HER ROUTINELY USING DILDOS AND VIBRATORS TO ACHIEVE THE ORGASMS THAT AL BUNDY COULDN'T PROVIDE FOR HER. THAT MIGHT NOT SEEM LIKE ANYTHING EYEBROW RAISING TODAY, BUT YOU HAVE TO REMEMBER THAT IN 1987 JOKES LIKE THAT SIMPLY DID NOT SHOW UP ON NETWORK TV OFTEN, IF EVER. THEN THERE WAS HER FRIENDLY N' FLIPPANT "WHO CARES" ATTITUDE THAT MADE IT SEEM ENTIRELY PLAUSIBLE THAT SHE COULD DECIDE TO GET NAKED RIGHT THERE AND BLOW THE MAILMAN ON THE COUCH JUST FOR THE FUN OF THE EXPERIENCE. PURE SEX IN MILF FORM! LITTLE KNOWN FACT: KATEY SAGAL BEGAN HER CAREER AS A SINGER/SONGWRITER, AND SANG BACKUP FOR BOB DYLAN, TANYA TUCKER, BETTE MIDLER, AND OLIVIA NEWTON-JOHN.

> THE #1 MOST FUCKABLE MOM IN SITCOM TV HISTORY: PEG BUNDY!

JUST AS I FINISHED INKING THIS REBECCA WALKED OVER AND SAID: ➡

I THINK YOU FORGOT ONE.

HUH?

I THOUGHT YOU LOVED PAMELA ADLON AS "KIM" ON LUCKY LOUIE (2006 TO 2007)?

AUGH!! THAT'S RIGHT! THEY HAVE A KID ON THAT SITCOM! HOW COULD I EVEN FORGET HER?! NOOO! BLAA! UGHH!

YOU'RE TOO LAZY TO GO BACK AND RELETTER THE WHOLE THING, AREN'T YOU?

I'LL DO A LITTLE COMIC!

APRIL 9TH 1980: THE DOA RESURRECTION BALL

CHEETAH CHROME WAS THE LEAD GUITARIST OF THE DEAD BOYS, ONE OF THE KEY BANDS OF THE OUTRAGEOUS MID-TO-LATE 1970S NEW YORK PUNK SCENE. HE LIVED AS WILD AS HIS MUSIC, AND OVERDOSED AND WAS PRONOUNCED DEAD THREE TIMES. THE DEAD BOYS ORIGINATED IN CLEVELAND, AND THEIR HIT "SONIC REDUCER" SOON BECAME A PUNK ANTHEM EVEN WHILE THEY NEVER QUITE GOT THE ACCOLADES AND FAME THAT THEIR PEERS IN OTHER MORE FAMOUS PUNK BANDS RECEIVED.

JUST BEFORE THE BAND IMPLODED IN THE EARLY 1980S, THEY WERE INVITED TO PERFORM AT AN APRIL 9TH 1980 RELEASE PARTY FOR A MOVIE ABOUT THE PUNK SCENE CALLED D.O.A. IT WAS A LEGENDARY NIGHT HELD AT THE RITZ (ONE OF THE FIRST CLUBS TO INCORPORATE VIDEO SCREENS INTO THE CLUB EXPERIENCE) IN THE EAST VILLAGE IN NEW YORK AT 119 EAST 11TH STREET, AND INCLUDED LIVE MUSIC ACTS AND A SCREENING OF THE MOVIE.

IN THOSE FIRST COUPLE OF YEARS THAT THE CLUB EXISTED, A LOT OF HISTORY WAS WAS GOING ON WITHIN ITS WALLS. THIS WAS THE SAME CLUB THAT TINA TURNER WOULD MOUNT HER INCREDIBLE SOLO COMEBACK IN 1981. THIS WAS THE FIRST MUSIC VENUE THAT MTV DID A LIVE BROADCAST FROM IN 1981. THIS WAS THE CLUB WHERE U2 PLAYED ITS FIRST LIVE SHOW IN THE US, ON DEC 6TH 1980. THIS WAS THE CLUB WHERE A RIOT BROKE OUT AT A PIL SHOW IN MARCH 1981, WHERE THE CROWD RUSHED THE STAGE, TEARING APART ONE OF THE HUGE VIDEO SCREENS BEFORE DISCO MUSIC WAS PLAYED TO DISPERSE THE ANGRY MOB.

BUT BACK TO THE NIGHT IN QUESTION: APRIL 9TH, 1980. IT WAS AN EVENING HOSTED BY JOEY RAMONE, IT COST $8 TO GET IN THAT NIGHT, AND WAS BILLED AS "THE PARTY OF THE YEAR". BUT BEFORE IT WAS DONE, CHEETAH WOULD LOSE A PINT OF HIS BLOOD ON STAGE, AND WOULD BE PERMANENTLY PHYSICALLY SCARRED. HERE NOW, IN A PASSAGE FROM HIS HIGHLY RECOMMENDED AUTOBIOGRAPHY, "CHEETAH CHROME: A DEAD BOY'S TALE: FROM THE FRONT LINES OF PUNK ROCK" (2010, VOYAGEUR PRESS), IS A FIRST HAND ACCOUNT:

SID+NANCY INVITE YOU TO...

THE D.O.A. RESURRECTION BALL

Celebrate D.O.A.'s World Premiere with —

- THE ORIGINAL DEAD BOYS – Stiv, Cheetah, Johnny and Jimmy reunited for a special resurrection performance.
- The Swinging Madisons
- Chris Salewicz's London Report featuring The Professionals
- An edited version of D.O.A. specially prepared for the party.
- Surprise guests and artists.
- More wierdness than you even want to think about

Thursday night, April 9th, at

and Joey Ramone — Your host for the evening.

Admission $8.00 per person. / Not much for the Party of the Year

RITZ
11TH STREET BETWEEN 3RD & 4TH AVENUES

"DURING THE SPRING OF 1980, THE MOVIE D.O.A. A RITE OF PASSAGE WAS RELEASED. THE DEAD BOYS WERE IN IT FOR ABOUT THIRTY SECONDS, WITH CRAPPY FOOTAGE FROM THE TORONTO REUNION SHOW BADLY SYNCHED TO THE WRONG SONG. THE PRODUCER OF THE FILM, TOM NORMAN, OFFERED THE DEAD BOYS A GOOD AMOUNT OF MONEY TO DO A ONE-OFF SHOW AT A NEW CLUB CALLED THE RITZ FOR THE PREMIER PARTY. WE WERE TO PUT IN AN APPEARANCE AT THE SCREENING AT THE WAVERLY THEATER, ATTEND A PRIVATE PARTY AT TOM'S LOFT, AND THEN DO THE SHOW THE NEXT NIGHT."

"THE FILM PREMIER WAS HILARIOUS. THEY SENT A LIMO TO PICK US UP AT THE GRAMERCY PARK HOTEL, WHERE WE'D ALL GOTTEN ROOMS AS PART OF THE DEAL. WE HAD BEEN PARTYING IN THE BAR BEFOREHAND, DRINKING A LOT AND DOING A TON OF BLOW. ALL WASN'T FORGIVEN AS FAR AS I WAS CONCERNED, BUT I BURIED THE HATCHET FOR THE DURATION OF THE GIG SO WE COULD MAKE SOME CASH. WE BEGAN GETTING VERY ROWDY ON THE RIDE OVER, MAKING OUR HANDLER, TOM NORMAN'S WIFE, VERY NERVOUS."

"AS WE PULLED UP IN FRONT OF THE THEATER, WE COULD SEE THERE WAS A GOOD CROWD OUTSIDE. I LED THE WAY AS WE ALL CLIMBED OUT OF THE SUNROOF AND WALKED ACROSS THE HOOD OF THE LIMO AND INTO THE THEATER. WE HAD A RESERVED ROW, AND WE IMMEDIATELY SAT DOWN AND PUT OUR LEGS OVER THE SEATS IN FRONT OF US, MAKING IT NECESSARY TO REARRANGE SOME OF THE SEATING. WHEN THE MOVIE CAME ON, WE HECKLED, CATCALLED, AND MADE SORT OF RUDE COMMENTS ABOUT THE BANDS, ESPECIALLY THE SEX PISTOLS. WE REALLY HAD FUN WITH THE SID AND NANCY INTERVIEW THAT WAS THE CLIMAX OF THE FLICK. A REVIEW OF THE MOVIE IN THE VOICE SAID THE BEST PART OF IT WAS OUR COMMENTS, WHICH TELLS YOU HOW GOOD THE MOVIE WAS."

"THE NEXT MORNING, STIV AND I WERE SCHEDULED TO DO AN APPEARANCE ON MIDDAY LIVE WITH BILL BOGGS, A TYPICAL DAYTIME TV INTERVIEW SHOW ON WNEW. ONE OF THE GUESTS WAS JIM BOUTON, A FORMER YANKEES PITCHER AND AUTHOR OF 'BALL FOUR', WHICH ODDLY ENOUGH, I HAD READ. THE OTHER GUEST WAS GORE VIDAL, AUTHOR OF A TON OF STUFF, NONE OF WHICH I HAD READ AT THE TIME."

"WE DID A FEW LINES, AND I DID A SPEEDBALL, BEFORE WE WERE PICKED UP IN THE LIMO, AND I MADE THE DRIVER STOP AT A DELI FOR BEER TO LOSE MY HANGOVER. WHEN WE GOT INTO THE GREEN ROOM, BOUTON WAS GETTING READY TO GO ON, AND HE AND I TALKED ABOUT HIS BOOK FOR A SECOND, HIM LOOKING AT ME LIKE I WAS A MARTIAN THE WHOLE TIME. WE WERE ON AFTER HIM, SO I KNOCKED BACK AS MANY BEERS AS I COULD IN THE TEN MINUTES THAT WE HAD, MAKING SMALL TALK WITH VIDAL, WHO WAS A PRETTY COOL OLD GUY... AND ACCEPTED AN INVITATION TO OUR SHOW. THAT NIGHT, THE DRESSING ROOM DOOR OPENED AND THERE HE WAS. HE HUNG OUT WITH US FOR QUITE A WHILE, AND REALLY THOUGHT THAT THE WHOLE THING WAS GREAT."

"MY EVENING WAS MARRED BY THE FACT THAT ON MY WAY DOWNSTAIRS, SOMETHING ON THE STAIR RAIL CUT THREE FINGERTIPS OF MY RIGHT HAND, BADLY. IT WAS TOO LATE TO STOP THOUGH, AS JOEY RAMONE WAS ALREADY INTRODUCING US, AND I WENT AHEAD AND PLAYED THE ENTIRE SHOW BLEEDING ALL OVER THE PLACE. I LOST ABOUT A PINT OF BLOOD ON THE STAGE, AND THERE WAS STILL A STAIN ON THE CARPET ABOUT THREE FEET IN DIAMETER WHEN WE PLAYED THERE FIVE YEARS LATER."

"MY ROADIE MADE ME UP A SHOT OF DOPE AND SKIN POPPED ME IN THE ASS ON STAGE WHILE PRETENDING TO FIX MY GUITAR STRAP. OTHERWISE, I PROBABLY WOULDN'T HAVE BEEN ABLE TO FINISH THE SET. WHEN WE WERE DONE, JOHN BELUSHI CAME BACKSTAGE WITH THE DOCTOR WHO HAD SAVED BLITZ' LIFE, AND AFTER INTRODUCING HIM TO JOHNNY, THEY BOTH RUSHED OVER TO ME AND LOOKED AT MY FINGERS."

"'C'MON, RIGHT NOW. YOU'VE GOTTA GO TO THE EMERGENCY ROOM!,' SAID JOHN. I ARGUED THAT I WAS OK. I WANTED TO RELAX A COUPLE OF MINUTES. THEN THE DOCTOR, WHOM I'LL CALL DOCTOR RICK, INSISTED I GO IMMEDIATELY. 'IF YOU DRINK ANYMORE BEFORE YOU GO, I CAN'T STITCH YOU.' HE SAID MATTER-OF-FACTLY."

"I GAVE IN TO HIS SUPERIOR KNOWLEDGE OF SUCH THINGS, AND THEY TOOK ME OUT TO JOHN'S LIMO. WE PROCEEDED TO BELLEVUE HOSPITAL, WALKING STRAIGHT THROUGH THE ER AND INTO THE BACK ROOM LIKE WE OWNED THE PLACE. SOME INTERN CAME RUSHING OVER AND SAID 'WHAT THE HELL DO YOU THINK YOU'RE DOING?'"

"DR RICK CAME AROUND ON HIM AND SAID 'I'M THE FUCKING HEAD SURGEON IN THIS ER, AND I'M GETTING READY TO WORK ON A PATIENT, THAT'S WHAT!,' THEN HE WHIPPED OUT AN ID THAT MADE THE POOR GUY'S EYES GO WIDE AND HIS FACE GO PALE. APPARENTLY HE DID OWN THE PLACE!"

"JOHN SAT ON THE TABLE NEXT TO ME WHILE RICK SQUIRTED SOME LOCAL ANESTHETIC ON MY FINGERS AND WENT TO WASH UP. HE CAME BACK AND SUTURED MY HAND, AND IT WAS ONLY AFTER HE WAS ON THE LAST ONE THAT IT OCCURRED TO ME TO ASK HIM 'WOAH DOC, HAVE YOU BEEN DRINKING?'"

"HE LAUGHED AND SAID 'OH YEAH, I'VE HAD QUITE A FEW. NO WAY I SHOULD BE DOING THIS."

"HE GAVE ME A NICE SHOT OF MORPHINE FOR THE ROAD, AND A PRESCRIPTION FOR SOME HEAVY DUTY FOLLOW UP MEDS, AND THEN HE AND JOHN GAVE ME A RIDE HOME. THE STITCHES CAME OUT A COUPLE OF WEEKS LATER, BUT THE TIPS OF MY MIDDLE, RING, AND PINKY FINGERS ON MY RIGHT HAND HAD NERVE DAMAGE AND STAYED NUMB UNTIL AROUND 2003. MY PINKY STILL FEELS WEIRD."

"WE NEVER DID FIND OUT WHAT I CUT MY FINGERS ON, FOR WHEN WE WENT TO LOOK THE NEXT DAY, THE RAIL HAD BEEN REPLACED, ODDLY ENOUGH. THE BAND WENT OUR SEPARATE WAYS AFTER THAT."

THE TOP 10 COOLEST WEAPONS IN FILM HISTORY!

ART BY: BEN JACQUES ☆ WRITING BY: BOUGIE!

JAPANESE HAND CANNON

WIELDED BY A CREEPY GUY WITH AN EYE-PATCH IN THE JAPANESE LOW-BUDGET SCI-FI SPLATTER FILM TOKYO GORE POLICE (2008), THE HAND CANNON IS A GIANT BAZOOKA THAT FIRES SEVERED HUMAN FISTS, WHICH THEN ATTACK/POKE/PUNCH THEIR VICTIMS. SADLY, THIS GROTESQUE AND RIGHTEOUS WEAPON WASN'T REALLY UTILIZED IN A VERY SATISFYING WAY AT ALL, WITH THE FISTS BEING SENT RIGHT BACK AT EYE-PATCH DUDE AFTER RUNNING INTO A DANGLING FLESH-STRING (??) THAT WAS HANGING IN THEIR WAY. YEAH, IT DIDN'T REALLY MAKE A LICK OF SENSE IN THE MOVIE, EITHER. OH WELL.

THE WEIRDING MODULE

A CRAZY SONIC WEAPON WHICH WAS INTRODUCED IN DAVID LYNCH'S SEMI-SATISFACTORY 1984 ADAPTATION OF DUNE. THIS FREAKY DEVICE SHOOTS A SONIC BEAM THAT TRANSLATES SPECIFIC SOUNDS INTO BRUTAL ATTACKS OF VARYING POTENCY. LYNCH IS SAID TO HAVE ADAPTED THE ORIGINAL NOVEL'S CONCEPT OF "THE WEIRDING WAY" INTO THE WEIRDING MODULE BECAUSE HE WASN'T KEEN ON THE CONCEPT OF "KUNG-FU ON SAND DUNES". AS SHOWN IN THE MOVIE, THE WORD "MUAD'DIB" TURNS OUT TO BE A POWERFUL "KILLING WORD" TRIGGER FOR THE MODULE, BUT I WOULD TOTALLY YELL "SWAG BALLER!" INTO IT, AND SEE WHAT THAT DID. THAT WOULD RULE.

FLYING CHROME PHANTASM BALLS

REMEMBER THAT CULT HORROR SERIES, PHANTASM? WELL, MORE ACCURATELY IT WAS A MIX OF HORROR, SCI-FI, AND FANTASY, BUT IT WAS PRETTY AWESOME. AS THE TAGLINE FOR DON COSCARELLI'S ORIGINAL 1979 FILM READ, "IF YOU'RE LOOKING FOR HORROR THAT'S GOT BALLS, IT'S FOUND YOU". THAT'S BECAUSE THE VILLAIN OF THE SERIES, THE TALL MAN, HAD ONE OF THE COOLEST AND WEIRDEST WEAPONS IN FILM HISTORY: FLYING CHROME BALLS WITH SPIKED METAL PRONGS THAT JUT OUT OF THEM. THROUGHOUT THE SERIES THESE SCARY-ASS THINGS SEEMED LIKE SENTIENT BEINGS, AND THEY STAPLED YOUR FUCKING HEAD TO THE WALL WHEN YOU GOT NAILED BY THEM.

FLYING GUILLOTINE

JIMMY WANG YU WRITES, DIRECTS AND STARS IN 1976'S MASTER OF THE FLYING GUILLOTINE, WHICH RANKS AS ONE OF THE MOST MEMORABLE CLASSIC MARTIAL ARTS MOVIES. AN OLD BLIND BEARDED DUDE WITH THE BIGGEST EYEBROWS IN FILM HISTORY TRIES TO AVENGE THE DEATHS OF HIS NEPHEWS WHILE ARMED WITH HIS SECRET WEAPON, A FLYING GUILLOTINE. THIS THING RULES, BROTHERS AND SISTERS. IT'S THIS WEIRD KINDA SPIKED HAT OR CLAW THINGEE ON A CHAIN, WHICH HE SWINGS AROUND AND PLOPS IT ON PEOPLE'S HEADS. ONCE THAT THING IS ON YOUR NOGGIN, SAY GOODNIGHT AND GOOD LUCK, BECAUSE YOUR HEAD IS ABOUT TO POP RIGHT OFF!

KEEP AN EYE OUT

FOR MY BALLS

DRAGON MISSILES

OK, MOST SHAW BROS FANS AND MARTIAL ARTS NERDS KNOW ALL ABOUT THE FLYING GUILLOTINE, BUT LESSER KNOWN IS LO LIEH AND HIS DRAGON MISSILES! IT'S NOT A GREAT MOVIE, BUT THE TITULAR WEAPONS WERE FUCKING AMAZING IN 1976'S DRAGON MISSILE. BASICALLY THEY WERE THESE CURVED MACHETTE BLADES, AND LO THROWS THEM LIKE A CHAMP WHO DEALS IN PURE RADNESS. THE DAMN THINGS WHIP ALL AROUND THE FUCKING PLACE LIKE HEAT-SEAKING ROCKETS UNTIL THEY VIOLENTLY CHOP EVERYONE'S HEAD OFF IN THE ROOM -- THEN THEY RETURN TO HIM LIKE OBEDIENT PUPS. THESE MISSILES DON'T MISS!

GRISTLE GUN

IN THE UNDERRATED CANADIAN SCI-FI/HORROR FILM EXISTENZ FROM 1999, JUDE LAW AND JENNIFER JASON LEIGH SIT DOWN IN AN ODD ASIAN EATERY AND ORDER "THE SPECIAL", AND WHAT ARRIVES IS A DISGUSTING PLATTER OF BOILED AMPHIBIAN-LIKE CREATURES. AS IF IN A TRANCE, LAW FINDS THE URGE TO EAT THE SICKENING MEAL AND ASSEMBLE THE VARIOUS

CHUNKS OF DETRITUS, BONE AND CARTILAGE INTO A GUN-SHAPED WEAPON THAT FIRES HUMAN TEETH. YOU'LL NEVER LOOK AT CHINESE FOOD THE SAME AGAIN!

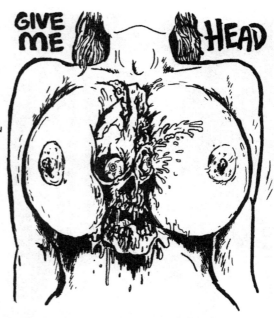

GIANT BOOBS

THIS ENTRY WOULDN'T BE ON THIS LIST IF THIS WERE FANGORIA OR RUE MORGUE MAGAZINE, BUT THIS IS CINEMA SEWER, AND HERE WE APPRECIATE IT WHEN BOUNCING BREASTS ARE UTILIZED AS KILLING MACHINES! IN THE MOVIES DEADLY WEAPONS (1974) AND DOUBLE AGENT 73 (1974), CHESTY MORGAN IS A SEXY SUPER-SPY WHOSE KILLER CLEAVAGE IS FAR MORE DANGEROUS THAN ANY LOADED PISTOL. THAT'S RIGHT, THIS CHUBBY, EXPRESSIONLESS DAME SEDUCES DUDES AND THEN WHEN THEY AREN'T EXPECTING IT, SHE TIT-SMACKS THEM IN THE YAPPER AND THEN SUFFOCATES THE POOR BASTARDS WITH HER INSANELY LARGE SNOOPIES. I CAN THINK OF WORSE WAYS TO DIE! AS A BODACIOUS BONUS, HER SWEATER-PUPPIES ALSO TAKE PICTURES. GO-GO GADGET MAMMARY GLANDS!

FREDDY'S CLAWS

THEY SEEM SOMEWHAT HOMOGENIZED AND TAME NOW SIMPLY BECAUSE OF HOW MANY TIMES WE'VE SEEN THEM, BUT TAKE YOURSELF BACK TO 1984 FOR A SECOND, AND THINK ABOUT HOW COOL FREDDY KRUEGER'S GLOVED SET OF CLAWS WERE WHEN WES CRAVEN'S A NIGHTMARE ON ELM STREET FIRST PREMIERED. HAD WE, AS HORROR FANS, EVER SEEN ANYTHING QUITE LIKE IT? METHINKS NOT. CRAVEN HAS STATED THAT HE WAS DESPERATE TO HAVE A WEAPON FOR HIS KILLER THAT WAS UNIQUE IN FILM HISTORY, AND WAS INSPIRED BY WATCHING HIS CAT SHARPEN ITS CLAWS ON THE SIDE OF HIS COUCH. I'LL SCRATCH YOUR BACK, AND YOU SHRED MINE!

FLYING MAGNETIC COMPACT DISC OF CARNAGE

IN 1990'S I COME IN PEACE (AKA DARK ANGEL) DOLPH LUNDGREN GOES UP AGAINST A BIG ALIEN GUY WHO SHOOTS FRIGHTENED PEOPLE WITH THESE CIRCULAR SILVER WEAPONS THAT LOOKED LIKE MUSIC CDS. THEY SHRED PEOPLE TO RIBBONS AS THEY BOUNCE ALL AROUND THE ROOM TO A JAN HAMMER SYNTHESIZED SCORE AND WITH A FIRST PERSON CAMERA VIEW. THIS, OF COURSE, IS RIGHTEOUS, AND WORTH THE PRICE OF ADMISSION IN A VERY UNDERRATED CRAIG BAXLEY MOVIE. NOW THOSE ARE SOME KILLER TUNES!!

ZORG ZF-1

AS OF THIS WRITING, THE GREATEST FIREARM IN SCIENCE FICTION FILM HISTORY HAS TO BE THE ZORG ZF-1, WHICH WAS CREATED FOR 1997'S THE FIFTH ELEMENT. THE WEAPON HAS ITS ATTRIBUTES APTLY DISPLAYED BY JEAN-BAPTISTE EMANUEL ZORG (GARY OLDMAN) AS HE DEMONSTRATES ITS CAPABILITIES TO A GROUP OF LARGE, GRUNTING MANGALORES. IT HAS ABOUT A DOZEN DIFFERENT FRIGHTENING FEATURES (RANGING FROM FLAME THROWER, TO ROCKET LAUNCHER, TO POISON DART SHOOTER), EACH MORE EYEBROW-RAISING THAN THE LAST. "A WORD ON FIREPOWER", ZORG CALMLY TELLS THE MANGALORES AS HE OPEN A MOONSHINE JUG OF ANUS-WHOOP ON A SOLITARY DUMMY. "TITANIUM RECHARGER, 3000-ROUND CLIP WITH BURSTS OF 3 TO 300. WITH THE REPLAY BUTTON, ANOTHER ZORG INVENTION, IT'S EVEN EASIER." THE SWISS ARMY KNIFE OF FICTIONAL FIREARMS,

BEHIND THE SCENES OF C.S:
MUCH OF THIS VOLUME WAS WRITTEN LATE AT NIGHT WHILE MY FURRY CO-PILOT SLEPT AND TIGHTLY HUGGED HIS OWN HIND LEGS -- WHICH IS HIS PREFERRED SNOOZING STANCE. HE'S ALWAYS RIGHT THERE, AND RARELY LEAVES MY SIDE...

TYPE TYPEY TYPE

HERBIE

BOUGIE 2014.

Making a No-Hatter: Sweet Smell of Sex
By Robin Bougie

WHEN YOU'RE IN THE MIDDLE OF THE ACT ITSELF, SEX SMELLS GREAT. YOUR NOSE IS ALL OPEN, YOUR ADRENALIN IS PUMPING, AND THE ONLY THING YOU CAN REALLY THINK ABOUT IS GETTING SOME. BUT IF WE'RE BEING HONEST, ASIDE FROM THAT PARTICULAR MOMENT OF TOTALLY PRIMAL ANIMALISTIC DESIRE, MOST OF US DON'T CARE MUCH FOR IT -- ANYMORE THAN WE'RE FOND OF SAY, THE SMELL OF A GYM LOCKER. THE PUNGENT AROMA OF SOMEONE ELSE'S FUNKY UNDERWEAR REGION IS, QUITE FRANKLY, SOMETHING YOU'VE GOT BE IN THE MOOD FOR.

ROBERT DOWNEY SR'S SWEET SMELL OF SEX (A CHEEKY PLAY ON THE TITLE OF THE 1957 FILM, SWEET SMELL OF SUCCESS) WAS A TITLE THAT PUT ALL OF THAT IN MIND, AND BECAUSE OF IT WAS CLEARLY FAR TOO RACY FOR NEWSPAPERS AT THE TIME. THEY INSTEAD RAN ADS FOR THE RELEASE UNDER THE AKA "THE SWEET SMELL OF PERFUME", BUT IT DIDN'T MAKE ANY DIFFERENCE IN ATTENDANCE. IT FLOPPED. DOWNEY SR. HOWEVER, WENT ON TO HAVE A SUCCESSFUL CAREER AS BOTH AN UNDERGROUND FILMMAKER (PUTNEY SWOPE, GREASER'S PALACE, POUND), ACTOR (TO LIVE AND DIE IN LA, BOOGIE NIGHTS, TOWER HEIST) AND A FATHER (ROBERT DOWNEY JR'S DAD).

AFTER THE MOVIE'S SHORT AND UNSUCCESSFUL RUN IN THEATERS (ONE OF WHICH WAS THE BRYANT THEATER AT 138 W. 42ND STREET IN NEW YORK) IT ALL BUT DISAPPEARED, AND BELIEVE ME, A GOOD NUMBER OF ROBERT DOWNEY SR. FANS WERE WONDERING WHERE IT WENT. DISAVOWED BY ITS CREATOR SWEET SMELL OF SEX WAS A "LOST FILM" FOR MANY DECADES. WHEN A PRINT WAS FINALLY LOCATED IN FEBRUARY 2014 (IT SHOWED UP ON EBAY, AND SOLD FOR OVER THREE GRAND), ROBERT BEGRUDGINGLY ALLOWED THE RARE PRINT TO BE SCREENED BY ITS PROUD NEW OWNERS, THE LOS ANGELES REP THEATER, CINEFAMILY.

"WE'VE FINALLY FOUND IT", HE SAID, EXASPERATED, TO JONATHAN MARLOW IN A DECEMBER 2014 INTERVIEW FOR FANDOR.COM. "IT'S ONE OF THE WORST FUCKING THINGS EVER MADE, AND I MADE IT! WHAT A PIECE OF SHIT THAT WAS. STAY AWAY FROM THAT ONE."

I CERTAINLY COULD NOT. GO AHEAD, TELL ME NOT TO SEE A RARE SEXPLOITATION MOVIE THAT HAS BEEN UNAVAILABLE FOR MY ENTIRE LIFETIME. UNLIKE SWEATY GROINS, THE SWEET SMELL OF CELLULOID IS SOMETHING YOU DON'T HAVE TO BE IN THE MOOD TO ENJOY. I LOVE THIS GENRE SO MUCH, THE FUCKING MOVIE DOESN'T EVEN HAVE TO BE GOOD FOR ME TO GET SOMETHING OUT OF IT. 1960S SEXPLOITATION, WITH ITS MURKY BLACK AND WHITE SHADOWS, IS AS CLOSE AS THE ADULT FILM INDUSTRY HAS GOTTEN TO FILM NOIR.

YES, SWEET SMELL OF SEX WAS SHOT IN BLACK AND WHITE WITH A 16MM CAMERA, WITHOUT THE USE OF SYNCH SOUND. THAT MEANS THE ENTIRE SOUNDTRACK (WHICH IN THIS CASE SIMPLY CONSISTS OF JAZZY INSTRUMENTATION AND THE NARRATION OF OUR LEAD CHARACTER) WAS DONE IN POST. IT'S TOTALLY UNLIKE THE WAY MOVIES ARE MADE NOW, BUT IT WASN'T UNUSUAL FOR SEXPLOITATION FILMS FROM THE 1960S, WHICH WERE ROUTINELY MADE ON SHOESTRING BUDGETS AND DESIGNED SOMEWHAT LESS AS A CINEMATIC

EXPERIENCE, AND MORE AS A DELIVERY SYSTEM FOR 30 FOOT TALL NAKED FEMALE FLESH FOR THE VARIOUS MEMBERS OF THE COMMUNITY WHO ENJOYED LOOKING AT IT WHILE IN A PUBLIC PLACE.

THE STAR OF THIS ONE IS CUTE. SHE WEARS A TIGHT WHITE ANGORA SWEATER, KEEPS HER SHORT BROWN HAIR CROPPED AND SPORTS BANGS. HER NAME IS BEBE KATSAFANNIS. LIKE MOST OF THE PLAYERS IN THE REST OF THE FILM IT'S A ROLE THAT GOES UNCREDITED, BUT IS COMMONLY ATTRIBUTED TO AN ACTRESS (SIMPLY KNOWN AS 'DOTTIE') WITH NO OTHER CREDITS THAT I'M AWARE OF. BEBE IS A SALES GIRL FOR "A BIG COMPANY IN INDIANA", AND AS A CYNICAL YOUNG WOMAN OF THE 1960S, SHE'S BORED AND UNIMPRESSED WITH PRACTICALLY EVERYTHING. SHE HAS HOOFED IT TO NEW YORK FOR HER ANNUAL WEEK-LONG HANG-OUT SESSION WITH HER SEXY BLONDE STRIPPER FRIEND, WHOSE STAGE NAME IS "SMOKEY LA BARE" (CHORTLE). TIGHT-LIPPED AND TIGHT-THIGHED WHEN BACK HOME AMONGST HER FRIENDS AND FAMILY, EVERY YEAR WHEN BEBE SETS FOOT IN THE BIG APPLE, SHE WHORES IT UP TO PAY HER WAY. CONSIDER IT A HEDONIST VACATION.

MISS SMOKEY LA BARE HAS GONE AND SHACKED UP WITH A BARTENDER, SO AFTER HITTING TIMES SQUARE (THE BRIGHTLY LIT MARQUEES REVEAL THAT THE AWFUL DOCTOR ORLOF, DANIELLA BY NIGHT, AND SLAVE TRADE IN THE WORLD TODAY ARE ALL ENJOYING THEIR FIRST RUN IN LEGENDARY 42ND STREET GRINDHOUSES LIKE THE RIALTO AND THE LYRIC) BEBE GOES TO SAID BAR AND WAITS THERE FOR HER BURLESQUE GAL-PAL TO FINISH SHAKING HER ALABASTER WHITE MONEY-MAKER. FOR NO REASON AT ALL THE BARTENDER SPIKES HER DRINK (SHE'S LATER TOLD BY SMOKEY NOT TO GET UPSET ABOUT IT, HE DOES THAT TO EVERY WOMAN) AND BEBE ENDS UP FLAT ON HER ASS BEFORE GETTING DRAGGED BACK TO MISS LA BARE'S UNASSUMING ROOST TO SLEEP IT OFF.

QUICKLY GETTING BORED OF WATCHING SMOKEY AND HER ASSHOLE RAPIST BOYFRIEND SMASH FACES THE NEXT DAY ON THEIR COUCH, BEBE SCREWS UP HER COURAGE AND ENDS UP TROLLING THE BAR FOR GUYS TO HAVE SEXUAL RELATIONS WITH. PAYING FOR HER VACATION FROM MIDWESTERN BOREDOM SHOULD BE EASY, BUT THE LOVELY BEBE WON'T LET IT BE SO. A CLEARLY FABULOUSLY WEALTHY AND DECENT LOOKING MAN SHE DUBS "BALDY" STALKS HER STREET SIDE FROM THE BACK SEAT OF HIS CHAUFFEUR-DRIVEN LIMO, BUT SHE'S ODDLY CONTENT TO "MAKE HIM WAIT" FOR REASONS THAT MAKE NO SENSE WHATSOEVER WHEN ONE TAKES INTO ACCOUNT THAT SHE'S MADE IT CLEAR THAT SHE'S FOCUSED ON GETTING SOME COIN. CLEARLY, AN INCREDIBLY STINKY FAT MAN SEEMS LIKE A BETTER PROSPECT FOR A HIP YOUNG WHORE.

"HE'S PATHETIC, BUT UNDERNEATH IT ALL HE SEEMS LIKE A HECK OF A NICE GUY", BEBE SARCASTICALLY NARRATES AS THE FOUL SMELLING FATSO TAKES HER TO HIS FLOPHOUSE DIGS. SHE'S UNIMPRESSED BY HIM, AND HIS APARTMENT FILLED WITH CATS, CHICKENS, DOGS, AND OTHER SMALL ANIMALS MAKES HER EVEN MORE SO. HE FUMBLES TOWARDS HER ON HIS RUMPLED BED, AND THE JAZZY SOUNDTRACK SUDDENLY GOES FRANTIC. OH SHIT -- HE'S HAVING A HEART ATTACK, AND THE CHICKENS, DOGS AND CATS RUN FOR COVER. BEBE GRABS SOME WATER AND SOME PILLS FROM HIS NIGHTSTAND AND SHOVES BOTH IN HIS GREASY YAPPER, AND GETS WHILE THE GETTING IS GOOD. HE LOOKS OK FOR A SECOND, BUT THEN GRABS HIS HEART AND KEELS OVER. "A HUNDRED DOLLARS, DOWN THE DRAIN", SHE LAMENTS.

BEBE GOES UPSTAIRS AND WATCHES A PHOTOGRAPHER TAKE PICS OF A BIKINI-ADORNED MODEL ON THE

ROOF AS SHE CAVORTS WITH A BOTTLE OF VODKA.
SENSING THAT BETTER PUSSY IS AFOOT, THE
PHOTOG SENDS THE FLOOZY PACKING. "ACT NAIVE
AND INNOCENT" SHE SAYS TO HERSELF AS SHE
DECIDES HOW TO TAKE ADVANTAGE OF THE
SITUATION FOR FINANCIAL GAIN. "I WONDER WHAT
HIS HANG-UP IS." THEY RETIRE TO HIS APARTMENT,
AND SHE ADMIRES HERSELF IN THE BATHROOM
MIRROR WHILE HE SNAPS PICS OF HER SCANTILY-
CLAD WITH A BOTTLE OF J&B. "WHAT A DRAG", SHE
NARRATES WHILE SMILING AND LIFTING HER LEG
COYLY FOR THE ENTHUSIASTIC SHUTTERBUG.

SUDDENLY THE CAMERA PLOWS CLOSE INTO HER FACE,
AND SHE LOOKS CONCERNED. AGAIN THE SOUNDTRACK
SKIDDLY-SCATS AND SKI-DOODLES AROUND, LETTING
US KNOW THAT SOMETHING UNKOSHER IS AFOOT. WE
AREN'T TOLD WHAT IT IS, BUT APPARENTLY MISTER
CAMERAMAN WANTS SOMETHING PERVERSE TO HAPPEN
AND BEBE ISN'T GAME. "I DON'T MIND SELLING
NORMAL MERCHANDISE, BUT WHAT HE WANTS ISN'T
WORTH $200." SHE CLEARS OUT, WANDERS OUT ON
TO 42ND STREET WHERE JOSE BENAZERAF'S MOODY
SIN ON THE BEACH (AKA L'ETERNITE PUR NOUS. 1963)
IS PLAYING AT THE VICTORY, AND WHERE BALDY'S
MOBILE BUTLER INFORMS HER THAT IT'S "WORTH
THOUSANDS" IF SHE "SPENDS AN HOUR" WITH HIM.
AGAIN, SHE DOESN'T LIKE THAT PLAN, BUT SHE'LL
CHANGE HER MIND.

BACK AT SMOKEY'S, SHE'S GIVEN HER WALKING
PAPERS BECAUSE THE APARTMENT IS GETTING "TOO
CROWDED". "I KNOW THIS LINE", SHE SCOFFS,
DISGUSTED WITH BEING OUSTED FROM THE FREE
ROOM AND BOARD. "ONCE I GET THE THOUSAND
FROM BALDY, I'LL CATCH THE FIRST BUS BACK TO
INDIANA". SURE THING, BUT NOT BEFORE MR. DATE-
RAPIST BARTENDER TRIES TO RAPE HER ONE MORE
TIME FOR GOOD LUCK. SHE GRABS HER SUITCASE,
AND JUMPS IN BALDY'S CAR. HE LOOKS AS DOUR AND
UNIMPRESSED AS USUAL. "HERE COMES A THOUSAND
DOLLARS" SHE SAYS TO HERSELF AS THEY BOTH
LOOK MISERABLE DURING THE RIDE BACK TO HIS
ELEGANT PENTHOUSE APARTMENT.

WITH THE RECENT DEATH OF THE STINKY FAT JOHN
STILL REELING IN HER MIND, BEBE REALIZES SHE
SHOULD GET PAID IN ADVANCE THIS TIME, SO BALDY
SITS DOWN AT HIS BIG OAK DESK UNDER A HUGE
PAINTING OF A DEMON ROOSTER (?) AND PENS HER
A CHEQUE FOR A GRAND. SATISFIED, SHE TAKES THE
COSTUME HE MOTIONS FOR HER TO WEAR TO A
NEARBY BEDROOM TO CHANGE INTO. IT'S A MEN'S
DRESS SHIRT AND NOTHING ELSE. WHEN SHE
RETURNS, HE'S SITTING AT HIS DESK IN A ROBE,
AND TAKES THE PHONE OFF THE HOOK, AND WE ALL
KNOW WHAT IT MEANS WHEN YOU TAKE THE PHONE
OFF THE HOOK. BALDY BITES HIS LIP AS SHE OPENS
THE SHIRT AND SHOWS HIM (BUT NOT US) WHAT
PRESUMABLY ARE HER BARE TITS.

"HE LOOKS LIKE A TURTLE", SHE LAMENTS, AS HE
STARES PAST THE CAMERA AND GETS INCREDIBLY
SWEATY AND DISORIENTATED WHILE STARING AT
HER UNCOVERED CHESTICLES. UH OH -- THE
SOUNDTRACK GOES INSANE AGAIN, BUT THIS TIME
IT'S BECAUSE BALDY IS CUMMING ALL OVER THE
INSIDE OF HIS ROBE. SHE JUST STOOD 3 FEET IN
FRONT OF HIM WITH HER SHIRT OPEN WHILE HE
JACKED OFF FOR 30 SECONDS. ADJUSTED FOR
INFLATION, THAT'S A PAYDAY OF $7,500.00 AND YOU
DIDN'T EVEN HAVE TO TOUCH THE DUDE? GOOD
WORK IF YOU CAN GET IT, BUT BEBE DOESN'T SEEM
EVEN REMOTELY TICKLED.

LAZILY STOPPING AT THE BAR ONE LAST TIME
BEFORE BEATING CHEEKS BACK TO THE BUS
STATION, BEBE IGNORES THE RAPIST BARTENDER,
AND TAKES NOTE THAT THE BIKINI MODEL FROM

THE ROOFTOP IS THERE, AND SHE'S ALL ABOUT FLIRTING AND SMOKING WITH A GOOD LOOKING YOUNG BLACK MAN. "SHE MUST BE ONE OF THOSE CIVIL RIGHTS-ERS", BEBE INTONES. "BACK IN INDIANA WE FROWN ON THAT, BUT WHAT THE HECK! THEY WANT ME TO GO TO SOME KIND OF MASQUERADE PARTY. FINE. I'LL GET THE BUS BACK TO INDIANA IN THE MORNING."

THE PARTY SEQUENCE IN THE SWEET SMELL OF SEX IS EASILY THE BEST SCENE. ROBERT DOWNEY SR. HAD CLEARLY INVITED ALL OF HIS PALS FOR A HOUSE PARTY, AND THE PLACE WAS JUMPING. CROSS DRESSERS, WEIRDOS, ARTISTS, BEATNIKS, A DROOLING BABY, LESBIANS, A HARP PLAYER, SATANISTS, SADISTS, PRIESTS, AND OTHER NEW YORK MALCONTENTS LIVE IT UP, AND THE SOUNDTRACK ISN'T SHY ABOUT LETTING US KNOW IT. THERE IS DRINKING, DOOBIE-SMOKING, A SLAPPY-FIGHT, A DRUNK ANNOYING GUY IN A SUIT CONTINUALLY SHRIEKING "FREAKY FREAKY FREAKY! YAAA! WAKA-WAKA-WAKA!".

PLENTY OF DANCING AND REVELRY GOES ON, WHICH BEBE REALLY SEEMS TO LOVE, (SHE'S SMILING FOR THE FIRST AND ONLY TIME IN THE MOVIE) BUT THE JOY OF TAKING PART IN THIS BONKERS EVENT IS SUDDENLY SPOILED FOR HER WHEN A BLINDFOLDED MIDDLE-AGED PERVERT IS DRAGGED OUT, TIED TO A BIG CHINESE GONG, AND BEATEN SENSELESS WITH A RIDING CROP BY THE PARTY-GOERS. HORRIFIED, SHE CLUTCHES HER FACE AS IF SHE WERE AFRAID IT WERE GOING TO FALL OFF, AND RUNS OUT ONTO THE SIDEWALK, WHERE SHE CATCHES A YELLOW CAB.

FREE OF THE RAW INSANITY THAT IS THE NEW YORK CREATIVE ARTS SCENE, BEBE BEGINS TO RELAX, WHICH HER CAB-DRIVER TAKES AS AN INVITATION TO FORCIBLY JAM HIS PENIS INTO HER VAGINA. SUDDENLY AND BRAZENLY JUMPING INTO THE BACK SEAT WITH HER WHEN STOPPED AT A GAS STATION, HE TAKES WHAT HE WANTS. "AT LEAST HE DIDN'T KEEP THE METER RUNNING", SHE SHRUGS, POST ASSAULT.

FINALLY MAKING HER WAY TO THE BUS STATION, BEBE HAS ONE FINAL CONFRONTATION WITH A CHARACTER THAT THE MOVIE ADDRESSES AS THE MOST AVERAGE, NORMAL FELLAH AROUND. HER ESCAPE FROM NEW YORK BACK TO INDIANA DOESN'T GO AS SHE PLANNED, BECAUSE, AS THE MOVIE'S ADVERTISING PUT IT: "FOR ALL THE WEIRDOS BEBE TOYED WITH, THE ORDINARY JOE -- WHO LOOKED SO STRAIGHT -- LEFT THE MOST LASTING IMPRESSION ON HER.

THIS IS A RESOLUTELY UNSEXY MOVIE, IN MORE WAYS THAN ONE. FIRST OFF, IT'S A TALE ABOUT A HOOKER WHO NEVER HAS SEX DESPITE SPENDING THE ENTIRE MOVIE TRYING TO (ASIDE FROM AN OUT-OF-LEFT-FIELD RAPE AT THE END THAT HAPPENS OFF CAMERA). THIS IS LIKE THE CINEMATIC VERSION OF BLUE-BALLS. SECONDLY (AND MOST SURPRISINGLY FOR THIS GENRE) THERE IS ALMOST ZERO NUDITY, WHICH WAS HIGHLY UNUSUAL FOR A SEXPLOITATION PICTURE. MID 1960S SEX FILMS ADMITTEDLY OFTEN HAD DEMURE NAKEDNESS, BUT DID HAVE SOME. A NOTABLE EXCEPTION IS RUSS MEYER'S FASTER, PUSSYCAT! KILL! KILL! (1965), AND WHILE JOE SARNO'S SIN IN THE SUBURBS (1964) IS VERY LIGHT ON NAKED FLESH, IT MAKES UP FOR IT WITH RAW PRIMAL SEXUALITY THAT REALLY MAKES YOU FORGET THAT YOU DIDN'T SEE MUCH. NOT SO WITH THIS PICTURE, WHICH CERTAINLY COULDN'T HAVE PLEASED MANY OF THE TIMES SQUARE RAIN-COATERS.

WHEN THE MOVIE WAS FINISHED, ROBERT GOT MANY OF HIS FRIENDS (AS WELL AS THE CAST AND CREW) TOGETHER, AND SCREENED THE FINAL CUT AT THE BLEEKER STREET CINEMA WITH NO SOUNDTRACK, AS ONE DIDN'T EXIST AT THAT POINT. INSTEAD, HE PUT ON BEATLES RECORDS, AND NOTED THAT HE AND HIS PALS HAD A REALLY GOOD TIME WITH THE MOVIE IN THIS FORM. HE LIKED HAVING A NIGHT OUT WITH HIS PALS, BUT THIS DIRECTOR CLEARLY WASN'T CONCERNED WITH THE INTERESTS OF THE AUDIENCE OF FILMS OF THIS SORT, NOR THE MAN WHO PAID HIM TO MAKE THE MOVIE.

"UNDERGROUND FILM NOTORIETY DIDN'T EXACTLY PAY THE BILLS, AND DOWNEY DESPERATELY NEEDED A GIG", CURATOR OF THE ANTHOLOGY FILM ARCHIVES, ANDREW LAMPERT, NOTED IN 2014. "LUCKILY (OR NOT) WRITER/PRODUCER BARNARD L. SACKETT APPEARED WITH A SCRIPT ABOUT BEBE... AD COPY AND PRESS NOTES DISCOVERED IN THE DOWNEY FILE AT ANTHOLOGY CLAIM THAT THE FILM 'TAKES YOU ONE STEP BEYOND REALITY' AND 'PROVOKES TORTURE IN THE CHAMBER OF THE MIND'."

"SACKETT WANTED A STRAIGHT, SOFT-CORE PORN FILM", AUTHOR WHEELER WINSTON DIXON WROTE IN HIS 2003 BOOK, STRAIGHT: CONSTRUCTIONS OF HETEROSEXUALITY IN THE CINEMA. "BUT DOWNEY REFUSED TO BE CO-OPTED BY THE PRODUCER'S DEMANDS. HE INSTEAD PRODUCED A FILM THAT CRITICIZED PERFORMATIVE HETEROSEXUALITY AND THE PORN INDUSTRY ITSELF."

"IT WAS SHOT ON 16MM, AND THEN BLOWN UP TO 35MM. IT PLAYED ON 42ND STREET AND PLACES LIKE THAT.", DOWNEY SR. EXPLAINED IN THE 2004 BOOK, FILM VOICES: INTERVIEWS FROM THE POST SCRIPT. "I ACTUALLY DID SWEET SMELL OF SEX TO PAY FOR THE BIRTH OF MY SON, ACTOR ROBERT DOWNEY JR... BECAUSE WHEN MY DAUGHTER WAS BORN, IT WAS TOUGH, IT WAS IN BELLEVUE. BECAUSE OF SWEET SMELL OF SEX, I WAS ABLE TO PUT HIS MOTHER IN A DECENT HOSPITAL, AND THAT IS WHAT IT WAS REALLY ABOUT. I DIDN'T MIND DOING IT FAST, EITHER... I HAD TO WRITE, DIRECT, AND DELIVER THE FILM IN A WEEK!"

BUILT LIKE A WRESTLER, JEWISH PRODUCER BERNARD (BARNEY) SACKETT WAS KNOWN FOR SUCH DEMANDS, AND PAID THE YOUNG DIRECTOR $750 FOR HIS WEEK-LONG EFFORT. UPON RECEIVING THE FILM, BARNEY (ALONG WITH THE ELDERLY CHARLES MARTIN) WROTE THE SNIDE, SARCASTIC NARRATION FOR THE BEBE CHARACTER, AND TRIED TO SALVAGE WHAT HE SAW AS $750 WASTED BY BRINGING IN TOM O'HORGAN (WHO PLAYED THE FAT STINKY MAN WHO HAD A HEART ATTACK) AT DOWNEY SR'S INSISTENCE. TOM AND A COUPLE OF HIS FRIENDS WOULD BE RELIED UPON TO DROP BY AND WING A JAZZ SCORE AFTER WATCHING THE MOVIE JUST ONCE, A SOUNDTRACK THAT ROBERT WOULD LAMENT AS "TERRIBLE". ONLY THREE YEARS LATER O'HORGAN WOULD BE NAMED "THEATRICAL DIRECTOR OF THE YEAR" BY NEWSWEEK AFTER HE TOOK BROADWAY BY STORM WITH THE MUSICAL 'HAIR' -- THE FIRST BROADWAY MUSICAL TO FEATURE FULL FRONTAL NUDITY.

BORN IN THE 1920S, SACKETT WROTE FOR RADIO, WAS SYLVIA SYM'S MANAGER, AND RAN AND PRODUCED PLAYS FOR 'PLAYHOUSE IN THE PARK' IN PHILADELPHIA BEFORE MAKING A HANDFUL OF SEXPLOITATION FILMS IN THE 1960S. SACKETT MADE EROTICON (1971) WITH HARRY REEMS AND HAD A SMALL ACTING PART IN THE DORIS WISHMAN SEX FILM, BAD GIRLS GO TO HELL (1965), BUT WHAT THE FAST-TALKING HUSTLER WAS REALLY KNOWN AROUND TOWN FOR WAS HIS ABILITY TO BED FORMER HOLLYWOOD STARLETS. BETTE DAVIS AND CORINNE CALVET WERE TWO OF THEM, AND THEN HE BEGAN DATING AN AGING HEDY LEMARR. IN THE

EARLY 1970S THE TWO MOVED IN TOGETHER -- A PENTHOUSE IN MANHATTAN'S EXPENSIVE UPPER EAST SIDE GRAMERCY PARK NEIGHBOURHOOD.

"THE PRODUCER WAS FURIOUS WITH WHAT I'D DONE", DOWNEY EXPLAINED IN AN INTERVIEW WITH PROFESSOR JOEL E. SIEGEL OF GEORGETOWN UNIVERSITY, THAT SAW PRINT IN THE 1974 BOOK, 'SINEMA: AMERICAN PORNOGRAPHIC FILMS AND THE PEOPLE WHO MAKE THEM.' "THE SEX THEATERS DIDN'T WANT TO SHOW IT BECAUSE IT DIDN'T HAVE THE KIND OF SEX THEY WANTED IN IT. I WAS DOING ALL THESE STRANGE, WILD THINGS WITH CHICKENS AND DOGS, AND IT WAS FUNNY. BUT THE PRODUCER, WHO HAD DONE OTHER SEX FILMS, KEPT REFERRING TO HIS PAST MOVIES AS ONE, TWO, AND THREE HATTERS. WHICH REFERS TO HOW MANY HATS THE OLD CREEPS WHO GO TO THESE MOVIES BRING INTO THE THEATER TO, LIKE, MAKE IT IN. THE PRODUCER SAW MY FILM, SAID IT WAS A NO-HATTER, AND THAT WAS THAT."

—BOUGIE 2016 ☆

INFERNO (1980 Dir: Dario Argento)

LACKING IN LOGIC BUT SOAKED IN STYLE, THERE ARE A FEW OTHER ARGENTO MOVIES THAT I PREFER TO THIS, BUT DURING ITS BEST MOMENTS IT IS AS POWERFUL AS ANYTHING THIS DIRECTOR EVER DID. UNFORTUNATELY, THOSE MOMENTS ARE ALSO SURROUNDED BY OTHER STUFF THAT DOESN'T HOLD UP NEARLY AS WELL, AND IS PROBABLY WHY IT WAS MOSTLY GIVEN A NEGATIVE RECEPTION BY THOSE THAT SAW IT WHEN IT APPEARED IN THE 1980S. I IMAGINE EXPECTATIONS WERE HIGH, GIVEN THAT THIS WAS HIS FOLLOW UP TO HIS MOST POPULAR FILM, 1977'S SUSPIRIA.

FOR REASONS UNKNOWN, 20TH CENTURY FOX DIDN'T THINK IT WAS PRUDENT TO PUT INFERNO INTO A WIDE THEATRICAL RELEASE IN THE US LIKE THEY HAD WITH SUSPIRIA. ARGENTO HIMSELF HAS SUPPOSED THAT FOX'S COLD FEET CAME BECAUSE OF AN ABRUPT CHANGE IN MANAGEMENT AT THE STUDIO, LEAVING HIS WORK AND ABOUT 30 OTHER FILMS THAT HAD BEEN GREENLIT, IN LIMBO. SO ON A SHELF IT SAT FOR FIVE LONG YEARS, UNTIL FOX'S KEY VIDEO SUBSIDIARY PUT OUT A STRAIGHT-TO-VHS VERSION. AS ARGENTO TOLD CINEFANTASTIQUE MAGAZINE IN 1983, "I THINK ANYBODY OUTSIDE OF ITALY WAS LUCKY TO SEE INFERNO."

NONETHELESS, THIS ATMOSPHERIC HORROR CLASSIC CERTAINLY DOES HAVE ITS FANS, ESPECIALLY AMONGST RESPECTED FILM CRITICS AND FILMMAKERS. IN FACT, WHEN TIME OUT COMPILED A LIST OF THE 100 GREATEST HORROR FILMS EVER MADE IN 2013, AND BASED THE RESULTS ON THE TOP TEN LISTS OF OVER ONE HUNDRED FILM DIRECTORS, SCREENWRITERS, AND CRITICS — INFERNO SLOTTED IN THE 92ND SPOT. NOT BAD.

IRENE MIRACLE STARS, BUT AS PER USUAL WITH ARGENTO, THE PERFORMER IN HIS CAST I WAS MOST TAKEN WITH WAS DARIA NICOLODI. SHE TURNS IN A COMPETENT PERFORMANCE HERE, PLAYING

THE KIND, BUT MENTALLY DISTRAUGHT, ELISE. BESIDES A TIGHT WORKING RELATIONSHIP THAT LASTED 30 YEARS, THE PAIR WERE LOVERS FOR ROUGHLY TEN YEARS AND GAVE BIRTH TO A LOVELY DAUGHTER, ASIA ARGENTO, IN 1975. BY THE TIME THIS MOVIE CAME AROUND, THEIR ROMANTIC DECADE LONG TRYST WAS OVER, HOWEVER.

REPORTEDLY, ARGENTO WROTE THE SCREENPLAY WORKING FROM NICOLODI'S ORIGINAL STORY NOTES WHILE RENTING A ROOM IN A NEW YORK HOTEL OVERLOOKING CENTRAL PARK. WHEN IT CAME TIME FOR CASTING, JAMES WOODS WAS SLATED TO PLAY ONE OF THE LEAD CHARACTERS, MARK, BUT THAT FELL THROUGH, SO 20TH CENTURY FOX GOT AMERICAN TV ACTOR, LEIGH "DALLAS" MCCLOSKEY, INSTEAD. I CAN'T HELP BUT THINK HOW MUCH COOLER IT WOULD HAVE BEEN TO SEE JAMES WOODS IN THIS, 3 YEARS BEFORE STARRING IN HIS LEGENDARY VIDEODROME ROLE. OH WELL.

AHHH, FUCK IT...
DISMANTLE THE HOLLYWOOD STUDIO SYSTEM

IT'S A BOUGIE RANT!

I HEAR OVER AND OVER AGAIN ABOUT HOW THE HOLLYWOOD STUDIO SYSTEM, AS IT IS SET UP CURRENTLY, IS DESIGNED SO THAT GOOD MOVIES ARE NEARLY IMPOSSIBLE TO MAKE. TOO MUCH MONEY IS RIDING ON EVERYTHING, SO THEY HAVE TO REWRITE AND FOCUS GROUP EVERYTHING INTO MOOSHY PABLUM. THEY ERASE THE VERY SOUL OF THEIR PRODUCT BEFORE IT EVER MAKES IT FROM SCRIPT TO SCREEN. PEOPLE KEEP SAYING, AND I AGREE WITH THEM, THAT IT IS NOW THE MEDIUM OF TELEVISION WHERE ALL THE EXPANSIVE STORYTELLING, HIGH QUALITY ACTING, AND ENTERTAINMENT IS HAPPENING. THEY SWITCHED PLACES AT SOME POINT WHEN WE WEREN'T PAYING ATTENTION. WHAT WENT WRONG?

THE THING THAT MAKES ME LAUGH IS HOW NONE OF THESE FILM STUDIOS WANT TO TAKE A "RISK" ON AN ORIGINAL, UNTESTED IDEA OR CONCEPT. THEY WON'T PUT A PENNY INTO SOMETHING THAT ISN'T "PROVEN" (THUS ALL THE REMAKES, SEQUELS, REBOOTS, AND BORING RETREADS) AND YET WHO AMONG US THOUGHT THE 2013 FLOP, THE LONE RANGER WAS GOING TO MAKE THE 250 MILLION IT COST? HOW IS THAT A SURE THING? THEY'RE TERRIBLE BUSINESS PEOPLE, AND THE MOVIE LOST WALT DISNEY A WHOPPING $161 MILL. THE CURRENT HOLLYWOOD STUDIO SYSTEM IS OVERDUE TO BE DISMANTLED, IF YOU ASK ME.

THINK ABOUT THAT FOR A SECOND. $250 MILLION. YOU CAN MAKE AN EXCELLENT FILM FOR $5 MILLION. IT WON'T LOOK CHEAP AT ALL. THEY COULD HAVE MADE 50 FILMS FOR THAT. PONDER THAT FOR A MINUTE. FIFTY FILMS. WHAT DO YOU WANT TO BET THAT FIFTY MOVIES MADE FOR $5 MILL EACH, AND MADE BY HUNGRY YOUNG TALENTED DIRECTORS WITH SMALL CASTS AND CREWS, WHO ARE FREE TO DO WHATEVER CRAZY UNPROVEN THING THEY WANT, ARE GOING TO EASILY OUTGROSS THE LONE RANGER? I SAID IT BEFORE, AND I'LL SAY IT AGAIN: TERRIBLE BUSINESS PEOPLE.

SURE, LONG GONE ARE THE DAYS WHEN A FILM LIKE LAST TANGO IN PARIS COULD BE AMONG THE TOP GROSSING FILMS OF THE YEAR, BUT THE STUDIOS WOULDN'T EVEN NEED THE GENERAL PUBLIC TO FLOCK TO A $5MILLION DOLLAR MOVIE. MAKING $5MILLION OR $10MILLION ISN'T MUCH OF A CHALLENGE GIVEN HOW MUCH MOVIES MAKE THESE DAYS, AND THE STUDIO WOULD HAVE 50 CHANCES OF LANDING THE NEXT BLOCKBUSTER, INSTEAD OF ONE. THESE ARE BASIC AND UNCOMPLICATED NUMBERS HERE, AND LITTLE INDIE FILMS STILL DO VERY, VERY WELL FROM TIME TO TIME.

I'M NOT EVEN TALKING ABOUT THE QUALITY OF THE LONE RANGER, OR IF DEPP IS GOOD AS TONTO, OR IF VERBINSKI IS A GOOD DIRECTOR, OR WHATEVER. THAT IS ALL TOTALLY BESIDE THE POINT AND IRRELEVANT. IT COULD HAVE BEEN THE GREATEST MOVIE EVER MADE, BUT IT WOULD STILL BE A TERRIBLE BET TO ASSUME IT WAS GOING TO BE THAT BANKABLE -- TAKING INTO ACCOUNT HOW MUCH WESTERNS TRADITIONALLY MAKE, AND WHAT THE PUBLIC SEEMS TO BE ENTICED BY. IT'S JUST ARROGANCE AND PURE AUDACITY.

FUCK, WHEN WAS THE LAST TIME A LONE RANGER MOVIE MADE MONEY, ANYWAY? THE YOUTH MARKET DOESN'T WANT TO SEE BIG LOUD ACTION MOVIES BASED ON CREAKY OLD FILM SERIALS FROM 60 YEARS AGO. YOU WOULD HAVE THOUGHT THEY WOULD HAVE LEARNED THEIR LESSON WITH HOW THE PHANTOM DID BACK IN 1996. IT COST $45 MILLION AND MADE $17 MILLION BACK. THE GREEN HORNET LOST $22 MILLION IN 2011. SO YEAH, DON'T BOTHER WITH $200 MILLION DOLLAR ADAPTATIONS OF SMILIN' JACK OR CONGO BILL, EITHER. MOST OF THE PEOPLE WHO WOULD BE ENTICED ARE EITHER DEAD, OR HAVE DEMENTIA.

BOUG GONE CRAY ZEE!

SQUAMISH 5 STYLE!

BLOW IT UP!

ANYWAY, ALL OF THIS JUST MAKES ME THINK OF CANNON FILMS. IMAGINE WHAT GOLAN AND GLOBUS COULD HAVE MADE WITH FIFTY $5MILLION DOLLAR FILMS? IT'S STAGGERING TO PONDER. THEY DID EVERYTHING ON A BUDGET, AND PUT NEARLY EVERY PENNY INTO THE MOVIE ITSELF SO THAT IT ALL SHOWED UP ON THE SCREEN. THEY WERE HANDS OFF, FOR THE MOST PART. THEY HIRED TALENTED PEOPLE, LET THEM DO WHAT THEY WERE GOOD AT, AND KEPT THEIR FUCKING NOSES OUT OF IT. IF YOU DIDN'T LET THEM DOWN, YOU GOT TO KEEP MAKING MOVIES. THEY KEPT THE CREATIVE TALENT HAPPY, AND FOCUSED ON GETTING THE MONEY FOR OVERSEAS RIGHTS UP FRONT TO BANKROLL THE BUDGET.

IT'S A BRILLIANT FUCKING SYSTEM THAT COULD WORK JUST AS WELL NOW, AND AS I'VE MENTIONED IN OTHER ARTICLES I'VE WRITTEN ABOUT THE STUDIO, IT MADE CANNON INTO THE BIGGEST INDEPENDENT IN HOLLYWOOD. THEY ONLY WENT OUT OF BUSINESS BECAUSE THEY STUPIDLY INVESTED ALL THEIR MONEY IN THEATER CHAINS, AND DID SO TOO FAST -- FREEZING ALL THEIR CASH IN INVESTMENTS. IF THEY HAD JUST STUCK TO THEIR MOVIE MAKING, THEY WOULD HAVE BEEN FINE..

BUT DON'T JUST TAKE MY WORD FOR IT: AT A UNIVERSITY OF SOUTHERN CALIFORNIA MEDIA EVENT IN JUNE 2013, STEVEN SPIELBERG OUTRIGHT PREDICTED THAT THE STUDIO SYSTEM IS SET TO IMPLODE OR FACE A "BIG MELTDOWN", WHICH HE CLAIMS WILL COME ABOUT WHEN THE RIGHT AMOUNT OF INSANELY-BUDGETED FILMS FLOP AT THE SAME TIME. ALSO AT THE SAME EVENT, GEORGE LUCAS ECHOED SPIELBERG'S OPINION, AND POINTED OUT THE CURRENT DIFFICULTIES FOR EVEN TWO THOROUGHLY ESTABLISHED FILMMAKERS TO GET A MOVIE OUT WITHOUT INTENSIVE STUDIO MEDDLING, AND PUSHING TO DUMB THE PRODUCT DOWN.

"THE PATHWAY TO GET INTO THEATERS IS REALLY GETTING SMALLER AND SMALLER", SPIELBERG COMPLAINED.

BURN IT DOWN, I SAY. START OVER. THIS SHIT IS BROKE, MAN. TRUST ME, IT'S FOR THE BEST.

- BONGIE - 2013

BROTHERS (1977)
DIRECTED BY: ARTHUR BARRON
WRITTEN BY: EDWARD AND MILDRED LEWIS
EXEC. PRODUCED BY: LEE SAVIN

A story of love...and hate

BROTHERS

EDWARD LEWIS PRODUCTION OF BROTHERS
STARRING BERNIE CASEY · VONETTA McGEE · RON O'NEAL
MUSIC COMPOSED AND PERFORMED BY TAJ MAHAL

STARTS FRIDAY

MATURE ENTERTAINMENT
warning: some violence
and coarse language R.W. McDONALD—B.C. DIRECTOR

Feature starts at: 1:45 3:50
5:55 8:00 10:05
Last complete show 9:45

▶ downtown 965 granville

WHEN I ORIGINALLY LOOKED TO TRACK THIS DOWN, I THOUGHT I WAS LOOKING FOR A BLAXPLOITATION PRISON FILM, BUT THE MOST INTERESTING THING ABOUT BROTHERS IS THAT IT WAS MADE AS A SEMI-FACTUAL ACCOUNT OF THE FASCINATING RELATIONSHIP BETWEEN RADICAL BLACK ACTIVIST ANGELA DAVIS AND A BLACK INMATE NAMED GEORGE JACKSON -- A MAN WHO WAS PUT IN JAIL AT AGE 18 FOR A ROBBERY, AND EVENTUALLY SHOT AND KILLED DURING A FAILED SOLEDAD PRISON BREAKOUT BACK IN 1971.

THE ALWAYS AWESOME VONETTA McGEE (RIP) IS THE OUTSPOKEN DAVIS, AND JACKSON IS PLAYED BY THE EQUALLY EXCELLENT ACTOR, BERNIE CASEY -- WHO GENRE FILM FANS WILL PROBABLY REMEMBER BETTER AS THE STAR OF DR. BLACK, MR. HYDE. HIS TRANSFORMATION FROM AN OUTRAGED HOODLUM TO A CALM AND INTELLIGENT MEMBER OF THE BLACK PANTHERS AFTER A HARROWING STINT IN A RACIST WHITE JAIL WHILE SHARING A CELL WITH HUEY NEWTON IS REPRESENTED IN THE FILM IN QUITE A FEW RATHER MOVING SCENES.

ANOTHER PART OF THE STORY THAT SEEMS WAY TOO CRAZY TO BE NON-FICTION (BUT THAT REALLY HAPPENED!) IS WHEN JACKSON'S HOT-HEADED 17-YEAR-OLD BROTHER JONATHAN GREW FRUSTRATED WITH THE RED TAPE INVOLVED WITH LEGALLY PURSUING JUSTICE FOR IMPRISONED BLACK FREEDOM FIGHTERS, AND INSTEAD GRABBED AN AUTOMATIC WEAPON AND ON AUGUST 7, 1970, BURST INTO A MARIN COUNTY COURTROOM. THERE, HE FREED PRISONERS JAMES McCLAIN, WILLIAM A. CHRISTMAS AND RUCHELL MAGEE, AND TOOK JUDGE HAROLD HALEY, DEPUTY DISTRICT ATTORNEY GARY THOMAS, AND THREE JURORS HOSTAGE. THE PLAN WAS TO USE THE HOSTAGES TO DEMAND THE RELEASE OF THE "SOLEDAD BROTHERS", WHO CONSISTED OF HIS BROTHER AND OTHER IMPRISONED BLACK PANTHERS, BUT IT ALL WENT AWRY IN A HAIL OF BULLETS OUTSIDE OF THE COURTHOUSE.. JACKSON, CHRISTMAS, McCLAIN AND JUDGE HALEY WERE ALL KILLED AS THE GETAWAY CAR WAS TURNED INTO SWISS CHEESE IN A HAIL OF GUNFIRE.

ANGELA DAVIS, A PROMINENT BLACK COUNTERCULTURE ACTIVIST AND RADICAL OF THE 1960S AND '70S, COMES INTO THE STORY BECAUSE SHE'D CORRESPONDED WITH AND VISITED GEORGE JACKSON IN PRISON (THE MOVIE SUPPOSES A ROMANTIC INTERMINGLING, WHICH WAS LATER CONFIRMED BY ANGELA HERSELF), AND WAS ALSO LINKED TO THE COURTHOUSE HOSTAGE TAKING WHEN IT WAS DISCOVERED THAT SHE HAD BOUGHT THE GUNS THAT THE YOUNG JONATHAN JACKSON HAD UTILIZED IN THE BLOOD-SOAKED MASSACRE. ANGELA FLED CALIFORNIA, AND BECAME THE 3RD WOMAN TO EVER APPEAR ON THE FBI'S "TEN MOST WANTED" LIST, AND INSPIRATION FOR ONE OF THE FEW POLITICAL SONGS THE ROLLING STONES EVER RECORDED ("SWEET BLACK ANGEL"). UPON HER CAPTURE THREE MONTHS LATER, RICHARD NIXON CONGRATULATED THE FBI ON ITS "CAPTURE OF THE DANGEROUS TERRORIST, ANGELA DAVIS", ALTHOUGH SHE WAS

- CONTINUED FROM THE PREVIOUS PAGE -

EVENTUALLY FOUND INNOCENT -- BY AN ALL-WHITE JURY, NO LESS.

JUST TO GIVE YOU AN IDEA OF THE TIME AND THE POLITICAL CLIMATE THIS MOVIE WAS RELEASED INTO, TV GUIDE LAMENTED THE FILMGOING EXPERIENCE FOR CAUCASIAN VIEWERS, WHEN THEY WARNED OF "PREACHINESS" AND "VIOLENCE" AND WROTE: "WOE TO THE WHITE PATRON WHO HAPPENS INTO A BLACK THEATER WHERE THIS FILM IS SHOWING". THINLY VEILED FEAR-MONGERING ASIDE, A STATEMENT BY A MAJOR ENTERTAINMENT MAGAZINE ABOUT HOW DANGEROUS BLACKS ARE TO WATCH MOVIES ALONGSIDE SPEAKS TO WHY A FILM LIKE THIS WAS SO IMPORTANT IN THE FIRST PLACE.

FOR HER PART, THE ACTUAL ANGELA DAVIS LOOKED PAST SOME OF THE DRAMATIC AND ROMANTIC LIBERTIES THAT BROTHERS TOOK WITH THE TRUTH (AS ALL CINEMA IS WONT TO DO) AND PRAISED IT AS A POSITIVE EXAMPLE OF "HOW TO SENSITIZE PEOPLE ABOUT THE NEED TO GET INVOLVED WITH A MOVEMENT."
— BOUGIE

RANDOM TRIVIA

ORIGINALLY, THE NASTY AND UPSETTING FAMILY MASSACRE SCENE IN 1986'S **HENRY: PORTRAIT OF A SERIAL KILLER** WAS MUCH LONGER -- AT LEAST IN SCRIPT FORM. DIRECTOR JOHN MCNAUGHTON DECIDED NOT TO FILM THE PART WHERE OTIS MOLESTS THE CORPSE OF THE FRESHLY MURDERED MOTHER, AND THEN FUCKS IT.

ACTRESS ERICA LEERHSEN WAS SO CONVINCING IN HER BLOOD-CURDLING SCREAMS DURING HER SCREEN TEST TO BE IN THE 2003 REMAKE OF **TEXAS CHAINSAW MASSACRE**, THAT PEOPLE IN OTHER PARTS OF THE BUILDING CALLED THE COPS AND REPORTED THAT A WOMAN WAS BEING MURDERED.

THE FAKE TESTICLES THAT WILL FERRELL PRESSES AGAINST THE DRUM KIT IN 2008'S **STEP BROTHERS** COST 20 THOUSAND DOLLARS TO MAKE, AND WERE GIVEN TO FERRELL AS A WRAP PARTY GIFT. HE AND JOHN C. REILLY PERFORM AN IMPROVISED SONG ABOUT THE MAKING OF THE FAKE BALLSACK ON THE AUDIO COMMENTARY FOR THE DVD!

IN **TARZAN THE APE MAN** (1981) BO DEREK LETS A CHIMP SUCK HER NIPPLE. THE ESTATE OF AUTHOR EDGAR RICE BURROUGHS WERE DISPLEASED BY THIS.

"I HAVEN'T FUCKED LINDA LOVELACE, AND SOMEHOW OR OTHER I'VE ALSO MANAGED TO MISS MARILYN CHAMBERS. THEY'RE THE ONLY TWO MAJOR FEMALE PORN STARS THAT I HAVEN'T MADE IT WITH. I'VE GOTTEN TO ALL THE OTHERS."

"I REALLY STARTED TAKING MY PORN CAREER MORE SERIOUSLY, WHEN MORE AND MORE PEOPLE WERE CALLING ME TO DO SEX FILMS. I BEGAN TO FEEL I HAD MADE A PLACE FOR MYSELF, THAT I WAS IMPORTANT. PEOPLE NEEDED AND WANTED ME. I WAS HAVING A BALL, AND THE MONEY WAS A LOT BETTER THAN WHAT I'D BEEN MAKING DRIVING A CAB. I USED TO FEEL THAT I WAS DOING SOMETHING QUITE MEANINGFUL.. I DON'T FEEL THAT WAY ANY MORE, I GUESS BECAUSE IT SEEMS TO ME THAT MY JOB IS DONE. I MEAN, I LIKE TO THINK THAT I MADE A CONTRIBUTION TO THE QUOTE-UN-QUOTE SEXUAL REVOLUTION, AND I'M VERY HAPPY ABOUT THAT. THE THING IS THOUGH, THIS BUSINESS OFFERS NO SECURITY -- IT DIDN'T THEN, AND IT DOESN'T NOW. I THINK I DID ABOUT 30 OR 40 LOOPS BEFORE I GOT INTO THE REAL FEATURE-LENGTH STUFF. HARRY REEMS HELPED ME OUT IN THAT DEPARTMENT. BUT THE PORN INDUSTRY IS FULL OF SURPRISES. I EXPECTED TO BE WORKING FOR FAT SLOBS WITH CIGARS HANGING OUT OF THEIR MOUTHS. I CAN'T BELIEVE HOW MANY BRIGHT, YOUNG, WELL-EDUCATED FILM MAKERS THERE ARE IN THIS BUSINESS."

"I DON'T REMEMBER THE NAME OF THE FIRST FEATURE FILM I WAS IN, BUT I REMEMBER THAT HARRY REEMS WAS IN IT. I DID SOMETHING IN IT THAT I RARELY DO IN MY FILMS -- I PROLONGED A PARTICULARLY ENJOYABLE SEX SCENE. THEY WERE WAITING FOR A CUM SHOT, YOU KNOW, AND I SAID TO MYSELF, 'FUCK THESE GUYS. I'M GOING TO STAY HERE AND FUCK THIS BITCH AS LONG AS I WANT, AND THEY CAN WAIT 'TIL DOOMSDAY'. HER NAME WAS LUCY, AND SHE WAS ABSOLUTELY LUSCIOUS".

"I REALLY LIKED TINA RUSSELL. SHE HAD A FLOWING, EASY SEXUALITY THAT REALLY TURNED ME ON. I CAN STILL REMEMBER A CERTAIN IMAGE OF HER ON FILM, SHOWING HER LITTLE ASSHOLE TO THE CAMERA. I TOOK ADVANTAGE OF EVERY OPPORTUNITY TO DO AS MUCH AS I COULD WITH HER. THE FLICK WE DID TOGETHER (FRENCH POSTCARD GIRLS FROM 1977 -ED) HAD A VERY THIN PLOT. THE ACTORS HAD TO AD-LIB THE DIALOGUE UNTIL THE SEX SCENE CAME ALONG. WE WORKED ABOUT 15 HOURS A DAY, FOR WHICH WE GOT PAID APPROXIMATELY TWO BILLS. AND I BROUGHT MY OWN LUNCH."

-- JAMIE GILLIS (PICTURED HERE WITH KEISHA) FROM A JULY 1983 INTERVIEW WITH KNAVE X STARS MAGAZINE. ONE OF THE MOST POPULAR MALE STARS WITH THE FEMALE PERFORMERS FROM THE 1970S AND '80S ERA OF ADULT FILMS, JAMIE GILLIS WAS RENOWNED FOR HIS KINKY EXCESS, ERECTILE DEPENDABILITY, AND HIS FINELY TUNED ACTING SKILLS EVEN UNDER LESS THAN EXEMPLARY CONDITIONS. HE MADE NEARLY A THOUSAND LOOPS AND FILMS IN HIS 30-YEAR CAREER, AND PASSED AWAY IN FEB 2010. HE'S MY PERSONAL FAVOURITE MALE PORN STAR OF ALL TIME, AND THE ONLY ONE THAT I EVER BECAME CLOSE WITH. REST IN PEACE, JAMIE. A LOT OF PEOPLE REALLY MISS YOU, BROTHER.

A PASSAGE THRU PAMELA

☆ BOUGIE 2013.

PAMELA IS AN ODD DUCK. SHE'S GOT A THICK PORTUGUESE ACCENT (SHE BARELY SPEAKS ENGLISH) A FUCKING TERRIBLE BOOB JOB, AND THE FACT THAT SHE'S ONE OF THE WORST ACTRESSES IN THE HISTORY OF A GENRE THAT WASN'T EXACTLY LEGENDARY FOR ITS TALENTED THESPIANS. WHAT PAMELA DOES HAVE GOING FOR HER, HOWEVER, IS HER SMOKING HOT ASS AND THE FACT THAT, FROM THE NECK UP, SHE'S EASILY THE MOST GORGEOUS WOMAN IN THIS 1985 PORN MOVIE.

JUST LOVELY EYES, MODEL-QUALITY BONE STRUCTURE IN HER FACE, AND I LOVE HER HAIR. USUALLY THAT WOULDN'T BE ENOUGH FOR A LEADING LADY, BUT HELL, I'VE SEEN A FEW STARS OF CLASSIC SMUT THAT ARE HARDLY ANYTHING TO NUT ABOUT, SO I'M NOT GOING TO GET RILED.

> PAMELA AND HER BOY-TOY, SNAPPER

THE MOVIE STARTS IN ARGENTINA WITH A TASTEFULLY FILMED SHOWER SESSION AS PAMELA SOAPS UP HER CUTE LITTLE ASS AND DAYDREAMS ABOUT HER BELOVED MANNY (PLAYED BY BISEXUAL PORN STAR, JOHNNY NINETEEN), WHO LATER HUMPS A HOOKER WITHOUT REALIZING HIS FUTURE WIFE HAD WALKED IN THE ROOM. HEARTBROKEN, PAMELA JETS OFF TO MANHATTAN WHERE TWO ELITE MODELLING AGENCIES WILL GO OUT OF THEIR MINDS TRYING TO COAX THE BEAUTY TO COME AND SIGN AN EXCLUSIVE CONTRACT. SHARON KANE'S CHARACTER, ASHLEY, WORKS AT THE AGENCY THAT LANDS THE FORMER MISS BUENOS AIRES, AND LOOKS FORWARD TO HER INEVITABLE SUPERMODEL WORLD DOMINATION. THE MOVIE INFORMS US, IN NO UNCERTAIN TERMS, THAT PAMELA IS YOUNG, CONFIDENT, AND THE WOMAN EVERY OTHER WOMAN WANTS TO BE. SHE'S THE CENTER OF ATTENTION.

PUT TO WORK ON A LINGERIE CAMPAIGN, PAMELA IS PHOTOGRAPHED BY A RESIDENT NYC HORNDOG NAMED "SNAPPER" (JOEY SANTINI), WHO CAN'T KEEP HIS GRUBBY MITTS OFF HER CURVY BUTT DESPITE ASHLEY'S DEMANDS THAT HE STAY PROFESSIONAL. PAMELA, HOWEVER, WELCOMES THE SHUTTERBUG'S LUSTY ADVANCES, AND TAKES A BREAK FROM THEIR PHOTO SESSION TO BEND OVER AND TAKE HIS DICK UP HER ASS RIGHT AS SOME CLIENTS FROM A PERFUME COMPANY WALK INTO THE STUDIO. NO HARM DONE THOUGH, AS THE TWO QUICKLY COVER UP AND THE BUSINESSMEN ARE JUST AS SUITABLY IMPRESSED AS THEY ARE SCANDALIZED BY HER OVERTLY SLUTTY BEHAVIOUR. "SHE'S THE PERFECT GIRL FOR OUR NEW PERFUME LINE!", THEY GUSH.

FOR HER PART, ASHLEY IS SUPER PISSED THAT SNAPPER COULD HAVE RUINED EVERYTHING WITH HIS WANDERING FINGERS (AND BUTT-HUNGRY WANG) SO SHE DEMANDS THAT PAMELA MOVES INTO HER NEW YORK PENTHOUSE SO SHE CAN KEEP HER EYE (AND TONGUE) ON THE AGENCY'S RAVISHING MEAL TICKET.

CAN PAMELA KEEP HER SHIT TOGETHER AND ROCK NOT ONLY THE FASHION INDUSTRY BUT HER CO-STARS GENITALS AS WELL? CAN HER EMPLOYER KEEP THE RIVAL AGENCY (HELMED BY CLASSIC PORN STUD ASHLEY MOORE) FROM EITHER STEALING PAMELA AWAY OR SETTING HER UP FOR A PUBLIC RELATIONS DISASTER? CAN SHE FIND A WAY TO SECURE HAPPINESS EVEN WITH ALL OF THIS SEXY DRAMA AND THE STRESS OF HAVING A SECRET THAT SHE CAN'T BEAR TO HAVE REVEALED?

☆☆ SPOILERS AHEAD ☆☆ (DON'T READ ON IF YOU'RE PLANNING ON WATCHING THE MOVIE!)

HERE'S THE THING...

PAMELA HAS A COCK AND BALLS. NO, FOR REAL. EVEN THOUGH IT HAS MOSTLY BEEN FORGOTTEN TODAY, SEVEN YEARS BEFORE **THE CRYING GAME** A PASSAGE THRU PAMELA WAS BLOWING MULTIPLE MASTURBATORS MINDS.

> RISING TO THE TOP OF THE MODELLING GAME, EVERYTHING IS GOING PAMELA'S WAY.

41

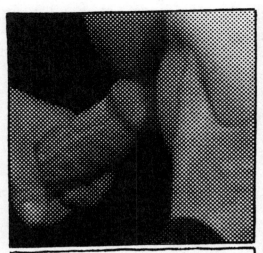

NOW, WHETHER YOU'RE INTO LADYBOYS AND TRANNIES IS TOTALLY BESIDE THE POINT. WHAT I LOVED ABOUT THE WAY PASSAGE THRU PAMELA HANDLED THE TOPIC WAS HOW DIRECTOR JOHN AMERO (UNDER THE NAME "LESLIE BROOKS") REVEALED IT AS A JAW-DROPPING PLOT TWIST MORE THAN HALFWAY THROUGH THE PICTURE WHEN SHARON KANE YANKED THOSE PANTIES DOWN WHILE SHE AND PAMMY WERE GETTING IT ON. WE'D ALREADY HAD THE PREVIOUS CAREFULLY STAGED SHOWER AND BUTTFUCK SCENES TO INSPIRE ONE TO WRESTLE THE CYCLOPS, AND NOW HERE WAS A VERY ROMANTIC LESBO LAY-ABOUT. OUT OF NOWHERE, THIS SUPPOSEDLY SAPPHIC SEX SUDDENLY GOT LAYERED WITH SOME FOREBODING MUSIC THAT DIDN'T SEEM QUITE RIGHT. THAT MUSIC SWELLED, AND WE WERE HANDED OUR SHOCK AT THE SAME TIME SHARON KANE'S CHARACTER WAS HANDED HERS -- JUST AS SHE WAS ABOUT TO START SLOBBERING ON WHAT SHE ASSUMED WAS GOING TO BE A STICKY SNATCH. AND HOW ABOUT THAT FINALE WHERE WE FIND OUT THAT PAMELA IS GOING TO BE THE FATHER TO SHARON KANE'S BABY? SAY WAAAA?! _AMAZING!_

IT'S CERTAINLY NOT THE BEST BONER-INDUCER I'VE EVER SAT THROUGH, BUT I ADORE THE WAY THIS FILM TROLLED THE AUDIENCE. IT'S LIKE THE FIRST PART OF THE STORY WAS ALL JUST A STRAIGHT-FACED PRANK ON INSECURE STRAIGHT MEN WITH RIGID IDEAS OF HOW WOMEN AND PORN SHOULD BE. I GRIN WHEN I THINK OF HOW THE RAINCOATERS MUST HAVE REACTED WHEN THIS PLAYED THEATERS IN A FAR LESS LIBERATED 1985, CONFUSED ABOUT HOW THE MOVIE HAD MADE THEM LUST OVER A TRANS MAN. I GIGGLE AT THE IDEA THAT IT MADE AS MANY PEOPLE UNCOMFORTABLE AS IT TURNED ON. THIS IS WHAT PORN SHOULD BE, I THINK. AMERICAN MAINSTREAM SMUT REALLY SHOULDN'T BE SO PREDICTABLE. IT SHOULDN'T BE SO FORMULAIC, AND IT SHOULDN'T BE SO GODDAMN SAFE.

NO ONE KNOWS WHAT BECAME OF PAMELA. HER ONLY OTHER SCREEN CREDIT WAS A BIT PART IN J. ANGEL MARTINE'S VIDEO **GIRL BUSTERS**, MADE THAT SAME YEAR. THE CREDITS OF P.T.P ANNOUNCE THAT PAMELA WILL BE GETTING HER SEX CHANGE, AND TO STAY TUNED TO SEE HER IN PART TWO. THIS, HOWEVER, WAS SADLY A SEGUEL THAT FAILED TO MATERIALIZE.

ACCORDING TO THE MAY 1986 ISSUE OF HUSTLER EROTIC VIDEO, AFTER PERFORMING IN THE FIRST FILM PAMELA GOT HER GENDER REASSIGNMENT SURGERY DONE IN SWEDEN, AND UPON RETURNING TO THE STATES, LOOKED TO ARRANGE AN ADVANCE ON THE ANNOUNCED SEGUEL TO HELP PAY FOR THE DEBT ACCRUED. APPARENTLY SHE ASSUMED THAT SHE WOULD LAND THE SAME $10,000.00 PAYDAY AS BEFORE, BUT WAS TOLD THAT PART TWO WASN'T GOING TO BE SHOT ON FILM OR PLAY IN THEATERS. IT WOULD BE A LOWER BUDGET SHOT-ON-VIDEO PRODUCTION, AND SHE'D BE PAID THE SAME $300.00 DAY RATE THE OTHER GIRLS IN THE MOVIE WERE GETTING. THE SURGERY HOPEFULLY MADE HER HAPPIER, BUT IT HAD ALSO ERASED WHAT HAD MADE HER BANKABLE IN THE WORLD OF XXX MOVIES.

—BOUGIE

.. AND PAMELA MOANS AND GROANS.

ICH LIEBE IHREN FETTEN TITTEN!
An Appreciation of Georgina Lempin
By Bill Adcock

EXCUSE ME, WHERE DO YOU GUYS WANT THESE BAGS?

BOUGIE '13

I'VE BEEN A CHUBBY-CHASER SINCE I DISCOVERED GIRLS WEREN'T ICKY ANYMORE. I LIKE BIG, SOFT, PLUMP, CURVY, VOLUPTUOUS, ZAFTIG WOMEN. IT'S SIMPLY HOW MY BRAIN AND MY COCK ARE WIRED. AND WHILE BBW PORN HAS IMPROVED BY TREMENDOUS LEAPS AND BOUNDS IN RECENT YEARS (THERE'S MINIMAL RISK OF SEEING A SHAPELESS, DUMPY WOMAN WITH DIRTY HAIR AND BEDSORES GETTING PLOWED BY SOME "LUCKY" GUY ANY MORE), I'M FINDING I REALLY PREFER VINTAGE PORN. I LOVE THE UNENHANCED BODIES, I LOVE PUBIC HAIR ON WOMEN, I LOVE THAT OLDER PORN JUST GENERALLY FEELS LIKE PEOPLE HAVING FUN WITH THEIR GENITALS. QUITE THE DILEMMA, TRYING TO SATISFY BOTH MY LUST FOR CHUBBY GIRLS AND MY APPRECIATION OF VINTAGE PORN.

YOU CAN IMAGINE THEN, MY DELIGHT WHEN I DISCOVERED GEORGINA LEMPIN, A HUNGARIAN HEFTY-HOOTERED HONEY WHO MADE A STRING OF MOVIES IN GERMANY IN THE EARLY '90S. WITH HER NATURAL FLAME-RED HAIR (CONFIRMED BY HER SILKY AND INVITING-LOOKING BUSH), SOFT TUMMY AND HUGE, BOUNCING, ALL-NATURAL PLEASURE ZEPPELINS, GEORGINA LOOKS LIKE SHE WAS BUILT IN SOME MAD SCIENTIST'S LAB TO MY EXACT SPECIFICATION. ADD HER WINNING SMILE AND EAGERNESS TO FILL HER MOUTH WITH WIENERSCHNITZEL AND WE HAVE A GODDESS ON OUR HANDS, FOLKS. NO TWO WAYS ABOUT IT.

I'M NOT KIDDING ABOUT THE SMILE AND THE EAGERNESS. UNLIKE FAR TOO MANY PORN ACTRESSES, GEORGINA NEVER APPEARED JADED OR BORED OR EVEN LIKE SHE WAS HAVING AN OFF DAY. IT DIDN'T MATTER IF SHE WAS DOING A SCENE WITH A MAN OR A WOMAN, OR TWO MEN, OR THREE MEN, OR THREE MEN AND TWO WOMEN, SHE APPROACHED EVERY SCENE THE SAME... LIKE SHE WAS RAPTUROUSLY IN LOVE WITH HER COSTARS AND ON THE FIRST NIGHT OF A HONEYMOON WITH THEM. SHE KNEW EXACTLY WHAT SHE WANTED IN THE BEDROOM AND MADE IT HAPPEN WITHOUT APPEARING AGGRESSIVE OR DEMANDING -- SHE JUST GENTLY GUIDES HANDS OR MOUTHS TO HER SWOLLEN PINK NIPPLES, OR EASES THE GUY ON TO HIS BACK AND MOUNTS HIM.

HER COWGIRL SCENES ESPECIALLY ARE A THING OF UNBELIEVABLE BEAUTY. SIMPLY PUT, SHE'S A BUNDLE OF ECSTATIC SEXUAL ENERGY. THERE'S AN OLD STEREOTYPE THAT YOU NEVER WANT TO HAVE A CHUBBY GIRL RIDE YOU COWGIRL BECAUSE SHE'S PRESUMABLY TOO FAT TO DO ANY OF THE WORK, MAKING THE ACT OF FUCKING HER SO MUCH MORE OF AN EFFORT. GEORGINA THROWS THAT MYTH RIGHT OUT THE WINDOW, BOUNCING SO HARD ON COCK AFTER COCK THAT HER BIG, PERFECT TITS PRACTICALLY SLAP HER IN THE FACE. IN MOST OF THESE SCENES, SHE DOES ALL THE WORK WHILE THE GUY JUST LAYS THERE, THE LAZY BUM!

ALSO APPEARING UNDER THE NAMES GEORGINA LEMPKIN, SUSIE BARD, GEORGIA KIST, TINA SAMPSON, GEORGINA EVANS, GORGLY, CHRISTINA SCHWARTZ AND GYORGYI KOPEKIN (WHICH MIGHT BE HER REAL NAME, BUT I HAVEN'T BEEN ABLE TO CONFIRM OR DENY THIS AS OF YET), GEORGINA MOVED FROM HUNGARY TO GERMANY SOME TIME AROUND 1990. THERE SHE SUPPORTED HERSELF AS AN EXOTIC DANCER BEFORE ENTERING THE ADULT FILM INDUSTRY IN 1991 WITH FILMS LIKE **SPRITZENDE COLTS** AND **LUST STATT FRUST** (THE LATTER RELEASED IN AMERICA IN 1995 AS **PLUMPER THERAPY**, AND FEATURING AN AMAZING GIRL-ON-GIRL BATHTUB SCENE BETWEEN GEORGINA AND FELLOW HUNGARIAN MAMMAZON ILDIKO) AND MADE AROUND 20 FILMS (NOT COUNTING RETITLINGS AND SCENES FROM EARLIER FILMS EDITED INTO NEW ONES) BEFORE RETIRING IN 1996. SOMEWHERE ALONG THE WAY, SHE DID A COUPLE SPREADS FOR SCORE MAGAZINE AS WELL, INTRODUCING HER LUSCIOUS LOVE-PILLOWS TO TIT-HOUNDS ON THIS SIDE OF THE ATLANTIC.

HOLY FUCK. THIS LAY-DAY IS TOO FINE.

ADCOCK 4 LYFE

ONE OF GEORGINA'S BEST ROLES (OTHER THAN THE AFOREMENTIONED BATHTUB SCENE IN **PLUMPER THERAPY**), COMES IN THE RIOTOUSLY FUN **SECRETS OF MOZART** (1992, RELEASED IN AMERICA, 1995). IN THIS HOT LITTLE NUMBER, A WOMAN (ANDREA MOLNAR) VISITS THE MOZART WOHNHAUS MUSEUM IN SALZBURG AND DISCOVERS A SECRET LETTER, IN WHICH GOOD OL' WOLFGANG DETAILS HIS SEXUAL ADVENTURES, WHICH THE FILM THOUGHTFULLY PLAYS OUT AS A SERIES OF FLASHBACKS. YES, READERS, IT'S POWDERED WIG PORN, WITH ALL THE PERFORMERS IN FULL 1780S GARB, WITH THE MEN IN BREECHES, FROCK COATS AND POWDERED WIGS, AND THE WOMEN SIMILARLY BEWIGGED WITH FRILLY POOFY DRESSES AND PLENTY OF PETTICOATS. PANCAKE MAKEUP ABOUNDS. GEORGINA (CREDITED HERE AS GEORGIA KIST) IS ONLY IN ONE SCENE, IN WHICH SHE, DAGMAR LOST AND AN UNIDENTIFIED PETITE GIRL TAKE TURNS PLAYING MOZART'S (CHRISTOPH CLARK, DOING A FAIR IMPRESSION OF TOM HULCE'S PERFORMANCE IN

AMADEUS) MAGIC SKIN-FLUTE. WHILE THE PETITE GIRL LETS MOZART PUSH IN HER STOOL, THE UNDENIABLE STARS OF THE SCENE ARE GEORGINA'S UNSTOPPABLE UDDERS. IT'S A SILLY MOVIE, BUT IT GOT ME HOTTER THAN ANYTHING COMING OUT OF THE ADULT INDUSTRY TODAY, BECAUSE IT'S JUST PLAIN FUN!

UNFORTUNATELY, THERE'S NOT A WHOLE LOT OF AVAILABLE, CONFIRMED INFORMATION OUT THERE ON THE WEB ABOUT GEORGINA AND QUITE A BIT OF WHAT'S OUT THERE IS WRONG! HER "OFFICIAL" WEBSITE (VERY CLEARLY A FAN-RUN OPERATION, NOT ENDORSED BY HER) HAS A BIOGRAPHY COPIED AND PASTED FROM THAT OF DONITA DUNES, WITH MOST (BUT NOT ALL, WHICH IS ALMOST MORE INSULTING IN ITS UTTER LAZINESS) INSTANCES OF THE NAME "DONITA" REPLACED WITH "GEORGINA." SEEING THE LOVELY AND ALL-NATURAL GEORGINA FALSELY DESCRIBED AS HAVING "INCREDIBLY MASSIVE FAKE BOOBS" GIVES ME HEARTBURN, READERS, LET ME TELL YOU. SO I HAVE NO IDEA WHEN GEORGINA WAS BORN, HER MEASUREMENTS, HEIGHT, WEIGHT, OR WHERE SHE IS NOW. RUMOUR HAS IT SHE'S MARRIED AND HAS TWO KIDS, BUT CONTINUED TO STRIP FOR SOME TIME POST-RETIREMENT AT A CLUB IN NUREMBERG. SCORE LISTS HER HEIGHT AND WEIGHT AS 5'5 AND 161 LBS, WHICH SEEMS A LOT MORE PLAUSIBLE, GIVEN HER BUILD, THAN THE 5'9 AND 127 LBS. LISTED ON HER "OFFICIAL" WEBSITE.

PEOPLE, THIS IS A TRAVESTY. THIS JAW-DROPPINGLY GORGEOUS WOMAN DESERVES A WHOLE HELL OF A LOT BETTER THAN A HALF-ASSED "BIOGRAPHY" COPIED AND PASTED OFF ANOTHER WOMAN. SOMETHING NEEDS TO BE DONE TO CORRECT THIS GLARING INJUSTICE AND SET MATTERS RIGHT, FOR GEORGINA AND FOR US RAINCOATERS WHO WANT TO GET TO KNOW THE WOMAN WE'RE FLOGGING THE BISHOP TO. I AM NOT GOING TO SETTLE FOR BEING TOLD GEORGINA LEMPIN HAS "INCREDIBLY MASSIVE FAKE BOOBS" AND IS CURRENTLY LIVING IN SOUTHERN CALIFORNIA. I'M NOT! AND I HOPE YOU PERVERTS (ESPECIALLY ANY OF YOU WHO SPRECHEN SIE DEUTSCHE BETTER THAN I DO) WILL JOIN ME IN THIS, BECAUSE THIS INJUSTICE CANNOT BE ALLOWED TO STAND!

RISE UP AND JOIN ME, PERVERTS! WRITE LONG, ANGRY LETTERS TO YOUR COUNTRY'S EMBASSIES IN GERMANY AND HUNGARY! DEMAND YOUR COUNTRY'S REPRESENTATIVES PLEDGE THEMSELVES TO WORK NIGHT AND DAY UNTIL GEORGINA IS FOUND AND HER STORY SET STRAIGHT! MARCH IN THE STREET! HANG FLYERS AND BANNERS OFF EVERY STREETLIGHT! WRITE "WHERE'S GEORGINA?" ON SCHOOL CHILDREN'S FOREHEADS IN PERMANENT MARKER! WE'RE GOING TO MAKE THIS A CRUSADE, PEOPLE-- GEORGINA'S CRUSADE! WE'RE GONNA HOLD MIDNIGHT JERK-OFF VIGILS EVERY NIGHT UNTIL THE TRUTH CAN BE TOLD! DON'T JUST DO IT FOR ME, OR FOR YOUR PENDULOUS PEARL-POUCHES, ACHING TO BE DRAINED! DO IT FOR GEORGINA LEMPIN, WHEREVER SHE MIGHT BE!!

—ADCOCK '13

Sadie (1980 Dir: Bob Chinn)

SET IN BORNEO IN 1971 AND BASED ON SOMERSET MAUGHAM'S "RAIN", SADIE FEATURES A LADY OF THE NIGHT WHO WORKS AS A NIGHTCLUB ENTERTAINER AT A SHITTY LITTLE ISLAND HOTEL BAR WHERE AMERICAN SOLDIERS ON SHORE LEAVE COME TO CALL ON HER. A GREGARIOUS AND REBELLIOUS WOMAN WHO LOVES TO BE THE LIFE OF THE PARTY, SADIE'S SIMPLE LIFE OF IMPOVERISHED SUCKS N' FUCKS IS TURNED UPSIDE DOWN WHEN, DURING A TORRENTIAL RAIN STORM, A SELF-RIGHTEOUS SENATOR, HIS WIFE, AND THEIR DAUGHTER DASH IN TO GET OUT OF THE ELEMENTS. SINCE IT'S A PORNO, THE WIFE AND DAUGHTER ARE BOTH SECRETLY BEDDED BEFORE LONG BY VARIOUS SEDUCTIVE MEN-FOLK WHO FREQUENT THE RUN DOWN RETREAT, BUT SADIE AND THE SENATOR HAVE A DIFFERENT RELATIONSHIP.

"THE GIFT OF GOD IS WORTH FAR MORE THAN MONEY. IT'S PRICELESS." HE PREACHES AT THE BLONDE SEXPOT IN HER MODEST ROOM. "YEAH", SHE REPLIES WITH A SNEER. "BUT IT DON'T PAY THE RENT, IF YOU KNOW WHAT I MEAN."

THIS FORMER MAN OF THE CLOTH EVENTUALLY WEARS SADIE DOWN WITH HIS PREACHING, ESPECIALLY AFTER THREATENING TO HAVE HER DEPORTED BACK TO THE U.S. TO STAND TRIAL FOR BEING A SEX WORKER. SHE'S READY TO REFORM AND PUT HER TRUST IN THE LORD FOR A BETTER LIFE, BUT WITH HER ABUNDANT CHARMS AND INTOXICATING PERSONALITY (THAT HAVE ALL THE LOCAL SAILORS WHIPPING OUT THEIR DICKS) SADIE HAS WORN HIM DOWN AS WELL -- ENOUGH SO THE FAT HYPOCRITICAL BASTARD CAN NO LONGER RESIST THE TEMPTATIONS OF THE FLESH.

"SOME FIGHT FOR THEIR HONOUR AND REPRESS THEIR FEELINGS", THE NARRATOR ON THE TRAILER INFORMS US AS SCENES FROM THIS HARDCORE PASSION PLAY FLASH ACROSS THE SCREEN. "WHEN THE TROPICAL HEAT OF THE ISLANDS WINDS DESIRES AND RAVAGES ONE'S BRAINS TO A FEVER PITCH, THE GIVING OF ONE'S SELF TO THE ONE YOU LOVE BRINGS THE FULFILLMENT YOUR BODY TINGLES FOR."

THERE IS A LOT TO LOVE ABOUT THIS MOVIE. SHOT IN 35MM EASTMANCOLOR BY SKILLED CINEMATOGRAPHER KEN GIBB, THE WHOLE PRODUCTION HAS A WARM INVITING FEEL ABOUT IT. THE SCRIPT IS BETTER THAN YOU WOULD EXPECT, AND DRAWS YOU RIGHT IN. THE SETS AND THE WAY THEY ARE LIT IS INCREDIBLE, AND THE WAY THE CAMERA INTERACTS WITH THEM GIVES THE EFFECT OF A STAGE PLAY. SADIE HAS A WONDERFUL POVERTY ROW FILM VIBE THAT STAYS TRUE TO THE ROOTS OF THE 1932 VERSION OF THE FILM (STARRING JOAN CRAWFORD IN THE ROLE OF THE PROSTITUTE) AND IF DIRECTOR BOB CHINN HAD FOUND EVEN SEMI-COMPETENT ACTORS, IT WOULD HAVE BEEN ONE OF THE BEST ADULT FILMS OF 1980, QUITE EASILY. THE MIDDLE-AGED ACTOR WHO PLAYED THE GOD-FEARING SENATOR WAS GOOD IN HIS NON-SEX ROLE (JOSEPH DARLING, WHO ALSO APPEARED ON THE 1980S TV SERIES FALCON CREST), BUT HE'S ABOUT IT, THOUGH.

THE THING IS... I DON'T EVEN MIND BAD ACTING IF THE PERSON HAS A LOT OF CHARISMA, LIKE JOHN HOLMES ALWAYS DISPLAYED FOR INSTANCE. BUT IT'S WHEN IT'S THAT SORT OF BLAND "BAD LINE READING" STUFF THAT I CHECK OUT, MENTALLY. SADLY, SADIE HAS A LOT OF THAT SORT OF THING, ESPECIALLY FROM ITS LEAD PERFORMER, CRIS CASSIDY, WHO JUST COULDN'T CARRY OFF A SCRIPT THIS ELABORATE WITH HER MEAGRE ACTING ABILITIES. WHEN A SCRIPT IS AS DIALOG HEAVY AS THIS ONE IS AND THE SEX SCENES DON'T REQUIRE ANY SEXUAL GYMNASTICS, THIS MOVIE PROVES THAT CASTING ACTORS WHO DON'T MIND FUCKING IS FAR SUPERIOR TO HIRING SEXUAL OLYMPIANS WHO CAN'T ACT THEIR WAY OUT OF A PAPER BAG.

THAT SAID, THE LIST OF AFOREMENTIONED PLUSES (AND SOME COOL PLOT TWISTS THAT I DIDN'T MENTION) ARE EASILY ENOUGH FOR ME TO SLAP DOWN A RECOMMENDATION FOR SADIE. IT'S JUST THAT IT'S, YOU KNOW, FRUSTRATING TO THINK OF WHAT COULD HAVE BEEN IF ONLY A LITTLE MORE EFFORT HAD BEEN PUT INTO THE CASTING. HEADS UP, THOUGH: IT'S BEEN RELEASED IN BOTH HARDCORE AND SOFTCORE VERSIONS. GET THE XXX ONE.   —BOUGIE

DID YOU KNOW?

SADIE STAR CRIS CASSIDY WAS A LESBIAN AWAY FROM PORN SETS, ALTHOUGH YOU WOULD NEVER KNOW IT FROM HER SIZZLING PERFORMANCES WITH THE DUDES. YOU KNOW, I THINK SHE WAS A FAR BETTER ACTRESS THAN I GAVE HER CREDIT FOR.

COOL BREEZE (USA . 1972)

"HE HIT THE MAN FOR $3 MILLION. RIGHT WHERE IT HURTS -- IN THE DIAMONDS. AND BABY, THAT'S COLD!"

THE BLAXPLOITATION GENRE WAS WELL KNOWN FOR TAKING PRE-EXISTING WHITE FILMS AND PUTTING AN URBAN SPIN ON THEM. BLACULA (1972) WAS THE BLACK DRACULA. HITMAN (1972) WAS A REMAKE OF THE GREAT BRITISH THRILLER GET CARTER. BLACK MAMA, WHITE MAMA (1973) WAS THE BLACK EXPLOITATION CINEMA VERSION OF THE DEFIANT ONES. ABBY (1974) RODE THE COAT TAILS OF THE EXORCIST. BLACK SHAMPOO (1976) WAS A VERY ENTERTAINING VARIATION ON WARREN BEATTY'S SHAMPOO. AND COOL BREEZE (1972) BROUGHT THE FILM NOIR THRILLS OF THE ASPHALT JUNGLE TO AFRO-AMERICAN AUDIENCES.

WRITTEN AND DIRECTED BY BARRY POLLACK, THE PLOT OF THE VERY BREEZY COOL BREEZE IS COOL ENOUGH. BEING A BLAXPLOITATION HEIST MOVIE, AN ASSORTMENT OF BLACK JEWEL THIEVES ARE PRESENTED. TO BE CLEAR, CAPER MOVIES ALWAYS HAVE THAT UNLIKELY COLLECTION OF EXPERTS AND ODDBALLS, AND COOL BREEZE IS CERTAINLY NO EXCEPTION.

THERE'S THE WEALTHY CRIMINAL BUSINESSMAN (RAYMOND ST. JACQUES), THE ALCOHOLIC RETAILER WHO RUNS A BOOKIE JOINT ON THE SLY (SAM LAWS), THE PREACHER (RUDY CHALLENGER) WHO OWNS A LASER BEAM (?), AND LEADING THEM IS THE VERY AUTHORITATIVE SIDNEY LORD JONES (THALMUS RASULALA) WHO HAS JUST GOTTEN OUT OF PRISON. THE PLAN IS TO STEAL THREE MILLION DOLLARS IN "WHITEY'S ICE", AND THEN FENCE THE DIAMONDS AND OTHER BAUBLES IN ORDER TO USE THE PROCEEDS TO START A BANK THAT WILL AID BLACK BUSINESSES. A NOBLE GOAL, BUT AS ALL HEIST MOVIES GO, THE SUCCESS THE CRIMINALS ENJOY IS SHORT-LIVED, AND EVERYTHING COMES CRASHING DOWN AROUND THE GANG IN A SERIES OF UNLIKELY ACCIDENTS AND DOUBLE CROSSES.

I HAD HIGH HOPES FOR THIS ONE, GOING IN. ACTUALLY, IT WASN'T EVEN THAT I HAD BIG EXPECTATIONS, IT'S JUST THAT I HAD ABSOLUTELY NO REASON TO THINK IT WOULDN'T BE ENTERTAINING. COOL BREEZE HAS THE BASIC CHECKLIST FOR GREAT 1970S GENRE CINEMA FILLED OUT: THE POSTER IS COOL, THE CHEEKY TRAILER IS ONE OF MY FAVOURITE BLAXPLOITATION PREVIEWS OF ALL TIME, IT'S A HEIST MOVIE (I LOVE THOSE), PAM GRIER IS NOT ONLY IN IT AS AN ABUSED PROSTITUTE -- SHE GETS NAKED TOO! IT WAS SHOT ON-LOCATION IN THE GRITTY PARTS OF 1970S LOS ANGELES, IT HAS A COOL SCORE BY SOLOMON BURKE, IT GETS PLENTY OF GREAT REVIEWS (JOSIAH HOWARD OF THE EXCELLENT 2008 BOOK BLAXPLOITATION CINEMA SAID IT WAS "HIGHLY RECOMMENDED"), IT DID VERY RESPECTABLE BOX OFFICE DURING ITS ORIGINAL RELEASE IN 1972, AND IT STARS THALMUS RASULALA -- WHO ON TOP OF HAVING AN AMAZING NAME, IS A GREAT ACTOR WITH A COMMANDING PRESENCE.

WHAT COULD GO WRONG? WELL DESPITE ALL THAT, THE FINAL PRODUCT -- SPECIFICALLY THE PARTS OF THE MOVIE PERTAINING TO THE SCRIPT AND THE PACING -- FAILS THE AUDIENCE IN JUST ABOUT EVERY WAY QUANTIFIABLE. HONESTLY, THIS SCREENPLAY IS A TOTAL FUCKING MESS, AND ITS MAIN PROBLEM IS THAT IT TAKES BLOODY FOREVER FOR ANYTHING TO START HAPPENING. 'LONG-WINDED' AND 'MUDDLED' ARE TERMS THAT COME TO MIND, AND THAT APPLIES NOT ONLY TO THE FIRST PART OF THE MOVIE, BUT DURING ITS ALL-IMPORTANT FINALE AS WELL. WHEN THE ROBBERY ITSELF TAKES PLACE, IT'S NOT INGENIOUS OR ANYTHING, BUT IT'S FAIRLY WELL DONE. THE PROBLEM IS THAT IT COMES IN THE MIDDLE OF THE MOVIE AND HAPPENS TOO FAST. THE WHOLE THING FEELS RIGHT OUT OF LEFT FIELD THANKS TO THE PREPARATION FOR IT NOT HAVING BEEN SHARED WITH THE VIEWERS -- AN INTEGRAL PART OF EVERY GREAT HEIST MOVIE.

AND THEN ONCE THE ROBBERY GOES DOWN WE ARE FACED WITH THE FILM EXCRUCIATINGLY SLOWING DOWN THE PACE ONCE AGAIN, MAKING ME LOOK AT MY WATCH MULTIPLE TIMES AND WONDER WHEN THIS CLUNKER WAS GOING TO FINALLY SPUTTER AND DRAG ITSELF TO A HALT DURING ITS INCOMPREHENSIBLE THIRD ACT. AN ANTICLIMAX IS NOT SOMETHING I'M USED TO SEEING IN BLAXPLOITATION PICTURES, A GENRE KNOWN FOR ITS TO-THE-POINT PLOTTING, BUT IT WILL REMAIN PERHAPS MY DEFINING MEMORY OF COOL BREEZE.

I'M FAIRLY EASY TO PLEASE WITH THESE TYPES OF MOVIES, BUT I'M HONESTLY NOT REALLY ALL THAT SURE WHY THIS BLAXPLOITATION PICTURE GETS SO MANY RAVE REVIEWS FROM OTHER CRITCS. CONSIDERING HOW HARD THE MOVIE WAS TO SEE (THERE WERE ONLY A FEW REMAINING PRINTS, NO VHS RELEASE, AND ONLY A WARNER "ON DEMAND" DVD-R EVENTUALLY MADE AVAILABLE IN 2012), IT MAKES ME WONDER IF MOST PEOPLE HAVE ACTUALLY EVEN SEEN IT, AND WEREN'T JUST REVIEWING THAT COOL-ASS TRAILER I MENTIONED EARLIER.

NOT THE WORST 1970S BLAXPLOITATION MOVIE BY ANY MEANS, BUT CERTAINLY ONE THAT WAS SUNK BY A POOR SCRIPT, BLAND DIRECTION, AND AWFULLY QUESTIONABLE EDITING THAT RESULTED IN DIRE PACING. A FRUSTRATING LITTLE MOVIE THAT SHOULD HAVE BEEN MUCH BETTER CONSIDERING ALL THE QUALITY ELEMENTS IT HAD GOING FOR IT. HAD POLLACK'S SKILLS AS A WRITER AND FILMMAKER BEEN SHARPER, THIS SAME CAST AND CONCEPT COULD HAVE EASILY COALESCED INTO SOMETHING TRULY OUTSTANDING IN THIS GENRE.

·BOUGIE 2015·

Light Blast (1985 Italy Dir: Enzo Castellari)

A VAN OWNED BY SOME BAD GUYS HAS A SUPER-LASER ATTACHED TO IT, AND THEY MELT SOME INNOCENT PEOPLE'S FACES WITH IT. THE EXECUTION OF THIS HAPPENS TO BE ONE OF THE MOST AWESOME THINGS IN THE HISTORY OF EVERYTHING, SO IF YOU ONLY HAVE A FEW MINUTES TO SPEND WITH LIGHT BLAST, BE SURE TO SKIP AHEAD TO THOSE SCENES AND THEN RUN OFF TO GO DO WHATEVER THE HELL WAS SO FUCKING IMPORTANT TO YOU. WHAT, YOU DON'T HAVE TIME TO SPEND WITH ERIK ESTRADA? YOU SHOULD BE ASHAMED OF YOURSELF.

WITH THREATS TO BLOW UP THE CITY OF SAN FRANCISCO IF THEIR RANSOM OF FIVE MILLION DOLLARS IS NOT PONIED UP, ESTRADA AND HIS PARTNER (PLAYED BY MICHAEL PRITCHARD) DO EVERYTHING THEY CAN TO BRING A HALT TO THE TERRORISTS' EVIL SCHEMES, WHICH INVOLVES LOTS OF FIGHTING, EXPLOSIONS, ELECTROCUTIONS, MESSY BLOOD SQUIBS, AND TOTALLY SWEET DUNE BUGGY CAR CRASHES — AS YOU CAN SEE FROM THE ITALIAN MOVIE POSTER DOWN BELOW. ESTRADA ALSO SHOOTS A MAN IN THE HEAD WITH A FUCKING TURKEY. YES, I SAID TURKEY. CAN HE SAVE THE DAY BEFORE HE GETS HIS FACE MELTED OFF? YOU'LL HAVE TO WATCH AND SEE!

THIS IS SUCH A DUMB, FUN MOVIE, AND YOU'LL WANT TO REVISIT IT MULTIPLE TIMES. ESTRADA IS PERFECTLY SUITED FOR DIRECTOR ENZO CASTELLARI'S INSANE COMIC-BOOK-STYLE ACTION, WHICH SPORTS AN AWESOME SCORE BY GUIDO AND MAURIZIO DE ANGELIS. ODDLY, WHEN THIS WAS RELEASED ON DVD IN 2010 BY CODE RED, THEY MARKETED IT AS A "POST APOCALYPSE" FILM, WHICH IS TOTALLY 100% FALSE, BUT THEN CODE RED IS A BIT OF A FUCKING GONG SHOW IN THE WAY IT IS RUN, SO NOTHING REALLY SHOCKS ME WITH THAT LABEL.

ERIK ESTRADA

PURE ACTION THRILLS!

COLPI di LUCE

ENNIO GIROLAMI · MICHAEL PRITCHARD · PEGGY ROWE · BOB TAYLOR

Regia di ENZO G. CASTELLARI

Musiche di GUIDO & MAURIZIO DE ANGELIS   una produzione FASO Film · METROFILM

Colore LUCIANO VITTORI

TOO NAUGHTY TO SAY NO

Director: Victor Nye and Suze Randall. 1985 (78min)

GOLLY GEE! WHEN YOU'RE A NAIVE CATHOLIC COLLEGE GIRL PLAYED BY ANGEL IT SURE IS A FUCKIN' BUZZKILL WHEN YOU'RE WAITING AROUND WITH THE NUNS AT SCHOOL FOR YOUR FRIEND TO SHOW UP SO YOU CAN GET THE WEEKEND STARTED. SO MUCH SO, THAT SHE NODS OFF AND WHEN SHE AWAKENS FROM HER NAP, THE WORLD IS A MUCH MORE SEXUALLY DEPRAVED AND KINKY-ASS PLACE. HANG ON TO YOUR SKIRTS AND YOUR UNWAVERING BELIEF IN THE OL' HOLY GHOST BECAUSE WE'RE IN FOR SOME DE SADE BY WAY OF ALICE IN WONDERLAND, HERE.

OUR ALICE IS THE ANGELIC ANGEL. OR MORE ACCURATELY I SHOULD SAY THAT THE PORN ACTRESS KNOWN AS ANGEL PLAYS "BETTY", AND HER GAL PAL IS "KATHY" (GINGER LYNN). GINGER IS ONE OF MY ALL TIME FAVES, AND HER KATHY CHARACTER DOESN'T HAVE TO WORK VERY HARD TO TALK BETTY INTO COMING ALONG WITH HER TO HAVE A GOOD TIME, AND I'M TALKING ABOUT THE KIND OF GOOD TIME WHERE A LEATHER-CLAD JAMIE GILLIS PULLS UP IN A ROCKIN TRANS AM, KICKS OFF HIS SNAKESKIN PANTS, AND FUCKS YOUR TEENAGE FACE RIGHT OFF.

BETTY, AS BEAUTIFUL AND INNOCENT AS SHE IS, DOESN'T KNOW HOW TO HAVE SEX, SO THE SMOOTH-TALKING PERV BANGS KATHY AS A HANDS-ON LESSON TO CORRUPT THE NEWB. "SEE WHAT YOUR NASTY FRIEND IS DOING, BABY?" GILLIS HISSES WHILE HE PRYS OPEN KATHY'S ASSCHEEKS. BEFORE LONG, BETTY IS FURIOUSLY MASTURBATING AND WE'VE GOT A SERIOUS CASE OF "GOOD TIMEZ" ON OUR HANDS. FROM DEMURE TO DEPRAVED IN JUST A FEW EASY LESSONS! BUT THAT'S NOT ALL. THIS DREAMY WEEKEND OF SIN IS JUST BEGINNING.

SEE WHAT YOUR NASTY FRIEND IS DOING BABY?

FROM THERE IT IS ON TO THE BROTHEL OF MADAME ROSE (LISA DE LEEUW) WHERE POOR BETTY IS AUCTIONED OFF TO THE HIGHEST BIDDER AN ORGY BUSTS OUT AMONGST THE WHORES (BUNNY BLEU, RAVEN, STEVIE TAYLOR AND HEATHER THOMAS) AND THE HIGH ROLLERS, AMONGST THEM A SENATOR (ERIC EDWARDS), A PRIEST (MICHAEL MORRISON), A NAZI COLONEL (KLAUS MÜLLER), AND A HOLLYWOOD MOVIE MOGUL (EDWARD LONGLY). I GUESS YOU COULD SAY THAT THIS SCENE IS THE PUNCHLINE TO THE OLD JOKE THAT BEGINS WITH "A NAZI, A PRIEST, A

SENATOR AND A DIRECTOR WALK INTO A BAR". RAVEN, FOR HER PART, IS ON ALL FOURS AND USED AS A TABLE TO HOLD A TRAY OF THE PRIEST'S SNACKS. INTERESTING WORK IF YOU CAN GET IT.

ESCAPING FROM THE BROTHEL, BETTY MUST EVADE THE CLUTCHES OF A UNSEEMLY PIMP NAMED MR. LOVE (RUFUS JEFFERSON) BEFORE BEING NABBED BY TWO SLEAZY COPS (RICK CASSIDY AND PAUL BARRESI) WHO INVESTIGATE HER CASE BY INVESTIGATING HER BOX. BEFORE THE MOVIE IS OVER, SHE'LL ALSO BE POTENTIALLY MOLESTED BY A FLASHER (CRAIG ROBERTS) AND EVEN TURN UP AS CORPSE THAT IS PREYED UPON BY A NEFARIOUS NECROMANTIC UNDERTAKER (HARRY REEMS). THIS FRESH STUFF REALLY GETS AROUND, MAN. AND I DIDN'T EVEN MENTION THE LESBO MAKE-OUT SESSION IN THE STATION WAGON WHILE A VILLAGE PEOPLE-SIZED GANG OF LEATHER BOYS OUTSIDE THE VEHICLE UNLOAD THEIR MAN GRAVY ON THE WINDOWS. MACHO, MACHO, MEN INDEED.

A BRITISH NURSE (TURNED-NUDE MODEL, AND THEN TURNED-PORNOGRAPHER), SUZE RANDALL SHOT PILES OF PHOTOGRAPHIC CONTENT FOR HUGH HEFNER AND LARRY FLYNT TO RUN IN THEIR WANK RAGS BACK IN THE DAY, AND DID SO EXPERTLY. SHE WAS AT THE TOP OF THE ADULT INDUSTRY IN THE 1970S AND 1980S FOR PRINT MEDIUM SMUT, BUT HERE SHE TEAMS UP WITH HER HUSBAND TO SHARE THE DIRECTORS CHAIR. HE WAS A SOUTH AFRICAN-BORN WRITER, WHO DIRECTED THE NON-PORN SCENES AS 'VICTOR NYE.' FOR HER PART, SUZE SHOOTS THE HARDCORE, AND EVERYTHING WORKS OUT PRETTY GOOD, ALTHOUGH SOME OF THE EDITING HINGING THE TWO ELEMENTS TOGETHER IS A TAD DODGY.

THE PHOTOGRAPHY, COSTUMES, AND SETS ARE ALL DESIGNED AND EXECUTED WITH TASTE AND UNCLUTTERED ELEGANCE, WHICH IS EXACTLY HOW SUZE RAN SHIT ON HER SHOOTS FOR HUSTLER AND PLAYBOY, AS EVIDENCED BY FOOTAGE OF HER IN DOCUMENTARIES OF THE ERA LIKE 'NOT A LOVE STORY.' WHEN I MET GINGER LYNN IN 2014, I HAD HER SIGN A HIGH SOCIETY MAGAZINE COVER SHE WAS ON, AND SHE GUSHED ABOUT HOW IT WAS A SUZE RANDALL PHOTO, AND HOW MUCH FUN IT WAS TO SHOOT WITH RANDALL, AND HOW LEGITIMATELY SEXY THE VIBE WAS ON HER SETS.

ON THE VINEGAR SYNDROME DVD, THE COUPLE TEAM UP FOR AN AUDIO COMMENTARY (ALONG WITH AN APPEARANCE BY THEIR PORN PHOTOGRAPHER DAUGHTER, HOLLY RANDALL -- THE FRUIT CLEARLY DOES NOT FALL FAR FROM THE TREE) TO TALK ABOUT HOW MUCH THEY LOVED WORKING FOR LARRY FLYNT, AND WHAT IT WAS LIKE MAKING XXX IN AMERICA IN THE MID 1980S WHILE TRYING NOT TO GET BUSTED BY THE VICE SQUAD FOR MAKING OBSCENE MATERIAL. OR WORSE YET, GETTING SADDLED WITH THE GREATER CRIME OF PIMPING AND PANDERING-- A REAL THREAT IN CALIFORNIA AT THE TIME BEFORE HAL FREEMAN TOOK HIS CASE TO THE SUPREME COURT AND NEUTERED THAT PARTICULAR LAW THAT WAS DESIGNED TO CRIMINALIZE THE MAKING OF PORNOGRAPHY IN 1980S LA-LA LAND.

"I NEVER SOCIALIZED WITH THE INDUSTRY" SUZE RANDALL TOLD THE RIALTO REPORT PODCAST IN 2014. "I KEPT MY FAMILY ASIDE. I MEAN, I DIDN'T CARE-- MY FAMILY KNEW WHAT I DID — BUT I KEPT MY PRIVATE LIFE SEPARATE, BECAUSE THERE IS NOTHING MORE BORING THAN A BUNCH OF PORNOGRAPHERS, LET ME TELL YOU!"

-BOUGIE '16

ART FOR THIS REVIEW WAS DONE BY THE TALENTED BEN NEWMAN:
GO TO: BENNEWMANART.BLOGSPOT.CA/

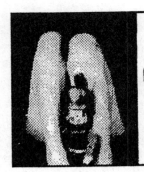

The shock has set in!

HARRY NOVAK PRESENTS
"toys are not for children"

Toys Are Not For Children (aka Virgin Dolls. 1972 Dir: Stanley Brassloff)

THIS MOVIE IS TOTALLY BIZARRE AND STRANGELY BEAUTIFUL IN ITS OWN WAY. THE PLOT CONCERNS A TROUBLED YOUNG WOMAN NAMED JAMIE (MARCIA FORBES) WHO WORKS IN A TOY STORE AND IS DEVASTATED BY THE FACT THAT HER FATHER GOT BANISHED FROM THE FAMILY BY HER MOTHER BECAUSE HE GOT BUSTED BANGING HOOKERS ON THE SIDE. DESPITE NOT SEEING HIM SINCE SHE WAS SIX YEARS OLD, JAMIE DOES HER BEST TO TRY TO LIVE A NORMAL LIFE, MARRYING HER CO-WORKER AT THE TOY SHOP. BUT WHEN IT COMES TIME TO CONSUMMATE HER MARRIAGE ON THE WEDDING NIGHT, HER VULVA CLAMPS SHUT LIKE A VICE GRIP AND WON'T LET HIM IN. MENTALLY, SHE'S NOT MUCH OLDER THAN WHEN HER FATHER ABANDONED HER, AND JUST CAN'T HANDLE THE CONCEPT OF AN ERECT, SWOLLEN DICK FLYING AT HER. HE'S UNDERSTANDING, BUT EVENTUALLY HE YELLS THAT HE'S "23", AND NEEDS TO "GET LAID".

CONSTANTLY OBSESSING ABOUT DADDY AND THE TOYS HE GAVE HER AS A LITTLE GIRL (SHE COYLY MASTURBATES WITH THEM), A PAINFUL PORTRAIT OF ARRESTED ADOLESCENCE IS PAINTED ON OUR MAIN CHARACTER, A FACT DRIVEN HOME BY HER EVENTUALLY HUNTING DOWN THE AGING HOOKER NAMED PEARL (EVELYN KINGSLEY) THAT HER FATHER USED TO SCREW, AND THEN MOVING IN WITH HER. LOOKING FOR A NEW MOTHER-FIGURE AND TO BE TAUGHT HOW TO PROPERLY SELL THE PUSSY THAT SHE CAN'T BRING HERSELF TO GIVE TO HER OWN HUSBAND, JAMIE LOOSENS UP AND BECOMES A PROSTITUTE SIMPLY AS A WAY TO CONNECT WITH HER LONG LOST PAPA. HE LOVED WHORES, SO MAYBE IF SHE'S A SKILLED WHORE, HE'D SOMEHOW APPROVE? I KNOW, IT'S STRANGE, BUT SOMEHOW THIS CRAZY MOVIE MAKES THE CONCEPT TOTALLY MAKE SENSE SOMEHOW!

DEPRESSING, SLEAZY, GRIMY, UNHINGED AND CREEPY AS SHIT, TOYS ARE NOT FOR CHILDREN GETS WILDER AS IT GOES AND CULMINATES IN A MUST-WATCH CINEMATIC EXPERIENCE FOR CINEMA SEWER READERS. THE POSTER THAT PRODUCER HARRY NOVAK USED TO SELL THE MOVIE WAS DESIGNED TO TRICK VIEWERS INTO THINKING IT WAS A SKIN FLICK, BUT EVEN WHILE LACKING ON-SCREEN SEX AND VIOLENCE, THE PLOT ACTUALLY MAKES THIS FAR DIRTIER AND SLEAZIER THAN MANY HARDCORE GONZO XXX I'VE SEEN, WHICH IS CERTAINLY A TESTAMENT TO THE POWER OF WRITING AND FILMMAKING.

AS SEXPLOITATION EXPERT CASEY SCOTT NOTED IN HIS REVIEW, "THIS IS A GRIPPING, WELL-ACTED DRAMA WITH AN EXCELLENT SCRIPT AND ACCOMPLISHED DIRECTING AND EDITING". HE WOULD ALSO GO ON TO CALL TOYS ARE NOT FOR CHILDREN "AN UNDERRATED GEM", AND "AN INCREDIBLE EXAMPLE OF AN HONEST-TO-GOD MOTION PICTURE, NOT JUST A SERIES OF SEX SCENES DRAPED ON AN INVISIBLE PLOT". HIGH PRAISE FOR A FILM FROM THE USUALLY DISRESPECTED EXPLOITATION GENRE, AND WORDS I WILL CERTAINLY SECOND AND BOLSTER WITH MY OWN UNRESERVED AND ENTHUSIASTIC THUMBS UP. CHECK THIS ONE OUT ASA-FATHER-FUCKING-P.

TRIVIA: JAMIE'S SHRILL, HAG-FACED MOTHER WAS PLAYED BY FRAN WARREN, WHO WASN'T KNOWN FOR BEING IN WEIRD 1970S DRIVE-IN MOVIES AT ALL. NO, SHE WAS ACTUALLY A MAJOR 'BIG BAND' MUSIC RECORDING ARTIST WITH RCA RECORDS IN THE LATE 1940S AND 1950S, APPEARING ON THE ED SULLIVAN SHOW, THE TONIGHT SHOW, AND THE COLGATE COMEDY HOUR. I CAN ONLY PONDER HOW SHE ENDED UP IN THIS MOVIE, AS IT HAD BEEN 20 YEARS SINCE SHE'D DONE ANYTHING ON TELEVISION OR ON THE BIG SCREEN.

– BOUGIE'S

JAMIE WITH HER BIG PILE OF SEX TOYS.

ART BY SCOTT "DADDY ISSUES" MILLER

REVIEW BY:
ERIC PERETTI
·2015·

IN THE '90S, THE FRENCH VIDEO CLUB WORLD WAS IN FULL MUTATION. HUNDREDS OF COPIES OF THE MAJORS' BLOCKBUSTERS WERE OVER-RUNNING THE PLACE, WHEREAS THE SUBVERSIVE EXPLOITATION FLICKS RELEASED AT THE DAWN OF THE VHS BY SMALL COMPANIES WERE BEING LOST IN A DUSTY OBLIVION ON THE BOTTOM SHELVES, JUST BEFORE THEY GOT KICKED OUT OF THE CIRCUIT. GRADUALLY SECOND HAND SHOPS AND FLEA MARKETS BECAME THE FERTILE FIELDS FOR A NEW GENERATION OF MOVIE ARCHEOLOGISTS IN FRANCE. YOU DIDN'T EVEN HAVE TO DIG DEEPLY TO EXHUME ODDITIES, AND USUALLY ONE TRIP WAS ENOUGH TO BRING BACK HOME TONS OF NEVER HEARD OF BEFORE MOVIES, JUST ON THE BASIS OF THEIR GREAT, BUT OFTEN MISLEADING, BOX COVERS.

MADE FOR THE HOMOSEXUAL MARKET AT THAT TIME AND DISTRIBUTED IN SELECTED AREAS, HAND BALLING (AKA POING DE FORCE) WAS RELEASED ON VHS IN THE EARLY 1980S BY GAY LABEL VIDEOMO, AND DID NOT LEAVE MUCH TO THE IMAGINATION REGARDING ITS CONTENT. THE MISTAKE, HOWEVER, WOULD BE TO ASSUME THAT THIS GAY PORNO WAS NOTHING BUT A PLOTLESS DIRECT-TO-VIDEO FEATURE. YOU WOULD BE MISSING OUT ON SOMETHING DISTURBINGLY ARTISTIC.

THE FIRST GRAINY IMAGES, SHOT IN GLORIOUS 16MM FILM, SET THE SCENE IN A FILTHY APARTMENT WHILE A NEUTRAL VOICE OVER INFORMS US THAT EVERYTHING WE'RE GOING TO WITNESS IS REAL. DRESSED IN A PAIR OF BLUE JEANS, BARE-CHESTED UNDER A LEATHER JACKET AND WEARING A MATCHING LEATHER HOOD, A MAN MAKES HIMSELF AN OMELETTE BEFORE HE SITS AT A TABLE AND STARTS TALKING DIRECTLY TO THE CAMERA. THE MAN EXPLAINS THAT HE IS NOT HIDING HIS FACE TO REMAIN ANONYMOUS, BUT BECAUSE HE WAS THE VICTIM OF A TERRIBLE MOTORCYCLE ACCIDENT IN WHICH HE RECEIVED THIRD DEGREE BURNS. DESPITE NUMEROUS PLASTIC SURGERIES, HE STILL CARRIES HORRIBLE SCARS.

THIS MAN DESCRIBES HIMSELF AS A MASTER OF DISCIPLINE AND BONDAGE, HIGHLY PRAISED BECAUSE OF HIS LEATHER LOOK, AND INFORMS US THAT A CLIENT IS ON HIS WAY. THEN THERE IS A CHANGE OF LOCATION TO A MESSY ROOM WHERE A MUSTACHED GUY IS WAITING. AS MUSIC FROM AN ELECTRONIC KEYBOARD FILLS THE AIR, THE NEWCOMER GETS ON HIS KNEES AND IS WHIPPED WITH A BELT. A MOTOR OIL CAN IS OPENED TO LUBRICATE A QUICK ANAL INTERCOURSE SESSION BEFORE OUR SUBMISSIVE LIES ON HIS BACK, SPREADING HIS LEGS. THE LEATHER FACED MONSTER GRABS A JAR OF CRISCO SHORTENING, BUT I CAN ASSURE YOU THAT NO BAKING IS GOING TO TAKE PLACE. WITH DISCONCERTING EASE, HE QUICKLY INTRODUCES A TOTALLY GREASED HAND INTO THE HUNGRY ASSHOLE IN FRONT OF HIM, RAPIDLY FOLLOWED BY A SECOND ONE.

THE URBAN DICTIONARY DENOTES THE TERM "HANDBALLING" AS "THE ART OF STUFFING YOUR HAND AND ARM INTO YOUR PARTNERS ANUS", AND TRUE TO THAT DEFINITION, THE MAN'S HANDS MOVE IN AND OUT LIKE PISTONS -- ROCKY BALBOA STYLE -- GIVING US THE IMPRESSION AN INTERNAL PUNCHING BAG IS BEING BOXED.

AFTER WHAT SEEMS AN ENDLESS TIME, AND HAVING BEEN SCREWED IN A MORE CONVENTIONAL METHOD, THE DILATED AND HAPPY FISTEE FINALLY EJACULATES ON THE LEATHER HOOD OF HIS MASTER. THE PREVIOUS VOICE OVER WARNS US TO GET READY FOR SOMETHING STRONG, AND OUR MYSTERIOUS HOST REVEALS HIS GRUESOME FACE IN A LAST, SILENT GAZE INTO THE CAMERA.

THANKS TO THE INTERNET, WE'RE CURRENTLY OVER-RUN WITH EXTREME HARDCORE PERFORMANCES POORLY RECORDED UNDER THE HARSH UNNATURAL LIGHT OF VIDEO AND DIGITAL. THESE XXX CLIPS DON'T CARE ABOUT BEING

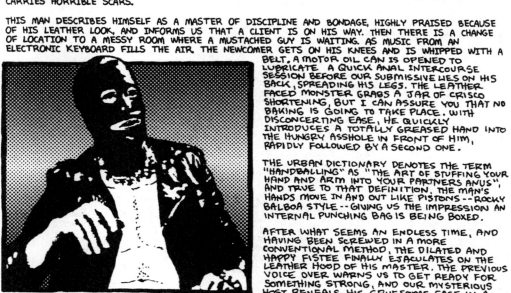

"DRESSED IN A PAIR OF BLUE JEANS, BARE-CHESTED UNDER A LEATHER JACKET AND WEARING A MATCHING LEATHER HOOD, THE MAN MAKES HIMSELF AN OMELETTE."

ARTISTIC, THEY ARE JUST JUNK FOOD FOR CONSUMERS WITH SHORT MEMORIES. HOWEVER, SHOT ALMOST FOUR DECADES AGO, HAND BALLING IS STILL, EVEN BY TODAY'S STANDARDS, STRONG ENOUGH TO REMAIN IMPRINTED ON THE MIND FOR A LONG TIME, PERHAPS BECAUSE IT WAS CREATED TO BE VIEWED ON A THEATER SCREEN, AND CONCEIVED BY TALENTED ARTISTS. DESPITE ITS SHORT RUNNING TIME OF 20 MINUTES, HAND BALLING IS NOT A LOOP, BUT THE UNCENSORED CLIMAX OF A FEATURE FILM INITIATED BY A PIONEER IN THE FRENCH GAY PORN MARKET: NORBERT TERRY.

FORMER ASSISTANT TO JACQUES TATI ON HIS MASTERPIECE **PLAYTIME** (1967), TERRY VENTURED INTO THE GAY SMUT BUSINESS IN THE MID '70S, REALIZING THERE WAS AN AUDIENCE SILENTLY SCREAMING TO SEE ALL MALE SEX MOVIES. HE WAS RIGHT AND QUICKLY MADE ENOUGH MONEY TO BUY SOME THEATERS. TO SATISFY A GROWING DEMAND AND FEED HIS OWN DISTRIBUTION CIRCUIT, HE STARTED TO SHOOT MOVIES. BUT IF TERRY WAS A DARING PIONEER, HE WAS A POOR FILMMAKER AND HIS MOVIES WERE CHEAPLY MADE, HIDEOUSLY PHOTOGRAPHED AND HECTICALLY EDITED. BUT AT LEAST THEY PROVIDED RAW SEX TO CLIENTS UNCONCERNED WITH QUALITY. LUCKILY, HE SOMETIMES TEAMED UP WITH ANOTHER KEY FIGURE OF THE ERA, JEAN-ÉTIENNE SIRY, THUS UPGRADING THE QUALITY OF HIS PRODUCTS.

WITH AN EYE FOR VISUAL ARTS, SIRY BEGAN HIS CAREER AS AN ARTWORK DESIGNER, GAINING NOTORIETY WITH THE PROMOTIONAL POSTER OF THE FRENCH CULT CRIME MOVIE **LES TONTONS FLINGUEURS** (1963), BEFORE DESIGNING MANY OTHER POSTERS FOR THE MAJORS' RELEASES IN FRANCE. IN THE '70S, SIRY BECAME FRIENDS WITH U.S. GAY PORN DIRECTOR JACK DEVEAU AFTER HE DESIGNED THE FRENCH ARTWORK FOR HIS MOVIE **GOOD HOT STUFF** (1975). THIS WAS THE FIRST HARDCORE GAY FILM THAT WAS RELEASED IN FRANCE, AS HISTOIRES D'HOMMES. WHEN DEVEAU CAME TO FRANCE TO SHOOT A MOVIE IN PARIS, SIRY MADE HIM A PROPOSITION OF A SCREENPLAY AND ASSISTED HIM ON THE SETS FOR WHAT WOULD BECOME **STRICTLY FORBIDDEN** (1976).

IN 1977, NORBERT TERRY AND JEAN-ÉTIENNE SIRY TEAMED TO DIRECT AN ANTHOLOGY CALLED **MÂLES HARD CORPS**, IN WHICH THE FICTIONAL DOCTOR NEXUS (SIRY HIMSELF) TELLS SIX STORIES DEPICTING THE LOVE LIFE OF MODERN URBAN HOMOSEXUALS. STARTING WITH AN ALMOST INNOCENT MASTURBATION SEQUENCE, THE MOVIE GETS WILDER AT EACH DIFFERENT SKETCH TO REACH ITS PEAK IN EXPLICITNESS DURING THE LAST ONE WITH THE DOUBLE FIST FUCKING SCENE. CONTRARY TO THE OTHER MOVIES PRODUCED BY TERRY, THIS ONE IS VERY WELL MADE, ESPECIALLY FOR ITS AESTHETIC APPEAL HIGHLY INSPIRED BY THE NEW YORK'S BDSM PRACTICES AND ALL THE ACCOMPANYING FETISH ACCESSORIES, SIRY PUSHES OUT THE ENVELOPE AS THE FILM ADVANCES BY BRINGING A DARKER AND HARDER IMAGERY THAN HAD BEEN PREVIOUSLY SEEN IN FRANCE, THUS OFFERING SOMETHING TOTALLY NEW TO HIS FRENCH AUDIENCE.

ALL CREDIT FOR THE INCREDIBLE AESTHETICS OF THE MOVIE MUST GO TO FRANÇOIS ABOUT, THE DIRECTOR OF PHOTOGRAPHY. HE WAS THE ONE WHO (UNDER)LIT THE DARK FANTASIES OF WHAT SIRY HAD IN MIND, AND BROUGHT THEM TO THE SCREEN.

WHEN THE MOVIE WAS SUBMITTED TO THE CLASSIFICATION BOARD, THINGS WENT WRONG. THE LEGALIZATION OF PORNOGRAPHY WAS QUITE NEW, AND IT WAS STILL DIFFICULT FOR THE COMMITTEE MEMBERS TO ALL AGREE TO SOME MOVIES. WHEN IT CAME TO GAY PORN, THEIR TOLERANCE WAS EVEN MORE CHALLENGED. THE BOARD REQUIRED HEAVY CUTS TO ALLOW THE SCREENINGS, AND CLEARLY EXPRESSED THEIR DISGUST CONCERNING THE FINAL SEGMENT WITH THAT INFAMOUS DOUBLE FIST FUCK SCENE. TO AVOID A TOTAL BANISHMENT OF THE FEATURE AND THUS A HUGE LOSS OF MONEY, NORBERT TERRY AGREED TO REMOVE IT.

IT IS THIS UNCENSORED SCENE THAT WAS DISTRIBUTED IN 1981 ON VHS AS **HAND BALLING**, BUT IT DIDN'T CATCH THE EYE OF GENERAL AUDIENCES DURING ITS ORIGINAL RELEASE. IT WAS MUCH LATER, WITH THE FALL OF THE ONCE POWERFUL VIDEO MARKET, THAT THE MOVIE WAS REDISCOVERED BY UNDERGROUND MOVIE LOVERS WHO WOULD RECOGNIZE IT FOR WHAT IT IS: A SUPREME ACT OF TRANSGRESSION. IN FACT, A CULT AROSE AROUND THIS TAPE AND INTEREST IN IT WENT FAR BEYOND ITS ORIGINAL INTENDED VIEWERSHIP. THE PEAK OF THAT VENERATION WAS A SCREENING OF HAND BALLING IN THE FORM OF A CINE-CONCERT, WITH A LIVE BAND, WHICH TOOK PLACE DURING THE LAUSANNE UNDERGROUND FILM FESTIVAL IN 2014, IN FRONT OF A BAFFLED CROWD.

— END

IN **CALIGULA** (1979) DURING THE WEDDING SCENE WHERE CALIGULA RAPES PROCULUS'S WIFE, DIRECTOR TINTO BRASS ORIGINALLY WANTED MALCOLM McDOWELL TO THEN ALSO RAPE PROCULUS. McDOWELL REFUSED TO MIME GAY SEX, BUT AGREED TO THE IMPLICATION THAT HIS CHARACTER THEN BENT PROCULUS OVER AND FORCIBLY FISTED HIM IN THE ASS.

The Bad Bunch (1973)

"SO REAL, SO HONEST, SO BRUTALLY VIOLENT, ONLY A FEW THEATERS DARED TO SHOW IT!" -BAD BUNCH TRAILER.

ALSO KNOWN AS **TOM** AND **NIGGER LOVER**, THE BAD BUNCH IS A LOW BUDGET RACEPLOITATION FILM SHOT IN THE WATTS NEIGHBOURHOOD OF LOS ANGELES OVER THE COURSE OF TWO WEEKS IN SEPTEMBER 1971 FOR FIFTEEN GRAND BY GENRE FILM LEGEND, GREYDON CLARK. NOT ONLY DID GREYDON DIRECT THIS SCATHING 82 MINUTE BUN-BURNER, BUT HE CO-WROTE IT (ALONG WITH ALVIN FAST), AND STARRED IN IT AS WELL. THE LINE BETWEEN SOCIAL COMMENTARY AND DRIVE-IN SLEAZE IS BLURRED IN THIS NIXON-ERA MELODRAMA, ESPECIALLY WHEN ONE CONSIDERS THE VIOLENT WATTS RACE RIOTS THAT TOOK PLACE IN THE FILM'S POVERTY-STRICKEN LOCATIONS ONLY A FEW YEARS EARLIER.

GREYDON PLAYS A WHITE VIETNAM WAR VET NAMED JIM WHO RETURNS HOME TO LOS ANGELES TO DELIVER A SOMBRE LETTER OF BAD NEWS TO THE GHETTO-RESIDING FATHER OF HIS BLACK BUDDY, CLAY, WHO DIED IN COMBAT. NONE TOO PLEASED AT THE WHITE MAN'S WAR MACHINE TAKING A MEMBER OF THE FAMILY IS MAKIMBA, THE FALLEN SOLDIER'S YOUNGER, ANGRIER AND MORE MILITANT BROTHER -- AND HE'S RUNNING WITH A REAL BAAAAAD BUNCH. AS GREYDON CLARK SUCCINCTLY SUMS UP THE PLOT ON HIS OFFICIAL WEBSITE: "A BLACK GANG OWNS THE STREETS OF WATTS. A WHITE VIETNAM VET TRIES TO BEFRIEND THEM. PREJUDICE STANDS IN THE WAY OF ANY FRIENDSHIP AND TURNS BLACK AGAINST WHITE."

"I CAME FROM A SMALL TOWN IN MICHIGAN WITH VERY FEW MINORITIES", GREYDON REVEALED IN AN INTERVIEW AT THEINDEPENDENTCRITIC.COM. "A VERY CONSERVATIVE AREA. I NEVER PAID MUCH ATTENTION TO POLITICS UNTIL JFK RAN FOR THE PRESIDENCY IN MY SENIOR YEAR IN HIGH SCHOOL, AND THEN MY COLLEGE YEARS WERE IN THE TURBULENT 1960S. SOCIAL CHANGE WAS EVERYWHERE: CIVIL RIGHTS, VIETNAM, AND POVERTY HEADLINED THE NEWS AND I RESPONDED TO THE CHANGES ON CAMPUS AND IN SOCIETY IN GENERAL. AS MY HORIZONS BROADENED I TURNED AWAY FROM THE CONSERVATISM OF THE AREA I GREW UP IN AND EMBRACED LIBERAL CAUSES. I WAS PARTICULARLY INTERESTED IN CIVIL RIGHTS."

BEING AN EXPLOITATION MOVIE FROM THE EARLY 1970S, THE BAD BUNCH ALSO HAS SOME OTHER ENJOYABLE ELEMENTS FROM THE ERA, INCLUDING HORRIBLY BIGOTED COPS, FREE-LOVE HIPPIES, A GREAT SKINNY-DIPPING SCENE AT A POOL PARTY (LOOK AT ALL THAT FULL FRONTAL BUSH), A SASSY BLACK PROSTITUTE, AND A TOPLESS BAR SCENE WITH THE PATRONS OF THE CLUB AND THE NAKED DANCERS ACTING AS EXTRAS. NOT TO MENTION THE ENTIRE CAST WEARING THEIR OWN CLOTHES, DOING ALL OF THEIR OWN STUNTS ON LOCATIONS WITHOUT PERMITS -- AND USUALLY IN A SINGLE GODDAMN TAKE. I LOVE THESE KINDS OF 1970S FLY-BY-THE-SEAT-OF-YOUR-PANTS GRINDHOUSE CLASSICS! I EAT 'EM RAW LIKE SUSHI.

GREYDON CLARK'S AUDIO COMMENTARY FOR THE

2010 DVD RELEASE OF THIS WAS COOL BEANS, WITH LOTS OF LITTLE TRIVIA TITBITS FLOWING FROM HIS MEMORY, INCLUDING A FUNNY ANECDOTE ABOUT HOW HE CONVINCED A LOCAL FISH AND CHIPS PLACE TO FEED THE ENTIRE CAST AND CREW FOR THE DURATION OF THE SHOOT, ONLY TO HAVE EVERYONE GET REALLY FUCKING SICK OF BATTERED FISH AND CHIPS AFTER ONLY A FEW DAYS OF CONSTANTLY INGESTING IT.

IT WAS ALSO NICE TO SPOT THE PIGTAILS OF SEXPLOITATION ACTRESS BAMBI ALLEN, WHOSE FAULTY SILICONE TIT ENHANCEMENTS WOULD UNFORTUNATELY KILL HER THE YEAR AFTER SHOOTING THIS MOVIE. SHE OFFERS A PAIR OF TOPLESS SCENES, HERE, WHICH ARE AWFULLY BITTERSWEET FOR A KNOWLEDGABLE AUDIENCE WHO KNOWS OF HER ULTIMATE FATE.

"THIS IS A BITTER AND ENTERTAINING CONFECTION OF RACIAL FEARS, SIMMERING VIOLENCE AND GRATUITOUS SEX" WROTE FANDOR REVIEWER, PINBALLMARS IN 2014. "IT'S ROUGH-EDGED AND SOMETIMES CLUMSY, BUT AN INTRIGUING SNAPSHOT OF THE TIMES FROM A DIRECTOR WHO'D GO ON TO BE A B-MOVIE MAINSTAY."

"THE BAD BUNCH IS NOT A HAPPY FILM", WROTE INSIDEPULSE.COM REVIEWER, ROBERT SAUCEDO. "THERE IS REAL EMOTIONAL WEIGHT BEING TOSSED AROUND LEADING UP TO A DEVASTATING ENDING TO THE FILM ... COLOR ME SURPRISED, BUT I FOUND *THE BAD BUNCH* TO BE A DAMN FINE MOVIE."

—END

THE BIG GUNDOWN (1966. IT./SP. DIR: SERGIO SOLLIMA)

EVERYONE CAN PRETTY MUCH AGREE THAT THE FINEST SPAGHETTI WESTERNS WERE MADE BY SERGIO LEONE WHEN HE WAS AT HIS BEST, BUT WHERE OPINIONS DIVERGE IS WHEN YOU ASK WHICH ARE THE FINEST OUTSIDE OF LEONE'S FILMOGRAPHY. A STRONG CASE COULD BE MADE FOR SERGIO SOLLIMA'S THE BIG GUNDOWN, AND I WOULD SAY AT THE VERY LEAST THAT NO 'TOP 10' OF THE GENRE WOULD BE COMPLETE WITHOUT IT.

THIS WAS THE FIRST MOVIE LEE VAN CLEEF MADE FOLLOWING HIS STAR-MAKING TURN IN **THE GOOD, THE BAD AND THE UGLY** (1966) AND WAS HIS FIRST LEADING MAN PERFORMANCE OF HIS CAREER AFTER DECADES OF PLAYING VILLAINS AND SECONDARY CHARACTER ROLES. HE'D THEN GO ON TO STAR IN MANY OF THE OTHER GREAT ITALIAN WESTERNS, SUCH AS **DEATH RIDES A HORSE, DAY OF ANGER,** THE **SABATA** TRILOGY, **THE GRAND DUEL,** AND A ITALIAN-AMERICAN CO-PRODUCTION KNOWN AS **TAKE A HARD RIDE.**

IN GUNDOWN, CLEEF PLAYS A BOUNTY HUNTER TRYING TO NAB THE ACCUSED RAPIST AND MURDERER OF A 12-YEAR-OLD GIRL, A MEXICAN (PLAYED BY TOMAS MILIAN) WHO IS IN THE PROCESS OF FLEEING AMERICA TO GET BACK TO HIS HOMELAND. THE SAVVY BLADE-WIELDING HISPANIC LEADS LEE'S CHARACTER IN A HARROWING GAME OF CAT AND MOUSE IN A COLOURFUL LANDSCAPE POPULATED BY CHARACTER TYPES THAT FANS OF THE GENRE KNOW AND LOVE.

THE KICK-ASS CHERRY ON THE TOP IS ONE OF THE FINEST SCORES OF ENNIO MORRICONE'S CAREER, WHICH INCLUDES A THEME SONG CALLED "RUN MAN RUN", WHICH WAS UTILIZED AS THE TITLE OF THE SEQUEL.

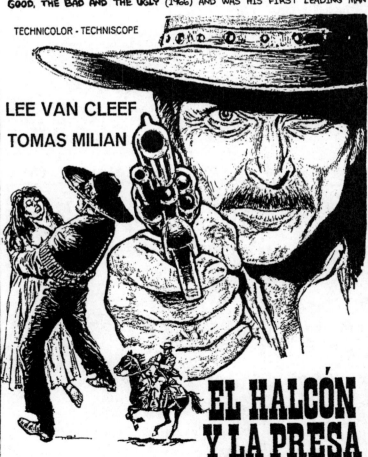

TECHNICOLOR - TECHNISCOPE

LEE VAN CLEEF

TOMAS MILIAN

EL HALCÓN Y LA PRESA

Dirigida por SERGIO SOLLIMA - Música de ENNIO MORRICONE

Mini-Skirt Love (1967 USA Dir: Lou Campa)

WOW, THIS IS TRASHY, CAMPY, WEIRDO SEXPLOITATION -- THE KIND THEY SIMPLY DON'T MAKE ANYMORE! MINI-SKIRT LOVE WAS PUT TOGETHER BY DIRECTOR/WRITER AND PRODUCER LOU CAMPA, AND OLD LOU WAS REALLY IN HIS ELEMENT MAKING MOVIES LIKE THIS. THAT FACT WAS EVIDENCED BY ADVICE HE PASSED ON TO THE NEXT GENERATION OF SMUT-MAKERS, SPECIFICALLY 1970S XXX DIRECTOR CARTER STEVENS:

"HE SAID SOMETHING TO ME I'VE NEVER FORGOTTEN", CARTER TOLD INTERVIEWER KEITH CROCKER FOR HIS ZINE, CINEFEAR. "HE SAID 'LOOK, YOU DON'T THINK THERE IS ANYTHING WRONG WITH WHAT WE ARE DOING AND NEITHER DOES ANYBODY WORKING ON THE FILM. BUT THE GUY WHO PAYS HIS 5 BUCKS AND IS SITTING IN THE THEATER WHACKING OFF -- HE KNOWS HE'S GOING TO BURN IN HELL BECAUSE OF IT, AND HE WANTS TO BE REMINDED OF THAT FACT EVERY ONCE IN A WHILE. KEEP IT SLEAZY.' IT TOOK ME A LONG TIME TO REALIZE HE WAS RIGHT."

BILLY (DONNY LEE) IS A MENTALLY CHALLENGED GROWN MAN WHO LIVES WITH HIS FAMILY IN THE SUBURBS, AND LIKES TO ROLL AROUND ON THE FRONT LAWN AND TAKE PICTURES OF THE SKY WITH HIS CAMERA. HIS MOM AND DAD ARE JUST LIKE YOURS AND MINE: POP GOES TO DINGY MOTELS DURING THE DAY AND BANGS A BLACK SHORT-HAIRED MOD HOOKER (MARIE CONTI), AND MA (BELLA DONNA) SPREADS FOR HER ACTING COACH WHO LIKES TO COME OVER AND MAKE RANDY HOUSE CALLS.

BUT THERE IS TROUBLE IN PARADISE. BILLY THINKS IT'S FUN TO SECRETLY TAKE BOUDOIR PHOTOS OF MOMMY GETTING NAILED BY STRANGE MEN, AND THINKS DAD WILL FIND IT JUST AS ENTERTAINING WHEN HE SHOWS HIM THE PICS. FAR FROM IMPRESSED, THIS SETS IN MOTION A VIOLENT PARENTAL ARGUMENT WHICH ENDS IN BILLY'S FATHER MURDERED BY HIS MOTHER, AND HIS MOTHER CARTED OFF TO THE FUNNY FARM. GOOD THING DAD HAS A SISTER NAMED JANET THAT CAN COME AND LIVE WITH THE POOR CLOD, AND MAKE SURE HE DOESN'T DO SOMETHING LIKE STAB HIMSELF IN THE EYE WITH HIS FORK WHILE EATING DINNER.

CAM-SCOPE PRODUCTIONS PRESENTS

A SHOCKING GLIMPSE INTO THE WARPED MORALS OF THE MOD WORLD

MINI-SKIRT LOVE

STARRING

MARIE BRENT · DONNY LEE · BELLA DONNA · GUY SINCLAIR · LOU CAMPA

PRODUCED & DIRECTED BY

A BOXOFFICE INTERNATIONAL RELEASE

BUT SINCE THIS IS A SEXPLOITATION MOVIE, LITERALLY FIVE MINUTES AFTER ARRIVING TO LOOK AFTER BILLY, AUNT JANET IS WASHING HIS BUTTCHEEKS IN THE SHOWER. "THANKS AUNT JANET!" BILLY SAYS ENTHUSIASTICALLY. "THAT FEELS GOOD!". SEXUALLY AWAKENED BY THIS INCIDENT, JANET ROLLS AROUND IN BED THAT NIGHT IN HER SHEER BLACK NIGHTY. WE KNOW SHE IS FURTIVELY MASTURBATING OVER THE MERE CONCEPT OF AN AFFAIR WITH HER MENTALLY CHALLENGED WARD, ALTHOUGH BECAUSE IT CAN'T BE EXPLICITLY SHOWN (REMEMBER, THIS IS 1967 AND IT'S A COUPLE YEARS BEFORE SUCH THINGS CAN OPENLY BE DEPICTED ON A BIG SCREEN), THE CONCEPT IS REALIZED FOR THE AUDIENCE SIMPLY BY ACTRESS JANET BANZET (AKA MARIE BRENT) ROLLING BACK AND FORTH AND MOANING. FOR GOOD MEASURE, SHE SPREADS THE PORN PHOTOS THAT BILLY TOOK OF HIS MOM ALL OVER THE BED, AND GETS WORKED UP OVER THOSE TOO.

FINALLY SHE FALLS ASLEEP AND DREAMS ABOUT SHE AND BILLY ROCKING OUT AT A DANCE IN THE LOCAL ICE CREAM PARLOUR, A GROOVY SCENE WITH A LIVE BAND WHICH FEATURES SOME OF MY FAVOURITE AND MOST AWKWARD LOOKING 'WHITE PEOPLE DANCING' EVER RECORDED TO CELLULOID. HERE IN HER FANTASY THE TWO STAR-CROSSED LOVERS GO HORSE BACK RIDING WHILE SOME PSYCHO-BILLY SURF GUITAR PLAYS, AND THEN THEY GIGGLE AS THEY THROW ROCKS IN A CREEK. SINCE IT'S A DREAM, HE IS NO LONGER INTELLECTUALLY DISABLED AND THE TWO HAVE A NORMAL HUM-DRUM ROMANTIC RELATIONSHIP COMPLETE WITH SMALL TALK.

WAKING FROM HER DREAM WITH A START, AUNT JANET GOES TO BILLY'S ROOM WHEN SHE HEARS HIM YOWLING LIKE HE SHOULD BE IN DIAPERS. "AUNT JANET! AUNT JANET! I HAD A BAD DREAM!" HE CRIES. FEELING HER MATERNAL INSTINCTS KICK IN SHE KISSES HIM SOFTLY AND THEN, SHOCKINGLY, SOME OTHER INSTINCTS KICK IN EVEN HARDER. BAFFLED BY GETTING A BIG SMOOCH RIGHT ON HIS KISSER BILLY LOOKS ON AS HIS SUBSTITUTE MOM BEGINS UNDRESSING SLOWLY IN FRONT OF HIM, COOING

"BILLY YOU'LL NEVER BE ALONE! HOLD ME, PLEASE HOLD ME!" HER ROUND, NAKED ALABASTER-WHITE ASS SHIMMERS IN THE MOONLIGHT FLOODING THROUGH THE BEDROOM WINDOW, LIGHTING IT AS IF IT WERE A CENTER-STAGE SPOTLIGHT AT MINSKY'S BURLESQUE. BILLY WILL LEARN HOW TO FUCK A WOMAN ON THIS NIGHT, MY FRIENDS.

CUT TO: 5 YEARS LATER. NOW THIS IS WHERE IT GETS AMAZING, BECAUSE THE SCENE BEGINS AS AUNT JANET IS KISSING WHAT WE LEARN IS A 20-YEAR-OLD BILLY, AN ASTUTE AND UPWARDLY MOBILE YOUNG GENTLEMAN WHO IS WEARING A PLAID SPORT COAT AND ROCKING A BRIEFCASE. HE STRUTS DOWN THEIR FRONT WALKWAY, GETS INTO HIS CAR AND STARTS HIS DAILY COMMUTE TO WORK, WITH NOT A CARE IN THE WORLD, LEAST OF WHICH BEING THAT BILLY AND JANET ARE NOW LIVING RIGHT OUT IN THE OPEN AS AN INCESTUAL COUPLE IN SUBURBIA.

THIS IS WHERE I SUDDENLY REALIZED THAT THIS MOVIE TOTALLY FUCKED WITH ME. THAT'S RIGHT, THROUGH THIS ENTIRE CINEMATIC EXPERIENCE, WHAT I THOUGHT WAS A THIRTY-YEAR-OLD ACTOR HAMMING HIS WAY THROUGH A ROLE AS A MENTALLY CHALLENGED MAN-CHILD WAS ACTUALLY A TERRIBLY MISCAST THIRTY-YEAR-OLD ACTOR LAUGHABLY FAILING AT PLAYING A 15-YEAR-OLD! WELL PLAYED, LOU! YOU SUCCESSFULLY SCREWED WITH MY HEAD! YOU HAVE WON ON THIS DAY, BUT I SHALL GET MINE, MR CAMPA.

BUT OL' LOU ISN'T DONE THERE! OH NO. NOW HE'S GOT A DOOR-TO-DOOR AVON LADY TRUDGING UP THE WALK TO SELL AUNT JANET SOME MAKE UP. OF COURSE, THEY QUICKLY TIRE OF THAT AND BEGIN DRINKING MARTINIS (AT 9 IN THE MORNING?!) AND THEN GET TO MAKING OUT. BILLY DRIVES BACK BECAUSE HE FORGOT SOMETHING AND WALKS IN ON THE TWO NAKED HORNY WOMEN GRABBING TIT AND ROLLING AROUND ON THE CARPET. AGAIN ARMED WITH A CAMERA (THIS TIME AN 8MM BOLEX), BILLY AGAIN TAKES SOME SAUCY FOOTAGE FOR LATER BEFORE HE'S INVITED TO PARTAKE WHAT IS QUICKLY BECOMING A LIVING ROOM ORGY. DOOR-TO-DOOR SALES? MORE LIKE DOOR-TO-DOOR PUSSY-MUNCHING.

BUT LOOK OUT BECAUSE MOM IS NOW OUT OF THE INSANE ASYLUM AND ON HER WAY BACK TO THE HOOD AS WE SPEAK! "IT'S SO GOOD TO BE HOME!" SHE SAYS, BEFORE BABBLING ABOUT HOW WELL BILLY'S DEAD FATHER IS DOING, AND HOW IT'S WEIRD THAT HE'S BEEN AWAY EVERY WEEKEND. CLEARLY OUT OF HER FUCKING MIND, BILLY AND JANET AREN'T QUITE SURE WHAT TO DO WITH MOMMA. "WE'LL JUST STICK HER IN MY OLD ROOM AND KEEP HER OUT OF THE WAY!" BILLY SAYS, FORGETTING THAT HIS OLD ROOM NOW HAS A BUNCH OF NUDIE PICS ALL OVER THE WALLS.

WILL BILLY'S MOTHER AGREE THAT INCEST IS BEST? WILL SHE WANT HER OLD ROOM BACK? WHAT THE SHIT IS SHE GOING TO DO TO THE MILK DELIVERY GUY (PLAYED BY LOU CAMPA HIMSELF)? YOU'LL JUST HAVE TO SEE THE MOVIE YOURSELF, YOU PERVERTS!

MAN THIS IS WONKY AS SHIT. IT'S A LITTLE ROUGH AROUND THE EDGES (WITH SOME EDITING MISTAKES, SOME SUSPECT CAMERA WORK, AND A FEW OTHER TECHNICAL ELEMENTS GONE AWRY), BUT THAT IS EASY TO DISMISS WHAT WITH THE INSANE PLOT AND CHARACTERS. I'D ALSO BE LEAVING A LOT OUT IF I DIDN'T MENTION THE ORIGINAL SOUNDTRACK PROVIDED BY A BAND CALLED "THE MUSICAL PROCESS". AN INCESSANT AND REPETITIVE DRUM BEAT DEEPLY DRONES THROUGHOUT EVERY SEX SCENE AND EVEN A BUNCH OF NON SEX SCENES THROUGH THE LAST HALF OF THE MOVIE. "BA DOOM BA DOOM BA DOOM" -- ALMOST AS IF IT WERE SCORED FOR A MOVIE ABOUT MARCHING CAVEMEN. THERE ARE OTHER ODD MUSIC CUES EARLY ON TOO, NEVER QUITE MATCHING WHAT IS HAPPENING ON SCREEN. YOU WOULD THINK THIS SORT OF AWKWARD SCORE WOULD TAKE AWAY FROM THE MOVIE AND MAKE IT HARD TO WATCH, BUT SOMEHOW IT ACTUALLY MAKES IT BETTER.

"THIS IS WITHOUT A DOUBT ONE OF THE MOST UNCOMFORTABLE SEXPLOITATION FLICKS EVER MADE", WROTE SEXPLOITATION EXPERT CASEY SCOTT. "LIKE A JOE SARNO FILM WITHOUT THE CLASS AND FINESSE."

HE AIN'T LYING, FOLKS. CHECK THIS ONE OUT FOR SURE! THE OUT OF PRINT SOMETHING WEIRD DVD MANAGED TO ELUDE ME FOR YEARS, GARNERING BETWEEN $40 AND $80 EVERY TIME I TRIED TO SNAG ONE ON EBAY. BUT THEN IN AUGUST 2015 SOMEONE TRADED IN A COPY TO THE DVD STORE WHERE I WORK, VIDEOMATICA, AND YOU CAN BET YOUR ANGRY AUNTIE THAT I DID A LITTLE SOMETHING WEIRD DANCE RIGHT THEN AND THERE! (IT INVOLVES LOTS OF SHIMMYING.)

END

JOHNNY CASTANO

'ATS RIGHT, YOU SWEET LIL' THING... PINCH THOSE NIPS FOR JOHNNY! PINCH 'EM!!

HEH HEH

SNAP SNAP

GOSH, JOHNNY! DO YA THINK PEOPLE'LL LIKE THESE KINDA PHOTOS?

I'M SURE OF IT!

JOHNNY CASTANO (AKA JOHN COSTANO) RETIRED IN 2000 AT THE AGE OF 69. BY THAT TIME HE WAS LIVING IN A SMALL APARTMENT ON THE OUTSKIRTS OF LAS VEGAS, AND HAD SPENT THE PREVIOUS 40 YEARS AS ONE OF THE PREMIER SHUTTERBUGS FOR ADULT MAGAZINES. JOHNNY WAS A VERY SKILLED PHOTOGRAPHER WHO SHOT TENS OF THOUSANDS OF DIRTY PICTURES AND WORKED WITH THE BEST IN THE BIZ. US SMUT HOUNDS, WE KNOW THE MODELS AND THE PUBLISHERS, BUT THE PHOTOGRAPHERS AREN'T REALLY KNOWN, SO LET ME TELL YOU ABOUT HIM FOR A MINUTE.

JOHNNY'S PHOTOS WERE GORGEOUS. HE MADE SPLAYED CUNT AND SPREAD ASS CHEEKS INTO AN ART FORM. THIGHS WERE CURVIER, LEGS LOOKED LEGGIER, HAIR WAS SOMEHOW MORE LUXURIOUS, AND TITS APPEARED ROUNDER AND MORE SUPPLE WHEN CASTANO SHOT THEM. HIS MENTOR AND TEACHER WAS FAMED CAMERAMAN OZZIE SWEET, A LAUDED PHOTOJOURNALIST AND EXPERT IN PORTRAITURE WHO HELPED USHER IN A NEW ERA OF PHOTOGRAPHY IN THE 1940S. CASTANO TOOK THE CONCEPTS HE LEARNED FROM SWEET, AND APPLIED THEM TO FILTH. THE RESULTS WERE OFTEN BREATHTAKING.

HIS PHOTOGRAPHY STUDIO WAS AT 16875 HART STREET IN VAN NUYS CALIFORNIA, AND THE CAR HE DROVE HAD A LICENCE PLATE THAT READ: "PHOTO1". PORN PERFORMER TONY MONTANA, WHO WAS DIAGNOSED WITH HIV IN 1999, SAID HE BEGAN HIS CAREER IN PORN BACK IN 1979 WHEN HE SHOT WITH CASTANO. MONTANA REMEMBERS A LOT OF PORN PERFORMERS GETTING THEIR START THROUGH THE GRUFF-BUT-KIND BALDING SPANISH PORNOGRAPHER, AND THEN MOVING UP THE RANKS VIA JIM SOUTH AND WORLD MODELING TO GET FAMOUS (OR AT LEAST MAKE A LIVING) IN FUCK MOVIES.

"I'M NOT SPEAKING ILL OF HIM WHEN I SAY THAT HE PRIDED HIMSELF ON BEING A CRANKY SON-OF-A BITCH", FELLOW CRANKY SON-OF-A-BITCH BILL MARGOLD TOLD ME IN NOVEMBER 2013. "HE WAS A WORLD CLASS PHOTOGRAPHER AND I HAD THE PLEASURE OF WORKING WITH HIM A FEW TIMES IN HIS STUDIO ABOVE THE MAGIC STORE IN HOLLYWOOD. HE HAD A GLORIOUS DOBERMAN NAMED MOMMA."

PRIMARILY JOHNNY WORKED ON DISREPUTABLE ADULT MAGAZINES, BUT HE ALSO WAS EMPLOYED AS A STILLS PHOTOGRAPHER FOR MANY XXX MOVIES. PRODUCTIONS SUCH AS LIPS (1981 DIR: PAUL VATELLI), THE MAGIC TOUCH (1985 DIR: JACK REMY), THE GENTLEMEN'S CLUB (1987 DIR: BRIAN JONES), AND DREAM JEANS (1987 DIR: DREA).

"IF I WAS SMART, I WOULD'VE GONE INTO THE VIDEO BUSINESS", CASTANO TOLD INTERVIEWER LUKE FORD IN OCTOBER 2002. "A FEW PEOPLE ASKED ME TO DO IT AND I SAID NO. I'M SORRY I DIDN'T DO THAT, BECAUSE I'D BE A MILLIONAIRE TODAY. I HAD CERTAIN SCRUPLES. I LOVE PHOTOGRAPHY."

"I USED TO KNOW EVERYONE IN HOLLYWOOD WHEN I HAD MY STUDIO ON HOLLYWOOD BLVD IN THE EARLY SEVENTIES. I KNEW EVERY PRODUCER. TELLY SAVALAS USED TO SEND ME SO MANY GIRLS TO DO PORTRAITS OF. I KNEW MELISSA PROPHET, WHO APPEARS IN GOODFELLAS... MELISSA WAS SMART. SHE KNEW HER WAY AROUND HOLLYWOOD BUT SHE COULD NEVER MAKE IT BIG IN THE MOVIES. I WONDER IF SHE EVER RUNS INTO MY OLD SIDEKICK, APOLLONIA? PRINCE'S CO-STAR IN PURPLE RAIN."

PROPHET AND CASTANO WERE CHUMMY BACK IN THE EARLY 1970S. HE'D HAD A TORRID AFFAIR WITH HER 19-YEAR-OLD BEST FRIEND, A "BEAUTIFUL MEXICAN PROSTITUTE" WHO LOVED GUAALUDES AND BROKE JOHNNY'S HEART WHEN SHE COMMITTED SUICIDE. PROPHET WOULD GO ON TO

BOTTOMS UP!

FOR JOHNNY!

BE A BEAUTY QUEEN, BECOMING MISS LOS ANGELES AND MISS CALIFORNIA, AND THEN APPEARED IN A NUDE PICTORIAL IN THE MAY 1987 ISSUE OF PLAYBOY, WHICH WAS SHOT BY KEN MARCUS (A FACT THAT PISSED CASTANO OFF). ACCORDING TO CHARLES FLEMING'S 1999 BOOK, HIGH CONCEPT, SHE'D GO ON TO BECOME ONE OF HOLLYWOOD'S BIGGEST MADAMES IN THE MID 1980S BEFORE GOING LEGIT AS A VERY SUCCESSFUL LOS ANGELES TALENT AGENT. BUT MELISSA WASN'T THE ONLY PIMP THAT JOHNNY WAS RUBBING ELBOWS WITH.

"WHEN I WAS IN HOLLYWOOD AND I HAD MY BIG STUDIO, RON VOGEL AND MARIO CASILLI (WHO SHOT MORE PLAYBOY PLAYMATES THAN ANYONE) USED TO COME UP. MARIO BROUGHT DOROTHY STRATTEN TO MY STUDIO. WE USED TO SIT AROUND AND DRINK COFFEE AND NICE WINE. I KNEW ALL THE PRODUCERS. ONE PRODUCER WOULD CALL ME AND SAY, 'HEY JOHNNY, I'VE GOT A REAL NICE ONE I'M GOING TO SEND YOU OVER. SHE NEEDS SOME HEADSHOTS. MAYBE YOU CAN WORK A DEAL OUT WITH HER. YOU KNOW WHAT I MEAN? WORK A NICE DEAL OUT?'"

"I KNEW RIGHT AWAY WHAT HE WAS TALKING ABOUT. I'D ASK 'WHO HAS SHE SEEN?' AND HE'D NAME OFF TWO OR THREE PRODUCERS SHE'D SEEN THAT DAY. THIS WAS AN EVERY DAY THING IN HOLLYWOOD. THEY USED TO PASS THE GIRLS AROUND LIKE THEY WERE NOTHING. I'D BE SECOND OR THIRD ON THE LIST."

MELISSA PROPHET IN INVASION USA (1985)

"THERE WAS THIS AGENCY RUN BY POLLY PELUSO. SHE USED TO SEND ME A LOT OF GIRLS. SHE'D COME RIGHT ON THE PHONE AND SAY, 'HEY MAN, FOR A $100, YOU COULD HAVE A REALLY GOOD TIME WITH THIS GIRL.' THE NEXT THING I KNEW, SHE WAS THE HEAD OF THE PLAYBOY TALENT AGENCY. A WEEK AGO, I'M READING THE LAS VEGAS PAPER, AND THERE SHE IS. SHE'S 74 YEARS OLD AND LIVING IN LAS VEGAS."

ONE OF THE MOST IMPORTANT ADULT MAGAZINE PHOTOGRAPHERS OF THE 1970S AND 1980S, WAS PAUL JOHNSON, AND HE REMEMBERED JOHNNY VERY WELL WHEN I TALKED TO HIM IN 2013.

"WHEN I WAS A TEENAGER I JACKED OFF TO JOHNNY'S PHOTOS IN MAGS THEN I FOUND MYSELF BECOMING FRIENDS WITH HIM AFTER I GOT IN THE BIZ," PAUL TOLD ME VIA EMAIL. "HIS STUDIO WAS ACROSS THE WALKWAY FROM MEL BLANC WHO I MET THROUGH JOHNNY. ONE DAY I WAS DOING A SHOOT IN JOHNNY'S STUDIO WHEN ONE OF MY MODELS FOUND A HUGE DILDO. SHE WAS SWINGING IT AROUND LAUGHING AND SAYING 'NOBODY COULD BE THIS BIG!' WHEN JOHNNY GRABBED IT OUT OF HER HANDS, UNZIPPED HIS FLY AND HAULED HIS COCK OUT AND HELD IT NEXT TO HIS SOFT DICK SAYING 'WHAT DO YOU MEAN NOBODY COULD BE THIS BIG? THEY TOOK THE MOLD OFF OF ME.'"

"YEAH, THAT WAS CASTANO", PERFORMER AND DIRECTOR RICK SAVAGE SAID. "I RECALL JOHNNY COMING UP TO ME AT A CONVENTION IN VEGAS ONE DAY AND SAYING, 'YOU HEARD ABOUT MY DICK, RIGHT? I GOT A DICK LIKE A CROWBARRRRRRRR.'"

"JOHNNY DID ME A HUGE FAVOUR BY TURNING ME ON TO CHARLES COTLAND OF GREENLEAF CLASSICS", SAID PAUL JOHNSON. "HE WAS CRANKY BUT HE HAD A HEART OF GOLD. OUR AGREEMENT WHEN HE TURNED ME ON TO GREENLEAF WAS THAT I WOULD PAY HIM 10% OF MY PROFIT FROM THEM. I SENT HIM A CHECK COVERING THE 1ST SALE AND

LATER I WENT INTO HIS STUDIO TO MAKE ANOTHER PAYMENT BUT BEFORE I COULD SPEAK HE SAID 'DON'T GIVE ME ANY MORE MONEY, I FELT TERRIBLE TAKING THAT LAST CHECK.'"

LIKE ALL OF HIS WORK, JOHNNY'S LAST PUBLISHED NUDES PASSED BY WITHOUT ANY FANFARE OR NOTICE FROM ANYONE. THEY WERE IN "GIRLS OF BARELY LEGAL" MAGAZINE ISSUE #10 FROM 1999. JOHNNY WAS DONE. HE WAS SIMPLY TOO SICK TO WORK ANYMORE, EVEN THOUGH HE STILL LOVED TAKING PHOTOS AND BEING AROUND NAKED GIRLS ALL THE TIME. THE KIND HEARTED DIRTY OLD MAN SAID

AFTER THIS. LET'S GO FOR A RIDE, JOHNNY!

GORGEOUS NAKED WOMEN POSING IN INTERESTING LOCATIONS: THE CASTANO RECIPE FOR GREAT PICS.

YOU GOT IT, BABY!

CALIFORNIA PHOTO 1

THAT WAS WHAT KEPT HIM FEELING YOUNG.

"I'M CRIPPLED" CASTANO LAMENTED TO LUKE FORD. "THEY SCREWED ME UP PRETTY BAD WITH BACK OPERATIONS. I GOT NOPROBYIA IN MY FEET. THEY GET NUMB. DIABETES. YOU DON'T GET GOOD CIRCULATION DOWN THERE. I TAKE A LOT OF MEDICINE. I'M PROBABLY A DRUG ADDICT. I'M LIVING ON MY SOCIAL SECURITY, MY VETERAN'S DISABILITY AND MY SAVINGS. I CAN WALK ON A WALKER. I GO DAY TO DAY."

JOHNNY CASTANO DIED IN 2006. HE WAS 75 YEARS OLD.

—BOUGIE '14

THE MAD BOMBER
(1973. AKA "THE POLICE CONNECTION")

I REALLY LIKE THIS SEVENTIES DRIVE-IN EXPLOITATION MOVIE. ITS DIRECTOR, BERT I. GORDON, IS FAR BETTER KNOWN FOR HIS G-RATED 1950S AND '60S GIANT MONSTER (AND PEOPLE) MOVIES, BUT BY 1973, AUDIENCES WERE DEMANDING A LITTLE MORE EDGE IN THEIR GENRE FILMS, AND THAT EDGE CAME IN THE FORM OF NAKED FEMALE FLESH, BLOOD AND GORE, AND EXCESSIVE CHARACTERS AND PLOT ELEMENTS. SO LOVEABLE OL' BERT SAID 'FUCK IT', AND JUMPED IN THE DEEP END OF THE GHOUL POOL WITH THIS R-RATED POLICE DRAMA ACTION FILM ABOUT A RAPIST (NEVILLE BRAND -- ONE OF THE MOST HIGHLY DECORATED SOLDIERS OF WWII) AND A TERRORIST (CHUCK CONNORS -- FAMOUS FOR HIS COWBOY ROLES IN WESTERNS) RAGING TWO SEPARATE ATROCITY CAMPAIGNS.

VINCE EDWARDS
THE PSYCHO COP -
He's got two jobs - find a mad bomber and find a rapist.

CHUCK CONNORS
THE BOMBER -
He's blowing up the town piece by piece.

NEVILLE BRAND
THE RAPIST-
The only man who can identify the bomber.

THE MAD BOMBER
—IT WILL BLOW YOUR MIND

DANGER DYNAMITE

JERRY GROSS Presents THE MAD BOMBER Starring VINCE EDWARDS • CHUCK CONNORS • NEVILLE BRAND Screenplay by BERT I. GORDON • Story by MARC BEHM • Produced and Directed by BERT I. GORDON

Distributed by CINEMATION INDUSTRIES   R RESTRICTED

CHUCK CONNORS'S CHARACTER IS A BIG SCARY GUY -- A "MAD BOMBER" IN EVERY SENSE. HE COLLECTS CLOCKS, HAS WEIRD LITTLE GLASSES THAT DON'T MATCH HIS BIG MEATY HEAD, AND HE'S A MAN TOTALLY UNABLE TO COME TO HEALTHY TERMS WITH THE WAY THE WORLD AROUND HIM IS CHANGING AND EVOLVING. THINGS LIKE FEMINISTS WANTING EQUALITY AND LITTERBUGS MAKE HIM GO FUCKING BALLISTIC. HE'S ALSO OBSESSED WITH ORDER AND COMMON COURTESY -- ALMOST LIKE A "GET OFF MY LAWN" TYPE OLD MAN WHO SAYS THE WORLD HAS GONE TO HELL IN A HANDBASKET, BUT TAKEN TO EXTREMES. CHUCK IS HANDING OUT EXCESSIVE PUNISHMENT TO TOTAL STRANGERS CONSTANTLY, AND FOR THE SLIGHTEST OF PERCEIVED INSULTS, HE EVEN BLOWS UP HIGH SCHOOLS AND MENTAL HOSPITALS, MURDERING COUNTLESS INNOCENTS FOR REASONS THAT ONLY MAKE SENSE IN OWN HIS DISTURBED MIND.

THE MAD BOMBER GETS FAIRLY GRAPHIC. IT'S NOT AN ITALIAN CANNIBAL FILM OR ANYTHING, BUT IT REALLY DOES GRAB YOU WITH SOME WELL PLACED RED STUFF AT KEY MOMENTS. THE VICTIMS OF CHUCK CONNORS ARE BLOWN UP (OFTEN IN SLO MO) AND BRAND'S HAPLESS RAPE VICTIMS DON'T GET OFF WITH A MUCH LIGHTER FATE. THE FRANTIC SCREAMING AND VIOLENTLY VIOLATED WOMEN GET THEIR TOPS RIPPED OFF, AND ONE EVEN GETS GAKKED VIA A DRAWN-OUT STRANGULATION SCENE. THEN THERE'S A PART WHERE BRAND JERKS OFF TO 8MM PORN LOOPS (!?) AND MAKE SURE YOU STICK AROUND FOR THE FINALE. IT'S FAIRLY SHOCKING IN ITS SUDDENNESS.

NOTE: IT'S AN ABSOLUTE MUST TO FIND THE UNCUT VERSION OF THIS ONE, AS THE MAJORITY OF DVD RELEASES HAD THE LAME-ASS CENSORED TV CUT, LACKING MOST OF THE VIOLENCE, SOME OF THE HILARIOUS DIALOG, AND ALL OF THE FULL FRONTAL NUDITY. THEY'RE TWO TOTALLY DIFFERENT MOVIES, QUITE FRANKLY.

RESTRICTED
limited admittance if under 18

RESTRICTED
limited admittance if under 18

RESTRICTED
limited admittance if under 18

RESTRICTED
limited admittance if under 18

JACKSON COUNTY JAIL (1976)

YVETTE MIMIEUX PLAYS A HEADSTRONG, TAKE-NO-BULLSHIT LOS ANGELES TV NEWS ANCHOR WHO SAYS "FUCK IT" AND PILES ALL HER BELONGINGS INTO HER GROOVY LITTLE AMC PACER AND HEADS FOR NEW YORK. WE GET THE FEELING IF SHE CAN JUST GET THERE, EVERYTHING IS GONNA BE ALL RIGHT FOR HER, BUT THAT'S JUST IT. SAYING HER ROAD TRIP DOESN'T GO SMOOTHLY WOULD BE AN UNDERSTATEMENT, AS EVERYONE YVETTE INTERACTS WITH ON THE JOURNEY IS OUT TO TAKE EITHER MILD ADVANTAGE, OR IN THE CASE OF HER SAVAGE JAIL CELL ABUSE AT THE HANDS OF A CROOKED DEPUTY WITH A HARD-ON, LAY SOMETHING DOWN FAR MORE SOUL-CRUSHING. DESPITE BEING MARKETED AS A TRASHY DRIVE-IN RAPE-REVENGE MOVIE, JACKSON COUNTY JAIL IS ACTUALLY MORE OF A DRAMATIC AND SOBERING MEDITATION ON THE UNFORTUNATE REAL-LIFE VULNERABILITY OF BEING A WOMAN AND TRAVELING ALONE.

WITH THE VILE RAPE, VENGEFUL MURDER, AND ALL OF THOSE JACKASS HILLBILLIES, ONLY A SLIGHT CHANGE IN TONE WOULD HAVE CATAPULTED THIS DEAD CENTER INTO THE HONKYSPLOITATION GENRE, SO IT'S INTERESTING AND LESS PREDICTABLE THAT DIRECTOR MICHAEL MILLER AND SCREENWRITER DONALD STEWART MAINTAINED A VERY SINCERE APPROACH WITH THE MATERIAL. WHAT YOU END UP WITH IS ONE OF THOSE EXCELLENT 1970S MIDDLE AMERICA BONNIE AND CLYDE-ESQUE MOVIES THAT IS BLEAK AS SHIT. THE PACING IS BRISK AND PROFESSIONAL, AND THERE IS A WORKING CLASS AURA THAT MAKES THE CHARACTERS FEEL VERY GROUNDED AND REAL. AS OKLAHOMA GAZETTE FILM REVIEWER ROD LOTT NOTED, "IF THIS WERE PRODUCED NOT BY CORMAN, BUT A HOLLYWOOD STUDIO, YVETTE MIMIEUX WOULD HAVE BEEN AN OSCAR CONTENDER FOR BEST ACTRESS. SHE'S THAT GOOD."

EQUALLY AS MESMERIZING IS HER CO-STAR. THIS WAS THE FIRST STARRING FILM ROLE FOR A VERY YOUNG TOMMY LEE JONES, WHOSE CHARACTER APTLY MUSES ABOUT WHAT IT MEANS TO BE A CRIMINAL WHEN "THIS WHOLE GODDAMN COUNTRY IS A RIP-OFF". THIS REALLY IS THE FILM THAT GOT HIM NOTICED BY CRITICS, ALONG WITH HIS PERFORMANCES SOON AFTER IN FILMS LIKE ROLLING THUNDER AND COAL MINER'S DAUGHTER. FILM JUNKIES WILL ALSO FIND VARIOUS LEVELS OF GLEE IN SPOTTING SUCH NOTABLES AS HOWARD HESSEMAN, BETTY THOMAS, ROBERT CARRADINE, MARY WORONOV AND SEVERN DARDEN IN BIT PARTS. THIS IS SOMETHING OF A MUST-SEE FOR 1970S CINEMA NERDS.

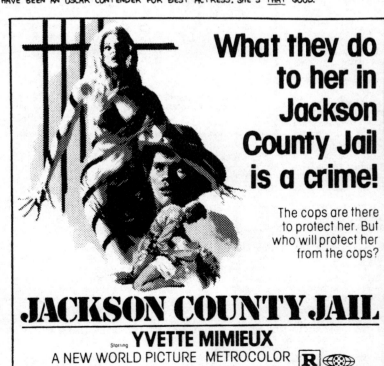

Fantasia

· FESTIVAL DIARY · JULY 2015 ·

I DON'T GET OUT TO THE FANTASIA FILM FEST IN MONTREAL, QUEBEC NEARLY AS MUCH AS I WOULD LIKE TO. THE 'FANTASIA FESTIVAL INTERNATIONAL DE FILMS' IS CONSIDERED BY MANY AS THE PREMIER GENRE FILM FESTIVAL ON THE CONTINENT, AND THE LAST TIME I'D GONE WAS BACK IN 2006, NINE YEARS PRIOR, ON A TRIP THAT CHANGED MY LIFE. THAT WAS WHERE I MADE CONTACTS WHICH LED TO VARIOUS JOBS DOWN THE ROAD, NOT TO MENTION THE PUBLISHING PARTNERSHIP WITH FAB PRESS THAT MAKES ALL OF THESE SOFT AND HARDCOVER BOOKS I DO POSSIBLE. I'D BEEN SEARCHING FOR A WAY TO GET CINEMA SEWER MAGAZINE INTO BOOK FORM, AND THIS HUB OF CINEMA WAS WHERE IT HAPPENED.

ZOOOM

QUEBEC, HERE I COME!

WEEEE!

BUT HERE I WAS -- THE BOUG -- GETTING ON A PLANE, AN $800 ROUND TRIP AND A 6-HOUR FLIGHT ACROSS THE CONTINENT -- ACROSS MOST OF THE ENTIRE COUNTRY OF CANADA. A FINANCIAL COMMITMENT TO A GUY LIKE ME ON A BUDGET. I'D HAVE A PRESS PASS SO THE MOVIES WOULD BE FREE TO WATCH, AND I HOPED I COULD MAKE BACK THE PLANE FARE VIA A MERCH TABLE THAT I'D BE SELLING MY WORK AT BETWEEN SHOWS IN THE MAIN FESTIVAL THEATER (CONCORDIA HALL) FOR THE 5 DAYS I'D BE THERE IN LATE JULY 2015. WITH NEARLY 800 SEATS, THE THEATER IS TRULY A PERFECT PLACE TO SEE A MOVIE, AND SCREENINGS ROUTINELY SELL OUT WITH LINES GOING AROUND THE BLOCK.

FANTASIA IS UNLIKE ANY OTHER FESTIVAL I'VE EVER BEEN TO, AND IT IS MY PERSONAL FAVOURITE. AS NOTED, THE FOCUS IS ON GENRE FILMS, BOTH MODERN AND VINTAGE, (BUT MOSTLY BRAND NEW STUFF). MONSTER MOVIES, POST APOCALYPSE FILMS, TRASHY AND WILD EXPLOITATION, SCI-FI, ACTION CINEMA, CRIME DRAMAS, ANIME FEATURE FILMS, AND OTHER GENRE FILM INSANITY. IT'S A SAFE HAVEN FOR CINEMA SEWER DEVOTEES, AND FANS OF ALL UNUSUAL INDEPENDENT, ORIGINAL FILMMAKING. YOU KNOW, THE KIND THAT IS HARDER AND HARDER TO FIND IN OUR MULTIPLEXES CRAMMED FULL OF REBOOTS, REMAKES, SEQUELS — AND OTHER "BLOCKBUSTER" GARBAGE PEOPLE ALWAYS SAY THAT THEY HATE, AND YET CONFUSINGLY SUPPORT WITH THEIR MONEY ANYWAY.

AFTER CABBING FROM THE AIRPORT I MET UP WITH SOME GREAT FILM JOURNALISM PUBLISHING PALS AND HAD SOME DRINKS (RICK TREMBLES OF 'MOTION PICTURE PURGATORY', AND MICHAEL HELMS OF THE INFAMOUS AUSSIE 'FATAL VISIONS' ZINE). THEN I WAS OFF TO SEE **LA LA LA AT ROCK BOTTOM** (JAPAN 2015. DIR: NOBUHIRO YAMASHITA). THIS WAS DONE IN A SIMILAR VEIN AS THE FILMMAKER'S EARLIER (AND BETTER) RELEASE FROM 10 YEARS PRIOR, **LINDA LINDA LINDA** (JAPAN 2005). LIKE THAT MOVIE, IT INFUSES MUSIC, JAPANESE CULTURAL MORES, AND A DRAMEDY TONE TO TELL THE STORY OF A MAN FRESH OUT OF JAIL WHO IS CONKED ON THE HEAD BY A STREET GANG AND GETS AMNESIA. A 17-YEAR-OLD ORPHAN GIRL WHO MANAGES A RECORDING STUDIO IS IMPRESSED BY HIS SINGING WHEN HE JUMPS ON STAGE AT A CONCERT AND GRABS THE MIC, AND THE MOVIE CHUGS ALONG IN FITS AND STARTS UNTIL THE MAN'S DARK PAST COMES BACK TO INTERFERE. NOT BAD, BUT CERTAINLY NOT THE BEST THING I'D SEE DURING MY STAY IN QUEBEC.

≡SIGH≡

SOMEBODY BETTER BUY THESE BOOKS, MAN.

RICK TREMBLES AND MOI

NEXT IT WAS TIME TO RUN ACROSS THE STREET FROM THE DE SEVE THEATER TO THE CONCORDIA HALL THEATER TO SET UP MY MERCH TABLE IN THE LOBBY, SELL SOME CINEMA SEWER VOLUME 5'S (MAKING THEIR WORLD DEBUT THAT DAY) AND THEN TOSS A BLANKET OVER THE TABLE AFTER THE CROWD HAD FILTERED IN AND TAKE IN **BIG MATCH** (KOREA 2014. DIR: CHOI HO). THE FANTASIA CROWD REALLY GOT INTO THIS ONE,

CHEERING DURING ALL THE ACTION SEQUENCES, LAUGHING UPROARIOUSLY FOR EVEN RATHER TEPID COMEDY ELEMENTS, AND CLAPPING ANYTIME THE FILM GOT UPBEAT AND OVER-THE-TOP. USUALLY I'M THE ONE ENJOYING THE THEATER-GOING EXPERIENCE MORE THAN MOST ANYONE IN THE THEATER, SO THAT WAS KIND OF STRANGE TO FEEL LIKE THE ODD MAN OUT IN TERMS OF EXCITEMENT LEVEL.

IN THIS PICTURE A FORMER SOCCER PLAYER BECOMES A MIXED MARTIAL ARTS SUPERSTAR, AND IS COACHED TO THE TOP OF HIS GAME BY HIS BROTHER WHO IS KIDNAPPED, AND THOUGHT TO BE DEAD. OUR HERO MUST NOT ONLY CONSTANTLY ELUDE THE COPS BUT ALSO FOLLOW A SERIES OF CLUES IN A GAMBLED-UPON GAME THAT WILL FIND HIM TRACKING HIS BROTHER'S KIDNAPPERS AND RISKING HIS LIFE AT EVERY TURN. IT WAS ONE OF THE BETTER KOREAN MOVIES I'VE SEEN IN A WHILE, ACTUALLY, WITH THAT COUNTRY NOT CONTINUALLY PUMPING OUT THE THEATRICAL BRILLIANCE THAT IT WAS IN THE EARLY 2000S, AND YET I WAS STILL LEFT WANTING SOMEWHAT. THE ACTION CHOREOGRAPHY WASN'T AT THE OH-SO IMPRESSIVE LEVELS I LIKE FROM ASIAN ACTION FESTS AND THE COMEDY SEEMED A BIT FORCED. BUT WHAT BIG MATCH DID HAVE GOING FOR IT WAS AN INCREDIBLE PACE, ENIGMATIC AND LIKEABLE CHARACTERS, AND K-POP STAR BOA'S FILM DEBUT. WORTH SEEING.

STAYING OVERNIGHT IN A SPARE BEDROOM BELONGING TO MY FRIEND CHRIS BAVOTA, THE NEXT DAY, THURSDAY THE 30TH OF JULY I GOT UP AT AROUND 1PM AND TOOK IN THE CANADIAN PREMIERE OF **PORT OF CALL** (HK. 2015. DIR: PHILIP YUNG). NOT A BAD GRITTY CRIME PROCEDURAL, BUT NOTHING WORTH WRITING HOME ABOUT EITHER, ESPECIALLY WHEN COMPARED TO SOME OF THE OTHER STANDOUTS WITHIN THAT GENRE. THEN I HAD SOME POUTINE AND CAUGHT THE WORLD PREMIERE OF **ANTISOCIAL 2** (CANADA. 2015 DIR: CODY CALAHAN). AS WITH A LOT OF MODERN NORTH AMERICAN LOW-BUDGET HORROR, IT DIDN'T DO MUCH FOR ME AND I FOUND MYSELF LOOKING AT MY WATCH. THE ENTHUSIASM OF THE CAST AND FILMMAKERS ON HAND WAS INFECTIOUS THOUGH, EVEN IF THE SCARES WEREN'T.

SPENDING THE NIGHT JUST FUCKING SWEATING MY ASS OFF IN MONTREAL.

WEST COAST BOY

HOLY CRAP! THE EAST IS SO FUCKING HOT IN JULY! HOW DO PEOPLE LIVE?

FINALLY AT 7PM I SAW WHAT I CONSIDERED MY FIRST GREAT FILM EXPERIENCE OF THE FEST, A SCREENING OF A PICTURE CALLED **SCHERZO DIABOLICO** (MEXICO/USA. 2015. DIR: ADRIAN GARCIA BOGLIANO). THIS WAS A REALLY SEVERE AND HORRIFIC BLACK COMEDY ABOUT THE KIDNAPPING OF A TEENAGE GIRL. YOU NEVER REALLY KNEW WHAT WAS GOING TO HAPPEN NEXT, AND ASIDE FROM A FEW TECHNICAL INCONSISTENCIES AND SOME TERRIBLE GORE FX IN THE LAST ACT, I LOVED EVERY MOMENT OF IT. IT'S BEEN A LONG TIME SINCE I'VE SEEN A VENGEANCE THRILLER AS STRONG AS THIS ONE, AND I LEFT THE THEATER FEELING EXHILARATED. THE Q+A WITH THE DIRECTOR WAS COOL, TOO.

I FINISHED THE NIGHT WITH **DARK PLACES** (USA 2015. DIR: GILLES PAQUET-BRENNER), A MOVIE THAT I ENJOYED WELL ENOUGH WHILE I WAS WATCHING IT, BUT AFTER I'D HAD TIME TO GO GET A BEER AND THINK ABOUT IT, SLOWLY FELL FROM GRACE IN MY MIND'S EYE. YOU EVER HAVE THAT HAPPEN? YOU LIKE A MOVIE WHILE YOU'RE INSIDE IT, BUT ONCE YOU PULL OUT YOU REALIZE IT WASN'T SUCH HOT SHIT AFTER ALL? ANYWAY, WITH A STRONG STARRING PERFORMANCE BY CHARLIZE THERON AND AN ADAPTED SCRIPT FROM GILLIAN "GONE GIRL" FLYNN, IT WAS PASSABLE GOTHIC CRIME FICTION, BUT NOTHING WORTH JUMPING UP AND DOWN ABOUT. IF ANYTHING AT LEAST IT WAS AN INTERESTING COMMENT ON TRUE CRIME NERD CULTURE.

THE NEXT DAY WAS FRIDAY THE 31ST OF JULY, AND I ROLLED ON DOWN TO THE FEST TO START WITH A BORING EXAMPLE OF IRISH HORROR CINEMA CALLED **CHERRY TREE** (IRELAND. 2015. DIR: DAVID KEATING). DURING THIS SCREENING I WAS CHECKING MY WATCH CONTINUALLY, AND REALLY STARTING TO TAKE NOTE OF THE FACT THAT I HADN'T SEEN MUCH TO REALLY FREAK OUT ABOUT THE WAY I HAD IN PREVIOUS YEARS AT FANTASIA FEST. "SHIT HAS GOTTEN STALE" I THOUGHT TO MYSELF. "THE QUALITY CONTROL IS NOT BEING TAKEN CARE OF". THANKFULLY, I SPOKE WAY TOO SOON, AS CHERRY TREE WOULD BE THE VERY LAST DISAPPOINTMENT OF THE FEST FOR ME. PRETTY MUCH EVERYTHING FROM HERE ON OUT WAS A+.

AFTER-
PARTIES
DISCUSSING
FILMS
AND
DRINKING
...

CLINK

A
MANDATORY
PART OF
THE
FESTIVAL
EXPERIENCE

CRUMBS (ETHIOPIA. 2015. DIR: MIGUEL LLANSO) WAS NEXT, AND WHAT A FUCKING WEIRD ONE THIS WAS. I'VE NEVER SEEN AN ETHIOPIAN GENRE MOVIE BEFORE, BUT IF THEY'RE ALL LIKE THIS, I'M REALLY LOOKING FORWARD TO MORE. FANTASIA WAS BILLING IT AS THE VERY FIRST SCI-FI MOVIE TO EVER BE MADE IN THAT COUNTRY, AND "PROBABLY THE SINGLE MOST UNUSUAL AND UNFORGETTABLE FILM YOU WILL SEE ANYWHERE THIS YEAR", AND WHILE THAT IS A BIT OF OVERHYPE TO GET BUMS IN SEATS, IT'S ALSO NOT FAR OFF FROM THE TRUTH. THIS OUTLANDISH STORY SET IN A DISTANT FUTURE WASTELAND HAS PLENTY OF WIT AND LAYERS OF SURREALISTIC IMAGERY MIXED IN AMONGST ITS UNEXPECTED AFRO-CENTRIC MEDITATIONS ON MAGIC, ALIEN RACES, RELIGION, AND ROMANCE. I HOPE IT GETS A DVD/BLU RELEASE.

H. (USA/ARGENTINA. 2014 DIR: RANIA ATTIEH / DANIEL GARCIA) WAS ONE OF THE BIG SURPRISES OF THE FEST FOR ME. THERE WAS LITTLE-TO-NO HYPE, NO ONE TELLING ME TO SEE IT (AS MOST OF THE FILMS DID), AND VERY LITTLE "I LOVED THAT ONE TOO!" FROM OTHER CINEMAGOERS AT THE BAR AFTERWARDS. AND YET, SOMEHOW, THIS WAS ONE OF THE BEST FILMS I SAW AT FANTASIA 2015. THE ENTIRE THING IS PRETTY DAMN MELANCHOLY, AND TAKES PLACE IN TROY, NEW YORK, AS VARIOUS RESIDENTS FROM ALL WALKS OF LIFE STRUGGLE TO COME TO GRIPS WITH MYSTERIOUS OCCURRENCES THAT SEEM TO BE HERALDING THE END OF THE WORLD. IT'S A HARD FILM TO PROPERLY DESCRIBE, BUT JUST TAKE MY WORD THAT IT'S SUPERBLY ACTED, DELIBERATELY PACED, AND INTRIGUING AS FUCK. AS THE OFFICIAL PROGRAM STATES, IT WILL LEAVE "BOTH ARTHOUSE AND GENRE FILM BUFF CROWDS ENCHANTED". A REAL SLOW BURNER.

ON SATURDAY I GOT SOME AMAZING SMOKED MEAT (MONTREAL IS FAMOUS FOR IT), AND FINALLY GOT SOME GREAT JAMAICAN ROTI (ANOTHER DISH THAT SEEMS TO BE BETTER HERE THAN ANYWHERE ELSE IN CANADA), AND GOT MYSELF READY TO TAKE IN SOME MORE MOVIES AND DRINK A LOT MORE BEER. FIRST UP WAS **MANSON FAMILY VACATION** (2015. USA DIR: J. DAVIS), WHICH WAS BETTER THAN EXPECTED, BUT DIDN'T BLOW MY MIND OR ANYTHING. IMAGINE A ROAD TRIP DARK COMEDY WITH...

YOU KNOW WHAT? LET'S JUST HOLD UP HERE FOR A SECOND. I SAW MORE MOVIES (**NINA FOREVER, TURBO KID, EXCESS FLESH, LUPIN THE THIRD, EXPERIMENTER,** ETC), MANY OF WHICH WERE FANTASTIC, BUT I'M ALREADY RUNNING A LITTLE LONG FOR THIS FEST DIARY TO BE DOING A PARAGRAPH LONG SYNOPSIS FOR EACH ONE, AND I'VE STILL GOT ONE MORE STORY I WANT TO TELL BEFORE WE WRAP THIS UP.

ONE NON FILM-RELATED HIGHLIGHT WAS VISITING MY FAVOURITE STRIP CLUB ANYWHERE, CAFE CLEOPATRA ON BOUL. ST-LAURENT. WHAT SETS CLEO'S APART IS HOW IT DOESN'T REALLY STICK WITH THE USUAL FAKE-TITTED "STRIPPER TYPE" OF WOMAN YOU SEE EXCLUSIVELY IN EVERY OTHER PEELER JOINT I'VE EVER BEEN TO. YOU SEE DIFFERENT AGES, DIFFERENT BODY TYPES, AND DIFFERENT FETISHES CATERED TO BY THE WOMEN WHO PERFORM. LIKE MY ABSENCE FROM THE FANTASIA FEST ITSELF, IT HAD BEEN 9 YEARS SINCE I'D BEEN BACK, AND I WAS PLEASED THAT THE VIBE WAS STILL JUST AS KINKY AND SLIGHTLY DANGEROUS AS IT ALWAYS WAS. AND PRIVATE LAP DANCES WERE STILL ONLY TEN MEASLY CANADIAN DOLLARS. THAT'S LIKE $7.50 AMERICAN THESE DAYS.

TWO OF MY COMPANIONS THAT NIGHT WERE FEST ORGANIZER MITCH DAVIS AND MY FRIEND CELIA POUZET, WHO WAS VISITING THE FESTIVAL FROM PARIS, FRANCE. SHE'S A VERY COOL WOMAN, AND NOTHING SHORT OF A CINEMA SEWER MEGA-FAN. ABLE TO QUOTE MY OWN WRITING BACK TO ME OVER DRINKS AND LAUGHS, POUZOT HAS GREAT TASTE IN MOVIES, AND APPARENTLY IN SHOES TOO. YES, LET'S JUST SAY THAT CELIA WAS MORE THAN A LITTLE OBSESSED WITH THE FOOTWEAR OF THE VARIOUS GIRLS PARADING IN FRONT OF US AS WE SAT UP IN THE FIRST SET OF CHAIRS, OR "GYNAECOLOGY ROW", AS I LIKE TO CALL IT.

PUSSY   HOUNDS

"DO YOU THINK THEY WOULD MIND IF I TRIED ON THEIR SHOES?" SHE KEPT ASKING ME, SHOUTING IN HER FRENCH ACCENT, DESPERATE TO BE HEARD OVER THE LOUD MUSIC. THINKING SHE WAS INSINUATING JUMPING UP AND MUGGING A STRIPPER FOR HER FOOTWEAR RIGHT IN THE MIDDLE OF A DANCE, I LAUGHED AND ASSURED HER THAT WAS SURELY NOT GOING TO BE LOOKED UPON FONDLY. MITCH AGREED. HUFFING HER DISAPPOINTMENT, SHE KNOCKED BACK ANOTHER BEER AND THE DANCERS KEPT DANCING.

A YOUNGER GUY WHO LOOKED LIKE HE MIGHT HAVE HAD SOME DOWNS SYNDROME OR SOME FORM OF MENTAL RETARDATION HAPPENING WAS LED ON STAGE AND SAT IN A CHAIR BY TWO CUTE GIRLS. HIS HANDLER (OR POSSIBLY FATHER?) HAD PAID FOR A SPECIAL DANCE FOR HIM, ONE THAT WAS TO BE PLAYED OUT FOR THE ENTIRE ROOM. HE WAS STRIPPED DOWN TO HIS TIGHTY-WHITIES, AND THE GIRLS RUBBED THEIR ASSES AND TITS ALL OVER HIM WHILE HE COOED HIS APPRECIATION AND THE REST OF US CHEERED.

"OH SHIT, I'VE SEEN THIS BEFORE", MITCH -- A VETERAN OF THE CLUB -- SUDDENLY WARNED. "THIS GUY'S GONNA GET IT!". CONFUSED ABOUT WHAT HE MEANT, I LOOKED ON. IN AN INSTANT, THE LAD WAS ON HIS STOMACH WITH ONE OF THE GIRLS SITTING ON THE BACK OF HIS HEAD, WHILE THE OTHER WHIPPED HIS UNDERWEAR DOWN AND BEGAN SPANKING HIS ASS WITH A LEATHER BELT. AND I DON'T MEAN CUTE LITTLE "NAUGHTY BOY" SPANKS. I MEAN FUCKING **WAILING** ON HIM WHILE HE TRIED TO WRESTLE FREE. CLEARLY DISTURBED, A FROWNING YOUNG COUPLE SITTING ACROSS FROM US GOT UP AND LEFT, BUT I COULD SEE FROM HIS HANDLER'S ENTHUSED REACTION AND HOW HE LAUGHED AS HE CAME DOWN FROM THE STAGE THAT THE PERVERTED SIMPLETON WAS NO WORSE FOR WEAR, AND SEEMED READY FOR MORE LESS THAN A SONG LATER.

A FEW DRINKS IN HER, CELIA HAD MOVED ON FROM GAUDY PLATFORM SHOE ENVY, AND WAS INSTEAD ITCHING TO GET ONSTAGE. "I CAN'T STAND IT ANYMORE!" SHE SHOUTED AT ME. THINGS WERE COMING TO A HEAD. SENSING SOMETHING AWESOME WAS ABOUT TO TRANSPIRE, I THREW $10 DOWN IN FRONT OF HER ON THE STAGE, WHICH GOT THE DANCER'S ATTENTION TO SLINK OVER TO US. IN THE SPAN OF MERE SECONDS THE GORGEOUS NAKED WOMAN IN THE SPOTLIGHT AND CELIA MADE EYE CONTACT, AND BEFORE I KNEW IT MY FILM-GOING COMPANION HAD SCRAMBLED OUT OF HER CHAIR AND UP ONTO THE STAGE, AND WAS NOW DOING DRUNKEN SPINS ON THE STRIPPER POLE MUCH TO THE DELIGHT OF THE PATRONS OF THE CLUB. CELIA IS QUITE PRETTY, SO AS YOU CAN IMAGINE NO ONE WAS UPSET TO SEE HER ONSTAGE AND HAPPILY KICKING HER HEELS UP.

DELIGHTED, THE STRIPPER WRESTLED CELIA'S SHIRT OFF, LAY HER DOWN ON HER BACK ON THE FLOOR, AND BEGAN WRITHING ALL OVER HER. MERE SECONDS EARLIER SHE'D BEEN MY DRINKING BUDDY, BUT NOW SHE WAS IN A 69 POSITION WITH A GORGEOUS NAKED WOMAN -- SHAVED BARE STRIPPER PUSSY AN INCH AWAY FROM HER NOSE. I CHEERED AND HOOTED MY DEBAUCHED DELIGHT. MORE BEER! MORE TIPS! THE NIGHT WAS SPINNING DELIRIOUSLY.

AS CELIA SLOUCHED BACK INTO HER CHAIR NEXT TO ME, HAIR TOUSLED, SHE LOOKED BLISSFULLY SATISFIED. SHE'D CONQUERED HER FEAR OF STRIP-DANCING ONSTAGE FOR A CROWDED ROOM OF CANADIANS, AND HER EXUBERANCE WAS CATCHING FOR MYSELF AND EVERYONE AROUND US, INCLUDING A STRANGER FROM HALIFAX THAT KEPT GIVING ME HIGH FIVES. ON A WHIM I HANDED HIM SOME OF MY SLEAZY SLICE COMICS I HAD IN MY BAG, AND HE WHOOPED WITH DELIGHT. WITH THAT, WE ALL DECIDED CHARGING OUT ON A HIGH NOTE WAS THE WAY TO GO. SCOOTING INTO A CAB, WE DRUNKENLY GIGGLED AS WE TOLD CELIA HOW AMAZING SHE WAS. MINUTES LATER WE WERE BACK AT THE OFFICIAL FESTIVAL BAR, BREATHLESSLY REGALING EVERYONE WITH STORIES OF WHAT THEY'D MISSED, AND PLANNING WHICH MOVIES TO GO SEE THE NEXT AFTERNOON -- STARTING THE WHOLE EXPERIENCE ALL OVER AGAIN.

SUCH IS THE FANTASIA FILM FEST. YOU CAN BET I'LL BE BACK.

— BOUGIE '15

MILEY CYRUS:
AMERICAN SLUT

BEFORE I START, I'M GOING TO SAY RIGHT OFF THE BAT THAT THIS IS **NOT** AN ARTICLE ABOUT POP STAR MILEY CYRUS. DESPITE THE TITLE, THIS REALLY DOESN'T HAVE MUCH TO DO WITH HER, SPECIFICALLY. SHE COULD HAVE BEEN ANYONE, BUT IT JUST SO HAPPENS THAT SHE WAS THE TOUCHSTONE THAT GOT A LOT OF PEOPLE TALKING IN 2013 ABOUT DEPICTIONS OF SEXUALITY IN MAINSTREAM POP CULTURE. I'M NOT IN THE HABIT OF WRITING ABOUT MUSIC PERSONALITIES (ESPECIALLY ONES LIKE CYRUS, WHOSE MUSIC I DON'T REALLY CARE ABOUT), BUT I AM VERY INTERESTED IN THE WAY SEXUALITY IS CONSUMED IN OUR MEDIA. I'M INTERESTED IN WHAT PEOPLE DEEM TO BE "TRASH CULTURE", AND HOW THEY REACT TO THAT. THAT IS ONE OF THE THINGS THAT CINEMA SEWER IS ALL ABOUT.

IT STARTED WITH AN AUGUST 2013 SHOW THE FORMER HANNAH MONTANA CHILD ACTRESS DID ON THE MTV VIDEO MUSIC AWARDS, WHERE SHE JUMPED AROUND DURING A MUSIC NUMBER IN A REVEALING OUTFIT AND RUBBED HER CROTCH A LITTLE. SHE TWERKED, STUCK OUT HER TONGUE LEWDLY, AND THEN ROBIN THICKE (FELLOW YOUNG CHART-TOPPER AND SON OF 1980S SITCOM STAR, ALAN THICKE) ARRIVED ON STAGE AND RUBBED HIS CROTCH AGAINST HER ASS. "MTV EDITED SO MUCH. THEY CUT ALMOST EVERYTHING I DID", CYRUS CONTESTED AFTERWARDS. "I FEEL LIKE MUSIC IS REALLY STALE RIGHT NOW. I COULD HAVE GUESSED WHAT A LOT OF ARTISTS WOULD HAVE DONE THAT NIGHT."

REGARDLESS OF HOW MUCH TONING DOWN MTV EXECS DID, THE FCC WAS FLOODED WITH COMPLAINTS. "HAD I WANTED MY FAMILY TO SEE A HOOKER PERFORM A LIVE SEX SHOW, I WOULD HAVE TAKEN HER TO TIJUANA," WROTE ONE BLUNT PARENT. THE RIGHT HALF OF AMERICA WAS SCANDALIZED, AND THE LEFT HALF MADE A BIG SHOW ON INTERNET SOCIAL MEDIA BY POSTING ABOUT HOW "BORING", "TACKY", "RACIST" AND "SEXIST" THE PERFORMANCE WAS. IN A MEDIA EXPLOSION, BOTH GROUPS COULD TALK OF LITTLE ELSE FOR A FEW DAYS. THE TWEETS FLOODED IN AT A RATE OF 306,000 PER MINUTE DURING THE EAST COAST AIRING OF THE VMAS.

THEN IN SEPTEMBER THE "WRECKING BALL" MUSIC VIDEO WAS RELEASED, WHICH FEATURED CYRUS FULLY NUDE (WITH NAUGHTY BITS OBSCURED BY PROPS), AND SWINGING AROUND ON A WRECKING BALL. SHE ALSO LICKED SOME SLEDGEHAMMERS AND ROLLED AROUND IN SOME DIRT. AGAIN, PEOPLE ACTED AS IF THEY'D NEVER SEEN A FORMER G-RATED CHILD STAR STRETCH BOUNDARIES LIKE SO MANY BEFORE HER HAD, AT THE RATE OF 1 OR 2 EVERY FEW YEARS SINCE THE 1960S. EVERY TIME FEELS LIKE THE FIRST TIME, DOESN'T IT?

THE FINAL STRAW CAME IN THE PHOTO SHOOT MILEY DID WITH PHOTOGRAPHER TERRY RICHARDSON, WHICH WAS RELEASED ONLINE THAT OCT. A LITTLE BIT OF NIPPLE APPEARED IN ONE PIC, AND SOME FABRIC WAS TIGHTLY BOUND AGAINST A SHAVED CROTCH. THIS PROMPTED ANOTHER OUTPOURING OF CONCERN, REVULSION, AND TITILLATION, AND SCADS OF ATTENTION FOR CYRUS'S FORTHCOMING ALBUM, "BANGERZ". CYRUS AND HER PUBLICISTS HAD MANUFACTURED THE ENTIRE SITUATION QUITE BEAUTIFULLY.

FROM THE RIGHT IT CAME FROM ALL OF THE USUAL SUSPECTS: THE DESK ANCHORS ON THE TODAY SHOW DISCUSSED THE CURRENT ONGOING TREND OF SEXUALIZATION OF YOUNG WOMEN IN POP CULTURE, AND YET TOTALLY IGNORED THE FACT THAT GUEST ANCHOR BROOKE SHIELDS DID UNDERAGE NUDITY 35 YEARS EARLIER IN THE FILM **PRETTY BABY**, WHERE SHE PLAYED A CHILD PROSTITUTE. SHIELDS HERSELF SAT THERE AND CONDEMNED CYRUS, WHILE SEEMING TO FORGET THAT HER OWN CAREER AS A MODEL AND ACTRESS WAS TOTALLY FOUNDED AND FOCUSED ON HER SEXUALIZATION AS A YOUNG WOMAN. I SAT THERE WITH MY MOUTH OPEN. IT WAS SURREAL -- KINDA LIKE WATCHING MR.T GET UPSET ABOUT ALL THE "FOOL PITYING" THAT THE KIDS ARE DOING THESE DAYS.

MANUFACTURED OUTRAGE
WAS THIS MOMENT REALLY AS SCANDALOUS AS AMERICA PERCEIVED IT?

BOOGA BOOGA BOOGA!

PFFTT

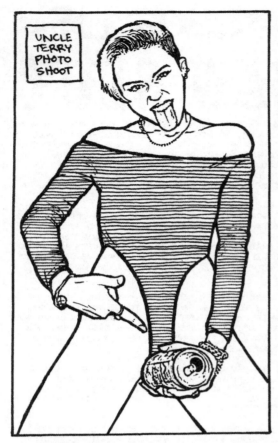

UNCLE TERRY PHOTO SHOOT

FROM THE LEFT, IT CAME FROM WHAT I WOULD CONSIDER TO BE AN UNLIKELY SOURCE, SINEAD O'CONNOR -- AN EARLY 1990s MUSIC STAR THAT MOST OF AMERICA HADN'T REALLY THOUGHT MUCH ABOUT SINCE SHE HAD GONE OFF SCRIPT AND FURIOUSLY SHREDDED A PICTURE OF THE POPE ON SNL IN 1992. NOW, INSTEAD OF SENDING A PRIVATE LETTER OF CONCERN, THE 46 YEAR OLD IRISH SINGER PENNED AN OPEN LETTER TO THE DAUGHTER OF COUNTRY STAR BILLY RAY CYRUS, WHERE SHE COMPLAINED THAT THE MUSIC INDUSTRY WAS "MAKING MONEY" OFF CYRUS'S "YOUTH AND BEAUTY". "NOTHING BUT HARM WILL COME IN THE LONG RUN, FROM ALLOWING YOURSELF TO BE EXPLOITED", O'CONNOR INFORMED MILEY. "YOU DON'T CARE FOR YOURSELF. THAT HAS TO CHANGE". "PLEASE IN FUTURE SAY NO WHEN YOU ARE ASKED TO PROSTITUTE YOURSELF. YOUR BODY IS FOR YOU AND YOUR BOYFRIEND. IT ISN'T FOR EVERY SPUNK-SPEWING DIRTBAG ON THE NET."

FRANKLY IT WAS SOME PRETTY PATRONIZING SHIT IN MY OPINION, BUT I WAS FIRMLY INFORMED BY VARIOUS SOCIAL MEDIA CONVERSATIONALISTS THAT THE TONE SINEAD TOOK WAS OBVIOUSLY "MOTHERLY", "CARING", AND THAT SHE WAS "TRYING TO LOVINGLY INFORM A 20-YEAR-OLD GIRL THAT SEEMS TO BE GOING OFF THE RAILS THAT SHE DOESN'T NEED TO EXPLOIT HERSELF IN ORDER TO GET ATTENTION AND LOVE, THAT HER STRONG TALENT IS MORE THAN ENOUGH."

OH, IS THAT WHAT SHE WAS DOING? "LOVINGLY" GIVING SOME ADVICE? GIMME A BREAK. WHAT A LOAD OF SHIT. THE SITUATION QUICKLY DEVOLVED ONCE SINEAD WROTE A SECOND OPEN LETTER WHERE SHE ANGRILY BARKED "CEASE BEHAVING IN AN ANTI-FEMALE CAPACITY. YOU WILL BECOME THE VICTIM OF IT SHORTLY" AND "..YOU COULD REALLY DO WITH EDUCATING YOURSELF, THAT IS IF YOU'RE NOT TOO BUSY GETTING YOUR TITS OUT TO READ", AND "TAKING ME ON IS EVEN MORE FUCKIN' STUPID THAN BEHAVING LIKE A PROSTITUTE AND CALLING IT FEMINISM".

SINEAD WAS CLEARLY MORE OF A CHILD THAN THE 20-YEAR-OLD GIRL SHE WAS BERATING WAS, AS PATHETIC AS THAT IS. UNABLE TO SHOW RESTRAINT, SHE STRAIGHT OUT CALLED MILEY A PROSTITUTE, AND ASSIGNED SOME NASTY INTENTION AND MEANING BEHIND SOME VERY BENIGN TWEETS COMPARING O'CONNOR TO ACTRESS AMANDA BYNES THAT CYRUS SENT OUT AS A REACTION TO THE FIRST LETTER. THE "MOTHERLY LOVE" SHIT WAS A SMOKE SCREEN. SINEAD WAS JUST BEING A JUDGEMENTAL DICK, ACTING AS IF BEING A SEXUAL BEING WAS WORTHY OF SHAME AND SCORN. ACTING LIKE SHE WAS SO MUCH MORE MORALLY SUPERIOR TO SOME OTHER PERSON SHE DIDN'T EVEN KNOW.

THIS WAS ALL A LAUGH, CONSIDERING I KNEW SINEAD HAD SPENT A FAIR PORTION OF 2011 TWEETING ABOUT HOW MUCH SHE WANTED TO GET FUCKED IN THE ASSHOLE. SHE'D TOLD HER FANS OVER AND OVER AGAIN HOW MUCH SHE LOVES GETTING FUCKED IN THE BUTT, OR IN THE "TRADESMAN'S ENTRANCE" AS SHE SOMETIMES CALLED IT. I LOVED SINEAD'S MUSIC DURING HER EARLY "LION AND THE COBRA" DAYS, BUT NOW ALL I COULD SEE IS WHAT A HYPOCRITE SHE WAS. SHE'S CALLING THIS OTHER WOMAN A "PROSTITUTE" FOR BEING SCANTILY CLAD IN HER VIDEOS? HOW WOULD SHE HAVE REACTED IF MILEY RECORDED A SONG CALLED "FUCK MY ASS"?

AGAIN, THIS WAS ABOUT MORE THAN MILEY VS SINEAD, OR HOWEVER ELSE THE MEDIA WANTED TO SPIN IT. THIS WAS ABOUT HOW SOCIETY AT LARGE VIEWS WOMEN AND THEIR SEXUALITY. WE -- NEITHER MEN NOR WOMEN -- AFFORD WOMEN THE SAME LEEWAY IN THIS AREA THE WAY WE DO FOR MEN, AND WE DON'T LIKE TO CONFRONT THAT BECAUSE WE LIKE TO THINK WE'RE ALL ABOUT EQUALITY. THIS KIND OF THING MAKES US CONFRONT THAT. WHEN WOMEN ARE SEXUAL, THEY ARE "VICTIMS" OR "SLUTS", AND WHEN MEN ARE, THEY'RE "SEXY" OR "CONFIDENT" OR "STUDLY" OR WHATEVER POSITIVE THING WE ATTRIBUTE TO THEM. WE FALL BACK ON THIS STUFF CONSTANTLY, AND DON'T EVEN NOTICE IT.

FOR THE MOST PART HER OPEN LETTER TO MILEY WAS RECEIVED VERY FAVOURABLY. I SAW SO MUCH SLUT-SHAMING GOING ON AROUND

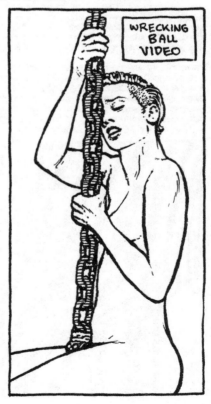

WRECKING BALL VIDEO

ON MY FACEBOOK WALL ANY TIME THIS TOPIC CAME UP, AND A LOT OF IT WAS COMING FROM PEOPLE WHO SEEM TO LIKE TO THINK OF THEMSELVES AS OPEN MINDED AND SEX-POSITIVE. OVER AND OVER MILEY WAS SCORNED FOR BEING "AN ATTENTION WHORE". CALLING HER AN ATTENTION WHORE AS A CRITICISM IS ACTUALLY DOWNRIGHT HILARIOUS. POP STARS (AND ALL CELEBRITIES, REALLY) ARE AS MUCH ABOUT VISUAL IMAGE AS THEY ARE ABOUT ANYTHING ELSE THEY DO. THEY ARE PERFORMERS. THEY VIE FOR OUR ATTENTION. IT'S THEIR JOB TO DO SO. AS ENTERTAINERS, THEY ARE PAID TO TITILLATE US, MENTALLY, EMOTIONALLY, AND PHYSICALLY. THERE ARE A THOUSAND LEGIT REASONS TO DISLIKE CELEBRITIES, BUT TO DIS THEM AS "ATTENTION WHORES" FOR DOING THE ONE THING WE DEMAND OF THEM IS LIKE COMPLAINING THAT MILK HAS TOO MUCH DAIRY IN IT. IT IS WHAT IT IS.

WHY SHOULD WE BE SHOCKED BY SOME GIRL IN THE ENTERTAINMENT INDUSTRY TRYING TO USE HER YOUTH AND CELEBRITY TO PUSH THE BOUNDARIES OF ACCEPTABLE SEXUAL EXPRESSION IN MAINSTREAM ENTERTAINMENT, OR ASSUME THAT SHE'S DOING IT AGAINST HER WILL? IT'S BEEN DONE THOUSANDS OF TIMES BEFORE, AND IT WILL BE DONE MANY TIMES IN THE FUTURE. THERE WAS JUST SOMETHING SO DISTASTEFUL ABOUT THE WAY PEOPLE JUMPED TO DISAPPROVE OF THIS KIND OF STUFF.

AND WHAT OF ROBIN THICKE, OH HE OF THE GRINDING COCK? HIS CHART-TOPPING "BLURRED LINES" SINGLE HAD A VIDEO JAMMED PACKED WITH FULL FRONTAL NUDITY, BUT NO ONE WAS WORRIED ABOUT HIM AT ALL. WHY WAS NOT ONE SINGLE PERSON CONCERNED ABOUT HOW THIS YOUNG MAN WAS BEING TAKEN ADVANTAGE OF BY THE MUSIC INDUSTRY? WHY DIDN'T ANYONE THINK HE WAS ACTING LIKE A PROSTITUTE? WHERE WAS THE OPEN LETTER OF CONCERN FOR THE MORAL SOUL OF ROBIN THICKE? OH RIGHT, THERE WASN'T ONE BECAUSE HE DIDN'T FUCKING NEED ONE, AND NEITHER DID CYRUS.

THERE IS AN IMBALANCE THAT COMPLICATES THIS ISSUE, IN THAT MEN DON'T GET NAKED OR ACT OVERTLY SEXUAL AS A MEANS TO VIE FOR OUR ATTENTION THE WAY WOMEN DO. YOU DON'T SEE DICKS, AND A CLOTHED MAN IS GENERALLY CONSIDERED MORE SEXY THAN A NAKED ONE. EVEN AS A STRAIGHT GUY, I'D LIKE TO SEE MORE NAKED MEN IN MY POP CULTURE TO EVEN THINGS OUT, BUT ULTIMATELY THE POINT IS THAT PEOPLE SHOULD GET TO WEAR WHATEVER THE FUCK THEY WANT WITHOUT BEING BRANDED AS A 'SLUT' OR A 'VICTIM'. WOMEN AREN'T AFFORDED THE SAME RIGHTS AND CONDITIONS AS MEN WHEN IT COMES TO THEIR SEXUALITY, AT LEAST NOT IN THE PUBLIC EYE, AND I'D LIKE TO FINALLY SEE MORE TRUE EQUALITY.

I MEAN IF I'M BEING HONEST, IT BASICALLY COMES DOWN TO THE FACT THAT I WANT CELEBRITIES TO BE ABLE TO GET TOTALLY NAKED AND DO HARDCORE PORN, AND NOT HAVE IT BE AN ISSUE, OR A CAREER-KILLER. NO ONE HAS EVER BEEN ABLE TO GIVE ME A GOOD REASON WHY WE NEED TO GHETTOIZE SEX IN ENTERTAINMENT CONSUMED BY ADULTS. I'M THE FAR EXTREME OF ONE SIDE, AND THE OTHER SIDE OF THE AISLE WANTS ALL OF THEIR CELEBRITIES TO BE CLOTHED AND SEXLESS, BUT IF WE HONESTLY BELIEVE THAT SEX IS NATURAL, AND A NORMAL PART OF THE HUMAN EXPERIENCE, THEN WHY THE CONSTANT NEED TO DISTANCE IT FROM LEGITIMACY? WHAT ARE WE AFRAID OF?

—BOUGIE 2015

BASKET CASE (1982. USA.)

SUPPOSE I TOLD YOU THERE WAS A CRAZY MOVIE OUT THERE WHERE THE LEAD VILLAIN WAS JUST A HEAD AND ARMS, AND LIVED IN A FUCKING BASKET. NO LEGS, NO TORSO. NADA. JUST A GROSS-LOOKING MELTED HEAD AND A PAIR OF ARMS. NOW AFTER THAT IMAGINE THAT THIS CREATURE WASN'T AN ALIEN OR SOME NIGHTMARE THAT ONE OF THE OTHER CHARACTERS DREAMT OF OR ANYTHING, BUT THE CHOPPED OFF PART OF A PAIR OF SIAMESE TWINS — A FREAKY, CHUNKY PILE OF DUDE WHO, VIA MENTAL TELEPATHY, MAKES HIS PERFECTLY NORMAL LOOKING BROTHER DO HORRENDOUS THINGS. I THINK YOU WOULD TELL ME "WHERE IS THIS MOVIE ABOUT A MAN WHO CARRIES HIS VINDICTIVE MUTATED CONJOINED BROTHER IN A BASKET, AND CAN WE FIGURE OUT A WAY THAT I CAN WATCH IT AT LEAST ONCE EVERY DAY BEFORE I SHUFFLE OFF THIS MORTAL COIL?"

FUCK YEAH, HOLMES. YOU CAN DO WHATEVER YOU WANT. LIVE IT UP.

THE MOVIE IS CALLED BASKET CASE. IT'S FROM 1982, AND IT WAS WRITTEN AND DIRECTED BY FRANK HENENLOTTER FOR $35,000. YEAH, POCKET CHANGE, BUT EVERY PENNY SHOWS UP ON SCREEN. COUNTRY BUMPKIN DUANE BRADLEY (KEVIN VAN HENTENRYCK) WANDERS AROUND TIMES SQUARE, PAST THE SKEEVY PEEP SHOW PALACES AND PORNO THEATERS. HE SEEMS ALONE, BUT HE'S GOT HIS MISSHAPEN BROTHER BELIAL UNDER HIS ARM IN THAT OLD WICKER BASKET. THEY'RE IN THE BIG APPLE ON A BLOOD-SOAKED

THE TENANT IN ROOM 7 IS VERY SMALL, VERY TWISTED AND VERY MAD.

BASKET CASE.

REVENGE MISSION TO GET EVEN WITH THREE QUACK DOCTORS, WHO, EIGHT YEARS PRIOR, WENT ALL JOSEF MENGELE OPERATING ON THE TWINS IN A SLOPPY SEPARATION.

YEAH, NOT ONLY DO WE GET ALL KINDS OF DOCUMENTARY STYLE OUTDOOR FOOTAGE OF THE GREASY AREAS OF EARLY 1980S NEW YORK, BUT THE LOCATION OF NEW YORK'S INFAMOUS HELLFIRE S&M CLUB FEATURES PROMINENTLY IN THE MOVIE TOO. OF COURSE, HENENLOTTER'S CREW HAD TO SQUIRREL AWAY ALL OF THE SEX TOYS, INCLUDING A LARGE SEX SWING (WHICH IS STILL IN THE CLUB TO THIS DAY). IT'S ALSO WORTH NOTING THAT THE BUZZ SAW USED TO KILL DUANE AND BELIAL'S FATHER USED TO HANG ABOVE THE DOOR OF THE HELLFIRE UNTIL IT WAS EVENTUALLY STOLEN BY SOME THIEVING KINKSTER.

"GROWING UP ON 42ND STREET IS ACTUALLY WHERE THE IDEA FOR THIS CRAZY MOVIE CAME FROM", HENENLOTTER TOLD SPLATTER CINEMA IN 2010. "BECAUSE, YOU KNOW, I JUST LIVED AND ATE UP EXPLOITATION FILMS ON THAT

STREET. BASKET CASE IS MY TRIBUTE TO THEM."

BEING A LOW-BUDGET SHOT-ON-16MM AFFAIR (OR AS SLANT MAGAZINE SAID "SHOT ON A BUDGET SO CONSTRAINED HENENLOTTER COULDN'T EVEN AFFORD A SHOESTRING"), THERE WASN'T MUCH MONEY PUT ASIDE TO HIRE A NORMAL SIZED CREW, SO A SKELETON STAFF OF ONLY A HANDFUL OF PEOPLE WERE UTILIZED. FRANKLY, MOST OF THE CREDITS THAT APPEAR AFTER THE FILM IS FINISHED ARE TOTALLY FAKE. HENENLOTTER JUST MADE UP NAMES SO AS TO MAKE THE FILM LOOK MORE LEGIT.

IT WAS PROBABLY DUE TO THOSE PALTRY WAGES THAT THE DIRECTOR FACED A MUTINY ABOUT HALFWAY THROUGH MAKING BASKET CASE. DURING THE SHOOTING OF SHARON'S (TERRI SUSAN SMITH) GORY DEATH SCENE THE CREW BECAME OFFENDED AND SIMPLY WALKED OFF OF THE PRODUCTION. THIS WOULD HAPPEN AGAIN DURING THE DIRECTOR'S NEXT FILM, THE EVEN BETTER **BRAIN DAMAGE** (1988).

IN AN INTERESTING TWIST, IF IT WEREN'T FOR TRASH FILM HISTORIAN AND ALL AROUND GENRE FILM NERD, JOE BOB BRIGGS, THE MOVIE WOULD NEVER HAVE BEEN THE LEGENDARY CULT FILM IT IS TODAY. INITIALLY, ANALYSIS FILM CUT ALL OF THE GORE OUT OF THE MOVIE AND MARKETED IT AS A COMEDY, MUCH TO HENENLOTTER'S HORROR. **BASKET CASE** MADE VERY LITTLE MONEY IN THIS INCARNATION, AND SEEMED AS IF IT WAS DESTINED TO QUICKLY DISAPPEAR, THAT IS UNTIL JOE BOB PLANNED A BIG SCREENING IN DALLAS, TEXAS. HE ONLY HAD ONE CONDITION: THAT ANALYSIS WOULD SEND HIM AN <u>UNCUT</u> PRINT TO PLAY.

JOE BOB'S CROWD IN DALLAS ATE IT UP. THEY <u>ADORED</u> THE MOVIE, SO HE PLANNED MORE SCREENINGS.

"IT WAS SELLING OUT EVERY NIGHT", SAID HENENLOTTER. "AND FINALLY ANALYSIS VERY QUIETLY REMOVED ALL THE OTHER PRINTS, THE ONE IN SAN FRANCISCO, THE ONE IN NEW YORK, AND THEY ONLY PLAYED THE UNCUT VERSION. I DIDN'T EVEN KNOW IT RIGHT AWAY, BUT ONCE IT WAS THE UNCUT VERSION PLAYING EVERYWHERE, THE WAVERLY THEATER ENDED UP PLAYING BASKET CASE AT MIDNIGHT FOR OVER TWO YEARS. IT DID WELL FOR ME. IT BOUGHT ME THIS APARTMENT."

— BOUGIE. 2014.

EVERYONE REMEMBERS BETA AS THE LOSER IN THE GREAT 1980S VHS/BETA TAPE WARS, BUT LESSER REMEMBERED IS THAT THERE WAS A **THIRD** FORMAT IN THAT WAR AS WELL. THE MOSTLY FORGOTTEN 3RD FORMAT IN THE BATTLE FOR HOME FORMAT SUPREMACY WAS CALLED VIDEO 2000. ALSO KNOWN AS VCC, VIDEO 2000 WAS PUT OUT IN 1979 BY PHILIPS TO COMPLEMENT THEIR LANDMARK AUDIO CASSETTE FORMAT WHICH CHANGED THE GAME BACK IN THE MID 1960S. THE VIDEO 2000 TAPES THEMSELVES KIND OF LOOKED LIKE WHAT YOU WOULD HAVE IF A VHS TAPE AND AN AUDIO CASSETTE HAD A LOVE CHILD, AND THEY REPORTEDLY HAD BETTER PICTURE QUALITY THAN VHS. I FOUND SOME OLD PHOTOS OF THE PHILIPS VIDEOWERK FACTORY IN VIENNA, WHICH WAS 40 ACRES AND EMPLOYED 2000 WORKERS MAKING VCC PLAYERS, WHICH WERE MOSTLY SOLD IN EUROPE. <u>HISTORY</u>, YO!

Highway to Hell (1991 Directed by Ate de Jong)

MIAMI VICE UBER-FANS KNOW THE SEASON 4 EPISODE, "MISSING HOURS" ALL TOO WELL. WITH ITS TEENAGE CHRIS ROCK GUEST APPEARANCE, JAMES BROWN PLAYING A FUNKY ALIEN, A PORNO DEALER WHO DIES OF FRIGHT, AND A WHOLE SECTION OF THE PLOT REVOLVING AROUND ALIEN ABDUCTION AND PEANUT BUTTER

THEMED ACID-TRIPS, THIS IS WIDELY CONSIDERED TO BE THE EPISODE WHERE THE SERIES JUMPED THE SHARK. UNEQUIVOCALLY AND INARGUABLY THIS IS THE WEIRDEST (AND MOST AGREE, WORST) EPISODE OF MIAMI VICE, AND PROBABLY THE STRANGEST HOUR OF DRAMA TO AIR ON NETWORK TV IN THE 1980S.

BUT WHAT NOT MANY REMEMBER IS THAT IT WAS DIRECTED BY A DUTCH ARTHOUSE FILMMAKER NAMED ATE DE JONG, WHO WAS DOING HIS BEST TO IMPRESS WHILE GETTING HIS VERY FIRST CHANCE TO MAKE A GO OF BEING A DIRECTOR IN AMERICA. NEEDLESS TO SAY AFTER THIS MISGUIDED EFFORT, IT WOULD BE A COUPLE YEARS BEFORE ANYONE WOULD LET HIM DIRECT ANYTHING AGAIN, AND THAT CHANCE CAME WITH HIS VERY FIRST NORTH AMERICAN THEATRICAL FILM -- A TRULY ODDBALL AND UNUSUAL GENRE FILM EFFORT WHICH HAS GONE ON TO SLOWLY GROW A CULT FOLLOWING DESPITE ONLY PLAYING IN 8 THEATERS DURING ITS RELEASE IN 1991, A FULL 2 YEARS AFTER IT WAS MADE.

THAT MOVIE IS THE SERIOUSLY STRANGE **HIGHWAY TO HELL**, AND I REALLY DIG IT.

"THE PRODUCTION COMPANY OF THE FILM WAS HEMDALE, WHO HAD JUST DONE THE FIRST TERMINATOR AND PLATOON", DE JONG NOTED IN HIS AUDIO COMMENTARY FOR THE 2016 BLU-RAY RELEASE OF THE MOVIE. "THOSE WERE BIG HITS, SO THEY WERE EAGER TO MAKE A NEW, HIP FILM, AND THIS WAS THAT FILM. THE SAD THING IS THAT AS WE WERE IN POST PRODUCTION, HEMDALE WENT BANKRUPT, AND THE FILM NEVER GOT THE RELEASE THAT IT DESERVED."

MADE FOR JUST 6 MILLION DOLLARS AND SHOT IN SEVEN WEEKS IN THE HIGH DESERT OF ARIZONA, HIGHWAY TO HELL WAS A TOTAL FLOP IN THEATERS, BUT DID FIND SOME FANS ON VHS BEFORE FALLING OUT OF PRINT AND OFF THE MAP. SOME HAVE CALLED THIS A HORROR GENRE FILM, BUT DIRECTOR DE JONG DOESN'T AGREE, AND THE PLOT IS STRUCTURED MUCH MORE LIKE AN ACTION/ADVENTURE FILM WITH SOME COMEDIC ELEMENTS. I THINK IT'S JUST THE SETTING OF HELL AND THE PRESENCE OF COOL DEMONS AND UNDEAD SPECIAL FX (NOT TO MENTION THAT IT WAS WRITTEN BY BRIAN HELGELAND, WHO PENNED A NIGHTMARE ON ELM STREET 4: THE DREAM MASTER AND FEATURES C.J. GRAHAM, THE GUY WHO PLAYED JASON IN FRIDAY THE 13TH PART VI: JASON LIVES) THAT MAKES IT SEEM LIKE HORROR FARE.

WHERE THE TOLL IS YOUR SOUL.

CHAD LOWE (LITTLE BROTHER OF ROB LOWE AND FORMER LONGTIME HUSBAND OF HILARY SWANK) AND KRISTY SWANSON (PRE BUFFY THE VAMPIRE SLAYER) ARE ON THEIR WAY TO ELOPE IN VEGAS, BUT HE'S NERVOUS ABOUT THE FACT THAT THEY'RE DOING SOMETHING REALLY WRONG, AND BECAUSE OF THAT SOMEONE MIGHT BE FOLLOWING THEM. SO IN ORDER TO STAY ON THE DOWN LOW HE SUGGESTS THAT THEY TAKE THE ROAD LESS TRAVELED, WHICH ENDS UP BEING "LESS TRAVELED" FOR A DAMN GOOD REASON. NOT EVERYONE WHO GOES DOWN THE CREEPY LITTLE SIDE ROAD THEY DETOUR ONTO EVER MAKES IT TO THEIR DESTINATION -- SOME OF THEM GET PULLED OVER ON THIS LONELY STRETCH OF HIGHWAY BY A SCAR-FACED FREAK WE'LL SOON REALIZE IS CALLED THE "HELL COP".

THE IDEA FOUND ITS GENESIS WHEN SCREENWRITER BRIAN HELGELAND AND HIS WIFE WERE DRIVING TO VEGAS ON A DESERTED STRETCH OF HIGHWAY AT NIGHT WHEN THEY WERE PULLED OVER AND HAD AN OFFICER OF THE LAW SHINE A FLASHLIGHT IN THEIR FACES, AND PACE AROUND THE CAR LIKE A COLD-BLOODED SHARK CIRCLING ITS PREY.

"IT WAS REAL CREEPY" HELGELAND TOLD FANGORIA WRITER MARC SHAPIRO IN THE EARLY 1990s. "HE DIDN'T SAY A WORD WHILE ALL THIS WAS GOING ON. FINALLY HE WENT BACK TO HIS CAR AND SPED OFF. I TURNED TO MY WIFE AND SAID 'HE WAS A COP OUT OF HELL'."

GOING LITERAL WITH THAT CONCEPT, HELGELAND CREATED A MONSTER COP (WITH A PAIR OF SEVERED ZOMBIE HANDS ON A CHAIN IN PLACE OF HANDCUFFS) THAT MUTELY PATROLS THE DESERT, AND WHEN HE FINDS THEM HE ESCORTS VIRGIN GIRLS TO THE NETHERWORLD SO THEY CAN BE TEENAGE FUCK-SLAVES FOR THE DEVIL. SINCE ADORABLE KRISTY DOESN'T LET STRESSED-OUT CHAD BUST HER CHERRY IN HIS NASTY LITTLE BOMBED OUT HATCHBACK, SHE'S STILL GOT A HYMEN FOR THE COURSE OF HER TRIP, AND SURE ENOUGH SHE'S YANKED RIGHT OUT OF THE CAR BY THE HELLCOP, AND KIDNAPPED, LEAVING THE WIMPIER OF THE TWO LOWES TO FOLLOW THE DEMONIC SQUAD CAR TO HADES IN ORDER TO TRY TO RESCUE HER.

NOW THIS ISN'T THE BIBLICAL REPRESENTATION OF HELL MOST EVERYONE WATCHING WOULD EXPECT. THIS MOVIE CONSISTENTLY SUBVERTS EXPECTATION, AND THERE ARE VERY FEW REFERENCES OF ANY SORT TO CHRISTIANITY AT ALL, WHICH MAKES IT VERY ORIGINAL, AESTHETICALLY. INSTEAD, THE MOVIE USES THE SURREAL "HELL" CONCEPTS FOUND IN CLASSIC ART LIKE THE WORK OF HIERONYMUS BOSCH AND ALBRECHT DURER, + THOSE WRITTEN ABOUT IN GREEK MYTHOLOGY -- SUCH AS CEREBUS THE THREE-HEADED DOG (AMAZING STOP MOTION EFFECTS!) AND THE RIVER STYX.

THERE ARE OTHER ODD TOUCHSTONES AS WELL, SUCH AS THE MASSIVE 13 LANE HIGHWAY THAT GOES THROUGH HELL, WHICH IS ONLY DRIVEN BY OLD VOLKSWAGEN BEETLES WHICH ARE CONSTANTLY SMASHING INTO EACH OTHER. "WE DID THIS AS A REFERENCE TO WORLD WAR 2", EXPLAINED DE JONG. "AND THE SPOT IN HELL RESERVED FOR JERRY LEWIS WAS AN IDEA THAT BEN STILLER CAME UP WITH. I DON'T KNOW IF IT WORKS, BUT WHEN SOMEONE THAT FUNNY TELLS YOU AN IDEA, YOU GO WITH IT."

THAT'S RIGHT, A VERY YOUNG BEN STILLER SHOWS UP IN THIS, MAKING HIS VERY FIRST BIG SCREEN APPEARANCE AS THE FRY COOK (WHO COOKS EGGS ON THE SIDEWALK OUT FRONT, BECAUSE — DUH — IT'S HOT IN HELL) AT A SHITTY DONUT SHOP CALLED PLUTO'S. THIS IS WHERE ALL THE CORRUPT COPS WHO HAVE DIED END UP, AND AS PUNISHMENT THEY NEVER GET SERVED COFFEE OR DONUTS, DESPITE DESPERATELY ORDERING BOTH FROM THE WAITRESS CONSTANTLY. BEN'S DAD PLAYS ONE OF THE FRUSTRATED COPS, AND HIS MOM PLAYS THE YAPPY WAITRESS. HIS SISTER SHOWS UP LATER ON, PLAYING A SASSY CLEOPATRA SITTING IN A STRIP CLUB WITH HITLER (GILBERT GOTTFRIED). SHIT, THIS MOVIE IS PRACTICALLY A STILLER FAMILY PHOTO ALBUM. 1980s ROCK GODDESS LITA FORD IS ANOTHER FUN CAMEO, AND SHE PROVIDES A SONG FOR THE SOUNDTRACK, TOO.

I RARELY DO BLIND BUYS ON BLU-RAYS I'VE NEVER HEARD OF, BUT THE COVER AND WRITE UP ON THIS JUST SEEMED TOO STRANGE AND MEMORABLE TO PASS UP, AND I'M GLAD THAT I TOOK A CHANCE ON IT. IT'S A TOTALLY ENTERTAINING AND STRANGE MOVIE THAT TV GUIDE CALLED "A GENUINE VIDEO FIND", AND BILLBOARD MAGAZINE CALLED "SMART, WITTY, AND INCREDIBLY IMAGINATIVE". "THERE ARE ZERO BORING MOMENTS FOUND IN THE 94 MINUTE RUNTIME" WROTE MARK TOLCH AT ROCKSHOCKPOP.COM. "IN THE WAY THAT LYNCH COMPOSES EVERY FRAME AS A BEAUTIFUL WORK OF ART, HIGHWAY TO HELL DELIVERS EVERY FRAME AS A WACKY NOVELTY POSTCARD."

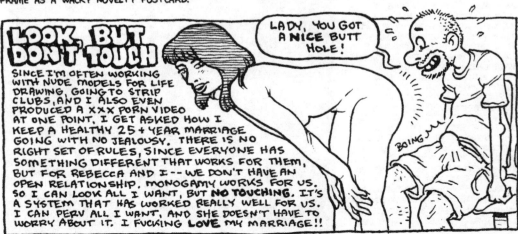

Watching Duck Dynasty Porno At The

art CINEMA

IN 2019 THE ART CINEMA (255 FRANKLIN AVE, HARTFORD, CT) WILL CELEBRATE ITS 100TH YEAR OF OPERATION. THIS HISTORICAL LANDMARK WAS OPERATED BY WARNER BROS CIRCUIT MANAGEMENT CORP IN 1941, AND THEN WHEN BUSINESS WANED IN THE 1950S, IT STARTED SHOWING A MIXTURE OF BERGMAN AND FELLINI ART FILMS AND BLACK AND WHITE SEXPLOITATION. HENCE THE NAME, "ART CINEMA", WHICH IT HAS CONTINUED USING TO THIS DAY, EVEN AFTER TRANSFORMING INTO A XXX FUCK FILM PALACE IN THE 1970S.

OWNED AND OPERATED BY ERNEST GRECULA JR. (HAVING PREVIOUSLY BEEN RUN BY HIS FATHER, KEEPING THIS HISTORIC VENUE IN THE FAMILY FOR 40 YEARS) THE THEATER SEATS 601 PATRONS (350 ON THE MAIN LEVEL, 251 ON THE BALCONY) AND STILL HAS A 35MM PROJECTOR WHICH IT HAS NOT UTILIZED IN DECADES, PREFERRING TO SHOW MODERN ADULT FILMS FOR ITS CLIENTELE VIA DVD AND BLU-RAY PROJECTION. MY RESEARCH TELLS ME THAT THE ART MAY WELL BE INDEED THE LONGEST RUNNING ADULT THEATER IN AMERICA, IF NOT THE WORLD.

THEATRICAL POSTERS FOR 1979'S SISSY'S HOT SUMMER (A PORN SPOOF OF THE THREE'S COMPANY SITCOM) AND 1980'S BALLGAME HANG IN THE LOBBY, AND THERE ARE PHOTOS OF MARYLIN MONROE AND RONALD REAGAN HANGING ABOVE THE WELL-STOCKED SNACK BAR. ERNEST STATES ON THE ART'S WEBSITE THAT THEY ARE THE HIGHEST RANKED ADULT THEATER IN THE U.S. BY "THE JOURNAL OF ADULT THEATERS", AND THAT THEY PROVIDE THEIR "GUESTS WITH A TRULY UNIQUE EXPERIENCE".

IN 2014, ONE OF THOSE GUESTS HAVING A UNIQUE EXPERIENCE WAS A REDDIT USER NAMED "BANGWHIMPER", WHO THEN WENT HOME AND REVEALED TO HIS FELLOW REDDITORS WHAT IT WAS LIKE TO SPEND AN EVENING WITH HIS BRIDE-TO-BE AT ONE OF THE VERY LAST REMAINING ADULT THEATERS IN THAT AREA OF THE USA. LET'S HEAR WHAT HE HAD TO SAY, SHALL WE?

• ——————————————— •

IT STARTED OUT AS A USUAL FRIDAY NIGHT. WE HAD BOTH WORKED ALL DAY, AND WE WERE LOOKING FOR A WAY TO UNWIND. I SUGGESTED GRABBING A BOTTLE OF SOMETHING AND JUST RELAXING AT HOME, BUT SHE WANTED TO GO OUT. I FIGURED, "YEAH, WHY NOT," AND WE HEADED TO A SUPER HIP SAKE BAR, WHERE THE DRINKS ARE CHEAP.

NOW, WHEN WE FIRST MOVED TO HARTFORD, WE QUICKLY LEARNED ABOUT THE ART CINEMA. WE ALWAYS TALKED ABOUT HOW WE SHOULD GO AT SOME POINT, BUT WE NEVER REALLY PUT ANY EFFORT INTO IT. IT WAS JUST ONE OF THOSE VAGUE IDEAS. BUT THE THEATER IS IN WALKING DISTANCE FROM THE BAR WE WERE AT, AND AS WE WERE WRACKING OUR BRAINS FOR THINGS TO DO BEFORE WE WENT HOME, IT JUST KIND OF HIT ME: LET'S GO TO THE PORN THEATER! I MENTIONED IT, AND SHE WAS DOWN.

WE ENTER AND THERE'S A WOMAN SITTING ON A STOOL RIGHT BY THE DOOR. I'M PRETTY SURE SHE WAS BLIND, BECAUSE SHE PAID NO ATTENTION TO US AND WAS HOLDING ONE OF THOSE LONG METAL CANE-TYPE THINGS BLIND PEOPLE USE TO GET AROUND. WE WALK PAST HER TO THE ELDERLY BOUNCER (I'D SAY ABOUT MY GRANDPA'S AGE — 72 OR SO), WHO STOPS ME AND ASKS FOR ID. I PROVIDE IT, AND HE'S SATISFIED, AND NEVER ASKS MY FIANCEE FOR PROOF OF AGE AT ALL. THE ENTRANCE FEE WAS 10 BUCKS A POP, AND THE EASTERN EUROPEAN CASHIER FOREBODINGLY SAYS TO ME AS WE ENTERED: "IF YOUR LADY NEEDS HELP, TELL HER TO COME GET ME. I WILL BE READY."

HAHA! OKAY! WHAT COULD GO WRONG?!

THE ART CINEMA IS FUCKING DECREPIT. THE CARPET STINKS; THE WALLS AND CEILING ARE PEELING, AND IT LOOKS LIKE NO ONE HAS CLEANED IT SINCE 1967. IF WE TRIED TO GO WHEN WE WERE SOBER, WE PROBABLY WOULD HAVE FROZE UP OUTSIDE THE DOORS AND NEVER GATHERED THE COURAGE TO ENTER IN THE FIRST PLACE.

I REALLY HAVE TO PEE AT THIS POINT, SO I NAIVELY GO TO THE BATHROOM AND LEAVE MY FIANCEE TO FIND A SEAT. THERE'S A GIANT SIGN OVER THE URINALS IN THE MEN'S BATHROOM ALL ABOUT HOW SEXUAL CONDUCT IS FORBIDDEN AND HOW PEOPLE MUST REMAIN FULLY CLOTHED AT ALL TIMES. THE SIGN LITERALLY SAYS, "SEXUAL ACTIVITY OF ANY KIND IS STRICTLY FORBIDDEN AND WILL RESULT IN REMOVAL FROM THE PREMISES", BUT OUTSIDE THE BATHROOM THE BOUNCER IS JUST STANDING THERE AND WATCHING AS A GUY MASTURBATES IN THE LOBBY.

AFTER I EMERGE, I FIND MY FIANCEE STILL WAITING, BUT NOW SHE'S SURROUNDED BY OLD GUYS WHO ARE ALL TRYING TO TALK TO HER. WE ARE, BY AND LARGE, THE YOUNGEST PEOPLE IN THIS THEATER. WE'RE IN OUR EARLY TWENTIES; THE CLIENTELE ARE, ON AVERAGE, 60 AT THE YOUNGEST. "I TRIED TO FIND A SEAT," SHE SAYS. "BUT A BUNCH OF DUDES SURROUNDED ME, SO I LEFT THE THEATER."

WELL, I FIGURE, NOW THAT I'M HERE, WE'LL HAVE NO PROBLEMS. WE WALK BACK INTO THE THEATER TOGETHER AND SIT DOWN, TOWARDS THE MIDDLE. IMMEDIATELY, A PACK OF OLD DUDES DESCENDS ON US. ONE SITS NEXT TO ME. ONE SITS BEHIND US. TWO SIT IN FRONT OF US. ONE SITS NEXT TO HER, HE SAYS, "HEY, HOW ARE YOU," THEN PROCEEDS TO PUT HIS HAND ON HER THIGHS. SHE'S FREAKED OUT. I REALIZE WE MADE A MISTAKE: CLEARLY, THE PROTOCOL IS THAT COUPLES WHO SIT IN THE MAIN THEATER ARE DOWN TO "PLAY," SO TO SPEAK.

I ASK HER IF SHE WANTS TO LEAVE. SHE SAYS 'YES.' WE GET UP AND WALK BACK TO THE LOBBY. WE CAN HEAR THESE MEN AUDIBLY SIGH. THEY ARE SO DISAPPOINTED THAT WE DIDN'T WANT TO PLAY.

BACK IN THE LOBBY, WE FIND THE STAIRS FOR THE COUPLES ONLY BALCONY, SO WE HEAD UP THERE. AS WE WALK WE REALIZE THE THEATER WAS NOT SO MUCH "STICKY" AS IT WAS "CRUSTY." SEE, THE WHOLE PLACE WAS CARPETED, WHICH I THINK MIGHT BE A BAD IDEA FOR A PORN CINEMA.

THE FIRST THING WE SEE IN THIS BALCONY? A 70+ YEAR OLD DUDE BUTT-ASS NAKED, FUCKING THE SHIT OUT OF A WOMAN WHO MUST BE IN HER FIFTIES. SHE'S SCREAMING, MOANING, LOVING IT. HE'S THRUSTING SLOWLY, METHODICALLY, DELIBERATELY. I AM ENTRANCED. MY FIANCEE PULLS ON MY ARM, DIRECTS ME TO THE ONLY UNOCCUPIED ROW.

WE TAKE OUR SEATS. ALL AROUND US: OLD PEOPLE FUCKING. WE HEAR THE SLAPPING OF SKIN ON SKIN. WE HEAR BELTS BEING UNDONE AND CAST TO THE FLOOR AS NEW COUPLES ENTER. WE HEAR THE MOANS OF PLEASURE, THESE PEOPLE OLD ENOUGH TO BE OUR GRANDPARENTS. THE UPPER BALCONY WAS LIKE A NIGHTMARISH NURSING HOME. JUST SO MANY NAKED OLD PEOPLE, TOTALLY NAKED, NO-HOLDS-BARRED, RAUNCHY FUCKING WITH WILD ABANDON.

PERHAPS YOU THINK WE WOULD HAVE LEFT. BUT, NO, WE COULDN'T, BECAUSE THE MOVIE THEY WERE PLAYING WAS A FUCKING DUCK DYNASTY PORNO PARODY, COMPLETE WITH FAKE BEARDS AND WEIRD PSEUDO-SOUTHERN ACCENTS! IT WASN'T CALLED 'DICK DYNASTY,' NOR WAS IT CALLED 'FUCK DYNASTY.' I FUCKING WISH. THEY WENT WITH THE GENERIC 'THIS AIN'T DUCK DYNASTY XXX'. REGARDLESS, WE WERE ENTRANCED. IT WAS DESPICABLE AND HILARIOUS.

IT BECAME CLEAR TO US THAT PEOPLE DIDN'T REALLY COME TO THIS PLACE WATCH THE MOVIES AT ALL: THEY CAME TO FUCK IN THE BALCONY. WE WERE THE ONLY PEOPLE WHO KEPT OUR CLOTHES ON -- MOSTLY BECAUSE WE WERE TOO NERVOUS TO DO ANYTHING, THOUGH I DID SPEND MOST OF THE MOVIE WITH MY HANDS DOWN HER SHIRT, BECAUSE, DUCK DYNASTY OR NOT, PORNO IS PORNO, MAN.

THERE WAS A COUPLE IN FRONT OF US IN THE BALCONY, A MIDDLE-AGED COUPLE, PROBABLY IN THEIR FORTIES. DUDE WAS SEATED, WOMAN WAS RIDING HIM COWGIRL STYLE. AFTER HE BUSTS, MAKING EXACTLY THE SORT OF NOISE YOU'D EXPECT, THE WOMAN CALMLY LIFTED HERSELF OFF OF HIM AND SAID, "HURRY UP AND CLEAN YOURSELF. WE HAVE TO GET GOING. I HAVE GIRLS' NIGHT TONIGHT."

MOST OF THE PEOPLE WERE WHITE, BUT THERE WAS ONE BLACK COUPLE IN THE BALCONY. AS THEY WERE FUCKING, SHE SHOUTED (YES, SHOUTED): "NIGGA, GIVE ME ALL OF THE DICK." (I KNOW THAT ONE SEEMS LIKE I'M MAKING IT UP -- I SWEAR I'M NOT.)

THE CAST OF CHARACTERS IN THAT BALCONY CHANGED AT 15-MINUTE INTERVALS: PEOPLE CAME, THEY FUCKED, THEY LEFT. BUT WE WATCHED THE WHOLE MOVIE, LIKE CHAMPS (OR CHUMPS, I GUESS). THE CROWD WAS DEFINITELY THE BEST PART. YOU CAN WATCH A DUCK DYNASTY PORNO ANY DAY. FINDING YOURSELF IN THE MIDDLE OF WHAT WAS BASICALLY AN ELDERLY ORGY IS MUCH HARDER TO DO.

-END

HUFF HUFF

UNGH! YES, FUCK ME! FUUCK MEEE!

PUMP PUMP

The Birth and Death of the Manic Pixie Dream Girl

NATHAN RABIN IS A FILM CRITIC. HE WROTE A BOOK CALLED 'MY YEAR OF FLOPS' THAT WAS BEAUTIFULLY ILLUSTRATED BY CINEMA SEWER CONTRIBUTOR, DANNY HELLMAN. HE ALSO USED TO BE THE HEAD WRITER FOR THE ONION AV CLUB WEBSITE, AND IT WAS THERE IN 2007 WHILE HE WAS WRITING A NOW-LEGENDARY REVIEW OF THE SHITTY CAMERON CROWE FLOP, ELIZABETHTOWN, THAT HE DID SOMETHING THAT VERY FEW FILM CRITICS CAN CLAIM TO HAVE EVER DONE.

WITHOUT EVEN TRYING TO, HE ALTERED THE WAY THAT MODERN SCREENWRITERS WRITE FEMALE CHARACTERS.

"KIRSTIN DUNST EMBODIES A CHARACTER TYPE I LIKE TO CALL THE MANIC PIXIE DREAM GIRL (SEE NATALIE PORTMAN IN GARDEN STATE FOR ANOTHER PRIME EXAMPLE)", WROTE RABIN CHEERFULLY AS HE OUTLINED WHY THE CHARACTERS IN THE MOVIE WERE NEEDY, ANNOYING TURDS. "THE MANIC PIXIE DREAM GIRL EXISTS SOLELY IN THE FEVERED IMAGINATIONS OF SENSITIVE WRITER-DIRECTORS TO TEACH BROODINGLY SOULFUL YOUNG MEN TO EMBRACE LIFE AND ITS INFINITE MYSTERIES AND ADVENTURES."

MPDG'S, AS RABIN DESCRIBED THEM, ARE ADORABLE, QUIRKY, PRECOCIOUS FANTASY GIRLS WHO, WITHOUT PURSUING THEIR OWN HAPPINESS OR CHARACTER ARC, ONLY EXIST TO HELP PONDEROUS, INTROSPECTIVE MEN REALIZE IMPORTANT LIFE LESSONS. SHE'S HERE TO LIVEN UP HIS LIFE, AND THAT SEXY LITTLE SPRITE IS GOING TO DO IT WHETHER HE LIKES IT OR NOT!

GOOD OL' NATHAN RABIN...

HEE HEE!

YOU KNOW, I THINK HE COULD USE A PERKY MANIC PIXY DREAM GIRL, HIMSELF.

ACCORDING TO THE BLOGGERS WHO PICKED UP RABIN'S MANTLE AND CARRIED ON WITH IT, WRITING COUNTLESS ESSAYS, LISTS AND CLICK-BAIT ABOUT THE CLICHE, HOLLYWOOD HAD BEEN WRITING THESE TYPES OF LOVE INTERESTS EVER SINCE KATHARINE HEPBURN'S CHARACTER IN 1939'S BRINGING UP BABY. THIS CONTINUED ON TO AUDREY HEPBURN IN 1961'S BREAKFAST AT TIFFANY'S, TO GOLDIE HAWN IN 1969'S CACTUS FLOWER, TO MELANIE GRIFFITH IN 1986'S SOMETHING WILD, TO CHRISTINA RICCI IN 1998'S BUFFALO '66, TO KATE HUDSON IN 2000'S ALMOST FAMOUS, AND THE HUNDREDS OF OTHER PRIME EXAMPLES IN BETWEEN.

WITH HIS DEFINITION HITTING HOME WITH FILM FANDOM, AND HIS CRITICISM CUTTING OH-SO DEEP, SCREENWRITERS, EN MASSE, BECAME ACUTELY AWARE THAT THIS SORT OF TROPE WOULD NOW BE DERIDED, MOCKED AND PICKED APART. ALMOST OVERNIGHT, THE CLICHE ALMOST TOTALLY DISAPPEARED FROM SCRIPTS, AND IN THE 10 YEARS SINCE RABIN PUT A SPOTLIGHT ON IT, ONLY A FEW MANIC PIXIES (SUCH AS THE OCCASIONAL SAUCER-EYED ZOOEY DESCHANEL FILM) WERE THERE TO STAND (AND PLAYFULLY DANCE) AS AN EXCEPTION.

"IS THE MANIC PIXIE DREAM GIRL DEAD?" QUERIED SLATE'S AISHA HARRIS IN 2012, AS SHE NOTED HOW "SELF-AWARE ABOUT SUCH CHARACTERS" MODERN SCREENWRITERS HAD BECOME. IN JULY 2013, KAT STOEFFEL POINTED OUT THAT THE TERM ITSELF HAD BECOME SEXIST, AND ACTRESS AND SCREENWRITER ZOE KAZAN CRITICIZED IT AS REDUCTIVE AND MISOGYNISTIC: "I THINK THAT TO LUMP TOGETHER ALL INDIVIDUAL, ORIGINAL QUIRKY WOMEN UNDER THAT RUBRIC IS TO ERASE ALL DIFFERENCE."

IN 2014, STANDING IN HORRIFIED AWE OF THE POWER HIS CASUAL WORDS HAD OVER AN INDUSTRY AND HIS CAREER, RABIN RETRACTED THEM AND DISOWNED THEM. "IN 2007, I INVENTED THE TERM IN A REVIEW," RABIN LAMENTED IN AN ARTICLE PUBLISHED BY SALON. "THEN I WATCHED IN QUEASY DISBELIEF AS IT SEEMED TO TAKE OVER POP CULTURE. I HONESTLY HATE THE TERM. I FEEL DEEPLY WEIRD, IF NOT DOWNRIGHT ASHAMED, AT HAVING CREATED A CLICHE THAT HAS BEEN TROTTED OUT AGAIN AND AGAIN IN AN INFINITE INTERNET FEEDBACK LOOP."

"LAST YEAR I HAD THE SURREAL EXPERIENCE OF WATCHING A MUSICAL CALLED 'MANIC PIXIE DREAMLAND,' ABOUT A FANTASY REALM THAT PRODUCES MANIC PIXIE DREAM GIRLS. SITTING IN THE DARK THEATER, I THOUGHT: 'WHAT HAVE I DONE?!' I WOULD WELCOME ITS ERASURE FROM PUBLIC DISCOURSE. I'D APPLAUD AN END TO ARTICLES ABOUT ITS COUNTLESS DIFFERENT PERMUTATIONS."

I DON'T KNOW IF YOU CAN ERASE HISTORY AS EASILY AS YOU CAN CREATE IT, AND I THINK NATHAN MAY FIND MORE FRUSTRATION COMING HIS WAY, BUT IF THIS OVERVIEW OF THE HISTORY OF THE TERM THAT YOU'RE READING RIGHT NOW IS THE LAST ARTICLE EVER WRITTEN ABOUT IT, THEN LET IT END WITH SOME APPROPRIATELY IDIOSYNCRATIC FEMININE PLAYFULNESS.

**HE'S TOO FAST...TOO QUICK...AND TWO FISTED —
HE'S "TOO SWEET" AND HE'S BACK FOR REVENGE!**

Leon
Isaac
Kennedy
is back!

PENITENTIARY II

JAMAA FANAKA (WHO PASSED AWAY IN 2012) WAS A UCLA FILM STUDIES STUDENT IN THE 1970S AND
MADE THE FIRST PENITENTIARY AS HIS SUBMISSION FOR HIS MASTERS THESIS IN 1979. A FEW
YEARS LATER AND WITH A BIGGER BUDGET, HE MADE THIS ENTERTAINING SEGUEL, WHICH I LIKE EVEN
BETTER THAN THE ORIGINAL. IT'S LACKING THE GRIM AND GRITTY VIBE THE FIRST WAS SO WELL
KNOWN FOR AND IS FRANKLY CHEESY AS FUCK, BUT SOMETIMES THAT'S EXACTLY WHAT YOU'RE IN THE
MOOD FOR.

HOW CORNBALL IS IT? WELL, IT HAS A WHOLE SERIES OF MUSICAL NUMBERS (INCLUDING A ROLLER
BOOGIE SEGUENCE), CRAZY CLOTHING, POTATO SALAD ABUSE, HORNY MIDGETS, PLENTY OF JIVE-TALKING,
OVERUSE OF THE WORD "SUCKA", EXTREMELY BLOODY BOXING MATCHES, BONG-HITS, TOILET-SWIRLIES,
A BIG BUNCH OF TERRIBLE ACTING FROM A PRE-FAME MR. T, A PRE-GHOSTBUSTERS ERNIE HUDSON,
AND A POST-DOLEMITE RUDY RAY MOORE. IF YOU CAN BELIEVE IT, THIS BAT-SHIT INSANITY (WHICH I
HONESTLY BELIEVE WAS MOSTLY WRITTEN ON THE SPOT) IS SOMEHOW **NOT** A COMEDY. IT DIDN'T
MAKE MUCH SENSE, BUT I FUCKIN' LOVED IT ANYWAY. WATCH IT WITH SOME BEER, PIZZA, AND A FEW
FRIENDS WHO LOVE SILLY GARBAGE LIKE THIS AS MUCH AS YOU DO.

-BOUGIE

CINEMA SEWER SNOPES:
The Urban Legend of the Fluffer

"I know it's supposed to be the most degrading job imaginable, but I wanna be a fluff girl. Seems like it's all the benefits of doing porn without having videos come and haunt you later. How much do fluff girls make? How much "fluffing" do you do in a day? It's totally legal, right? Do the guys wear condoms for fluffing, or no? Would I have to be AIM tested?"

THIS POST WAS MADE BY A YOUNG WOMAN ON STRIPPERWEB.COM IN 2007, AND I'M REPOSTING IT BECAUSE I THINK THE QUESTIONS IT ASKS ARE QUITE TELLING WHEN IT COMES TO WHAT PEOPLE WHO AREN'T IN PORN THINK FLUFFING IS AND HOW ONE GOES ABOUT BECOMING AN INDIVIDUAL THAT PARTAKES IN THE ACT OF DOING IT. PEOPLE ARE TURNED ON BY THE DEGRADING ASPECT AND TITILLATED BY THE BACCHANALIAN IDEA THAT THERE IS SO MUCH SEX HAPPENING ON A PORN SET THAT MUCH OF IT DOESN'T EVEN SHOW UP ON-CAMERA. IT GIVES YOU SOME SMALL IDEA WHY THIS URBAN LEGEND IS BELIEVED BY SO MANY.

YES, AFTER YEARS OF RESEARCH I BELIEVE THAT THE VOCATION OF FLUFFER IS MERELY THE WORK OF OVERACTIVE IMAGINATIONS. THE MISCONCEPTION COMES FROM THE FACT THAT FLUFFING IS SOMETHING THAT HAPPENS ON PORN SETS FROM TIME TO TIME (A CO-STAR HELPING A WOODSMAN GET HARD), BUT THEN SOMEONE CONFLATED THAT TO MEAN THAT A "FLUFFER" WAS PRESENT -- SOMEONE WHO ISN'T SEEN IN THE MOVIE, WHOSE SOLE PURPOSE IS TO GET PERFORMERS HARD AND READY TO GO.

"NON PORN PEOPLE LOVE TO TALK 'KNOWINGLY' TO ME ABOUT FLUFFERS." LONGTIME PORN INDUSTRY SCREENWRITER HART WILLIAMS MENTIONED TO ME IN 2014. "AND I GENERALLY ROLL MY EYES AND INTONE 'RIGHT' IN A VERY NON COMMITTAL MANNER."

WHEN FLUFFING DOES HAPPEN, IT'S ONLY IN EXCEEDINGLY RARE SITUATIONS AND CERTAINLY DOESN'T DESERVE TO BE AS TIED TO THE IDEA OF PORN AS IT IS. AND YET LIKE HART NOTES, IT'S ONE OF THE MOST FAMOUS, APPEALING ASPECTS OF PORN TO PEOPLE OUTSIDE OF THE ADULT INDUSTRY. BUT THAT'S JUST SILLY. HOW SILLY? IT WOULD BE LIKE SOMEONE WHO ISN'T A MUSICIAN ALWAYS TALKING ABOUT HOW MUSIC BEING PLAYED IN OUTER SPACE IS SUCH A HUGE PART OF THE MUSIC INDUSTRY. I'M SURE AN ASTRONAUT HERE AND THERE HAS DONE SO AT SOME POINT, BUT IT DOESN'T MEAN IT DESERVES TO BE A TALKING POINT WHENEVER THE TOPIC OF LIVE MUSIC PERFORMANCE IS DISCUSSED, DOES IT?

THE WAY PEOPLE TALK ABOUT THE WHOLE IDEA OF FLUFFERS, YOU WOULD THINK THEY WERE KEPT IN CAGES AND ON LEASHES, LIKE SOME KIND OF...

ANIMAL

I MEAN, LETS GET REAL.

♥ BOUGIE '11

"IN TEN YEARS, 99.9% OF WHICH WAS ON THE LEFT COAST, I WORKED WITH ONLY ONE FLUFFER", RICHARD PACHECO SAID IN 2014. "IT WAS IN CANDY GOES TO HOLLYWOOD. I'D GET HARD WITH THE FLUFFER (ORAL) AND THEN LOSE IT WHEN I TRIED TO INSERT INTO THE "STAR" (DOGGY). BACK TO THE FLUFFER AGAIN — HARD AGAIN — BACK TO THE STAR AND LOSE IT AGAIN. THIS UNCHARTERED EPISODE OF THE THREE STOOGES WENT ON FOR ABOUT AN HOUR BEFORE THEY GAVE UP ON ME ENTIRELY AND PUT OUT A CALL FOR WOODSMAN SUPREME JON MARTIN TO STAND IN FOR ME. I BELIEVE IT TOOK HIM ALL OF FIVE MINUTES TO FINISH THE SCENE."

ASIDE FROM THE UNFORTUNATE INCIDENT ON CANDY GOES TO HOLLYWOOD (1979), AND A STORY RON JEREMY TOLD ABOUT GETTING FLUFFED ON THE SET OF TIGRESSES (1979), THE ONLY SOLID EVIDENCE I'VE FOUND ON THIS TOPIC HAVING REAL WORLD IMPLICATIONS WERE THE HANDFUL OF TIMES THAT FLUFFERS WERE UTILIZED IN THE SHORT-LIVED "WORLD'S BIGGEST GANGBANG" ORGY SUBGENRE THAT WAS POPULAR FOR A FEW YEARS IN THE 1990S. THERE WERE LITERALLY HUNDREDS OF GUYS AND ONLY ONE WOMAN TO SERVE THEM, SO IT IS UNDERSTANDABLE WHY IT MIGHT TO GOOD TO HAVE SOME PAID RELIEF PITCHERS WAITING IN THE DUGOUT. HOWEVER, THAT DOESN'T

EXPLAIN WHY THE CONCEPT OF FLUFFING WAS SO INTRINSICALLY LINKED TO THE GENRE OF ADULT ENTERTAINMENT FOR SO MANY YEARS BEFORE THE NINETIES, ESPECIALLY WHEN NOTORIOUSLY CHEAP PORNOGRAPHERS WEREN'T EXACTLY WORKING WITH LARGE CASTS AND CREWS, OR SPENDING AN EXTRA PENNY ON ANYTHING OR ANYONE THAT THEY DIDN'T HAVE TO.

THE EARLIEST REFERENCE I HAVE FOUND TO FLUFFING IS THE JUNE 1974 ISSUE OF BACHELOR MAGAZINE WHERE THEY CALLED THE WOMEN WHO DO IT "MUFFERS", AND ANNOUNCE THAT THEY HAVE AN INTERVIEW WITH A REAL, LIVE "MUFFER" AKA "A GET-EM-UP EXPERT". SHE'S A WOMAN NAMED DALE MARIS, EXCEPT WHEN THEY SAT DOWN TO INTERVIEW HER ABOUT IT, THE PART OF THE INTERVIEW PERTAINING TO "MUFFING" SORTA GOT MUFFED ITSELF. LET'S LISTEN IN, SHALL WE?

Bachelor: Now, how long have you been doing muffing?
Maris: Doing what?
B: Do they call you a muffer?
M: What's a muffer?
B: What the hell do you do?
M: I don't do much of anything, really.
B: But you've worked on porn movies?
M: I've done five loops.
B: You've done five loops. Now I've heard you were one of those girls that is in movies, but is never seen. That it's your job to get people ready to ball. Is that true?
M: No. What they were talking about was a time that I did a thing with Marc Stevens. We did a layout for a sex magazine. He was trying on rubbers, and they had to have a girl there to get him hard. So there's pictures of me sucking Marc Stevens.

"THERE IS NO DEDICATED FLUFFER ON A PORN SET." GAY PORN STAR JESSE JACKMAN WROTE ON HIS WEBSITE IN JULY 2012. "THE TERM WAS ORIGINALLY USED TO REFER TO THE PERSON ON SET WHO WOULD 'CLEAN UP' A PORNOGRAPHIC ACTOR BETWEEN TAKES (APPLY MAKE-UP, SUPPLY LUBE, WIPE AWAY SWEAT ETC.) SO THAT THE ACTOR WOULDN'T NEED TO CHANGE POSITION – KIND OF LIKE 'FLUFFING THE PILLOWS' WITHOUT REARRANGING THE FURNITURE. THE JOB IS NOW MORE COMMONLY REFERRED TO AS 'PRODUCTION ASSISTANT', BUT THE URBAN LEGEND OF KEEPING THE ACTOR AROUSED PERSISTS TO THIS DAY. THE TRUTH IS THAT WE ACTORS KEEP EACH OTHER AROUSED."

HURRY UP!! WE NEEDED HIM ON SET 15 MINUTES AGO!

LOVE LETTER TO C.J. LAING

MY LONGSTANDING CRUSH ON THE FOXY MISS LAING FIRST INITIALIZED IN THE VERY FIRST MOVIE I PEEPED HER IN, 1977'S *WATERPOWER*. BUT I HAPPEN TO THINK C.J. IS AT HER SEXY BEST IN *SWEET PUNKIN'* (1976), *ANYONE BUT MY HUSBAND* (1975) AND *BARBARA BROADCAST* (1977).

LAING REMEMBERS HER INFAMOUS KITCHEN SCENE IN THE FILM AS "INTENSE", AND RECALLS THAT IT WAS DONE IN ONE TAKE. IT'S A RIGHTEOUS WAD OF FUCKS, AS C.J. PISSES IN A POT AND TAKES WADE NICHOLS UP HER ASS LIKE A WANTON SUPERCHAMP!

AT A TIME WHEN SCRIPTS AND NAKED BODIES WITH BACKGROUNDS IN ACTING WAS A PRIMARY CONCERN, C.J. WAS A PERFORMER THAT PUT THE EMPHASIS ON SEXUAL SKILLS RATHER THAN THESPIAN ONES, EVEN GOING SO FAR AS TO CALL ACTING IN ADULT FILMS "ABSURD" AND TELLING TIME MAGAZINE IN 2005 THAT SHE "DESPISED" CO-STARS FOR CLAIMING THEY WERE "ACTORS".

GETTING HER START IN XXX AFTER WALKING INTO THE MITCHELL BROS. O'FARRELL THEATER IN SAN FRANCISCO IN 1974, LAING WAS IN OVER 50 PORN MOVIES AND LOOPS IN THE 1970S. SURE, SHE WAS "SHOOTING COCAINE DAILY", AND WAS A SELF DESCRIBED "PHYSICAL AND EMOTIONAL MESS" BY 1977, BUT SHE CAME OUT THE OTHER SIDE INTACT AND BETTER FOR THE EXPERIENCE.

WHAT A GAL!

The most iconic Drive-in theater of all time:
THE PICKWICK

A MAY 12, 1949, FLYER ADVERTISED THE GRAND OPENING OF THE PICKWICK DRIVE-IN THEATER ON 1100 WEST ALAMEDA AVENUE IN BURBANK CALIFORNIA. "CLEAN, HEALTHFUL ENTERTAINMENT UNDER THE STARS FOR THE ENTIRE FAMILY," THE AD BOASTED, ALL FOR JUST 65 CENTS. A HANDSOME DRIVE-IN VENUE, THE PICKWICK HAD SPACE FOR 781 CARS ON ITS 9 ACRES, AND WAS A FAVOURITE FOR LOS ANGELES TEENS FOR GENERATIONS.

THE PICTURES FEATURED ON THE THEATER'S OPENING NIGHT WERE THE ACTION ADVENTURE **RED STALLION IN THE ROCKIES**, AND THE DOROTHY LAMOUR COMEDY, **THE LUCKY STIFF.** "WE HAD BANNERS, FREE DRINKS AND POPCORN. . . . I REMEMBER NATALIE WOOD WAS ON HAND FOR THE OPENING," VETERAN EMPLOYEE FRANK DIAZ TOLD LOS ANGELES TIMES REPORTER CARLOS LOZANO IN 1989. WOOD WAS ONLY 12 AT THE TIME BUT ALREADY A MOVIE STAR.

"I FREQUENTED (IT) AS OFTEN AS THE APPROPRIATE DOUBLE FEATURE WOULD ALLOW", LONGTIME CUSTOMER TOM KACHLER EXPLAINED. "SUCH WONDERFUL EVENINGS WATCHING (AND SOMETIMES RE-WATCHING) SUCH GLORIOUS CHEESE AS **INFRA-MAN, FEAR NO EVIL, FRIDAY THE 13TH, LIFEFORCE,** AND TOO MANY OTHERS TO REMEMBER PRESENTLY. OF COURSE I ALSO VIEWED OTHER MORE MAINSTREAM FILMS TOO, BUT THE DRIVE IN FOR ME WAS A HOME FOR HORROR AND NECKING -- AND NOT ALWAYS IN THAT ORDER."

MORE THAN JUST A POPULAR COMMUNITY HUB, THE PICKWICK WAS A POP CULTURE PINNACLE THANKS TO IT BEING A POPULAR LOCATION FOR SHOOTING TV AND FILMS. THAT'S BECAUSE OF HOW CLOSE IT WAS TO BURBANK STUDIOS, WHICH IS WHERE WALT DISNEY, COLUMBIA PICTURES AND WARNER BROS RESIDE. "IT WAS CONVENIENT, JUST A FEW BLOCKS AWAY," RON CHAN, FIELD PUBLICIST FOR WARNER BROS SAID. "IT WAS EASIER TO GO THERE THAN OTHER PLACES."

LOCATION, LOCATION, LOCATION. AND ITS PROXIMITY TO HOLLYWOOD MEANT THAT THE PICKWICK REALLY BECAME THE PLACEHOLDER FOR WHAT THE ENTIRE WORLD THINKS OF WHEN THEY THINK OF THE VISUAL AESTHETICS OF A DRIVE-IN MOVIE THEATER. INDEED, SOME OF THE MOST ICONIC SCENES AND IMAGES EVER TO BE SHOT AT A DRIVE-IN WERE FILMED HERE -- SCENES THAT WILL LIVE ON FOR GENERATIONS, LONG AFTER EVERY DRIVE-IN IS GONE.

FIRST AND FOREMOST: THE FAMOUS DATE SCENE AT THE DRIVE-IN WITH JOHN TRAVOLTA AND OLIVIA NEWTON-JOHN IN 1978'S **GREASE**, WHERE DANNY GETS RAPEY WITH SANDY, THEN GOES AND FEELS SORRY FOR HIMSELF ON THE SWINGS AND WAILS OUT THE SONG "SANDY" WHILE CARTOON ICE CREAMS DANCE ON THE BIG SCREEN BEHIND HIM. WE ALSO GET TO SEE THE INSIDE OF THE WOMEN'S BATHROOM, WHERE STOCKARD CHANNING ADMITS THAT SHE GOT KNOCKED UP.

YOU CAN GET A REAL SENSE OF THE SIZE OF THE PLACE WITH IT'S APPEARANCE IN A 1976 EPISODE OF THE TV SERIES **THE ROCKFORD FILES** CALLED "THE NO-CUT CONTRACT". AS JAMES GARNER DRIVES BY THE MARQUEE, WE SEE THAT THE GAMBLER WITH JAMES CAAN IS CURRENTLY PLAYING.

THE PICKWICK PLAYS IN ROLE IN A ROBBERY SCENE IN 1976'S **ST. IVES**, WHICH STARRED CHARLES BRONSON AND JACQUELINE BISSET. GOOD LITTLE MOVIE. CHECK IT OUT.

SOME EXCELLENT AERIAL FOOTAGE OF THE THEATER AND ITS GROUNDS ARE VISIBLE IN THE 1983 ROY SCHEIDER HELICOPTER-THEMED THRILLER, **BLUE THUNDER**.

THE EXCELLENT DRIVE-IN SCENE IN JOHN CARPENTER'S **CHRISTINE** (1983) GOES DOWN AT THE PICKWICK. THE ONE WHERE THE NEFARIOUS CAR NEARLY GAKS THE LOVELY GIRLFRIEND OF ITS OWNER, PLAYED BY KEITH GORDON. ALTHOUGH HOW THE CAR MAKES HER CHOKE ON HER OWN FOOD IS STILL A MYSTERY TO ME, EVEN WITHIN THE CONFINES OF THE MAGICAL LOGIC OF A HAUNTED CAR THAT CAN REPAIR ITSELF.

WHAT 1980S KID DIDN'T WATCH **KNIGHT RIDER**? THE EPISODE "SKY KNIGHT" FEATURED THE PICKWICK, AS DID THE 1985 MOVIE **EXPLORERS**, AND THE 1980S TV SERIES **T.J. HOOKER**, STARRING WILLIAM SHATNER -- SPECIFICALLY THE EPISODE ENTITLED "STREET BAIT".

THE VERY LAST THING TO FILM ON LOCATION HERE WAS THE LITTLE-REMEMBERED 13-EPISODE TV SERIES **THE OUTSIDERS**, WHICH WAS A SMALL SCREEN ADAPTATION OF THEATRICAL FILM, AND DAVID ARGUETTE'S FIRST ACTING ROLE. "I HAD TO HOLD UP DEMOLITION FOR A WEEK SO THEY COULD COME IN HERE AND DO THEIR FILMING," SAID A. TERRANCE DICKENS, DIRECTOR OF REAL ESTATE FOR PACIFIC THEATRES CORPORATION, WHICH OWNED THE PICKWICK.

BUT PERHAPS THE MOST LEGENDARY EVENT TO HAPPEN ON THIS SITE WAS THE OFT-CITED WORLD PREMIERE OF MEL BROOKS'S **BLAZING SADDLES**, AN EVENT THAT WARNER BROTHERS HELD. MAKING IT ESPECIALLY NOTEWORTHY WAS THAT THE GUESTS ATTENDING WERE MOSTLY ON HORSEBACK. "THE WORLD'S FIRST MOVIE PREMIERE FOR HORSES IS FREE TONIGHT AT THE PICKWICK DRIVE-IN", READ ADS THAT RAN IN LOCAL PAPERS. "OTHER FORMS OF HORSEPOWER REQUIRE GENERAL ADMISSION".

250 MEMBERS OF THE AUDIENCE, INCLUDING THE STARS OF THE FILM, CLEAVON LITTLE AND GENE WILDER, ARRIVED AND WATCHED THE MOVIE ON THEIR HORSES, AND DRIVE-IN SPEAKERS WERE ATTACHED TO THEIR SADDLE POMMELS. TO MAKE SURE THE PONIES DIDN'T GET HUNGRY, A "HORSEPITALITY BAR" WAS SET UP IN FRONT OF THE HUGE OUTDOOR SCREEN. THE UNUSUAL PREMIERE WAS THE BRAINCHILD OF THE LATE WARNER BROS. PUBLICIST MARTY WEISER, AND SO PLEASED DIRECTOR MEL BROOKS, THAT HE SENT MARTY A LETTER PRAISING HIM FOR HIS BRILLIANT IDEA.

CONT. FROM PREVIOUS PAGE

THE PICKWICK HOSTED ITS LAST PREMIERE IN 1987, WHICH WAS A SCREENING OF ALEX COX'S CULT FAVORITE, **STRAIGHT TO HELL**. THE SCREENING DREW SUCH STARS AS DENNIS HOPPER AND EMILIO ESTEVEZ, BOTH OF WHOM CAME WITH SOME FRIENDS IN A 1960S FORD FALCON. ACTORS BUCK HENRY, SHELLEY DUVALL AND ED HARRIS ALSO ATTENDED. REPORTEDLY THE FILM'S PREMIERE WAS A TOTAL FIASCO, WITH A NUMBER OF PEOPLE DRIVING OUT THROUGHOUT THE MOVIE, LEAVING ITS STAR, A YOUNG COURTNEY LOVE, VISIBLY UPSET. BUT THEN, WHEN ISN'T COURTNEY LOVE UPSET ABOUT SOMETHING?

"AT THE PICKWICK, YOU NOT ONLY SAW THE SCREEN BUT THE ROLLING HILLS ALL AROUND IT. NOWHERE ELSE IN THE VALLEY CAN YOU GET THAT KIND OF VIEW," BURBANK RESIDENT LESLIE BROGAN TOLD THE LOS ANGELES TIMES IN 1989. BROGAN ADMITTED THAT THE OLD DRIVE-IN WAS NOT AS POPULAR IN RECENT YEARS AS IT ONCE HAD BEEN. SHE SAID "ONLY ABOUT 25 CARS SHOWED UP" AT THE THEATER'S VERY LAST SCREENING, A DOUBLE FEATURE OF **TURNER & HOOCH** AND **INDIANA JONES AND THE LAST CRUSADE**.

IN THE MID TO LATE '80S, ONE DRIVE-IN CLOSED PER DAY ACROSS THE US, FROM OVER 5800 DOWN TO THE OVER 300 THAT EXIST TODAY. THE PICKWICK DRIVE-IN ITSELF WAS CLOSED AND TORN DOWN IN OCTOBER OF 1989 TO MAKE WAY FOR A STAPLES OFFICE SUPPLY STORE AND A SUPERMARKET, ALTHOUGH THE GRAND PICKWICK GARDENS ENTERTAINMENT COMPLEX (BANQUET ROOMS, SWIMMING POOL, BOWLING LANES, ICE SKATING RINK, ETC) IS STILL IN OPERATION JUST TO THE SOUTH (BEHIND THE SHOPPING CENTER) ON RIVERSIDE DRIVE.

AND YES, STUFF STILL GETS FILMED THERE! THE GIANT 24-LANE PICKWICK BOWLING ALLEY RECENTLY HOSTED THE TV SERIES **PARKS AND RECREATION** FOR FILMING OF A SEASON 4 EPISODE CALLED "BOWLING FOR VOTES".

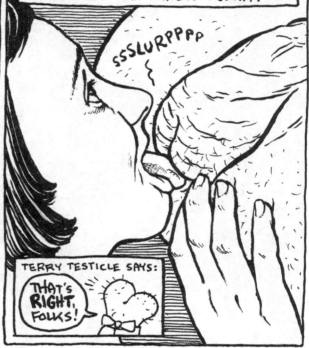

BALL-SACKERS BALL-SNACKERS

WHAT'S THE BIG DEAL, PORNOGRAPHERS? YOU GOT NOTHING FOR THOSE OF US WHO LOVE TO HAVE OUR BALLS MUNCHED, AND THOSE OF US WHO LOVE TO SNACK ON BALLS? YOU GIVE US ENDLESS BLOWJOB FOOTAGE THROUGHOUT THE HISTORY OF XXX, BUT ONLY A FEW SECONDS OF SCROTUMSUCKIN' HERE AND THERE. YOU DON'T NEED TO THROW US A BONE, BUT YOU DO NEED TO TOSS US A TESTICLE! I DON'T CARE HOW CLOSE THEY ARE TO OUR BUTTHOLES, STOP IGNORING THE MARBLE POUCH!!

SSSLURPPPP

TERRY TESTICLE SAYS: THAT'S RIGHT, FOLKS!

Warbus (1985. Philippines/Italy. Dir: Ferdinando Baldi)

NEVER GET OUT OF THE BUS! A GROUP OF THREE GRITTY U.S. ARMY GREEN BERET MARINES COMMANDEERS A YELLOW SCHOOL BUS DRIVING THROUGH THE MIDDLE OF THE JUNGLE. THE INHABITANTS OF THE BUS ARE DO-GOODER CHRISTIAN MISSIONARIES, A SOUTH VIETNAMESE GENERAL, A BROTHEL'S MADAM, AN AUSSIE OUTBACKER, AND A FEW OTHER RANDOM TAG-ALONGS TRYING TO ESCAPE FROM THE VIETCONG. A MIXED BAG TO BE SURE, BUT THESE TYPES OF MOVIES THRIVE ON CONFLICTING PERSONALITIES. IT'S KEY TO THE GENRE.

NOW PROTECTED BY THE HEAVILY-ARMED AMERICANS, THE WHEELS ON THIS BUS REALLY START TO GO ROUND AND ROUND. FACED WITH THE NEAR-IMPOSSIBLE TASK OF MAKING IT OUT OF ENEMY TERRITORY ALIVE, THE RAG-TAG GROUP SOON REALIZE THAT THEY'RE RUNNING OUT OF GAS. A QUICK EXPLOSION-FILLED RAID AT AN ENEMY CAMP GETS THEM REFILLED, BUT BEFORE LONG THEY'RE STUCK ON ONE SIDE OF A BRIDGE, WITH A SMALL ARMY STANDING IN THEIR WAY ON THE OTHER SIDE. CAN THEY MAKE IT TO THE OTHER SIDE?

OF COURSE THEY FUCKING CAN. DON'T ASK STUPID QUESTIONS. THEY CAN ALSO EASILY ACHIEVE THE HALF DOZEN OTHER MISSIONS-WITHIN-THE-MISSION THEY TAKE ON IN THIS HOUR AND A HALF OF CHUTZPA. THEY'LL GRIT THEIR TEETH AND LOOK ANGRY, BUT NO ONE SAID TRAVELLING TO DISTANT LANDS AND SLAUGHTERING THE LOCAL INHABITANTS WOULDN'T MAKE YOU GRUMPY. AND WHEN YOU'RE GRUMPY, YOU BLOW SHIT UP.

THE EXPLOSION PYROTECHNICS ARE REALLY SOMETHING TO WRITE HOME ABOUT. HOUSES, GUARD TOWERS, BUNKERS, CORPSES THEY FIND BY THE SIDE OF THE ROAD, AND VEHICLES ALL BLOW UP REEEEAL GOOD. THESE REALLY ARE SOME OF THE BEST 'BOOM'S OF ANY OF THE MID-1980S ITALIAN RAMBO RIP-OFFS, AND

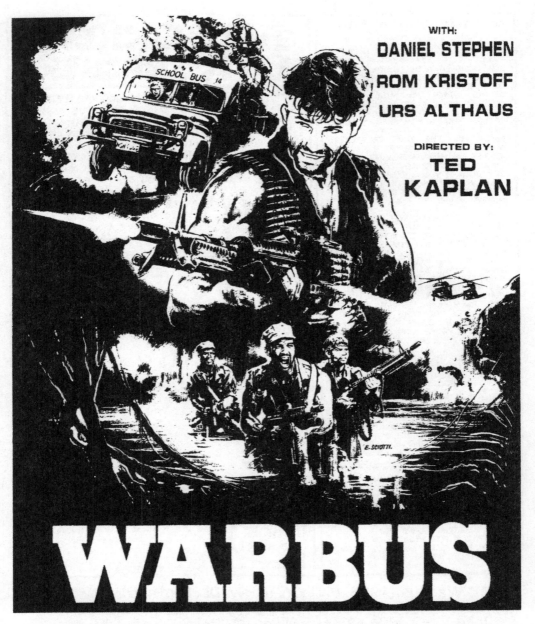

WITH:

DANIEL STEPHEN

ROM KRISTOFF

URS ALTHAUS

DIRECTED BY:

TED
KAPLAN

E. SCIOTTI.

WARBUS

THAT'S SAYING SOMETHING SINCE THAT'S WHERE THESE MOVIES USUALLY PUT MOST OF THEIR BUDGET.
ORANGE FIREBALLS AND FLAMING DEBRIS ROUTINELY FLY HUNDREDS OF FEET IN THE AIR THROUGHOUT
THIS TRASHY LITTLE NUT-HUGGER, THE EXTRAVAGANCE OF WHICH SHOULD HELP ONE FORGET HOW MANY
BRAINLESS WAR-MOVIE CLICHES WERE LAYERED UPON EACH OTHER IN ORDER TO BUILD THE SIMPLISTIC
PLOT.

ITALIAN FILMMAKER FERDINANDO BALDI CLEARLY GOT A KICK OUT OF SERVING UP SOME JINGOISTIC
AMERICAN WAR-MACHINE FUN-TIMES. FOR INSTANCE, HIS MARINES ARE NOTHING SHORT OF SUPER-SOLDIERS.
EVEN WHEN THEY'RE SEEMINGLY SHOOTING THEIR GIANT MACHINE GUNS WILLY-NILLY -- NOT EVEN BOTHERING TO
AIM — THEY SOMEHOW NAIL EVERY TARGET NO MATTER HOW FAR AWAY IT IS. THEY EVEN SEEM TO BE
KILLING MULTIPLE VIET CONG DUDES WITH EACH BULLET -- GUYS WHO FALL OVER, INSTANTLY DEAD,
EVERY TIME. AMERICA: FUCK, YEAH.

STEELY-EYED OVERACTING, SWEATY HEADBANDS, EPILEPTIC SEIZURES, GORGEOUS PALM-TREE-FILLED
LOCATIONS IN THE PHILIPPINES, AND VERY COMPETENT DIRECTION FROM BALDI IS WHAT YOU HAVE TO
LOOK FORWARD TO, HERE. FREDINANDO WAS SOMEWHAT INFAMOUS FOR HIS 3-D GENRE FILMS *COMIN' AT
YA* (1981) AND *TREASURE OF THE FOUR CROWNS* (1983), BOTH OF WHICH STARRED TONY ANTHONY. A
THIRD 3-D OUTING (A SPACE OPERA ALSO STARRING ANTHONY) NEVER GOT PAST THE PLANNING STAGES.
BALDI'S BEST FILM WOULD BE THE HIGHLY UNDERRATED SPAGHETTI WESTERN, *BLINDMAN*, FROM 1971, AND HE'S
NOTABLE FOR HAVING ONE OF HIS LAST PRODUCTIONS, *MISSIONE FINALE* (1988) FUNDED BY AND FILMED IN
NORTH KOREA. FERDINANDO BALDI PASSED AWAY IN ROME, ITALY IN NOVEMBER OF 2007.

-BOUGIE · '16

ADULT INDUSTRY LEGEND BILL MARGOLD ONCE SAID THAT SHE "IS WITHOUT A DOUBT THE BEST SPOKESPERSON THAT THE ADULT ENTERTAINMENT INDUSTRY HAS EVER HAD". STARTING HER CAREER IN 1984 WITH THE THEATRICAL FEATURE, EDUCATING NINA, HARTLEY REMAINS ONE OF THE MOST ENDURING AND RECOGNIZABLE FEMALES IN ADULT FILMS AND VIDEO — AND THAT'S A FACT SUPPORTED BY HER TROPHY CASE. HARTLEY HAS WON MORE AVN AWARDS THAN ANY PORN STAR IN HISTORY. SHE'S ALSO WIDELY CONSIDERED TO BE THE OWNER OF ONE OF THE NICEST BUTTS IN PORN HISTORY, AND IS NOTEWORTHY FOR GENUINELY BEING VERY INTO FUCKING GIRLS. MANY XXX "LESBIANS" ARE MERELY GAY-FOR-PAY.

"I DON'T HAPPEN TO BE A SURVIVOR OF SEXUAL ABUSE, DRUG ABUSE, OR INCEST", NINA TOLD FILMMAKER R.C. HORSCH, RESPONDING TO THE ASSUMPTIONS THAT MANY PEOPLE HAVE ABOUT SEX WORKERS, STRIPPERS, AND PERFORMERS IN HARDCORE PORN. HE MADE A DOCUMENTARY ABOUT HER, APTLY TITLED NINA. IT INTIMATELY CAPTURED HER LAST YEARS ON THE ROAD AS A STRIPPER IN THE LATE 1990S AND EARLY 2000S, AND IN THIS LITTLE-SEEN MOVIE SHE CLEARLY DISPLAYS THAT SHE IS EVERY BIT AS INTELLIGENT AS SHE IS FOXY AND OVERSEXED.

"ONE OF THE REASONS I GOT INTO PORN WAS TO HONOUR MY FEMINIST RIGHT TO SEXUALITY ON MY OWN TERMS", HARTLEY TOLD THE LA WEEKLY IN 2014. "IT'S TAKEN ME 25 YEARS TO FINALLY BE OK WITH, LIKE, ANDREA DWORKIN. I HONESTLY DID TRY TO LOOK AT IT FROM THEIR POINT OF VIEW. WAS I REALLY BEING EXPLOITED?"

IT'S A QUESTION THAT EVERY PORN PERFORMER MUST ASK THEMSELVES. IT'S SOMETHING EVERYONE WHO WORKS FOR A LIVING SHOULD PROBABLY ASK THEMSELVES, ACTUALLY. HAVING A BOSS OR DOING THE BIDDING OF CLIENTS HAS ALWAYS BEEN A SYSTEM OF CHECKS AND BALANCES.

"I HAVE DONE MY REFLECTION, AND NO, I'M NOT BEING TAKEN ADVANTAGE OF", NINA STATED MOST UNEQUIVOCALLY. "AND NO, I'M NOT DOING THIS FOR THE PATRIARCHAL PRIVILEGE AND FOR THE MALE GAZE. I AM A BISEXUAL EXHIBITIONIST VOYEURISTIC NON-MONOGAMOUS QUEER BUTCH TOP, NURSE AND FACILITATOR, AND SEX IS MY THANG!"

LIKE ANNIE SPRINKLE, NINA REALLY CARVED AN INTERESTING NICHE FOR HERSELF IN THE LATER YEARS OF HER CAREER AS A SEX EDUCATOR AND SEX-POSITIVE FEMINIST WHO IS ENTHUSED ABOUT TAKING WHAT SHE'S LEARNED WORKING IN FOUR DIFFERENT DECADES IN THE TRENCHES OF THE ADULT INDUSTRY, AND TEACHING THAT TO PEOPLE WHO CERTAINLY HAD NEVER HAD ANYTHING LIKE THOSE KINDS OF EXPERIENCES. EVEN NOW, IN 2014, AS A GRADUATE WITH HONOURS FROM SAN FRANCISCO STATE UNIVERSITY AND THE AUTHOR OF SEVERAL PUBLISHED BOOKS AND DOZENS OF SELF-HELP SEX DVDS, NINA IS A 54-YEAR-OLD MILF PORN PERFORMER WHO REGULARLY UPDATES HER WEBSITE (NINA.COM) WITH ORIGINAL CONTENT LABELED AS "LESSONS". NOT ONLY IS IT PORN DESIGNED TO GET YOU OFF, BUT IT'S ALSO A PLACE WHERE ALL MANNER OF KINK IS HAPPILY SCHOOLED TO GUEST STARS (AKA STUDENTS) OF ALL AGES, RACES, SEXES AND BODY TYPES.

OOHHH LA LA!

HEH HEH

NINA AND ANNIE

LEGENDARY SUPER SEX GODDESSES!

BOUGIE 2014

WOW

REWIND THIS!

(2013, USA)

THE FORMAT WARS CONTINUE!

BACK IN THE OLD DAYS VCRs (NOT BLU-RAY PLAYERS OR DVRs) REIGNED SUPREME, AND MOM N' POP RENTAL STORES WERE WHERE YOU GOT YOUR FIX. TAPES WERE COVERED WITH STICKERS THAT SAID "BE KIND, REWIND," A SIMPLE COMMON COURTESY THAT WAS REQUESTED FROM SHOPKEEP TO CONSUMER, ALTHOUGH THE MAKERS OF THIS 2013 DOCUMENTARY HAVE FOUND FURTHER MEANING IN THE PHRASE. THAT FRIENDLY FACE STICKER ADORNING THOSE DUSTY OL' TAPES NOW APPEARS TO BE A REQUEST TO TAKE THE TIME TO LOOK BACK AND REFLECT. PONDER HOW WE GOT TO WHERE WE ARE CURRENTLY.

LIKE COLLECTORS OF 8 TRACK TAPES (REMEMBER THE DOCUMENTARY ABOUT THEM FROM '95 CALLED **SO WRONG THEY'RE RIGHT** ?) THESE ARE PASSIONATE FANS WHO ADORE A FORMAT WHOSE TIME HAS PASSED, AND YET SEEMS PRIMED TO LIVE ON VIA CULT FILM FANS WITH AN EYE TOWARDS NOSTALGIA AND A BURGEONING COLLECTORS MARKET. EXPECT A HOST OF NEW, YOUNGER VHS FANS, ESPECIALLY IF THE LINE UP OF DOCUMENTARIES FOCUSED ON VHS SUBCULTURE (CHECK OUT **ADJUST YOUR TRACKING** FROM 2013 AS WELL) CONTINUE ON UNABATED.

THE DIRECTOR AND EDITOR OF **REWIND THIS** HAD THEIR SHIT TOGETHER. TIGHT SKILLS. FROM THE HISTORY OF THE FORMAT ITSELF (AND ITS RISE OVER BETAMAX), THE WAYS IN WHICH IT WAS DISTRIBUTED AND MARKETED TO THE PUBLIC, THE WAYS IN WHICH IT DIRECTLY AFFECTED THE ART OF FILMMAKING, THE RISK OF LOSING CONTENT FOREVER DUE TO THE LACK OF VHS ARCHIVING AND THE UNSTABLE NATURE OF MAGNETIC TAPE, TO THE CURRENT ARGUMENT ABOUT THE PROS AND CONS INVOLVED WHEN COMPARING PHYSICAL MEDIA TO STREAMING/DIGITAL. THE PAST, PRESENT, AND FUTURE OF THE VHS FORMAT ARE REVELLED IN, AND THERE AREN'T MANY TAPES UNTURNED.

A SHITPILE OF (IN)FAMOUS PERSONALITIES GIVE FACETIME. **GHOST IN THE SHELL** CREATOR MAMORU OSHII, ELVIRA, DIRECTOR FRANK HENENLOTTER, DIRECTOR ATOM EGOYAN, SEVERIN FILMS' DAVID GREGORY, SOMETHING WEIRD'S MIKE VRANEY (REST IN PEACE), TROMA'S LLOYD KAUFMAN, SYNAPSE'S DON MAY, PORN ICON BILL MARGOLD, AND THE THEATER PROGRAMMERS FROM THE ALAMO DRAFTHOUSE AND CINEFAMILY ARE ALL HERE––AND SO ARE THE LESSER KNOWN BUT NO LESS IMPORTANT VOICES. I'M TALKING ABOUT MY FELLOW ZINESTERS AND BLOGGERS, BOOTLEGGERS, MIXTAPE MAKERS, VIDEOSTORE EMPLOYEES, AND OF COURSE, PLENTY OF RABID VHS COLLECTORS. MY DEARLY DEPARTED PEN PAL, ANDY COPP, RANKS AMONGST THEM AS WELL, AND THE FILM IS DEDICATED TO HIM.

THE GUY FROM **EVERYTHING IS TERRIBLE** IS PROBABLY A WONDERFUL FELLOW AND ALSO DISHES A COUPLE GREAT SOUND BITES FOR THIS FILM, BUT IF I'M BEING BRUTALLY HONEST HE ALSO GIVES OFF THE STINKING AURA OF THE SMIRKING, BLACK-FRAME-GLASSES-WEARING ELITIST FROM CHICAGO. MAYBE THAT IS BECAUSE HE'S BUILT HIS ENTIRE BRAND ON THE BASIC CONCEPT OF ENJOYING EVERYTHING FROM THE '70s, '80s, AND '90s IRONICALLY, BUT AS ONE OF THE TWO GUYS BEHIND A SIMILAR VENTURE IN THE **RETARD-O-TRON** MIXTAPE SERIES, I'M HARDLY ONE TO PRESUME TO JUDGE HIM, AM I?

THIS MOVIE RULES. I LOVED WATCHING SO MANY OF MY ONLINE FRIENDS AND PEERS (BOTH LIVING AND PASSED ON) TALK ABOUT THE VHS FORMAT, BUT WHEN IT COMES RIGHT DOWN TO IT, I HAVE TO CONFRONT SOMETHING THAT WAS TUMBLING AROUND IN THE MACHINE DRYER THAT IS MY HEAD THE WHOLE TIME I WATCHED THIS DOCUMENTARY. WHILE I'M FASCINATED AND ENTHUSED BY THE RESURGENCE IN VHS CULTURE, I ALSO HAVE MY RESERVATIONS. WHILE I'M ON SOCIAL MEDIA IN THESE VHS FAN GROUPS I FEEL WAY MORE LIKE DIAN FOSSEY WATCHING THE APES FIGHT OVER THEIR RARE AND OBSCURE VHS TAPES, THAN I FEEL

ROBIN, WHY_

WHY DID YOU GET RID OF ME?

BECAUSE! I LIVE IN A TINY 700 FT CONDO AND YOU FUCKERS TAKE UP SO MUCH ROOM!

LIKE ONE OF THE APES.

I MEAN, FUCK -- C'MON. THE IDEA OF WARRING OVER OR PLEDGING ALLEGIANCE TO A FORMAT (DYING OR NOT) SEEMS SO IRRELEVANT TO ME. IT'S LIKE TAKING A STAND ON WHICH IS BETTER, COKE OR PEPSI, WHILE IGNORING THAT, WHILE DELICIOUS, BOTH ARE LOADED WITH HIGH AMOUNTS OF GLUCOSE-FRUCTOSE CORN SYRUP DESIGNED TO MAKE YOU FAT AND DEAD. I'M NOT GONNA BE PRECIOUS ABOUT THE DELIVERY PROCESS, SIMPLY GIVE ME A WAY TO HAVE THESE MOVIES I LOVE SO VERY MUCH, AND IM IN. AND I DON'T MEAN DIGITALLY FLOATING IN AN IMAGINARY "CLOUD" WHERE A COMPANY CAN DELETE THEM AT THEIR OWN DISCRETION AFTER I "BUY" THEM -- I MEAN ACTUALLY **HAVE** THEM.

AND "HAVING" THEM BRINGS US TO ANOTHER ELEMENT OF WHAT KINDA TORTURES ME ABOUT THIS WHOLE THING. PLENTY OF THE PEOPLE ON THE FRONT LINES OF THE VHS COMEBACK MOVEMENT CONSISTENTLY DISPLAY THAT COLLECTOR MINDSET THAT I SO ABHOR IN THE WORLD OF COMICS FANDOM. WHERE SIMPLY COLLECTING AND DISPLAYING AN ITEM ENDS UP MEANING SO MUCH MORE TO THE COLLECTOR THAN READING/WATCHING/ENJOYING IT THE WAY IT WAS DESIGNED TO. WHERE JUST HAVING IT BECOMES SO MUCH MORE IMPORTANT TO YOU THAN ENGAGING WITH IT. IT'S ONE OF THE MOST UNAPPEALING MINDSETS DISPLAYED IN FANDOM.

OF COURSE, I'M CONFLICTED ABOUT THAT LAST THOUGHT AS WELL, THOUGH, BECAUSE THE LAST THING I WANT TO BE IS THAT ANNOYING GUY WHO TELLS EVERYONE THE "RIGHT" WAY TO ENJOY THINGS. **FUCK** THAT ATTITUDE AND THE KILL-JOYS WHO TROT IT OUT RIGHT WHEN YOU'RE IN THE MIDDLE OF LOVING SOMETHING WITH ZERO PRETENSIONS. WHAT I TRY TO DO IS TAKE CARE OF MY OWN SHIT, AND MAKE SURE I DON'T BECOME THAT KIND OF COLLECTOR -- BECAUSE ONCE THAT HAPPENS THE EXPERIENCE BECOMES VERY HOLLOW, I DON'T WANNA LOSE MY PASSION.

NOT PUTTING MUCH IMPORTANCE ON FORMAT ENDS UP MAKING ME FEEL REMOVED FROM THE RETRO VHS CELEBRATION. FORMATS AND MEANS OF CONSUMPTION OF THE ART FORM WILL COME AND GO THROUGHOUT OUR LIFETIMES, BUT THE MOVIES THEMSELVES WILL BE FOREVER. IN FACT, I RARELY MENTION FORMAT AT ALL WHEN I'M REVIEWING MOVIES FOR CINEMA SEWER, AND THAT IS PRIMARILY BECAUSE OF HOW TEMPORARY ITS NATURE IS. I WANT MY WRITING TO REMAIN RELEVANT AND READABLE DECADES FROM NOW, AND NIT-PICKING OVER RUN TIMES ON THE CURRENT DVD/BLU/WHATENER WORKS ENTIRELY AGAINST THAT GOAL. CONTENT OVER FORMAT HAS **ALWAYS** BEEN MY MANDATE.

BUT ONCE AGAIN -- I'M CONFLICTED. HOW CAN I NOT BE? I TOO AM A NOSTALGIA-BASED CREATURE. I FULLY UNDERSTAND THAT THE TEMPORARY NATURE OF VHS, DVD, OR ANY FORMAT, IS ONE OF THE VERY THINGS THAT MAKES IT INTERESTING. IT IS WHAT GROUNDS US TO THAT TIME, THAT TIME THAT VIDEO RENTAL STORES WERE A PART OF OUR LIVES. IT HELPS US RETAIN OUR CONNECTION WITH THE PAST. 20 YEARS FROM NOW PEOPLE ARE GOING TO BE ALL NOSTALGIC FOR NETFLIX. _SAME_ THING.

OBVIOUSLY, I'M OF TWO MINDS ON THIS TOPIC, AND A DOC LIKE REWIND THIS IS INCREDIBLY VALUABLE BECAUSE IT ALLOWS YOU AND I TO REALLY CONFRONT WHY WE ARE FANS, AND WHY WE OBSESS OVER THIS STUFF. IT'S A MUST-SEE FOR ALL CINEMA SEWER READERS.

ARE THESE TAPES I'VE GOT, RARE? HUH, HUH! JUST KIDDING, I **KNOW** THEY'RE RARE. I ONLY COLLECT RARE VHS.

FUCK THIS NON SENSE

VHS
IS HAPPINESS

T-SHIRT SOLD BY LUNCHMEAT CULT FILM/VHS FANZINE.

85

Run Out and Rewind

By Billy Burgess

STANDING IN A ROOM STACKED WALL TO WALL WITH VHS CASSETTES, THE SMELL OF THOUSANDS OF MILES OF MAGNETIC TAPE SPOOLED TIGHT, HIDDEN, WAITING. NOTHING BEATS THAT RUSH. DEEP WITHIN THESE VOLUMES LIE SOME OF THE FINEST SPECTACLES OF OUR TIME, THE EXPERIMENTAL FILM ELEMENTS WHICH FLASH THROUGHOUT EXPLOITATION CINEMA UNNOTICED BY FILM HISTORIANS.

DAY FOR NIGHT WITH CLOUDS. NIGHT SHOOTS WITH NO FILL LIGHT. ACTORS IN REGIONAL THEATRE MAKEUP. DIALOGUE DELIVERED AS THOUGH THERE WERE NO ONE ELSE IN THE ROOM. SLOPPY OPTICAL PRINTING. SPROCKET HOLES SNAPPING IN THE GATE. TITLE SEQUENCES SO CHEAP THE TEXT UNDULATES OVER THE FILM. CUTS SO DIRTY THEY LOOK LIKE THEY WERE DONE WITH A BUTCHER KNIFE AND MODEL GLUE. A PRINT BEAT-UP FROM RUNNING BEFORE HUNDREDS OF SWEATY EYEBALLS IN RAUNCHY, CRUMBLING THEATRES. WORK PRINTS THAT BECOME THEATRICAL PRINTS. PRINTS SO FADED THEY'RE PURPLE. PRINTS SO OLD THE PETROLEUM PRODUCT OF THE FILM ITSELF SLOWLY RETURNS TO ITS NATURAL STATE.

DIALOGUE WRITTEN WHILE DRUNK. ACTORS WHO ARE DRUNK. THE BEAUTIFUL DECAY OF JOHN CARRADINE, CAMERON MITCHELL, ALDO RAY AND BELA LUGOSI. SINGLE WEEK PRODUCTIONS. SINGLE DAY PRODUCTIONS. CONTINUITY THAT COULDN'T GIVE TWO FUCKS. SHOT BY SHOT CIGARETTE CONTINUITY. SHOT BY SHOT HAIR CONTINUITY. A LONG BIT OF EXPOSITIONAL DIALOGUE INTERRUPTED BY SUDDEN ACTION. HORRIFIC DUBBING. RAGGED PANS. FOG MACHINES. CULT INITIATIONS. GANG FIGHTS. EVIL GRAVEDIGGERS. OUT OF CONTROL TEENAGERS. LONG TAKES. SINGLE TAKES. TORTURE-OBSESSED MIDGETS. LIVE MUSICAL INTERLUDES. STAGE BLOOD. FETID ALLEYWAYS. NAZIS. DUMB PUNKS. VIGILANTES. HALLOWEEN MASKS. THUNDERSTORMS. LEERING HOBOES. LEERING PIMPS. LEERING COPS. PRISON DYKES. SWITCHBLADE DRAGGING GREASEBALLS.

THE STRANGE MACHISMO OF DORIS WISHMAN. THE SINGLE DIRECTION LIGHTING OF GEORGE KUCHAR. THE RISING PHOENIX OF EDWARD D. WOOD JR. AND THOSE NAMES WHICH ARE STILL TO RISE. THE SEXUAL EXPLOSIVENESS OF ALEX DE RENZY. THE FUNKY FX OF DON DOHLER. THE AUDACITY OF H.G. LEWIS. THE THREE-DOLLAR CHARM OF ARCH HALL JR. THE CASTING OF TED V. MIKELS. THE HOLY NAMES REGAL, PARAGON, CAMP, CONTINENTAL, MYSTIC FIRE, EMBASSY, GORGON.

THE SEEMING INDESTRUCTIBILITY OF BETA. THE TOTAL DESTRUCTIBILITY OF VHS. THIRD GENERATION MASS MARKET VHS. FIVE GENERATION TAPE-TRADE VHS. SLOPPILY PHOTOCOPIED VHS TAPE-TRADING CATALOGUES. EP MODE 6-HOUR BLANK CASSETTES. TOP LOADING VHS PLAYERS. AMATEUR, HAND-PAINTED COVER ART. "EXTREME CONTENT" WARNING LABELS. WEIRD TITLES. WEIRD FONTS. JANKY DISTRIBUTOR LOGOS. COVERS WITH VAGUE SCENE RE-ENACTMENTS CHEAPLY PHOTOGRAPHED WITH RANDOM MODELS. BACK COVER STILLS PHOTOGRAPHED FROM TELEVISIONS. BACK COVERS WITH A SINGLE BLOCK OF JUSTIFIED TEXT. RENTALS THAT SMELL LIKE CIGARETTES. RENTALS WITH SILVER FOIL SECURITY STICKERS. RENTALS THAT COME IN BROWN OR CLEAR CLAMSHELLS.

THE MECHANICAL SONG OF THE VCR ENGAGING THE THREAD OF AN OLD CASSETTE. ALTERNATE OPENING TITLES TYPED ON ANALOG BOARDS THAT APPEAR OVER TREMBLING STILL FRAMES. FILM GRAIN COALESCING WITH TAPE GRAIN. TAPE-TO-TAPE EDITS WITH REEL JUMPS, SOUNDTRACK JUMPS AND CRUNCH LINES. WHITE SUBTITLES EVAPORATING INTO THE SHIFTING FORMS OF AN OVEREXPOSED SHOT. THE SUN RISING OUT MY WINDOW AS THE LAST OF THE CREDITS FADE.

I SHAMBLE TOWARDS THAT ROOM FILLED WALL-TO-WALL WITH VHS. BALANCING THE WEIGHT OF A FRESH TAPE IN MY HAND, THE SPOOLS *KA-CHUNK* AS I TURN IT OVER. WHAT WERE THEY THINKING WHEN THEY MADE THIS THING?

WHEN IT GETS A LITTLE LESS BUSY I'LL TAKE YOU BACK THERE. YOU GOTTA SEE THIS TAPE.

BILLY BURGESS IS FOUNDER OF THE DRUID UNDERGROUND FILM FESTIVAL: WWW.DRUIDUNDERGROUNDFILMFESTIVAL.COM

STATIC LINES OF HARD LIVING

BY DANIEL "FRESH FELLOW" BERNARDI

STEP UP

A RETRO BOUTIQUE FILM STORE TRANSPLANTED INTO ONE OF THE MOST CONSERVATIVE AND AFFLUENT WASP SUBURBS IN MELBOURNE, MAROONED FROM FELLOW COGNATES THAT ARE WELL SUPPORTED IN THE PRETENTIOUS NORTH-EASTERN SUBURBS -- HOME OF BOHEMIAN CULTURE. INVARIABLY DRESSED IN BLACK, THE OWNER, JAMES, IS A TALL, SKINNY AND BESPECTACLED FIRST WAVE GENERATION X FILM MAVEN -- A POST-PUNK BUDDY HOLLY -- WHO SITS MEEKLY BEHIND THE COUNTER. HE IS SURROUNDED BY A GREAT SELECTION OF DVD IMPORTS, MEMORABILIA, VINTAGE FILM POSTERS AND A MODEST GROUPING OF VHS. SORELY MISSING THE HEYDAY OF VIDEO CASSETTES, JAMES SAYS "DVD LIBERATED FILM BUT THEN DESTROYED IT."

MANY TITLES WERE DIFFICULT TO COME BY ON VHS IN AUSTRALIA. THE SELL-THROUGH MARKET WAS A VERY LIMITED ONE AS WE WEREN'T YET A 'BUYING FILMS TO OWN' CULTURE AS MUCH AS WE WERE A 'TAPING THINGS OFF TELEVISION' CULTURE. THE AVERAGE HOUSEHOLD WAS AT BEST ADORNED WITH MAYBE A HALF DOZEN OFFICIAL VHS TITLES, THE REST BEING BLANK TAPES. TITLES WERE HELD BACK A LITTLE MORE IN THOSE DAYS. SOME FILMS WOULD PLAY AT THE CINEMAS FOR A LONG TIME AND WOULDN'T SEE A VIDEO RELEASE FOR AT LEAST A YEAR AFTER THE END OF ITS THEATRICAL RUN. ADD TO THAT ANOTHER YEAR UNTIL BRAND NEW SELL-THROUGH COPIES OF THE TITLE WERE AVAILABLE, WHICH WAS USUALLY ONLY A SMALL SELECTION OF THE BIGGER RELEASES. THEN THE WORLD OPENED UP TO EVERYBODY WHILE THE DOOR IMMEDIATELY IN FRONT OF THEM WAS BOARDED SHUT.

CONSUMER DEMANDS HAVEN'T CHANGED DRASTICALLY SINCE THE VIDEOTAPE FORMAT WAR BETWEEN BETAMAX AND VHS. ALTHOUGH BETAMAX TAPES WERE SIGNIFICANTLY SMALLER IN SIZE THAN THE MORE CUMBERSOME VHS AND HAD A REPUTATION FOR BETTER PICTURE QUALITY, IT MAY BE LOST ON FUTURE GENERATIONS AS TO HOW THE MORE PETITE AND SUPERIOR OF THE TWO COULD

FAIL. THE BIGGEST MISTAKE THAT CAUSED BETA TO CAPITULATE WAS THAT THEIR STANDARD TAPES ONLY HAD A MAXIMUM OF ONE HOUR RECORDING LENGTH, WHILE VHS MANUFACTURED TWO HOUR TAPES WHICH INGRATIATED ITSELF TO MEET THE DEMANDS OF THE STUDIOS AND CONSUMERS ALIKE. AT THE HEIGHT OF THE BATTLE THIS WAS A SIGNIFICANT WIN FOR VHS MANUFACTURERS, AND EVEN THOUGH BETAMAX INCREASED THE LENGTHS OF THEIR TAPES TO MEET THAT OF THEIR CHIEF COMPETITOR, CONSUMERS NOT USUALLY KNOWN FOR GIVING SECOND CHANCES TO EQUIVALENT ALTERNATIVES THAT WEREN'T NE PLUS ULTRA -- EXPEDIENTLY REMAINED LOYAL TO VHS.

ANOTHER SIGNIFICANT FACTOR AS TO WHY VHS MAY HAVE PREVAILED WAS THAT THE ADULT FILM INDUSTRY SET UP THEIR BIVOUACS IN THE VHS CAMP, FOR THE MOST PART. THEIR DESPOTIC CARNAL GOVERNANCE ALWAYS PROMISES TO USHER IN THE PURIENT PUBLIC WHO NEVER FAIL TO OBSEQUIOUSLY FOLLOW THEIR LEAD. PORN AND ITS CONSTITUENTS PULLED VHS

THROUGH ON ITS WINNING TICKET IN A LANDSLIDE VICTORY THAT CAN BE COMPARED ONLY TO THAT OF NIXON'S WIN OVER McGOVERN.

VHS WILL FOREVER BE KNOWN AS HAVING THE LONGEST REIGN OF ALL PRIMARY HOME VIDEO FORMATS. IT FOUGHT WITH GALLANTRY RIGHT TO THE END -- GLIBLY SQUELCHING PUTSCHES FROM SUPER-VHS AND LASERDISC. AS SENESCENT BATTLE-WEARINESS CREPT IN, VHS ABDICATED TO DVD AFTER HOLDING SWAY FOR ALMOST A QUARTER OF A CENTURY.

WITH THE EXCEPTION OF A SMALL SUBCULTURE OF HORROR FANS WHO HAVE FETISHIZED THE "BIG BOX" PACKAGING OF OBSCURE HORROR TITLES OF THE 1980s, THE VIDEO CASSETTE IS YET TO ENTER THE REVERENT ORBIT OF THE CULTIVATED COLLECTOR. WITHOUT FURTHER BREEDING PROGRAMS TAKING PLACE, THE SCARCELY EXTANT VIDEO CASSETTE BETTER GET A MOVE ON AND FIND A WAY TO MAKE ITSELF DIGNIFIED AND WORTH SAVING BEFORE THE FINAL WORDS OF ITS SWAN SONG ARE UTTERED.

AS SVENGALI-LIKE MAGNATES CONVERGE ON THE MASSES DURING EXTENDED HIGHWAY HYPNOSIS, THE UNASSAILABLE FEW WHO HAVE COME INTO UNSHAKABLE CONSCIOUSNESS, WITH PRESCIENCE FROM EXTRAPOLATION -- ESCHEW ADVANCEMENT. THERE ARE THOSE WHO GENUINELY PREFER TO DIVEST THEMSELVES OF PHYSICAL MEDIA FORMATS IN THE NAME OF SPACE AND NEATNESS NOW THAT THE MODERN APARTMENT RESEMBLES SOME KIND OF SARCOPHAGUS. OTHERS DO SO FROM THE PARALYSING FEAR OF MODISH EXCLUSION.

BY ATOMIZING MEDIA HARDCOPY INTO THE DIGITAL ETHER, TAKING THE SHRINKING RAY TO THE WAY IN WHICH WE CONSUME FILM, IT'S ERASING A PAST THAT MOST COULD NOT POSSIBLY CATCH UP WITH IF THEY ARE TO REMAIN IN-STEP WITH THE PRESENT. WE CAN'T COMPETE WITH THE MONOLITHIC EARTHLY MEMOIRS OF WHAT CAME BEFORE US WITH ITS TOWERING OVERARCHING HEIGHT IN PHYSICAL FORM.

THE PHILISTINES ARE THE RULING CLASS -- TRANMOGRIFYING AN OLD TELEVISION SET INTO A FISH TANK, OR GUTTING A VINTAGE TURNTABLE CABINET AND RETROFITTING IT WITH A DOCKING STATION. IT'S A THROWBACK TO OLD TIMES WITHOUT VALORIZING ITS SIGNIFICANCE AND FUNCTION. PERHAPS THE MOST ODIOUS OFFENCE OF THEM ALL -- TO BE USED AS A CONVERSATION PIECE FOR HOUSEHOLD KLATCHES PARADING CARRIONS OF RETRO CHIC AS A VERITABLE SIDESHOW ATTRACTION.

RECENTLY YOUTUBE ADDED A TRANSITORY "TAPE MODE" FUNCTION FOR SELECTED VIDEOS TO MARK THE 57th BIRTHDAY OF THE VCR, WHICH SEEMS TO BE MET WITH THE SAME KIND OF PERVERSELY DERISIVE CURIOSITY AS SOMEONE LIKE PRINCE RANDIAN HAD TO ENDURE AS "THE HUMAN TORSO". IT IS INCREDIBLE TO IMAGINE YOUNGER GENERATIONS WERE ONCE THANKFUL THAT THEY DIDN'T LIVE IN THE TIME BEFORE ELECTRICITY AND ANTIBIOTICS, OR DURING CONSCRIPTION. NOW MOPPETS AND YOUNG ADULTS LOOK AT THE STANDARD DEFINITION FULL SCREEN GRAIN AND LINES AND SIMILARLY THANK THEIR HIGH DEF DEITIES THAT THEY NEVER HAD TO SUFFER SUCH HARDSHIP -- BECOMING MORE THANKFUL FOR A LOT LESS.

EMPTY VIDEO STORES ABOUND, AKIN TO WHAT ONE WOULD IMAGINE A POST APOCALYPTIC WORLD MIGHT LOOK LIKE. IT'S DEEPLY HEART-RENDING, AS I WAS PRETTY MUCH RAISED AT MY LOCAL VIDEO STORE, AND VOLUNTEERED THERE AS A KID JUST TO HANG AROUND THE FILMS. THIS CULMINATED IN AN ACTUAL JOB THERE WHEN I FINALLY REACHED THE LEGAL AGE OF 14. FIRST THE NATIVE

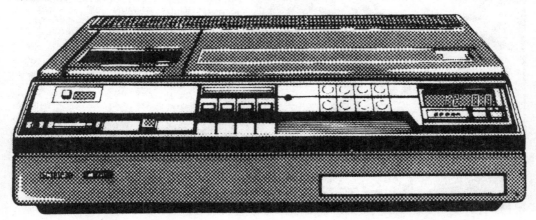

AMERICANS SAW THEIR WORLD DISAPPEAR RIGHT IN FRONT OF THEIR EYES BECAUSE OF MANIFEST DESTINY AND NOW THAT SAME SENSE OF ENTITLEMENT IS FIGHTING ITSELF IN A CULTURAL CIVIL WAR.

PEOPLE DON'T WANT TO PAY FOR THEIR FILMS ANYMORE. AND WHY SHOULD THEY? A TERRIBLE INSECURITY BEFALLS INDIVIDUALS WHO HAND OVER CASH IN RETURN FOR A SPECTRAL FILE THAT IS AS TANGIBLE AS THE AKASHIC RECORDS. BECAUSE IT NEVER ENTERS THE MATERIAL WORLD IT BECOMES A FRAGMENTED RECOLLECTION -- A FEVER DREAM. IN THIS COMATOSE CONSUMPTION OF MEDIA THERE IS NO SENSE OF OWNERSHIP WITHOUT ANY KEEPSAKES, ONLY A PIRATED MEMORY OF A DISEMBODIED EXPERIENCE -- AS IN DEATH -- THE END OF OUR PHYSICAL LIVES. THE PRESENT HAS BECOME JUST AS IMPALPABLE AS THE PAST AND FUTURE ALIKE.

OBFUSCATING ANY DISCERNIBLE ANATOMY, A DIGITAL FILE IS GESTALT IN ITS CONSTITUTION. UNLIKE A DIGITAL FILE, THE VIDEO CASSETTE IS SEEN AS GROTESQUELY GAUCHE INSOFAR AS ONE CAN SEE ALL ITS PRIVATE PARTS -- LIKE A NATIVE SAVAGE WITHOUT A LOIN CLOTH. THE VIDEO CASSETTE AND THE VCR, WITH ALL THEIR BULK AND WEIGHTINESS, ARE THE ULTIMATE SYMBOL OF MASCULINITY. THE COMBATANT OUTLAW WITH ATTITUDE TO BURN BUSTING THROUGH THE SWINGING SALOON DOOR, THE CLANK OF SPURS WITH EACH SLOW STEP. TECHNOLOGY HAS BEEN EMASCULATED MUCH LIKE THE ALPHA MALE, NOW A GENDERLESS AND UXORIOUS NONENTITY.

QUIRKS IN THE VHS FORMAT ADDED SOFTNESS AND HUMANITY TO THE MEDIUM. IT WAS TRACTABLE AND ENDURED THE WEAR AND TEAR OF A SOUL WITHIN A FUNCTIONING EXTERIOR THAT GROWS OLD AND WEARY AND CAN'T PARRY INELUCTABLE DEMISE. THE ULTIMATE MIRRORING OF LIFE AND DEATH. THE DIGITAL REVOLUTION HAS AN ERSATZ IMMORTALITY TO IT WHERE EVEN AN ORIGINAL IS LIKE A FACSIMILE FIVE TIMES REMOVED THROUGH MARRIAGE FROM BARREN LINEAGE. FOR WEAR IMPLIES LIFE -- THE STATIC LINES OF HARD LIVING. THE VICISSITUDES OF PERSONALITY AND MOOD WOULD HAVE GEPPETTO TURN PINOCCHIO BACK INTO A WOODEN BOY OPTING TO TRADE IN HIS LIVING, BREATHING CATAMITE FOR THE UNREACTIVE ALACRITY OF A WOODEN SEX TOY FOR AN ALWAYS RELIABLE, HO-HUM FUCK.

MOST OF THE VIEWING PUBLIC VAUNTS NANOTECHNOLOGY TO THE POINT THAT SPEAKING OUT AGAINST IT IS MET WITH A KIND OF REPROACH THAT CAN ONLY BE COMPARED TO THE DEBASING OF A CLOSE FRIEND OR FAMILY MEMBER. ONE IS LIKELY TO VERILY ELICIT BILIOUS SCOWLS -- SET UPON BY VIRTUAL DEMAGOGUES AND THEIR PUGNACIOUS ACOLYTES AT EVEN THE SLIGHTEST INFERENCE OF DISLIKE AT THE DIRECTION FILM SPECTATORSHIP IS HEADING. TECHNOLOGY HAS FORMED SUCH A MAJOR PART OF THE MODERN IDENTITY -- A STOPGAP FOR A REAL ONE -- WHICH HAS REVERTED FULL CIRCLE BACK TO THE KINETOSCOPE WHICH DEMONSTRATES THAT IT TOOK OVER ONE HUNDRED YEARS TO FIGURE OUT HOW TO GET THAT CONCEPT INTO OUR POCKETS. SPECTATOR--SHIP HAS BECOME AN INDIVIDUAL EXPERIENCE, ANALOGOUS TO EDISON'S NASCENT VISION.

WE ARE SPOILING AS OUR EXPIRATION DATE APPROACHES -- LOOTED WITH NOTHING LEFT TO WIPE OUT. THE PEANUT GALLERY WILL HECKLE AND THROW BEER BOTTLES AT THE SEVEN TRUMPETERS DURING THEIR PERFORMANCE

AND AT THAT MOMENT WHILE THE SUPERNAL BAND LUMBER OFF THE STAGE WITH THEIR HEADS HUNG LOW, GOD TRIES TO FIND ANOTHER GIG FOR THEM, AS IT IS CLEAR THAT NOT EVEN THE APOCALYPSE CAN PENETRATE THE INTRANSIGENT CONCEIT OF THIS AUDIENCE.

-END-

THE ANUS FAMILY (1991)

THE ADDAMS FAMILY: XXX (2011) AND THE MADDAMS FAMILY (1991) ARE BOTH FAIRLY SERVICEABLE PORN PARODIES. THEY AREN'T LEGENDARY, BUT THEY DO WHAT THEY SET OUT TO DO MODERATELY WELL, AND FANS OF THE ORIGINAL SHOW WILL FIND THINGS TO LIKE ABOUT THEM. NOT SO WITH A LESSER KNOWN ADDAMS FAMILY PORN SPOOF FROM 1991. IT'S CALLED THE ANUS FAMILY, AND IT'S A BUTT-LOAD.

HOW BAD IS IT? THE ON-SET SOUND QUALITY IS SO POORLY DONE, I CAN BARELY MAKE OUT THE DIALOG. THE SHOT-ON-VIDEO CAMERA WORK IS SO AMATEURISH IT SEEMS LIKE SOMEONE IS FILMING THEIR VACATION (THEY CONSTANTLY GO IN AND OUT OF FOCUS AND ACCIDENTALLY-- YET ROUTINELY-- FILM THE LIGHTING AND SOUND EQUIPMENT), AND THE ACTORS STEP ON EACH OTHERS' DIALOG AS IF THEY WERE IN A GRADE SCHOOL PLAY. LISTEN, I HAVE SEEN SOME SHITTY PORN PARODIES IN MY TIME, BUT THIS ONE TAKES THE CAKE... AND THEN ACCIDENTALLY DROPS IT IN THE CATBOX. HONESTLY, YOU CAN EVEN CLEARLY HEAR THE DIRECTOR SAY "... AAAAND ACTION" IN A SHOT TOWARDS THE END. I WISH I WAS SHITTING YOU.

THE THING THAT MADE THE ADDAMS FAMILY TV SHOW AND MOVIES ENTERTAINING WAS THAT THE SET ITSELF WAS ONE OF THE CHARACTERS. THAT GETS TOSSED OUT COMPLETELY HERE. INSTEAD OF A CREEPY COBWEB-COVERED CASTLE RESPONSIBLE FOR COUNTLESS KOOKY SIGHT GAGS, WE GET SOMEONE'S MODERN (AND MUNDANE) SUBURBAN HOUSE. THEY DIDN'T EVEN BOTHER WITH THE BARE MINIMUM OF EFFORT, THAT IS: TO LITTER THE PLACE WITH SOME CRUDDY PLASTIC HALLOWEEN DECORATIONS LIKE THEY DID FOR THE OTHER ADDAMS FAMILY PORN PARODIES.

THIS HALF-SHAT PILE OF BUNG-MUD DOESN'T EVEN HAVE COMMON SENSE ENOUGH TO CASH IN ON ITS SPOOF TITLE. LOOK ELSEWHERE, BUTT-LOVERS. THERE IS 14 SECONDS (I TIMED IT) OF TOTALLY UNEXCEPTIONAL CORN-HOLING, ZERO ASSLICKING, AND NO SPREAD CHEEKS TO BE SEEN. JUST FAKE TITS EVERYWHERE, CONDOMS, BY-THE-NUMBERS SUX N' FUX, AND LOUSY EARLY 1990S CANNED CASIO KEYBOARD MUZAK PIPED THROUGH THE WHOLE THING TO MAKE IT EVEN MORE EXCRUCIATING.

BILL MARGOLD PLAYS GONZO ANUS, BUT IT'S A NON-SEX ROLE, SO HE JUST SORT OF STROLLS THROUGH VARIOUS SCENES, SAYS "HEY" OR WHATEVER, AND LEAVES. WHAT THE FUCK? SEAN MICHAELS PLAYS LETCH, THE BLACK ZOMBIE BUTLER WHO LISTENS TO A SONY WALKMAN. RON JEREMY PLAYS 'THING,' WHICH OF COURSE MEANS WE JUST SEE HIS HAND (AND HEAR HIS VOICE?), WHILE HE SITS UNDERNEATH A TABLE AND PASSES PEOPLE DILDOS. MADISON PLAYS TUSHY ANUS. SHE'S TOLERABLE, BUT AS MENTIONED EARLIER THE SOUND IS SO BAD AND ECHO-Y, I CAN'T REALLY MAKE OUT MUCH OF WHAT SHE SAID IN HER VARIOUS OVERLY TALKY SCENES. UNCLE FELTCHER DOESN'T DO ANY FELTCHING, AND WEARS ALL WHITE. FROM BOTH A PARODY AND A PORNO STANDPOINT, THAT JUST AIN'T RIGHT, MAN. WHITE AIN'T GOTH.

IF YOU NEEDED YET ANOTHER REASON TO NOT WATCH THIS, TAKE NOTE THAT THERE IS NO WEDNESDAY ADDAMS CHARACTER. THAT'S RIGHT, NOT A SINGLE KINKY AND EVIL-LOOKING TEENAGE GOTH GIRL TO BE SEEN THROUGH THE HOUR AND A HALF RUNTIME. THAT'S LIKE MAKING STAR WARS PORN AND NOT BOTHERING TO INCLUDE PRINCESS LEIA! IT'S LIKE MAKING SCOOBY DOO PORN AND LEAVING OUT VELMA! IT'S LIKE MAKING MEGAFORCE PORN AND LEAVING OUT PERSIS KHAMBATTA! IT IS SUCH A GRIEVOUS ERROR, IT HONESTLY MAKES ME FRUSTRATED THAT THIS EVEN EXISTS.

THE ANUS FAMILY IS NOT EVEN BAD ENOUGH TO BE UNINTENTIONALLY FUNNY, IT'S JUST BORING. SIMPLY PUT, THIS IS ONE OF THE MOST DISAPPOINTING MOVIES EVER TO BE REVIEWED IN CINEMA SEWER. IT'S SO LAME, I'M NOT EVEN GOING TO DO A DRAWING BASED ON IT. HERE INSTEAD IS A DRAWING OF WHAT THIS MOVIE SHOULD HAVE BEEN LIKE.

MAY I HAVE THE DICK?

WHAT DO WE SAY?

NOW.

DOIN' IT ADDAMS STYLE

KEEP IT IN THE FAMILY

UGH!

BOUGLE '13

POM POM & HOT HOT (1992) Dir: Joe Cheung
(aka FRIED CURRY & TOP MARKSMEN
aka HARDBOILED KILLERS)

REVIEW BY: GIGANTOR

NOT TO BE CONFUSED WITH OR ASSOCIATED WITH DIRECTOR JOE CHEUNG'S OTHER 4 FILMS IN HIS POM POM FILM SERIES, I FIRST CAME ACROSS THE NOTEWORTHY POM POM & HOT HOT AFTER SEEING A VCD IN A MONSTER PILE OF VCDS IN THE CRAP BIN AT ONE OF THE LOCAL DVD SHOPS IN VANCOUVER'S CHINATOWN. IT WENT FROM IN MY HAND, TO BACK IN THE BIN, TO BACK INTO MY HAND SEVERAL TIMES. KEEP IN MIND THAT I HATED VCDS WITH A PASSION AT THAT TIME, AND COULD BARELY LOOK AT THEM UNLESS THEY WERE SUPER CHEAP. YEARS AFTER, I CHANGED MY MIND AND WARMED UP TO THE FORMAT AS I REALIZED IT HAD BECOME THE ASIAN EQUIVALENT TO THE VHS FORMAT, WITH SEVERAL HONG KONG FILMS ONLY GETTING A VCD RELEASE.

A WHILE BACK I WAS DOING SOME LATE NIGHT SHOPPING FOR DVDS IN A SHOP IN HONG KONG, AND I STUMBLED ACROSS 2 DIFFERENT DVD VERSIONS OF THIS MOVIE AND PROCEEDED TO STARTLE THE SHOP KEEPER WITH MY LOUD YELP OF HAPPINESS. THE COVERS ON EVERY RELEASE OF THIS PICTURE DON'T DO THE MOVIE ANY JUSTICE, AND ONLY ADD TO THE DISJOINTED NATURE OF THE WHOLE THING. ONE DVD COVER MAKES THIS FILM LOOK LIKE A WAR FLICK, THE OTHER SUGGESTS A SUPERNATURAL PLOT, WHILE THE VCD COVER LOOKS LIKE A CORNBALL COMEDY. ANYWAY, MY HAPPINESS OVER THIS DVD DISCOVERY DID NOT LAST AS LONG AS I WOULD HAVE LIKED, AS I QUICKLY REALIZED THAT THE LOWLY VCD OF THIS FILM THAT I'D PREVIOUSLY BOUGHT WAS FAR SUPERIOR IN QUALITY.

IT HAD BEEN PUT ON MY SHELF AND BURIED UNDER A SMALL MOUNTAIN OF UNWATCHED MOVIES, AND THERE IT COLLECTED DUST. THEN ONE DAY I SAW IT LISTED ON A FELLOW FILM COLLECTOR'S TRADE LIST, WHERE IT WAS DESCRIBED AS A "SLOW HONG KONG COP FLICK WITH A CRAZY ENDING". EVEN WITH THAT MUNDANE REVIEW, SOMETHING GOT IN MY HEAD ABOUT WANTING TO WATCH IT. I DUSTED IT OFF, AND PUT IN THE FIRST DISC. I WOULDN'T SAY THIS FILM WAS AS TEDIOUS OR AS PAINFUL TO WATCH AS SOME PEOPLE CLAIM IT TO BE, BUT AS PROMISED, IT WAS SLOW. NOTHING TERRIBLE, JUST GENERIC.

JACKY CHEUNG AND TUNG WEI PLAY A COUPLE OF ZANY COPS OUT TO CATCH THE BAD GUYS. THE FILM STARTS AS YOUR TYPICAL HONG KONG BUDDY COP MOVIE, LOOKING LIKE IT'S GOING TO BE AN ACTION PICTURE, THEN DECIDES IT'S GOING TO BE A COMEDY. THEN, OUT OF NOWHERE AN INANE SUBPLOT POPS IN THAT DOES NOTHING BUT SLOW DOWN THE FILM AND COMES OFF AS PURE FILLER. THERE IS ONE SCENE, FOR INSTANCE, OF THE CHARACTERS PLAYING MAHJONG THAT SERVES NO PURPOSE. HOW THIS SCENE DIDN'T END UP ON THE CUTTING ROOM FLOOR (OR AS THEY CALL IT, "THE NG SECTION") IS BEYOND ME. EVERY SO OFTEN THE FILM HINTS THAT SOMETHING BIG IS GOING TO HAPPEN AND SOME MAJOR ACTION IS ABOUT TO KICK IN, BUT THEN JUST AS QUICKLY IT SLUMPS BACK.

NONCHALANTLY, I GOT UP AND PUT IN THE SECOND VCD DISC, WHICH CONTAINED THE SECOND HALF. WOW. WHAT A DIFFERENCE! IT'S ALMOST IF I WAS WATCHING A COMPLETELY DIFFERENT MOVIE. RIGHT OFF THE BAT THE PRODUCTION PICKS RIGHT UP AND TOWARDS A COMPLETELY DIFFERENT NIPPLE-TWISTER OF AN ENDING, ONE SURE TO PLEASE ACTION FANS. JUST AFTER THE ONE HOUR MARK WE GET AN AMAZING STUNT (WHERE A GUY GOES ONE-ON-ONE WITH A CAR ON THE HIGHWAY, AND USES A STREET SIGN CONNECTED WITH CHAINS SO HE CAN RAMP THE CAR IN THE AIR, AND BLAST IT WITH A SHOTGUN) WHICH REALLY SETS THE TONE. FROM THAT POINT ON, POM POM AND HOT HOT KICKS INTO HIGH GEAR, AND BEGINS ITS STEADY MIGRATION TOWARDS ITS EPIC AND STYLIZED FINALE THAT CALLS BACK TO THE GREATEST IN HEROIC BLOODSHED FROM HONG KONG. I'M NOT GOING TO SPOIL IT FOR YOU BECAUSE IT NEEDS TO BE SEEN TO BE BELIEVED. FRANKLY, THAT FIRST HALF JUST RELAXES YOUR SENSES AND THROWS YOU IN A FALSE SENSE OF TRANQUILITY, AND REALLY MAKES THE FILM'S EXPLOSIVE ENDING POP EVEN HARDER.

I REALIZE THIS IS FROM THE SAME DIRECTOR AS THE CRITICALLY THRASHED 'MY DAD IS A JERK' (1997), BUT WHAT GETS ME IS THAT 'POM POM AND HOT HOT' NOT ONLY GETS NO LOVE FROM ASIAN ACTION FILM FANS, IT HAS NEVER GOTTEN ATTENTION OF ANY KIND. WITH ALL MY FRIENDS AND OF ALL THE CONVERSATIONS I HAD WITH THEM ABOUT MOVIES OVER THE YEARS, I HAVE ONLY HAD TWO FRIENDS MENTION THIS FILM. THE FIRST ONE WAS VIA A SNIDE COMMENT ABOUT "MOVIE TITLES YOU WOULD ONLY SEE IN HONG KONG", AND THEN YEARS LATER THE SECOND ONE WAS FROM SOME EDITOR OF A LOCAL SMUT RAG ABOUT HOW GREAT THE ENDING WAS. (EDIT: HEY! THAT'S ME! — RB)

IT'S NO HARD TASK FOR A FILM TO GET LOST IN THE SURPLUS OF FILMS BEING MADE IN THE EARLY 1990S HONG KONG FILM BOOM. FROM THE LATE '80S UP TO THE EARLY '90S, THE INDUSTRY REACHED ITS PINNACLE. THE AMOUNT OF MOVIES MADE IN THE EARLY PART OF THAT DECADE WAS TRULY AMAZING, AND EVEN WITH MY OBSESSION FOR ASIAN CULT MOVIES, TO THIS DAY I'M STILL FINDING STUFF WAS MADE DURING THIS TIME THAT I NEVER HEARD OF BEFORE. UNFORTUNATELY THE BOOM DIDN'T LAST MORE THAN A FEW YEARS, AND WITH POOR DISTRIBUTION AND TERRIBLE HOME FORMAT RELEASES, 'POM POM AND HOT HOT' CLEARLY STRUGGLED TO GET ANY OF THE ATTENTION IT DESERVED.

WHEN FANS OF HONG KONG CINEMA TALK ABOUT LEGENDARY ACTION FILMS, THINGS LIKE TIGER ON BEAT (WITH ITS CHAINSAW-PACKED ENDING), THE WHOLE SLEW OF JOHN WOO AND JACKIE CHAN FILMS, AND THE ACTION CHOREOGRAPHY OF YUEN WOO PING ALWAYS GET BROUGHT UP. WHILE THESE OBVIOUSLY DESERVE THE RESPECT THEY ARE GIVEN, IT'S ANNOYING THAT SOMETHING AS EXCITING AS 'POM POM & HOT HOT' REMAINS SO NEGLECTED (AND ALMOST SHUNNED) BY THE FANS OF THE GENRE. CHECK OUT THE IMDB (GO AHEAD, I'LL WAIT). IT'S THE SO-CALLED MOVIE INFO HQ OF THE INTERNET AND WHAT IS THERE ABOUT THIS MOVIE? A WHOPPING TWO REVIEWS. IT DESERVES TO BE GIVEN SO MUCH MORE CREDIT.

—BOUGIE— 2014

SEMICORE

IN 1972'S PRIVATE PLEASURES OF A WOMAN, LYNN ROGERS (LYNN HARRIS) IS A SWEET LITTLE BRUNETTE TART THAT SHOWS UP IN SAN FRANCISCO TO GRIEVE AT THE FUNERAL OF HER UNCLE BRIAN. HIS BUXOM THIRD WIFE, THE PREDATORY SWISS "PHOTO MODEL", MARTINE (RUSS MEYER INGENUE, USCHI DIGARD) "ISN'T THE TYPE OF PERSON THAT PEOPLE LIKED. NOT OTHER WOMEN, AT ANY RATE." BUT AS IT TURNS OUT, BRIAN LEFT LYNN A RATHER LARGE SUM OF MONEY AND WHILE SHE'S WAITING FOR THE READING OF THE WILL, SHE DECIDES TO SHACK UP FOR A FEW DAYS AT MARTINE'S PAD. THAT IS WHEN THE TWO WOMEN REALIZE THEY HAVE SOMETHING IN COMMON.

WHILE LYNN IS SLEEPING, MARTINE SNEAKS INTO HER ROOM, STEALS ONE OF HER SHOES, AND THEN MASTURBATES WITH IT. (GOD, I HATE IT WHEN MY ROOMMATES CAN'T KEEP THEIR HANDS OFF MY STUFF) INTRIGUED BY THIS ODD BEHAVIOUR, LYNN FOLLOWS MARTINE BACK TO HER ROOM AND PEEPS ON THE OVER-SEXED HARLOT IN THE MIDST OF HER BIZARRE HUSH PUPPY SHOE-LOVE SESSION. AND IT'S WHILE LYNN IS STANDING AROUND GAWKING AT THIS, THAT WE GET SOME OF MY FAVOURITE NARRATION IN THE MOVIE:

"IMAGINE, THAT SEXY DARLING WAS AFRAID TO MAKE HER DESIRES KNOWN. I GUESS SHE WAS AFRAID I'D BE SHOCKED. LITTLE DID SHE KNOW WE BOTH CAME FROM THE SAME GUTTER. IN COLLEGE I WAS ONE OF THE FOUNDING MEMBERS OF THE SEXUAL FREEDOM LEAGUE. SHE WAS A BIZARRE CREATURE INDEED, MOVING WITH HOT, QUICK ANIMAL-LIKE PASSION. A BITCH SET ON FIRE BY HER OWN STRANGE DEVICES. HOT, HOT, HOTTER! SOON THE VOLCANO WOULD GO OFF. THE TOP WOULD BE BLOWN SKY HIGH! GO, MARTINE! GO! GO! GO! GO!"

THE LESBIAN PULP NOVEL NARRATION (WITH ITS MANY LANGUID DESCRIPTIONS OF THE DEPRAVITY PLAYING OUT ON SCREEN) MAY OCCASIONALLY BE LAUGHABLE, BUT DIRECTOR NICK PHILLIPS IS SERIOUS WITH HIS CAMERA. HE UNDERSTANDS WHAT IS SEXY, AND TEASES US WITH IT. A FREE FORM JAZZ SCORE BOBS ALONG WITH THE NARRATION OF THE MOVIE, VERY MUCH IN THE STYLE OF THE BLACK AND WHITE SEXPLOITATION SHOT IN NEW YORK A DECADE EARLIER. THESE VISUALS MAY BE POST-HIPPIE CALIFORNIA, BUT THE BREATHY AUDIO IS POST-BEATNIK VIA A LITTLE BASEMENT CLUB IN GREENWICH VILLAGE.

PRIVATE PLEASURES OF A WOMAN IS OFTEN REFERRED TO AS A HARDCORE PORN MOVIE, BUT IT'S TECHNICALLY SOFTCORE -- SEEING AS IT LACKS GRAPHIC PENETRATION. BUT I ALSO CAN'T DENY THAT IT CROSSES OVER WITH THE COPIOUS AMOUNT OF GENITALS ON DISPLAY AND HOW THE PERFORMERS TAKE PART IN THE SO-CALLED "SIMULATED" SEX. LOOK, IT'S TOTALLY OBVIOUS THAT THEY'RE ACTUALLY GOING AT IT, BUT IN THE EARLY 1970S THERE WAS A LOT OF CONCERN FOR THE QUESTIONABLE LEGALITY OF SHOWING EVERYTHING TOO BLATANTLY. IN THAT RESPECT, THIS FALLS INTO A HALF-HARD SUBGENRE I'VE DUBBED "SEMICORE". IT'S SOMETHING THAT NEEDED A NAME, SO I'VE GONE AHEAD AND NAMED IT.

WHAT IS "SEMICORE"? NO, IT'S NOT PORN FILMS ABOUT TRUCK DRIVERS. A "SEMI" IS SLANG FOR AN ERECT PENIS THAT ISN'T ALL THAT HARD, OR A SOFT DICK THAT IS ONLY PARTIALLY ERECT. SO WITH THAT IN MIND, SEMICORE IS A SOFTCORE FILM THAT DOESN'T QUITE GO ALL THE WAY IN SHOWING GRAPHIC PENETRATION, BUT DOES SHOW PRETTY MUCH EVERYTHING ELSE. SOME SEMICORE EFFORTS EVEN GO SO FAR AS TO SHOW FLEETING IMAGERY OF A GRAPHIC BLOWJOB, BUT NONE OF THE OTHER DIRTY DETAILS ARE PUT ON OVERT DISPLAY.

BOUGIE
2013

PRIVATE PLEASURES OF A WOMAN

SO YEAH, SEMICORE: ABOUT AS HARD AS A SOFTCORE SEX FILM CAN GET. IT'S A SEX FILM SUBGENRE PERFECTLY SUITED TO LADIES (OR SENSITIVE GENTLEMEN) WHO ARE A LITTLE TURNED OFF BY THE GYNECOLOGICAL ASPECTS OF XXX, BUT FIND THE SOFTCORE FILMS A LITTLE SILLY WITH ALL THEIR OVERTLY FAKE LOVE SCENES WHERE THE GUY KEEPS HIS UNDERWEAR ON, OR WHERE SIMPLY RUBBING NAKED TORSOS TOGETHER SEEMS TO BE USED AS A SUBSTITUTE FOR FUCKING. I LIKE THESE MOVIES, BECAUSE THEY ARE A HAPPY MEDIUM BETWEEN THE TWO, BUT THEY ARE ALSO A TYPE OF SEX FILM THAT HAS NEVER BEEN REALLY DISSECTED. UNTIL NOW, THAT IS.

"WHEN BRITISH DISTRIBUTORS WERE FIRST STARTING TO GET BRIEF MOMENTS OF HARDCORE PASSED BY THE CENSORS IN THE LATE '90S (NO CLOSE-UPS, BRIEF SHOTS, ETC) THE TERM THEY USED WAS MEDIUMCORE", SLEAZE FILM EXPERT DAVID FLINT INFORMED ME IN 2014. "BUT YOUR TERM, SEMICORE, HAS A BIT MORE SNAP TO IT!"

SEMICORE MOVIES HAD THEIR HEYDAY IN THE LATE 1960S AND EARLY '70S, AT A TIME WHEN FILMMAKERS WERE JUST ON THE CUSP OF BEING ABLE TO MAKE HARDCORE MOVIES WITH LITTLE FEAR OF BEING LOCKED UP FOR IT, BUT WEREN'T ENTIRELY SURE IF THEY HAD THE LEGAL RIGHT TO DO SO. THEY WERE OFTEN EVIDENCE OF A MOVIE MAKER TESTING THE WATER, DIPPING HIS/HER TOE IN THE HARDCORE POOL BEFORE DIVING IN. IN OTHER CASES, THEY WERE MADE IN THE LATE '70S OR '80S, AND RELEASED TO GRAB SOME OF THAT SWEET SEXY MONEY, BUT CAME JUST SHORT OF HARDCORE IN ORDER NOT TO KILL THEIR ABILITY TO BE EASILY DISTRIBUTED VIA DRIVE-INS AND GRINDHOUSES THAT DIDN'T SHOW PORN.

"THERE IS AN INTRIGUING TRANSITION ERA IT SEEMS", ADULT FILM HISTORIAN AND JOURNALIST DIMITRIOS OTIS MENTIONED TO ME. "A TIME WHEN THERE WAS EXPLICIT SEX SHOWN BUT IT HADN'T GONE FULLY HARDCORE -- BLOW-JOB BUT NO PENETRATION, OR PENETRATION BUT NO MONEYSHOT. THIS ALSO HAPPENED LATER WITH RADLEY METZGER'S THE IMAGE. AND I WAS ALWAYS FASCINATED BY HOW RUSS MEYER MANAGED TO GET SO CLOSE TO XXX, ESPECIALLY IN BENEATH THE VALLEY OF THE ULTRA VIXENS, WITHOUT IT BEING AT ALL HARDCORE."

DESPITE BEING AN OUTSPOKEN CRITIC OF HARDCORE MOVIES IN THEIR EARLY YEARS, PRODUCER DAVE FRIEDMAN EVENTUALLY RELENTED AND RELEASED PORN FILMS SUCH AS 7 INTO SNOWY AND MATINEE IDOL ONCE HE REALIZED HOW MUCH MONEY COULD BE MADE. BUT BEFORE THAT, HE DABBLED IN THE ART OF HARDENING HIS SOFTCORE FARE, AS IS EVIDENCED BY MOVIES LIKE THE EROTIC ADVENTURES OF ZORRO.

HE ONCE SAID "ONE ALMOST HARDCORE SCENE COULD SELL A MOVIE BACK THEN. EVERYONE WOULD BE TALKING ABOUT IT. DID THEY OR DIDN'T THEY SEE? THEY HAD TO GO BACK AND SEE IT AGAIN TO FIND OUT." HE MADE A GOOD LIVING ON THAT CONCEPT IN THE 1970S.

THERE ARE ALSO A DECENT AMOUNT OF SEMICORE RELEASES FROM THE 1990S AND BEYOND AS WELL, ALTHOUGH I'M GOING TO FOCUS MORE HERE ON THE CLASSIC MATERIAL. BESIDES, MANY OF THE SO-CALLED SOFTCORE MOVIES ONE COULD FIND ON AMERICAN CABLE TV DURING THAT ERA WERE IN FACT, RE-EDITS OF HARDCORE RELEASES. THERE WERE ALSO THE MOVIES OF EURO SEX MAVENS ERWIN DIETRICH, JESS FRANCO AND JOE D'AMATO, AND A LARGE AMOUNT OF THE 1970S AND '80S JAPANESE NIKKATSU PINK SEX FILMS ARE ALSO REALLY EXCELLENT EXAMPLES OF SEMICORE.

IF YOU DUG PRIVATE PLEASURES OF A WOMAN, THE ORGY MACHINE (1972) IS YET ANOTHER SEMICORE FILM STARRING MASSIVE-CHESTED USCHI DIGARD. YES SIR, SHE WAS INFAMOUS AS A DYNAMITE SOFTCORE PERFORMER WHO WORKED WITH THE BEST DIRECTORS IN THAT GENRE, BUT LOOK CAREFULLY AT HER FUCK SCENE IN THIS LOOP-CARRIER. IT'S PRETTY OBVIOUS THAT HER COSTAR BANGS HER BUT GOOD, AND EVEN FINISHES INSIDE HER. STEAMY, STEAMY STUFF. WITH A CAPITAL 'S', MAN...

'THE PIGKEEPER'S DAUGHTER'

She brought new meaning to the phrase "DRIVING A HARD BARGAIN"!

SOME OTHER NOTEWORTHY AND RECOMMENDABLE VINTAGE AMERICAN SEMICORE ARE AS FOLLOWS: A SCREAM IN THE STREETS (AKA GIRLS IN THE STREETS 1973) BY DIRECTOR CARL MONSON, THE PIGKEEPER'S DAUGHTER (1972) AND THE DIRTY MIND OF YOUNG SALLY (1973) BY BETHEL BUCKALEW, THE LOVE GARDEN (1971) AND THE ALL-AMERICAN GIRL (1973) BY MARK HAGGARD, AND THERE IS ALSO ROBERT CARAMICO'S SEX RITUALS OF THE OCCULT (1970).

BAT PUSSY (1973), WHICH WAS BY AN ANONYMOUS DIRECTOR, IS AN INTERESTING EXAMPLE OF A HOMEMADE LOOP-STYLE SEMICORE RELEASE. AS MY ONLINE PAL JOHN KOSTKA SO APTLY PUT IT "IT'S OSTENSIBLY HARDCORE, BUT 90% OF IT IS ORAL SHOT FROM HALFWAY ACROSS THE ROOM WITH THE CHICK'S HEAD IN THE WAY, SO IT ENDS UP BEING BARELY EVEN A PORNO MOVIE."

"IT'S BEEN SAID THAT THIS IS THE WORST PORN FLICK OF ALL TIME, AND WHILE THAT'S ONE HELL OF A BOLD STATEMENT I CAN'T HELP BUT AGREE." WROTE DRIVE-IN FREAK IN 2012. "UGLY PEOPLE TOO DRUNK TO GET IT ON AND NOT INTO EACH OTHER AT ALL ARGUE FOR THE VAST MAJORITY OF THIS FLICK'S RUNNING TIME. YOU HEAR A BELCH IN THE BACKGROUND AT ONE POINT, AND OCCASIONALLY THE 'ACTOR' LOOKS UP AND ASKS THE DIRECTOR, 'WHAT?' THEN THE SOUND GOES BLANK."

AND THAT'S BEFORE A CHICK IN A BATMAN COSTUME SHOWS UP

(AFTER RIDING ACROSS TOWN ON ONE OF THOSE HIPPITY-HOP BOUNCY BALLS KIDS USED TO BOUNCE AROUND ON IN THE OLD DAYS) AND HAS SEX WITH A GUY WHILE HIS WIFE WHINES ABOUT IT. "IT'S A BONER-KILLER" WROTE ADRIAN MACK IN 2009. "MORE THAN THAT, IT'S THE BONER-KILLER OF ALL TIME. THE FILM THE CELLULOID UPON WHICH THE IMAGE SITS ACTUALLY APPEARS TO BE STAGNANT OR MOLDY, AND SO DO THE PERFORMERS. IF YOU COULD CALL THEM 'PERFORMERS'. WHICH YOU CAN'T, SINCE THEY'RE INCAPABLE OF EITHER ACTING OR FUCKING. BUT THAT ASIDE, IT'S THE WRETCHED QUALITY OF THE PICTURE THAT HITS YOU FIRST, LIKE A WAVE OF NAUSEA UNDERWRITTEN BY AN ATTACK OF HYGIENE PANIC."

AND FROM ONE OF THE WORST SEMICORE MOVIES OF ALL TIME WE BOUND RIGHT OVER TO ONE OF THE ALL-TIME BEST. BUTTERFLIES (AKA BUTTERFLY, AKA BABY TRAMP, 1975) IS CERTAINLY ONE OF THE PINNACLES OF DIRECTOR JOE SARNO'S CAREER AS A PORNOGRAPHER, AND HE'S A MAN WHO IS UNIVERSALLY ACCLAIMED AS ONE OF THE FIVE MOST ACCOMPLISHED SEX-FILM DIRECTORS OF THE 1960S

BAT PUSSY

AND 1970S. IT'S REALLY A GORGEOUS MOVIE (WHICH WAS ORIGINALLY SHOT HARDCORE, AND THEN TRIMMED IN POST BY SARNO, SO AS TO PUT MORE OF A FOCUS ON THE ACTING AND STORYLINE), AND ONE THAT I WOULD RECOMMEND TO EVERYONE WITH EVEN A PASSING INTEREST IN EROTIC MOVIES FROM THIS ERA.

THE MOVIE INTRODUCES A 19-YEAR-OLD BLONDE MARIE FORSA (AKA MARIA FORSA) "THE NEW SWEDISH TEENAGE SEX GODDESS", WHO STARS AS BIBI, THE OVER-SEXED RESTLESS COUNTRY GIRL WHO TIRES OF HER BOYFRIEND (ERIC EDWARDS), AND YEARNS FOR SOMETHING MORE EXCITING. YES, IT'S THAT CLICHE STORY OF THE RURAL GIRL WHO WANTS TO BE A MODEL AND TRAVELS TO THE BIG CITY, BUT THE CLICHE IS AT ITS BEST HERE -- AND THAT DOES COUNT FOR SOMETHING. BESIDES, IN 1975 I DON'T KNOW THAT THIS STORYLINE WAS QUITE SUCH A STANDARDIZED PART OF PORN YET, AND ITS IMPORTANT TO JUDGE THESE THINGS IN CONTEXT.

PACKING HER BAGS AND SETTING OUT FOR MUNICH VIA HER HITCHHIKED RIDES WITH STRANGERS, BIBI MEETS AMERICAN STUD, FRANK (PLAYED BY HARRY REEMS) WHO PLAYS A WOMANIZING NIGHTCLUB OWNER WHO IS UP TO HIS ARMPITS IN PUSSY BUT STILL CAN'T SEEM TO GET ENOUGH. HIGHLY SKILLED IN THE ART OF CHARMING YOUNG GIRLS, BIBI IS NO MATCH FOR HARRY, AND SHE FALLS UNDER HIS SPELL. AT THIS POINT THE FILM CHANGES AND BECOMES ABOUT REEMS'S CHARACTER. IT'S AN INTERESTING NARRATIVE CHOICE, BECAUSE IT REVEALS HOW A LIFE LED WITH NOTHING BUT LUST-FILLED ONE NIGHT STANDS BECOMES FRUITLESS AND BORING. YOUNG BIBI BECOMES JUST ONE MORE PRETTY CONQUEST THAT IS USED AND TOSSED AWAY BY THE

TODAY THE MEN & BOYS... TOMORROW THE WORLD!

The All-American Girl

Starring
PEGGY CHURCH

IN COLOR

Directed & Written by
MARK HAGGARD

Produced by
ROLAND MILLER

Executive Producer
ROBERT C. CHINN

Music by
DON DUNN

ADULTS ONLY
NO ONE UNDER
18 ADMITTED

A
MANUEL S. CONDE
RELEASE
HOLLYWOOD, CALIF. U.S.A.

ULTIMATELY UNHAPPY REEMS, AND IT MAKES FOR THOUGHT-PROVOKING VIEWING SEEING THE TWO OF THEM COME TO THAT DISILLUSIONED REALIZATION. IT'S A SORT OF DOWNBEAT FINALE, BUT IT FEELS RIGHT. IT FEELS APPROPRIATE TO ME.

THE SEX SCENES (FEATURING FORSA'S UNFAKED ORGASMS) GRACEFULLY UNSPOOL WITHOUT MUSIC TO COVER UP THE LEGIT SEXY FUCK SOUNDS TAKING PLACE, A SMART IDEA THAT MOST PORNOGRAPHERS NEVER SEEM TO FIGURE OUT. BESIDES, THERE IS PLENTY OF OTHER PLOT-HEAVY SCENES WHERE MUSIC CAN BE APTLY USED. SARNO MAKES THE MOST OF THAT OPPORTUNITY TO PIPE IN SOME COOL GERMAN ROCK MUSIC. ON TOP OF THAT, THE CINEMATOGRAPHY IS IMPECCABLE, AND THE LIGHTING AND STYLISH COSTUMES ARE ALSO TOP NOTCH. THE CRITICS AT THE TIME WENT WILD, RIGHTFULLY IGNORING THE FACT THAT AUDIENCES WEREN'T EXACTLY GOING TO FLOCK TO SEE A NON XXX ADULT FILM NOW THAT WET GRAPHIC CONTENT WAS IN THEATERS.

"SUPERB!!! MILES APART FROM THE REST. RATED 92%!" —AL GOLDSTEIN'S MAG.

"AN ACHIEVEMENT!!!" —MOVIE WATCH/ CHANNEL J

"WINS BEST PERFORM- ANCE!" — WHBI RADIO

"RARE!!!" —HIGH SOCIETY

"A MASTER- PIECE!" —ELITE MAG.

"THE FINEST PORNO MATCH-UPS OF ALL TIME. RATED FULL!" —HUSTLER

"MOST DESIR- ABLE WOMEN OF THE YEAR!" —GALLERY

OPENS TOM'W

Butterfly

INTRODUCING **MARIA FORSA** THE NEW SWEDISH TEENAGE SEX GODDESS

X
IN COLOR FOR LADIES AND GENTLEMEN OVER 21 BOX OFFICE OPENS 9:45 A.M. LATE SHOW EVERY NIGHT

EXCLUSIVELY AT **PUSSYCAT CINEMA** THE "COUPLES" THEATER BROADWAY AT 49th ST. 582-2725 —FULLY AIR-CONDITIONED— —NOT TO BE CONFUSED— WITH ANY OTHER THEATER IN THE UNITED STATES

LAST DAY China de Sade

FORSA IS MAGNIFICENT -- PURE FEMALE SEXUALITY PERSONIFIED. SHE IS TENDER-YET-INSATIABLE WITH ALL OF HER PARTNERS IN THIS FILM, BUT ESPECIALLY IN THE SEQUENCES WITH ERIC EDWARDS. IT'S APPARENT TO ANYONE WHO WATCHES BUTTERFLIES THAT THE TWO OF THEM FELL DEEPLY IN LUST OFF SCREEN AS WELL, A FACT VERIFIED BY EDWARDS IN LINDA J. ALEXANDER'S 2003 BOOK, DOROTHY FROM KANSAS MEETS THE WIZARD OF X. "MARIA AND I HAD A FLING", EDWARDS WAS QUOTED AS SAYING. "IT WAS WONDERFUL. SHE WAS JUST MY STYLE. WHENEVER I'D GO BACK TO EUROPE, WE COULDN'T HELP OURSELVES. WE SCREWED EVERYWHERE -- OUT IN THE BUSHES, IN THE JACUZZI, ANYWHERE WE COULD, EVEN IN DANGEROUS PLACES WHERE YOU COULD GET CAUGHT SUCH AS IN A PUBLIC POOL WHERE PEOPLE COULD WALK IN AT ANY TIME. WE'D DO IT FIVE OR SIX TIMES A DAY."

A YEAR EARLIER, AUDIENCES WERE TREATED TO SCORE (1974) BY WAY OF MASTER EROTICA DIRECTOR RADLEY METZGER. WHAT HE PRODUCED HERE IS ONE OF THE HARDER SEMICORE FILMS -- IN FACT THE UNCUT VERSION IS HARD ENOUGH THAT ONE COULD CONFUSE IT RATHER EASILY WITH A HARDCORE MOVIE. BY 1974, RADLEY'S NAME WAS SYNONYMOUS WITH HIGH END SMUT, AS HE'D FOUND MAINSTREAM SUCCESS AND CRITICAL RECOGNITION BY EVEN ART-HOUSE CRITICS, AND A PERMANENT HOME FOR HIS FILMS IN THE COLLECTION OF THE NEW YORK MUSEUM OF MODERN ART. BUT THEN IN THE EARLY 1970S, ALL THE RULES WERE CHANGED. DEEP THROAT WAS RELEASED, WAS ONE OF THE BIGGEST THEATRICAL BLOCKBUSTERS IN FILM HISTORY, AND THE EROTIC FILMMAKING LANDSCAPE TRANSFORMED. SOFT CORE CUDDLING WOULDN'T CUT IT ANYMORE. METZGER WAS FORCED TO ADAPT OR DIE.

BEFORE LEAPING INTO SHOOTING UNCENSORED FUCKY-SUCKY CINEMA UNDER HIS NOM-DE-PORN, HENRY PARIS, METZGER WOULD TEST THE WATERS UNDER HIS REAL NAME WITH SCORE. HE'D INCLUDE A COUPLE SHOTS OF HARDCORE TO HELP ENSURE DECENT BOX OFFICE, BUT FOR THE MOST PART THE PROJECT WOULD DELVE INTO THE MORE CEREBRAL POLITICS OF SEXUAL CONQUEST. IT IS TODAY RECOGNIZED AS ONE OF HIS FINER ACHIEVEMENTS, BUT RADLEY REMEMBERS IT PLAYING TO POORLY ATTENDED GRINDHOUSES IN TIMES SQUARE WHILE THE NEW WAVE OF WALL-TO-WALL FULL-PENETRATION XXX PACKED THEM IN RIGHT NEXT DOOR. DESPITE DECENT REVIEWS, THE MOVIE TANKED.

A SEX-OBSESSED PAIR OF MARRIED SWINGERS NAMED ELVIRA (CLAIRE WILBUR) AND JACK (GERALD GRANT) ARE INTO BEDROOM CONQUESTS AND CONCOCT A GAME TO SEE WHICH OF THE TWO OF THEM CAN BED THE MOST SAME-SEX PARTNERS. THERE IS A TIME LIMIT SET IN WHICH THEY HAVE TO SEDUCE A TARGET, AND A POINT IS SCORED WHEN THE PREY IS FELLED. STRAIT-LACED VANILLA-TYPES ARE THE FAR BIGGER CHALLENGE, AND ELVIRA AND JACK HAVE BEEN PLAYING THIS GAME LONG ENOUGH THAT THE CHALLENGE IS HALF THE FUN.

YOU SEE, ELVIRA HAS SET HER SIGHTS ON A NAIVE NEWLYWED NAMED BETSY (LYNN LOWRY). A VIRGINAL WIDE-EYED DOE, BETSY'S CHILD-LIKE INNOCENCE PROVIDES A SERIOUS OBSTACLE, BUT LEADING BY EXAMPLE -- FUCKING A TELEPHONE REPAIR MAN (CARL PARKER) ON THE LIVING ROOM FLOOR RIGHT IN FRONT OF THE ASTONISHED YOUNG WOMAN -- PLAYS THE SLUTTY FREE-LOVE CARD, FOR BETTER OR WORSE.

NOT JUST SEX SIMPLY FOR THE SAKE OF SLIPPERY BLOOD-ENGORGED GENITALS, METZGER'S MOVIE IS AN ABSOLUTE LOVE LETTER TO THE BISEXUAL LIFESTYLE, AND INDEED, IT WAS ONE OF THE FIRST FILMS TO EVER EXPLORE BISEXUAL

TOTALLY DIFFERENT!

Come to a deliciously wild weekend of "mixed doubles!"

"SCORE"

with Claire Wilbur / Calvin Culver / Lynn Lowry / Gerald Grant / Carl Parker
screenplay by Jerry Douglas / Eastmancolor / directed by Radley Metzger
an Audubon Films Release

RELATIONSHIPS. BASED ON AN OFF-BROADWAY STAGE PLAY THAT RAN FOR 23 PERFORMANCES AT NEW YORK'S MARTINIQUE THEATRE FROM OCTOBER 28 TO NOVEMBER 15, 1971, METZGER MOVED THE SETTING FROM A SHABBY QUEENS APARTMENT TO A MYSTERIOUS AND ELEGANT EUROPEAN SEA-SIDE COMMUNITY (WHICH WAS IN ACTUALITY, YUGOSLAVIA).

LYNN LOWRY, AS THE PURE AND VIRTUOUS LITTLE LAMB, IS THE GLUE THAT HOLDS THIS MOVIE TOGETHER. 24 AT THE TIME OF FILMING, LOWRY HAD A PERSONAL GOAL TO VISIT EUROPE BEFORE SHE HIT 25, SO WHEN THE ATLANTA, GEORGIA NATIVE GOT THE NEWS THAT SHE'D LANDED THE PART, IT WAS A DREAM COME TRUE. THAT DREAM WOULDN'T TAKE LONG TO SOUR, THOUGH. SHE WOULDN'T EVEN GET TO TOUCH DOWN BEFORE THE DRAMA STARTED. SHE AND THE ACTRESS THAT SHE WAS SCRIPTED TO BE SO INTIMATE WITH, CLAIRE WILBUR, HAD A FALLING OUT ON THE PLANE RIDE OVER WHEN LOWRY REVEALED THAT SHE WAS MAKING MORE THAN THE REST OF THE CAST, WHILE NAIVELY THINKING THEY WERE BEING PAID AN EQUAL SALARY.

"WE HAD A LOT OF TROUBLE IN THE LOVE SCENES," LOWRY REVEALED TO INTERVIEWER MICHAEL BOWEN. "BECAUSE SHE DIDN'T WANT ME TO TOUCH HER, AND YOU KNOW, WE'RE SUPPOSED TO BE HAVING ORAL SEX... THEN RADLEY ASKED ME IF I WANTED TO DO SOME AMYL NITRATE, WHICH WAS PART OF THE WHOLE SCENE, I HAD NEVER DONE IT, AND I THOUGHT 'OH, WHAT COULD IT BE? IT'LL BE FUN'. SO I TOOK IT, AND OF COURSE IT MAKES YOU REALLY ABANDONED AND KINDA WILD. WE WERE KISSING AND I GOT MY HANDS ALL TANGLED UP IN HER HAIR, AND REALLY MESSED IT UP. SHE WAS FURIOUS WITH ME. IT MADE EVERYTHING BETWEEN US A LOT WORSE. THE WHOLE SEX SCENE TOOK DAYS TO SHOOT, AND IT WAS REALLY UNPLEASANT BECAUSE WE HATED EACH OTHER."

A LOVELY, CLASSY WOMAN THAT IMPRESSED METZGER GREATLY, CLAIRE WILBUR WAS THE ONLY MEMBER OF THE ORIGINAL CAST OF THE STAGE PLAY BROUGHT OVER TO REPRISE HER ROLE FOR THE FILM VERSION. EVEN ORIGINAL CAST MEMBER SYLVESTER STALLONE (YEARS BEFORE HIS SUPERSTARDOM) DIDN'T MAKE THE CUT, AS RADLEY FELT HIS ELEGANCE-FREE BROOKLYN-ESQUE PERSONA AND ACCENT DIDN'T FIT THE CONTINENTAL EUROPEAN SETTING. SADLY, CLAIRE WILBUR WAS DIAGNOSED WITH LUNG CANCER IN 2003 AND PASSED AWAY IN HER UPPER EAST SIDE APARTMENT IN MANHATTAN ON MAY 20, 2004.

LOOKING BACK ON MAKING SCORE TODAY, LYNN LOWRY IS ALL SMILES. SHE HAS FOND MEMORIES AND HEAPS OF PRAISE FOR HER CO-STARS AND HER DIRECTOR, BUT AT THE TIME IT WAS A VERY DIFFERENT SITUATION:

"ON 42ND STREET, IN THE PORNO DISTRICT, SCORE CAME OUT AND WAS AN X-RATED FILM. I WENT TO SEE THE MOVIE AND WAS SHOCKED. AT THAT POINT I WANTED TO BECOME A LEGITIMATE ACTRESS, AND I DIDN'T WANT ANYONE TO EVER SEE ANY OF THESE MOVIES WHERE I HAD DONE NUDITY. SUDDENLY, NOT ONLY AM I SEEING THIS MOVIE WITH ME DOING ALL THIS NUDITY, BUT I'M SEEING THE TWO MEN ACTUALLY HAVING SEX, AND I WAS JUST SO UPSET, BECAUSE I NEVER THOUGHT THE FILM WAS GOING TO BE THAT WAY."

AHH YES, THE UGLY SOCIAL STIGMA OF HARDCORE HAD REARED ITS UGLY HEAD ONCE AGAIN. THAT CAN BE A TOUGH PILL TO SWALLOW. IF ONLY THE CONCEPT OF SEMICORE AS A GENRE HAD EXISTED IN 1975, PERHAPS IT WOULDN'T HAVE TAKEN LOWRY 20 YEARS TO GET COMFORTABLE WITH HER APPEARANCE IN THE FILM.

— BOUGIE 2014

TURKEY SHOOT (AKA "ESCAPE 2000. AUSTALIA. 1982)

"FREEDOM IS OBEDIENCE, OBEDIENCE IS WORK, WORK IS LIFE." -- CHARLES THATCHER

IT'S THE WRETCHED TOTALITARIAN FUTURE, AND YOUNG "SOCIAL DEVIANTS" ARE ROUNDED UP, PUT IN MATCHING YELLOW JUMP SUITS, AND DRIVEN TO A REMOTE, NIGHTMARISH, CO-ED PRISON CAMP (YES, THEY SHOWER TOGETHER) AS PUNISHMENT FOR THEIR VARIOUS MINOR INDISCRETIONS. HERE THEY ARE TORTURED AND MISTREATED, AND IF SOMEONE STEPS OUT OF LINE, THE POMPOUS CAMP COMMANDER CHARLES THATCHER (YEAH, THEY NAMED HIM AFTER MARGARET THATCHER) GOES AHEAD AND -- PURELY FOR SHITS AND GIGGLES -- RELEASES THE MALCONTENTS INTO THE NEARBY WILDERNESS WHERE HE AND HIS HIGH CLASS PALS HUNT THEM FOR SPORT. THE RULES ARE PRETTY SIMPLE: IF THE CHARACTERS PLAYED BY STEVE RAILSBACK, OLIVIA HUSSEY, LYNDA STONER, AND JOHN LEY CAN RUN FAST ENOUGH AND MAKE IT OUT OF THE WOODS, THERE WILL BE A FULL PARDON FOR ALL THEIR "CRIMES". IF THEY'RE CAUGHT, THEY'RE DOG FOOD.

THE HUNTING OF HUMAN PREY AS PART OF AN ORGANIZED GAME IS A TIME HONOURED GENRE FILM STAPLE, AND IS OFTEN QUITE ENTERTAINING AS A PLOT DEVICE, BUT TURKEY SHOOT MAKES THINGS EVEN MORE INTERESTING BY GIVING THE FIVE HUNTERS THEIR OWN CARTOONISHLY WILD WEAPONRY AND DIFFERENT PERSONALITIES ONLY BROUGHT TOGETHER BY THEIR WILLINGNESS TO PAY BIG BUCKS FOR HUMAN TARGET PRACTICE. THERE'S THE SNOTTY, UPPER-CRUST

STEVE RAILSBACK GETS STABBY WHEN HE MEETS THE WOLFMAN

OLIVIA HUSSEY AND ROGER WARD

LESBIAN WHO CARRIES AROUND A CROSSBOW THAT SHOOTS EXPLOSIVE ARROWS, A FAT POLITICIAN WHO ONLY LIKES HUNTING DEFENCELESS WOMEN, THE HULKING PRISON GUARD PLAYED BY ROGER WARD, AND THE DOUCHE-NOZZLE NAMED 'TITO' THAT TOOTLES AROUND IN THE AUSTRALIAN OUTBACK IN A FUCKING MINI-BULLDOZER, RIDING UPON WHICH IS HIS PET WOLF-MAN. YOU READ THAT RIGHT... HIS PET WOLF-MAN ~ AND OL' WOLFY EATS HUMAN TOES LIKE YOU AND I EAT DORITOS. (BOUGIE STOPS WRITING TO SQUEAL WITH GLEE).

THE FIRST THIRD OF TURKEY SHOOT IS FAIRLY SLOW GOING SO DON'T GET DISTRACTED AND START TEXTING OR SOMETHING STUPID. THIS IS TIME USED (AND WELL SPENT) TO REALLY GET ACROSS JUST WHAT OUR MAIN CHARACTERS ARE ABOUT AND HOW NASTY THE VILE PIGS WHO RUN CAMP THATCHER ARE. OF COURSE, ONCE THE "MOST DANGEROUS GAME" BEGINS, THE PACE QUICKENS AND EVERYTHING GETS 5X MORE RIDICULOUS. I'VE READ/HEARD MULTIPLE SUPPOSEDLY INTELLIGENT GENRE FILM CRITICS COMPLAIN ABOUT THE SLOW START IN THIS ONE, BUT PERSONALLY I REALLY FUCKING LIKE THAT SORT OF BUILD UP IN EXPLOITATION FILMS. IF IT'S JUST PURE CRAZINESS FROM BEGINNING TO END, IT'S TOO MUCH LIKE EATING ALL YOUR HALLOWEEN CANDY IN ONE SITTING OR READING A BOOK WHERE EVERY SENTENCE ENDS IN AN EXCLAMATION POINT. A LITTLE LESS OF A GOOD THING IS SOMETIMES EXACTLY WHAT THE (MAD) DOCTOR ORDERED FOR EFFECTIVE CINEMATIC DELIRIUM, ESPECIALLY IF IT ALL COMES TO A GLORIOUS GORE-SOAKED FINALE LIKE TURKEY SHOOT DOES. Yummy.

THERE ARE A LOT OF GREAT TRIVIA TITBITS ABOUT THIS MOVIE IN MARK HARTLEY'S INCREDIBLE 2008 DOCUMENTARY ABOUT AUSTRALIAN GENRE FILMS ENTITLED NOT QUITE HOLLYWOOD, BUT MY FAVOURITE ARE THE ONES ABOUT SHY BRITISH STAR OLIVIA HUSSEY, WHO WAS TOTALLY MISERABLE WHILE ON LOCATION. OLIVIA WAS TOTALLY STRESSED THAT THE WILDLIFE IN AUSTRALIA WAS GOING TO KILL HER AT ANY MOMENT IF SHE LET HER GUARD DOWN. I LOVE THE AMAZING ANECDOTE ABOUT WHEN SHE NEARLY CUT OFF ACTOR ROGER WARD'S HANDS IN

A SCENE WHERE EXACTLY THAT WAS SUPPOSED TO HAPPEN -- BUT WITH EFFECTS AND THE MOVIE MAGIC OF TRICK EDITING. UNFORTUNATELY FOR ROGER, WHEN DIRECTOR BRIAN TRENCHARD-SMITH YELLED "CUT!" AT THE END OF THEIR SCENE, HUSSEY THOUGHT HE MEANT TO DO SO WITH HER MACHETE, LEAVING HER UNFORTUNATE AND UNPREPARED CO-STAR TO PULL HIS HANDS OUT OF THE WAY WITH BARELY A SECOND TO SPARE. THE CAST INTERVIEWS AND AUDIO COMMENTARY FROM NOT QUITE HOLLYWOOD ALSO PROVIDES DETAILS ABOUT THE MANY OTHER RISKY MOMENTS THE CAST WENT THROUGH INCLUDING (ALLEGEDLY) GETTING SHOT AT WITH REAL BULLETS TO ADD AUTHENTICITY (!!!).

SADLY, THIS VIOLENT CAMPY CLASSIC WAS NOT A BIG SUCCESS ON ITS HOME TURF, AND WAS SAVAGED BY CRITICS AT THE TIME OF ITS RELEASE. TO THIS DAY IT CONTINUES TO GET SHIT FOR BEING EXPLOITIVE AND CRASS IN THE WAY IT GETS BORDERLINE PORNOGRAPHIC IN ITS WILD DEPICTIONS OF THE EVILS OF FASCISM, BUT THESE ARE PRECISELY THE REASONS ANY CINEMA SEWER FAN WILL ADORE THIS MOVIE AS MUCH AS I DO. THAT AND THE ABSOLUTELY JAW-DROPPING HEAD EXPLOSION (THEY BLEW IT UP REAL GOOD) PERPETRATED ON THE EVIL THATCHER CHARACTER. IT SHOULD GO WITHOUT SAYING THAT THIS IS A TOTALLY SATISFYING WATCH IF YOU'RE IN THE MOOD (AS I OFTEN AM) FOR THIS KIND OF MEAN-SPIRITED SCHLOCK. A MUST-SEE.

ILLUSTRATIONS BY BEN NEWMAN! 2014©

JOHN LEY

NEWPORT KENTUCKY RESIDENT ANNETTE HEINZ WAS BORN ON APRIL 25, 1953 IN CINCINNATI, OHIO. SHE DROPPED OUT OF HIGH SCHOOL IN THE 11TH GRADE TO ATTEND COSMETOLOGY SCHOOL, AND WHILE HEINZ WAS WAITING ON HER LICENSE TO ARRIVE SHE SAW AN AD PLACED IN THE SUNDAY CINCINNATI ENQUIRER BY A LOCAL 28-YEAR-OLD ENTREPRENEUR NAMED LARRY FLYNT. HE WAS LOOKING FOR GO-GO DANCERS FOR A VENUE CALLED THE HUSTLER CLUB. HER LIFE CHANGED THAT DAY. SHE WAS JUST SIXTEEN YEARS OLD.

IN 2013 I STRUCK UP A FRIENDSHIP WITH ANNETTE ON FACEBOOK, AND WE WOULD OCCASIONALLY CHAT BACK AND FORTH, TELLING EACH OTHER ABOUT DUMB LITTLE THINGS THAT WERE GOING ON IN OUR DAY-TO-DAY LIVES. I'D SEND HER MY BOOKS AND ZINES, WHICH SHE SEEMED TO ENJOY VERY MUCH, AND SHE'D TICKLE ME BY CASUALLY REMINISCING ABOUT THE GOOD OLD DAYS IN THE GOLDEN AGE OF PORN -- WHICH OF COURSE I WAS BORN TOO LATE TO HAVE TAKEN PART IN FIRST HAND. RECENTLY, IN 2015, WE DECIDED TO DO A PROPER MINI-INTERVIEW FOR CINEMA SEWER, SO MORE PEOPLE COULD ENJOY HER SASSY TALES OF TRASHY ADVENTURE. HERE'S HOW IT WENT:

CINEMA SEWER: HI ANNETTE! THANKS FOR CHATTING WITH ME. LET'S START AT THE BEGINNING, SHALL WE?

ANNETTE HEINZ

I'LL BE UPSTAIRS IN A MINUTE, LARRY!

IT'S MISS HEINZ CIRCA 1983 ...

THEY DON'T MAKE 'EM LIKE THIS ANYMORE FELLAHS!

ANNETTE HEINZ: I WAS BORN IN CINCINNATI, OHIO TO A CARPENTER AND A SEAMSTRESS. IN SCHOOL, I WAS THE MENSA CLASS CLOWN. I WAS ASKED TO LEAVE THE ROOM ON MANY AN OCCASION. HAHA! I GUESS THAT 'MISCHIEVIOUS' WOULD HAVE BEEN A GOOD CATCH ALL ADJECTIVE FOR ME. GOOD OF HEART, I ALWAYS HAD A DOG, AND I WAS RAISED AS AN ONLY CHILD. I ALWAYS HAD 4 OR 5 BOYFRIENDS... MAYBE IT WAS BECAUSE I PLAYED BASEBALL WITH THEM. PERHAPS I WAS 'BOY CRAZY', AND NOT MUCH HAS CHANGED, BECAUSE I STILL HAVE AN EYE FOR THE FELLOWS AND I STILL HAVE A DOG. AHH... THE CYCLE OF LIFE.

LEST I FORGET, I AM FROM A HIGHLY RECOGNIZABLE FAMILY IN SOUTH CENTRAL KENTUCKY... BLUEGRASS COUNTRY. WE DON'T SPEAK. I LOVED THEM AND THE VISITS TO GRANDMA'S HOUSE. THE SOUTHERN FOOD. THEY HAD A WORKING FARM WITH HOGS, HORSES, AND GARDENS. IN ALL THE YOUNG PICS OF ME I HAVE A WATERMELON OR AN ANIMAL IN MY ARMS. AGAIN, THE CYCLE OF LIFE, AS I BECAME A CERTIFIED CHEF. LIFE IS STRANGE AND GOOD.

CS: I LOVE THAT YOU DANCED AT THE ORIGINAL HUSTLER CLUB THAT LARRY FLYNT OPENED IN 1968, AND BEGAN PUBLISHING HIS LITTLE HUSTLER NEWSLETTER OUT OF -- WHICH OF COURSE BECAME ONE OF THE MOST FAMOUS ADULT MAGAZINES OF ALL TIME. WHAT WAS THAT LIKE? ESPECIALLY COMPARED TO HOW IT WAS PORTRAYED IN THE 1996 BIOPIC, THE PEOPLE VS. LARRY FLYNT.

AH: I BEGAN DANCING FOR LARRY'S HUSTLER CLUB IN CINCINNATI, OHIO. THE ORIGINAL CLUB HAD A HUGE GLASS WINDOW THAT WE DANCED IN AND A SMALL STAGE. SOMETIMES WE WOULD WALK

AROUND THE BLOCK IN OUR SLINKY COSTUMES WITH LARRY IN OUR MIDST, AND THE CUSTOMERS FOLLOWED US BACK TO THE CLUB. FLYNT KNEW HOW TO MAKE MONEY. I REMEMBER THE BEGINNING OF HUSTLER MAGAZINE. IT WASN'T EVEN THAT. I WAS STILL AT THE HUSTLER CLUB IN 1972 WHEN IT STARTED PUBLICATION. THIS "MAGAZINE" WAS JUST ONE SHEET OF PAPER FOLDED IN HALF. THEY WERE FREE AND SAT BY THE DOOR.

CS: I BET YOU WISH YOU GRABBED A HANDFUL OF THOSE OLD NEWSLETTERS TO SAVE, ANNETTE! THEY'RE SO RARE NOW. YOU COULD PROBABLY PAY YOUR RENT FOR A YEAR SELLING THEM ON EBAY! I ALSO BET THAT CLUB WAS A REAL HAVEN FOR SWINGERS AND OTHER WILD CHARACTERS.

AH: WE HAD MANY ORGIES, UPSTAIRS, IN THE APARTMENT. ONE NIGHT, WE WERE GOING TO HAVE A WILD PARTY BUT I HAD TO EXCUSE MYSELF AS I HAD DRANK SO MUCH WINE. THE THING IS THAT MY NAUSEA SAVED ME FROM GETTING A DOSE OF THE CLAP. EVERYONE HAD IT BUT ME! THANK YOU, CHEAP WINE, "COLD DUCK." THE PEOPLE VS. LARRY FLYNT IS ACCURATE BUT A TAMED-DOWN VERSION OF OUR ANTICS. WE WERE PAID TO PARTY. I LOVE LARRY FLYNT. <u>GREAT</u> BOSS.

CS: AS FAR AS I'M CONCERNED, YOU ARE A QUEEN OF BURLESQUE, AND WITH IT MAKING A COMEBACK WITH THE YOUNGER GENERATION IN THE LAST DECADE, I REALLY THINK YOUR NAME SHOULD BE KNOWN ALONG WITH THE MORE FAMOUS PERSONALITIES. I'D LOVE TO HEAR ABOUT THAT TIME IN YOUR LIFE. I IMAGINE THERE WERE A LOT OF UPS AND DOWNS.

AH: THERE IS NO GREATER ART THAN REAL BURLESQUE. THE BOOM-CHICKA-BOOM IS BURLESQUE, WHICH IS WHAT I DID. NOT POLE DANCING. THEY ARE ENTIRELY DIFFERENT. I DANCED FOR A QUARTER CENTURY. THERE IS NO FINER ZEN THAN A STANDING OVATION. SOME GIRLS THINK THAT FANS AND FRIENDS ARE SEPARATE BEINGS, BUT I ALWAYS WELCOMED SEEING FAMILIAR FACES WHEN I WAS ON THE CIRCUIT. NICE FELLOWS BUYING ME A

ANNETTE, FROM THE MARCH 1984 ISSUE OF VIDEO-X MAGAZINE. IT'S THE ONLY ADULT MAGAZINE I'VE FOUND WHERE SHE WAS THE COVER MODEL...

SEAFOOD DINNER, AND SOME HELPING ME TO UNLOAD MY GEAR. THE ROAD IS NOT GLAMOROUS. IT IS LONELY AND TIRING WITHOUT MY LOVING FANS AND FRIENDS. AS A HEADLINER I DROVE ALL OVER THE COUNTRY. I HAD TO FINALLY GET A ROADIE AS I NEEDED A SPOTLIGHT AND PYROTECHNICS. THE SHOWS BECAME FANTASIES, AND I HAD VARIOUS CHARACTERS. THERE WAS AN S & M FRENCH MAID WHO BEGAN DANCING "THE ROBOT". SHE WAS, AFTER ALL, A TOY. SHE WAS IN VELVET AND LACE, AND THAT RIPPED OFF INTO ALL LEATHER AND CHAINS — SHE HAD TRANSFORMED AND BECOME THE DOMINATRIX. YEAH, I'LL MAKE YOU THINK AND JERK. <u>THAT</u> IS BURLESQUE.

CS: THE THINKING MAN'S BONER! I'D LOVE TO HEAR ABOUT THE OTHER CHARACTERS YOU PLAYED IN YOUR SHOWS.

AH: 'CLEOPATRA' WAS ALL METAL AND SWAROVSKI CRYSTALS, AND I HAD A SNAKE THAT WAS USED FOR HER LETHAL BITE. I REMEMBER BEING IN COUNCIL BLUFFS, IOWA AND THEY HAD HAD THE DOOR OPEN DURING A BLIZZARD! THE METAL COSTUME WAS FREEZING AND THE SNAKE CONSTRICTED. GOOD GRIEF. ANOTHER NIGHT, TWO DRUNKS WERE RIDICULING MY "FAKE SNAKE". MR. COOPER HISSED AND THEY RAN LIKE HELL. NOTHING WAS FAKE HERE. OH, AND MY CIRCÈ HAD A BATHTUB. I GOT PAID TO TAKE A BATH! HAHA! ANYWAY, AFTER TWO YEARS OF HEADLINING THE CIRCUIT, I WAS TIRED. NEW YORK CITY WAS THE MOST SPLENDID OF ALL CITIES. I SETTLED THERE FOR 10 YEARS. NEW YORK, I LOVE YOU.

CS: NEW YORK MUST HAVE BEEN AMAZING BACK THEN. I CAN SEE WHY YOU SETTLED DOWN AND TOOK UP ROOTS. SO HOW DID YOU FIRST GET INVOLVED WITH PERFORMING IN ADULT FILMS? WHAT ARE SOME OF YOUR MEMORIES OF YOUR EARLIER EXPERIENCES ON SET?

AH: ONCE I GOT TO NEW YORK I HAD EXPRESSED AN INTEREST IN FILMS TO ANNIE SPRINKLE AND MARC STEVENS. I DANCED WITH MARC AT MAGIQUE MONTHLY. BOTH ANNIE SPRINKLE AND MARC STEVENS TALKED DAMIANO INTO VISITING MY SHOW. DAMIANO SAYS TO ME, FROM THE FRONT ROW, "I AM DAMIANO." YEAH RIGHT BUDDY, "I AM MORGANNA." THEN MARC JOINS HIM AND I JUST SAT DOWN ON THE STAGE. WE WERE ALL LAUGHING. DAMIANO IS KNOWN AS "THE KING OF PORN." ONCE HE CAST YOU, THE XXX INDUSTRY WOULD OFFER YOU MANY ROLES. DAMIANO EQUALS STAR-MAKER.

CS: AH YES! THIS WAS AT THE INFAMOUS MELODY BURLESQUE AT 48TH AND BROADWAY. I'VE HEARD THE LEGENDS. I BELIEVE YOU DANCED THERE FOR ABOUT TEN YEARS, RIGHT? AND THAT'S WHILE YOU WERE MAKING YOUR HARDCORE FILMS.

AH: THAT'S RIGHT.

CS: I'VE SEEN A BUNCH OF YOUR MOVIES, AND I'M LOOKING FORWARD TO DRAWING YOU! I LIKE DRAWING BUTTS, SO I'M PROBABLY GOING TO DRAW YOUR ASS -- SO GET READY FOR THAT! HAHA, WHICH MOVIES OF YOURS ARE YOU THE MOST PROUD OF?

AH: MY FAVORITE CHARACTER I GOT TO PLAY WOULD BE JODEE IN PUBLIC AFFAIRS, WHICH WAS BY HENRI PACHARD. PAUL THOMAS MAKES A FABULOUS CORRUPT POLITICIAN VS MY INNOCENCE. I WAS IN FOUR ROBERT HOUSTON FILMS WITH ALL-STAR CASTS. BE SURE TO CATCH PIGGY'S.

CS: I REMEMBER PIGGY'S! THAT WAS THE PORKY'S SPOOF FROM 1983. WHO COULD FORGET THAT ONE. YOU WERE THE SOUTHERN BELLE, "SYLVIA"! I REMEMBER YOU SITTING ON GEORGE PAYNE'S FACE WHEN HE TRIED TO DELIVER YOUR MAIL, AND THEN LATER YOU SAT ON JERRY BUTLER'S FACE WHEN HE WAS LAYING ON THE FLOOR BEHIND THE BAR TRYING TO FIX THE FAUCET. YOU WERE SITTING ON EVERY ONE'S FACE IN THAT ONE! HAHA!

AH: HAHA, YES! AND I PLAY AN INSANE TRANNY NAMED MARGARITA IN HYPERSEXUALS. WELL, SHE WAS SUPPOSED TO BE A TRANNY. THE WORLD WAS NOT READY FOR IT, SO A LOT OF THE TRANNY DIALOGUE WAS LEFT ON THE EDITING FLOOR. ROBERT HOUSTON, AHEAD OF HIS TIME! ROBERT HOUSTON'S FILMS NEED TO BE MADE AVAILABLE ON DVD AND BLU-RAY. HE NEEDS A BOX SET, ACTUALLY. ON THE SET OF HOT LIPS IN 1984 I MET MICHAEL GAUNT, AKA MICHAEL DATTORE. WE WERE LOVERS FOR A HOT WHILE. I THANK THE BIZ FOR GIVING ME THAT JOYOUS TIME WITH HIM. WOODSTOCK WAS A JOY WITH MICHAEL.

CS: DID YOU EVER HAVE ISSUES WITH PUSHY FANS? I'VE HEARD SOME HORROR STORIES ABOUT SOME OF THESE FUCKIN' GUYS.

AH: I REMEMBER TAKING MY DOG TO DO HER BUSINESS, AND I HAD NO MAKEUP, SUNGLASSES, AND MY HAIR IN A PONYTAIL. HERE I AM WITH A BAGGIE FULL OF STEAMING DOGGIE DOO, AND A FAN THAT WAS ATTACHED TO MY ARM WITH A BARRAGE OF QUESTIONS. I HAD TO SWING THE CRAP BETWEEN US AND YELL AT HIM. SOME ARE MORE THAN PUSHY. AND BESIDES ME WALKING THE DOG, I HAD TO GO ONSTAGE! "I'VE GOT TO GET TO WORK", JUST DIDN'T WORK! HE WASN'T LISTENING, AND I STILL HAD HAIR AND MAKEUP TO DO. NO, WE DON'T WAKE UP LOOKING LIKE FANTASIES! HAHA!

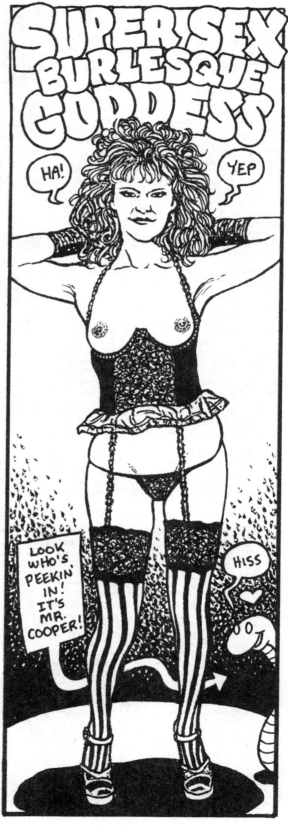

CS: IT'S A PROCESS! SO YOU DID ABOUT 30 MOVIES OR SO. HOW DO YOU FEEL ABOUT THE SWITCHOVER FROM SHOOTING ON FILM TO SHOOTING ON VIDEO THAT THE ADULT INDUSTRY DID IN THE MID 1980S? DID IT TAKE AWAY OR ADD SOMETHING TO THE PRODUCT? I'M ALSO CURIOUS ABOUT YOUR FEELINGS ON MODERN PORN.

AH: IT IS MY UNDERSTANDING THAT SOME OF TODAY'S XXX PARODIES ARE OKAY. I DON'T WATCH IT. WE HAD BIG GALAS FOR THE OPENING OF A FILM. WE'D GET ALL DRESSED UP AND HAD A BLAST OR TWO ;-) LARRY REVENE SHALL ALWAYS BE THE GREATEST CINEMATOGRAPHER, EVER. VIDEO KILLED THE GOLDEN AGE OF PORN. I REMEMBER WHEN SARNO CAME TO NYC. HECK, THE GREAT SARNO, RIGHT? OF COURSE I WAS GOING TO SAY 'YES' TO DOING FILMS FOR HIM. WRONG! HE WASN'T SHOOTING ON FILM ANYMORE. IT WAS NOW CHEAP VIDEOS WITH NO SCRIPTS. I KEPT ASKING FOR A COURIER TO BRING OVER MY SCRIPT. NOPE, THERE WAS NONE. JUST A PIECE OF PAPER HANDED TO ME. THE LAST REAL 'REEL' I DID WAS FOR CANDIDA ROYALLE. THREE DAUGHTERS.

CS: IT'S SUCH A SHAME WE LOST CANDIDA RECENTLY. I KNOW HER PASSING REALLY AFFECTED YOU.

AH: HER WORKS ARE FOR ETERNITY -- A BRIGHT LIGHT IN A DARK WORLD. CANDIDA KNEW HOW TO THROW A PARTY, TOO. SHE FLEW A CHEF IN TO FEED US ON THREE DAUGHTERS. SHE RENTED A LOVELY HUGE HOME, AND THE DAUGHTER OF THE OWNER CAME IN DRUNK. SHE AND HER BOYFRIEND KEPT CALLING EACH OTHER AND CUSSED FOR HOURS! I LEFT THE BEDROOM AND CRAWLED IN BED WITH JOHNNY NINETEEN. HE WAS THE MANAGER OF THE MEZZALUNA RESTAURANT, WHERE NICOLE BROWN SIMPSON DINED ON THAT FATEFUL NIGHT. I SOMETIMES WONDER IF HE SENT POOR RON GOLDMAN TO DELIVER NICOLE'S GLASSES.

CS: I'M GOING TO REVIEW THREE DAUGHTERS FOR THE MAGAZINE ONE OF THESE DAYS, AND HOPEFULLY I CAN GET SOME QUOTES FROM YOU THEN ABOUT THE EXPERIENCE OF BEING ON SET TO WORK INTO MY REVIEW. AND SO AFTER BEING IN THE ADULT ENTERTAINMENT BIZ, WHERE DID LIFE TAKE YOU THEN?

AH: I LEFT NEW YORK TO DANCE FOR 8 MORE YEARS AS ''KENTUCKY'S ONLY XXX STAR.'' I DID PACK THE NIGHTCLUBS. THEY ALL WANTED TO SEE THE NAUGHTY LOCAL GAL. I AM STILL FRIENDS WITH A FEW CUSTOMERS OF THAT ERA, BUT WHEN THE LAW MADE AREOLAS AND ALCOHOL ILLEGAL, IT WAS OFF TO COLLEGE I GO. I RECEIVED TWO DEGREES, CULINARY ARTS AND HOTEL RESTAURANT MANAGEMENT. GRADUATED CUM LAUDE. FOOD IS ANOTHER SOUL PLEASURE FOR THIS HEDONIST. I'M OFF TO FULFILL MYSELF RIGHT NOW.

CS: HAVE A NIBBLE FOR ME! THANKS ANNETTE.

·END·

PRESENTS SEPTEMBER RELEA...

ANNETTE HAVEN

KELLY NICHOLS

...is Make Strange Bedfell...

PUBLIC Affairs

1983's PUBLIC AFFAIRS, WHERE HEINZ WAS FORCED TO SHARE THE SPOTLIGHT WITH THE OTHER ANNETTE -- HAVEN.

THIS PAGE REPRESENTS A MAJOR SHIFT IN HOW CINEMA SEWER IS CREATED. EVERY PAGE AFTER THIS IS PART OF THE NEW ERA. WHY'S THAT? WELL UP UNTIL NOW, EVERY LINE OF LETTERING AND EVERY DRAWING I'VE DONE FOR THIS PUBLICATION WAS DONE AT MY DESK IN OUR BEDROOM, OR AT THE KITCHEN TABLE WHERE THE COMPUTER IS. THAT'S 18 YEARS AND THOUSANDS OF PAGES IN ONE PLACE. BUT AS OF THIS PAGE, AND AS OF OCTOBER 22ND 2015, I'M NOW MAKING THIS MAG AT MY NEW STUDIO SPACE I'M SHARING WITH COMIC BOOK ARTIST JAMES LLOYD, AND ILLUSTRATORS, PRISCILLA YU AND ZED ALEXANDRA. (EDIT: ZED MOVED OUT...) IT'S 7 BLOCKS FROM MY APARTMENT, IN THE 'WEDGE BUILDING' WHERE MAIN AND KINGSWAY MEET HERE IN VANCOUVER, BC CANADA. MY FAVE SHIT IS EVERYWHERE! DOWNSTAIRS IS MY FAVE COMIC BOOK STORE (RX COMICS), MY FAVE BOOK STORE (PULP FICTION BOOKS), MY FAVE ART SUPPLY STORE (RATHS), AND BUDGIES BURRITOS -- WHICH IS MERELY "OK" IN TERMS OF BURRITOS. I'M SO EXCITED ABOUT THIS NEW HOME FOR C.S. AND ABOUT SURROUNDING MYSELF WITH OTHER TALENTED PROFESSIONALS!

Dum DEEE DUM

A NEW BEGINNING

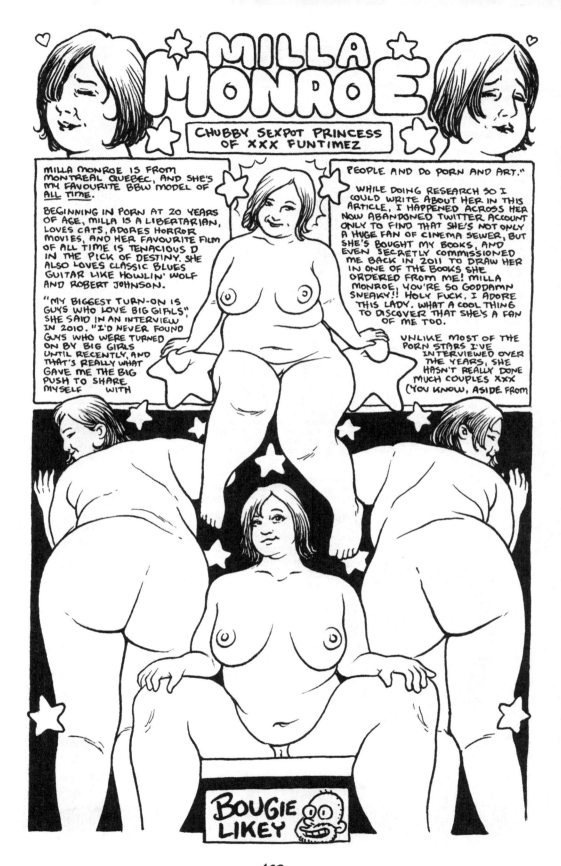

MILLA MONROE

CHUBBY SEXPOT PRINCESS OF XXX FUNTIMEZ

MILLA MONROE IS FROM MONTREAL QUEBEC, AND SHE'S MY FAVOURITE BBW MODEL OF ALL TIME.

BEGINNING IN PORN AT 20 YEARS OF AGE, MILLA IS A LIBERTARIAN, LOVES CATS, ADORES HORROR MOVIES, AND HER FAVOURITE FILM OF ALL TIME IS TENACIOUS D IN THE PICK OF DESTINY. SHE ALSO LOVES CLASSIC BLUES GUITAR LIKE HOWLIN' WOLF AND ROBERT JOHNSON.

"MY BIGGEST TURN-ON IS GUYS WHO LOVE BIG GIRLS" SHE SAID IN AN INTERVIEW IN 2010. "I'D NEVER FOUND GUYS WHO WERE TURNED ON BY BIG GIRLS UNTIL RECENTLY, AND THAT'S REALLY WHAT GAVE ME THE BIG PUSH TO SHARE MYSELF WITH PEOPLE AND DO PORN AND ART."

WHILE DOING RESEARCH SO I COULD WRITE ABOUT HER IN THIS ARTICLE, I HAPPENED ACROSS HER NOW ABANDONED TWITTER ACCOUNT ONLY TO FIND THAT SHE'S NOT ONLY A HUGE FAN OF CINEMA SEWER, BUT SHE'S BOUGHT MY BOOKS, AND EVEN SECRETLY COMMISSIONED ME BACK IN 2011 TO DRAW HER IN ONE OF THE BOOKS SHE ORDERED FROM ME! MILLA MONROE, YOU'RE SO GODDAMN SNEAKY!! HOLY FUCK, I ADORE THIS LADY. WHAT A COOL THING TO DISCOVER THAT SHE'S A FAN OF ME TOO.

UNLIKE MOST OF THE PORN STARS I'VE INTERVIEWED OVER THE YEARS, SHE HASN'T REALLY DONE MUCH COUPLES XXX (YOU KNOW, ASIDE FROM

BOUGIE LIKEY

103

SOME GIRL-ON-GIRL STRAP-ON), AND HER CAREER IN THE SKIN-BIZ MOSTLY JUST CONSISTED OF SOLO MASTURBATION STUFF WHERE SHE FUCKS HERSELF WITH DILDOS, AND A LOT OF NUDE MODELLING. "I'VE NEVER ONCE WATCHED ONE OF MY OWN VIDEOS, EVER", SHE STATED ON TWITTER IN 2012. "I WAS ALWAYS TOO SHY TO ACTUALLY SEE MYSELF ON FILM."

WE FINALLY CONNECTED IN NOVEMBER 2015, AND SHE GRACEFULLY AND KINDLY CONSENTED TO AN INTERVIEW. IT WENT LIKE THIS:

CINEMA SEWER: HI MILLA! THANKS FOR TALKING WITH ME!

MILLA MONROE: HEY!

CS: LET'S START AT THE BEGINNING. THE EARLY YEARS OF YOUR SEXUALITY.

MM: WELL, I HAD A PRETTY SKEWED VIEW OF SEX AND SEXUALITY AS A YOUNG PERSON. I ACTUALLY LOST MY VIRGINITY TO A GUY WHOM I WAS IN GROUP THERAPY WITH, WHERE THE NUMBER ONE RULE WAS NO OUTSIDE CONTACT. WE FUCKED FOR WHAT MUST HAVE BEEN A GOOD SOLID 3 MINUTES IN A GARAGE. I HAD CONFESSED THIS TO SOMEONE AROUND ME AND PROMPTLY I WAS KICKED OUT OF THE THERAPY GROUP, WHILE HE STAYED AND THAT REALLY MARKED ME TO NOT BE OPEN ABOUT MY SEXUALITY FROM THAT POINT ON. I NEVER HAD A STEADY BOYFRIEND UNTIL I WAS INTO MY 20S, SO SEX WAS SPORADIC AND MOSTLY A NEGATIVE EXPERIENCE TO SAY THE LEAST. AT ONE POINT I WAS DATING A COUPLE, ALTHOUGH IT WAS A VERY STRANGE FEW MONTHS AND WE NEVER ALL SLEPT TOGETHER, BUT I DID FINGER HER A FEW TIMES UNTIL SHE SQUIRTED EVERYWHERE. ANOTHER QUASI RELATIONSHIP THAT REALLY MARKED ME WAS THE ONE I STARTED WHEN I WAS 19 OR SO WITH A MUCH OLDER MAN. HE WAS IN AN OPEN RELATIONSHIP, SO WE DID FOOL AROUND A FEW TIMES. HE HAD A VERY STRONG PERSONALITY AND WAS WICKED SMART WHILE I ON THE OTHER HAND, WAS FRAGILE IN MY ESTEEM. PLUS, HE WAS AN AMAZING BLUES MUSICIAN *SWOON* (I HAD NO CHANCE!) I PINED FOR HIM HARD. FOR YEARS. IT WAS A VERY CONCRETE MOMENT OF UNREQUITED AFFECTION THAT LEFT ME BROKEN IN THE LONG RUN. I COULDN'T SAY HE WAS RESPONSIBLE FOR IT IN ANY WAY, BECAUSE I WAS A TOTAL MESS BACK THEN IN TERMS OF MY BELIEFS, VIEWS AND MISPLACED ATTENTION SEEKING FROM A 'FATHER FIGURE'.

CS: TELL ME ABOUT YOUR FIRST YEARS OF GETTING INTO THE INDUSTRY. ARE YOU BISEXUAL? WHAT PROMPTED YOU TO GET STARTED WITH MODELLING? WAS IT A GOOD EXPERIENCE?

MM: I DIPPED MY TOE INTO THE WATERS OF SEX WORK THAT SAME YEAR OF 19 BY WEB-CAMMING FOR A SITE CALLED IFRIENDS. THIS WAS BACK IN 2006. THE SETUP WAS IN AN OFFICE BUILDING ABOVE A MEDICAL CLINIC. THERE WERE FOUR ROOMS WITH FOUR KEYBOARDS AND FOUR CLUNKY MONITORS STARING BACK AT YOU FROM FOUR AWKWARDLY CHOSEN SCREEN NAMES IN FOUR SEPARATE CHAT ROOMS. I DON'T REMEMBER PERFECTLY, BUT ONE OF MINE WAS SOMETHING LIKE 'BOOTYFULBBW'. I WAS CERTAINLY NOT ONE OF THE TOP MONEY EARNERS, BUT I DID ENJOY IT AT THE TIME. I DEVELOPED A GENUINE FRIENDSHIP WITH A CLIENT OVER THE INTERNET WELL PAST MY EXPIRATION DATE ON THAT JOB. HE WAS SUCH A SWEET GUY, I FELL INTO THE TRAP OF NOT WANTING TO CHARGE HIM FOR ONLINE SHOWS, BUT WE BOTH UNDERSTOOD THE BASIS OF OUR FRIENDSHIP AND IT WAS VERY LUCRATIVE FOR ME. I GENERALLY DIDN'T USE TOYS OFTEN FOR MY PRIVATE SHOWS AND DID ANAL PLAY VERY FEW TIMES. BOY, HOW TIMES HAVE CHANGED FOR CAM GIRLS TODAY IN THE SHORT 10-YEAR SPAN!

CS: I'LL SAY. THOSE GIRLS JUMP THROUGH HOOPS THESE DAYS. I'VE SEEN SOME SHIT, I'LL TELL YOU. I'M ON THAT CHATURBATE SITE SOMETIMES, AND IT GETS PRETTY WILD DEPENDING ON WHO THE GIRL IS. GAPED BUTTS AND ROBOTIC FUCKING MACHINES, AND THE WHOLE DEAL. SO, HOW DID THAT END FOR YOU?

MM: WELL, I WAS BANNED FROM THE WEBSITE AT SOME POINT BECAUSE OF A DISGRUNTLED EX-CLIENT,

"I CUM REALLY EASILY, REALLY FAST WITH MY OWN HAND."

"LIKE 'ONE MINUTE' KIND OF FAST."

WHO WANTED MORE FROM ME THAN AN ONLINE PRESENCE, HAD SET UP A FAKE EMAIL UNDER MY REAL NAME (I MADE THE MISTAKE OF TELLING HIM MY FIRST NAME) AND HE SENT THREATS TO HIMSELF FROM THAT ACCOUNT. THOSE FEW EMAILS WERE SO FULL OF SPELLING AND SYNTAX ERRORS, THAT I WAS ALMOST MORE OFFENDED THAT I WAS BEING ACCUSED OF ACCOSTING THE ENGLISH LANGUAGE THAN I WAS OF LOSING MY JOB.

CS: FUCK, WHAT A MOULDY DICKHOLE! AND FROM THERE WHERE DID YOU GO?

MM: I BUMMED AROUND A FEW JOBS IN 2007 UNTIL I FOUND A NOW DEFUNCT CAM STUDIO CALLED KAMERIX, WHICH WAS RUN BY THREE GUYS IN THEIR MID-TWENTIES. I HAD SOME FUN TIMES AT THAT STUDIO AND THAT'S WHERE MY PORN CAREER STARTED, PRETTY MUCH. I DON'T REALLY CONSIDER IT A CAREER IN PORN, BECAUSE I NEVER DID BOY/GIRL, AND IN MY GIRL/GIRL SCENES I WAS JUST TOO PAINFULLY SHY TO TOUCH THEM. THEY ARE PRACTICALLY MORE MUTUAL MASTURBATION SCENES. I CAN'T SAY I'M ACTIVELY BISEXUAL, TO ANSWER YOUR EARLIER QUESTION, BUT I WAS ATTRACTED TO WOMEN. PERHAPS IT WAS IN A MORE VOYEURISTIC WAY.

CS: SO LOTS OF THESE CAM SESSIONS WERE RECORDED AND ENDED UP AS ONLINE CONTENT. HOW WOULD YOU DESCRIBE YOUR SCENES YOU DID FOR THEM?

MM: I'VE ALWAYS JOKED AROUND THAT MY SCENES WERE 'ARTSY AND TASTEFUL', PARTICULARLY THE 'PIZZA DELIVERY' ONE. I CONTINUED TO CAM ON A FEW OTHER SITES AT THIS PLACE. IT WAS IN A COMMERCIAL BUILDING, FULL OF MOSTLY COMPANIES FROM THE GARMENT INDUSTRY AND AGAIN, MY PAYOUTS SUCKED COMPARED TO OTHERS AND MORE WAS EXPECTED OF ME IN PVT'S AS THE CLIENTELE ON THESE SITES WERE EUROPEAN. ONE OF THE OWNERS, AN OVERLY CAFFEINATED FELLA NAMED ALEX RACO ASKED ME IF HE COULD TAKE A FEW PICTURES OF ME AND WHAT HE DID WAS POST THEM UP ON GFY.COM AND SEE IF ANYONE WAS INTERESTED IN SHOOTING ME. FROM THERE I DID TWO SOLO SETS FOR WHO KNOWS WHO AND I WAS TOTALLY INTO IT. THE OWNER OF PLOMPERS SHOWED INTEREST IN STARTING A SOLO SITE WITH ME AND I WAS OFFERED A DEAL, WHICH I WAS MORE THAN HAPPY TO TAKE. I WOULDN'T OWN THE CONTENT AND WOULD GET PAID BASED ON SHOOTS. I WAS OFFERED 30% OF THE SITE BUT WOULD HAVE TO FORFEIT ANY PAY FOR THE SHOOTS THEMSELVES AND HINDSIGHT BEING 20/20, I WOULD HAVE ACTUALLY MADE SOME REAL COIN HAD I TAKEN THE PERCENTAGE. THEN AGAIN, I FEEL VERY CONFIDENTLY, HAD THEY GOTTEN 'FREE' CONTENT, THE SITE WOULD HAVE TAKEN TRIPLE THE AMOUNT OF TIME TO LAUNCH. FROM THERE, THE REST IS HISTORY (OR A RECENTLY DELETED BROWSER HISTORY, IF YOU WISH).

CS: IT'S A DIFFERENT HISTORY THAN MOST OF THE CLASSIC PORN STARS THAT I USUALLY FEATURE IN THESE PAGES. WOULD YOU DESCRIBE YOURSELF AS AN EXHIBITIONIST?

MM: I WOULDN'T EVER CALL MYSELF AN EXHIBITIONIST, BUT WITHIN THE COMFORT OF MYSELF AND A PHOTOGRAPHER, I FELT COMFORTABLE.

CS: SO MOST OF YOUR PORN CAREER WAS CAMMING, UNTIL THE MILLA MONROE WEBSITE STARTED UP IN 2008, AND THAT HAD NEW CONTENT GOING UP UNTIL 2011. WHAT BROUGHT THAT TO AN END? DID YOU GET INTO OTHER TYPES OF SEX WORK?

MM: NO, I NEVER GOT INTO OTHER TYPES OF SEX WORK. I JUST NEVER HAD THE INTEREST. I DEVELOPED A FOND HATRED FOR CAMMING AND THE WEBSITE SHOOTS JUST DISSIPATED ONCE THE NETWORK MY

SITE WAS PART OF WAS SOLD TO A NEW OWNER. AT FIRST, WE WERE IN TALKS TO SHOOT MORE CONTENT, AND POSSIBLY BOY/GIRL STUFF, BUT HE COMPLETELY FLAKED AND DISAPPEARED INTO THIN AIR. SINCE THEN, THE ORIGINAL OWNER OF THE SITE HAD RETAKEN CONTROL OF THE PLOMPERS/CAM NETWORK AND HAS PERIODICALLY CONTACTED ME TO WORK FOR HIM AGAIN. UNFORTUNATELY, WE COULD NEVER REACH ANY AGREEABLE TERMS, AS HE WAS REALLY PUSHING ME TO DO WEBCAM FOR HIM AND I COULDN'T MAKE AMENDS WITH IT BEING WORTH THE MONEY/TIME/TOTAL MIND-FUCKING ANGER.

CS: DEALING WITH THE PUBLIC CAN BE INFURIATING, EVEN WHEN THEY AREN'T HORNY GUYS WHO BARELY SPEAK ENGLISH BARKING ORDERS AT YOU WHILE YOU ROLL AROUND NAKED IN FRONT OF THEM. I CAN ONLY IMAGINE SOME OF THE DIPSHITS YOU'VE HAD TO DEAL WITH. YOU MENTIONED THAT YOU'RE SHY. I THINK A LOT OF PEOPLE WOULD FIND IT HARD TO BELIEVE THAT SOMEONE WHO IS CONFIDENT ENOUGH TO TAKE OFF THEIR CLOTHES AND SPREAD 'EM AT WORK WOULD BE SHY. CAN YOU TALK A LITTLE ABOUT THAT?

MM: WELL, EVERY SHOOT WAS SHOT BY ONE OF THREE GUYS: ALEX, THE OWNER OF KAMERIX; ANDERS, A SWEET AMAZING GUY WHO WORKED THERE FOR A TIME; AND MY CURRENT BEAU, WHO WORKED THERE AS A DESIGNER AND TALENT. MY BF AND I ONLY DID TWO SETS TOGETHER WHILE WE WERE DATING (THE HANGMAN ONE AND CHOCOLATE MILK ONE, SHOT IN MY APARTMENT, WE TOTALLY FUCKED AFTER THEM...A FEW TIMES) ALSO, I WAS NEVER GIVEN DIRECTION, I WAS DOING WHATEVER I WANTED. IT WAS REALLY JUST MYSELF AND WHAT I CALLED A 'CAMERAMONKEY'. I WAS INCREDIBLY SHY AT FIRST WITH ALEX TOO. THE FIRST VIDEO WE SHOT, I WAS MASTURBATING AND I HAD AN ORGASM. I WAS EMBARRASSED I HAD A REAL ORGASM! I GOT ALL RED IN THE FACE, SAID 'SORRY' AND SAID I NEEDED A SEC.

CS: AWW! THAT'S CUTE! YOU'RE THE BEST!

MM: HAHA! I CUM REALLY EASILY, REALLY FAST WITH MY OWN HAND. LIKE 1 MINUTE KIND OF FAST. IT'S A BIT RIDICULOUS. I'M TOTALLY DONE WITH SEX EASILY, IN 5 MINUTES.

CS: WOW! WHAM-BAM-THANK-YOU-HAND! SO ALL THE ORGASMS IN YOUR MASTURBATION VIDEOS ARE REAL?

MM: YES, PRETTY MUCH EVERY ORGASM IN MY VIDS IS REAL! AND LUCKILY THE SHYNESS WITH ALEX FADED QUICKLY. I WAS QUITE SHY WITH SOME OF MY SHOOTS WITH ANDERS, SINCE HE WAS A GOOD LOOKING GUY I WAS ATTRACTED TO, PLUS I WAS VERY SINGLE AT THE TIME. HE WAS INCREDIBLY INTELLIGENT AND SOFT SPOKEN, AND SOME OF THE BETTER PHOTOS OF ME CAME FROM HIM BECAUSE HE WAS VERY ATTENTIVE. I WAS ONLY EVER EXPOSED IN FRONT OF TWO GUYS I HADN'T SLEPT WITH, REALLY. I GOT OVER THOSE SHYNESS HUMPS, BUT OVERALL, I'M VERY SOCIALLY AWKWARD IN PUBLIC AND USED TO HAVE A KNACK OF SAYING THE WRONG THING TO THE WRONG PERSON AT THE WRONG TIME. IN FACT, I HAD A REAL TALENT FOR IT! AT THE SAME TIME, I AM ALSO A VERY SILLY PERSON AND I LOVE TO MAKE PEOPLE AROUND ME LAUGH WHEN I KNOW THEM AND FEEL AT EASE. I ONLY HAVE A FEW FRIENDS, IN CONSEQUENCE OF MY TROUBLE BREAKING THE ICE WITH NEW PEOPLE. NONE THE LESS, I'M A PRETTY GOOD FRIEND. THROUGH ALL THIS, I'M PRETTY SHY WHEN IT COMES TO MY SEXUALITY. PERHAPS PRIVATE WOULD BE A BETTER WAY TO DESCRIBE. IT'S ALSO HARD TO GAUGE AS WELL, SINCE THE PERSON I WAS YEARS AGO WAS LITERALLY 4 LIFETIMES AGO.

CS: 4 LIFETIMES AGO? HOW SO?

MM: I'VE HAD 4 KIDS SINCE THEN!

CS: WOW! I HAD NO IDEA! BACK TO THE THE WHOLE CONCEPT OF SHYNESS AND CONFIDENCE, THAT'S SOMETHING I'VE ALWAYS LOVED ABOUT YOU. EVEN IN SOME OF YOUR VIDEOS WHERE IT'S CLEAR THAT YOU'RE NERVOUS (SUCH AS THE STRAP-ON SCENE YOU DID WITH THAT SKINNY BLONDE CHICK) THERE IS A WONDERFUL AURA ABOUT YOU THAT JUST GLOWS, AND I THINK THAT STEMS FROM YOUR CONFIDENCE. THAT GLOWING CONFIDENCE IS SOMETHING THAT NOT ENOUGH PLUS-SIZED WOMEN HAVE, AND IT'S BECAUSE THEY'VE HAD IT SLOWLY FORCED OUT OF THEM BY OUR FAT-SHAMING SOCIETY. WITH SLUT-SHAMING BEING YET ANOTHER COMMON MINDSET, THAT COUNTS AS TWO BATTLES MILLA MONROE HAS TO FIGHT, AND I CAN IMAGINE YOU MUST HAVE TO TOUGHEN UP AND BE STRONG TO DO WHAT YOU DO.

AS FAR AS I'M CONCERNED, YOU'RE SUPER-WOMAN. YOU'RE A FUCKING HEROINE. YOU SHOULDN'T BE SHAMED, YOU SHOULD BE ADMIRED AND EXTOLLED!

MM: WELL, FIRST OFF, THANK YOU KINDLY! I OVERALL HAVE NOT EXPERIENCED MUCH 'FAT SHAMING' MYSELF BEYOND MY CHILDHOOD YEARS AND THE OCCASIONAL TROLL ON CAM-SITES, BUT I CERTAINLY HAVE HAD MY STRUGGLES, LIKE ALL YOUNG GALS, IN ACCEPTING MYSELF. IN ALL HONESTY, AT THAT POINT, FAT ISN'T EVEN THE ISSUE. I'VE RARELY MET A PERSON, MALE OR FEMALE, WHO WHOLEHEARTEDLY HAD ACHIEVED BODY ACCEPTANCE EARLY IN LIFE. I WAS CERTAINLY FEELING INSECURE ABOUT MYSELF AT TIMES BUT LUCKILY HAD A POSITIVE OUTLET THROUGH THESE SHOOTS AND FOR A TIME, WITH THE WEBCAM. I HAD BEEN TOLD MANY TIMES I WAS PRETTY, EVEN RANDOM STRANGERS WOULD COME UP TO ME TO SAY THAT. IT WAS SO STRANGE. RECENTLY I WAS DISCUSSING WITH MY BOYFRIEND ABOUT HOW SOME PEOPLE AT WORK MENTIONED MEETING ME FOR THE FIRST TIME AT LAST YEAR'S COMPANY CHRISTMAS PARTY. SO MANY COLLEAGUES WOULD SAY, 'SHE'S SO PRETTY!' WHICH WAS UNCALLED FOR, AND UNNECESSARY. BECAUSE I AM FAT, THEY FEEL OBLIGED TO SEEM COOL WITH IT, LIKE IT MEANS SOMETHING.

CS: THAT'S A REALLY INTERESTING PERSPECTIVE. I SURE HOPE YOU DON'T THINK I WAS TOOTING YOUR HORN SIMPLY AS SOME SELF-SERVING WAY TO SHOW YOU THAT I'M "COOL" WITH FAT CHICKS. I THINK PROSTITUTES, STRIPPERS AND PORN PERFORMERS IN GENERAL SHOULD BE ADMIRED AND CELEBRATED, NOT JUST THE FAT ONES! HAHA! I HEAR SOME PORN STARS TALKING ABOUT BEING EMPOWERED BY THEIR JOB, SEXUALLY. DID THAT HAPPEN FOR YOU?

MM: YEAH, THOSE VIDEOS, IN NO SMALL TERMS, EMPOWERED ME! I WAS MOSTLY IN CONTROL OF THE MAJOR ASPECTS OF THE SHOOTS AND WITH THAT COMES A LEVEL OF COMFORT. I DO FEEL AT EASE IN FRONT OF THE CAMERA AND I AM VERY HAPPY TO HEAR YOU SAY YOU CAN SENSE THAT. ALSO, AT THIS POINT IN MY LIFE, I CAN HONESTLY SAY I JUST DON'T GIVE A FUCK ABOUT SHAME IN GENERAL, BECAUSE I LIVE MY LIFE WITH INTEGRITY, I TAKE RESPONSIBILITY FOR WHO I AM AND WHAT I DO. BUT IT TOOK ME A FEW YEARS TO REALLY ABSORB THAT ONE. I HAPPENED TO BE AT THE RIGHT PLACE, AT THE RIGHT TIME, AROUND THE RIGHT PEOPLE WHEN MY SITE WAS DONE. I DID IT BECAUSE I WAS SURROUNDED BY A GOOD GROUP OF PEOPLE, HAVING FUN AND GETTING PAID. IT JUST MADE SENSE FOR ME.

CS: AWESOME. THAT'S GOOD TO HEAR. I LOVE YOUR POSITIVITY. IT'S FUCKING SEXY AS HELL.

MM: THANK YOU! I DO BELIEVE IN BEING OPTIMAL AND ALWAYS STRIVING TOWARDS THAT GOAL. WHETHER THAT IS AT 120 LBS OR 220 LBS, WHATEVER IS THE NORM FOR THAT PARTICULAR PERSON. NO ONE IN MY LIFE JUDGES ME FOR MY PANTS SIZE OR HOW I HAVE CHOSEN TO SPEND THE ACCUMULATION OF SEVERAL HOURS OF MY LIFE, BUT RATHER BY THE CONTENT OF MY CHARACTER, MY KINDNESS AND MY GOODNESS. IF THEY DIDN'T, THEY'D BE PRETTY SHITTY PEOPLE AND I'D LIMIT CONTACT WHETHER ONLINE OR IN PERSON.

CS: SO, YOUR BOYFRIEND — I'D LIKE TO HEAR ABOUT HIM AND HOW THAT WORKS WHEN YOU'RE WORKING IN YOUR INDUSTRY. YOU'VE BEEN WITH THE SAME GUY FOR A WHILE NOW, HAVEN'T YOU?

MM: MY BOYFRIEND (OR AS I LIKE TO DESCRIBE HIM: MORE THAN BOYFRIEND BUT LESS THAN HUSBAND) IS A REALLY GREAT GUY! WE'VE BEEN TOGETHER FOR 6 YEARS NOW. WE ACTUALLY MET AT KAMERIX, WHERE HE WAS DOING WEBSITE DESIGN AND WAS MALE TALENT FOR THE COMPANY. HE WAS DATING A VERY BEAUTIFUL GIRL AT THAT POINT AND THERE WAS ZERO INTEREST ON MY PART. FAST FORWARD A YEAR AND HE WAS SINGLE. I HAPPENED TO HANG OUT WITH HIM IN A GROUP, THEN INVITED HIM TO A BLUES SHOW AND WE HIT IT OFF. WE ENDED UP SKINNY DIPPING ON OUR FIRST DATE, WHICH IS TOTALLY OUTSIDE OF MY USUAL CHARACTER! WE LIKE TO JOKE THAT DESPITE THE SHIT SHOW THAT KAMERIX BECAME, OUR FAMILY IS THE ABSOLUTE BEST THING TO COME OUT OF IT. WE OWN A HOME OUTSIDE OF MONTREAL, AND AS I MENTIONED, WE HAVE 4 CHILDREN TOGETHER.

CS: YES, TOTS! AND THAT IS WHY YOU GOT OUT OF THE SMUT BIZ?

MM: YEAH, THAT'S WHY I 'DISAPPEARED', MORE OR LESS. MY FOCUS AND PRIORITIES DRASTICALLY SHIFTED, AND ALTHOUGH WE OFTEN DISCUSSED PERHAPS RETURNING TO SOME KIND OF SHOOTING (AND HE WAS VERY ENCOURAGING), I NEVER FELT I COULD GIVE IT THE ATTENTION THAT IT WOULD NEED, NOR GET INTO THE HEADSPACE FOR IT. THAT'S JUST MYSELF. THERE ARE PLENTY OF GIRLS

BOUGIE! I DIDN'T AGREE TO THIS SHIT! WHERE DID YOU DIG THIS FELLAH UP? I MEAN, JEEZ!

HAHAHA!

BLORT

THAT ARE ABLE TO MANAGE THAT BALANCE. I'M JUST NOT ONE OF THEM. IF IT WAS UP TO HIM, I'D BE IN THE MIDDLE OF A 6-WAY IR GANGBANG AND BLOWBANG.

CS: HAHA! I'LL BET! I WOULDN'T BE AVERSE TO WITNESSING SUCH AN EVENT, MYSELF!

MM: HAHA YEAH, I'M PRETTY MUCH A ONE COCK AT A TIME KIND OF GAL. POOR HIM. THE LAST TWO EVER SHOOTS I EVER DID WERE DONE WITH HIM. THEY ARE PROBABLY MY FAVOURITE BECAUSE HE WAS HARD AS A ROCK WHILE FILMING THEM AND THE SEXUAL ENERGY WAS INTOXICATING! I REALLY WISH I COULD HAVE DONE MORE AT THAT TIME, IT WAS VERY MUCH THE HONEYMOON PERIOD OF OUR RELATIONSHIP AND IT WAS SO MUCH FUN!

CS: SO WHAT ARE YOU DOING THESE DAYS, MISS MONROE?

MM: WELL, ONCE KAMERIX HIT THE FAN IN 2010 I WAS PERUSING ONLINE ADS AND FOUND A JOB WITH GAMMA ENTERTAINMENT. MY HUSBAND HAS BEEN A BRAND ARCHITECT FOR SITES LIKE EVILANGEL.COM AND NOW THE INCREDIBLY SUCCESSFUL GIRLSWAY.COM. I'VE ALSO PICKED UP THE GIG OF SOCIAL MEDIA MANAGER FOR WEBSITE ACCOUNTS UNDER THE EVIL ANGEL BRAND FOR A LITTLE OVER A YEAR NOW. I DO IT PART TIME FROM HOME, IN THE MOMENTS AMID THE MADNESS AND INSANITY OF LIFE. I SPEND MY DAYS BETWEEN DIRTY DIAPERS, ENDLESS DISHES -- AND WHEN A NEW JAY SIN MOVIE COMES OUT, ANAL PROLAPSES AND MILK ENEMAS.

CS: HAHA! WHO DOESN'T? I'M SHOOTING MILK OUT OF MY BUMHOLE RIGHT NOW.

MM: HAHA! WELL, I ABSOLUTELY LOVE MY JOB AND THE COMPANY I WORK FOR! I'M PART OF AN AMAZING TEAM AND FEEL SO FORTUNATE TO BE ABLE TO STILL WORK IN AN INDUSTRY I LOVE SO MUCH IN AN INTERESTING WAY. I HAVE SUCH A PROFOUND RESPECT AND ADMIRATION FOR JOHN STAGLIANO AND HIS VALUES. I FEEL QUITE PRIVILEGED TO BE DIRECTLY RESPONSIBLE, IN PART, FOR THE PUBLIC IMAGE OF HIS COMPANY.

CS: AWESOME POSSUM. ANY FINAL THOUGHTS BEFORE WE WRAP THIS UP?

MM: I'LL CONCLUDE WITH THIS STATEMENT: PORN HAS VEERED ME INTO A DIRECTION IN MY LIFE THAT HAS GIVEN ME THE SOURCE OF UNLIMITED HAPPINESS. IT'S RESPONSIBLE, IN PART, FOR MY FOUR AMAZING, BEAUTIFUL CHILDREN, AND IT CURRENTLY PUTS FOOD ON OUR TABLE. TO ME, PORN ACTUALLY REPRESENTS WHAT IS BEAUTIFUL IN THE WORLD, AS WELL AS FREEDOM AND LIBERTY OVER ONE'S SELF IN ITS MOST RAW FORM. I LOVE IT.

CS: THANK YOU! THAT'S A GREAT NOTE TO LEAVE ON. WHAT A TREAT TO GET TO TALK WITH YOU!

IT'S THE END, AND IT'S A PICTURE OF MY BUTT!

GET IT?

GET AHOLD OF YOURSELF, WOMAN!

AH, THE HYSTERICAL WOMAN CLICHE! IT HAS TO BE ONE OF THE MOST TIME-HONOURED TROPES IN CINEMA HISTORY. DATING BACK TO THE ORIGINATION OF FILMED NARRATIVES, IT'S A PLOT ELEMENT AND CHARACTERIZATION THAT SUPPOSES THAT FEMALES ARE LESS RATIONAL, PRONE TO UNDISCIPLINED OUTBURSTS, AND LESS EMOTIONALLY STABLE THAN MEN ARE. A KEY PART OF THIS IS TO SEE FEMALE OPINIONS UNDERVALUED BY THE OTHER CHARACTERS, WHILE ALSO BEING CONDESCENDED TO, CODDLED, AND ULTIMATELY STRAIGHTENED OUT WITH A HARD SLAP TO THE FACE -- WITH PERHAPS THEN SOME THROTTLING FOR GOOD MEASURE. THIS IS ALMOST ALWAYS FOLLOWED BY THE PHRASE "GET AHOLD OF YOURSELF, WOMAN!" OR PERHAPS A LOUD "SNAP OUT OF IT!".

FALLING OUT OF FAVOUR SOMEWHAT IN RECENT DECADES, IT IS REGARDLESS AN ENTERTAINMENT

GODDAMN IT!!

TROPE/CLICHE THAT ENJOYED A VERY LONG RUN OF POPULARITY ON BOTH THE SMALL AND BIG SCREEN, WITH VARIATIONS OF IT MEMORABLY BEING USED IN **JAWS 2** (1978), AND **THE FUGITIVE** (1993). BUT MY FAVORITE USE OF THIS HACKNEYED DEVICE WAS WHEN IT WAS SPOOFED AND MADE FUN OF IN THE EXCELLENT ABRAHAMS/ZUCKER BROS FILM **AIRPLANE!** (1980), WHERE A LONG PARADE OF VARIOUS PASSENGERS PAUSE AND LINE UP TO TAKE THEIR TURN SLAPPING A SINGLE HYSTERICAL WOMAN ACROSS THE FACE. THE GAG WAS LATER RECYCLED IN **AIRPLANE II** (1983), WHERE THE SAME LADY IS TESTIFYING IN COURT, AND AGAIN GOES HYSTERICAL UPON REMEMBERING WHAT HAPPENED TO HER IN THE FIRST MOVIE. THIS, OF COURSE, RESULTS IN EVERYONE IN THE COURT ROOM TAKING TIME TO GIVE HER A SLAP ACROSS THE FACE.

-BOUGIE '16

ORGANIZING THE ARCHIVES AT THE CINEMA SEWER HQ

Born Innocent (1974)

FRESH OFF HER MASSIVE STAR-MAKING TURN AS THE POSSESSED YOUNG THANG IN THE SMASH HIT THE EXORCIST, A 14-YEAR-OLD BABY-FACED LINDA BLAIR STARRED IN THIS CONTROVERSIAL (AT THE TIME, AND NOW VIRTUALLY FORGOTTEN) 1974 TV MOVIE.

SHE PLAYS CHRIS PARKER, AN INTELLIGENT YOUNG RUNAWAY WHOSE PARENTS (ASSHOLE FATHER AND ALCOHOLIC MOTHER) HAND HER OVER TO THE STATE. SHE'S PLACED IN A DETENTION HOME FOR NEGLECTED TEENS, A PLACE WHERE THE ABUSED GIRL IS CONFRONTED WITH THE HELLISH REALITIES OF WHAT IT MEANS TO BE LOCKED UP WITH OTHER TROUBLED KIDS.

THE DIFFERENCES IN THE WAY THIS FILM WAS MARKETED WHEN IT WAS RELEASED ON DVD IN THE 2000S GIVES YOU AN IDEA OF JUST WHAT KIND OF A SPLIT PERSONALITY THE MOVIE HAS, AND WHAT A CONFUSING MELDING OF GENRES IT IS. THE COVER OF THE HEN'S TOOTH RELEASE FROM 2011 LOOKS LIKE A LIFETIME OR HALLMARK CHANNEL MOVIE, WITH LINDA'S FACE FLOATING IN THE CLOUDS ABOVE A BEAUTIFUL RURAL AREA WITH ROLLING HILLS. THERE SHE IS WITH HER SUITCASE, AN INNOCENT COUNTRY GAL, READY TO LEAVE HOME FOR THE FIRST TIME. THE DESIGN FEELS AS HOMESPUN AND SAFE AS A CROCHET BLANKET ON GRANDMA'S SOFA.

MEANWHILE THE VCI DVD RELEASE FROM 2004 SCREAMS AT YOU IN YELLOW ANGRY LETTERS ("GRAPHIC! RAW! UNCOMPROMISING REALISM!") AND SPORTS A 1970S STYLE PAINTED GRINDHOUSE POSTER WITH BLAIR COWERING IN FEAR AGAINST A WALL. THE TOP BUTTONS ON HER SHIRT ARE UNBUTTONED, AND HER 15-YEAR-OLD HEAVING CLEAVAGE IS A FOCAL POINT OF THE IMAGE. I'M SURE I DON'T HAVE TO TELL YOU WHICH OF THESE TWO RELEASES IS MORE POPULAR, AND ROUTINELY SELLS FOR 3X WHAT THE OTHER DOES WHEN THEY SHOW UP USED ON EBAY.

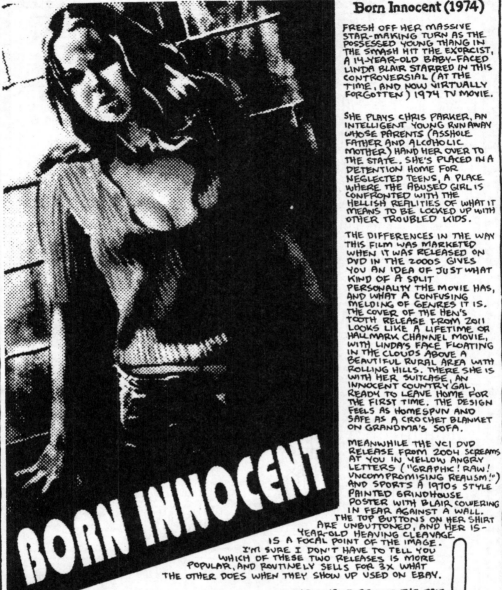

THERE IS ONE SCENE IN PARTICULAR THAT WENT BEYOND THE PALE OF PRETTY MUCH ANYTHING THAT HAD BEEN MADE SPECIFICALLY FOR TV AT THE TIME, AND IT HAPPENS TO LINDA BLAIR'S CHARACTER WHILE SHE IS IN THE COMMUNAL SHOWER AREA. NAKED AND HAPPILY THINKING SHE'S ALONE, LINDA OPENS HER EYES TO SEE TWO OTHER GIRLS STANDING THERE WATCHING HER LIKE CREEPS. UH-OH.

"COME OUT HERE" THE ONE WITH THE BROWN FEATHERED HAIR SAYS. SHE'S HOLDING A TOILET PLUNGER. A BUTCH BLONDE BITCH WEARING DENIM OVERALLS BACKS HER UP AND SNEERS. LINDA LOOKS JUSTIFIABLY WORRIED AND STEPS FORWARD, ONLY TO BE JUMPED FROM BEHIND BY TWO SHORT HAIRED GIRLS THAT HAD BEEN HIDING. THEY CLAMP THEIR HANDS OVER HER MOUTH SO HER ANGUISHED SCREAMS WILL BE MUFFLED.

"JOHNNY" LINDA BLAIR'S CO-STAR

BEFORE SHE IS HELD DOWN ON THE COLD BLUE-TILED FLOOR AND FUCKED WITH THE WOODEN HANDLE OF THE TOILET PLUNGER, ONE OF THE ADORABLE LIL' RAPISTS LETS US KNOW THAT "JOHNNY LIKES THE NEW GIRLS". THIS IS AN EXCEEDINGLY DISTURBING LINE OF DIALOG, BECAUSE IT TELLS THE AUDIENCE THAT 1) THEY DO THIS TO A LOT OF INNOCENT GIRLS, AND 2) THAT THEY'VE DONE IT ENOUGH TIMES THAT THEY'RE ACTUALLY GETTING KINDA CHUMMY WITH THE TOILET PLUNGER ITSELF -- INSOFAR AS TO GIVE IT A MASCULINE NICK-NAME THAT OPERATES AS A PLAYFUL NOD TO A TOILET BEING KNOWN AS A "JOHN".

"YOU GO THROUGH ALL THE MOTIONS OF BEING RAPED", BLAIR NOTED IN A 2003 INTERVIEW WITH E! WHILE CONFESSING THAT BORN INNOCENT WAS VERY DIFFICULT FOR HER TO SHOOT. "YOU COME OUT OF IT FEELING PRETTY RAPED. THAT DID NOT SIT WELL WITH ME AT ALL." IT IS WORTH NOTING THE OTHER ACTRESSES IN THIS INCENDIARY SCENE WERE ALL PLAYING MUCH YOUNGER CHARACTERS THAN THEY ACTUALLY WERE. JANIT BALDWIN WAS 19. NORA HEFLIN AND TINA ANDREWS WERE 24 AND 23, RESPECTIVELY.

THE VCI DISC PROUDLY ANNOUNCED THAT ITS VERSION WAS "DIGITALLY MASTERED AND UNCUT" AND "CONTAINS ORIGINAL GRAPHIC RAPE SCENE!" NOW WHILE THE ASSAULT IS NOT ACTUALLY THAT GRAPHIC IN ITS EXECUTION COMPARED TO WHAT ONE WAS SEEING IN SOME OF THE RAPE-REVENGE FILMS OF THE 1970S, YOU CAN SURPRISINGLY SEE LINDA'S EXPOSED NIPPLE FOR ABOUT A HALF SECOND DURING THE ATTACK.

LET THAT SETTLE IN FOR A SECOND. WHO DECIDED IT WAS NECESSARY FOR A 15-YEAR-OLD TO BE TOPLESS ON A TV MOVIE FILM SET? SINCE IT IS VERY FLEETING, ONE CAN ASSUME IT WASN'T INTENTIONAL OR NOTICED INITIALLY, BUT WHY TAKE THAT KIND OF CHANCE? IT'S WORTH NOTING THAT IT ONLY APPEARED ON THE ORIGINAL 1974 PRIMETIME TELECAST AND THE ENTIRE SCENE WAS CUT WHEN THE FILM WAS REPLAYED.

THAT THERE WASN'T ANY PUBLIC OUTCRY OVER THIS SCREW UP IS EVEN MORE SHOCKING THAN THE TOILET PLUNGER VIOLATION ITSELF. AN UNDERAGE NIPPLE ON NETWORK TV? DURING A HARROWING GANG RAPE SCENE, NO LESS?! ARE YOU FUCKING KIDDING ME?

ANYONE ELSE REMEMBER THE JOBS LOST AND THE MILLIONS OF DOLLARS IN FINES HANDED OUT BY THE FCC IN THE WAKE OF JANET JACKSON'S PARTIALLY EXPOSED ADULT NIP MAKING AN APPEARANCE AT THE SUPERBOWL IN 2004? YOUTUBE CO-FOUNDER JAWED KARIM CLAIMED IN 2015 THAT THE DIFFICULTY INVOLVED IN FINDING AND WATCHING CLIPS OF MISS JACKSON BEING NASTY (OFTEN REFERRED TO AS "NIPPLEGATE") IS WHAT DIRECTLY LED TO THE CREATION OF HIS TREMENDOUSLY POPULAR VIDEO SHARING WEBSITE. IT ALSO MADE "JANET JACKSON" THE MOST SEARCHED TERM AND IMAGE IN INTERNET HISTORY UP TO THAT POINT.

NO, BORN INNOCENT'S PUBLIC OUTCRY CONCERNING THIS SCENE CAME FOR AN ENTIRELY DIFFERENT REASON: A COPYCAT CRIME THAT HAPPENED THAT SAME YEAR AND REACHED THE SUPREME COURT IN 1978. NBC WAS BLAMED FOR THE RAPE OF A 9-YEAR-OLD GIRL, A TRAGIC INCIDENT -- A CRIME COMMITTED BY A FEMALE CLASSMATE WITH A GLASS COKE BOTTLE.

IN THE CASE OF OLIVIA N. VS. THE NATIONAL BROADCASTING COMPANY, THE SUIT ALLEGED THAT SEVERAL GIRLS HAD SEEN BORN INNOCENT, AND DECIDED TO REENACT THE ATTACK AT A BEACH IN SAN FRANCISCO. FURTHERMORE, THE SUIT ALLEGED THAT THE PRODUCERS AND DISTRIBUTORS OF ANY MEDIA -- BE IT TV, MOVIES, BOOKS, OR MAGAZINES -- SHOULD BE HELD LEGALLY RESPONSIBLE FOR ANY VIEWER WHO WAS STIMULATED TO INFLICT INJURY ON AN INNOCENT PERSON UPON COSUMING MEDIA THAT CONTAINED ANY DEPICTION OF SEXUALIZED VIOLENCE.

NBC'S LAWYERS CONTENDED THAT THEIR BROADCAST DID NOT INTEND ANY SUCH ACTION, NOR ON THE BASIS OF PSYCHOLOGICAL RESEARCH COULD THEY HAVE REASONABLY FORESEEN VIOLENCE TAKING PLACE FOLLOWING A SCREENING OF THEIR PROGRAM. THE CALIFORNIA SUPREME COURT RULED THAT THE FILM WAS NOT OBSCENE, AND THAT THE NETWORK THAT PRODUCED AND AIRED IT WAS NOT LIABLE FOR THE ACTIONS OF THE PERSONS WHO COMMITTED THE CRIME. OLIVIA N. AND HER FAMILY WERE UNABLE TO RECOVER ANY DAMAGES OR LEGAL FEES THEN, NOR IN 1981 WHEN THEY TOOK THE CASE TO THE CALIFORNIA COURT OF APPEALS.

"THE TELEVISION BROADCAST OF 'BORN INNOCENT' DOES NOT FALL WITHIN THE SCOPE OF UNPROTECTED SPEECH" THE JUDGE STATED UNEQUIVOCALLY IN THE 1981 APPELLANT COURT DECISION. "NOTWITHSTANDING THE PERVASIVE EFFECT OF THE BROADCASTING MEDIA AND THE UNIQUE ACCESS AFFORDED CHILDREN, THE EFFECT OF THE IMPOSITION OF LIABILITY COULD REDUCE THE U.S. POPULATION TO VIEWING ONLY WHAT IS FIT FOR CHILDREN."

BORN INNOCENT WAS PRESENTED AS A CAUTIONARY TALE OF HOW HORRIBLE THINGS CAN HAPPEN TO GOOD KIDS THAT MAKE THE MISTAKE OF ACTING OUT IMPULSIVELY. 'ACTING OUT' SPECIFICALLY BEING: DEFYING THE WHIMS OF YOUR SHITTY PARENTS, SMOKING,

WHY ISN'T THIS FILM BETTER REMEM-BERED? NONE OF MY PALS SEEM TO KNOW IT.

LINDA BLAIR HAS NO PALS IN THIS PEN

Linda Blair learns about life the hard way behind bars.

BORN INNOCENT MONDAY 8PM

FOX WNYW 5

DRINKING, EXPERIMENTING WITH DRUGS, SHOPLIFTING, AND DRESSING PROVOCATIVELY. IT WAS CLEARLY DESIGNED TO WARN YOUNG VIEWERS FROM GOING DOWN THAT PATH. THEN, LIKE NOW, TV AUDIENCES ATE FEAR-MONGERING UP, BUT IN THE 1970s IN PARTICULAR, THE AFTER SCHOOL SPECIALS AND TV MOVIES SPECIFICALLY MADE TO SCARE PARENTS ABOUT THE VARIOUS SOCIAL ILLS AND DILEMMAS OF THE DAY WERE FUCKING HUGE. BORN INNOCENT WAS, IN FACT, THE HIGHEST RATED TV MOVIE TO AIR IN THE UNITED STATES IN 1974.

BUT AS I NOTED EARLIER, THIS MOVIE HAS A SERIOUS SPLIT PERSONALITY, BECAUSE IT IS ALSO UNABASHEDLY WORKING AS EXPLOITATION, LOOKING TO SELL AD TIME AND COLLECT RATINGS USING THE PROMISE OF ABUNDANTLY VIOLENT AND PRURIENT CONTENT. A VIOLENT SHOWER RAPE IN THE GRIM SETTING OF A FEMALE PRISON WAS MOST CERTAINLY INFLUENCED BY THE THEN-POPULAR WOMEN-IN-PRISON DRIVE-IN FARE LIKE **WOMEN IN CAGES** (1971), **THE BIG DOLL HOUSE** (1971), **SWEET SUGAR** (1972), AND **CAGED HEAT** (1974). IT WAS PROVEN AND BANKABLE.

CASTING LINDA BLAIR (KNOWN ONLY AT THAT TIME FOR A ROLE IN WHICH SHE WAS DEPICTED AS FUCKING HER TWAT WITH A CRUCIFIX AND SCREAMING IN A DEMON VOICE ABOUT SUCKING COCKS IN HELL) WAS NOT MERE HAPPENSTANCE, EITHER. IT WAS DELIBERATE. NBC KNEW THAT LINDA BLAIR'S NAME WAS SHORTHAND FOR "YOUNG GIRL THAT DOESN'T SHY AWAY FROM ADULT CONTENT" AND THE PERFORMER'S SCREAMS WHILE BEING ATTACKED WERE PROMINENT IN THE PROMOS AIRED ON NBC LEADING UP TO THE BROADCAST -- WITH A STERN VOICE ANNOUNCING "SHE WAS BORN INNOCENT -- BUT THAT WAS FOURTEEN YEARS AGO!"

"AS THE 1970s PROCEEDED, THE MADE-FOR-TV MOVIE WAS QUICKLY BECOMING A MAJOR SITE FOR TELEVISION'S REPRESENTATION OF SEX", AUTHOR ELANA LEVINE WROTE IN HER BOOK, 'WALLOWING IN SEX: THE NEW SEXUAL CULTURE OF 1970s AMERICAN TELEVISION.' "THE ISSUES THAT TV MOVIES BEGAN TO COVER BY THE MID 1970s TENDED TOWARD THE SALACIOUS, INCLUDING PROSTITUTION, WHITE SLAVERY, DOMESTIC VIOLENCE, AND RAPE -- ISSUES THAT HAD SEXUAL AND VIOLENT ELEMENTS AT THEIR CORE. IN CONTRAST, LESS DRAMATICALLY REALIZABLE ISSUES -- SUCH AS POVERTY OR WAGE DISCRIMINATION -- WERE RARELY TOUCHED."

THEY CERTAINLY DON'T MAKE TV MOVIES LIKE BORN INNOCENT ANYMORE. IN SO MANY WAYS, THE 1970s WERE UNLIKE ANY DECADE BEFORE OR SINCE.

– BOUGIE '16

TARD HARGET...

HA HA!

I WAS BORED ONE EVENING ON FACEBOOK, SO I AND SOME CINEMA SEWER READERS DECIDED TO GO AND SWITCH THE FIRST LETTERS AROUND IN SOME MOVIE TITLES, VERY SIMILAR TO GOOFING AROUND WITH SPOONERISMS (ALTHOUGH WE WERE ONLY CHANGING THE FIRST LETTER, AND NOT ALSO SWITCHING THE OTHER WORD SOUNDS OR SYLLABLES), IT WAS FUNNY FOR A SHORT WHILE BEFORE WE GOT BORED WITH IT. EVEN SOME OF THE BETTER ONES ARE PRETTY LAME, BUT THEY COULD BE GOOD FOR A LIGHT LAUGH OR THREE IF YOU'RE PERHAPS SUICIDAL AND JUST HORRIBLY DESPERATE FOR ONE.

OR NOT.

To Mill A Kockingbird
Casket Base
Paster, Fussycat! Kill! Kill!
Card Handy
Ringing in the Sain
Noogie Bights
Railhouse Jock
Lanufactured Manscapes
Mat Ban
Rurple Pain
Wood Hill Gunting
Bitty Bitty Chang Chang T.E.
Muppet Paster
Sad Banta
Flood Beast
Bill Kill
Won't Do in The Goods
Horno Polocaust
Dot Hog: The Movie
Dear Nark
Wong Leekend
Dullholland Mr.
Feet The Mockers
Dive and Let Lie
Roon Maker

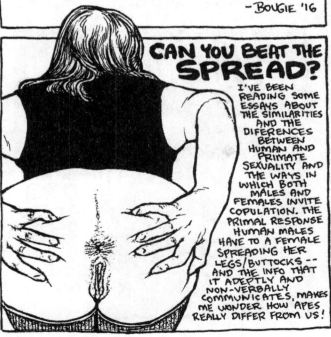

CAN YOU BEAT THE SPREAD?

I'VE BEEN READING SOME ESSAYS ABOUT THE SIMILARITIES AND THE DIFERENCES BETWEEN HUMAN AND PRIMATE SEXUALITY AND THE WAYS IN WHICH BOTH MALES AND FEMALES INVITE COPULATION. THE PRIMAL RESPONSE HUMAN MALES HAVE TO A FEMALE SPREADING HER LEGS/BUTTOCKS -- AND THE INFO THAT IT ADEPTLY AND NON-VERBALLY COMMUNICATES, MAKES ME WONDER HOW APES REALLY DIFFER FROM US!

20 NON-PORN FILMS THAT FEATURED ACTUAL SEX

BY: ROBIN BOUGIE '16

YOU CAN RELAY A LOT OF INFORMATION TO THE AUDIENCE ABOUT A CHARACTER IN A SEX SCENE, BECAUSE AT ITS BASIS SEX IS SIMPLY TWO PEOPLE INTERACTING. IN A COUPLE MINUTES OR LESS, YOU CAN IMPRESS UPON YOUR VIEWER IF YOUR CHARACTERS ARE INHIBITED, PASSIONATE, DOMINANT, SUBMISSIVE, IMPULSIVE, ADVENTUROUS, OR DIABOLICAL -- AND YOU CAN DO ALL OF THAT WORDLESSLY. SEX IS INCREDIBLY PERSONAL, AND THERE ARE COUNTLESS WAYS IN WHICH YOU CAN DEPICT IT. WE JUDGE THE PEOPLE ON SCREEN, BOTH CONSCIOUSLY AND UNCONSCIOUSLY, DEPENDING ON HOW THEY CHOOSE TO BE SEXUAL -- AND THROUGH THAT JUDGEMENT, WE CAN BETTER UNDERSTAND OUR OWN SEXUALITY.

BACK IN THE DAYS BEFORE THE INTERNET, IT WASN'T ALL THAT EASY TO SEE ACTUAL SEX IF YOU DIDN'T HAVE UNHINDERED ACCESS TO PORN, WHICH NOT EVERYONE HAD. EVERY SO OFTEN, THOUGH, A FEW SECONDS OR MINUTES OF IT WOULD POP UP IN THE MOST UNEXPECTED OF PLACES, IN CULT OR ARTHOUSE MOVIES. IN THE MAINSTREAM. IN STUFF THAT WASN'T SEEN AS PORN.

HERE, WITHOUT FURTHER DELAY, IS A LIST OF THEATRICAL FILMS WITH SOME OF (IN MY OPINION) THE MOST MEMORABLE AND/OR GRAPHIC NON-SIMULATED FUCK SCENES IN FILM HISTORY. NOTE: I'VE LEFT OUT MOVIES LIKE PARADISE, POLA X, ANTICHRIST, AND NYMPHOMANIAC WHERE THE STARS USED BODY DOUBLES OR CGI TO DO THE SEX SCENES. GET THE HELL OUTTA HERE WITH THAT. WE AIN'T PLAYING, HERE.

MELVIN VAN PEEBLES IN 1971'S SWEET SWEETBACK'S BAADASSSSS SONG
ACCORDING TO MELVIN, NOT ONLY DID HE FUCK FOR REAL DURING A FEW OF THE UNSIMULATED SEX SCENES IN THIS LEGENDARY BLAXPLOITATION FILM, HE EVEN GOT AN STD FOR HIS TROUBLE. (CASUAL THOUGHT: I BET IT WAS THAT REDHEAD IN THE SCENE WHERE ALL THE BIKERS ARE WATCHING AND CHEERING.) AFTER THE FILM WAS COMPLETED, VAN PEEBLES SUED THE PRODUCTION FOR WORKER'S COMPENSATION, ON ACCOUNT OF THE STD. AND GUESS WHAT? HE WON. A "SWEETBACK" IS 1970S SLANG FOR A BIG COCK, BY THE WAY.

DIVINE IN 1972'S PINK FLAMINGOS
INFAMOUS DRAG QUEEN DIVINE AND HER BIZARRE FAMILY OF MISFITS COMPETE TO BE NAMED THE FILTHIEST PEOPLE ALIVE IN JOHN WATERS' PINK FLAMINGOS. IF THE PART WHERE SHE EATS DOG POOP ISN'T WILD ENOUGH, IN ONE PARTICULARLY UNAPPEALING SEQUENCE DIVINE BLOWS A YOUNG BEARDED GUY. NOT THAT BLOWING A YOUNG BEARDED GUY IS GROSS, BUT IN THE WORLD OF THE FILM, THAT MAN IS HER SON, "CRACKERS".

CAROLE LAURE IN 1974'S SWEET MOVIE
SWEET MOVIE IS A 1974 AVANT-GARDE ART HOUSE ODDITY BY YUGOSLAVIAN DIRECTOR DUSAN MAKAVEJEV. THE FILM MOSTLY FOLLOWS A CANADIAN BEAUTY QUEEN, ALTHOUGH THE FRENCH-CANADIAN ACTRESS PORTRAYING HER, CAROLE LAURE, QUIT DURING THE LEGENDARY COMMUNE DINNER SCENE WHERE OTTO MUEHL AND HIS FABLED VIENNA ACTIONISTS WENT FUCKING NUTS AND STARTED VOMITING AND SHITTING ON THE TABLE, AND DRINKING EACH OTHER'S PISS. BEFORE THAT, THOUGH, CAROLE BREASTFEEDS FROM A BLACK MOTHER'S MILKY BOSOM, NUZZLES A FLACCID COCK, AND GETS NAKED AND PLAYS WITH HERSELF WHILE COVERED IN CHOCOLATE. BECAUSE OF HER ROLE IN THE FILM, ANNA PRUCNAL WAS EXILED FROM HER NATIVE POLAND FOR 7 YEARS, AND EVEN DENIED A VISA TO SEE HER DYING MOTHER.

MICK JAGGER AND ANITA PALLENBERG IN 1970'S PERFORMANCE
YOU DON'T SEE IT IN THE FINISHED PRODUCT, BUT NOT ONLY DID MICK HAVE REAL SEX ON THE SET OF THIS CULT FILM WITH ANITA PALLENBERG (THE SONG "ANGIE" WAS WRITTEN FOR HER), SHE WAS ACTUALLY GUITARIST KEITH RICHARDS' GIRLFRIEND AT THE TIME. AS PAUL GALLAGHER NOTED AT DANGEROUSMINDS.COM "WHILE JAGGER AND PALLENBERG PERFORMED IN FRONT OF THE

CAMERA, RICHARDS SAT OUTSIDE THE LOCATION CHAIN SMOKING, DRINKING AND FUMING OVER WHAT HIS FELLOW STONE AND WOMAN WERE GETTING UP TO. THE FOOTAGE OF JAGGER'S SEXUAL HI-JINKS WITH HIS CO-STARS NEARLY HAD THE FILM PROSECUTED AND SHUT DOWN. WHEN THE RUSHES WERE SENT OUT, THE LAB REFUSED TO PROCESS THE FOOTAGE AS IT WAS CONSIDERED PORNOGRAPHIC. THE FOOTAGE WAS DESTROYED. BUT SOME OF IT-- OR SO IT HAS LONG BEEN RUMOURED -- SURVIVED AND WAS EDITED TOGETHER (ALLEGEDLY BY CAMMELL HIMSELF) INTO A SHORT PORN MOVIE WHICH WON FIRST PRIZE AT SOME UNDERGROUND PORN FESTIVAL IN AMSTERDAM."

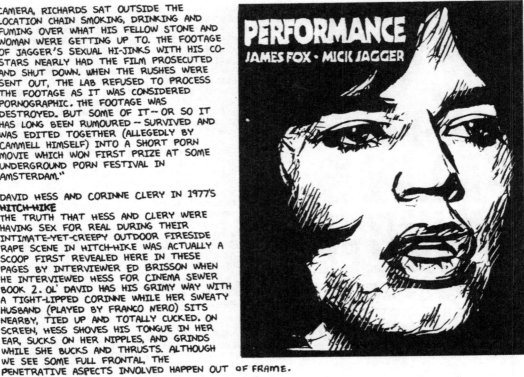

DAVID HESS AND CORINNE CLERY IN 1977'S HITCH-HIKE
THE TRUTH THAT HESS AND CLERY WERE HAVING SEX FOR REAL DURING THEIR INTIMATE-YET-CREEPY OUTDOOR FIRESIDE RAPE SCENE IN HITCH-HIKE WAS ACTUALLY A SCOOP FIRST REVEALED HERE IN THESE PAGES BY INTERVIEWER ED BRISSON WHEN HE INTERVIEWED HESS FOR CINEMA SEWER BOOK 2. OL' DAVID HAS HIS GRIMY WAY WITH A TIGHT-LIPPED CORINNE WHILE HER SWEATY HUSBAND (PLAYED BY FRANCO NERO) SITS NEARBY, TIED UP AND TOTALLY CUCKED. ON SCREEN, HESS SHOVES HIS TONGUE IN HER EAR, SUCKS ON HER NIPPLES, AND GRINDS WHILE SHE BUCKS AND THRUSTS. ALTHOUGH WE SEE SOME FULL FRONTAL, THE PENETRATIVE ASPECTS INVOLVED HAPPEN OUT OF FRAME.

FIONNULA FLANAGAN IN 1985'S JAMES JOYCE'S WOMEN
MISS FLANAGAN WROTE AND PRODUCED THIS FEATURE FILM ABOUT SIX WOMEN IN THE AUTHOR JAMES JOYCE'S LIFE, AND THEN PROCEEDED TO PLAY ALL OF THEM IN A CINEMATIC ONE-WOMAN-SHOW. "THE CENTERPIECE OF THE FILM IS MOLLY'S MASTURBATION", WROTE GREG WROBLEWSKI IN HIS REVIEW FOR SCOOPY.COM. "THE ENTIRE SCENE, INCLUDING FINGER-TO-GENITAL CONTACT, IS PICTURED ON

CAMERA. THIS IS AN EXTRAORDINARY MOMENT IN CINEMA, BECAUSE THE NAKED WOMAN PLAYING WITH HER PRIVATES IN FRONT OF YOU IS NOT A B-MOVIE STARLET, A STRIPPER, A PORNO STAR, OR A FADING MOVIE QUEEN MAKING A FINAL GRASP FOR ATTENTION, BUT A LEGITIMATE CLASSICAL ACTRESS, ALA DAME EDITH EVANS OR MERYL STREEP. SINCE SHE IS AN EXCELLENT ACTRESS AND A NATURAL LOOKING WOMAN, THE SCENE CREATES THE IMPRESSION THAT WE ARE ACTUALLY WATCHING A WOMAN MASTURBATE, AND THAT SHE IS UNAWARE OF OUR PRESENCE."

CAROLINE DUCEY IN 1999'S ROMANCE
DIRECTED BY CATHERINE BREILLAT, THIS FRENCH FILM'S SEX SEQUENCES ARE COMPLETELY UNSIMULATED. THE PLOT FOCUSES ON MARIE (CAROLINE DUCEY) WHO CAN'T GET HER BOYFRIEND TO HUMP HER, SPURRING HER INTO A JIZZ-COATED JOURNEY OF EROTICISM WHERE EURO PORN STUD ROCCO SIFFREDI DRILLS HER FROM BEHIND. BREILLAT LATER ADMITTED TO CASTING ROCCO BECAUSE SHE WANTED A WELL-ENDOWED LEAD MALE PERFORMER TO BE THE SWINGING DICK IN HER THEATRICAL FEATURE. SEEMS REASONABLE.

JULIA LEMMERTZ AND ALEXANDRE BORGES IN 1999'S A FIT OF RAGE
HERE'S A BRAZILIAN RARITY WHERE A YOUNG COUPLE GO TO A HOUSE OUT IN THE RURAL COUNTRYSIDE AND HASH OUT

THEIR RELATIONSHIP PROBLEMS IN AN ANIMALISTIC WAY -- WHICH INCLUDES ARGUING, FIGHTING AND PRIMAL FUCKING. THE TWO ACTORS WERE MARRIED IN REAL LIFE, SO DIRECTOR ALUIZIO ABRANCHES JUST HAD THEM GRIND GEARS FOR REAL. JULIA'S A LITHE SEXY REDHEAD WITH A FULL BUSH, AND, I FELT NO PAIN WHATSOEVER WATCHING HER GET HER MUFFIN STUFFED. ALEXANDRE ALSO IS KIND ENOUGH TO SHOOT A CREAMY GUNK-LOAD ON HER TITS.

RAFFAELA ANDERSON AND KAREN LANCAUME IN 2000'S **BAISE-MOI**
BAISE-MOI, THE TITLE OF THIS SOMEWHAT ENJOYABLE FRENCH ART-HOUSE EXPLOITATION RAPE-REVENGE FILM, CAN BE LOOSELY TRANSLATED TO EITHER "KISS ME", "FUCK ME", OR "RAPE ME", SO IT'S RATHER APPROPRIATE THAT THE INFAMOUS BRUTAL RAPE SCENE IN IT WOULD FEATURE ACTUAL PENETRATION. THIS IS A VERY DISTURBING SCENE, ESPECIALLY IF YOU'VE EVER BEEN RAPED OR MOLESTED, SO I WOULDN'T RECOMMEND IT FOR ANYONE WITH AN UNFORTUNATE HISTORY IN THAT DEPT. THERE IS ALSO QUITE A BIT OF CONSENSUAL MASTURBATION, FUCKING, SUCKING AND PUSSY-EATING THAT GOES ON IN SOME LATER SCENES. IN FACT, THIS AND SHORTBUS PROBABLY HAVE THE MOST ON-SCREEN SEX ON THIS ENTIRE LIST, ALTHOUGH ANDERSON STATED IN AN INTERVIEW THAT "THE MOVIE IS NOT FOR MASTURBATION, SO IT'S NOT PORN." BOTH OF THE LEAD ACTRESSES/CO-DIRECTORS PREVIOUSLY WORKED AS XXX PORN PERFORMERS PRIOR TO MAKING THIS FEATURE. LANCAUME COMMITTED SUICIDE A FEW YEARS LATER IN 2005, A DEATH THAT THE MEDIA IGNORED.

MARK RYLANCE AND KERRY FOX IN 2001'S **INTIMACY**
PLAYING TWO STRANGERS WHO ENGAGE IN ANONYMOUS SEX IN WEEKLY MEETINGS AND SLOWLY DEVELOP AN EMOTIONAL ATTACHMENT, MARK AND KERRY DID ALL OF THE SEX TOTALLY UNSIMULATED (INCLUDING A NICE BLOWJOB) WHICH IMMEDIATELY GAINED THE FILM NOTORIETY AND ARGUABLY STALLED FOX'S PROMISING CAREER. DESPITE BEING BETTER KNOWN FOR HER EARLIER ROLE IN DANNY BOYLE'S SHALLOW GRAVE, FOX STILL CONTENDS THAT THIS PATRICE CHÉREAU FILM IS THE FILM SHE IS THE MOST PROUD OF.

VARIOUS IN 2002'S **KEN PARK**
LARRY CLARK IS OBSESSED WITH THE SEXUALITY OF TEENAGERS, AND IT WAS NEVER BROUGHT TO THE FORE AS MUCH AS IT WAS IN HIS 2002 MOVIE, KEN PARK. OVER AND ABOVE THE STORYLINE ABOUT RATHER BANAL RELATIONSHIPS AND HOW MUCH IT SUCKS TO BE A TEENAGER, WE'VE GOT ALL KINDS OF SEX GOING ON HERE, THE MOST MEMORABLE OF WHICH IS A LONG AND INVOLVED CUNNILINGUS SCENE BETWEEN AN 18-YEAR-OLD BOY AND HIS FRIEND'S MOM. THERE IS ALSO GOBS OF NUDITY, SPITTING INTO EACH OTHER'S MOUTHS, SOME LIGHT BONDAGE, IMPLIED INCEST, NAKED TICKLING, NAKED PILLOW FIGHTS, A BLOW JOB, A VERY STEAMY THREESOME, LABIA FONDLING, PEE COMING OUT OF A DICK, AND IF YOU LIKE WATCHING A DUDE JERKING HIMSELF OFF FOR THREE MINUTES WHILE GETTING CHOKED, THEN HERE'S YOUR MOVIE, BUCKAROOS. I SHOULD ALSO MENTION THAT THIS FILM IS NOTEWORTHY FOR BEING BANNED IN AUSTRALIA, AMONG OTHER LESS NOTABLE COUNTRIES.

CHLOË SEVIGNY SLURPS VINCENT GALLO'S MEAT

CHLOË SEVIGNY AND VINCENT GALLO IN 2003'S THE BROWN BUNNY
CHLOË SHOCKED FESTIVAL GOERS AT CANNES WHEN SHE GAVE BLATANT SLOPPY ORAL PLEASURE TO HER CO-STAR VINCENT GALLO IN THE BROWN BUNNY WHILE IT WAS RECORDED WITH REMOTE CAMERAS. CRITIC ROGER EBERT THEN ANNOUNCED THAT GALLO'S FEATURE WAS "THE WORST FILM IN THE HISTORY OF CANNES", AND IN SNIDE RETALIATION, GALLO TOLD A REPORTER HE "CURSED" EBERT WITH CANCER. WITHIN WEEKS, IT WAS REVEALED THAT EBERT HAD COLON CANCER, WHICH WOULD EVENTUALLY TAKE HIS LIFE TEN AGONIZING YEARS LATER IN 2013. WHEN SEVIGNY WAS ASKED ABOUT WHAT IT WAS LIKE TO SUCK GALLO'S COCK ON CAMERA BY PLAYBOY MAGAZINE IN 2010, SHE RESPONDED BY SAYING "THERE ARE A LOT OF EMOTIONS. I'LL PROBABLY HAVE TO GO TO THERAPY AT SOME POINT." JIM MCBRIDE AKA "MR. SKIN" NAMED THIS THE 49TH MOST IMPORTANT NUDE SCENE OF ALL TIME, AND "THE MOST SEXUALLY EXPLICIT ACT EVER IN A COMMERCIAL FILM WITH A MAINSTREAM HOLLYWOOD ACTRESS."

KIERAN O'BRIEN AND MARGO STILLEY IN 2004'S 9 SONGS
MICHAEL WINTERBOTTOM'S 9 SONGS WAS CONTROVERSIAL AT THE TIME OF ITS RELEASE DUE TO THE DEPICTION OF REAL SEX BETWEEN HIS ACTORS. THE TITLE REFERS TO THE NINE SONGS PLAYED BY EIGHT DIFFERENT ROCK BANDS (LIKE FRANZ FERDINAND, THE DANDY WARHOLS, AND BLACK REBEL MOTORCYCLE CLUB) THROUGHOUT THE MOVIE. NOT ONLY ARE THERE SEQUENCES OF GENITAL FONDLING AND MASTURBATION, THERE'S ALSO ONE FULL-ON EJACULATION.

AMIRA CASAR IN 2004'S ANATOMY OF HELL
AMIRA BANGS A GONG, AND LOOK -- AGAIN IT'S WITH ITALIAN PORN STAR ROCCO SIFFREDI. DUDE DIDN'T GET ENOUGH PORN STAR PUSSY, HE'S GOTTA GO FUCKING ALL THE FOXY FRENCH ACTRESSES, TOO? CAN YOU SMELL MY JEALOUSY? YOU DON'T SEE THE PENETRATION HERE, BUT YOU DO SEE THE ENGORGED GENITALIA FROM BOTH PARTIES, AND IT'S PRETTY OBVIOUS THAT THINGS ARE GOING INTO THINGS. AGAIN DIRECTED BY CATHERINE BREILLAT, THE PLOT CONCERNS A LONELY YOUNG THANG WHO PAYS A GAY DUDE TO ACCOMPANY HER FOR A FOUR-DAY EXPLORATION OF EACH OTHER'S LOINS WHILE SHACKED UP ON AN ISOLATED ESTATE.

GRY BAY IN 2005'S ALL ABOUT ANNA
DIRECTED BY JESSICA NILSSON (AND PRODUCED BY LARS VON TRIER, WHO IS CERTAINLY NO STRANGER TO REQUESTING SEX FROM ACTORS), ALL ABOUT ANNA IS A DANISH MOVIE STARRING PRETTY BLONDE ACTRESS AND SINGER, GRY BAY. THERE ARE VARIOUS SCENES WHERE REAL VAGINAL POUNDAGE TAKES PLACE AND THERE'S EVEN A LITTLE MUTUAL MASTURBATION FOR GOOD MEASURE. I PARTICULARLY LIKE THE PART WHERE BAY GETS HERSELF SOME COCK FROM BEHIND WHILE STANDING AGAINST A WALL COVERED IN WET PAINT DURING SOME HOME RENOVATIONS. BONUS POINTS FOR SHOWING US THE CONDOM FULL OF JIZZ AFTER HER COSTAR EMPTIES HIS BALLS AND PULLS HIS STILL ERECT SHLONG OUT OF HER. <u>GREAT</u> SCENE.

LORI HEURING IN 2005'S 8MM 2
8MM 2 HAS LITERALLY NOTHING TO DO WITH THE ORIGINAL 8MM WITH NICOLAS CAGE. THE MOVIE WAS ORIGINALLY TITLED 'THE VELVET SIDE OF HELL' BEFORE IT WAS THEN DISINGENUOUSLY REBRANDED. I'M NOT ENTIRELY SURE THAT LORI EVEN GETS ACTUAL DEEP DICKING IN THIS MOVIE, OR IF SHE'S JUST GRINDING HER NAKED PUSS AGAINST HER COSTARS, BUT THERE IS DEFINITELY HARDCORE WHERE THE CHARACTERS ARE WATCHING PORN ON A COMPUTER, AND ALSO WHEN TWO BLONDE AND LEGGY LESBIAN EXTRAS MUNCH EACH OTHERS' RUGS.

SOOK-YIN LEE IN 2006'S SHORTBUS
A WIDE RANGE OF SEXUALLY ECCENTRIC CHARACTERS FREAK DURING WEEKLY SEX/ART PARTIES INSPIRED BY SOME LEGENDARY UNDERGROUND GATHERINGS THAT TOOK PLACE IN NEW YORK IN THE EARLY 2000S. NEVER MIND NON-PORN ACTORS, DIRECTOR JOHN CAMERON MITCHELL EVEN WENT SO FAR AS TO UTILIZE NON-ACTORS TO EMBARK ON THEIR OWN JOURNEY OF SEXUAL EXPERIMENTATION, JUST AS THEIR CHARACTERS DID. ONE DUDE SUCKS HIMSELF OFF AND CUMS IN HIS OWN MOUTH, AND LOOKS A FUCK OF A

SOOK-YIN GETS FUCKED RIGHT IN THE OL' SHORTBUS

LOT BETTER THAN RON JEREMY WHILE DOING SO. THE REAL HIGHLIGHT THOUGH, IS ACTRESS (AS WELL AS RADIO HOST, MUSICIAN, AND FORMER GIRLFRIEND OF COMIC ARTIST CHESTER BROWN) SOOK-YIN LEE, GETTING HER PUSSY EATEN OUT WHILE SITTING ON A PIANO, GETTING SCREWED IN ABOUT 6 DIFFERENT POSITIONS (INCLUDING A WEIRD BACKWARDS WHEELBARROW STANCE), JERKING A COCK, BOUNCING HER NAKED ASS UP AND DOWN ON A YOGA BALL WHILE SUCKING DICK, AND RAMMING HER COOCHIE WITH A BLACK VIBRATOR WHILE LAYING ON THE BATHROOM FLOOR. <u>VERY</u> ENTERTAINING. CHECK THIS ONE OUT.

RODLEEN GETSIC -- THE ABUSED PROSTITUTE IN 'THE BUNNY GAME'

ROBERT PATTINSON IN 2008'S **LITTLE ASHES** FEELING THAT IT WOULD LOOK STUPID TO FAKE HIS O-FACE (ESPECIALLY WHILE HE HAD A DOPEY LITTLE PENCIL MOUSTACHE ON HIS UPPER LIP), PATTINSON (AS SALVADOR DALI) DECIDED TO MASTURBATE HIMSELF TO COMPLETION FOR REAL IN FRONT OF THE CAMERA, WITH THE AGREEMENT THAT THEY WOULD ONLY SHOOT ABOVE THE WAIST. SO YUP, WHEN YOU SEE ROBERT CUMMING IN LITTLE ASHES, HE'S <u>REALLY</u> DOING IT.

RODLEEN GETSIC IN 2011'S **THE BUNNY GAME**
GOING ONE BETTER THAN THE BLOWJOB SCENE IN THE BROWN BUNNY, IS THIS HARDCORE FELLATIO SCENE THAT LASTS FOR ABOUT 2 MINUTES, AND THE LEAD ACTRESS NOT ONLY SUCKS AND SLURPS LIKE HER LIFE DEPENDED ON IT, SHE'S ALSO CHOKED ON THE COCK, WHICH SHOULD PLEASE THE PERVERTS IN THE AUDIENCE. FILMED IN BLACK AND WHITE, THIS EXCELLENT TRANSGRESSIVE INDIE MOVIE

STARS A BLEACHED BLONDE DRUG-ADDICTED HOLLYWOOD PROSTITUTE CHARACTER PLAYED BY RODLEEN GETSIC. EVENTUALLY SHE IS ABDUCTED BY A CRAZY TRUCK DRIVER, TAKEN OUT TO THE DESERT, AND HARROWINGLY SUBJECTED TO EXTREME, BRUTAL ABUSE. SCARIEST OF ALL, THE PLOT WAS REPORTEDLY INSPIRED BY A REAL LIFE EXPERIENCE BY ITS STAR. SPEAKING OF EXTREME, JUST BEFORE THE MOVIE WAS RELEASED, RODLEEN SLIPPED ON A MAT IN A VEGAN RESTAURANT IN WEST HOLLYWOOD, AND LANDED ON THE BACK OF HER HEAD, SUSTAINING A TRAUMATIC BRAIN INJURY THAT HAS ENDED HER CAREER AND HAS LEFT HER WITH SEVERELY REDUCED MOBILITY AND CHRONIC DISABLING PAIN. AWFUL.

A BUNCH OF DUDES IN 2013'S **WETLANDS** HELEN (CARLA JURI), THE FILM'S 18-YEAR-OLD HEROINE, IS INTO ALL KINDS OF DIRTY, AND I MEAN DIRTY, STUFF. THIS IS A FILTHY, FILTHY MOVIE, BUT WHAT MOST REVIEWERS DON'T TELL YOU IS THAT THE SEXY STUFF IS SIMULATED AND ISN'T HARDCORE. THAT IS, UNTIL YOU REALIZE THAT THE FILM INCLUDES A TOTALLY REAL SCENE OF A GROUP OF MEN STANDING AROUND, SQUIRTING THEIR CUM ONTO A SPINACH PIZZA. I'LL HAVE MINE WITHOUT SPECIAL SAUCE, PLEASE!

·END·

RANDOM ★ TRIVIA

IN THE SEMINAL 1976 BOOK, "THE HISTORY OF SEXUALITY VOL 1: THE WILL TO KNOWLEDGE", MICHEL FOUCAULT NOTES THAT "WHAT IS PECULIAR TO MODERN SOCIETIES, IN FACT, IS NOT THAT THEY CONSIGNED SEX TO A SHADOWY EXISTENCE, BUT THAT THEY DEDICATED THEMSELVES TO SPEAKING OF IT AD INFINITUM, WHILE EXPLOITING IT AS THE SECRET."

THE FOLLOWING CRITERIA ARE DESIGNED TO FACILITATE SHOOTING

CAST: REHEASE DIALOG SCENES AND DEVELOP "CHARACTER" BITS.

DO NOT: LOOK AT CAMERA OR OFF SET, EXCEPT AS DIRECTED.
DO NOT: MAKE LARGE OR FAST MOVEMENTS IN EXTREME CLOSE UP.
DO NOT: CHANGE POSITION @ "CUT", ONLY @ "STRIKE".
DO NOT: MOVE OR TOUCH ANYTHING ON SET, EXCEPT ON CAMERA.

KEEP SOUND GOING – ABOUT WHAT IS HAPPENING OR COMING UP. YOUR
DIRECTION DURING SOUND TAKES WILL BE SHORT COMMENTS.

PLAN YOUR MOVE, THEN MAKE ADJUSTMENTS IN NATURAL RHYTHM.

WORKING WITH FELLOW ACTORS SHORTENS SET TIME REQUIRED. (CONVINCE
YOUR PARTNER, THEN THE AUDIENCE WILL BE CONVINCED).

MOVE MOUTH ON DIALOG. AVOID MUMBLING OR COVERING LINES. IF A SCRIPTED
LINE IS BLOWN, REPEAT IT. AVOID MENTAL BLOCKS.

HOLD FOR "ACTION", EVEN IF THE CAMERA IS RUNNING. BE AWARE OF CAMERA
POSITION. OPEN UP AND PLAY TO CAMERA. WATCH YOUR SHADOWS. DO NOT
COVER WITH HAIR, ARMS, HANDS.

BE WELL GROOMED EXCEPT AS SCRIPTED OTHERWISE.

RESERVE "VISTITING" FOR GREEN ROOM.

"CAST CALL" TIME MEANS ON SET IN WARDROBE AND MAKE UP, READY TO
PERFORM.

USE YOUR "OFF CAMERA" (AWAY FROM CAMERA) HAND FOR ALL ACTION
EXCEPT AS DIRECTED.

LISTEN TO DIRECTOR, ASK QUESTIONS, BLOCK DIFFICULT MOVES, AVOID QUICK,
UNNATURAL MOVEMENTS, AND BE SENSUAL.

1/2 DAY = 5 TO 6 SHOOTING HOURS – MINIMUM 60.00 TO 80.00
1 DAY = 6 TO 10 SHOOTING HOURS – MINIMUM 100.00 TO 130.00

THE ABOVE MAY DEPEND ON PERFORMANCE, COMPATABILITY, AND THE
OBSERVANCE OF THE ABOVE TECHINQUES.

THE ABOVE WAS AN INSTRUCTION SHEET GIVEN OUT TO CAST MEMBERS WHEN THEY WERE HIRED TO WORK ON A PORN SET BY 1970S SAN FRANCISCO XXX COMPANY "AVENTURA PICTURES", WHICH WAS OWNED AND OPERATED BY A MYSTERIOUS MAN NAMED RIK TAZINER. BASED IN LOS ANGELES, AND THEN LATER SAN FRANCISCO, RIK DABBLED IN BOTH THE GAY AND STRAIGHT PORN INDUSTRIES, PROMPTING SOME (SUCH AS PORN ACTOR JOHN SEEMAN) TO THINK THAT HE MIGHT HAVE ACTUALLY HAVE BEEN TWO PEOPLE.

THE INSTRUCTION SHEET COMES FROM THE COLLECTION OF PORN ACTOR RAY WELLS, WHO RECEIVED IT FROM RIK WHEN HE GOT A PART IN 1977'S TEENAGE DESIRES, WHERE HE DOUBLE-TEAMED SEKA ALONG WITH MIKE RANGER. "I REMEMBER HIM TELLING HIS ACTORS TO 'NEVER LOOK INTO THE CAMERA', RAY TOLD ME VIA EMAIL IN JULY 2015. "HE WOULD STOP SHOOTING IF SOMEONE DID AND DO A RETAKE."

THEY AREN'T PARTICULARLY GOOD ADULT MOVIES, IN MY OPINION. TAZINER WAS A TEDIOUS, CRUDE, SLOPPY AND ALTOGETHER UNTALENTED FILMMAKER, BUT HE DID GET THE JOB DONE, SO I HAVE TO GIVE HIM CREDIT FOR THAT I SUPPOSE. MAYBE IT WAS ALL OF THAT REFUSING TO LET THE CAST "VISIT FOR THE GREEN ROOM" THAT KEPT HIM ON BUDGET AND ON TIME. OTHER PORN MOVIES PRODUCED BY AVENTURA AND DIRECTED BY TAZINER INCLUDE:

South of the Border (1974), The Winter of 1849 (1976), Devil's Playground (1976), Ski Hustlers (1976), Cherry Truckers (1976), Teenage Madam (1977), Love Notes (1977), Inside Baby Sister (1977), House of Sir (1978).

SAHARA

BORN YVONNE WELDON IN PARIS FRANCE, SAHARA GREW UP IN SAN FRANCISCO AND MOVED TO LOS ANGELES IN 1982 TO TRY TO FURTHER HER MODELLING CAREER. VERY ACTIVE IN PORN FROM 1984 TO 1988 (NOT COINCIDENTALLY BEING THE YEARS THE AMERICAN PORN INDUSTRY FIRST KINDA REALIZED THAT BLACK AUDIENCES HAD MONEY TO SPEND, TOO), SAHARA WORKED AT A FEVERISH PACE, APPEARING IN MOST OF THE POPULAR INTERRACIAL-THEMED XXX VIDEOS RELEASED DURING THOSE 4 YEARS. EVEN WHILE SHE WAS DOING FUCK FILMS SHE ALSO RAN A SUCCESSFUL FINE ART DEALERSHIP, WHICH REPORTEDLY IS WHAT SHE CONCENTRATED UPON AFTER GETTING MARRIED AND RETIRING FROM THE JIZ-BIZ.

SAHARA DIDN'T HAVE THE STEREOTYPICAL BODY THAT HAS COME TO BE ASSOCIATED WITH FEMALE BLACK PORN STARS -- WITH THE CURVES AND THE BA-DONKA-DONK ASS. SHE WAS QUITE LITHE, AND HAD THE KIND OF TRIM FRAME THAT ONE EXPECTS TO SEE IN NON-PORN MODELLING, WITH HER AIR OF QUIET SOPHISTICATION AND ELEGANCE LEAVING THAT IMPRESSION AS WELL. "ONLY KAY PARKER, THE ORIGINAL 'CLASS ACT' OF PORN, CARRIES HERSELF WITH COMPARABLE DIGNITY" TRUMPETED ADAM FILM WORLD IN THEIR MARCH 1987 ISSUE. "WHAT'S MORE, SHE COMMUTES BETWEEN EUROPE AND THE UNITED STATES AS FREQUENTLY AS YOU OR I WASH THE FAMILY CAR."

SAHARA'S LARGE MOUTH AND BIG FULL LIPS HELPED HER GAIN A REPUTATION AS A COCK-SUCKING SPECIALIST. ALL THE LIP WAS UPSTAIRS ON THIS ONE, THOUGH. SAHARA'S LABIAS WERE SO SMALL THEY WERE VIRTUALLY NON-EXISTENT, AND UNLIKE A LOT OF WOMEN IN THE LATE 1980S PORN SCENE, SHE WASN'T INTERESTED IN SHAVING HER CUNT. IN EVERY VIDEO OF HERS I EVER SAW, SHE ALWAYS HAD AN ABUNDANCE OF AFRO-PUBES FRAMING HER VULVA. IN ONE FILM I SAW WHEN I WAS A TEENAGER, SHE THRUST FORWARD HER SOAPED UP HER PUBIC BRILLO PAD, LITERALLY USING IT TO SCRUB THE WINDOWS OF A WHITE LIMO PARKED IN THE DRIVEWAY OF A CALIFORNIA TOWNHOUSE.

THIS WAS NOT A SUBMISSIVE PERSONALITY. SHE OFTEN GAVE THE PRESENCE OF DRIVING AND DIRECTING HER OWN SCENES, AND SHE DID THAT WITH HER CONFIDENT BODY LANGUAGE, AND SOMETIMES VOCALLY. "I WANT YOU TO FINGER MY PUSSY WHILE YOU SUCK MY CLIT. ARE YOU LISTENING TO ME?", SHE FIRMLY ASKED BLAKE PALMER DURING THEIR SCENE TOGETHER IN 1985'S FIREFOXES. "HEY. I WANT YOU TO FINGER MY PUSSY. PUT IT A LITTLE IN MY ASS, TOO."

HER MOST INFAMOUS SCENE CAME IN LET ME TELL YA 'BOUT BLACK CHICKS. LIKE SO MANY OF THE FILMS PRODUCED BY GREGORY DARK (AKA GREG BROWN, THE BADBOY OF 1980S XXX), LET ME TELL YA 'BOUT BLACK CHICKS IS KNOWN FOR BEING CONTROVERSIAL. ONE SCENE IN PARTICULAR LED TO THE VIDEO'S

INDICTMENT DURING THE REAGAN ERA, AND ITS WITHDRAWAL FROM THE HOME VIDEO MARKET. IT'S A MEMORABLE SHOT-ON-VIDEO SEQUENCE THAT VIDEOTRAMP.COM CALLS "ONE OF THE MOST CONTROVERSIAL SCENES IN ADULT FILM HISTORY".

"PEOPLE HAD A FIT WHEN THAT CAME OUT," SAHARA'S LET ME TELL YA 'BOUT BLACK CHICKS COSTAR, JEANNIE PEPPER SAID. "BUT IT SOLD LIKE HOTCAKES."

IN THE 1990S, ANOTHER OF SAHARA'S COSTARS IN THE MOVIE, ANGEL KELLY, APPEARED ON THE BLACK ENTERTAINMENT TELEVISION SERIES CALLED 'OUR VOICES.' HOST BEV SMITH GRILLED HER AND QUESTIONED SAHARA'S ROLE IN THIS SCENE, ASKING "ISN'T IT PLAYING TO ALL THE STEREOTYPES THAT WHITE MEN HAVE ABOUT WOMEN?".

"BACK THEN, ALL BLACK ACTRESSES COULD ONLY GET PARTS AS MAIDS OR WHORES, OK?" ANGEL, RESPONDED. "AND THE PEOPLE THAT PRODUCED THIS PARTICULAR VIDEO WERE THE BIGGEST PEOPLE TO WORK FOR, SO I'M SURE WHEN THEY APPROACHED HER AND SAID, LIKE 'HEY, WE WANT TO USE YOU', IT'S LIKE SHE THOUGHT TO HERSELF, 'DO I WORK OR NOT?'"

AS THE SCENE OPENS, SAHARA LAYS IN BED WEARING A BLUE NIGHTIE, COMPLETE WITH FURRY HIGH HEELS. SHE'S MASTURBATING TO GOSPEL MUSIC, AND INTO THE ROOM TROT STEVE POWERS AND MARC WALLICE, DRESSED IN BLEACHED KLAN BED SHEETS AND HOODS. NOW AMONGST THE GOSPEL MUSIC IS THE INTRUDERS' RACIST VERBAL BANTER -- A SLEW OF HILLBILLY-STYLE REMARKS THAT CONTINUES UNTIL THE SCENE IS DONE. SAHARA BEGINS BY BLOWING THEM BEFORE THEY MOUNT HER, AND THIS DOUBLE PENETRATION PLOW-FEST IS ONE OF THE HOTTEST SEX SCENES OF SAHARA'S CAREER -- AND THAT'S SOMETHING I'VE EVEN SEEN REVIEWERS WHO DISLIKE THIS VIDEO ADMIT TO. THE KLANSMEN STAB AT HER PUCKER AND PUSSY IN UNISON, AND SHE GRINDS AND BUCKS AGAINST THEM AND GROANS TO BE SCREWED HARDER.

"YOU LIKE IT, DONCHA?" THEY GROWL AT HER. "YEAAAAH!!" SHE MOANS IN THE AFFIRMATIVE.

THEY WHOOP IT UP AND IT ENDS WITH WALLICE PULLING OUT OF HER ASSHOLE AND BLOWING A WHITE CREAMY LOAD ACROSS SAHARA'S BACK. SAHARA THEN SETS TO RIDING POWERS AS HARD AS SHE CAN, MILKING HIS SPUNK RIGHT OUT OF HIM SEEMINGLY BY HER OWN FORCE OF WILL. LATER, SAHARA GUSHES ABOUT THE ENCOUNTER TO THE OTHER MAIDS, DESCRIBING THE EXPERIENCE AS "TOO GOOD", AND SUGGESTING TO THE OTHER GIRLS THAT THEY GET THEMSELVES SOME "HONKEYS" TO FUCK.

ACCORDING TO SCRIPT WRITER ANTHONY R. LOVETT (AKA ANTONIO PASSOLINI, WHO PASSED AWAY IN 2014) THE INTENTION WITH LET ME TELL YA 'BOUT BLACK CHICKS WAS TO BE AS POLITICALLY INCORRECT AS POSSIBLE. IN 1987, JAMES WOLCOTT, WHO PENNED A FEATURE STORY ON GREGORY DARK CALLED "A WALK ON THE DARK SIDE" FOR VANITY FAIR, SAID ABOUT THE FILMMAKER AND HIS WRITING PARTNER: "THEY ATTEMPT TO BRING TO PORN WHAT SAM KINISON BRINGS TO STAND-UP COMEDY: SACRILEGE, NO APOLOGY, HOSTILE PATHOLOGY, HOARSE GUSTS OF LAUGHTER FROM THE JAWS OF HELL".

IN 2014, MIREILLE MILLER-YOUNG WROTE SPECIFICALLY ABOUT THIS INFAMOUS RACIALLY-CHARGED SCENE IN HER ACADEMIC BOOK ABOUT BLACK WOMEN IN PORNOGRAPHY, ENTITLED 'A TASTE FOR BROWN SUGAR.'

"SAHARA'S CHARACTER ATTEMPTS TO SUBVERT THE KLANSMEN'S SENSE OF MANHOOD AND ABILITY TO CONTROL HER SEXUALITY BY QUESTIONING THEIR GENITAL SIZE AND SEXUAL PROWESS. BY ATTACKING THEIR SEXUAL ABILITIES IN A MEAN, TAUNTING MANNER, THE BLACK WOMAN CHARACTER THREATENS WHITE MEN'S UNDERSTANDING OF POWER AND CAUSES POTENT FEELINGS OF   ANXIETY AND SHAME, WHICH, SET

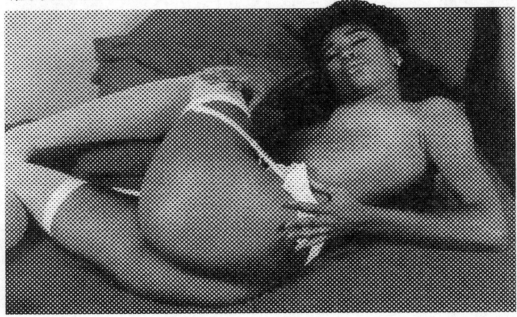

ALONGSIDE TITILLATION, EROTICALLY CHARGE THE SCENE. THE MEN RESPOND WITH A THREAT OF VIOLENCE, YET SAHARA'S MAID CONTINUES TO UNDERMINE AND PROVOKE THE MEN BY INTENTIONALLY REFUSING TO SEE THEM AS DANGEROUS. IN CONFIDENTLY ASSERTING THAT SHE "AIN'T AFRAID OF NO GHOSTS", HER CHARACTER DENIES THEM POWER AND POINTS TO THE HOLLOWNESS OF THEIR THREAT. DECLARING THEM GHOSTS, SHE MOCKS THE KLANSMEN'S ATTEMPT TO DISGUISE THEMSELVES IN THEIR RIDICULOUS WHITE SHEET COSTUMES."

"IN THE SEX SCENE THAT ENSUES BETWEEN THE THREE PERFORMERS, INCLUDING DOUBLE PENETRATION, THE BLACK WOMAN WOULD SEEM TO BE DOUBLY EXPLOITED BY AN UGLY FANTASY THAT RECALLS A HISTORY OF BLACK WOMEN'S ABUSE AT THE HANDS OF WHITE MEN. THIS INTERRACIAL SEX FANTASY APPEARS TO BE AUTHORED SO AS TO AROUSE FEELINGS OF NOSTALGIA FOR THE EROTIC FORCE OF WHITE SUPREMACY. SAHARA'S COMPLICITY DOES NOT ENDORSE WHITE SUPREMACY, AND SHE DOES NOT TAKE UP A PURE VICTIM STATUS EITHER. INSTEAD, IN THIS SCENE -- WHICH IS ONE OF THE MOST EXTREME SCENES I HAVE VIEWED IN MY RESEARCH, AND CERTAINLY THE MOST EXPLICITLY RACIST I HAVE OBSERVED FROM THE 1980S -- SAHARA'S PERFORMANCE GOES BEYOND REPRESENTING AND SUBMITTING TO BLACK WOMAN'S ABUSE. HER SEX PERFORMANCE IS FULL OF VOCALIZATIONS, EXPRESSIONS OF PLEASURE, AND GESTURES TO AFFIRM THAT SHE IS IN CONTROL OF THE SCENE. THIS IS NOT A FILMED RAPE. SAHARA'S REPRESENTATIONAL LABOR IS MORE COMPLEX: SHE PROVIDES A POTENTIAL DISRUPTION IN THE EROTICISM OF WHITE SUPREMACY BY ARTICULATING AN AGENTIVE SEXUAL PERFORMANCE THAT PRESENTS THE POSSIBILITY OF BLACK WOMEN'S OWN FANTASIES OF RACIAL SEXUAL DOMINATION. THIS SCENE EXPOSES THE WAYS IN WHICH FANTASIES OF INTERRACIAL SEX, BY WHITE MEN OR BLACK WOMEN, ARE INFORMED BY OUR COLLECTIVE HISTORY OF RACIAL AND SEXUALIZED VIOLENCE."

IN HIS KISS-AND-TELL MEMOIR, 'RAW TALENT', 1980S WOODSMAN JERRY BUTLER DIDN'T HAVE MUCH NICE TO SAY ABOUT WORKING WITH SAHARA ON THE SET OF 1985'S STRANGE BEDFELLOWS. "SAHARA WAS AS DRY AS THE DESERT", HE SNIPED, BEFORE NOTING THAT SHE WAS "ABUSIVE" AND "DISPLAYED AN UNNECESSARY AMOUNT OF STANDOFFISHNESS".

STRANGE BEDFELLOWS IS A SHOT-ON-VIDEO PRODUCTION ABOUT ROOMMATES (PLAYED BY SAHARA AND JEANNIE PEPPER) WHO HAVE A TWO-WEEK VACATION AND HEAD UP TO TOPANGA CANYON AND WORK AT GETTING AS MUCH NOOKIE IN THAT TIME AS POSSIBLE. THEY FUCK EACH OTHER, KIMBERLY CARSON, KEVIN JAMES, ERIC EDWARDS, AND OF COURSE, JERRY BUTLER. SAHARA AND BUTLER'S SCENE TAKES PLACE OUTSIDE BY A SWIMMING POOL, AND AS DICTATED BY THE SCRIPT, SHE HATES HIS GUTS BUT HAS SEX WITH HIM BECAUSE HE USES HIS MASTERY OF SCIENCE TO TURN HER ON AGAINST HER WILL.

"YOU ARE THE LEAST SEXUALLY AROUSING FUCKFACE I'VE EVER SEEN!" SAHARA SNAPS AT HIM BEFORE TELLING HIM TO "FUCK OFF!" JERRY DOES A REALLY GOOFY JERRY LEWIS IMPERSONATION WHILE PLAYING A NERDY SCIENTIST, AND I CAN'T HELP BUT THINK THAT HIS MEMORY OF SAHARA BEING "STANDOFFISH" AND "ABUSIVE" WAS UNDULY TAINTED BY THE ROLES THEY PLAYED. HE'S REMEMBERING HER NASTY CHARACTER, BUT NOT HER. AFTER BUTLER UNLOADS GLOBS OF CUM ON HER ASS, HE SLIDES INTO THE HOT TUB, FARTS, AND SAYS "OH LOOK! BUBBLES!!".

121

IN THE MAY 1986 ISSUE OF PLAYERS MAGAZINE, SAHARA WAS DUBBED "THE REIGNING QUEEN OF BLACK ADULT VIDEOS", AND WAS INTERVIEWED BY JOURNALIST/EDITOR H.L. SORRELL IN HER "WARM AND ARTFULLY DECORATED MALIBU BEACH HOUSE". IT WOULD STAND AS ONE OF THE ONLY INTERVIEWS SHE EVER CONSENTED TO IN HER CAREER.

PLAYERS: WHAT KIND OF CHILD WERE YOU?

SAHARA: I WAS AN INDIVIDUALIST. I BELIEVED VERY STRONGLY IN MY INDIVIDUALITY. I WANTED TO TRY TO DISCOVER EVERYTHING MY OWN WAY. IT WASN'T LIKE I WAS THE BLACK SHEEP OR ANYTHING. BUT I'VE ALWAYS HAD MY OWN LITTLE QUIRKS ABOUT ME. BUT MY FAMILY UNDERSTOOD ME AND I'VE ALWAYS HAD THE SUPPORT OF MY FAMILY TO GO OUT AND DO WHATEVER I WANTED TO DO.

P: SO WHEN DID YOU GET THE INKLING TO BECOME A PERFORMER?

S: I DIDN'T START OUT WITH THE IDEA OF BEING AN EROTIC FILM ACTRESS. IT JUST KINDA FELL INTO PLACE. I ALWAYS HAD BEEN SEXUALLY AWARE. I ALWAYS HAD THE DESIRE TO TRY DIFFERENT THINGS. I WAS NEVER INHIBITED, NEVER. SO BEING THAT WAY, IT BECAME EASY FOR ME TO "DO IT" IN FRONT OF OTHER PEOPLE. THE FIRST TIME I WAS EXPOSED TO A SITUATION THAT WASN'T A PERSONAL ONE ON ONE, WAS AT A SWING PARTY. I DIDN'T KNOW ABOUT IT IN ADVANCE, I WAS TAKEN THERE BY A DATE. WHEN I GOT THERE, PEOPLE WERE RUNNING AROUND WITH NO CLOTHES ON! I SAID TO MYSELF "WOW, I HAD HEARD ABOUT THESE THINGS, BUT THIS IS WILD!"

P: OKAY, HOW LONG AGO WAS THAT?

S: (SMILES) IT WAS ABOUT SIX YEARS AGO. BUT I WASN'T FREAKED OUT BY IT. I JUST THOUGHT IT WAS REALLY WILD. IT WAS LIKE ALL THE FANTASIES YOU'VE EVER HAD WHEN YOU'RE GROWING UP. YOU ALWAYS READ A DIRTY BOOK SOME POINT IN LIFE AND THERE ARE PICTURES OF PEOPLE FREAKING. I SAW THAT PEOPLE REALLY DO THESE THINGS, THE STRANGE POSITIONS ON THE ZODIAC CALENDAR, YOU KNOW WHAT I MEAN?

P: SO WHAT WAS THE NEXT STEP?

S: I HAD GOTTEN INTO FASHION MODELING. AND I WAS HIRED TO DO AN EROTIC SHOOT THAT WASN'T SUPPOSED TO BE NUDE, BUT IT TURNED OUT THAT WAY. BUT THE NUDITY WAS VERY SENSUOUS, WITH LOTS OF EROTICISM.

P: WAS THAT FOR A MAGAZINE LAYOUT?

S: YES. THAT WAS FOR A EUROPEAN MAGAZINE LAYOUT, FOR A PHOTOGRAPHER I HAD WORKED WITH ON STRAIGHT THINGS. ONE OF THE SETS WE SHOT WAS A BODY PAINTING LAYOUT. MY WHOLE BODY WAS PAINTED IN VERY EROTIC DESIGNS SO I KIND OF GOT INTO MY BODY. AFTER THAT, ONE THING LEAD TO ANOTHER. I WAS ASKED "DO YOU WANT TO DO THIS, DO YOU WANT TO DO THAT?" AND THAT WENT ON UNTIL I WAS OFFERED MY FIRST X-RATED VIDEO. SOMEONE ASKED ME IF I COULD PERFORM SEX ACTS ON VIDEO WITHOUT FREAKING OUT. I SAID I DON'T KNOW. BUT I TRIED IT AND I GUESS I DID OKAY.

P: WHAT WAS YOUR FIRST ADULT VIDEO?

S: BLACK TABOO WAS MY VERY FIRST VIDEO. I MIGHT ADD A HORRIBLE VIDEO. IT TOOK ME A FEW YEARS AFTER BEFORE I COULD DISTINGUISH BETWEEN A BAD SCRIPT AND ONE THAT WAS GOOD.

P: AND YOU STARRED IN BLACK TABOO WITH JEANNIE PEPPER?

S: YES, AND WITH TONY EL-AY. TONY EL-AY WAS THE FIRST MALE I WORKED WITH. YES, THAT WAS THE FIRST VIDEO BUT I DIDN'T FIND IT DIFFICULT. I WAS A LITTLE NERVOUS IN THE BEGINNING SIMPLY BECAUSE I DIDN'T KNOW THOSE PEOPLE VERY WELL. THEY TOO WERE NOT ACCUSTOMED TO MAKING VIDEOS. IN FACT, IT WAS THE FIRST VIDEO FOR MANY OF THAT CAST. IT WAS DIFFICULT BECAUSE I DIDN'T HAVE VERY MANY PROFESSIONALS TO PLAY OFF.

P: SPEAKING OF TONY EL-AY, HE'S ALWAYS SPOKEN VERY HIGHLY OF YOU. HE'S DESCRIBED YOU AS "A REAL GO-GETTER", ALTHOUGH HE OBVIOUSLY INTENDED IT AS A COMPLIMENT, WHAT DO YOU THINK HE MEANT BY THAT?

S: I THINK HE MEANT THAT I'M ONE OF THOSE PEOPLE WHO REALLY MEMORIZED THEIR LINES. I BELIEVE THAT I'M ON THE SET TO PERFORM A SPECIFIC TASK; THAT TASK IS TO EXCITE PEOPLE, TO ENTERTAIN PEOPLE IN A SENSUAL WAY. SO I COME IN WITH THE ATTITUDE, I'LL TALK AND LAUGH WITH YOU BUT WHEN IT'S TIME TO WORK, IT'S TIME TO WORK. I WANT TO SHOOT AND I WANT TO GET IT DONE. I DON'T TOLERATE PEOPLE JUST SCREWING UP BECAUSE IT'S NOT NECESSARY. I COME IN FOR A REASON, I DO MY JOB AND I GO ABOUT MY EVERYDAY LIFE.

P: YOU ARE CONSIDERED THE LEADING BLACK ACTRESS IN THE ADULT ENTERTAINMENT INDUSTRY. HOW DOES IT FEEL TO HAVE THAT KIND OF STAR STATUS AND HAVING GOTTEN IT SO QUICKLY?

S: IT'S NICE, IT'S REAL SWEET! (LAUGHS) I'LL BE STRAIGHT UP. TO HAVE PEOPLE CALL ME AND ASK ME CAN I DO THIS OR THAT, IT'S NICE. IF I DON'T WANT TO DO IT, I HAVE THE OPTION TO SAY NO. HOWEVER, IF I WERE A PERSON JUST STARTING OUT, IN JUST TO MAKE MONEY, I'D HAVE TO TAKE EVERYTHING THAT CAME ALONG. IT'S NICE BECAUSE I GET RECOGNITION. I GET MY NAME PUT FIRST ON THE VIDEO BOX COVER (GIGGLES) I KNOW THAT'S SILLY BUT IT'S FUN TOO. I DON'T LIKE THE RECOGNITION ALL THE TIME, WHEN I'M WITH FRIENDS FOR EXAMPLE. I'VE HAD PEOPLE COME UP TO ME IN SMALL TOWNS HERE, EVEN IN EUROPE, AND SAY "DIDN'T YOU DO SO AND SO?" OR "I SAW YOU IN SUCH AND SUCH, YOU WERE GREAT." AND I'LL SAY "OH, REALLY. PLEASE TAKE YOUR HAND OFF MY SHOULDER NOW." (LAUGHS).

P: BUT THAT'S THE PRICE YOU PAY FOR BEING A STAR. THERE ARE A GROWING NUMBER OF BLACK PERFORMERS IN ADULT VIDEOS, YET FEW BLACKS ARE CAST IN X-RATED FILMS THAT GET THEATRICAL RELEASE, WHY?

S: THE MARKET NOW IS IN VIDEO. PEOPLE ARE INTO SEX MOVIES AT HOME RATHER THAN GOING TO A THEATER TO SEE AN X-RATED MOVIE. FILMS DON'T PAY FOR THEMSELVES AS MUCH AS VIDEOS DO AND THAT HAS A LOT TO DO WITH IT.

P: MANY OF THE ROLES YOU BLACKS ARE ASKED TO PLAY SEEM TO BE RACIAL JOKES. FOR EXAMPLE, IN ONE OF YOUR RECENT VIDEOS, LET ME TELL YA 'BOUT BLACK CHICKS, YOU HAD SEX WITH TWO WHITE GUYS WEARING KLU KLUX KLAN HOODS. HOW DID YOU COME TO GRIPS WITH THAT?

S: IT WASN'T EVEN A MATTER OF COMING TO GRIPS WITH IT. I WAS CALLED TO PLAY A SPECIFIC PART. EVERYTHING IN THOSE VIDEOS IS THE INVENTION OF SOMEBODY'S MIND, IT'S NEVER BASED ON FACT. THE ROLE WASN'T SOMETHING THAT OFFENDED ME, AND I DON'T FEEL PEOPLE SHOULD BE OFFENDED BY IT. ESPECIALLY BLACK PEOPLE. IT WAS SOMETHING DONE TO ENTERTAIN -- NOT TO OFFEND -- AND THAT'S EXACTLY HOW I LOOKED AT IT. IF I GET A PART I FEEL IS DEGRADING THAN I'M NOT GOING TO DO IT. IN THAT SENSE IT WASN'T DEGRADING. I MEAN I DIDN'T HAVE TO CALL ANYBODY "MASSAH". I WILL NOT DO THAT. I THINK OF ALL THE THINGS THAT I'VE DONE, I'VE PLAYED A MAID CHARACTER MAYBE A TOTAL OF THREE TIMES. BUT THEY'VE BEEN THE TYPE OF MAIDS THAT ARE LIKE EUROPEANS/FRENCH CUTIE MAIDS, NOT SOMEBODY WITH A TURBAN ON HER GOD-DAMN HEAD. I WOULDN'T DO THAT, THAT'S NOT MY STYLE.

P: THERE ARE OTHER THINGS ACTRESSES ARE ASKED TO DO IN ADULT MOVIES. ONE IS THE OBLIGATORY GIRL/GIRL SCENE. NOW, YOU'VE PERFORMED A FEW OF THOSE ON-CAMERA YOURSELF. DID YOU EVER ENGAGE IN THAT KIND OF SEXUAL ACTIVITY BEFORE YOU GOT INTO ADULT MOVIES?

S: YEAH, SURE I DID. I'VE BEEN BISEXUAL FOR A LONG TIME.

P: ADULT MOVIES ARE OBTAINING A GREAT DEAL OF POPULARITY. SOME LEGAL FACTIONS IN OUR SOCIETY ARE SAYING THAT ACTRESSES WHO PERFORM ACTS OF SEX IN ADULT MOVIES FOR PAY ARE SIMPLY PROSTITUTES. HOW DO YOU REACT TO THAT?

S: (LAUGHTER) I'M LAUGHING AS YOU CAN SEE BECAUSE — NUMBER ONE — I AM NOT A PROSTITUTE, OKAY? NUMBER TWO: IT IS MY OCCUPATION TO EXCITE, JUST AS IT'S SOMEONE ELSE'S OCCUPATION AS AN ATTORNEY TO DEFEND A PERSON WHO CANNOT DEFEND HIMSELF, THE SAME AS A DOCTOR WHO IS HIRED TO HELP A PATIENT. A WIFE IS A PROSTITUTE WHEN YOU LOOK AT IT, ONE THAT DOESN'T WORK, ONE THAT TAKES THE KIDS SHOPPING. SHE HAS A BABY AND THAT'S A FORM OF PROSTITUTION THAT ENABLES HER TO KEEP MONEY COMING IN. SO DON'T GET DOWN ON AN ACTRESS WHO'S GETTING PAID TO HAVE RELATIONS WITH OTHER PEOPLE. IT'S DONE IN PRIVATE. WHAT DOES A WIFE DO? HER MAN COMES HOME, SHE COOKS AND SHE SCREWS HIM AT NIGHT. IS THAT NOT A FORM OF PROSTITUTION? SHE'S NOT WORKING BUT SHE'S GETTING MONEY, HER EXPENSES ARE TAKEN CARE OF. SO IF THEY WANT TO CALL ME A PROSTITUTE, THEN CALL HALF THE WOMEN IN MIDDLE AMERICA PROSTITUTES.

P: HAVE YOU CONSIDERED CROSSING OVER INTO GENERAL FILMS?

S: NO. I'M NOT REALLY INTERESTED IN BEING AN ACTRESS. I'M INTERESTED IN BEING EROTIC.

P: AS AN EROTIC SUPERSTAR IN THE X-RATED GENRE, DO YOU FEEL YOU OWE A DEBT OF GRATITUDE TO PREDECESSORS, SUCH AS SPARKY VASC AND DESIREE WEST, FOR PAVING THE WAY FOR YOU?

S: (SILENCE, THEN A PENSIVE SIGH) NO. I BELIEVE THAT EVEN IN STRAIGHT FILMS WHEN THERE WAS A LONG TIME WHEN BLACK PEOPLE WEREN'T ALLOWED, THAT PEOPLE PAVED THE WAY, SURE. BUT I DON'T BELIEVE THAT THE PEOPLE THAT FOLLOWED THEM OUGHT TO BE GRATEFUL. I BELIEVE I AM WHERE I AM BECAUSE I JUST WENT OUT AND DID SOMETHING BECAUSE THE MOOD HIT ME, NOT BECAUSE THE WORK OF SOMEONE ELSE HELPED ME ALONG THE WAY.

P: DO YOU HAVE TIME TO ENJOY THESE LOVELY SURROUNDINGS?

S: OH YEAH, NOT ALL THE TIME BUT WHENEVER I CAN. I'M A HOMEBODY. I DON'T GO OUT TO PARTY THAT MUCH AT ALL, BECAUSE I'M CONTENT IN MY HOME. I ENJOY SPENDING A LOT OF TIME HERE, BUT I RARELY INVITE PEOPLE HERE. EVERY BLUE MOON SOMEONE WILL COME BY HERE. THIS IS MY SPACE, I LIKE BEING HERE. I CONDUCT A LOT OF BUSINESS HERE, MY OFFICE IS HERE. I HAVE TO BE HERE A LOT TO CONDUCT BUSINESS OUTSIDE OF MAKING MOVIES.

P: GETTING BACK TO THE MOVIES, WHAT IN THE ADULT INDUSTRY DO YOU THINK REQUIRES THE MOST IMPROVEMENT OR CHANGE?

S: THE SCRIPTS. WE COULD USE SOME BETTER WRITERS. WE COULD USE SOME BETTER ACTORS AND ACTRESSES. THAT'S NOT TO SAY THAT THEY AREN'T SEXUALLY EXCITING. BUT WE NEED TO PORTRAY THEM A LITTLE MORE INTELLIGENTLY.

P: SOME OF THE FEMALE PRODUCERS I WAS REFERRING TO WHILE AGO ARE RESPONSIBLE FOR A TREND TOWARDS SOFTER X-RATED MOVIES. DO YOU FEEL THIS TREND TOWARDS SOFTCORE PORN WILL BE A STEP UP FROM THE HARDCORE PREDOMINATELY OFFERED NOW?

S: NO. I BELIEVE WE'VE ALREADY HAD SOFT PORN. IT DOESN'T TAKE A STEP UP OR A STEP BACK. IT'S POSSIBLE TO HAVE BOTH WITHOUT SACRIFICING ONE FOR THE OTHER.

I LIKE SOFT PORN. I LIKE NICE SLOW EROTIC MOVIES. BUT WHEN I WANT TO BE EXCITED I LIKE TO TURN ON THE VCR AND GET HOT. I WANT TO SEE STUFF! SO I BELIEVE IT'S POSSIBLE TO HAVE THE TWO.

P: WHAT OTHER TALENTS DO YOU HAVE THAT YOUR FANS MAY NOT BE AWARE OF?

S: UMMMM, PROBABLY THE FACT THAT I SPEAK FRENCH FLUENTLY. I WAS GOING TO STUDY LANGUAGES TO BE AN INTERPRETER FOR THE UNITED NATIONS. IT WOULD HAVE BEEN A LOT OF TIME INVOLVED, THOUGH.

P: THIS RECENT TRIP YOU HAD TO EUROPE, WHAT WERE YOU DOING THERE?

S: I WAS MODELLING DESIGNER FASHIONS. RUNWAY MODELLING, WHICH I LIKE A LOT BECAUSE THERE'S A LIVE AUDIENCE IN FRONT OF YOU. I GET TO SEE FIRST HAND THEIR REACTION TO THE CLOTHES AND TO ME.

P: SO WHAT KIND OF PERSON IS SAHARA? HOW WOULD YOU BEST DESCRIBE YOURSELF?

S: I WOULD DESCRIBE SAHARA AS BASICALLY A REALLY WARM PERSON WITH A WONDERFUL SENSE OF HUMOUR, VERY EARTHY AND STRAIGHTFORWARD. SHE'LL GET PISSED OFF IF THERE'S A REASON FOR IT, BUT OTHERWISE SHE'S THE MOST PLEASANT PERSON YOU'LL EVER WANT TO KNOW.   ·END·

JAILED FOR SHOWING TEENAGERS A HORROR MOVIE

IN MARCH 2015 A SUBSTITUTE TEACHER IN COLUMBUS, OHIO WAS CONVICTED OF A FELONY, SPECIFICALLY FOUR COUNTS OF DISSEMINATING MATTER HARMFUL TO JUVENILES. THIS WAS DETERMINED IN A COURT OF LAW AFTER MRS. SHEILA KEARNS SHOWED THE ANTHOLOGY FILM THE ABCS OF DEATH TO FIVE OF HER HIGH-SCHOOL SPANISH CLASSES (AGED 14 TO 18 IN APRIL 2013.)

AT THE TIME, SHEILA KEARNS' LAWYERS ARGUED THAT SHE HAD NO CLUE WHAT THE MOVIE WAS ABOUT (THE DVD CASE IMPLIES THAT IT IS A HORROR MOVIE, BUT GIVES NO IMPLICATION AS TO HOW GRAPHIC THE UNRATED FILM MAY OR MAY NOT BE) AND ASSUMED THAT THE ENTIRE MOVIE WAS IN SPANISH -- AS THREE OUT OF THE 26 SHORTS THAT MAKE UP THE FILM INDEED ARE. THEY ALSO NOTED THAT SHE HAD HER BACK TURNED TO THE TV FOR THE WHOLE DAY, AND DIDN'T TAKE NOTE OF THE ACTED OUT SCENES THAT FEATURED SEXUAL SITUATIONS, NUDITY, AND DEPICTIONS OF VIOLENCE. IN ESSENCE, HER LAWYERS ARGUED THAT SHE WASN'T GOOD AT HER JOB. SOMEHOW IT NEVER OCCURRED TO THEM THAT PERHAPS THEY SHOULD ARGUE THAT INCARCERATING SOMEONE AND ENDING THEIR TEACHING CAREER FOR SHOWING A COMMERCIALLY AVAILABLE FILM THAT ANY ONE OF THE TEENS COULD HAVE WATCHED ON NETFLIX OR BOUGHT FROM AMAZON.COM -- NO MATTER HOW INAPPROPRIATE IT WAS -- WAS FUCKING BONKERS.

DETECTIVE LOLITA PERRYMAN TESTIFIED KEARNS SEEMED UNCONCERNED WHEN THE MOVIE'S CONTENT WAS DESCRIBED TO HER. "SHE TOLD ME," PERRYMAN SAID, "THOSE KIDS SEE WORSE THAN THAT AT HOME." ANOTHER WITNESS FOR THE PROSECUTION WAS ONE OF KEARN'S STUDENTS IN THE CLASS THAT DAY. HE TESTIFIED THAT SOME OF THE OTHER STUDENTS IN THE CLASS WENT "CRAZY" WHILE WATCHING IT.

UNIMPRESSED, COMMON PLEAS JUDGE CHARLES A. SCHNEIDER PROCEEDED TO THROW THE BOOK AT KEARNS AFTER A JURY FOUND HER GUILTY OF FOUR FELONY COUNTS. THE 58-YEAR-OLD WAS SENTENCED TO 90 DAYS IN JAIL, AND PLACED ON PROBATION FOR 3 YEARS AS WELL AS HAVING HER TEACHING LICENCED PERMANENTLY REVOKED. THAT SHE WAS HIRED TO TEACH A SPANISH CLASS DESPITE BEING TOTALLY CLEAR TO HER EMPLOYERS THAT SHE DIDN'T SPEAK A WORD OF SPANISH SEEMED TO MATTER VERY LITTLE. SHE WAS THE ONE HELD WHOLLY RESPONSIBLE.

THREE MONTHS IN JAIL FOR A GRANDMOTHER BECAUSE SHE SHOWED SOME TEENAGERS A MOVIE. YOU KNOW, WITH ACTORS DOING ACTING. JUST LET THAT SINK IN... 90 DAYS, BEHIND BARS, FOR AN OLD WOMAN WITH NO CRIMINAL HISTORY... FOR WATCHING A MOVIE. I MEAN CHRIST, SHE SAID SHE WAS SORRY FOR HER MISTAKE. WOULDN'T A FIRING, A SUSPENSION, OR EVEN A STERN "TALKING TO" HAVE BEEN A FAR MORE APPROPRIATE PUNISHMENT FOR THIS "CRIME"? WHAT GOOD DOES JAILTIME AND TAKING HER CAREER AWAY, DO? IT'S SHOCKINGLY DRACONIAN TO SAY THE LEAST, AND COULD ONLY HAPPEN IN A COUNTRY WITH THE SORT OF INCARCERATION EPIDEMIC THAT THE U.S. HAS. I MEAN, I KNOW THE AMERICAN PRISON SYSTEM IS SIMPLY A BUSINESS, AND THE MORE PEOPLE IN THERE, THE BETTER IT IS FOR THE PROFIT MARGINS. I'M WELL AWARE THAT TOO MANY PEOPLE ARE PROFITING OFF THE JAILING OF THE POPULACE FOR THIS GROSSLY UNJUST AND CORRUPT GARBAGE TO END ANY TIME SOON, BUT THAT DOESN'T MEAN WE CAN'T CALL BULLSHIT WHEN WE SEE IT.

AND YET MOST PEOPLE THOUGHT SHEILA KEARNS WAS THE BULLSHITTER. AMONGST THE MOVIE GEEKS I KNOW, KEARNS WAS MOCKED AND THERE WAS A LOT OF DISBELIEF THAT SHE DIDN'T REALLY KNOW WHAT SHE WAS SHOWING TO THE TEENS. THERE WERE A GREAT NUMBER OF SNEERING COMMENTS AND OPINIONS ON SOCIAL MEDIA AND IN THE VIDEO/DVD STORE THAT I WORK IN -- ALL OF WHICH SEEMED

SHEILA KEARNS AND HER LAWYER

Hmmm THIS DOES **NOT** LOOK GOOD.

NO SHIT.

TO IGNORE THAT SHE WASN'T A COLLECTOR OR FAN OF HORROR MOVIE DVDS. NO ONE SEEMED ABLE TO FORGIVE HER FOR THE GRAVE OFFENSE OF NOT BEING AT ALL SAVVY ABOUT MODERN HORROR MOVIES AND THEIR PACKAGING. SHIT, MODERN HORROR MOVIES SUCK SO BAD, I HONESTLY WISH I WAS A LITTLE LESS SAVVY ABOUT THEM, MYSELF.

BEING DUMB ABOUT SOMETHING LIKE THIS SHOULDN'T BE A CRIME. IT JUST ISN'T AS OBVIOUS AS MANY OF YOU THINK AS TO HOW GRAPHIC THIS PARTICULAR MOVIE IS, ESPECIALLY TO SOMEONE WHO HAS NO FUCKING CLUE ABOUT THE GENRE. FOR ALL SHE KNEW, IT WAS LIKE GHOSTBUSTERS OR SOMETHING. I MEAN, THAT HAS "GHOST" IN THE TITLE, RIGHT? ISN'T THAT JUST AS SCARY A WORD AS "DEATH"? YOU CINEASTES COULD STEP OUT OF YOUR OWN SKIN FOR A SECOND AND LOOK AT THIS THROUGH THE EYES OF A 58-YEAR-OLD GRANDMOTHER WHO DOESN'T KNOW SHIT ABOUT THE GENRE. FOR INSTANCE, THE DVD COVER FOR MANY MOVIES (LIKE THE THE ORIGINAL RELEASE OF THE HAUNTING, FOR INSTANCE) DOESN'T LOOK ANY 'WORSE' (AS IN, SCARY AND GORY) THAN THE ONE FOR ABCs OF DEATH — AND IT'S RATED G.

AND I DON'T THINK IT'S MUCH OF A COINCIDENCE THAT ALL OF THE MOVIE NERDS I'VE DEBATED ABOUT THIS CASE WITH HAVE BEEN A BUNCH OF WHITE GUYS. AS A WHITE DUDE MYSELF, I THINK IT'S PRETTY FUCKIN' EASY TO SCOFF AND WAVE YOUR HAND AND SAY THIS IS ALL MUCH ADO ABOUT NOTHING, BUT I JUST KEEP THINKING ABOUT THE MULTITUDES OF STUDIES THAT HAVE SHOWN THAT BLACK PRISONERS ARE GIVEN MUCH STIFFER SENTENCES IN AMERICA THAN CAUCASIANS FOR THE EXACT SAME CRIMES, AND ARE OFTEN FOUND GUILTY AND GIVEN JAIL TIME FOR INFRACTIONS THAT WHITES ARE ROUTINELY GIVEN STERN WARNINGS FOR. THIS CASE IS A PERFECT EXAMPLE OF THAT KIND OF INJUSTICE IN ACTION.

DON'T AGREE? A QUICK GOOGLING FOUND MULTIPLE WHITE TEACHERS WHO HAD BEEN FIRED OR GIVEN DISCIPLINARY ACTION BY SCHOOL BOARDS FOR SHOWING SIMILAR R-RATED MOVIES TO THEIR CLASSES IN THE LAST 10 YEARS, NONE OF WHICH WERE GIVEN JAILTIME, A CRIMINAL RECORD, OR HAD THEIR CAREERS RUINED. I ALSO DIDN'T NOTICE ANYWHERE NEAR THE SAME LEVEL OF PUBLIC SCORN LEVIED AGAINST THEM ONLINE, FOR THAT MATTER. HELL, A CANADIAN TEACHER IN MONTREAL SHOWED THE INCREDIBLY GRAPHIC LUKA MAGNOTTA DEATH/CANNIBALISM FOOTAGE TO HIS GROUP OF 16-YEAR-OLD STUDENTS IN 2012, AND DIDN'T GET ARRESTED. THAT WAS AN ACTUAL STABBING, MUTILATION AND RAPE OF THE RAPIDLY COOLING CORPSE, WHILE THE ABCs OF DEATH IS SIMPLY A MOVIE STARRING ACTORS. IT'S NO COMPARISON AT ALL.

A LOT OF PEOPLE HAVE GIVEN ME EXCUSES AS TO WHY SHE DESERVES TO "DO THE TIME BECAUSE SHE DID THE CRIME". EVERYTHING FROM "TEACHERS AREN'T PAID TO SHOW KIDS HORROR FILMS", TO "SHE HANDED THE COURT A PIECE OF PAPER WITH A BIBLE QUOTE ON IT AND SAID LITTLE ELSE DURING HER SENTENCING." LOOK, I DON'T CARE IF SHE RAN UP THE SIDE OF THE COURTROOM WALL AND SANG THE FINNISH NATIONAL ANTHEM WITH HER BUTT, PUTTING PEOPLE IN JAIL FOR WATCHING MOVIES IS UNJUST.

IS IT KIND OF WEIRD THAT SHE PLAYED THE FILM FOR 5 DIFFERENT CLASSES OF KIDS AND CLAIMS NOT TO HAVE SEEN ANY OF IT? ABSOLUTELY THAT IS WEIRD, BUT IT IS NOT UNFATHOMABLE. SHE HAD HER BACK TO THE CLASS. IF YOU'VE SEEN THE WORK LOAD THAT TEACHERS ARE SADDLED UP WITH IN TERMS OF GRADING PAPERS AND STUFF, IT DOESN'T STRIKE ME AS UNLIKELY THAT SHE COULD HAVE HER NOSE IN THOSE PAPERS FOR MOST OF THE DAY. I MEAN, I DO REALIZE I AM REACHING TO SOME EXTENT WITH MY DEFENCE OF THIS TEACHER WHO VERY OBVIOUSLY MADE A REGRETTABLE MISTAKE, BUT THAT IS JUST TO ILLUSTRATE MY POINT THAT THERE IS MORE THAN ENOUGH DOUBT HERE, DOUBT THAT JUDGE SCHNEIDER DID NOT TAKE INTO ACCOUNT BEFORE SENDING YET ANOTHER AFRICAN AMERICAN TO PRISON FOR A PISS-POOR REASON. SHE SHOULDN'T HAVE BEEN FOUND CRIMINALLY LIABLE, MUCH LESS PUNISHED WITH THAT KIND OF SENTENCE.

SHEILA KEARNS DID HER 90 DAYS IN JAIL AND WAS NEVER ABLE TO TEACH AGAIN, ALTHOUGH THE PRODUCERS OF ABCs OF DEATH, ANT TIMPSON AND TIM LEAGUE, WERE KIND ENOUGH TO START A CROWD-SOURCING CAMPAIGN TO HELP PAY FOR A FEW THOUSAND DOLLARS OF HER LEGAL FEES. AS OF THIS WRITING THE COLUMBUS METROPOLITAN LIBRARY HAS THE ABCs OF DEATH AVAILABLE FOR LOAN TO ANYONE WITH A LIBRARY CARD -- INCLUDING TEENAGERS -- JUST AS IT DID BEFORE THE KEARNS CASE. IT CURRENTLY HAS 23 REQUESTS.

— BOUGIE '15

QUITE SURPRISINGLY (TO ME, ANYWAY) THE PREVIOUS ARTICLE, "JAILED FOR SHOWING TEENAGERS A HORROR MOVIE" ENDED UP BEING ONE OF THE MOST CONTENTIOUS CINEMA SEWER PIECES OF THE LAST FIVE YEARS WHEN IT FIRST SAW PRINT IN ISLAND #7, FROM IMAGE COMICS IN 2016. HERE ARE A FEW OF THE MORE NOTEWORTHY BITS OF FEEDBACK I GOT:

I just read Island #7 and I gotta say your article "Jailed" is incredibly wrong-headed. I've taught for 10 years, and I've shown some fairly questionable stuff to high schoolers in film studies (Shining, Tangerine) when I thought it was worthwhile, but the teacher in that case showed irredeemably poor judgement, was obviously lying about not knowing the content of the film (was she deaf as well as having her "back turned" for 6 hours? bullshit), and should absolutely never work with children again. Whether or not she deserved jail time is another question, but laws like that do have a valid purpose. Trust me, when the kids themselves feel their class time is being wasted and are disturbed enough to snitch on a teacher, that teacher deserves to be fired... Have you ever been an educator? I hope not. Your argument seemed to come strictly from a free speech perspective, but that freedom must be secondary to professional ethics in a classroom setting. -- gdkeen

You got it so back-asswards, Bougie-boy. I bet you think this is journalism, don't you? You're just another social justice warrior, and SJWs are the biggest fascists and sheeple there are. She was a bad, bad, bad teacher and shady as fuck and I guess you couldn't deal with that, and got triggered because she's black. Boo hoo. Cry harder. She got what she deserved. She should have gotten a lot worse, actually. -- Anon

What is this, 'black lives matter', or something? Sheila Kearns got off easy. So you found some evidence of white teachers who showed worse stuff and didn't get punished? All that proves is that the book needs to be thrown at these idiots more often. Congratulations on proving that, because that's all you proved. Stick to reviewing movies, Rob, and leave the social commentary to someone who is better at it. -- palgip1

I couldn't disagree more with your piece on Sheila Kearns. You obviously don't have kids, and have no understanding of what it's like to raise one or console a child who has just had a nightmare. I would be furious if my teenager came home and told me they watched a horror movie in class. They affect everyone differently, you know. Being forced to watch that kind of movie is not a victimless crime. -- A. Leeds

IN 2009, GRINDHOUSEDATABASE.COM INTERVIEWED QUENTIN TARANTINO AND ASKED HIM WHAT HIS TOP 20 GRINDHOUSE MOVIES OF ALL TIME WERE. THE DIRECTOR/WRITER CAME UP WITH HIS LIST, AND IT'S ONE THAT I THINK IT INTERESTING ENOUGH TO PRINT HERE, AS WELL. IT HAS THE STANDARDS THAT YOU WOULD EXPECT TO SEE MAKE AN APPEARANCE, BUT THERE ARE SOME UNUSUAL PICKS TOO.

20. The Pom Pom Girls (1976)
19. The Savage Seven (1968)
18. The Hammer of God (1970)
17. Suspiria (1977)
16. They Call Her One Eye (1973)
15. The Lady in Red (1979)
14. The Psychic (1977)
13. The Streetfighter (1974)
12. The Boss (1973)
11. Master of the Flying Guillotine (1976)
10. The Last House on the Left (1972)
9. Girl from Starship Venus (1975)
8. The Mack (1973)
7. Five Fingers of Death (1972)
6. Rolling Thunder (1977)
5. Coffy (1973)
4. Halloween (1978)
3. Night of the Living Dead (1968)
2. Dawn of the Dead (1978)
1. The Texas Chain Saw Massacre (1974)

TARANTINO'S TOP 20

What ever happened to

Ronnie Dickson?

I STOLE THE VERY FIRST ADULT MAG I EVER OWNED AS A 13-YEAR-OLD. I STOLE IT FROM A USED BOOKSTORE ON 14TH STREET IN CALGARY, BACK IN 1986. IT WAS THE DECEMBER 1986 ISSUE OF VELVET. THE OWNER OFTEN HIRED LOCAL KIDS TO HELP OUT IN EXCHANGE FOR USED COMICS/BOOKS/CASSETTE TAPES THAT WE WANTED AND COULDN'T AFFORD. I CAN'T TODAY REMEMBER THE NAME OF THIS STORE, BUT IT HAD A MURAL OF SOME PEOPLE ON THE SIDE OF THE BUILDING, WHICH ALWAYS PROMPTED MY MOM TO CALL THE PLACE "FACES ON THE WALL". AN ODD NAME, BUT IT STUCK, AND THAT'S WHAT MY FRIENDS AND I WOULD CALL IT.

IT WAS A HEIST, AND I PLANNED IT ALL OUT IN ADVANCE. THE SCAM WAS THAT AS I WAS HELPING CLEAN OUT A BACK ROOM IN THE STORE, I SNUCK THE ISSUE OF VELVET OUT THE BACK DOOR TO THE GARBAGE CAN IN THE ALLEY AMONGST A PILE OF OLD NEWSPAPERS, AND THEN PICKED IT OUT OF THERE LATER WHEN I WAS DONE HELPING CLEAN. KIDS ARE SO UNTRUSTWORTHY! I'VE NEVER SHOPLIFTED AFTER I BECAME AN ADULT, BUT I WAS ALWAYS DOING STUFF LIKE THAT AS A KID. I JUST DIDN'T KNOW ANY BETTER, I GUESS.

AS AN ASIDE: I ALSO FOUND AN OLD DILDO IN THAT SAME DUMPSTER MONTHS LATER, AND TOOK IT HOME AND HUNG IT ON MY BEDROOM WALL. MY MOTHER MUST HAVE THOUGHT I WAS INSANE. MY FRIEND LEON (WHO PULLED THE SAME SNEAKY AFOREMENTIONED SCAM TO ALSO PROCURE SOME PORN FROM THE SAME STORE) WAS UTTERLY HORRIFIED THAT I WOULD HANDLE A USED DILDO, AND FRANKLY I'M AGHAST IN HINDSIGHT THAT I DID, TOO. I WAS TOTALLY PREOCCUPIED WITH ANYTHING SLEAZY, SO FINDING AN OLD DILDO FOR ME WAS LIKE FINDING HIDDEN TREASURE! I WAS A WEIRD KID.

ANYWAY, IT WAS A GREAT ISSUE TO HAVE AS YOUR FIRST PORN MAGAZINE. THE LEGENDARY GINGER LYNN ON THE BACK COVER, HEADLINE NEWS OF THE INCREDIBLE SEKA'S "CARNAL COMEBACK" ON THE FRONT COVER. COLOURFUL PHONE SEX ADS IN THE BACK SECTION, WITH ABOUT HALF OF THEM SCANDALOUSLY BLACKED OUT (COMMON IN THE CANADIAN CENSORED EDITIONS OF AMERICAN STROKE MAGAZINES IN THE MID 1980S), WHICH ONLY MADE THEM SEEM SO MUCH DIRTIER. THEN THERE WERE AMATEUR POLAROID PORN OF THE WINNERS OF THE "NAUGHTY NEIGHBOR" CONTEST, SPREADS FEATURING THE AMAZING TISH AMBROSE AND SWEET KRISTARA BARRINGTON, AND A 5-PAGE FULL COLOUR PORN COMIC BY BRIAN FORBES.

NESTLED IN THERE AMONGST ALL THAT WAS A SECTION OF THE MAGAZINE CALLED "FANTASY OF THE MONTH", WHERE A READER NAMES A FANTASY (IN THIS CASE A PERSONAL TRAINER FROM A GYM WHO WANTED TO BE SEDUCED BY A WOMAN WHILE HE WOULD BE GIVING HER A MASSAGE AT WORK) AND VELVET WOULD HIRE SOME PHOTOGRAPHER TO TAKE SOME PICS OF SOME MODELS ACTING IT OUT. I WAS STUNNED, BECAUSE THE SHORT-HAIRED BRUNETTE GIRL IN THE PHOTO SHOOT LIT UP THE SYNAPSES OF MY BRAIN SOMETHING FIERCE. I DON'T KNOW WHAT IT WAS ABOUT HER, BUT I CRUSHED HARD. OVER THE FOLLOWING MONTHS I'D VISIT HER ROUTINELY EVERY EVENING FOR A MASTURBATION SESSION. I DIDN'T EVEN PAY ATTENTION TO THE REST OF THE MAGAZINE AFTER AWHILE. SHE WAS MY JAM.

A YEAR LATER AS A 14-YEAR-OLD I WOULD GET ANOTHER ISSUE OF VELVET MAGAZINE (I DON'T REMEMBER HOW I CAME TO ACQUIRE THIS ONE, YOU ONLY REALLY REMEMBER YOUR FIRST TIME, I GUESS), AND MUCH TO MY DELIGHT THERE WERE EVEN MORE PHOTOS OF THIS SAME ADORABLE GIRL, WEARING THE SAME PINK-ISH PURPLE

RONNIE ROCKS MANY COCKS!

LEOTARD -- BUT THIS TIME DOING A COUPLES SHOOT WITH A DIFFERENT STUD. FRUSTRATINGLY, SHE WAS YET AGAIN NOT EVEN SO MUCH CREDITED TO A FAKE NAME. THIS WAS THE FEB 1987 ISSUE OF VELVET. MORE MATERIAL FOR THE SPANK BANK.

ANYWAY, FLASH FORWARD NEARLY 30 YEARS TO SEPTEMBER 2015, WHEN I WAS PUBLICLY LAMENTING ON FACEBOOK ABOUT HOW I'D NEVER BEEN ABLE TO IDENTIFY THE SHORT-HAIRED PURPLE-LEOTARD GIRL. I SPOKE IN THAT POST ABOUT THE MASSIVE CRUSH I'D HAD ON HER AS A YOUNG PUP, AND HOW I WAS REALLY INTO HER SHORT HAIR AND ALL THOSE "NEW WAVE" LOOKING GIRLS. YOU BETTER BELIEVE I HAD ALL THE ALBUMS BY THE GO-GOS. OH HELL YES.

WHILE RESPONDING TO COMMENTS I WAS THUMBING THROUGH THAT OL' MAGAZINE FOR WHAT MUST HAVE BEEN THE 900TH TIME, AGAIN POURING OVER THE MYSTERY WOMAN'S PHOTOS WHEN SUDDENLY I HAD A LIGHTBULB MOMENT. I STARED AT THE PAGES INTENTLY. RECOGNITION. DON'T LOOK AT HER, LOOK AT HIM. THE MASSEUSE DUDE IN THE PHOTOSPREAD THAT WAS YANKING HER LEOTARD BETWEEN HER PERFECT ASSCHEEKS, RUBBING HER TITS, AND GRINDING HIS COCK AGAINST HER PUBIC MOUND WAS SOMEONE I FUCKING KNEW! WHY, THAT THERE WAS THE AWESOME RICK SAVAGE, ONE OF MY FACEBOOK FRIENDS! MY HEART THUMPING, I QUICKLY TAGGED HIM ON THE POST, AND WITHIN 15 MINUTES HE'D REPLIED WITH INFORMATION I'D BEEN HOPING TO FIND MY ENTIRE ADULT LIFE. THIS TECHNOLOGICAL WORLD WE LIVE IN NEVER CEASES TO AMAZE.

HERE'S WHAT RICK SAID. BLESS HIM AND BLESS HIS STILL-WORKING MEMORY: "IN 1986 I MET HER ON AN R-RATED PLAYBOY CABLE SHOOT. I HAD THE MALE LEAD. NEAR THE END OF THE DAY, SHE CAME UP TO ME AND SAID, SOMEWHAT INCREDULOUSLY, 'DO YOU KNOW, MOST OF THE GIRLS ON THIS SHOOT HAVE DONE PORN MOVIES?' I SAID YES, AND EXPLAINED THAT I'D DONE SEX SCENES WITH MOST OF THEM. I GAVE HER MY PHONE NUMBER AND TOLD HER IF SHE EVER WANTED TO GIVE IT A TRY, TO LET ME KNOW. 3 DAYS LATER, SHE GIVES ME A CALL. THE CAR PAYMENT ON HER BRAND NEW HONDA CIVIC WAS DUE."

"I THOUGHT SHE WAS EXTREMELY HOT SO I CALLED JIM SOUTH AND ASKED IF THERE WAS ANY DIRECTORS SHOOTING WITHIN THE NEXT FEW DAYS, BECAUSE I REALLY WANTED TO DO A SCENE WITH HER. OF THE 2 OR 3 DIRECTORS THAT WERE SHOOTING, ONE WAS CHARLIE BIGGS (AKA CHARLIE DIAMOND). NOW CHARLIE AND I GOT ALONG JUST FINE. SO I CALLED BIGGS AND SAID, 'CHARLIE, YOU HAVE ANY INTEREST IN HAVING A FORMER CONTESTANT IN THE MISS AMERICA CONTEST IN YOUR SHOOT THIS WEEKEND IN BIG BEAR?' OH, I FORGOT TO MENTION THE PART WHERE SHE WAS 19 AND SAID SHE'D BEEN A CONTESTANT IN THE MISS AMERICA PAGEANT WHEN SHE WAS 16 OR 17 AND HAD MOVED TO HOLLYWOOD TO "MAKE IT BIG." WELL-- SHE MADE MINE BIG, SO I TOLD CHARLIE I'D ONLY GIVE UP HER NAME IF HE HIRED ME TO WORK WITH HER. WELL, I'M SURE YOU CAN GUESS CHARLIE'S ANSWER. SO, ONE "RONNIE DICKSON" MADE HER FIRST MOVIE, "RIDE A PINK LADY" FOR CHARLIE BIGGS. SHE DID ONE SCENE WITH ME AND ONE WITH RANDY WEST."

RONNIE DICKSON! NOW THAT I HAD HER NAME, I COULD RESEARCH HER, AND FIND HER MOVIES. AND SO I DID OVER THE COMING DAYS, WITH RICK EMAILING ME EVERY SO OFTEN TO TELL ME MORE MEMORIES AS

THEY CAME TO HIM. HE TOLD ME ABOUT THAT FIRST SHOOT UP AT BIG BEAR, FILMING RONNIE'S FIRST MOVIE, RIDE A PINK LADY. ABOUT HOW IT WAS MADE IN A BIG 6-BEDROOM SKI LODGE, WHERE THE CAST AND CREW ALSO SPENT THE NIGHT.

"I KNEW THE DRILL", RICK NOTED. "SO, AS SOON AS I GOT THERE, I THREW MY BAG DOWN ONTO A QUEEN-SIZE BED IN ONE OF THE BEDROOMS, TO INDICATE THAT BED WAS TAKEN. AT THE END OF THE NIGHT, RONNIE SAYS TO ME, 'WOW, I'M NOT SURE WHERE I'M GOING TO SLEEP. I THINK ALL THE BEDS ARE TAKEN.' AND ROBIN...THIS IS WORD FOR WORD HOW IT HAPPENED... I SAID TO HER, 'WELL, I HAVE A HUGE BED AND I'M THE ONLY ONE IN MY ROOM. YOU'RE WELCOME TO SHARE IT WITH ME,' SAYING IT IN ALL POLITENESS, NO SLEAZY IMPLICATIONS. SO, WE GET INTO BED, AND AFTER A FEW MINUTES OF SILENCE, SHE SAYS TO ME, 'I DON'T KNOW HOW I'M EVER GOING TO GET TO SLEEP. I'M SO HORNY.' AND THAT WAS THE BEGINNING OF A 4-MONTH FLING THAT RONNIE AND I HAD."

RICK WOULD TAKE RONNIE'S PORNO CHERRY THE NEXT DAY, FUCKING HER EARLY ON, AND THEN SWITCHING OFF TO NAIL TIFFANY STORM IN A SCENE SHOT LATER IN THE DAY. CO-STAR AND CAPABLE WOODSMAN RANDY WEST SADDLED UP TO RONNIE'S BUM AND FUCKED HER IN THE ASS IN THE SAME SCENE. NOW THAT MAY NOT BE ALL THAT UNUSUAL IN TODAY'S ANAL-OBSESSED XXX INDUSTRY, BUT IT WAS EXCEEDINGLY RARE FOR A FIRST-TIME PORN ACTRESS TO DO ANAL RIGHT FROM THE GET-GO IN 1986 ON HER VERY FIRST DAY ON THE JOB IN THE INDUSTRY. FROM WHAT SAVAGE WOULD REVEAL TO ME, RONNIE WAS ACTUALLY QUITE FOND OF ANAL PENETRATION, SOMETIMES REQUESTING IT FROM HIM DURING THEIR PRIVATE LOVEMAKING, WITH THAT REQUEST USUALLY COMING IN THE FORM OF PLAYFUL BANTER.

"WE WOULD BE FUCKING LIKE CRAZY," SAID SAVAGE, "AND I REMEMBER HER WHISPERING, 'IF I GIVE YOU AN EXTRA HUNDRED, CAN I GET AN ANAL?' BEING THE GENTLEMAN THAT I AM, I OBLIGED."

I THINK RICK FELT A LITTLE AWKWARD KISSING AND TELLING, EVEN ABOUT SEXUAL CONQUESTS THAT HAD HAPPENED SO LONG AGO, BUT I WAS SO EXCITED TO HEAR FIRST HAND ACCOUNTS ABOUT THE MYSTERIOUS MISS RONNIE, AND CONTINUED TO GOAD HIM AND PROMPT HIM TO SPILL MORE BEANS. "ANOTHER TIME WE WERE ON THE 405 FREEWAY", RICK EVENTUALLY TOLD ME, "WE WERE STUCK IN BUMPER TO BUMPER TRAFFIC, SUDDENLY, WITHOUT ME ASKING OR SAYING A WORD, SHE JUST REACHED OVER, TOOK OUT MY DICK AND GAVE ME A BLOWJOB WHILE WE CRAWLED ALONG IN TRAFFIC."

"SHE WAS METICULOUS ABOUT HER APPEARANCE. SHE ACTUALLY HAD A BIT OF A FETISH FOR BLACK GUYS WITH VERY LARGE PENISES, BUT THAT'S A FETISH SHARED BY MANY A WOMAN, I SUPPOSE. YEAH, I GUESS PERSONALITY WISE, SHE DIDN'T SHOW MUCH OF HERSELF. SHE WAS A VERY HORNY 19-YEAR-OLD. I WAS 35 AT THE TIME, AND STILL YOUNG-LOOKING AND PRETTY IN THOSE DAYS. I DON'T REMEMBER MUCH ABOUT HER TASTE IN MUSIC OR MOVIES, I MOSTLY JUST REMEMBER THAT SHE LIKED TO FUCK."

"I KNEW A LOT OF DIRECTORS SO I COULD TURN HER ON TO A LOT OF JOBS. PART OF WHY SHE WAS WITH ME MIGHT HAVE BEEN FOR THE WORK I COULD GET HER. I SUSPECTED THERE WAS A BIT OF A GOLD DIGGER IN HER WHEN ONE DAY SHE TOLD ME THAT HER IDOL WAS THE CHARACTER OF ERICA (PLAYED BY SUSAN LUCCI) ON THE SOAP OPERA 'ALL MY CHILDREN'. ALL I REMEMBER ABOUT THE ERICA CHARACTER WAS (I REALLY DIDN'T WATCH THE SHOW) THAT SHE WAS A VERY CONNIVING WOMAN. AND THIS WAS RONNIE'S IDOL? YEAH, RONNIE WAS PLEASANT ENOUGH AND I REALLY ENJOYED HAVING SEX WITH HER. BUT I BEGAN TO WONDER IF SHE WAS LOOKING FOR A SUGAR DADDY. I MEAN, SHE WAS NICE, BUT JUST A LITTLE SUPERFICIAL

FOR EARTHY OLD HIPPIE ME. I WAS SAD TO SEE IT END, THOUGH. I WANTED TO GO BACK AND WORK IN JAPAN. SHE DECIDED SHE DIDN'T WANT TO GO, SO I TOOK LITTLE KNOWN ACTRESS, ELAINE SOUTHERN, WHO'D BEEN MY GIRLFRIEND BEFORE I MET RONNIE. AND THAT WAS IT."

ALSO IN 1986, RONNIE WAS ONE OF THE FEATURED PLAYERS IN A VIDEO CALLED BACKDOOR BRIDES 2: THE HONEYMOON. IT WAS YET ANOTHER ANAL OUTING, WITH RONNIE DOING A COUPLING WITH THE NOW-LEGENDARY TOM BYRON. IT'S A REALLY NICE SCENE -- SHE SUCKS OFF TOM AND THEN COWGIRLS HIM WHILE HE ROMANTICALLY FINGERS HER ASSHOLE. THEN SHE PASSIONATELY IMPALES HER BUTT ON HIS DICK, STILL IN COWGIRL POSITION, AND JUST RHYTHMICALLY MILKS IT. BOTH OF THEM SEEM TO REALLY ENJOY THEMSELVES, WHICH IS ALWAYS GOOD TO SEE. SINCE THIS VID GOT BETTER DISTRIBUTION THAN MOST OF HER MOVIES, IT'S ONE OF THE FEW THAT I'VE EVER FOUND EVIDENCE OF PORN FANS ACTUALLY CRITIQUING HER AND HAVING AN OPINION ON THIS MOSTLY IGNORED AND FORGOTTEN PERFORMER. ALMOST WITHOUT EXCEPTION, IT ISN'T VERY KIND.

"RONNIE DICKSON, THE WOMAN WITH THE SHORT BROWN HAIR AND THE NOT-SO-GREAT LOOKS", CHORTLED REVIEWER SERGEJ KRAVINOFF. "HER ASSHOLE, LIKE MANY OTHER ASSHOLES IN THIS VIDEO, IS VERY GREASY. THAT'S ANOTHER DIFFERENCE BETWEEN THE ANAL EROTICA OF THE LATE NINETIES AND THAT OF THE MID-EIGHTIES."

"(SHE WAS) PLAIN LOOKING WITH A SLIM BODY", WROTE AN UNIMPRESSED REVIEWER WHO SIGNED HIS WORK 'JMT'. "A SHORT HAIRED BRUNETTE A ONE-HIT WONDER. I NEVER HAVE SEEN HER IN ANYTHING ELSE."

NOR DID MOST PORN FANS. SHE WENT UNRECOGNIZED AND UNHERALDED THROUGHOUT HER SHORT ONE-YEAR CAREER AS RONNIE DICKSON, EARNING NO AWARDS OR ACCOLADES. EROTIC X-FILM GUIDE DID, HOWEVER, NAME HER FOUR-WAY SCENE WITH TOM BYRON, DON FERNANDO, AND MIKI KUROSAWA (IN WHICH RONNIE WAS DOUBLE-PENETRATED AND TOOK A CUM FACIAL) AS THEIR "SEX SCENE OF THE MONTH" FOR APRIL 1987. IN TRUE UNDERDOG FASHION, HOWEVER, SHE WAS AGAIN DENIED ANY SORT OF RESPECT OR JUSTICE WHEN SHE WAS MIS-IDENTIFIED AND INCORRECTLY CREDITED IN THE MAGAZINE AS FELLOW CAST-MEMBER BARBIE DOLL.

PERHAPS SENSING THAT HER XXX CAREER HAD SORT OF STALLED, SHE SUDDENLY DISAPPEARED. OR DID SHE?

RONNIE AS TIANA CAMBRIDGE, ROPED TO FELLOW 'BONDAGETTE' GERI ALCOTT IN THE 1987 CALSTAR VIDEO "KIDNAPPED SECRETARY CAPER"

BASED IN LANCASTER, CA, CALSTAR HAVE BEEN MAKING BDSM PORNO FOR 42 YEARS.

AFTER WORKING IN XXX PORN FOR ALL OF 1986, A FEW MONTHS INTO 1987 RONNIE SHIFTED GEARS. THE SHORT-HAIRED BRUNETTE THAT SEEMINGLY FAILED TO REALLY CAPTURE THE FULL ATTENTION OF ANYONE ASIDE FOR A 13-YEAR-OLD ME AND A 35-YEAR-OLD RICK SAVAGE STARTED FROM SCRATCH AND GAVE IT ANOTHER SHOT AS ANOTHER WOMAN. SHE GREW HER HAIR OUT, AND SHE CHANGED HER NAME. SHE WOULD NOW BE TIANA CAMBRIDGE (AND OCCASIONALLY: MONICA FRAGGI) AND SHE WOULD PRIMARILY NOW DO NON-HARDCORE SCENES IN BONDAGE AND KINK VIDEOS AND MAGAZINES.

IT WAS CLEAR THE LONG HAIR WENT OVER BETTER WITH MASTURBATORS, AND SHE NEVER WENT BACK TO THAT CUTE SHORT STYLE AGAIN. SHE INSTANTLY COMMANDED A BIGGER AND MORE APPRECIATIVE AUDIENCE, AND EVEN TODAY ONLINE TIANA HAS VASTLY MORE FANS THAN RONNIE DOES, WITH FEW OF THEM (AS OF THIS WRITING) REALIZING THEY ARE THE SAME WOMAN. EVEN IN A THREAD ABOUT TIANA CAMBRIDGE ON THE POPULAR PORN NERD MESSAGE BOARD, VINTAGE EROTIC FORUM, THE GUY WHO STARTED THE OFFICIAL THREAD DESIGNATED TO CELEBRATE THE CULT FAVE BONDAGE MODEL, MADE SURE TO ''CLARIFY'' THAT CAMBRIDGE AND DICKSON AREN'T THE SAME PERSON. IT'S QUITE CLEAR THAT THEY MOST CERTAINLY ARE ONCE YOU IGNORE THE LONGER HAIR STYLE.

IN 1987 SHE WAS IN TIGHT FIT, IN YET ANOTHER ONE OF HER MANY NON-SEX ROLES OF 1987. IN FACT, EVERYONE IN THE VIDEO WAS IN A NON-SEX ROLE. THERE'S ABSOLUTELY NO HARDCORE SEX TO SPEAK OF,

BECAUSE IT'S A FOOT-FETISHIST RELEASE. INSTEAD, RONNIE AND CO-STARS DANA LYNN, BARBII, AND LAUREL CANYON TICKLE EACH OTHER'S FEET, KISS AND SUCK EACH OTHER'S TOES, AND TRY ON DOZENS OF PAIRS OF SEXY SHOES WHILE MODELLING THIGH-HIGH STOCKINGS. THIS TITLE WAS PUT OUT BY PRESTIGE VIDEO, WHO WERE FAIRLY WELL KNOWN AT THE TIME AS A FOOT-FETISH AND CAT-FIGHTING VIDEO COMPANY, AND RONNIE APPEARED IN OVER A DOZEN OF THEIR VARIOUS RELEASES. OR SHOULD I SAY, TIANA DID.

BUT WITH THAT PILE OF TICKLING AND CAT-FIGHTING CONTENT ASIDE, IT WAS UNUSUAL TO SEE RONNIE FOR THE REST OF HER ADULT ENTERTAINMENT CAREER (WHICH LASTED UP UNTIL 1989) WITHOUT A GAG IN HER MOUTH, A MOURNFUL LOOK IN HER EYES, AND TIGHTLY TIED UP IN VARIOUS SEXY, DEFENCELESS POSES. TIANA CAMBRIDGE WAS BOUND TO BEDS, CHAIRS, MOTORCYCLES, TABLES, COUCHES AND OTHER WOMEN. SHE APPEARED IN MAGAZINES SUCH AS KNOTTY, BONDAGE PARADE, AND VARIOUS OTHER SLEAZY SLICKS, MOST OF WHICH WERE PUBLISHED BY CALIFORNIA KINK-KINGS HARMONY CONCEPTS INC, AND HOUSE OF MILAN (AKA HOM).

ARMED WITH THE INFO FROM RICK, I WAS ABLE TO SOLVE A BIT MORE OF THE MYSTERY. I MET PHOTOGRAPHER MICHAEL KEYE ONLINE AFTER HAPPENING UPON SOME OF HIS BONDAGE PHOTOS ON DEVIANTART.COM, AND BY CHANCE HAPPENED TO SEE HIM MENTION RONNIE/TIANA IN THE COMMENTS SECTION. HE WAS PONDERING A BONDAGE SHOOT THAT HAD BEEN DONE IN HIS HOME IN GLENDALE CALIFORNIA BACK IN THE DAY, AND IT SEEMED THAT HE KNEW HER PERSONALLY. AFTER CONTACTING HIM IN OCT 2015, IT WAS CLEAR TO ME THAT HE DID.

"IT WAS SOMETIME DURING THE FALL OF 1987 I CAME TO KNOW TIANA CAMBRIDGE", KEYE TOLD ME VIA EMAIL. "I ALREADY KNEW HER AS A FAN FROM HER HOUSE OF MILAN PHOTO SETS AND VIDEOS. AT HOM SHE WENT BY THE STAGE NAME RONNIE DIXON. AT THAT TIME I WAS APPEARING IN THE ROLE OF DIRK FOR THE STORYLINE PHOTO MAGAZINE SET TITLED THE PERILS OF TOPANGA TESS. THE HUSBAND AND WIFE TEAM JAYDEE HAD CREATED THE CONCEPT, INSPIRED BY THEIR APPRECIATION OF THE FREQUENT BONDAGE CONTENT FOUND IN THE CLIFFHANGER REPUBLIC SERIALS FILMED IN THE 30S, 40S, AND 50S. I HAD COME TO AUDITION FOR THE ROLE VIA REFERRAL FROM KIRI KELLY, WHO I HAD BECOME FRIENDS WITH IN 1986 DUE TO OUR FREQUENT RENDEZVOUS AT THE HOLLYWOOD BONDAGE BORDELLO CALLED PRIVATE QUARTERS."

"IT TOOK US ABOUT 2 MONTHS AND 3 OR 4 WEEKEND SHOOTS IN TOPANGA CANYON ABOVE MALIBU TO COMPLETE THE PROJECT. DURING THAT TIME I HAD BEEN INVITED TO HELP ON OTHER SHOOTS AT THE JAYDEE HOME STUDIO IN THE AREA OF LOS ANGELES COUNTY REFERRED TO AS SOUTH BEACH. ON ONE OF THOSE OCCASIONS TIANA CAMBRIDGE WAS BOOKED. WE HIT IT OFF AS FRIENDS, AND NEEDLESS TO SAY I BECAME QUITE SMITTEN. SHE EXPRESSED A RESERVED LEVEL OF FLIRTATIOUS TENDERNESS TOWARD ME AS WELL."

"I WAS WORKING A PROFESSIONAL VANILLA JOB AT THE TIME I DECIDED TO TAKE A STAB AT RUNNING MY OWN BONDAGE PHOTO SHOOT. WORKING WITH JAYDEE PROVIDED ME WITH THE EXPERIENCE TO BELIEVE I COULD DO IT ON MY OWN. I CHOSE TIANA TO BE MY FIRST MODEL IN THE SPRING OF 1988, AND SHE WAS HAPPY TO ACCEPT THE BOOKING. TIANA COULD TELL I WAS NERVOUS, BUT BEING A PROFESSIONAL SHE WAS VERY PATIENT WITH ME. HARMONY EDITORS WERE NOT PLEASED THAT I ONLY GOT 3 SCENES SHOT BUT NEVERTHELESS ENCOURAGED ME TO CONTINUE."

"THAT FIRST OF QUITE A FEW SHOOTS I DID FOR HARMONY AS AN INFREQUENT INDEPENDENT CONTRACTOR OVER A 4-YEAR PERIOD WAS THE ONLY ONE I DID WITH TIANA ON MY OWN. IF I HAD KNOWN SHE WOULD BE GONE SOON I WOULD HAVE MADE SURE TO SECURE ADDITIONAL PRIVATE SHOOT ENCOUNTERS WITH THIS FABULOUSLY ATTRACTIVE AND PERSONABLE WOMAN."

"THE REST OF 1988, UNTIL TIANA LEFT FOR A NEW LIFE ON THE EAST COAST, DID FIND US WORKING TOGETHER OFTEN AT JAYDEE'S, WHERE I CONTINUED TO BE A HELPER ON THEIR PRODUCTIONS. WE BOOKED A LOT OF STILL AND VIDEO SHOOTS, AND THE LADIES GRAVITATING TO JAYDEE SHOOTS, AND WE TO THEM, TENDED TO BE REAL LIFE ADVOCATES, AND THUS THE SHOOTS WERE OFTEN QUITE SEXUALLY CHARGED. AT THE VERY LEAST WE WERE ALL GREAT FRIENDS AND THE SHOOTS WERE AS MUCH A PARTY AS PROFESSIONAL ENDEAVOR. SOME OF THE STUFF WE SHOT, INCLUDING A TIANA CAMBRIDGE AND KIRI KELLY VIDEO, WAS TOO RISQUE FOR HARMONY TO RELEASE AT THE TIME."

"MY PERSONAL RELATIONSHIP WITH TIANA NEVER WENT BEYOND THE MUTUAL FRIENDS FLIRTING STAGE. PERHAPS SOMETHING MORE COULD HAVE HAPPENED, BUT IT WOULD HAVE TAKEN TIME AND PATIENCE, AND I KNOW HER SIGHTS BY THE TIME I MET HER WERE ALREADY SET ON MOVING BACK EAST. I DID HOWEVER HAVE THE PRIVILEGE OF BECOMING TIANA'S DESIGNATED "FIX MY NIPPLES" PERSON DURING SHOOTS AT WHICH I WAS PRESENT. HER NIPPLES TENDED TO STAY IN IF IT WAS COLD IN THE ROOM, AND SHE WANTED THEM TO STICK OUT FOR THE CAMERAS. SHE WOULD LET ME USE MY FINGERS AND MOUTH TO BRING THEM TO ATTENTION. ALL FOR THE SAKE OF ART, MIND YOU."

IN SOME OF THE LAST PHOTOS SHE EVER POSED FOR IN CALIFORNIA BEFORE SHE PACKED IT IN, RONNIE GOT INTO A WHITE CORSET, SOME WHITE HIGH HEELS, AND WAS TIED UP FOR SOME PICS THAT ARE CREDITED TO BONDAGE PHOTOGRAPHER MARK MARR (WHOSE WORK FROM THE LATE 1980S AND EARLY 1990S CAN BE FOUND AT HIS WEBSITE, WWW.CBTHEATER.COM), BUT LITTLE INFO ABOUT HER WHEREABOUTS AFTER THAT HAVE TURNED UP. AGAIN HER HAIR WAS DIFFERENT (THIS TIME RED), BUT MY DICK WILL TELL YOU THAT IT WAS RONNIE.

AS A WOMAN WHO WAS THERE AT THE VERY BEGINNING OF MY SEXUAL AWAKENING AND WAS CLEARLY VERY GOOD AT REINVENTING HER IMAGE AND PERSONA, I WOULDN'T BE SHOCKED TO FIND OUT THAT SHE WENT ON TO OPERATE AS SOMEONE ELSE YET AGAIN -- MAYBE EVEN SOMEONE I'M ALREADY A FAN OF! MAYBE SHE EVEN LIVES HERE IN MY CITY, OR COULD EVEN BE MY NEXT DOOR NEIGHBOUR. MAYBE I ACCIDENTALLY MARRIED HER. MAYBE SHE'S ME. MAYBE SHE NEVER EXISTED, AND I DREAMT THIS WHOLE THING. MAYBE RONNIE DICKSON IS EVERY SINGLE ONE OF US.

MAYBE IT'S REALLY FUCKING LATE, AND I SHOULD STOP WRITING AND GO TO BED. MY PORN COLLECTION WILL STILL BE THERE IN THE MORNING.
                                    -END-

•TIANA CAMBRIDGE CHECKLIST•

(AT LEAST, THE ONES I'M AWARE OF, ANYWAY)

BEAUTIFUL BONDAGE SCENES #10, 11, 12, 13 (1988)
BONDAGE ADVENTURES #1 (1989)
BONDAGE BY BRODY #9 (1989)
BONDAGE CLASSICS #35
BONDAGE IN CHICAGO #1 (1988)
BONDAGE PARADE #27, 28, 29, 30, 31 (1988/'89)
BONDAGE PHOTO TREASURES #21, 22, 23, 24, 28 (1988/'89)
BONDAGE GALLERY #5 (1988)
BONDAGE WORLD #3 (1988)
KNOTTY #5 (1987)
LOU KAGAN'S GLAMOUR IN BONDAGE #4 (1987)
LOVE BONDAGE GALLERY #15 (1990)
LOVE BONDAGE TREASURES #48 (1997 REPRINTS)
TIGHT ROPES VOL2 N #1 (1992)

10 - THE NEW YORK RIPPER (1982)
THIS JAW SMASHINGLY BRUTAL HEAD EXPLOSION OCCURS IN THE FINAL MINUTES AS THE DONALD DUCK IMPERSONATING KILLER IS ABOUT TO PLUNGE HIS BLADE INTO THE FLESH OF ANOTHER NUBILE YOUNG LADY. ONE SHOT FROM A COP'S GUN SENDS A BULLET SPLATTERING THROUGH THE PSYCHO KILLER'S CHEEKBONES IN SLO-MO. PROBABLY THE NASTIEST GIALLO EVER MADE, FULCI'S NO-HOLDS-BARRED APPROACH TO CINEMATIC VIOLENCE REALLY DELIVERS THE CRIMSON GOODS HERE AS WE ARE ALSO TREATED TO SOME HORRIFICALLY REALISTIC STABBINGS, A BROKEN BOTTLE RAMMED INTO A HOOKER'S CUNT, AND A RAZOR BLADE SPLITTING A WOMAN'S EYEBALL AND NIPPLE IN EXCRUCIATING CLOSE-UP!

9 - NIGHT OF THE LIVING DEAD (1990)
TOM SAVINI DIRECTED THIS EXCELLENT REMAKE BUT HANDED SPECIAL EFFECTS DUTIES TO JOHN VULICH AND EVERETT BURRELL. THE ZOMBIE MAKE UP IN THIS IS PARTICULARLY EFFECTIVE — FOR RESEARCH VULICH AND BURRELL ATTENDED MANY REAL AUTOPSIES TO ENABLE THEM TO ACHIEVE REALISTIC RESULTS. THE HEAD EXPLOSION IN THIS COMES AT AROUND THE HOUR POINT WHEN OUR PROTAGONISTS MAKE A RUN TO THE FUEL PUMPS TO ENABLE THEM TO GAS UP AND ESCAPE. HORDES OF ZOMBIES ATTACK AND ONE GETS ITS HEAD EXPLODED VIA SHOTGUN IN A FLOOD OF BLOOD AND SOGGY BRAINS! HOWEVER, MOST VERSIONS HAVE THIS SCENE REMOVED (ALONG WITH MOST OTHER BULLET IMPACT TO THE HEAD SHOTS AND A MESSY CROWBAR IN THE FOREHEAD EFFECT). THE UNCUT FOOTAGE CAN BE READILY SEEN IN THE WORKPRINT, WHICH FEATURES AN ALTERNATIVE SCORE.

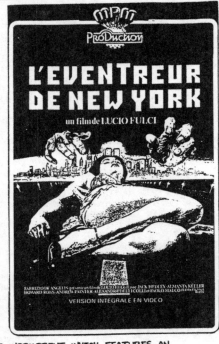

MPM ProDuction

L'EVENTREUR DE NEW YORK

un film de LUCIO FULCI

FABRIZIO DE ANGELIS présente un film de LUCIO FULCI avec JACK HEDLEY ALMANTA KELLER HOWARD ROSS·ANDREW PAINTER ALEXANDRA DELLI COLLI et PAOLO MALCO ainsi que

VERSION INTEGRALE EN VIDEO

8 - DAWN OF THE DEAD (1978)
THE TENEMENT SCENE IN WHICH A DEMENTED SWAT OFFICER KICKS DOWN A DOOR TO BLOW THE HEAD OFF OF AN UNSUSPECTING CITIZEN. THIS INCREDIBLY JOLTING MOMENT IS MISSING FROM MANY VERSIONS OF THE MOVIE SO MAKE SURE YOU GET AN UNCUT VERSION. SPECIAL EFFECT ONCE AGAIN COURTESY OF TOM SAVINI.

7 - THE PROWLER (1981)
THE FINALE WHEN THE KILLER GETS HIS HEAD BLOWN OFF AT POINT BLANK RANGE WITH A SAWN OFF SHOTGUN. HIS HEAD SHATTERS AND HIS BRAINS EJECT HIS SKULL IN A SHOWER OF SLOW MOTION GORE. AWESOME EFFECTS WORK BY MR SAVINI, WHO IS CLEARLY VERY GOOD AT SIMULATING THIS PARTICULAR EFFECT!

6 - HALLOWEEN 6 (1995)
OKAY, DEPENDING WHICH VERSION YOU SEE OF THIS FILM WILL DETERMINE WHETHER YOU GET TO SEE THIS MEMORABLE SPECTACLE OF BLOODSHED. AFTER SEVERAL GORY MURDERS MICHAEL MYERS HEADS TO HIS OLD HOMESTEAD TO FIND A THOROUGHLY UNPLEASANT FAT DUDE RESIDING THERE. MICHAEL TAKES A SPIKE AND RAMS IT THROUGH FATSO PINNING HIM TO THE

134

YOU WILL LIVE IN TERROR!

THE BEYOND

catriona macColl   david warbeck
cinzia monreale   antoine saint-john
music by fabio frizzi
director of photography sergio salvati
directed by lucio fulci
produced by beyond horror design

ELECTRIC METER CAUSING THOUSANDS OF VOLTS TO LIQUEFY HIS HANDS AND EXPLODE HIS HEAD INTO A MILLION BLOODY PIECES. A DEFINITE HIGHLIGHT IN THIS VERY GORY AND ENTERTAINING SEQUEL FROM GOOD OL' DIMENSION FILMS. THE BODY COUNT IS HIGH AND KILL SCENES ARE WELL EDITED TO MAXIMIZE THE GORY DETAILS OF JOHN CARL BUECHLER'S GRUESOME SPECIAL EFFECTS.

5 - DUST DEVIL (1992)
ANOTHER SLOW MOTION SHOCKER AND ONE OF THE MOST IMPRESSIVELY SPLATTERIFIC AND NAUSEATING HEAD EXPLOSIONS EVER AS ROBERT BURKE LOOSES HIS HEAD IN A SHOWER OF GORE VIA SHOTGUN BLAST, FOLLOWED BY HIS HEADLESS BODY FALLING TO THE GROUND TO EMPTY ITS FLUIDS INTO THE CAMERA LENS!

4 - THE BEYOND (1981)
A GENUINELY JOLTING MOMENT OF VIOLENCE OCCURS IN THE FINAL REEL OF FULCI'S ZOMBIE MASTERPIECE. AS THE DEAD RISE FROM MORGUE TABLES IN A ZOMBIE INFESTED HOSPITAL, A LITTLE GIRL HAS HER ENTIRE FACE BLOWN OFF IN SICKENING DETAIL FROM A CLOSE RANGE BULLET. DRESSED IN HER SCHOOL UNIFORM, HER HEAD SNAPS BACK AND THEN LURCHES FORWARD IN A DELUGE OF BRAINS AND BLOOD! UNFORGETTABLE AND ASTONISHING SPECIAL EFFECTS WORK BY GIANNETTO DE ROSSI.

3 - DEADLY FRIEND (1986)
OKAY, SERIOUSLY, WHAT THE FUCK? IN THIS DEMENTED EXERCISE IN 1980S EXCESS A NASTY OLD WOMAN GETS HER HEAD BLOODILY SMASHED LIKE A PIECE OF POTTERY BY A BASKETBALL THROWN BY A TEENAGE GIRL WITH A COMPUTER CHIP IN HER HEAD! WHAT THE HELL WAS WES CRAVEN THINKING? THIS TURD OF A MOVIE IS WORTH SEEING FOR THIS BIZARRE SIGHT ALONE. BUY IT NOW!

2 - SCANNERS (1981)
LIKE YOU DIDN'T KNOW THIS WOULD BE IN HERE! MOST OF YOU THOUGHT THIS WOULD BE NUMBER 1 THOUGH, RIGHT? HEAD EXPLOSION VIA TELEKINESIS. THIS SHOW-STOPPING EFFECT BY GARY ZELLER WAS CREATED BY FIRING A 12-GAUGE SHOTGUN AT A LATEX HEAD FILLED WITH RABBIT LIVERS AND DOG FOOD. LEGENDARY.

1 - MANIAC (1980)
TRULY AWE-INSPIRING SPLATTER FROM THE MASTER TOM SAVINI AS HE LITERALLY BLOWS HIS OWN HEAD OFF FROM A DOZEN FUCKING ANGLES IN SLOW-MOTION! THIS IS ONE OF THOSE MOMENTS IN THE HISTORY OF HORROR FILMS THAT WILL LEAVE YOUR JAW ON THE FLOOR! I SHIT YOU NOT! THIS MOVIE IS A CLAS-SICK AND ONE OF THE GREATEST GRINDHOUSE HORROR FILMS EVER MADE. GRUELLING, INTENSE, CLAUSTROPHOBIC AND UNRELENTINGLY GRIM. JOE SPINELL GIVES THE BEST PERFORMANCE OF HIS LARGE CAREER AS THE SWEATY MANIAC. A MUST-SEE FOR FANS OF SERIAL KILLER AND SLASHER FLICKS!

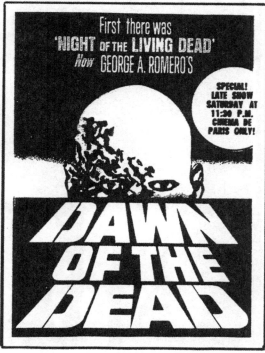

First there was 'NIGHT OF THE LIVING DEAD' Now GEORGE A. ROMERO'S

SPECIAL! LATE SHOW SATURDAY AT 11:30 P.M. CINEMA DE PARIS ONLY!

DAWN OF THE DEAD

BAD TASTE (1987)
IN THE OPENING MOMENTS AN ALIEN IN HUMAN DISGUISE HAS HIS HEAD BLOWN TO BITS WITH A
HANDGUN.

THE HILLS HAVE EYES - ALEXANDRE AJA REMAKE (2006)
A VERY FRIGHTENED OLD MAN BLOWS HIS BRAINS SKYWARDS VIA POINT-BLANK SHOTGUN SUICIDE.

ZOMBIE (1979)
PLENTY OF GORY DAMAGE TO ZOMBIE HEADS IN THIS. MOST MEMORABLE BEING A ZOMBIE HAVING
ITS CRUSTY HEAD BURST LIKE A BALLOON WITH A CROSS IN A CEMETERY! KERSPLATTT!

ANGEL OF DEATH: FUCK OR DIE (1998)
A NAKED WOMAN ON A RAPE-REVENGE KILLING SPREE IS SHOT THROUGH THE PUSSY AND THE
BULLET EXITS THROUGH THE TOP OF HER HEAD! NO SHIT! ONLY IN GERMAN. ULTRA-GORE, MY
FRIENDS...

TURKEY SHOOT (1982)
THIS BONKERS OZSPLOITATION HUNTING HUMANS CLASSIC DEPICTS A BAD GUY BEING LITERALLY TORN TO PIECES WITH A HIGH POWERED MACHINE GUN WHICH BURSTS HIS NOGGIN!

CHOPPING MALL (1986)
THIS FUN SLICE OF GOOFY TRASH DEPICTS A GROUP OF PEOPLE TRAPPED IN A SHOPPING MALL BEING PURSUED BY PSYCHOTIC SECURITY ROBOTS. THESE DROIDS DON'T TAKE ANY SHIT AND IN ONE UNFORGETTABLE SCENE A YOUNG WOMAN IS BLASTED WITH LASERS BEFORE HER HEAD IS LITERALLY BLOWN TO PIECES. ALSO STARS MARY WORONOV, AND LATE, GREAT PAUL BARTEL.

ILSA, SHE WOLF OF THE SS (1974)
OH MY, OH MY! I LOVE THIS FILM. MAYBE A LITTLE TOO MUCH! BUXOM DYANNE THORNE IS EASILY ONE OF THE HOTTEST WOMEN TO GRACE THE GRINDHOUSE SCREEN. HER DEMISE AT THE END OF THE FILM IS PRICELESS... THORNE IS DRESSED IN BALL-DRAINING LINGERIE AND TIED SPREAD-EAGLED TO A BED AS A SLOBBERING SYPHILIS INFECTED WOMAN CRAWLS OVER HER BARE FLESH. A NAZI SOLDIER ENTERS AND PROCEEDS TO BLOW HER HEAD TO PIECES WITH A LUGER. BLONDE HAIR, BITS OF BRAIN AND FRAGMENTS OF SKULL SHATTER THE SCREEN. A GENUINE GUILTY PLEASURE!

"Now . . . aren't you glad I refused to go to that nasty old X-rated movie tonight?"

THE HANG UP

THE LATE DIRECTOR JOHN HAYES DESERVES TO BE BETTER KNOWN AMONGST FILM NERDS. HE MADE ONE OF MY ALL-TIME FAVORITE 1960S SEXPLOITATION FILMS (1968'S HELP WANTED FEMALE), AND ONE OF MY ALL-TIME FAVORITE 1970S HARDCORE MOVIES (1976'S BABY ROSEMARY). IN BETWEEN THOSE TWO RELEASES HE MADE VARIOUS TRASHY GENRE MOVIES WITH MARGINAL ART-HOUSE ASPIRATIONS. I'M TALKING ABOUT: THE CUT-THROATS (1969), WALK THE ANGRY BEACH (1969), THE HANG UP (1970), SWEET TRASH (1970), DREAM NO EVIL (1970), FANDANGO (1970), GARDEN OF THE DEAD (1972), GRAVE OF THE VAMPIRE (1972), CONVICTS' WOMEN (1973), AND MAMA'S DIRTY GIRLS (1974).

AFTER 45 YEARS OF OBSCURITY FOLLOWING VERY SHORT THEATRICAL RUNS, TWO OF THOSE MOVIES FINALLY SAW THEIR FIRST WIDE-RELEASE IN THE FORM OF A DRIVE-IN COLLECTION DOUBLE BILL DVD IN JULY 2015 FROM VINEGAR SYNDROME RELEASING, ONE OF THE MOST IMPORTANT GENRE FILM LABELS ON THE PLANET. SWEET TRASH AND THE HANG UP WERE EDITED, WRITTEN, DIRECTED, AND PRODUCED BY HAYES, AND RELEASED VIA HIS LOW-RENT PRODUCTION COMPANY, CLOVER FILMS, WHICH HE STARTED BACK IN 1965 WITH A FRIEND NAMED DANIEL CADY. THEIR RECENT HOME FORMAT UNVEILING SEEMS TO HAVE BEEN MOSTLY OVERLOOKED, BUT I CAN TELL YOU UNEQUIVOCALLY THAT THIS DVD IS TOTALLY WORTH CHECKING INTO.

JOHN HAYES BEGINS THE HANGUP (1970) IN A TRANSVESTITE BAR WITH A NAUTICAL THEME, A UNIQUE CAMPY LOCATION THAT GRABS YOUR ATTENTION RIGHT OUT OF THE STARTING GATE. THE OVERTLY OUTRE CLIENTELE OF THIS COLORFUL LOS ANGELES BAR COLLECT TO WATCH A TRULY HEAD-TURNING, ORGASMIC PERFORMANCE FROM VINTAGE ADULT MAGAZINE CENTERFOLD AND SEXPLOITATION STARLET, BAMBI ALLEN. AN EARLY ADOPTER OF BREAST IMPLANTS, BAMBI WOULD -- LIKE MANY OF THE SILICONE-INJECTED GUINEA PIGS OF THE VERY FLAWED COSMETIC PROCEDURE -- BE KILLED BY COMPLICATIONS DIRECTLY RELATED TO HER HARD, AWKWARD-LOOKING CHEST AUGMENTATION.

PAN OVER TO THE TWO MOST UNCONVINCING SHOE-FACED CROSS-DRESSERS IN THE ROOM, AND SURE ENOUGH -- THEY ARE UNDERCOVER LAPD VICE DETECTIVES, WHO ARE OF COURSE, IN HIGH DEMAND AMONGST THE ELIGIBLE HORNY BACHELORS IN THE AREA. AFTER JETTING BACK TO A SKEEZY MOTEL AND REVEALING THAT IT'S A BUST, THE LEAD VICE COP, ROBERT WALSH (CLOVER FILMS REGULAR, TONY VORNO, WHO ALSO STARRED IN HELP WANTED FEMALE) ANGRILY HEAD-BUTTS ONE OF THE FRIENDLY JOHNS INTO SUBMISSION. OUCH.

"I SPIT ON SCUM. I'M A COP!", WALSH WILL LATER BARK AT HIS PARTNER (ERIK STERN) AS THEY TAKE OFF THEIR MAKE-UP. "IT'S BAD ENOUGH THESE WEIRDOS RUN FREE IN THIS TOWN WITHOUT HAVING TO IMPERSONATE THEM!"

AFTER A WEARY DAY SMASHING HEADS AND PUTTING THE FEAR OF GOD INTO SEXUAL DEVIANTS RESIDING IN THE CITY OF ANGELS, WALSH TRUDGES HOME TO HIS DINKY ROOMING HOUSE FLAT, WHERE HE WHINES TO HIS BUXOM REDHEAD LANDLADY, MISS HOWARD, ABOUT ALL THE CLOWNS THAT MAKE HIS EXISTENCE SO TRYING. "I CATCH QUEERS!", HE EXPLAINS AS IF HE WISHED THE WHOLE WORLD WOULD JUST EXPLODE. "I CATCH HOMOSEXUALS, TRANSVESTITES, CHILD MOLESTERS, PIMPS, PUSHERS, WHORES..."

138

SEEMINGLY WOOED BY HIS HOMOPHOBIA, GRATED NERVES AND LACK OF PATIENCE FOR ANYTHING OTHER THAN 1950S SUBURBAN VALUES, SHE TAKES IT UPON HERSELF TO TRY TO BED HIM. HE'S OBVIOUSLY HESITANT, BUT THE FLESH IS WEAK, AND AFTER SOME SKILFULLY STAGED SCENES OF AWKWARD ENTICEMENT, AN AVOCADO-GREEN BATHROOM TRYST WITH MISS HOWARD TAKES PLACE AS HE GRINDS AGAINST HER ON THE FILTHY FLOOR NEXT TO HER TOILET. SOON DISGUSTED WITH THE ENTIRE SCENE, HE GETS UP, LEAVES HER THERE TO WRITHE, AND GOES BACK TO HIS ROOM WHERE HE RUBS ONE OUT AWKWARDLY WHILE STANDING IN A CLOSET DOORWAY. IT WAS AT THIS PRECISE MOMENT THAT I FELL IN LOVE WITH THIS BITTER, BITTER MOVIE.

THE NEXT EVENING HE'S OFF TO ANOTHER DEN OF DEBAUCHERY TO USHER SOME MORE PERVERTS INTO JAIL CELLS. THIS TIME HE STRAPS ON HIS LEATHERS AND ROARS HIS MOTOR BIKE ON OVER TO A COSTUME PARTY ORGY AT A FANCY WHOREHOUSE MANSION OUT IN THE COUNTRY. WITH A CULT VIBE IN FULL EFFECT, CONSIDER THIS PART OF THE MOVIE A SORT OF WELFARE EYES WIDE SHUT. TAKEN INTO A BACK ROOM FOR EXTREME HUMPY-PUMPY, WALSH MEETS OUR LEAD ACTRESS, A YOUNG PROSTITUTE RUNAWAY FROM SALINAS NAMED LAURIE (SHARON MATT). DESPITE CLEARLY BEING THERE TO BRING IN THE WHORES AND PIMPS HE DESPISES SO MUCH, AFTER A QUIET, MEANINGFUL BEDSIDE CONVERSATION WITH THE WIDE-EYED AND INNOCENT LAURIE, WALSH HAS A SUDDEN CHANGE OF HEART.

"I DON'T KNOW WHY I'M DOIN' THIS", THE LAPD VICE OFFICER HISSES, NOT JUST AT HER, BUT AT HIMSELF AS HE SHAKES HIS HEAD AND ESCORTS HER OUT A BACK DOOR, JUST AS THE POLICE RAID OF THE PALATIAL BAWDY HOUSE GOES INTO FULL EFFECT. WITH NOWHERE ELSE TO TAKE HER, HE ESCORTS THE GIRL BACK TO HIS SMELLY, DUMPY BACHELOR APARTMENT AND STARTS CALLING HER 'ANGEL'. LAURIE DOES HER BIT TO MAKE HERSELF USEFUL (SHE'S CONCERNED ABOUT HIS SEEMING INABILITY TO DO HOUSEHOLD CHORES) AND BEING A CHILD OF THE SEXUAL REVOLUTION, SHE DOES THAT WHILE MOSTLY NAKED. THE TWO OF THEM SEEM MUCH LIKE FATHER AND DAUGHTER (BOTH IN AGE DISCREPANCY AND ATTITUDE) THROUGHOUT MOST OF THEIR INTERACTIONS, BUT FASCINATINGLY ALSO QUICKLY START ACTING LIKE A MARRIED COUPLE. AND BEFORE LONG THAT INCLUDES THE...UM, MORE INTIMATE ELEMENTS OF MARRIAGE AS WELL. (SLIDE WHISTLE SOUND FX)

IN HIS SEMINAL 2007 HARDCOVER TOME DEDICATED TO THE WILDEST VINTAGE AMERICAN EXPLOITATION FEATURES, NIGHTMARE USA, AUTHOR STEPHEN THROWER WONDERS OPENLY IF SCREENWRITER PAUL SCHRADER MAY HAVE BEEN HIGHLY INSPIRED BY A VIEWING OF THE HANG UP. "THE SIMILARITIES TO TAXI DRIVER ARE UNCANNY", THROWER WRITES. "WALSH'S LINES ABOUT HATRED OF PERVERSION ARE A VIRTUAL RINGER FOR TRAVIS BICKLE'S MUSINGS, AND WHEN WALSH DECIDES TO RESCUE ANGEL FROM THE IMMINENT VICE-BUST BECAUSE HE BELIEVES SHE'S AN INNOCENT IN NEED OF HIS PROTECTION, WE SEE THE RELATIONSHIP BETWEEN TRAVIS AND IRIS IN NASCENT FORM."

LIKE BICKLE, WALSH IS THE EPITOME OF A DAMAGED, CONFLICTED CHARACTER. HE MAKES EFFORTS TO IDENTIFY WITH THE FRESH-FACED GIRL, SUCH AS WHEN HE BUYS A GIANT BAG OF CELERY — "ORGANIC STUFF" HE GRUFFLY CALLS IT -- BUT THEN HE WEIRDLY EATS THE STALKS LIKE HE'S EATING A COB OF CORN, SEEMINGLY NEVER HAVING PUT A GREEN VEGETABLE IN HIS MOUTH BEFORE. WITH NOTHING BUT CONTEMPT FOR THE YOUNGER GENERATION, SEXUAL DEVIANCY AND HIS OWN URGES, HE HAS TROUBLE COMING TO TERMS WITH ANY OF IT. WALSH FEELS MORALLY IN THE RIGHT FOR RESCUING A TEENAGE RUNAWAY FROM THE STREETS, BUT KNOWS HE'S STEPPED FAR OVER THE LINE BY TAKING HER ON AS HIS LIVE-IN LOVER RATHER THAN PLACING HER IN PROTECTIVE CUSTODY OR GETTING HER BACK HOME. HE'S IN OVER HIS HEAD.

HE CAN'T SEEM TO HELP HIMSELF, THOUGH, AND WE WITNESS HIM -- VIA THE POWER OF PUSSY -- SHED HIS SKIN. AT WORK IS ONE THING, BUT IN PRIVATE THE HARDENED DEBAUCHERY-HATING URBAN VICE COP MELTS AWAY, REPLACED BY A FREE SPIRIT WHO LIKES GOING OUT INTO THE COUNTRY WITH HIS SUPPLE, PINK-NIPPLED FLOWER CHILD. TRANSFORMED, HE LITERALLY FROLICS THROUGH OPEN PASTURES WITH HER BEFORE SETTLING DOWN TO BOFF ON A PICNIC BLANKET AMONGST OTHER NAKED 20-SOMETHING BACK-TO-NATURE ORGYISTS. CONSIDERING THAT WALSH LOOKS LIKE AN ANGRIER MR HOWELL FROM GILLIGAN'S ISLAND CROSSED WITH GLENN FORD, THIS IS NOT JUST A COP GOING OUTSIDE HIS COMFORT ZONE WITH A FORBIDDEN AFFAIR, THIS IS A MOTHERFUCKIN' MID-LIFE CRISIS DIALED UP TO 11.

WITH HIS LIFE TURNED UPSIDE DOWN, WALSH IS UTTERLY UNPREPARED FOR WHAT HAPPENS NEXT. IN A GREAT TWIST THAT I DIDN'T SEE COMING AT ALL, THE BEAUTIFUL YOUNG PROSTITUTE IS REVEALED TO HAVE A SECRET THAT WILL CHANGE EVERYTHING. IT'S A REVELATION THAT WILL USHER THE WALSH CHARACTER EVEN FURTHER DOWN HIS SPIRAL OF DESTRUCTION AND THE MOVIE INTO WHAT THE DVD PACKAGING APTLY DESCRIBES AS "A POWERFUL INDICTMENT OF LAW-ENFORCEMENT HYPOCRISY" AND "A CREATIVE COMMENTARY ON THE SEXUAL REVOLUTION AND HUMAN NATURE." SURE IT WAS MADE QUICKLY AND ON A TIGHT BUDGET, BUT THIS IS BOLD, SOLIDLY-PACED, IMPRESSIVE AUTEUR SHIT, MAN. THIS IS WHAT FILM NOIR WOULD HAVE BEEN LIKE IN THE 1940S IF THEY WERE ALLOWED TO HAVE NUDITY AND OVERT SEXUAL SITUATIONS. THIS IS JOHN HAYES BRINGING HIS 'A' GAME.

SPEAKING OF OVERT SEXUALITY, IT'S WORTH NOTING THAT THE TRAILER FOR THE MOVIE INCLUDED ON THE DVD HAS FULL FRONTAL BEAVER SHOTS THAT NEVER APPEAR IN THE MOVIE, WITH SOME SCENES IN THE PREVIEW CLEARLY RESTAGED WITH THE ACTORS NOW UNCLOTHED. WONDERING IF PERHAPS A DIFFERENT, HARDER, VERSION OF THE MOVIE IS OUT THERE SOMEWHERE, I CONTACTED VINEGAR SYNDROME'S JOE RUBIN, WHO EXPLAINED THAT THE BEAUTIFUL PRINT ON THEIR DVD CAME DIRECTLY FROM THE ORIGINAL CAMERA NEGATIVE FOR THE HANGUP. "HOTTER OUTTAKES WOULD BE USED IN THE TRAILER TO SELL THE FILM", RUBIN NOTED. "THAT WAS COMMON. HARRY NOVAK DID THAT A LOT TOO."

GREAT SCOTT

☆ STATS ☆
BORN: 1983
FAVE SONG:
"KOZMIC BLUES"
BY J. JOPLIN
FAVE PORNO:
THE DEVIL IN
MISS JONES
FAVORITE FILM:
NASHVILLE
FAVE COLOR: GREEN

CASEY SCOTT IS ONE OF PORN FILM FANDOM'S MOST INTERESTING CHARACTERS NOT TO MENTION ONE OF THE MOST KNOWLEDGEABLE

INTERVIEW BY ROBIN BOUGIE '14

WHO IS CASEY SCOTT, AND WHY SHOULD YOU GIVE A CRAP? WELL, TO BE HONEST I OFTEN WONDER THE SAME THING ABOUT MYSELF. I GET LOTS OF FAN MAIL AND PLENTY OF COMPLIMENTS FROM TOTAL STRANGERS ABOUT WHAT I DO, AND WHAT IS IT THAT I REALLY DO, EXACTLY? WELL, I'VE WATCHED MOVIES AND WRITTEN ABOUT THEM IN AN ENTERTAINING WAY. I INTERVIEW PEOPLE WHO MAKE THEM. I STRIVE TO GROW AN ENCYCLOPEDIC KNOWLEDGE FROM YEARS OF RESEARCHING THEM, AND TAKE PRIDE IN BEING AWESOME TO OTHER PEOPLE IN THE SCENE — INSTEAD OF BEING A SNOTTY LITTLE KNOW-IT-ALL PRICK.

GUESS WHAT? CASEY SCOTT IS ANOTHER CAT WHO DOES ALL OF THOSE THINGS TOO! WHY SHOULD I HOG THE SPOTLIGHT ALL FOR MYSELF WHEN THERE ARE AMAZING DUDES AND DUDETTES WHO DESERVE TO HAVE THEIR VOICES HEARD? IT'S DAMN TIME CASEY SCOTT GOT HIS DUE FOR HIS YEARS OF HARD WORK IN CULT AND VINTAGE PORN FANDOM. LET'S HAVE A TINY CHAT WITH HIM AND SEE WHAT'S COOKIN'!

ROBIN BOUGIE: OK, SO HERE WE ARE! CASEY, JUST RIGHT OFF THE BAT I'D LIKE TO SAY THAT THE MAIN REASON I WANTED TO INTERVIEW YOU IS BECAUSE I THINK YOU ARE ONE OF THE MOST UNDERRATED WRITER/JOURNALIST/FILM CRITICS WITH A FOCUS ON VINTAGE ADULT FILMS, BOTH SOFTCORE AND HARDCORE. AND COME TO THINK OF IT, YOU'RE NO SLOUCH HOLDING YOUR OWN WHEN IT COMES TO DROPPING SCIENCE ABOUT OTHER CULT FILM GENRES. MAD PROPS, MY BROTHER!

Casey Scott: Wow, thank you Robin! That means a lot coming from you. Underrated! I do love that word, and apply it to a lot of films and performers, but haven't heard it said about me, so that's a nice surprise. Ha! In that regard, I've always been terrible at self-promotion and pursuing outlets for my work. But better to be underrated than overrated, I guess, just like a film.

RB: I COULD HAVE JUST HAD YOU CONTRIBUTE AN ARTICLE OR A REVIEW AND LET YOUR TALENT SPEAK FOR ITSELF (AND COME TO THINK OF IT, LET'S DO THAT TOO) BUT MOSTLY I WANTED TO SAY THAT IT JUST KILLS ME THAT THERE ARE PEOPLE OUT THERE THAT HAVE WRITTEN BOOKS ON THIS CLASSIC PORN JAZZ THAT CLEARLY DON'T HAVE HALF THE KNOWLEDGE AND CONNECTIONS THAT YOU DO. I'VE BEEN FOLLOWING YOUR WORK ONLINE ON VARIOUS SITES FOR A DECADE NOW — SEEING IT APPEAR HERE AND THERE — BUT AS FAR AS I CAN TELL YOU HAVEN'T HAD MUCH IN PRINT. I MEAN, CORRECT ME IF I'M WRONG, BUT THAT'S JUST PLAIN FUCKED. I'D LIKE TO HEAR ABOUT YOUR HISTORY WRITING ABOUT THESE MOVIES. HOW DID YOU GET STARTED? HOW LONG HAVE YOU BEEN WORKING AT THIS?

CS: Yeah it's been a while since I was last in Cinema Sewer. I remember you re-printed a review of The Candy Snatchers I did several years ago, which was my first time being in print in a magazine, so thank you for that. Sigh, yeah...the simple answer for my work not being in print or really anywhere on the web is that I have been working on a long-term book project for several years now. I work in stops and starts. I get really involved in a project and then something will go wrong or another opportunity will present itself and things go by the wayside. I stopped work on the book for a while after another researcher convinced two directors not to speak to me, which threw my concept into a tailspin. I had to regroup and start over, especially after one of those directors passed away. But I'm kinda back on track at this point. And you've been very supportive in pushing me to get something published, which means a lot. At this point I have a lot of stuff ready to go or about 3/4 finished, but no real outlets for it. It's not a proper book yet, and there's still so many people to get the full story on, so maybe a series of books or journals that when put together can create the best history of adult film auteurs imaginable. I did publish a rough draft of the book's introduction on my blog, to give an idea of what to expect.

GAWD-DAMN! THIS CAT KNOWS HIS SHEEEEIIT!

THE BOUG AND THE SCOTT— ONLINE CHAT

On a related note, I have to say, when you told me you were doing a book on the history of adult film poster artwork, I breathed a huge sigh of relief! Because that was one less thing for me to dig into and I knew that particular history was in the right hands. You're the person to cover that history! Honestly, I feel that way about a lot of topics in the classic adult film world! I don't feel like I'm the ONE historian to tell the entire story, but in many cases, no one else is writing the book I'd want to read about certain directors or performers or sub-genres so it gets added to the pile of things I passionately research. Of course I have my personal favourites that demand more attention.

RB: I'M GLAD TO HEAR THAT. I THINK THAT IS THE RIGHT SORT OF MENTALITY TO HAVE. THERE WAS ANOTHER BOOK ABOUT HARDCORE MOVIE POSTERS FROM THE 1970S THAT CAME OUT WHILE MY BOOK, GRAPHIC THRILLS, WAS JUST NEARING COMPLETION. SOME OF MY CLOSE FRIENDS SAW THIS, AND SAID THAT I MUST BE PRETTY PISSED OFF AND FRUSTRATED, CONSIDERING THERE HAD NEVER BEEN A BOOK LIKE THIS, AND SUDDENLY THERE ARE TWO. IT WASN'T THE CASE AT ALL. I DON'T THINK THERE IS ANY ROOM IN THIS LITTLE NICHE WORLD OF FANDOM WE EXIST IN TO BE COMPETITIVE. I SEE IT HAPPEN IN THE WORLD OF COMICS FANDOM, AND IT'S SO UGLY AND REALLY TAKES THE FUN OUT OF IT. I MEAN, I WAS THRILLED TO SEE THAT OTHER BOOK COME OUT. WE NEED TO SUPPORT ONE ANOTHER, INSPIRE ONE ANOTHER, AND HELP EACH OTHER. AS A FAN AND A HISTORIAN OF THESE MOVIES, I LOVE THAT THERE IS MORE THAN ONE BOOK ABOUT THIS SUBJECT I'M SO PASSIONATE ABOUT. AND THAT'S HOW WE SHOULD APPROACH THIS, I THINK.

CS: The more the merrier, I say! Of course some projects are going to cover similar, if not the exact same territory. But we all have different points of view, different approaches, and the history is so vast that it can't have enough books and magazines and films about it! It also saves me the worry of that history vanishing without anyone getting to it! Great, someone was

able to cover it, lemme get to reading so I can learn from this person! My only disdain is for projects that cover the exact same territory that has been covered elsewhere. It just adds nothing to the conversation, but it does light a fire under my ass to get back to work on my projects. The real danger is when someone feels that classic porn is their territory, and it can't be shared, and there are a few people who do feel that way and it's counterproductive and frankly very toxic to our little niche community in general. We writers need to be supportive of one another, and I can say that for the most part we do a good job of that with one another. If someone needs some facts checked or for me to reach out to someone I'm in touch with to inquire about an interview, I'm happy to do that. I'd want the same thing if I asked for help.

RB: SO HOW DID YOU FIRST GET INTO THIS STUFF? ON THE WRITING END OF IT, I MEAN.

CS: I started writing about "cult" or exploitation films when I was in high school, first on IMDB as so many of us and then for a few sites. One went defunct soon after, DVD Unleashed was the name I believe, then George Reis at DVD Drive-In asked me to join his crew. I started off doing just about anything he would send me screeners of, but

really found my niche in covering Something Weird Video's releases. And because softcore so often bleeds into hardcore it was a natural progression to start covering those films as well. Because I wanted to add some historical info to my reviews that wasn't included on the DVDs themselves, I started researching the films, their producers, their stars, and release histories. I can't say there aren't inaccuracies in those older reviews that I've since corrected in my personal files, but I can say that there really weren't any other web reviewers doing this for cult DVD releases. I'm sure it led to my working with a few DVD companies on extras and liner notes.

RB: VERY MUCH LIKE ANOTHER TALENTED AND UNDERRATED WRITER THAT I FEATURED IN THESE PAGES A FEW ISSUES AGO -- DRIES VERMEULEN FROM BELGIUM -- YOU'RE A GAY MAN WHO GENERALLY FOCUSES HIS ATTENTION ON THE HISTORY OF HETERO PORN MOVIES. I'D LIKE TO HEAR ABOUT THAT. I DON'T THINK A LOT OF FANS OF THESE OLD FUCK FILMS REALLY REALIZE HOW MANY GAY DIRECTORS THERE WERE MAKING THEM, AND HOW MANY GAY GUYS ARE SCHOOLING THEM ABOUT THE HISTORY OF THIS STUFF TODAY. MAKING THAT APPARENT IS NOT REALLY PART OF YOUR WRITING STYLE. IS THAT ON PURPOSE?

CS: Ah Dries, yes, we're good friends! We're also similar in that we do research in both classic gay and straight films, but I'd definitely agree that our general focus is more intently on the straight side. Yeah I think a number of people are surprised to learn that I'm gay. I can also see why it's confusing to anyone who's read my fevered odes to Uschi Digard or Sharon Kelly or Sue Nero or Lisa De Leeuw (if you couldn't tell from that list, I do adore breasts, just to confuse you more). I don't actively hide it in my writing, it just doesn't happen to apply to many of the films I write about. But in my reviews on DVD Drive-In, I was always sure to point out any instances of male nudity or shirtless hot hairy guys or surprising homoerotic content, because I know there are gay men and women who watch these films and like getting a heads-up for anything they might find erotic amidst all the naked ladies. For a long time, I kept a list of homoerotic scenes in straight X-rated movies, like Eric Edwards getting "pegged" in Midnight Desires or Bobby Astyr getting rimmed in Outlaw Ladies or DPs in movies where one of the guys would pull out and jerk off onto the other guy's balls or legs. But in general, good sex is good sex. I can't lie and say I'm grossed out by straight sex; if the guy is attractive, the heat is there, and the gal is skilled, it's a turn-on. Actually, right now I'm working on a study of gay male viewers in the classic adult film audience of today. It may startle you how many there really are!

RB: I REALLY THINK IT PROBABLY WOULD! ALTHOUGH MY MANY VISITS TO THE LOCAL FOX THEATER HERE IN VANCOUVER IN THE LATE 1990S AND EARLY 2000S GAVE ME A REAL STRONG INKLING. THE MAJORITY OF THE AUDIENCE THERE FOR THOSE STRAIGHT SEX MOVIES WERE GAY MEN. IT WAS CRUISING CENTRAL AROUND HERE!

CS: I'm also trying to research the history of classic gay straight films. The gay histories are so much more difficult to obtain, with the majority of filmmakers and performers dying

WANDA WHIPS WALL STREET AND HIGH RISE -- JUST TWO OF THE MANY CRITICALLY ACCLAIMED XXX CLASSICS THAT CASEY HAS BEEN SCREENING FOR AUDIENCES IN NEW YORK.

of AIDS in the 80s and 90s and records vanishing with companies that went under or were absorbed by other distributors. What's more, even though I'm gay myself, the survivors of this industry generally won't talk to me, with a few special exceptions like Tom DeSimone, Michael Zen, and Pat Rocco. I'm not sure how to change that. I'm much more embraced and encouraged by the straight industry participants who value what I'm doing and are sometimes titillated by the novelty of my not being a member of the films' target audience. Actresses especially feel comfortable with me, perhaps for obvious reasons.

RB: WHERE ARE YOU LIVING? WHAT ARE YOU WORKING ON THESE DAYS? WHAT GETS YOU OUT OF BED IN THE MORNING?

CS: Right now I'm going back and forth between New York City and Washington D.C. Trying to find permanent work in film distribution or programming, or even something challenging in research and organization. In the meantime most of my energy is spent programming "In the Flesh", a series of 35mm screenings of classic adult films at Anthology Film Archives. It's a lot of fun putting together themed weekend programs, securing prints, inviting guests. The two mandatory elements of the series are the films have to be shown on film and they must be accompanied by guests. So for each film I try to invite as many people involved with the film's production as possible, with one or two central guests for an audience Q&A, trying to create a "re-premiere" event for everyone to reunite and see each other again. The first series was in December 2013, and it would not have happened without Steve Morowitz at Distribpix or Joe Rubin at Vinegar Syndrome! We had composer Jack Urbont speak about his infectious original score for High Rise and director Jonas Middleton made his first public appearance in years for Through the Looking Glass (Pepe Valentine joined us in the audience). The Take Off screening had a lot of surprises, as Larry Revene did a Q&A about Armand Weston and a large number of cast and crew members attended to see their work on the big screen The Wanda Whips Wall Street screening was especially packed with industry friends. Veronica Hart flew out from the west coast to join director Larry Revene, Candida Royalle, Veronica Vera, Rick Savage, and Josey Duval came out in support, we had a great group of adult film screenwriters join us in the audience. We have a "porn noir" series in March 2014 and then June 2014 will feature some very in-demand films with some sure to be major cast and crew reunions! Thankfully the series has also led to other programming opportunities in the city at other venues, most adult film-oriented but some venturing out into other exploitation genres.

WE ♥ USCHI

143

RB: ALL OF THAT WILL HAVE COME AND PASSED BY THE TIME THIS SEES PRINT, SO I'LL JUST GO AHEAD AND SAY NOW THAT IT WAS ALL AWESOME! EVERYONE READING THIS MISSED OUT! HAHA! I THINK SOMETIMES ABOUT THE PREVIOUS GENERATION OF GUYS AND GALS DOING THIS, SOMETIMES. THE FANZINE AUTHORS, I MEAN. COULD YOU DO WHAT YOU DO WITHOUT THE INTERNET? HOW WOULD IT BE BETTER OR WORSE?

CS: I think about the people before us all the time! For me, it's more about researchers like Jim Holliday and Mark Kernes who were there within the business or Dr. Stetson, God rest his soul, and Bill Cates. Bill Landis paved the way for a lot of us to start writing about the "undesirable films" of the genre. I'm pretty sure Avon would have remained buried a lot longer without Landis. And "Sleazoid Express" and later Michelle Clifford's "Metasex" really kept that dialogue going, as did your Cinema Sewer, Scott Aaron Stine's very brief run of "Filthy Habits". The Internet has been a true godsend for anyone working on this history. It makes finding people easier, obviously, but it also connects you with people with similar interests or with potential publishing sources. I mean, virtually every step of my path in this field has been courtesy of the Internet. My web reviewing led to working on DVD extras, my relationship with Distribpix began through the Internet, I've connected with other researchers, I've maintained friendships with performers and directors across the country through e-mails that then lead to phone conversations. In this way I guess I'm part of that next generation of researchers who has things far easier...but not the easiest it could possibly be. There are still very human barriers that no electronic or digital gadget can kick out of the way.

⸺⸺⸺⸺⸺⸺

THANKS TO CASEY FOR CHATTING AND FOR ALL OF HIS HELP OVER THE YEARS WHEN IT COMES TO FACT CHECKING. DOING RESEARCH IS WAY EASIER WHEN YOU HAVE A NETWORK OF KNOWLEDGEABLE PALS!

BZZT. BEEP.

BZZT. BORP.

CINEMA SEWER

WHY IS NEARLY EVERY MOVIE THAT HAS EVER HAD "ROBOT" IN ITS TITLE TOTALLY TERRIBLE? THERE ARE A COUPLE OF SO-SO EIGHTIES MOVIES THAT PROVIDE THE EXCEPTION (ROBOT CARNIVAL FROM 1987 AND ROBOT JOX FROM 1989), BUT OTHER THAN THOSE, THERE ARE LITERALLY HUNDREDS OF REALLY TERRIBLE MOVIES THAT INCORPORATE THE WORD. I'M TALKING DOLLAR STORE BINS FULL OF THESE FUCKING FILMS. PILES OF THEM. (AND NO, ROBOCOP DOESN'T COUNT. CLOSE, BUT NO COOKIE.) SERIOUSLY, IF YOU'RE TRYING TO CURSE YOUR MOVIE DURING THE SCREENWRITING PROCESS, JUST GO AHEAD AND NAME IT ROBOT SOMETHING-OR-OTHER. I DARE YOU.

MAYBE "ROBOT" AND MOVIE TITLES GOT OFF ON THE WRONG FOOT WITH 1953'S ROBOT MONSTER (YOU KNOW, THE MOVIE WITH THE GUY IN THE APE SUIT WITH THE FISHBOWL ON HIS HEAD), AND NEVER REALLY RECOVERED. IT IS, AFTERALL, CONSIDERED TO BE ONE OF THE 5 WORST MOVIES OF ALL TIME BY MOST FILM SCHOLARS.

Hardgore (1975. Dir: Michael Hugo)
Cast: Dianne Galke, John Seeman, Turk Lyon, Joan Devlon, Bunny Savage, Justina Lynne

GUEST REVIEW BY CASEY SCOTT

CUTIE DIANNE GALKE STARS AS MARIA, A YOUNG NYMPHOMANIAC SHUT AWAY IN A MENTAL HOSPITAL RUN BY SHADY DR. GEORGE (JOHN SEEMAN), HIS ASSISTANT (TURK LYON) AND HIS STAFF OF BEAUTIFUL LESBIAN NURSES (INCLUDING JOAN DEVLON). MARIA FINDS PLENTIFUL OPPORTUNITIES TO INDULGE IN SEXUAL SHENANIGANS WITH THE NURSES, BUT EACH ONE SHE BEDS DIES A HORRIBLE DEATH. EVERY NIGHT SHE WANDERS FROM HER ROOM, SHE FALLS INTO A DREAMLIKE NETHERWORLD OF SATANISTS, ORGIES AND BLOODLETTING! WHAT DOES DR. GEORGE PLAN TO DO WITH HER YOUNG NUBILE BODY, AND HOW CAN SHE ESCAPE HER FATE? MORE IMPORTANTLY, HOW MUCH OF THE INSANITY SHE EXPERIENCES IS PART OF HER FEVERED IMAGINATION?

HARDGORE PLAYS LIKE A LOW-BUDGET REGIONAL HORROR FILM WITH THE ADDITION OF EXTENDED HARDCORE SEX SCENES. THE ATMOSPHERIC MENTAL HOSPITAL, DARKLY LIT CHASE SCENES AND RITUALISTIC SEX OVERSEEN BY A MASKED, CHANTING SATAN HIMSELF ALL WOULD FIT PERFECTLY IN A RACIER VERSION OF WILLIAM GIRDLER'S ASYLUM OF SATAN (1972). ACCORDING TO STAR SEEMAN, THE FILM WAS PRODUCED BY HOLLYWOOD PROS WHO WANTED TO TAKE A STAB (BAD PUN INTENDED) AT MIXING HORROR AND SEX, TWO LOW-BUDGET FILM GENRES THAT WERE GENERALLY

SUREFIRE BOX OFFICE WINNERS. THESE TWO ELEMENTS MAKE STRANGE BEDFELLOWS, HOWEVER, WHICH THE PRODUCERS LEARNED WHEN THEY HAD GREAT DIFFICULTY TRYING TO SELL THE FINISHED ODDITY.

WITH THE CREW'S MAINSTREAM BACKGROUND, IT'S NOT SURPRISING THAT THE FILM HAS A STRIKING VISUAL POLISH THROUGHOUT. ONE PARTICULARLY INVENTIVE SEQUENCE FEATURES MARIA GLIDING DOWN A HALLWAY TOWARDS A KALEIDOSCOPIC COLORED DOORWAY. THE GORE EFFECTS ARE APPROPRIATELY MOIST AND EYE-CATCHING: A NURSE'S THROAT SPRAYS BLOOD APLENTY WHEN IT IS SLIT, A SATANIST'S DICK IS SLICED OFF IN GLARING CLOSE-UP AS MARIA SUCKS ON IT, A NURSE'S VAGINA IS SCORCHED BY AN ELECTRIFIED DILDO (YES, PLENTY OF SMOKE COMES BILLOWING OUT AS SHE SCREAMS "CALL THE DOCTOR! CALL MY MOTHER! CALL THE FIRE DEPARTMENT!"), AND AN INNOCENT GIRL IS BEHEADED AS SHE IS TAKEN FROM BEHIND BY A HOODED CULT MEMBER. JUST AS BIZARRE AS THE RITUAL SEQUENCES IS A SCENE IN "THE ROOM", A BLOOD-SPATTERED HIDEAWAY WHERE THE DEAD BODIES OF NURSES HANG ON HOOKS AND LAY ON SHEETS, REVEALING ALL THE EFFECTS OF THEIR DEMISES. WHILE A HOSPITAL ATTENDANT HAS SEX WITH ONE OF THE CARCASSES, DR. GEORGE HAS HIS WAY WITH MARIA, WHO IN HER SEX-CRAZED IMAGINATION WHISKS THE TWO OF THEM AWAY TO AN ALL-WHITE ROOM WHERE THEY HAVE SEX ON A SPINNING TABLE. LATER, AS MARIA HANGS IN "THE ROOM" AS PUNISHMENT, SHE HAS A VISION OF FLOATING RED DILDOS SPRAYING GALLONS OF SEMEN ALL OVER HER NUDE BODY!

AS EROTIC AS HAVING YOUR LIVER REMOVED AND AS FRIGHTENING AS "THE PAUL LYNDE HALLOWEEN SPECIAL", HARDGORE IS ONE OF THE MOST FASCINATING MISFIRES IN THE ADULT FILM GENRE, WORTH WATCHING SPECIFICALLY FOR ITS SHEER WRONG-HEADED AMBITION, RARELY MATCHED BY ANY OTHER PORNO FILM YOU'LL EVER SEE.

- FIN -

HARD GORE

COLOR

X

Starring: Diane De Leigh & John Seeman

THIS HARDGORE REVIEW CAME OUT IN C.S. #28 IN FEB 2015 AND ABOUT A WEEK BEFORE I WENT TO PRINT WITH THIS, MUSLIM EXTREMISTS BURST INTO THE OFFICES OF CHARLIE HEBDO MAGAZINE IN PARIS FRANCE AND MURDERED FOUR CARTOONISTS, AS WELL AS 13 OTHER INNOCENT VICTIMS. SO IT WAS WITH HEAVY HEART THAT I PUBLISHED THE MAG. IT'S NOT OFTEN I HAVE TO PONDER IF I'M GOING TO GET VIOLENTLY GAKKED FOR DOING WHAT I DO, BUT WHEN YOUR FELLOW CARTOONISTS ARE KILLED IN THE LINE OF DOODLEY, IT SOBERS YOU UP A LITTLE.

BOUGIE JAN 2015 ☆

"FOR ME, IT WASN'T EVEN A DECISION TO BE A DIRECTOR. THERE WAS NO OTHER ROAD. UNLESS YOU'RE INDEPENDENTLY WEALTHY AND YOU DON'T MIND GOING OUT AND BLOWING MONEY, YOU NEED TWO THINGS: FIRST OF ALL, YOU NEED A BACKER WHO IS WILLING TO PUT UP THE MONEY, AND YOU NEED AN AUDIENCE WHO IS WILLING TO PAY THE MONEY TO SEE WHAT YOU HAVE DONE."

"THE DEVIL IN MISS JONES WAS SHOT IN THE APARTMENT OF MY PRODUCTION MANAGER. THERE WAS NO FURNITURE. IN THE OPENING SEQUENCE, SHE'S SITTING IN FRONT OF A BUREAU THAT WAS A COCKTAIL TABLE PILED ON TOP OF TWO APPLE BOXES, WITH A MIRROR STUCK ON THE WALL. IN THE SUICIDE SCENE, I HAD A SPECIAL EFFECTS MAN WHO JUST COULDN'T DO WHAT I WANTED. HE WAS TRYING TO CONCEAL A PACKET OF STAGE BLOOD, AND IT JUST DIDN'T WORK. BUT WHAT I DID WAS GO IN TIGHT AND FILL AN ENTIRE SCREEN WITH A RAZOR BLADE AND SLOWLY, DELIBERATELY, CUT A WRIST. THERE WAS NO WAY IN THE WORLD YOU COULD DO THAT UNLESS YOU SAID TO YOURSELF, 'I CAN DO IT.' AND IT WAS DONE SO SIMPLY. I TOOK SOME MORTICIAN'S WAX, APPLIED IT TO THE WRIST, AND THE RAZOR BLADE ACTUALLY CUT INTO THE MORTICIAN'S WAX. AND THEN IT WAS SIMPLY A MATTER OF PUTTING BLOOD ON THE OPPOSITE SIDE OF THE RAZOR, SO THAT WHEN THE RAZOR WENT IN, IT RUBBED OFF. IT WAS ALMOST LIKE JELLY ON A KNIFE WHEN YOU WIPE IT OFF. IT WASN'T A FAKE SHOT, BUT IT WAS DAMN SIMPLE, AND I KNOW THAT HOLLYWOOD WOULDN'T HAVE DONE THAT. THEY WOULD HAVE SPENT OVER $10,000 ON IT. BUT FOR ME THAT SUICIDE SCENE WAS IMPORTANT BECAUSE THE FILM TAKES PLACE AFTER SHE DIES. IT WAS ALSO VERY HORRIFIC. THIS WAS AN OBSCENE THING -- TO SEE A WOMAN SLICE HER WRIST THAT REALISTICALLY. BUT BECAUSE OF IT, YOU THEN BELIEVE EVERYTHING ELSE. THE PSYCHOLOGY BEHIND THE VULNERABILITY OF BEING NAKED IN A TUB IS DEVASTATING. THERE'S NO WAY OUT. YOU GET THAT TRAPPED FEELING BECAUSE THERE IS NO WAY OUT OF A TUB, AND PEOPLE PSYCHOLOGICALLY FEEL VERY VULNERABLE IN BATHROOMS."

-- GERARD DAMIANO, FROM AN INTERVIEW IN THE AUGUST 1975 ISSUE OF FLICK MAGAZINE. GERRY CAST MISS GEORGINA SPELVIN IN THE DEVIL IN MISS JONES, WHO WAS ORIGINALLY DESIGNATED AS THE CATERER FOR THE PICTURE -- AND IN FACT SHE KEPT THAT JOB FOR THE FILM AS WELL, PERFORMING AS WELL AS FEEDING EVERYONE. THE MOVIE WENT ON TO BE ONE OF THE MOST CRITICALLY BELOVED THEATRICAL FEATURES OF PORN'S GOLDEN AGE, AND ALONG WITH DEEP THROAT, CEMENTED DAMIANO AS ONE OF THE FOREMOST DIRECTORS WORKING AT THE TIME.

FIGHTING MAD (1976. USA)

SHOT IN 5 AND A HALF WEEKS, JONATHAN DEMME MADE THIS REALLY COOL AND VERY POWERFUL TRASH CLASSIC ABOUT A ARKANSAS FARMER (PETER FONDA) WAGING A ONE-MAN WAR AGAINST A CROOKED STRIP-MINER WHO NOT ONLY KILLS HIS FATHER, BUT WANTS TO STRONG ARM HIM INTO SELLING THE FAMILY FARM AS WELL. CUE THE FURIOUS RETRIBUTION.

ACCORDING TO CHRISTOPHER KOETTING'S 2009 BOOK, MIND WARP, CORMAN CLOSELY STUDIED THREE DRIVE-IN THRILLERS THAT HAD BEEN SMASH HITS IN THE EARLIER PART OF THE DECADE. THOSE MOVIES WERE BILLY JACK (1971), WALKING TALL (1973) AND DIRTY MARY CRAZY LARRY (1974). ROGER DEDUCED THAT THEY HAD THREE THINGS IN COMMON: A NO-NONSENSE HERO WITH AN OFF-BEAT SIDEKICK, AN UNUSUAL MODE OF TRANSPORT AND AN INTERESTING WEAPON. IN RESPONSE HE INSTRUCTED DIRECTOR JONATHAN DEMME TO MAKE SURE PETER FONDA'S CHARACTER WOULD HAVE A MOTORCYCLE, A TODDLER SON, AND A CROSSBOW.

HEY, I DON'T KNOW ABOUT YOU CATS AND KITTENS, BUT I LOVE INDIGNANT FILM REVIEWS ON IMDB WHERE CONSERVATIVE-TYPES GET ALL UPSET ABOUT NUDITY AND SWEARS. ONE OF MY FAVES IS FOR THIS MOVIE. A USER NAMED "INSPECTORS71" PENNED THIS NEGATIVE LITTLE GEM:

"STEER CLEAR...HAVING THE LOVE INTEREST OF PETER FONDA SCOLD HIM NOT TO GO OUT THERE AND GET HISSELF DEAD WHILE AIRING OUT HER MOMMY PARTS AFTER SEX ISN'T WORTH MY TIME. I MUST BE GETTING OLD. IN 1976, I WOULD HAVE ELBOWED MY BEST FRIEND TO MAKE SURE HE WAS GROOVING TO THE BOOBS ON SCREEN, THE ORANGEY BLOOD BEING SPILLED, AND THE BAD WORDS THAT THE THREE NETWORKS WOULD HACK OUT FOR BROADCAST. NOW, I LOOK FOR THINGS LIKE ORIGINALITY, DIALOGUE, DEPTH AND BREADTH OF VISUALS, AND INTELLECTUAL STIMULATION. YOU KNOW...THE STUFF YOU WOULD NEVER FIND IN ANYTHING LIKE FIGHTING MAD."

-BOUGIE '14

King Dong (Aka Lost on Adventure Island)
1984 Dir: Yancey Hendrieth

HAWAII-BASED DIRECTOR YANCEY HENDRIETH AND HIS WIFE DEE HENDRIETH (WHO CALLED THEIR COMPANY 'MOONCHILD VIDEO') ONLY EVER MADE ONE MOVIE, AND IT'S THIS ONE. I MEAN, WHAT IS TO BE MADE OF THIS, REALLY? I'M HALFWAY SURE IT WAS RELEASED IN THEATERS BECAUSE I'VE SEEN REFERENCES TO THAT FACT IN ADULT MAGAZINES IN 1985, AND YET ABOUT 50% OF THIS WAS SHOT ON A CAMCORDER, MAKING A THEATRICAL RUN SEEM AWFULLY UNLIKELY. ALL THE SEX, AND EVERY INDOOR SCENE -- SHOT ON VIDEO. CONVERSELY, PRETTY MUCH EVERY OUTDOOR SEQUENCE IS SHOT ON 16MM FILM.

SPLICED TOGETHER, THEY MAKE FOR A VERY JARRING AND ODD MOVIE VISUALLY, AND THAT'S EVEN BEFORE YOU NOTICE THAT THIS IS A HARDCORE SEX FILM WHERE A GIRL NAMED ANNA (CRYSTAL HOLLAND) AND HER BOYFRIEND ALEX (CHAZ ST. PETERS) GET SHIPWRECKED ON AN ISLAND WHERE THE FIRST INHABITANT THEY MEET IS A 3-STORY-TALL DINOSAUR THAT TRIES TO EAT THEM. ITS HORRIFIC SNARL IS PROVIDED BY A GUY GOING "BLAUGH. AHHRGG" INTO A MIC, AND SOMEHOW NOT BUSTING UP AFTERWARDS.

"WHAT IS THIS PLACE? WHERE ARE WE!?" ANNA YELLS. ALEX DOESN'T HAVE A CLUE, SO THEY ADVENTURE INTO THE JUNGLE TO FIND OUT. HERE THEY FIND TWO GORILLAS, ONE OF WHICH IS DIRECTOR YANCEY HENDRIETH IN AN APE SUIT (HIS CHARACTER IS NAMED "BUDDY"), AND THE OTHER IS ANOTHER 3-STORY-TALL STOP MOTION MONKEY (8 INCHES TALL, IN REALITY) WITH PUFFY, QUIZZICAL EYEBROWS. LATER, ALEX GETS GRABBED BY ITS GIANT RUBBER HAND, AND THEN KINDLY RELEASED, WHICH PROMPTS MY FAVOURITE LINE OF DIALOG: "THAT'S SUPER NICE OF YOU, BIG APE. I GOT A SUPER NICE NAME FOR YOU: SUPER SIMIAN!" JUST THE WAY IT'S DELIVERED IS SO STUPID, I LAUGHED FOR ABOUT 5 MINUTES.

ON TOP OF THAT, WE'VE GOT "OOGA BOOGA" STYLE PRIMITIVE CANNIBAL TRIBESMEN WHO DO EVERYTHING SHORT OF COOKING OUR HEROINE IN A POT, A BUNCH OF SKULLS ON STICKS, A LOT OF WOMEN SUCKING FLACCID WIENERS (CAN SOMEONE GET A BONER, PLEASE?), VOICE DUBBING OVER THE SEX SCENES THAT DOESN'T MATCH UP WITH THE MOUTH MOVEMENTS WHEN PEOPLE TALK, A MAN NEARLY FED TO A HUNGRY T-REX, A WITCH DOCTOR WHO SPENDS THE ENTIRE MOVIE SCREWING, A CLAN OF SWORD-WIELDING WARRIOR-WOMEN WHO RIDE ON HORSEBACK AND FORCE ALEX AT KNIFEPOINT TO BREED WITH CHAINED UP BITCHES, AND A HILARIOUS MARITIME COLLISION IN THE OPEN SEA PERFORMED WITH LITTLE TOY BOATS. IF WE LIVED IN A REALITY WHERE LITTLE KIDS WERE LOOKED UPON TO SCRIPT OUR HARDCORE PORN, MAYBE IT WOULD END UP LOOKING A LOT LIKE THIS. ALSO: THAT'S A REALLY STRANGE THOUGHT.

I'M ALMOST POSITIVE WHAT HAPPENED HERE WAS THAT OL' YANCEY MADE HIMSELF A LOW-BUDGET RIP-OFF OF KING KONG ON 16MM, FOUND THAT HE DIDN'T HAVE ANY VIABLE MEANS OF DISTRIBUTING IT OR MAKING BACK HIS INVESTMENT, AND SO WENT BACK WITH A VIDEO CAMERA AND SHOT LOTS OF HARDCORE INSERTS WITH THE SAME ACTORS. I'M NOT SURE HOW HE TALKED THEM INTO THAT.

BUT MY THEORY DOES SUDDENLY BRING ALL OF THOSE FLACCID DICKS INTO FOCUS --CONSIDERING THAT THESE WOULD HAVE NOT BEEN MALE ACTORS SUITED TO PLY THEIR TRADE IN XXX -- AND IN AN ERA BEFORE VIAGRA EXISTED CLEARLY. WITH THAT SMUT FACTOR IN PLACE, HE THEN GOT THIS SHIT OUT THERE BY SOME MINOR MIRACLE, AND I'M GLAD HE DID, BECAUSE IT WAS FUCKING HILARIOUS.

HAW HAW! GO GET 'EM, SUPER SIMIAN! WEE!!

CLEARLY I AM SO INTO THIS ONE

CRYSTAL HOLLAND Goes Ape in...

KING DONG

A YANCEY HENDRIETH FILM

I NEED SOME PUZZ ZAY!

LILI MARLENE:
THE FORGOTTEN ANAL PRINCESS

LILI MARLENE WAS A NATURAL DISHWATER BLONDE 1980S PORN STAR WITH TRIMMED WISPY WHITE PUBES THAT ENCIRCLED HER PETITE VULVA. TO ME SHE ALWAYS SORT OF LOOKED LIKE BLONDIE LEAD SINGER DEBBIE HARRY, BUT MAYBE HER TASTE IN MUSIC WAS A LITTLE MORE STAID CONSIDERING THE INSPIRATION FOR HER PORNO NOM DE PLUME. THE SONG "LILI MARLENE" WAS MADE FAMOUS BY THE LEGENDARY 1930S AND '40S GERMAN-BORN AMERICAN ACTRESS, MARLENE DIETRICH. IT WAS BASED ON A POEM FROM 1918 BY A GERMAN SOLDIER IN WORLD WAR 1 NAMED HANS LEIP, AND LILI WAS THE GIRL WAITING FOR HIM. SET TO MUSIC IN 1938, THE SONG BECAME VERY POPULAR WITH BOTH THE GERMAN AND ALLIED TROOPS IN 1944, AND AGAIN HIT THE CHARTS IN 1968. IT WAS SAID (ALTHOUGH NOT IN THE SONG ITSELF) THAT THE LOVELY GIRL THE LONELY GERMAN SOLDIER PINED FOR WAS ACTUALLY A PROSTITUTE.

THE MODERN LILI ALSO CAME TO THE RESCUE OF A LOT OF HORNY, LONELY MEN, AND QUIETLY PLIED HER TRADE IN THE JIZZ BIZ FROM EARLY 1982 (AT THE AGE OF 28) TO LATE 1987. FIVE YEARS ISN'T VERY LONG, BUT IT WAS ENOUGH TIME TO CARVE OUT A NICHE FOR HERSELF IN 8MM LOOPS, THEATRICAL PORN FILMS, VHS VIDEO RELEASES, AND MANY HARDCORE AND SOFTCORE MAGAZINE PHOTO SHOOTS. UNFINISHED MOVIES AND SCENES THAT SHE'D DONE DURING THAT TIME WOULD GET SPLICED INTO OTHER FILMS AND CONTINUE TO BE RELEASED UNTIL THE MID 1990S, YEARS AFTER SHE'D LEFT ADULT MOVIES -- AND YET SHE NEVER REALLY BECAME A WELL-KNOWN NAME AMONGST PORNO Film CONSUMERS OR GOT THE PROPS THAT HER VERY SMALL CIRCLE OF DEDICATED FANS BELIEVE SHE WAS OWED. SHE WAS GIVEN NO AWARDS AT THE TIME, NOR HAVE THERE BEEN ANY INVITES TO ENTER HER NAME INTO THE PORN HALL OF FAME TODAY.

"IF YOU'RE TALKING ABOUT THE MOST UNDERRATED SEX PERFORMER IN PORN HISTORY, I'D VOTE LILI MARLENE", LEGENDARY PORN STUD, RICHARD PACHECO, TOLD ME IN OCTOBER 2013. "SHE SHOULD HAVE BEEN A SUPERSTAR. SHE DESERVES TONS OF RESPECT."

THERE WAS NO HALF-ASSING IT WITH THIS SEXUALLY-SKILLED WOMAN WHEN IT CAME TO FUCKING ON A PORN SET. THE ORIGINATOR OF THE "CRYING ORGASM" (WHICH WAS LILI'S TRADEMARK MOANING GRIMACE WHEN SHE WAS HAVING SEX) MARLENE WAS FAMOUS FOR HER DOUBLE PENETRATIONS, ANAL SCENES, AND ASS-TO-MOUTH IN AN ERA WHEN NONE OF THESE KINKS WERE COMMON IN AMERICAN XXX. HELL, NO ONE HAD EVEN SEEN ATM'S BEFORE LILI STARTED IMPROVISING THEM IN HER SCENES, OFTEN CATCHING GUYS SEEMINGLY BY SURPRISE AS SHE WOULD TURN AROUND AND GOBBLE THEIR DICKS FRESH OUT OF HER BUTT. SHE WAS ALSO ONE OF THE FEW WOMEN WHO TOOK JOHN HOLMES'S GIANT COCK IN HER REAR.

LILI AND THE MAN SHE WAS PAIRED WITH IN MULTIPLE MOVIES, JON MARTIN. "LILI WAS SPECTACULAR" HE TOLD ME IN 2014.

"I HAVE THAT OLD VHS OF HER TAKING ON JOHN HOLMES", FAN DALE E TOLD ME IN 2014. "SHE SEEMED TO BE IN ECSTASY. AFTERWARDS SHE'S KISSING AND LOVING HIS MEMBER LIKE IT'S A SEPARATE PERSON."

"LILI WAS SPECTACULAR AND SHE DID LOVE HOLMES' LARGE MEMBER", LILI'S CO-STAR JON MARTIN NOTED WHEN I ASKED HIM ABOUT HER IN 2014. THAT AFOREMENTIONED ANAL SCENE WITH HOLMES IN THE 1985 VIDEO ENTITLED "BACKDOOR ROMANCE" WAS A THREE-WAY, AND MARTIN WAS THE UNNOTICED THIRD. IT WAS HARD TO BE IN THE SPOTLIGHT WHEN YOU SHARED A WOMAN WITH JOHNNY 'THE WAD' HOLMES.

"WHEN FEW WOULD TAKE IT IN THE BACK DOOR, SHE NEVER BACKED AWAY", MARTIN REMINISCED, WISTFULLY. "I KNEW HER BOTH IN FRONT OF THE CAMERA

AND PRIVATELY. LILI WAS WITH A RATHER OBNOXIOUS BOYFRIEND, BUT GOT RID OF HIM EVENTUALLY. I MISS HER AND WOULD LOVE TO HEAR FROM HER."

"THE MOVIE I'LL ALWAYS REMEMBER LILI FOR IS THE YOUNG LIKE IT HOT", CINEMA SEWER READER GEORGE P. WROTE ME IN 2013. "SHE PLAYED A NERVOUS VIRGIN, AND SHE DID THAT WHIMPERING SHE ALWAYS DID WITH HER FACE ALL SCRUNCHED UP. LILI MARLENE WAS THE BEST WHIMPERER IN THE

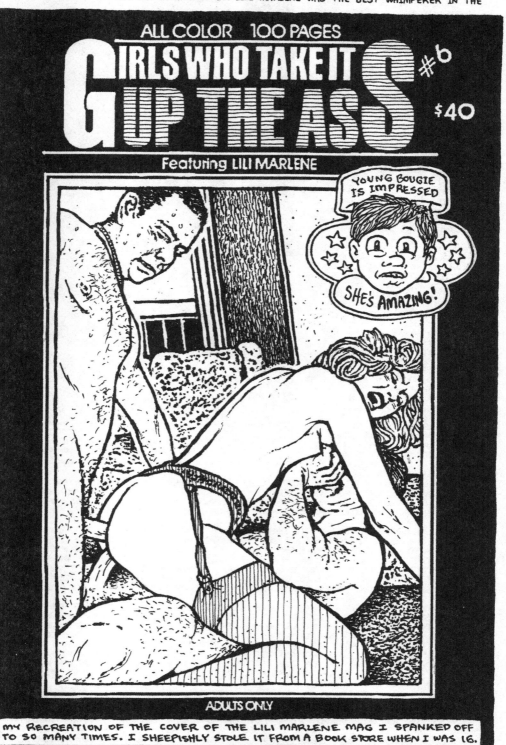

MY RECREATION OF THE COVER OF THE LILI MARLENE MAG I SPANKED OFF TO SO MANY TIMES. I SHEEPISHLY STOLE IT FROM A BOOK STORE WHEN I WAS 16.

BUSINESS. I SAW IT AT THE PUSSYCAT THEATER IN LOS ANGELES IN 1983, AND THERE WASN'T ANY WAY YOU COULD MISS HER. THERE WASN'T A DRY DICK IN THE HOUSE. ERIC EDWARDS HAPPILY DRILLING MARLENE'S PUCKER WAS ENOUGH TO MAKE ANYONE'S EYES WIDEN, EVEN IF YOU WEREN'T INTO ANAL. THESE NEW GIRLS NOWADAYS THINK THEY'RE SUCH ANAL PROS, BUT LILI WAS THE ORIGINAL. I BET SHE COULD STILL KEEP UP WITH THESE MODERN SLUTS IF SHE WAS STILL IN THE BUSINESS BECAUSE SHE MADE SOME OF THE BEST FACES. YOU DIDN'T EVEN NEED TO SHOOT THE PENETRATION WITH LILI, JUST KEEP IT ON HER FACE AND THE WHOLE THEATER WOULD GO HOME WITH STICKY PANTS."

SHE WAS CLEARLY AHEAD OF HER TIME, AND ALL OF THIS TALK OF LILI'S MESMERIZING FACIAL EXPRESSIONS PUTS ME IN MIND OF A MAGAZINE, A HARDCORE SLICK I OWNED WHEN I WAS 16 YEARS OLD. IT HAD THE RATHER TO-THE-POINT TITLE OF "GIRLS WHO TAKE IT UP THE ASS #6", AND SURE ENOUGH, THERE WAS NAUGHTY LILI RIGHT ON THE COVER WITH HER NAME PLASTERED RIGHT ACROSS THE FRONT OF THE MAGAZINE. THE MEMORABLE PHOTO WAS OF HER DOING A DOUBLE PENETRATION WITH TWO UNCREDITED HIMBOS, AND SHE'S HAVING ONE OF HER TITS TWISTED BY THE STUD BELOW HER WHILE THE GUY BEHIND IS GRINDING INTO HER BACKSIDE.

WHEN I WAS YOUNGER, TO ME THE LOOK ON HER FACE WAS ONE OF "I CAN WITHSTAND THIS. THIS IS AN ORDEAL, BUT I'M STRONGER THAN THIS", AND I FOUND THAT FASCINATING SOMEHOW — AS IF I WAS LOOKING AT AN ATHLETE MEETING A CHALLENGE HEAD ON AND WITHOUT FEAR. A SEXUAL OLYMPIAN. TO ME WOMEN LIKE LILI WEREN'T PATHETIC WHORES OR LOWLY SLUTS TO BE DISMISSED, THEY WERE <u>HEROINES</u>, MASTERS OF A CRAFT THAT WAS SO MYSTERIOUS TO TEENAGE VIRGINS LIKE ME, AND STILL SEEM LIKE SUPER HEROES EVEN NOW WHEN I'M FAR MORE

PHOTO BY PAUL JOHNSON. PLEASE VISIT HIS COOL WEBSITE: PAULSFANTASY.COM FOR MORE.

SEXUALLY KNOWLEDGABLE. OF COURSE, AFTER SEEING SOME OF HER MOVIES YEARS LATER I REALIZED THAT MEMORABLE GRIMACE FROM THE MAGAZINE COVER FLASHED ACROSS HER FACE REGUENTLY DURING SEX, REGARDLESS IF SHE WAS PERFORMING ADVANCED SPHINCTER GYMNASTICS WITH A GIANT BLACK STUD OR GETTING SOME GENTLE CUNNILIGUS FROM A LITHE, TENDER PLAYMATE.

BUT DESPITE HER HEADLINE BILLING ON THAT SLICK AND BEING A PERFORMER THAT ALWAYS SEEMED TO DO WHAT SHE COULD TO MAKE SURE EVERY SCENE SHE WAS IN WAS REMARKABLE, SHE WASN'T REALLY EMBRACED BY THE INDUSTRY. EVEN WHEN I GO THROUGH MY LARGE COLLECTION OF ADULT MOVIE MAGAZINES FROM THE YEARS SHE WAS MOST PROLIFIC, 1983 TO 1987, THERE WAS ALMOST NOTHING WRITTEN ABOUT THIS LOVELY BLONDE SEXUAL OLYMPIAN. IT WAS LIKE THEY IGNORED HER. MEANWHILE, I'VE FOUND DOZENS OF INTERVIEWS AND FEATURES ON GIRLS WHO DID FAR FEWER MOVIES, HAD LESS STARRING ROLES, AND WEREN'T THE SORT OF SKILLED SEXUAL ATHLETE LILI WAS.

ANOTHER MARLENE MOVIE THAT WAS MEMORABLE WAS LILI'S 3-WAY IN THE 1984 SHOT-ON-FILM RELEASE, PASSIONS. IT'S A GREAT LOOKING SCENE THANKS TO DIRECTION BY ALEX DE RENZY, AND LOVELY LILI DOES HER USUAL ANAL ANTICS, DOUBLE PENETRATION WIZARDRY, AND SOME GREAT FILTHY TALK WHILE LOOKING RIGHT INTO THE CAMERA. BUT THIS TIME IT'S HER TWO CO-STARS THAT I GET THE BIGGEST KICK OUT OF. WITH THEIR PERFECTLY TRIMMED BEARDS AND FEATHERY WELL-GROOMED HAIR, DAN T. MANN AND NICK NITER (AKA "SLY PUTZ", NO I'M NOT MAKING THAT UP) ARE DEAD RINGERS FOR TWO OF THE GIBB BROTHERS FROM THE BEE-GEES. IF ONLY A MUZAK VERSION OF "HOW DEEP IS YOUR LOVE" WAS PIPED IN OVER THIS JUICY PLOWING, IT WOULD HAVE BEEN JUST KNEE-SLAPPINGLY PERFECT.

"I SAW LILI MARLENE IN THE '80S AT SHOW WORLD ON 42ND/8TH", LOU LOOMIS WROTE IN 2009 AT THE VINTAGE EROTICA FORUM. "LET ME TELL YOU, I'LL NEVER FORGET IT. ONSTAGE, SHE WAS LIKE A WOMAN POSSESSED AND 'WORKED OUT' TO A POINT OF EXHAUSTION WITH A DOUBLE-HEADED DILDO, RAMMING IT DOWN HER THROAT AND IN HER PUSSY. BOTH ACTIVITIES OCCURRED WHILE SITTING ON A CHAIR. EVEN THOUGH IT WAS A LONG TIME AGO, I REMEMBER THAT SHE WAS COMPLETELY SLOBBERING ALL OVER THE DILDO WHEN SHE RAMMED IT DOWN HER THROAT LIKE A DEMON, AND

LILI AND FELLOW SEX STAR MIKE HORNER SHARE A TENDER MOMENT.

THAT I WAS SO CLOSE TO THE STAGE THAT I COULD SEE HER PORES THROUGH HER WHITE STOCKINGS. IT WAS UNFORGETTABLE, FOR SURE. I WAS STUNNED, MESMERIZED, AND MADE A BELIEVER FOREVER."

"SHE WAS A LOVELY, WARM AND SENSUAL WOMAN WHO WAS ALWAYS NICE TO BE AROUND", PHOTOGRAPHER AND FRIEND OF LILI, PAUL JOHNSON SAID IN 2014. "I NEVER (HAD SEX) IN FRONT OF THE CAMERA WITH LILI BUT WE HAD OUR ADVENTURES -- LIKE IN THE BACK OF A VAN DRIVEN BY MAI LIN'S HUSBAND, DEAN, WITH MIKE HORNER RIDING SHOTGUN. WE WERE ON THE WAY TO THE SWING HOUSE THAT DEAN AND MAI LIN LIVED IN AND MANAGED. DEAN ASSISTED ME IN SHOOTING LILI & MIKE FOR A MAGAZINE CALLED 'THE GIRL WITH THE GOLDEN BOX'."

HER CO-STAR IN THE 1984 MOVIE EDUCATING NINA WAS LEGENDARY PORN INDUSTRY LESBIAN (AND ACCOMPLISHED SEX EDUCATOR) NINA HARTLEY. THEY ALSO DID A FUN 1985 MUSIC INDUSTRY THEMED PORNO THAT WAS GEARED TO CASH IN ON THE POPULARITY OF MTV. IT WAS CALLED ROCK HARD. HARTLEY PLAYED A MEMBER OF THE UP AND COMING ROCK GROUP "THE SEXOLETTES", AND LILI PLAYED A PROMOTER WHO WAS ALSO A WHIP-WIELDING LESBIAN DOMINATRIX THAT LOVED PUTTING DESPERATE YOUNG MUSICIANS THROUGH THEIR PACES. IT'S A FUN LITTLE TIME WASTER.

"LILI MARLENE. NOW, THERE WAS A HOT WOMAN!", NINA WROTE ON HER WEBSITE IN 2007. "I LOVED HER A LOT. SHE HAD A BEAUTIFUL, RESPONSIVE PUSSY AND ALWAYS CAME FOR REAL. UNFORTUNATELY, SHE DEVELOPED A DRUG PROBLEM, AS HER HUSBAND WAS A USER, AND ABRUPTLY RETIRED IN ABOUT '87.

IT WAS BOTH TO SAVE HER LIFE AND TO TAKE ADVANTAGE OF THE GI BILL AND GO TO COLLEGE. SHE LEFT HIM (AND THE BUSINESS) COLD TURKEY AND THAT WAS THAT FOR THAT. SHE MOVED BACK HOME TO OHIO AND CUT OFF CONTACT WITH ANYONE FROM THE BUSINESS. I TRIED SENDING A LETTER A COUPLE OF TIMES, BUT GOT NO ANSWER. I WAS SAD, BUT I DO UNDERSTAND HOW ONE MUST SOMETIMES CUT OFF CONTACT COMPLETELY WITH THINGS OR PEOPLE WHOM ONE FEELS ARE DANGEROUS TO ONE'S SOBRIETY. I HOPE SHE IS WELL AND HAPPY. I THINK OF HER EVERY SO OFTEN AND WONDER HOW SHE'S DOING."

IF SHE'S ALIVE NOW IN 2014, LILI WOULD BE 60 YEARS OLD. MISS MARLENE (OR WHATEVER NAME YOU WERE BORN UNDER OR GO BY NOW) -- IF YOU ARE SOMEHOW READING THIS -- KNOW THAT YOU ARE REMEMBERED, AND VERY FONDLY.

—BOUGIE '14

PORN: MAKING IT UP

TALENTED MAKE-UP ARTIST MELISSA MURPHY, 36, TOILED IN OBSCURITY FOR 8 YEARS WHILE DOING MAKE-UP ON PORN SETS IN LOS ANGELES. SHE'D RIDE TO WORK ON THE 101 FREEWAY ON HER MOTORCYCLE, JUST ANOTHER TATTED-UP BEHIND-THE-SCENES PERSONALITY WHOSE WORK WASN'T RECOGNIZED OR APPRECIATED BY THE PUBLIC. THEN SHE STARTED TAKING BEFORE-AND AFTER PHOTOS OF HER FAMOUS SUBJECTS, AND POSTING THEM (WITH PERMISSION) ON HER INSTAGRAM ACCOUNT JUST FOR FUN.

"WHEN I FIRST STARTED DOING THE 'BEFORE AND AFTERS' IT WAS EVEN SHOCKING FOR ME, BECAUSE I'D NEVER SEEN MY WORK PRESENTED IN THAT WAY", SHE TOLD INTERVIEWER MARIKA GUTMANN FOR A PIECE AIRED ON GERMAN TV IN 2013.

THE IMAGES WERE TRULY STARTLING IN WHAT THEY REVEALED ABOUT WHAT PORN STARS LOOK LIKE UNDER THEIR PERFECTLY APPLIED SLUT-MASK. THE PROFESSIONAL TRANSFORMATIONS FOUND MANY OF THE VERY NORMAL PIMPLY-FACED, FRIZZY-HAIRED GIRLS UTTERLY UNRECOGNIZABLE IN THEIR AFTER PICS, AND WHILE THIS SERIES OF IMAGES RECEIVED MILLIONS OF HITS AND A LOT OF ATTENTION, MUCH OF IT (ESPECIALLY ONLINE) WAS NOT POSITIVE. IT SEEMED LIKE MANY MALE PORN FANS REALLY DIDN'T LIKE TO DISCOVER THAT THEIR FANTASY GIRLS LOOKED

BOUGIE

UTTERLY AVERAGE IN REAL LIFE, AND MANY WOMEN WERE VERY CRITICAL OF MELISSA FOR PERPETRATING UNACHIEVABLE BEAUTY MYTHS THAT MADE WOMEN SEEM LIKE LOOKALIKE BARBIE DOLLS.

"I TOOK IT REALLY HARD", MELISSA SAID OF THE EXPERIENCE OF HER BEFORE-AND-AFTER MAKE UP PICS GOING VIRAL. "I LOCKED MYSELF IN MY APARTMENT FOR A FEW DAYS, DELETED INSTAGRAM AND TWITTER OFF MY PHONE, AND CRIED A LOT. UM, BUT THEN I WAS GETTING A LOT OF POSITIVE ON THE BACK SIDE. YOU KNOW, EMAILS FROM WOMEN SAYING THAT WHAT I DO IS AN INSPIRATION, AND ALL THESE NEWS PEOPLE TALKING ABOUT HOW I'VE HUMANIZED PORN."

"BESIDES FOR THE FACT THAT THE GIRLS ARE HAVING SEX, FOR ME THERE REALLY ISN'T MUCH DIFFERENCE IF I'M DOING MAKE UP FOR A WEDDING OR DOING MAKE UP FOR AN ADULT FILM", SHE ADMITTED. "THE IDEAL THAT EVERYONE IS TRYING TO ACHIEVE IS FAKE. IT'S FAKE, PEOPLE. IT'S NOT REAL."

Monkey Shines (1988. Dir: George Romero)

THE CREDITS ROLL, THE TITLES COME UP, AND OUR MAIN CHARACTER, ALLAN MANN (PLAYED BY JASON BEGHE) DOES SOME NAKED STRETCHING ON THE FLOOR AFTER SOME HOT MORNING-TIME SEX WITH HIS CUTE GIRLFRIEND (JANINE TURNER, WHO LATER STARRED IN CLIFFHANGER). HE THEN PROCEEDS TO GET DRESSED, HAPPILY STRAP ON A BACKPACK FULL OF BRICKS, GO FOR A JOG, GET A HIGH FIVE FROM A RANDOM DUDE ON A TEN-SPEED, AND THEN JUMP INTO THE STREET TO AVOID A DOG. IT'S AT THIS POINT WHEN THE POOR SCHMUCK GETS SCHMUCKED BY A TRUCK (MAN, THOSE BRICKS FLEW SO BEAUTIFULLY) AND ENDS UP A BEARDED, SELF-PITYING VEGETABLE IN A HIGH TECH MOTORIZED WHEELCHAIR. THE ACCIDENT LEAVES HIM PARALYZED FROM THE NECK DOWN, NOT TO MENTION BITTER, PISSED OFF, AND STUCK WITH AN OVERBEARING MOM (JOYCE VAN PATTEN) AND A CRANKY, NAGGING NURSE (CHRISTINE FORREST). THIS

Once there was a man whose prison was a chair,
The man had a monkey, they made the strangest pair.

The monkey ruled the man, it climbed inside his head,
And now as fate would have it, one of them is dead.

SHITTY SITUATION IS FURTHER EXACERBATED BY HIS GIRLFRIEND BEING TOTALLY TURNED OFF BY HIS PERMANENTLY LIMP DINGUS, WHICH PROMPTS HER TO SNEAK OFF AND PLAY SWEATY CUM DUMPSTER FOR THE VERY SURGEON (STANLEY TUCCI) WHO FAILED TO PUT HER ONCE ATHLETIC BOYFRIEND BACK ON HIS FEET.

THAT IS WHEN ALLAN'S BEST PAL, GEOFFREY (JOHN PANKOW), DECIDES TO HELP OUT BY GIFTING HIM A TRAINED CAPUCHIN HELPER MONKEY HE'S SECRETLY BEEN INJECTING WITH MELTED DOWN CHUNKS OF A DEAD GIRL'S BRAIN. WHY? WELL, DUH -- TO TRY TO MAKE IT SMARTER, OF COURSE. THE PARALYZED MAN AND HIS LITTLE BRAINY FRIEND PROCEED TO BOND IN AN ALMOST OTHERWORLDLY WAY, WHICH OF COURSE RESULTS IN TRAGEDY, HORROR, AND BLOOD-SOAKED INSANITY.

THE BEHIND-THE-SCENES ANECDOTE I LIKE THE MOST ABOUT THIS UNDERRATED MOVIE (WHICH IN MY OPINION IS JUST BEHIND CREEPSHOW AS THE BEST FILM GEORGE ROMERO EVER DIRECTED OUTSIDE OF HIS ORIGINAL LIVING DEAD TRILOGY) CAME TO MY ATTENTION VIA THE COOL MAKING-OF DOCUMENTARY THAT APPEARS ON THE 2014 BLU-RAY RELEASE FROM SHOUT! FACTORY. IT'S A STORY THAT STAR JASON BEGHE TELLS ABOUT WORKING CLOSELY WITH THE MAIN CAPUCHIN MONKEY IN THE FILM, WHO PLAYS HIS HELPER, "ELLA". BEGHE, PLAYING A MAN UNABLE TO MOVE ANYTHING OTHER THAN HIS HEAD AND NECK, WAS CLOSELY WORKING WITH HIS FURRY NIMBLE-FINGERED CO-STAR WHILE CAMERAS WERE ROLLING, TRYING TO GET IT TO FEED HIM GRAPES AS PREPARATION FOR THEIR NEXT INTIMATE SCENE TOGETHER. WITH EACH PROMPT, THE CAPUCHIN WOULD ACT AS IF IT WAS ABOUT TO POP A GRAPE IN JASON'S YAPPER, AND THEN AT THE LAST MOMENT, TOSS IT ON THE GROUND. ON THE THIRD TRY, THE NAUGHTY SIMIAN PAUSED, AGAIN SENT THE GRAPE FLYING IN THE OPPOSITE DIRECTION, AND QUICKLY SCOOPED UP ONE OF ITS TURDS INSTEAD AND STUFFED IT IN THE SURPRISED ACTOR'S GAPING MOUTH.

"SOMEWHERE, THAT FOOTAGE EXITS", BEGHE SAID WITH A LAUGH. "AND MONKEY POOP TASTES SORT OF LIKE GRAPES."

AS I GUSHINGLY WROTE IN CINEMA SEWER #24, "IN 1987, WHEN I WAS 14 -- AND BEFORE I'D EVEN SEEN A PORN MOVIE -- I KNEW WHO GINGER LYNN WAS". FORGIVE MY REVERENCE, BECAUSE THIS 1980S SEX GODDESS IS DIRECTLY TIED TO MY MEMORIES OF HOW EXCITING, NEW AND MYSTERIOUS PORN IS WHEN ONE FIRST DISCOVERS IT. BEING AS SHE WAS A DISTINCT PART OF MY ADOLESCENT SEXUALITY, I HAVE ALL OF THIS GOOD-WILL (AND GOOD-BONERS) TOWARDS HER, SOMETHING THAT I WAS ABLE TO EXPRESS IN PERSON AT 2014'S SHOCK STOCK CONVENTION IN LONDON ONTARIO. THE CONVENTION ORGANIZERS SEATED US NEXT TO EACH OTHER, SO I HAD PLENTY OF TIME TO GET TO KNOW HER AND I FOUND HER TO BE EVERY BIT AS PLEASANT AS I FANTASIZED SHE WOULD BE WHEN I WAS 14, NOT TO MENTION CHARMING AND ARTICULATE. EVEN THOUGH I WAS LIKE A NERVOUS KID AT FIRST, WE HIT IT OFF REALLY WELL! WHAT WITH THE RIGOURS OF MEETING THE PUBLIC AND SELLING OUR MERCH, WHAT THE TWO OF US UNFORTUNATELY DIDN'T HAVE TIME TO DO WAS AN INTERVIEW.

LUCKILY, I MADE A GOOD FRIEND AT THE CONVENTION, JEREMY HOBBS, A LOCAL LONDON WRITER WHO HAD FORESIGHT ENOUGH TO INTERVIEW GINGER BEFORE THE CONVENTION KICKED OFF, AND SO THANKS TO HIM I CAN SHARE THAT WITH YOU GUYS NOW. THANKS JEREMY, AND THANK YOU GINGER LYNN.

JH: AS A YOUNG LADY, WHAT DID YOU DREAM OF DOING WHEN YOU GREW UP?

GL: I grew up in Rockford, Illinois – which is the home of the famous band Cheap Trick. My girlfriend and I thought we were gonna be the next Heart. I wanted to be a lyricist, to write music and perform onstage. I wanted to be a rock 'n' roll star. I used to put on plays in my garage. I'd get the neighbourhood girls to be my back-up dancers, and I would sing along to Mr. Bojangles and Cher songs and whatever I put on my little record player.

☆ STATS: ☆
- BORN: DEC. 14th 1962
- RANKED #7 BY AVN IN A LIST OF THE GREATEST PORN STARS
- 166 FILMS
- SURVIVED CERVICAL CANCER

GINGER

We would play these songs and charge the neighbourhood kids ten cents to come and watch. We had an old car seat set up, which is where the audience sat. So I always thought I was going to be a famous rock 'n' roll star.

JH: WHEN DID YOU FIRST CONSIDER MAKING ADULT FILMS, AND SUBSEQUENTLY HOW DID YOU GET INVOLVED IN THE INDUSTRY?

GL: You know, it wasn't so much a consideration as I kind of fell into it. I moved from Illinois to California in late 1982, and had the impression that California was going to be a very fun, inexpensive, carefree place to live. I had a job waiting for me because I was the manager of a record store. I became a troubleshooter, and I had nine stores in the California area that I was in charge of, so I had to move around and meet a lot of different people and work a lot of hours. I was working approximately 70 hours a week, and when you're the boss and you're going in and hiring/firing people, you don't make a whole lot of friends. I had a boyfriend in Illinois that decided he was in love with me, and that he was going come out to California as well. So he moved out, and I'm working 70 hours a week, and I've got this really expensive dump of an apartment, and a boyfriend with car payments – so I answered this ad in the newspaper and ended up posing for Penthouse magazine. Within a day of walking into my agent's office, I was approached for months and months to do 'commercial' work. I thought commercial work meant commercials for toothpaste and that sort of thing, so when I found out that it actually meant adult movies I thought to myself – that's not quite the girl that I am. Back in the eighties if you wanted to see an adult movie you had to go to the theatre. I had this image in my head of the guy in the raincoat with the popcorn, and the girls who did it were these mysterious bad girls, and I didn't see myself as that of type of girl. When I finally made the decision to say yes, there was a company that came in who wanted someone who'd never made a film before, that had that 'girl next door' look, and was willing to shoot on the island of Kauai for two weeks.

JH: AND THIS BECAME YOUR FIRST FILM SURRENDER IN PARADISE?

GL: That was Surrender in Paradise. I came back and said that I wanted script approval, I wanted cast approval, and I wanted this much per scene – and we worked out a deal, so I thought I would make Surrender in Paradise along with A Little Bit of… Hanky Panky, and that those would be my first and only two movies. Obviously that wasn't the case. [laughs]

JH: YOU WERE STILL QUITE YOUNG WHEN YOU MADE THESE FILMS. WERE YOU NERVOUS, AND HOW DID YOU FEEL AFTER HAVING PERFORMED YOUR FIRST SCENE?

GL: It was an amazingly beautiful, freeing experience. I mean – imagine turning 21 on the island of Kauai. I'd only been on an airplane once in my life. That was the second time. And with a bunch of people with great personalities, and an amazing crew and director. It was the director and his wife, much like somebody's mom and dad (only younger and hotter) telling you we want this, we want that. There was so much enthusiasm. Everybody was so excited

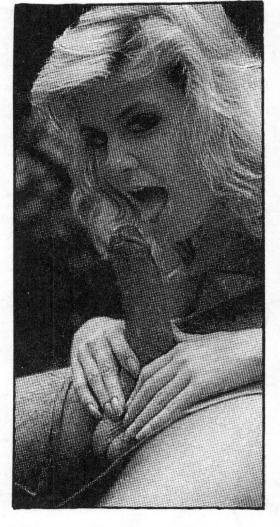

about what we were doing. It was a really big deal, and it could not have been a better experience for me. My leading man was wonderful, and we wound up falling in lust for a bit of a time. Those things never last, but…

JH: IT SOUNDS LIKE A TOTAL BLAST.

GL: It was illegal as well, so there was an outlaw element that went along with it. It was illegal until, I believe, 1988 or 1989. I did all of my initial films from December '83 until February '86. I was in it for a very short period of time – two years, three months. I did all of my filming when it was illegal to do, so there was this other whole element to it. It was a very exciting time, it was a very glamorous time, it was a very rebellious time – and we had a really great group of people.

JH: AT WHAT POINT DID PEOPLE START RECOGNIZING YOU IN YOUR REGULAR LIFE, AND WHAT WAS IT LIKE DEALING WITH THAT?

GL: It didn't take long at all. I made my first film in December '83, and it was 1984 when VCRs really came into play. Everyone was getting a VCR, and it just so happened to be the year that I signed a contract with Vivid Video, and all of the films had my name in the title. So when you walked into the video store, and went behind the curtain into that back room, there was a Ginger section. [laughs]

JH: I TOTALLY REMEMBER THOSE LITTLE BACK ROOMS, WITH THE BLUE CURTAINS.

GL: Yeah, and sometimes they couldn't even have the movie boxes out. They would have a book with the box covers in them. And you had to have a membership too. It was like $100 for a movie – and I think the rewind fee was $50! It's so different now.

GL: I appreciate every award I've been given, but I've never felt like 'Oh, I'm gonna get this award!' or 'Oh, I should have gotten that award!' or 'Dammit, I deserved that! That was mine!' The awards that I've been given, I've been humbled by all of them. My first awards show was the very first XRCO Awards, and that will be 30 years ago next month. I was up for three awards – Video Vixen, Female Performer of the Year, Best New Starlet – and I was up against Traci Lords. I didn't even wear makeup, I wore this little dress from Sears with yellow and black polka dots. Traci came in in her beaded gown, and I won all three awards. So it was really exciting, it was really wonderful, but it didn't change how I felt about myself. And so when I won the AVN award it was the same feeling, and I think it's been that way every time I've won one. I've never had a sense of entitlement, it's always just been icing on the cake.

JH: I THINK THERE'S AN HONESTY IN YOUR PERFORMANCES, A SENSE THAT YOU'RE GENUINELY PRESENT. YOU ALWAYS LOOK YOUR CO-STARS IN THE EYES.

GL: Thank you. I think that a lot of performers perform for the camera, and I performed with my partner (or partners) with the knowledge that the crew was watching. Not the camera, not the audience, not the final fan that got to see the movie. I knew that if I was turning on my leading man or woman, as well as the crew – because they're the most jaded of all – I knew I was in the right place. I was lost in what I was doing, but aware enough that the voyeuristic aspect of it was a turn-on.

JH: I READ THAT YOU ONCE PERFORMED A SCENE IN YOUR ACTUAL PROM DRESS. IS THIS TRUE?

GL: My very first scene in Surrender in Paradise, with Jerry Butler, is in my prom dress. I didn't have a whole lot of clothes, I was just out of high school.

JH: YOU'VE BEEN QUOTED AS SAYING THAT IT WAS EASIER TO DELIVER A BABY THAN TO ACCOMMODATE JOHN HOLMES'S LEGENDARY MEMBER. HOW DID YOU MANAGE?

GL: Um… [laughs] A lot of practice. Actually, I was talking to the makeup artist before the actual scene, letting her know that I was petrified and didn't think I was going to be able to do it. Amber Lynn was working on this film as well. So the makeup artist took myself, Amber Lynn, and John into the closet, and showed me that things weren't as scary as I thought they were gonna be.

JH: JOHN HOLMES DIED TRAGICALLY IN 1988. HOW DID THE ADVENT OF AIDS IN THE MID-'80S AFFECT THE INDUSTRY? WAS THERE A LOT OF FEAR IN THE AIR IN TERMS OF PERFORMING?

GL: I've always been very hygienic. When I got into the business there weren't any big scares, there weren't any big diseases, there weren't things that were going around. It was a very small gene pool, but at the same time I still went to the doctor's office every month. I began getting tested in 1986, and was getting tested on a regular basis, so I didn't have that big fear factor. It had been years since I'd worked with John. It was very sad, very tragic. Sex isn't like it used to be. It's not the '60s anymore. Or the '70s, or even the '80s. Things are different now, and you have to be so careful. There are strains of things out there that can crawl on their own.

JH: PAUL THOMAS ANDERSON'S PORN OPUS BOOGIE NIGHTS DOES A WONDERFUL JOB OF ILLUSTRATING HOW THE MORE PASSIONATE, ARTISTIC ADULT FILMS OF THE '70S AND EARLY '80S GAVE WAY TO THE GONZO, VIDEO-SHOT MOVIES OF THE LATE '80S AND BEYOND. WHAT ARE YOUR THOUGHTS ON HOW THE BUSINESS HAS CHANGED OVER THE YEARS?

GL: Change is inevitable. Within the adult film industry, I tend to romanticize the days when I was in it. I think that the

☆ JERRY BUTLER ☆

time period I was fortunate enough to be involved with the industry in was definitely the Golden Age. It was when the stars were treated like stars, when there were stars, when people did it because they wanted to and because they enjoyed it. It was not popular; it was not cool to be in the industry. It was, as I said, against the law. It became more and more popular as time went on.

JH: IN 1986 YOU RETIRED FROM THE ADULT FILM INDUSTRY TO PURSUE A CAREER IN MAINSTREAM MOVIES. WHAT ARE SOME HIGHLIGHTS FROM THAT PERIOD?

GL: I had a blast doing the Vice Academy series. They were so campy. They were the best worst movies ever made. Just wonderful, big, bad, B-movies. But my best experiences would definitely be doing the Metallica video. Working on the Viacom series Super Force was pretty amazing. NYPD Blue was a huge thrill – not only that I was in an episode, but it was nominated for five Emmys (three of which it won).

JH: YOU TURNED IN A HEARTBREAKINGLY GREAT PERFORMANCE IN THE METALLICA "TURN THE PAGE" VIDEO. HOW DID YOU GET INVOLVED WITH THAT, AND WHAT WAS IT LIKE WORKING WITH DIRECTOR JONAS AKERLUND?

GL: I'm very proud of my performance in the Metallica video. I was asked to be in the video for several months before I actually said that I would. I didn't want to be just another B-movie bimbo, portrayed as the girl with her clothes off again in a video. I had not read the script. When I finally met with Jonas, he was one of the most amazing men that I've ever met. I had no idea that he was such a big director. I met him in overalls and a ponytail, with a wife beater T-shirt and no makeup – and I had my baby, my nanny, and my bodyguard in tow! [laughs] And the way that he told me the story, he really made me relate to the character, and it was one of the most amazing experiences I've ever had. I've heard that Lars was a big influence on me getting the role, but unfortunately I didn't get to meet any of the band members.

JH: SPEAKING OF MUSIC, YOU CUT YOUR OWN 12" SINGLE 'FANTASY WORLD' IN 1986. EXPLAIN.

GL: [laughs] That was a big accident. I had a producer by the name of Bobby Gallagher come to me and say that he wanted me to sing a song and be in a video. I said 'I can't sing'. He said 'I don't care.' I said 'I do!' I took vocal lessons for about six months, and although I grew up playing guitar and singing, I'm really not good at it at all. I'm pretty awful, to tell you the truth. As my father puts it, I'm like a cat scratching its claws on a naily board. Rick Nelson's father said that I had an interesting voice that was off key, like Neil Young.

JH: A LOT OF MY FAVOURITE SINGERS CAN'T ACTUALLY SING.

GL: Yeah, well – I had fun doing it, but it didn't work out for me. I studied for about six months with my vocal coach, and I never got any better. She went with me to New Jersey, and actually did the recording at Jon Bon Jovi's cousin's studio. And as it turned out – they moved all of my singing into the background, and put the backing vocalist's singing in front. If you listen to the album you'll hear a little bit of [sings] 'Fantasy girl…' in the background. The really bad, really high little voice that squeaks in the back during the chorus – that's me.

JH: YOU HAVE A HILARIOUS CAMEO IN ROB ZOMBIE'S RETRO SLAUGHTERFEST THE DEVIL'S REJECTS. WHAT WAS IT LIKE WORKING WITH HIM?

GL: It was a wonderful little cameo. I was originally cast as one of the women in the motel room scene – one of the wives – but I broke my leg. I'd been a martial artist for years, and I busted out my ACL, my MCL, and my meniscus – all of them within weeks of filming!

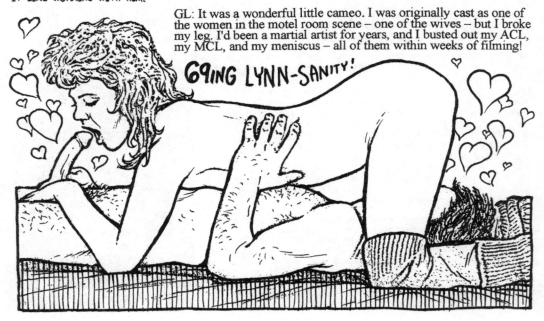

69ING LYNN-SANITY!

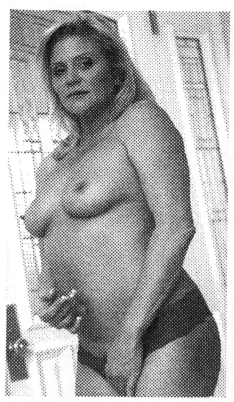

My agent had to call up and say 'Ginger can't run.' So Rob, wanting me to be in the film, wrote me the whole new role of Fanny. And I had to be carried onto the set because I couldn't walk.

JH: IF I REMEMBER CORRECTLY, YOU DID THE ENTIRE SCENE IN A CAST?

GL: I did the entire scene in a cast. Rob was so fabulous. I was afraid that he was going to be one of those tough directors, one of those cool rock 'n' roll people – and I'm much more of a down-to-earth Midwest girl, and don't deal well with hardcore people – but he was not that way at all. He was absolutely wonderful. One of the best experiences that I've ever had. Unfortunately I only worked for one day, and didn't get to meet everybody until the cast party – but over the years I've become good friends with Bill Moseley, Sid Haig, Michael Berryman, E.G. Daily. They're all wonderful. A lot of the cast, we do appearances together. It's one of those things that I'll take with me forever.

JH: IN THE EARLY '90S, YOU DATED THE INFAMOUS, BI-WINNING BAD BOY CHARLIE SHEEN. WHAT WAS THAT LIKE?

GL: Yes I did. We met on the set of Young Guns II. We dated for several years. It was fun, it was fantastic, it was wild and wonderful – and it was a long time ago.

JH: WHAT IS THE STRANGEST THING THAT'S EVER HAPPENED TO YOU ON A PORN SET?

GL: I don't know if it's strange or not, but one of the funniest stories is when I was working on The Grafenberg Spot with Jim and Artie Mitchell. And Artie was playing jokes, and always messing with people. He was the one that was killed, the younger one. He was such a goofball. And there was a scene where Annette Haven (who played the doctor) is supposed to find my G-spot, and I accidentally squirt. It was propped, because you can't do that ten times in a row…

JH: TODAY IT WOULD PROBABLY BE CGI SQUIRTING.

GL: That would be so funny. I wonder if they do that now? They must. So anyway, the big joke was that Annette Haven had never taken a cumshot in the face. That was her rule. She refused to do it. She was not allowed to do it. And so Artie came up to me and said 'I'll give you $1000 if you can hit her in the face.'

JH: AND YOU DID?

GL: [laughs] I did. And as far as I know, it's the only cumshot she's ever taken in the face to this day.

JH: IF I SHOULD BE SO LUCKY. WHAT IS YOUR FAVOURITE ADULT FILM YOU'VE MADE, AND WHO WAS YOUR FAVOURITE ACTOR TO WORK WITH?

GL: The Pleasure Hunt would be my favourite. It's hard to find, I don't know if it's even out there anywhere. It was just a very well made adult film. If I had to pick a second, I'd go with Trashy Lady. New Wave Hookers is always up there, as well as The Grafenberg Spot and Surrender in Paradise. Any of the ones I did in Hawaii. All of the ones that were shot on film I'm proud of. And when I made my comeback and did Taken, which I won AVN's Best Actress award for, I'm proud of that.

JH: WHAT TURNS YOU ON THE MOST?

GINGER AT AGE 50. STILL A FINE FOXY FEMALE WITH SEX APPEAL TO SPARE! GODDAMN, WOMAN! YOU LOOKIN' GOOOOD! ♡

YOU GOT THAT RIGHT!

GL: It may sound silly, but I'm gonna go with intelligence. I'm lucky enough to have been in a great relationship for quite a few years now, and one of the things that keeps it going is that we talk, and we have conversations. Don't get me wrong – we have the best sex I've ever had. It's amazing. But the fact that we can communicate and laugh and be best friends – those are the things that really get me going, that turn me on. When I look at him I get turned on too, but if he was stupid it wouldn't work. [laughs]

JH: I WHOLEHEARTEDLY AGREE. INTELLIGENCE IS VERY SEXY.

GL: You can only fuck so much.

JH: TELL ME SOMETHING MOST PEOPLE DON'T KNOW ABOUT GINGER LYNN.

GL: I'm an artist. I knit, I design jewelry, I sew. I have 24 years of martial arts training. I started with Shotoshinkai, which is a combination of Shotokan and Shintai. I studied with Jerry Bell for eight years, then I moved on to Mr. B and went into Tae Kwon Do, and finally ended up (after my fourth knee surgery) in MMA.

JH: SO ESSENTIALLY YOU COULD BEAT ME UP?

GL: On a good day. I know how to hurt you really bad, really quickly, and then get the fuck out. I'm not sticking around. I'm 5'2 – I'm gonna take you down, and I'm getting away. Unless I'm in a bar fight.

JH: THEN IT'S JUST A FREE-FOR-ALL?

GL: Let's go for it, yeah. Do not give me hard alcohol, do not give me any shots – there will be a fight. [laughs]

JH: I'LL KEEP THAT IN MIND. WHAT WOULD YOUR ADVICE BE TO YOUNG PEOPLE TODAY WHO MIGHT BE CONSIDERING A CAREER IN THE ADULT FILM INDUSTRY?

GL: Don't. Period. I still see it on a regular daily basis, and there is a place for it, and there are still good films being made – but I don't think anybody can really mentally know what they're gonna be in for. Don't get me wrong – I wouldn't change a day of my life, a day of my career – but it took me a long time to meet the right guy. And it doesn't go away. It's there forever, and you'd better find that right person who is not going to have difficulty with it. The older I get, the more I know that the people in my life are the best part of it.

JH: AMEN TO THAT. NOW MY FINAL QUESTION: YOU ONCE REMARKED THAT YOUR ULTIMATE SEXUAL FANTASY WOULD BE TO BANG AN ENTIRE FOOTBALL TEAM. DID THAT EVER HAPPEN, AND IF NOT, WOULD THE CAST AND CREW OF SHOCK STOCK 2014 BE AN ACCEPTABLE SUBSTITUTE?

GL: Still haven't done it! And if you're all wearing uniforms – yes.

- - - - -

TUNE INTO TO GINGER'S RADIO SHOW BLAME IT ON GINGER, LIVE MON-FRI 4-6PM PST AT SKIDROWSTUDIOS.COM, OR ANYTIME ON ITUNES -- AND IF YOU'RE STILL CURIOUS, CHECK OUT GINGER'S NAUGHTY ANSWER TO EBAY AT THE WEBSITE:

GINGERLYNNAUCTIONS.COM

I'M LOOKING AT IT RIGHT NOW. GINGER HAS GOT HER USED PANTIES UP FOR SALE, HER USED DILDOS -- YOU NAME IT! IT'S PRETTY FREAKIN' AWESOME.

JULIE DARLING (1983)

HEY KIDS, REMEMBER HOW FLIPPIN' GREAT THE NAKED CAGE (1986) AND CHAINED HEAT (1983) WERE? WELL, THE DIRECTOR OF THOSE MOVIES, PAUL NICHOLAS, DID ANOTHER COOL MOVIE JUST BEFORE THOSE CAME OUT. JULIE DARLING ISN'T A WOMEN IN PRISON FILM LIKE THE AFOREMENTIONED PAUL NICHOLAS DIRECTORIAL EFFORTS, BUT HE DOES GET TO EXERCISE HIS EXPLOITATION, HORROR AND SUSPENSE MUSCLES EVERY BIT AS MUCH. FUNDED BY WEST GERMANS (NICHOLAS IS GERMAN, HIMSELF), PRODUCED BY A CANADIAN, AND FILMED IN TORONTO AND BERLIN, JULIE DARLING FEATURES A CONNIVING AND DEVIOUS YOUNG GIRL AS AN APPLE-CHEEKED, INNOCENT THAT NO ONE WOULD SUSPECT OF BEING CAPABLE OF THE HEINOUS CRIMES SHE TAKES PART IN. THIS IS THE KIND OF GIRL THAT HIRES A KILLER TO SNUFF OUT HER MOM, AND CASUALLY MENTIONS THAT HE'S WELCOME TO "RAPE HER ALL YOU WANT BEFORE YOU KILL HER".

THE YOUNG STAR OF THE MOVIE, ISABELLE MEJIAS, IS TERRIFIC IN HER ROLE. CANADIANS MIGHT REMEMBER HER ON CRUDDY 1980S SHOWS LIKE THE EDISON TWINS, DANGER BAY, AND NIGHT HEAT. SHE HAS VERY LITTLE NICE TO SAY ABOUT THE EXPERIENCE OF MAKING THIS PICTURE ON THE CODE RED DVD THAT CAME OUT IN 2011, THOUGH, AND BOTH HER INTERVIEW AND COMMENTARY TRACK ARE EXCLUSIVELY DEVOTED TO SHITTING ALL OVER JULIE DARLING. SHE COMPLAINS ABOUT THE ELITIST ATTITUDE OF HER CO-STAR SYBIL DANNING, AND COMPLAINS BITTERLY ABOUT THE WARDROBE STAFF, SCREENWRITER, AND MAKEUP ARTISTS. SHE FEELS SORRY FOR HERSELF AND HER CAREER, AND SAVES SOME OF HER DEEPEST DISSES FOR DIRECTOR PAUL NICHOLAS. "HE'S WALKING AROUND LIKE HE'S THIS BIG-SHOT ARTIST AND, LOOK AT THIS CRAP!", MEJIAS SNARKS ON THE AUDIO COMMENTARY. "MY GOD, IT'S LIKE, 'YEAH, I'M A DIRECTOR.' WELL, YEAH. MY FIVE-YEAR-OLD CAN DO THIS TOO."

SURE, THE MOVIE HAS ITS SHORTCOMINGS, BUT FRANKLY I THINK MEJIAS IS JUST BEING A TOTAL BITCH. I HAVE NO IDEA WHAT IS UP HER ASS ABOUT THIS MOVIE, BUT IT'S NOT NEARLY AS BAD AS HER PISSING AND MOANING WOULD SUGGEST. MAYBE SHE THOUGHT SHE WAS SUPPOSED TO DO THE COMMENTARY IN CHARACTER AS JULIE, THE EVIL CUNT?

She's Getting Rid of Mommy to have Daddy all to Herself.

Julie Darling

Starring ANTHONY FRANCIOSA SYBIL DANNING ISABELLE MEJIAS
Written by PAUL NICHOLAS and MAURICE SMITH Executive Producer JOHN C. POZHKE
Produced by ERNST VON THEUMER and MAURICE SMITH Directed by PAUL NICHOLAS

Inter-Ocean Film Sales, Ltd.

LEE FROST AS "LEONI VALENTINO"

The not-so-sweet cinema of LEONI VALENTINO

ARTICLE BY CHRIS POGGIALI OF TEMPLE OF SCHLOCK

SIMILAR TO NATIONAL SCREEN SERVICE, CONSOLIDATED POSTER SERVICE, DONALD VELDE, BARTCO, AND MOTION PICTURE ACCESSORIES, UNITED THEATRICAL AMUSEMENTS (UTA) WAS A COMPANY THAT HANDLED ADVERTISING MATERIALS (ONE-SHEETS, STILLS, TRAILERS, AD MATS, ETC.) FOR VARIOUS INDIE DISTRIBUTORS AS WELL AS MAJOR STUDIOS. LOCATED AT 1644 CORDOVA STREET IN LOS ANGELES, UTA'S MAIN CLIENTS WERE DAVID F. FRIEDMAN, "MIGHTY MONARCH OF THE EXPLOITATION FILM WORLD," WHOSE OFFICES WERE NEXT DOOR AT 1654 CORDOVA STREET, AND FRIEDMAN'S FRIENDLY COMPETITOR — THE NOTORIOUS BOB CRESSE. WHERE UTA DIFFERED FROM THE OTHERS WAS IN THE FACT THAT ITS OWNER, ARMAND ATAMIAN, REALLY WANTED TO BRANCH OUT INTO PRODUCTION AND DISTRIBUTION AND BECOME AN EXPLOITATION MINI-MOGUL LIKE HIS FRIENDS FRIEDMAN AND CRESSE — AND HE HAD THE FACILITIES AND THE CONNECTIONS TO ACTUALLY MAKE THAT POSSIBLE.

IN 1970, ATAMIAN FORMED PHOENIX INTERNATIONAL FILMS WITH CRESSE'S FORMER PARTNER, LEE FROST. THEIR FIRST PRODUCTION WAS THE SNIPER-ON-THE-RAMPAGE ROUGHIE ZERO IN AND SCREAM (1970), WHICH FROST DIRECTED AS "LES EMERSON." THAT WAS QUICKLY FOLLOWED BY A TRIO OF SICK QUICKIES — RIDE HARD, RIDE WILD (1970), THE CAPTIVES (1971), AND SLAVES IN CAGES (1971) — THAT FROST SHOT MOS ON SHORT-END SCRAPS OF FILM AND ATAMIAN SOLD TO MOVIEGOERS AS BADLY-DUBBED IMPORTS FROM DENMARK. SLEAZY RIDER (1973) WAS HELMED BY FROST ASSOCIATE ROGER GENTRY, WHILE POOR CECILY (1973) AND THE IMPOSTER (1973) WERE DIRECTED BY FROST HIMSELF UNDER THE PSEUDONYM "FRANKLIN C. PERL". THE LATTER FILM WAS SPICED UP WITH HARDCORE FOOTAGE AND REISSUED TWO YEARS LATER AS A CLIMAX OF BLUE POWER.

CONCURRENT WITH HIS FROST COLLABORATIONS, ATAMIAN STARTED A SECOND COMPANY, FREEWAY FILMS CORPORATION, WITH UTA VICE PRESIDENT RICHARD ALDRICH ("DAMON CHRISTIAN") TO PRODUCE AND/OR DISTRIBUTE ADDITIONAL SEXPLOITATION TITLES LIKE DR. MASHER (1970), THE MERMAID (1972) AND GARY GRAVER'S THERE WAS A LITTLE GIRL (1973). BY THIS TIME, ALL THREE COMPANIES (PHOENIX, FREEWAY, UTA) WERE UNDER THE SAME ROOF AT 1658 CORDOVA STREET, BUT THAT CHANGED WHEN FREEWAY ENTERED THE HARDCORE MARKET IN 1974 AND RELOCATED TO 6331 HOLLYWOOD BOULEVARD. FREEWAY PRODUCED ALL OF THE COMPANY'S HARD-X HITS FOR THE NEXT FIVE YEARS, BEGINNING WITH HIGH SCHOOL FANTASIES (1974) AND BEACH BLANKET BANGO (1975) — BOTH DIRECTED BY JAMES BRYAN UNDER THE PSEUDONYM "MORRIS DEAL" AND CONFESSIONS OF A TEENAGE PEANUT BUTTER FREAK (1975). HOWEVER, ALDRICH FOUND HIS BIGGEST BOX-OFFICE SUCCESS AT FREEWAY WITH THE FIVE "JOHNNY WADD" FILMS STARRING JOHN C. HOLMES AND DIRECTED BY BOB CHINN: TELL THEM JOHNNY WADD IS HERE (1976), LIQUID LIPS (1976), THE JADE PUSSYCAT (1977), THE CHINA CAT (1978) AND BLONDE FIRE (1979).

AFTER A STRING OF HITS THAT ALSO INCLUDED 1977'S HARD SOAP, HARD SOAP (A SPOOF OF THE POPULAR DAYTIME TV SERIES MARY HARTMAN, MARY HARTMAN) AND 1978'S DISCO LADY (NAMED AFTER JOHNNIE TAYLOR'S #1 CERTIFIED PLATINUM SINGLE), ALDRICH AND CHINN PARTED WAYS WITH FREEWAY, STRIKING OUT ON THEIR OWN WITH LIPPS & McCAIN (1978) AND PIZZA GIRLS (1979).

AS A FAVOR TO ATAMIAN, WHO WAS NOW WITHOUT A PRODUCER AND DIRECTOR (AND WHOSE HEALTH WAS IN SERIOUS DECLINE BY THE CLOSE OF THE DECADE), FROST AGREED TO DIRECT TWO HARDCORE CHEAPIES FOR FREEWAY (UNDER THE PSEUDONYM "LEONI VALENTINO"), BOTH STARRING RHONDA JO PETTY, THE BALLYHOOED "FARRAH FAWCETT LOOK ALIKE" WHO HAD STARRED IN DISCO LADY THE PREVIOUS YEAR. THE RESULTING FEATURES, SWEET CAPTIVE (1979) AND SWEET DREAMS, SUZAN (1980), LEAVE A LOT TO BE DESIRED BOTH AS FREEWAY PRODUCTIONS AND AS LEE FROST MOVIES.

SWEET CAPTIVE BEGINS ON A PROMISING NOTE, WITH SUZAN (PETTY) DRIVING UP INTO THE HOLLYWOOD HILLS TO THE HOME OF DOUG (JOHN HOLMES) AND KEN (PAUL THOMAS) AND THEIR SHARED LIVE-IN GIRLFRIEND ANNE (DENISE O'BRIAN). A DOLLY SHOT THAT FOLLOWS DOUG PADDLING ON AN INFLATABLE POOL RAFT ALONGSIDE SUZAN AS SHE WALKS OVER TO KEN AND ANNE, LOUNGING POOLSIDE, NICELY ESTABLISHES THE LOCATION (PROBABLY FROST'S OWN HOUSE) WHILE LENDING THE CHEAPJACK PRODUCTION A FLEETING AIR OF PROFESSIONALISM. FROM THE ENSUING CONVERSATION, WE LEARN THAT SUZAN'S BOYFRIEND (NEVER SEEN) HAS STOLEN SOMETHING FROM DOUG AND KEN (NEVER EXPLAINED), AND NOW SHE MUST SUBMIT TO THE DUO'S EVERY WISH, WHIM AND PERVERSION FOR AN ENTIRE WEEKEND IN EXCHANGE FOR THEIR PROMISE NOT TO TURN HER BOYFRIEND OVER TO THE POLICE.

A DECADE EARLIER, FROST WOULD'VE TAKEN A SETUP LIKE THIS AND WHIPPED TOGETHER A SICK, SLEAZY AND SATISFYING PSYCHODRAMA, BUT SWEET CAPTIVE IS THE LAZIEST BIT OF BUSINESS IN HIS ENTIRE CANON. AFTER A LITTLE VERBAL ABUSE ("PIG BITCH!"), KEN AND DOUG FORCE SUZAN TO PERFORM CUNNILINGUS ON ANNE. KEN THEN STICKS A FINGER UP HER ASS AND MAKES HER COOK DINNER. LATER, WE SEE HER FLAT ON

HER BACK WITH HER LEGS IN THE AIR AND A LIT CANDLE PROTRUDING FROM HER VAGINA WHILE KEN AND DOUG BANG AWAY AT ANNE FROM BOTH ENDS. THERE'S A LESBIAN SCENE BETWEEN SUZAN AND ANNE, A TAME BONDAGE AND WHIPPING SCENE, AND A FOURSOME THAT CLOSES WITH KEN EJACULATING IN SUZAN'S MOUTH, FOLLOWED BY A SLOW-MOTION PAYLOAD TRANSFER TO ANNE'S MOUTH. AROUND THE 30-MINUTE MARK, SUZAN REVEALS TO ANNE THAT SHE'S REALLY A SEX FREAK WHO CAN TAKE ANYTHING THESE BUSH LEAGUERS CAN DISH OUT. TEN MINUTES LATER, KEN FIGURES THIS OUT ALL BY HIMSELF, AND THEN STRUGGLES TO THINK UP MORE DEGRADING SEX ACTS FOR SUZAN TO PERFORM (HE'S NOT VERY IMAGINATIVE). BY THE 50-MINUTE MARK, DOUG AND ANNE GET BORED AND GO TO THE MOVIES: "I'M TIRED," DOUG MUTTERS ON HIS WAY OUT, "I DON'T EVEN WANT TO SEE A PORNO."

KEN CALLS IN REINFORCEMENTS -- TOM (JON MARTIN) AND JACK (JESSE ADAMS) AND THEIR GIRLFRIENDS WILMA ("BONITA DYAN" A.K.A. BROOKE WEST) AND JANET (DOROTHY LE MAY) -- AND THEY PROVE TO BE JUST AS LAME AS DOUG AND KEN WHEN IT COMES TO PUTTING THE SCREWS TO SUZAN. AFTER A GROUP SEX SEQUENCE BETWEEN THE THREE COUPLES, WHICH DRAGS ON FOR ALMOST 15 MINUTES, SUZAN LEAVES. THAT'S IT. THERE'S NOTHING AT STAKE, NO DRAMA TO SPEAK OF, NO CHARACTERS TO CARE ABOUT -- JUST 71 MINUTES FROM AN UNDERCOOKED SCREENPLAY BY "ARMAND EASTON," WHO THE IMDB SEEMS TO THINK IS ACTUALLY ARMAND WESTON, BUT I DOUBT IT. SURELY HE WOULD'VE COME UP WITH SOMETHING BETTER THAN THIS (EASTON, MORE LIKELY FROST, IS CREDITED WITH WRITING BOTH VALENTINO FILMS). REPORTEDLY DRUNK ON THE SET AND THOROUGHLY UNINSPIRED WITHOUT HIS USUAL MUSES/ENABLERS HANGING AROUND (CRESSE, GENTRY, WES BISHOP, PHIL HOOVER), FROST CLEARLY DIDN'T GIVE A FIDDLER'S FUCK ABOUT THIS PROJECT, AND IT'S PAINFULLY OBVIOUS IN ALMOST EVERY FRAME.

SWEET DREAMS, SUZAN IS A SLIGHT IMPROVEMENT, IF ONLY BECAUSE IT FALLS BACK ON AN ANTHOLOGY FORMAT THAT DOESN'T BURDEN FROST WITH IRRITATING LITTLE DETAILS SUCH AS STORY STRUCTURE, CHARACTER DEVELOPMENT, AND OVERALL COHERENCY. FILMED MOSTLY MOS IN AND AROUND THE SAME HOUSE USED IN SWEET CAPTIVE, IT WAS NO DOUBT A MUCH CHEAPER FILM TO MAKE, ESPECIALLY WITHOUT MALE STARS LIKE HOLMES AND THOMAS AROUND TO COMMAND TOP DOLLAR. SUZAN MITCHELL (PETTY, AGAIN) CALLS HER SHRINK, DR. HENDERSON (HAMMY AARON STEWART), TO TELL HIM ABOUT THE FOUR EROTIC DREAMS SHE JUST WOKE UP FROM HAVING, ALTHOUGH ONLY THREE ARE ACTUALLY SHOWN. THE FIRST DREAM IS REMINISCENT OF FROST'S SLAVES IN CAGES FROM 10 YEARS EARLIER: SUZAN ATTENDS AN OUTDOOR PARTY AT HER COUSIN'S HOUSE AND FINDS EVERYONE THERE WEARING MASKS AND WATCHING A BEAUTIFUL WOMAN ('LAILANI' A.K.A. LAURIEN DOMINIQUE) DANCE NAKED ON A STAGE. WE LEARN FROM THE FEMALE NARRATOR -- SUPPOSEDLY SUZAN RELATING EACH DREAM TO DR. HENDERSON, ALTHOUGH IT SURE AS HELL ISN'T PETTY'S VOICE WE'RE HEARING -- THAT SUZAN'S UPTIGHT BROTHER EVAN (MICK SOUTH) AND HIS WIFE TERRY ("SHIRLEY WOODS" A.K.A. SHARON KANE)

ARE IN THE AUDIENCE, TOO. EVAN GETS UP ON STAGE AND HAS SEX WITH THE DANCER IN FRONT OF EVERYONE, MUCH TO SUZAN'S SHOCK-- UNTIL SHE FINDS HERSELF SO TURNED ON THAT SHE JOINS THEM. AFTER PERFORMING FELLATIO ON HER OWN BROTHER, SUZAN SEES HERSELF IN THE AUDIENCE, WATCHING THE SHOW. "ALL OF A SUDDEN I WANTED MYSELF!" SHE SAYS. "THE ULTIMATE DESIRE: MAKING LOVE TO YOURSELF! LICK YOUR OWN PUSSY, TASTE YOUR OWN JUICES, AND HAVE A DOUBLE CLIMAX!"

CUT TO DR. HENDERSON ON THE PHONE WITH SUZAN, SO TURNED ON BY HER DREAM THAT HE'S MASTURBATING AT HIS DESK, WHILE IN THE RECEPTION AREA HIS BEAUTIFUL SECRETARY (DOROTHY LE MAY) LISTENS IN ON THEIR SESSION AND DOES THE SAME. IN THE SECOND DREAM, SUZAN LOOKS OUT HER LIVING ROOM WINDOW AND SEES THREE WOMEN SHE KNOWS RELAXING AROUND HER SWIMMING POOL. THE FIRST WOMAN IS HER JUNIOR HIGH SCHOOL NURSE, JANIE (PENELOPE JONES). THE SECOND IS HER SISTER-IN-LAW TERRY, FROM THE PREVIOUS DREAM ("WOODS"/KANE). THE THIRD IS HER MOTHER'S HOUSEKEEPER, NAN (STAR WOULD). SUZAN GOES OUTSIDE AND HAS A LESBIAN SCENE WITH ALL THREE AT THE SAME TIME, PHOTOGRAPHED IN THE SAME UNFLATTERING WAY THAT FROST SHOT MOST OF THE MULTIPLE PARTICIPANT SEX SCENES IN HIS OEUVRE: THE FEMALE FORMS RESEMBLE BONELESS CHICKEN BREASTS PILED ON A PLATE, WAITING TO BE CLEANED.

CUT BACK TO DR. HENDERSON, STILL HOLDING THE PHONE TO HIS EAR AND TELLING SUZAN "YOUR DREAMS ARE PERFECTLY NORMAL" WHILE HE EATS OUT HIS SECRETARY. FOR THE THIRD DREAM, SUZAN IS A PIGTAILED 14-YEAR-OLD STUMBLING THROUGH A PIANO LESSON WITH HER HANDSOME TEACHER (BLAIR HARRIS) WHEN A SEXY GIRL SCOUT ("BONITA" A.K.A. BROOKE WEST) WITH COOKIES IN HAND RINGS THE DOORBELL. THE TEACHER PROCEEDS TO TEAR INTO HER COOKIE BOX A FEW FEET FROM SUZAN, WHO WATCHES WHILE STILL TRYING TO PLAY A PIANO THAT SOUNDS MORE LIKE A POORLY TUNED HARPSICHORD, THANKS TO THE DEEPLY CONTEMPTUOUS FROST AND HIS PROPENSITY FOR UNDERMINING ANY SCENE'S EROTICISM IN THE MOST OBNOXIOUS WAY

IMAGINABLE. THE HORRID CLANGING
STOPS WHEN SUZAN JOINS HER
TEACHER AND THE GIRL SCOUT ON
A COUCH FOR A LITTLE
AFTERNOON DELIGHT.

THERE IS NO FOURTH DREAM TO
GET SUZAN OFF THE PHONE SO HE
CAN ENJOY THE COMPANY OF HIS
SECRETARY. DR. HENDERSON TELLS
HER TO "JUST DO IT" -- IN
OTHER WORDS, PURSUE IN
REALITY THE KIND OF SEXUAL
FREEDOM SHE ONLY EXPERIENCES
IN HER DREAMS. SUZAN FOLLOWS
HIS ADVICE AND ENDS UP GETTING
BOUND WITH ROPES, STAKED TO
THE GROUND AND GANG-RAPED BY
THREE SWEATY, SKUZZY
GARDENERS (JON MARTIN, MICHAEL
MORRISON, JESSE ADAMS), A
CLASSIC FROST TABLEAU THAT IS
OCCASIONALLY INTERRUPTED BY
THE DOCTOR AND HIS SECRETARY
GOING AT IT IN A MORE
TRADITIONAL MANNER. AT THE
END, THE (S)EXHAUSTED DR.
HENDERSON BREATHLESSLY
EXPLAINS TO THE AUDIENCE THAT
HE ONLY BECAME A PSYCHIATRIST
BECAUSE OF THE SEX, AND THAT
HE REALLY ALWAYS WANTED TO BE
A MISSIONARY. FREEZE-FRAME
OVER A SHOT OF SUZAN IN HER
LIVING ROOM, LAUGHING. CUE
MUSIC. ROLL CREDITS.

SWEET CAPTIVE AND SWEET
DREAMS, SUZAN WERE THE LAST
MOVIES PRODUCED AND RELEASED
BY FREEWAY FILMS. ATAMIAN DIED
ON MARCH 16, 1980 AT AGE 49.
HIS NIECE, JULIA ST. VINCENT,
TOOK CONTROL OF THE COMPANY

AND MADE THE JOHN HOLMES DOCUMENTARY EXHAUSTED THE FOLLOWING YEAR, WHICH UTILIZED CLIPS FROM
THE FIVE JOHNNY WADD MOVIES BUT NOTHING FROM SWEET CAPTIVE OR THE COMPANY'S BEST MOVIE, HARD
SOAP, HARD SOAP. FROST SHOULD'VE GONE ON TO BIGGER AND BETTER THINGS, ESPECIALLY DURING THE
VIDEO BOOM OF THE MID '80S AND EARLY '90S, BUT HE NEVER RETURNED TO THE SAME LEVEL OF
CREATIVITY -- OR PRODUCTIVITY -- THAT HE HAD REACHED DURING THE 1960S AND '70S.

SPECIAL THANKS TO STEVE FENTON FOR THE R.J.P. ADMATS.

162

THE _{TRUE} ADVENTURES OF JODOROWSKY

REALLY REAL!

JA JA! HOLA!

ADAPTED FROM HIS BOOK: "THE SPIRITUAL JOURNEY OF ALEJANDRO JODOROWSKY"

THE STORY SO FAR: ALEJANDRO HAS MET THE ACTRESS REYNA D'ASSIA AT A PRESS CONFERENCE IN MEXICO AND, PRESENTLY, ARE SPEEDING IN A CAB TO A NEARBY HOTEL.

TAXI

THEY IMMEDIATELY PROCEED TO COUPLING, DURING WHICH REYNA AMAZES AND DRAINS ALEJANDRO WITH HER SEXUAL PROWESS, LEADING ALEJANDRO TO EXCLAIM:

NEVER HAVE I MET A WOMAN OF SUCH MASTERY!

SHE EXPLAINS: "I HAD A GREAT MASTER MYSELF. I WISH YOU TO KNOW I AM THE DAUGHTER OF GURDJIEFF, THE RUSSIAN PHILOSOPHER.

'HE SEDUCED MY MOTHER AND TAUGHT HER THESE VAGINAL TECHNIQUES.'

'GURDJIEFF SAID THAT THROUGH LAZINESS, MOST WOMEN HAVE A DEAD 'ATHANOR'. FROM CHILDHOOD ON, GIRLS ARE TAUGHT THAT ONLY THE PHALLUS IS POWERFUL, ACTIVE, AND VITAL.'

BAPIDA BAPIDA BAPIDA

R.I.P

'PEOPLE TAKE IT FOR GRANTED THAT THE VAGINA IS A PASSIVE ORGAN. GURDJIEFF TAUGHT MY MY MOTHER TO AWAKEN AND DEVELOP HER SOUL BY DEVELOP-ING HER VAGINA.'

"REYNA SPREAD HER LEGS BY WAY OF DEMONSTRATION, CONTRACTED THE LIPS OF HER VULVA, AND, WITH A SOFT AIRY SOUND, BEGAN TO PUMP AIR INTO HER VAGINA.

"SHE SET FOUR OLIVES IN A ROW AND, SCOOTING UP TO THEM WITH HER PERINEUM ON THE FLOOR, SHE SWALLOWED THEM ONE BY ONE."

AAIEE! THING COME!

"THEN SHE LAY ON HER BACK AND EXPELLED THEM WITH SUCH FORCE THAT THEY BOUNCED AGAINST THE CEILING."

PANG!

PAF

ROUP!

"SHE LIT SEVERAL CANDLES AND BLEW THEM OUT WITH A GUST FROM HER VAGINA."

FOOMF

"SHE DREW A THREAD UP INTO HER ORGAN AND THEN DEPOSITED IT, KNOTTED, IN MY HAND."

"'MY VAGINA HAS THE SAME AGILITY OF MOVEMENT AS MY TONGUE. WHAT'S MORE, I CAN WILL MY LUBRICANT SECRETIONS TO INCREASE OR DIMINISH,' SAID SHE."

SO IF YOU MEET ME HAVE SOME COURTESY

"SHE CONCENTRATED WITH EFFORT, THEN EXPELLED AN OVAL OF SMALL, TRANSPARENT JETS OF FLUID, WHICH COVERED HER THIGHS."

"FINALLY, KNEELING, SHE INHALED A LARGE QUANTITY OF AIR INTO HER VAGINA. WHEN SHE EXPELLED IT, A QUASIMUSICAL SOUND WAS HEARD, WHICH RECALLED THE SOUND OF WHALES."

BUH-MOO

"MY HAIR STOOD ON END AS I THOUGHT OF THE LEGEND OF THE SIRENS OF HOMER'S ODYSSEY, WHO ATTRACTED SAILORS WITH THEIR WAILS IN ORDER TO SHIPWRECK THEM."

BUH-MOOOOO

OH YEAH A WHALE LET'S HIT THAT!

CEASE FOOL! IT IS BUT A WOMAN WITH A WONDROUS VAGINA

"IN A VERY SOFT VOICE, SHE SAID, 'IN ANCIENT TIMES, WOMEN CHANTED LULLABIES WITH THEIR VULVAS TO MAKE THEIR BABIES SLEEP...'

OH BABY BABY IT'S A WILD WORLD

'... BUT AS THIS ART BECAME LOST AND FORGOTTEN, CHILDREN CEASED TO FEEL THEY WERE LOVED.'

IT'S NOT THE SAME!

'AN UNCONSCIOUS ANXIETY SETTLED IN THE SOULS OF HUMAN BEINGS. THAT WHIMPERING OF YOURS EXPRESSES THE PAIN OF HAVING A MOTHER WITH A MUTE VAGINA.'

ASOMBRO

'BUT WE ARE GOING TO RESOLVE THAT.'

TO BE CONTINUED...
(MAYBE)

CREATED BY CINEMA
The Enigma of Ajita Wilson

ARTICLE BY JOHNNY STANWYCK
GRINDHOUSESCHOOLHOUSE.COM
ART AND LETTERING   BY MR.
ROBIN
BOUGIE '15

AJITA
LAID
BARE

INHABITANTS OF THE 21ST CENTURY LIVE IN THE ABYSS OF A CELEBRITY-SATURATED CULTURE. WE KNOW EVERYTHING ABOUT OUR MODERN DAY DEMIGODS, FROM WHAT CAR THEY DRIVE TO HOW MANY FRECKLES THEY HAVE ON EACH BUTTOCK. WE'VE SQUEALED AT THEIR TRIUMPHS, WEPT AT THEIR MANY DIVORCES AND MEMORIZED THEIR O-FACES THROUGH THE MIRACLE OF "STOLEN" SEX TAPES. LONG GONE ARE THE PUFF PIECES OF THE CLASSIC MOVIE RAGS, REPLACED BY TABLOID TV TO DETAIL THE COMINGS, GOINGS, TOILET HABITS AND SEXUAL PECCADILLOES OF THE RICH AND FAMOUS. WITHOUT SALACIOUS PUBLICITY OOZING FROM EVERY ORIFICE, TODAY'S BIGGEST STARS WOULD SOON FADE FROM CONSCIOUSNESS AND INTO THE LAND OF ALSO RANS.

IN THIS WORLD OF CELEBRITY OBSESSION, IT IS INTERESTING TO KNOW THERE IS A STAR WHO CONTINUES TO ENTICE, TO FASCINATE, TO INTRIGUE, AND TO PIQUE OUR CURIOSITY LONG AFTER HER DEATH -- AND DOES SO WITHOUT TABLOIDS OR GOSSIP COLUMNISTS TO STOKE THE PUBLIC'S APPETITE FOR MORE. NEITHER THE PASSING OF TIME NOR THE MYSTERY SURROUNDING HER LIFE HAS DIMMED HER LIGHT OR MANAGED TO SNUFF OUT FILM FANS' LONGING TO KNOW MORE ABOUT THE STATUESQUE, ENIGMATIC BEAUTY KNOWN AS AJITA WILSON.

"A sculptural beauty. Tall and fascinating." -Tina Aumont

AJITA WILSON SEEMINGLY APPEARED OUT OF NOWHERE. IN 1976, STROLLING ACROSS THE SCREEN IN CESARE CANEVARI'S **THE NUDE PRINCESS**, SHE BECAME AN OVERNIGHT SEX STAR. LONG AND LANKY, WITH THE SCULPTURED FEATURES OF A STATUE COME TO LIFE, WILSON EFFORTLESSLY HOLDS THE VIEWER'S ATTENTION. ONE CANNOT LOOK AWAY WHEN SHE IS ON SCREEN. HER PIERCING EYES, DEWY LIPS AND LARGE HANDS -- MANICURED BEYOND ALL REASON -- HAD AN UNEARTHLY QUALITY THAT WAS IMPOSSIBLE TO RESIST. SHE WAS, SOMEHOW, MORE THAN HUMAN. HER FIGURE DISPLAYED A STRENGTH AND GRACE, LIKE A GAZELLE IN HUMAN FORM. AS DIRECTOR JESS FRANCO HAS SUGGESTED, SHE WAS MORE A PRESENCE THAN AN ACTRESS. WILSON'S MOST ARRESTING ONSCREEN MOMENTS ARE ONES OF STILLNESS, WHERE SHE COMMANDS ATTENTION SIMPLY WITH HER PRESENCE. SHE POSSESSES AN AURA OF DIGNITY, EVEN WHEN SURROUNDED BY THE MOST DIABOLICAL OF CINEMATIC PERVERSIONS.

"Ajita had that naivete, like she belonged to a world less perverted than our own."
- Jess Franco

WHERE DID THIS ENIGMATIC BEAUTY COME FROM? THAT QUESTION HAS HAUNTED THE HALLS OF ONLINE FANDOM SINCE THE DAWN OF THE INFORMATION SUPERHIGHWAY. IF THE PUBLICITY PIECES OF THE 1970s ARE TO BE BELIEVED, SHE WAS BORN IN NEW YORK CITY IN 1950 AND WAS ONE OF AMERICA'S

BIGGEST SEX STARS. TRUTH BE TOLD, AJITA WILSON WAS ALL BUT UNKNOWN IN THE USA UNTIL WELL INTO THE VIDEO AGE, SAVE FOR AN APPEARANCE IN A 1981 ISSUE OF JET MAGAZINE AS A "BEAUTY OF THE WEEK". EVEN THOSE WHO KNEW HER BEST WERE UNSURE OF HER ORIGINS. JESS FRANCO SUGGESTED IN THE 2003 DOCUMENTARY **SADOMANIAC**, THAT THE MYSTERIOUS STAR HAILED FROM ETHIOPIA. ONLINE SPECULATION SUGGESTS RIO DE JANEIRO, OR ELSEWHERE IN SOUTH AMERICA. ONE PARTICULARLY AMUSING TAKE ON THE STORY IS THAT AJITA WAS BORN IN FLINT, MICHIGAN AND WORKED AS A FIREFIGHTER BEFORE RUNNING AWAY FROM HOME. MOVING TO NEW YORK CITY, THE STORY GOES, SHE BEGAN PERFORMING AS A DRAG ENTERTAINER AND PROSTITUTE BEFORE UNDERGOING SURGERY TO BECOME A WOMAN.

THAT'S RIGHT, IT HAS LONG BEEN SUGGESTED THAT AJITA WILSON, TOUTED BY FILM POSTER TAG LINES AS "ALL WOMAN TO ALL MEN", WAS BORN MALE. IN KEEPING WITH HER ENIGMATIC ALLURE, THESE RUMORS DIDN'T BEGIN TO CIRCULATE UNTIL AFTER HER DEATH. IN LIFE SHE WAS PROCLAIMED THE ULTIMATE SEX GODDESS. HER IMAGE APPEARED IN COUNTLESS NUDIE MAGAZINES ACROSS EUROPE AND SHE ATTAINED A STATUS RIVALING OTHER SEX STARS SUCH AS LAURA GEMSER, PARTICULARLY IN ITALY AND GREECE.

FOLLOWING HER 1976 DEBUT IN CANEVARI'S AFOREMENTIONED POLITICAL SEX-FARCE, WILSON WORKED NEARLY NON-STOP FOR A DECADE. THERE WERE STOP-OFFS IN LURID SOFT-CORE FLICKS SUCH AS **BLACK DEEP THROAT** (1977) AND **THE PUSSYCAT SYNDROME** (1983) AS WELL AS MORE HIGH-GLOSS PRODUCTIONS LIKE THE GERMAN SEX COMEDY **THE JOY OF FLYING** (1977) OPPOSITE GIANNI GARKO. SHE WAS ALSO A FREQUENT VISITOR TO THE WORLD-OF-WOMEN-IN-PRISON FILMS WITH ROLES IN SUCH TITLES AS **HOTEL PARADISE** AND **ESCAPE FROM HELL** (BOTH 1980.) 1981 SAW HER PROMOTED FROM PRISONER-IN-PERIL TO SADISTIC WARDEN IN FRANCO'S INSANE **SADOMANIA**, A ROLE SO OVER THE TOP THAT WILSON'S PERFORMANCE ASSURED HER A PLACE AMONG CULT SIRENS EVER AFTER. HER ONSCREEN PERSONA WAS ONE OF STRENGTH, BEAUTY, AND UNINHIBITED SEXUALITY.

HER STAR ROSE AT A DIZZYING PACE. A PRODUCER ONLY NEEDED TO PLACE WILSON'S NAME AND IMAGE ON A POSTER TO ENSURE BOX OFFICE RETURNS. CERTAINLY PROLIFIC, WILSON SEEMED TO HAVE BEEN MORE INTERESTED IN THE WORK THAN THE ROLE AND APPEARED IN FEATURES THAT ARE THE VERY DEFINITION OF DIVERSIFIED. THERE WERE COMEDIC SEX ROMPS SUCH AS **MY NIGHTS WITH MESSALINA** (1982), ACTIONERS LIKE **LA BRAVATA** (1977) AND **CONTRABAND** (1980) ALONGSIDE EROTIC SOAP OPERAS **LOVE, LUST AND ECSTASY** (1981) AND **THE AMBITIOUS LOVER** (1982). SOME OF THE NUTTIEST FILMS IN WILSON'S CANON WERE TWO CO-STARRING ROLES OPPOSITE FELLOW GENDER-BENDER AND SINGER EVA ROBINS IN **EVA MAN** (1980) AND **EL REGRESO DE EVA MAN** (1982).

WHILE ACHIEVING FAME AMONG THE PATRONS OF STICKY-FLOORED THEATERS IN EUROPE, WILSON WAS PROBABLY MOST POPULAR IN GREECE. SHE FILMED A NUMBER OF SEXUAL POTBOILERS ON THE ISLAND, MOST NOTABLY AS A GUN-TOTING HOT MAMA IN THE CLEOPATRA JONES MOLD FOR **BLACK APHRODITE** (1977).

"STRENGTH, BEAUTY, AND UNINHIBITED SEXUALITY."

WHILE HER IMAGE MAY HAVE GRACED MAGAZINES AND FILM POSTERS APLENTY, INTERVIEWS WITH WILSON ARE SCARCE. FEW OF HER CONTEMPORARIES ARE LIVING AND ACTIVE IN THE INDUSTRY, BUT THOSE WHO HAVE BEEN INTERVIEWED SPEAK OF WILSON'S KINDNESS AND

PROFESSIONALISM ON SET. JESS FRANCO, LINA ROMAY AND TINA AUMONT ALL SPOKE FONDLY OF HER. WHILE AUMONT, INTERVIEWED FOR THE DVD RELEASE OF **THE NUDE PRINCESS** IN 2003, EXPRESSED SURPRISE AT THE SUGGESTION THAT WILSON WAS NOT BORN FEMALE, FRANCO AND ROMAY DID NOT. "SHE WAS DEFINITELY TRANSSEXUAL" SAID ROMAY OF WILSON IN A DOCUMENTARY FEATURETTE, **VOODOO JESS** (2006), TRACING THE MAKING OF FRANCO'S **MACUMBA SEXUAL** (1983).

AS THE LATE '70s/EARLY '80s SOFTCORE BOOM FADED AWAY AND THE AMERICAN HARDCORE FILMS FLOODED THE WORLDWIDE MARKET, WILSON'S STAR BEGAN TO DESCEND. WHILE A FEW HIGHER-PROFILE FILMS CAME HER WAY, WILSON INCREASINGLY FOUND HERSELF CAST IN BOTTOM-OF-THE-BARREL HARDCORE FEATURES. WHILE NOT A STRANGER TO PERFORMING SEX ON SCREEN, WHICH SHE HAD DONE OCCASIONALLY, HER HARDCORE APPEARANCES IN THE LATE 1980s WERE GENERALLY SORDID, GRIMY AFFAIRS WITH ZERO BUDGET OR MUCH TALENT ON EITHER SIDE OF THE LENS. IT WAS AROUND THIS TIME THAT WILSON'S PHYSICAL APPEARANCE BEGAN TO CHANGE.

HER EYES, ONCE ALLURING, BEGAN TO TAKE ON A SADNESS THAT SHE NEVER SEEMED TO SHAKE, NO MATTER WHICH CHARACTER SHE WAS PLAYING. HER BREASTS, ONCE PERT AND ROUND, BECAME HARDENED AND FLAT, WHILE HER FACE BEGAN TO TAKE ON A MORE MASCULINE APPEARANCE. WAS HER BODY BEGINNING TO REJECT THE MANY PROCEDURES IT MUST HAVE UNDERGONE TO TRANSFORM AJITA INTO A WOMAN? WE CAN NEVER KNOW FOR SURE, BUT THE LIVELY SPARK SHE ONCE DISPLAYED WAS ALL BUT GONE. FILM OFFERS DRIED UP AND SHE FOUND HERSELF GOING BACK TO HER ROOTS IN THE WORLD OF PROSTITUTION.

'ALLO 'ALLO

HER FINAL FILM TO BE RELEASED IN HER LIFETIME WAS 1986's SORDID **WHITE MOUTH, BLACK MOUTH** OPPOSITE THE "ANYTHING WITH A PULSE" SLUTTY PORN STRUMPET MARINA HEDMAN. IN THE FILM, WILSON SEEMS DETACHED, HARDENED AND UNCOMFORTABLE. SHE ENGAGES IN SEX ACTS SHE OBVIOUSLY DOES NOT ENJOY, AND ONE CAN'T HELP BUT NOTICE THAT THE LIGHT IN HER EYES THAT WAS DIMMING SEEMS TO HAVE GONE OUT COMPLETELY.

SOFTCORE CINEMA WAS DEAD AND IN MANY WAYS THAT WAS THE END OF AJITA WILSON. THE QUESTION LINGERED, THOUGH: WHO WAS SHE? DID SHE REALLY EXIST OUTSIDE OF THE CINEMA? WAS SHE MERELY A CREATION OF THE SCREEN, WITH THE REAL WOMAN UNDERNEATH FOREVER REMAINING AN ENIGMA? IT SEEMS AS IF THAT WAS THE CASE. ON MARCH 26th, 1987, THE WOMAN WE KNEW AS AJITA WILSON WAS TRAGICALLY KILLED IN A CAR ACCIDENT IN ROME.

IN A WORLD WHERE THE PUBLIC NEEDS TO BE CONSTANTLY FED SENSATIONALISM IN ORDER TO REMAIN ENGAGED, AJITA WILSON'S STORY SHOULD HAVE ENDED THERE. WITH NOTHING BUT RUMOR AND SPECULATION, AND WITH TRANSGENDER CELEBRITIES BEING FAR-FROM-SHOCKING IN THE ERA OF MAINSTREAM FAME FOR CAITLYN JENNER, WILSON COULD BE EXPECTED TO FADE FROM MEMORY ENTIRELY. HOWEVER, HER ENIGMATIC QUALITIES MAY WELL BE WHY SHE IS STILL REMEMBERED AND TALKED ABOUT AMONGST CULT FILM FANS TODAY. AJITA WILSON'S SCULPTURAL BODY, UNMISTAKABLE SCREEN PRESENCE AND PENETRATING EYES, SHROUDED HER IN THE MYSTERY OF WHO SHE WAS AND WHERE SHE CAME FROM, AND MAKES HER SEEM ALIVE STILL WHENEVER HER IMAGE APPEARS ONSCREEN.

WHEN YOU GET HOME FROM SCHOOL YOU KNOW WHAT WOULD RULE? READING CINEMA SEWER NAKED IT'S A WAY TO KEEP COOL!

READ CINEMA SEWER NUDE AT LEAST FROM THE WAIST DOWN WHETHER YOU'RE A GAL OR DUDE OF ILL REPUTE OR GREAT RENOWN

I'M NOT SAYING IT'S SMART OR A WAY TO IMPRESS BUT WHEN YOU'RE A SWEET LITTLE TART ROCK THAT STATE OF UNDRESS!

IS THERE ANYTHING IN HERE ABOUT RYAN GOSLING? HE'S HOT...

AN INTERVIEW WITH:
DAVID CHRISTOPHER

- -

"SOME PEOPLE FALL BETWEEN THE CRACKS OF CONTEMPORARY HISTORY, AND SOME PEOPLE FILL THEM...DAVID CHRISTOPHER FILLED MANY CRACKS WHICH MAY HAVE SLIPPED, AND THAT IS WHY HE'S NOW INDISPENSABLE."
-- NICK DOUGLAS

DAVID IN 1985 ...

HE STARTED WORKING IN ADULT FILMS IN 1974, DIRECTING IN THE EARLY 1980s, AND CONTINUES SLOGGING THROUGH THE PORN INDUSTRY TO THIS DAY. HE'S BETTER KNOWN NOW AS THE VAGINA-WORSHIPPING "PUSSYMAN" THANKS TO A LONG RUNNING VIDEO SERIES FROM THE NINETIES THAT LANDED HIM IN THE AVN HALL OF FAME, BUT DAVID CHRISTOPHER STARTED OUT BY GETTING HIS FIRST BREAK WITH THE BIGGEST DIRECTOR IN THE EARLY YEARS OF AMERICAN XXX FILMS — DEEP THROAT'S GERARD DAMIANO.

THE EARLIER PROJECTS WITH DAMIANO MAY HAVE BEEN MORE NOTEWORTHY AT THE TIME, BUT IT WAS WITH HIS ADVENT TO BECOMING A REGULAR PLAYER IN THE INFAMOUS LOW-BUDGET NEW YORK AVON FILMS THAT CHRISTOPHER SOLIDIFIED HIS LEGEND AMONGST VINTAGE SMUT FANS. THESE ARE THE MOVIES THAT STAND THE TEST OF TIME WHILE MUCH OF THE REST OF CHRISTOPHER'S LATER FILMOGRAPHY LANGUISHES, SOMEWHAT FORGOTTEN. DIRECTOR CARTER STEVENS DIRECTED 1982'S HOUSE OF SIN FOR AVON FILMS, WHO WOULD CHURN OUT THEIR LINE OF BIZARRE RAPE-PORN TO PLAY IN THEIR VARIOUS PORN THEATERS IN TIMES SQUARE.

"MISTRESS CANDICE WAS HIS LIVE-IN GIRLFRIEND", CARTER TOLD ME VIA EMAIL IN NOVEMBER 2013. "SHE WAS A REAL LIFE DOMME IN HOUSE OF SIN, AND LEAD HIM IN BY A DOG CHAIN AROUND HIS JUNK. SHE LAID HIM DOWN ON THE HARD WOOD FLOOR AND STARTED WHACKING THE HELL OUT OF HIS NUTS. HE HAD A RAGING HARD-ON, BUT EVERY OTHER GUY IN THE ROOM FLINCHED EACH TIME SHE HIT HIM. AS SOON AS I YELLED 'CUT!', HE STARTED TO COMPLAIN LIKE A BABY THAT HE DIDN'T HAVE A PILLOW UNDERNEATH HIS *HEAD*. THAT WAS WHEN I REALLY UNDERSTOOD BDSM. THE LITTLE BIT OF PRESSURE ON THE BACK OF HIS HEAD WAS NOT ALLOWING HIM TO FULLY ENJOY WHAT SHE WAS DOING TO HIS NUTS — WHICH TO HIM WAS NOT PAIN, BUT EROTIC STIMULATION."

WHILE HE WAS AN ABUSED SUBMISSIVE IN HOUSE OF SIN, HE ALSO SHOWED THAT HE COULD TURN THE TABLES ON HIS CO-STARS IN 1982'S THE TAMING OF REBECCA. RIGHT OUT OF THE GATE, CHRISTOPHER ABSOLUTELY OWNS A YOUNG SHARON MITCHELL WITH A COMMANDING PERFORMANCE AS A VILE DIRTY-TALKING FATHER WHO TAKES HIS DAUGHTER INTO THE BATHROOM AND SEXUALLY ABUSES HER. SHARON WAS OBVIOUSLY AN ADULT, BUT THE TWO OF THEM GOT SO INTO THE DERANGED ONSCREEN FANTASY, THAT NO ONE WHO SEES THE TWISTED COUPLING -- REGARDLESS IF THEY FIND IT TITILLATING OR RESOLUTELY AWFUL -- WILL FORGET IT.

"HE WAS *VERY* CREEPY AS SHARON MITCHELL'S INCESTUOUS FATHER", CLASSIC PORN HISTORIAN TONY COOPER REMARKED AS WE AGREED ON THE MEMORABLE TURN DAVID DID IN THE DERANGED PHIL PRINCE PRODUCTION. "HE NEARLY OUT-CREEPED GEORGE PAYNE. NO EASY FEAT."

... AND DAVID IN 2013

BORN BERNARD COHEN, ONE OF THE LESSER KNOWN HIGHLIGHTS OF HIS LONG CAREER IS THAT DAVID WAS ONE OF THE VERY FIRST TO CONCENTRATE ON RELEASING INTERRACIAL PORN IN AMERICA WITH VIDEOS LIKE BLACK SISTER, WHITE BROTHER (1984) CHOCOLATE BON BONS (1985), HOT FUDGE (1985), AND BLACK GIRLS IN HEAT (1985). THE SALT N' PEPPER PORKING SEEMS PRETTY BORING TODAY, BUT IT WAS OFF-THE-WALL STUFF AT THE TIME, AND IT WASN'T UNTIL HIS AWARD WINNING PUSSYMAN VIDEOS HIT VIDEO RENTAL SHELVES IN 1993 THAT HE BECAME A MAINSTREAM PORN INDUSTRY SUPERSTAR.

"IT WAS STRANGE TO WATCH HIM PERFORM", ADULTDVDTALK BOARD MEMBER DRAXXX SAID OF DAVID'S LATER OUTPUT IN THE LATE 1990S AND BEYOND. "HE WOULD START EATING A GIRL AND HIS EYES WOULD BUG OUT, AND HE'D GET A LOOK LIKE HE WAS A MADMAN. IT ALWAYS LOOKED ODD. HE USUALLY CAME ACROSS LIKE A STRANGE HORNY DUDE WHO HAD SOMEHOW TRICKED THESE GIRLS INTO LETTING HIM HAVE SEX WITH THEM."

ON AUGUST 22ND 2013, DAVID WAS KIND ENOUGH TO TAKE SOME TIME OUT OF HIS BUSY SCHEDULE BEING A BIG OL' PERVERT, AND SHARED SOME STORIES WITH ME ABOUT HIS LONG CAREER IN ADULT MOVIES. THAT LITTLE CONVERSATION FOLLOWS ON THE NEXT 5 PAGES. LET'S LISTEN IN, SHALL WE?

No matter what your fantasies might be...

PORTRAIT

CINEMA SEWER: WHO WAS DAVID CHRISTOPHER IN THE EARLY 1980S, AND WHO IS DAVID CHRISTOPHER IN THE EARLY 2010S?

DAVID CHRISTOPHER: I AM THE SAME PERSON THEN AS NOW AS FAR AS MY PHILOSOPHICAL BELIEFS, ATTITUDES, AND BELIEFS IN THE COMMUNICATION OF THE ART OF SEXUALITY. I HAVE ALWAYS BELIEVED IN THE SEXUAL POWER OF THE FEMALE, AND ALL MY WORK AND MOVIES HAVE TENDED TO SWAY IN THAT DIRECTION. I AM JUST MORE EXPERIENCED NOW IN THE ART OF MAKING AN EROTIC STATEMENT, AND IN GETTING THE MOST INTENSE AND BELIEVABLE PERFORMANCES FROM THE TALENT. I WAS ALSO IN THE KINK WORLD, AND MADE MANY MOVIES GEARED TO THAT CROWD. WHICH, BY THE WAY, GAVE ME A REP FOR A WHILE AS BEING ONE OF THOSE 'WEIRDOS' WHO DOESN'T LIKE HIS SEX 'VANILLA'.

CS: I GUESS THAT LEADS US TO THE NEXT AND RATHER OBVIOUS QUESTION, BUT HOW DID YOU GET YOUR START IN ADULT FILMS? WHAT LED YOU TO THAT MEANS OF MAKING A LIVING?

DC: I ALWAYS WAS ENGROSSED BY WATCHING THE FEMALE FORM AND WAS WORKING AS A PRODUCTION ASSISTANT ON CREWS THAT WERE COMMERCIALS, LOW-BUDGET MOVIES, AND PORNOS. COMPANIES AND PEOPLE WORKED ON ALL KINDS OF SETS. ACTORS IN NEW YORK WENT TO ACTING SCHOOL HOPING TO BREAK OUT. ANYHOW, I'M WORKING ON A DAMIANO FILM CALLED PORTRAIT (1974), STARRING THE SINGING COCKSUCKER FROM KANSAS CITY, JODY MAXWELL. YOU HAVE TO UNDERSTAND THAT DAMIANO IS A CULT HERO FROM DOING DEEP THROAT (1972) AND DEVIL IN MISS JONES (1973). PORTRAIT IS TWO PICTURES AFTER HE MADE DEVIL, AND FREE LOVE AND SEXUALITY ARE IN FULL BLOOM.

ANYWAY, ONE OF THE PERFORMERS LEAVES TOWN, LEAVING AN OPENING. I APPLY FOR THE JOB, AND AM VERY CONFIDENT THAT I WILL HAVE NO TROUBLE. WELL, THIS IS A GOOD ONE: FIRST OF ALL, JODY IS FAMOUS FOR SINGING 'HOW MUCH IS THAT DOGGY IN THE WINDOW' WHILE BLOWING 2 GUYS SIMULTANEOUSLY, AND MY FIRST SCENE IS THAT I COME IN TO THE BATHROOM WHERE SHE IS SITTING ON A TOILET READY TO GIVE ME HEAD. WELL, I WAS PETRIFIED. I WAS USED TO HIPPIE OR COLLEGE GIRLS, NOT SOME SEXPOT SITTING ON A TOILET BOWL. I CAME IN 2 SECONDS WITH A HALF A HARD ON. I THOUGHT MY CAREER WAS OVER, BUT THE DIRECTOR CAME TO ME AND SAID 'I LIKE YOU KID. WE'LL BREAK FOR LUNCH AND I'LL PUT YOU ON A BED FOR THE SCENE'. WELL, THE REST IS HISTORY. NOW-A-DAYS I WOULD INSIST ON THE GIRL BEING ON THE TOILET WHILE I WALKED INTO THE BATHROOM. I WOULD HAVE MANY MORE THINGS TO PERFORM THAN I DID BACK THEN.

CS: I LOVE JODY! SHE AND I CHAT OFTEN, ACTUALLY. PORTRAIT WAS HER FIRST MOVIE TOO, AND SHE REMEMBERS YOU FONDLY. SHE TOLD ME SHE THOUGHT YOU WERE 'VERY SWEET' AND 'VERY HORNY'. SHE ALSO TOLD ME A FUNNY STORY ABOUT HOW WHEN SHE AND DAMIANO WERE IN CHICAGO TO PROMOTE THE MOVIE IN 1974, A YOUNG ROGER EBERT CAME UP TO THEIR SUITE FOR AN INTERVIEW, AND WAS QUITE SWEET ON HER. TELLING JODY SHE REMINDED HIM OF A 'YOUNG LANA TURNER', AND WROTE IN THE PAPER THAT SHE WAS A 'A DARK-HAIRED, DARK-EYED, PNEUMATIC BEAUTY'. HE ALSO PUBLISHED THAT HER FATHER WAS A PROSECUTOR, AND THEN AFTER THAT CAME OUT IN THE CHICAGO TRIBUNE, JODY'S DAD HAD HUNDREDS OF CALLS FROM THE PRESS, AND HIS OFFICE PHONE LINE WAS TIED UP FOR NEARLY A WEEK!

THE STORY OF PRUNELLA (HERE UNDER ITS AKA OF "THE PUNISHMENT OF PRUNELLA) FEATURES CHRISTOPHER AS VICTOR 'THE KNIFE' DELGADO!

THIS IS UNRELATED TO HER, BUT I REALLY AM FASCINATED BY THE AVON MOVIES. PERHAPS MY FAVE ADULT FILM OF ALL TIME IS THE TAMING OF REBECCA FROM 1982. I JUST LOVE HOW SLEAZY AND LOW-BUDGET IT FEELS, AND ALSO SO MUCH LIKE A WEIRD CULT FILM BUT WITH HARDCORE SEX ADDED. YOU REALLY SET THE STAGE FOR WHAT IS TO COME IN THAT MOVIE WITH YOUR SCENE WITH SHARON MITCHELL. I'D LOVE TO HEAR ANY MEMORIES YOU HAVE ABOUT IT.

DC: I HAVE TREMENDOUS MEMORIES OF THOSE MOVIES. I WROTE AND CO-WROTE A NUMBER OF THOSE FILMS. MY GIRLFRIEND WAS MISTRESS CANDICE, A BLONDE BOMBSHELL THAT I TRIED TO PUSH INTO BEING A STUNNING DOMINATRIX THAT WOULD CROSS OVER. UNHEARD OF IN THOSE DAYS. THE SCENE WITH MITCH WAS HOT. WE HADN'T DONE A SCENE TOGETHER, AND I JUST LOVE THE END WHERE AFTER I COME, SHE PEES ALL OVER HER DAD'S COCK. (AVON'S FILMS) WERE LIKE AN ENSEMBLE. THEY WERE WILD, KINKY, SORT OF B-MOVIES WITH ALL KINDS OF FETISH ACTION, VIOLENCE AND HOT SEX. THEY HAD A THEATRE CALLED THE AVON WHICH SHOWED THE MOVIES, AND HAD THE STARS PERFORM THEIR SCENES LIVE ON STAGE. ALWAYS STANDING ROOM ONLY. THAT'S ENOUGH SAID. NO PORN THEATRES IN THOSE DAYS WERE STANDING ROOM ONLY, EXCEPT FOR SCREENINGS OF THE CLASSICS LIKE DEEP THROAT, AND BEHIND THE GREEN DOOR. THE IDEA WAS TO MAKE OUTLANDISH, WILD SEX MOVIES. GEORGE PAYNE WAS GREAT AS THE WILD AND OUT OF CONTROL

IN SWEET THROAT, DAVID PLAYS A MOVER WHO (ALONG WITH ROGER CAINE) FUCKS CLEA CARSON.

SEX MANIAC IN A NUMBER OF THE MOVIES. THE STUFF WAS REAL. PEOPLE CARED, SO THEY STAND OUT IN PORN HISTORY!

CS: PHIL PRINCE'S SON TELLS ME THAT PHIL WASN'T REALLY TURNED ON BY ANY OF THE "PERVERSION" OR FORCED SEX FANTASIES INVOLVED IN THE MOVIES HE MADE FOR AVON, AND THAT IT WAS ALL JUST A BIG JOKE TO HIM. IS THAT WHAT YOU REMEMBER ABOUT HIM? DID YOU APPROACH IT THAT WAY AS WELL?

DC: HE JUST WANTED TO MAKE MONEY FOR THE MOST PART. ONCE IN A WHILE HE WOULD GET INTO THE WILD ACTION. HE KNEW HE HAD A WINNER IN THIS FORMULA, AND WENT WITH IT. HE USED MISTRESS CANDICE IN A NUMBER OF FILMS TO HUMILIATE AND USE HER SLAVES. HE WOULD HAVE HER PEE ON THE SLAVES AND THEN AT TIMES SHOW THEM THEIR TRUE PLACE! I NEVER

COMING WED. MARCH 31
★ DOMINATRIX WITHOUT MERCY ★

ONE OF THE EARLIER AVON PRODUCTIONS WAS THIS JOE DAVIAN FILM WHICH HAS A SATANISM/VOODOO THEME. DAVID PLAYS A WEIRDO CULT MEMBER.

THOUGHT THEY WERE A JOKE. SOME WERE SOMETIMES OVER THE TOP, BUT THEY WERE AN ALTERNATIVE SORT OF ADULT MOVIE. THE FACT THAT YOU COULD THINK THEY WERE A JOKE IS GULLIBLE ON YOUR PART. REMEMBER HOW INTENSE THE MOVIES WERE, IF YOU HAVE SEEN THEM. RELATIVES SAY THINGS LATER ON. REMEMBER THAT!

CS: HAHA! NO NO, I DON'T MEAN THAT I THINK THE AVON FILMS WERE A JOKE -- LIKE I SAY, TAMING OF REBECCA IS MY FAVE ADULT FILM OF ALL TIME. I'M JUST TELLING YOU WHAT PHIL PRINCE TOLD HIS SON, AND IF YOU THINK ABOUT IT, IT REALLY MAKES SENSE. OF COURSE HE'S GONNA DOWNPLAY THESE INTENSE MOVIES TO HIS FAMILY, AND ACT LIKE IT WASN'T A BIG THING. I JUST WISH I COULD TALK TO PHIL ABOUT IT, AND HEAR HIS STORY DIRECTLY, BUT HE WON'T ADDRESS IT. HE'S PUT THIS PORN MOVIE STUFF BEHIND HIM, AND WON'T TALK ABOUT IT, AND IT'S A REAL SHAME BECAUSE WHEN THESE GUYS DIE, THEY TAKE THEIR STORIES WITH THEM. ANYWAY, I'M GOING OFF ON A TANGENT. SO YOU FUCKED IN LOTS OF LOOPS AND SOME THEATRICAL FILMS, AND YOU ALSO GOT INTO DIRECTING FILMS BACK IN THE EARLY 1980S, IS THAT CORRECT?

DC: YES. THE FIRST MOVIE I DIRECTED WAS CALLED SECLUDED PASSION (1983). IT WAS ABOUT A MALE STRIPPER WHO IS TURNED ON BY HIS SISTER TO PERFORM IN A STRIP CLUB WHERE WOMEN WATCHED. IT WAS THE TOTAL REVERSAL OF THE NORMAL FEMALE DANCER PERFORMING FOR MALES FANTASY. IT STARRED KELLY NICHOLS AS THE CLUB OWNER, AND SHE WAS THE NUMBER ONE STAR OF THE DAY. ALSO THERE WAS MISTRESS CANDICE, SUSAN NERO, SANDRA KING, HELEN MADIGAN, MYSELF, GEORGE PAYNE, AND A FEW OTHER STARS THAT I CAN'T REMEMBER. AT THE TIME RON JEREMY AND MYSELF WERE THE ONLY ACTORS WHO WERE ALLOWED TO DIRECT, ESPECIALLY IN NEW YORK. THE EARLY '80S WHEN VIDEO TAPE TOOK OVER IS WHEN ACTORS WERE FINALLY ALLOWED TO DIRECT, AND A FLOOD OF THE TOP ACTORS EVENTUALLY ALL BECAME DIRECTORS. NOW ACTORS OF BOTH SEXES (ESPECIALLY MEN) BECOME BOTH ACTORS AND DIRECTORS SIMULTANEOUSLY. PEOPLE COULD NOT BELIEVE IT WHEN I STARTED DIRECTING, BECAUSE I WAS AN ACTOR WHO WAS MOSTLY KNOWN FOR SHOOTING LOOPS AND NOT HAVING LARGE DIALOGUE ROLES IN THE SO CALLED 'REAL' MOVIES.

CS: YEAH, SHOOTING ON VIDEO CHANGED EVERYTHING IN A LOT OF WAYS, DIDN'T IT? GETTING BACK TO SECLUDED PASSION, I HAVE TO SAY THAT WHAT YOU'RE DESCRIBING HERE IS VERY DIFFERENT FOR STRAIGHT PORN IN THE 1980S, A FILM ABOUT MALE EXOTIC DANCERS! TURNED OUT BY HIS SISTER? WOW. THAT WAS REALLY UNTAPPED TERRITORY FOR FILMS BACK THEN. I'M SAD TO SAY I'VE NEVER SEEN IT, DAVID.

DC: I HAVE ALWAYS BEEN INTO THE POWER OF THE PUSSY, AND THE

IN 1980'S TRAMP, DAVID AND RON HUDD PLAYED A COUPLE OF SAILORS WHO DOUBLE TEAM GLORIA LEONARD AND SAMANTHA FOX! A **WILD** SCENE!

172

AGGRESSIVE WILD WOMEN WHO NEED TO GET OFF. THAT IS ONE REASON THAT MY STUFF IS DIFFERENT FROM MOSTLY EVERY OTHER MALE DIRECTOR WHO HAS EVER MADE ADULT FILMS. ALL THROUGH THE YEARS, AS PRODUCER AND CREATOR, MY MOVIES HAVE CENTERED ON SUPREME FEMALE SEXUAL GODDESSES. WOMEN WITH VOLUPTUOUS FIGURES AND BIG PUSSY LIPS, WHEN POSSIBLE. I'VE DIRECTED OVER 500 MOVIES RIGHT TO THE PRESENT DAY, WHERE I SPECIALIZE IN FEMDOM, FACE-SITTING, PUSSY AND ASS WORSHIP, AND OF COURSE GIANT TIT WORSHIP. BACK IN THE DAYS OF FILM, KINKY SCENES AND REGULAR SEX SCENES WERE MIXED TOGETHER IN THE SAME MOVIE, AND IT WAS NO BIG DEAL. TODAY, FETISHES ARE FULLY SPECIALIZED. I BASICALLY STARTED THE IDEA OF WOMEN SMOTHERING AND SITTING ON MEN'S FACES, AND GETTING OFF BY CUMMING IN THEIR MOUTH!

CS: AS LONG AS I'VE GOT A FACE, SHE'LL HAVE A PLACE TO SIT, RIGHT? SPEAKING OF DIRECTORS, I'D LOVE TO HEAR SOME OF YOUR THOUGHTS ABOUT WORKING WITH SOME OF THE OTHER DIRECTORS FROM BACK IN THE DAY WHOSE FILMS YOU WERE IN. SPECIFICALLY CHUCK VINCENT, JOHN CHRISTOPHER, AND JOE DAVIAN.

DC: I LIKED JOHN CHRISTOPHER, HE WAS CHUCK'S PROTÉGÉ. HIS PICTURES WERE FLUFF AND CUTE WITH NO INTENSITY. CHUCK VINCENT CARED ABOUT HIS MOVIES AND WAS A SERIOUS DIRECTOR OF REALLY EROTIC FILM. JOE DAVIAN WANTED TO MAKE SICK AND DEVILISH SORTS OF MOVIES. HE WAS VERY CREEPY. I DID WRITE A FEW MOVIES FOR HIM, AS I HAVE ALWAYS BEEN INTO KINKY, WILD STUFF. NOT YOUR NORMAL STUFF. I SHOT LOTS OF LOOPS. I DID NOT GO TO ACTING SCHOOL. I WANTED TO BE A DIRECTOR AND PROMOTE THE SEXUAL POWER OF THE FEMALE AND THE PUSSY!! I ALSO HAD VERY LONG HAIR IN THOSE DAYS, AND THEY WANTED YOU TO CUT IT OFF FOR BIG FEATURES, SO I PERFORMED IN TONS OF LOOPS AND WAS GIVEN HIPPIE ROLES OR ROLES THAT CAME ALONG ONCE IN A WHILE WHERE A CHARACTER COULD HAVE LONG HAIR.

CS: DO YOU HAVE ANY MEMORIES OF MOB VIOLENCE TIED TO THE ADULT INDUSTRY IN NEW YORK IN THE 1970S?

DC: I NEVER SAW ANY ACTUAL VIOLENCE. THERE WERE ALWAYS RUMOURS AND DIFFERENT STORIES OF GUYS BEING PUSHED AROUND, BUT THE FILMMAKING WAS BASICALLY ALL PROFESSIONAL. SURE, A COUPLE OF LOOP MAKERS DISAPPEARED AND WERE NEVER SEEN AGAIN, BUT OF COURSE IT WAS ALL JUST RUMOURS THAT IF YOU PRODUCED LOOPS OR MOVIES THAT YOU BETTER GIVE YOUR SHARE TO THE MOB. I WAS AN ACTOR BACK THEN, AND THE ACTORS WERE NEVER INVOLVED WITH THE MOB. THEY WERE JUST TRYING TO CROSS OVER AND BECOME GREAT ACTORS, AND BE KNOWN TO THE GENERAL PUBLIC. REMEMBER, NAMES WERE ON MOVIE MARQUEES IN LARGER THAN LIFE LETTERS, AND THEY GAVE THE ILLUSION THAT YOU WERE SOME KIND OF MOVIE STAR! I STILL REMEMBER WALKING INTO ONE OF THOSE ADULT THEATRES AND BEING PLEASED THAT MY COCK LOOKED GIANT. THAT IT WAS ON BIG SCREENS IN NYC AND THROUGHOUT THE COUNTRY TURNED MY EXHIBITIONISTIC TENDENCIES ON TO NO END.

CS: I BET! I REMEMBER ANNIE SPRINKLE TALKING ABOUT HOW MUCH SHE LOVED SEEING HER NAME ON MARQUEES IN TIMES SQUARE, TOO. SHE SAID IN NO UNCERTAIN TERMS THAT IT MADE HER PUSSY ALL WET. HEY, SPEAKING OF WET PUSSY, 1993 IS WHEN YOU STARTED THE PUSSYMAN SERIES. HOW MUCH DID THAT CHANGE YOUR CAREER GOING FORWARD?

DC: THE PUSSYMAN SERIES WAS AN EVOLVEMENT OF MY PUSSY POWER SERIES FROM BIG TOP, AND REALLY AN EVOLVEMENT OF MY FASCINATION WITH PUSSY, AND THE WORSHIP OF FEMALE CULTS AND RELIGIONS. IT JUMP STARTED MY CAREER INTO THE UPPER ECHELON OF THE ADULT FILM BUSINESS. RIGHT BEFORE THAT I WAS THE CREATIVE DIRECTOR FOR SEVEN YEARS AT COAST TO COAST, WHICH WAS, AT THE TIME, ONE OF THE TOP THREE COMPANIES IN THE BUSINESS.

CS: I HAVEN'T SEEN AS MUCH OF THE PUSSYMAN STUFF AS I SHOULD HAVE. I'M OBSESSIVE ABOUT THE 1970S AND 1980S ADULT MOVIES MORE THAN ANYTHING.

DC: AS FAR AS I AM CONCERNED, THE GOLDEN AGE OF PORN MOVIES WAS NOT THE 1970S OR EVEN THE 1980S, BUT THE 1990S -- SO MAYBE YOU SHOULD TAKE A LOOK AT A FEW FROM THAT ERA. THE 1990S BROUGHT PORN TO A NEW LEVEL WITH THE CAMERA WORK,

DAVID PLAYED A BURGLAR WHO GETS HIS WANG SUCKED BY BLACK PORNSTAR MOUSIENDI IN VISIONS.

ANGLE SHOOTING, TALKING TO THE CAMERA AND JUST PLAIN GREAT STUFF!

CS: INTERESTING, BECAUSE THE 1990S IS MY PICK FOR WEAKEST DECADE FOR QUALITY ADULT FILMS SINCE, WELL...SINCE THE 1950S. BUT I'LL CERTAINLY BE CHECKING OUT MORE OF YOUR STUFF AT THE VERY LEAST. JOHN LESLIE DIRECTED SOME STUFF THAT I LIKE IN THE 1990S, TOO.

DC: DON'T GET ME WRONG. THERE WERE SOME GREAT SCRIPTS AND TALENTED PERFORMERS IN THE OLD DAYS, BUT THE LACK OF QUALITY EQUIPMENT AND NOT REALLY UNDERSTANDING THE BEST WAY TO SHOW SEX ON CAMERA TO THE AUDIENCE WAS A PROBLEM. THE SEXUAL

Let's get sex out of the streets and onto the playing fields where it belongs!

GERARD DAMIANO presents
THE OLDEST SPORT OF ALL

JOINT VENTURE

WORLD PREMIERE

2ND SMASH WEEK

Starring VANESSA SHARON BOBBY MICHAEL
DEL RIO MITCHELL ASTYR DAYTORE

FOR LADIES AND GENTLEMEN OVER 21 YEARS

Guest Starring GERARD DAMIANO

X

Cine Lido 48th St.&B'way 757-4228
Door Open 9:45

JOINT VENTURE WAS A NOD TO THE 'SEX OLYMPICS' WHICH WERE HELD ANNUALLY BACK IN THE 1970S IN NEW JERSEY. THE "WIDE WORLD OF SPURTS", INDEED.

REVOLUTION HAD JUST STARTED, AND AS LONG AS PEOPLE WERE HAVING SEX ON CAMERA, THAT WAS GOOD ENOUGH. BUT I REMEMBER NOT BEING ABLE TO JERK OFF TO MANY OF THE SO-CALLED 'MASTERPIECES'. THE CAMERA WORK DURING THE SEX WAS PLAINLY AWFUL, AND PEOPLE WEREN'T SEX PERFORMERS SOLELY FOR THE MONEY LIKE THEY ARE TODAY. THEY DID IT 'CAUSE THEY WANTED TO HAVE SEX, AND YOU COULD SIT AROUND ALL DAY ON A SET AND HAVE SEX THREE TIMES WHILE WAITING FOR YOUR SCENE. THEN, FINALLY, IF YOUR SCENE CAME AND YOU HAD BEEN 'BAD', YOU COULD REALLY CAUSE THE DIRECTOR SOME PROBLEMS AND A BIG HEADACHE.

CS: NOTHING LIKE SELLING THE WINE BEFORE ITS TIME! SEE, I THINK THE PERFORMERS BEING LEGITIMATELY INTO THE SEX WAS ABSOLUTELY A POSITIVE, AND CERTAINLY NOT A NEGATIVE. I GUESS I'M JUST MORE INTO THE CINEMATIC ASPECT OF THE WHOLE THING, AND WHEN YOU TAKE THAT AWAY, I THINK YOU'RE TAKING AWAY A LOT. ANYWAY, THANKS A BUNCH, DAVID! I APPRECIATE YOU PUTTING ASIDE YOUR TIME FOR AN INTERVIEW.

PERHAPS HE DOESN'T THINK TOO MUCH OF THEM, BUT I SURE DO. HERE IS A SELECTED FILMOGRAPHY OF THE BEST AND MOST WATCHABLE VINTAGE MOVIES THAT DAVID APPEARED IN:

Portrait (1974)
Sharon (1975)
Night of Submission (1976)
She's No Angel (1976)
Untamed Vixens (1976)
French Teen (1977)
Heat Wave (1977)
High School Bunnies (1977)
Visions (1977)
Final Test (1978)
Here Comes the Bride (1978)
Joint Venture (1978)
Take Off (1978)
Blonde Ambition (1980)
Den of Dominance (1980)
Savage Sadists (1980)
Seduction of Cindy (1980)
Swedish Sorority Girls (1980)
Sweet Throat (1980)
Tramp (1980)

Twilite Pink (1981)
Angel in Distress (1982)
House of Sin (1982)
The Story of Prunella (1982)
The Taming of Rebecca (1982)
Kneel Before Me (1983)
Oriental Techniques in Pain and Pleasure (1983)
Secluded Passion (1983)
Smoker (1984)
Daughters of Discipline (1984)
Pain Mania (1984)
Bordello (1985)
Vasoline Alley (1985)
Down and Dirty Scooter Trash (1985)
Romancing the Bone (1985)
A Passage Thru Pamela (1985)
69th Street Vice (1986)
The Oddest Couple (1986)

MAN, I STILL CAN'T BELIEVE HE SAID THE 1990S WERE THE BEST DECADE FOR QUALITY PORN. IF HE'D TOLD ME HE BLOWS HIS DOG, I WOULD HAVE BEEN LESS SHOCKED. WHAT DO YOU GUYS N' GALS THINK OF THE NINETIES xxx?

BOUGIE '13

SPECIAL THANKS TO MY PAL STEVE FENTON FOR THE USE OF THE ADMATS. MOST OF THE ONES USED TO ILLUSTRATE THIS INTERVIEW ARE FROM HIS COLLECTION.

HOT DOG!

THAT'S SOME GOOD ADMAT.

STEVE IS THE ONLY ONE I KNOW WHO HAS A BIGGER COLLECTION OF THESE THAN I DO!

WHICH IS WHY HE MUST BE DESTROYED

END

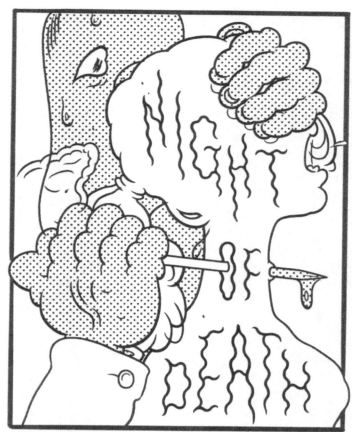

BETWEEN 1897 AND 1962 THE GRAND GUIGNOL THEATER IN THE PIGALLE AREA OF PARIS, FRANCE OFFERED GORY LIVE (ALTHOUGH FAKED) EVISCERATION AND DISMEMBERMENT TO ITS SPECTATORS, AND YET HORROR MOVIES DID NOT GO ON TO BE ONE OF THE COUNTRY'S SPECIALTIES. DESPISED BY THE CRITICS AND THE INDUSTRY ITSELF, THE GENRE HAS ALWAYS BEEN CONSIDERED AS VULGAR AND DUMB IN FRANCE, AND ONLY A FEW MOVIES (SUCH AS FRANJU'S EYES WITHOUT A FACE FROM 1960 OR THE 1965 TV SERIES BELPHEGOR) EVER MANAGED TO EMERGE FROM THE SEWER INTO WHICH THEY WERE FLUSHED.

THOSE WHO DARED TO VENTURE INTO THE DARK SIDE OF HORROR WERE VIVIDLY REJECTED AND BECAME OUTCASTS. DIRECTORS LIKE JEAN ROLLIN OBTAINED (AND STILL BENEFITS FROM) A MUCH MORE FAVORABLE RECEPTION OUTSIDE FRANCE, BUT AT LEAST HAS A NAME KNOWN AMONGST THE FRENCH UNDERGROUND INTELLIGENTSIA. DIRECTOR RAPHAEL DELPARD, ON THE OTHER HAND, REMAINS ONE OF THE UNSUNG HEROES OF FRENCH HORROR MOVIES. HIS FILM, NIGHT OF DEATH (1980) IS USUALLY LEFT OUT WHEN FRENCH GORE CINEMA HISTORY IS RECOUNTED, AND IT WOULD SEEM AS THOUGH THE PRODUCTION HAS DISAPPEARED FROM THE COLLECTIVE MEMORY OF MOVIE-GOERS. HOW COULD THAT HAVE HAPPENED?

THE PLOT FOLLOWS AN UNEMPLOYED WOMAN NAMED MARTINE WHO LEAVES HER BOYFRIEND SERGE TO TAKE UP A JOB AS A LIVE-IN NURSE IN AN OLD PEOPLE'S HOME. ARRIVING ONE DAY EARLY, SHE MAKES THE ACQUAINTANCE OF NICOLE, THE CURRENT NURSE, WHO SEEMS PRETTY SURPRISED TO SEE HER. ON THE JOB FOR THE LAST TWO MONTHS, NICOLE IS MEAN AND TOUGH WITH THE PENSIONERS AND SEEMS UNCARING. THAT SAME EVENING, NICOLE IS ABDUCTED BY THE ELDERLY RESIDENTS, STRIPPED, HAS HER THROAT SLIT, AND IS ULTIMATELY EVISCERATED AND PARTIALLY EATEN. THE FOLLOWING MORNING, WHEN MARTINE ENQUIRES ABOUT HER CO-WORKER'S ABSENCE, SHE IS TOLD THAT NICOLE HAS QUIT HER JOB AND LEFT. MORE APPRECIATED BY THE RESIDENTS, MARTINE WORKS CONTENTEDLY, BUT ALL THE SAME A FEW THINGS BOTHER HER -- SUCH AS THE NEWSPAPERS REPORTING A SERIAL KILLER ON THE LOOSE, THE WEIRD AND CREEPY HANDYMAN FLAVIEN WHO STALKS HER, AND THAT STRANGE MIXTURE SHE HAS TO DRINK EVERY DAY MAKING HER PUT ON WEIGHT...

ATYPICAL OF THE FRENCH CULTURAL SCENE, NIGHT OF DEATH IS ALSO A KIND OF AN ANOMALY IN CO-PRODUCER CLAUDE PIERSON'S FILMOGRAPHY. AT THE TIME PIERSON WAS WELL KNOWN FOR HIS ABOVE AVERAGE SEX MOVIES, AND THE CONCEPTION OF NIGHT OF DEATH WAS THE FRUIT OF A HAPPY ACCIDENT AS DIRECTOR RAPHAEL DELPARD EXPLAINED TO ME WHEN I MET HIM IN 2012.

"CLAUDE PIERSON WAS APPROACHED BY AN ITALIAN PRODUCER WHO WAS LOOKING FOR A PARTNERSHIP WITH A VIEW TO MAKING A MOVIE STARRING DALILA DI LAZZARO (FLESH FOR FRANKENSTEIN BY PAUL MORRISSEY) AND HE WAS INVITED TO ITALY TO SCOUT FOR LOCATIONS. CLAUDE PROPOSED THAT I JOIN THEM AND SO THERE WE WERE, THE THREE OF US, CLAUDE, MYSELF AND THAT OBESE PRODUCER, CROSSING ITALY IN A SMALL CAR."

"ON THE WAY BACK (BY PLANE), CLAUDE ASKED ME IF I KNEW ANYTHING ABOUT FANTASY MOVIES. IT WAS NOT HIS CUP OF TEA. HE WAS FROM THE OLD SCHOOL AND PREFERRED WRITERS LIKE SADE, DIDEROT AND VOLTAIRE. HE DIDN'T HAVE A PARTICULAR LOVE FOR THRILLERS. ANYWAY, HE ASKED ME IF I WAS CAPABLE TO WRITE A SCRIPT OF THAT TYPE. OF COURSE, I IMMEDIATELY SAID YES, AND IN THE PLANE, I HAD A FLASH OF THE OLD MOVIE WITH LOUIS JOUVET IN A RETIREMENT HOUSE, LA FIN DU JOUR AKA THE END OF THE DAY, AND EVERYTHING STARTED TO FALL INTO PLACE. IN THE END, THE MOVIE WITH DALILA WAS NEVER MADE, BUT I TOLD TO CLAUDE THAT IF HE WAS READY TO PUT MONEY INTO SUCH A PROJECT, I WAS WRITING A HORROR MOVIE THAT I'D PRODUCE WITH HIM!"

IN ALL HONESTY, THE SCREENPLAY OF NIGHT OF DEATH IS NOT FINELY CHISELED. APART FROM AN

ENJOYABLE TWIST, THE STORY UNFOLDS WITHOUT SURPRISES AND NEVER TRIES TO USE A WHODUNIT PROTOTYPE. DESPITE THE FACT THAT ITS FRAMEWORK IS CLEARLY UNVEILED FROM THE BEGINNING, THE MOVIE IS A PLEASURE TO WATCH BECAUSE OF THE MARTINE CHARACTER. SHE IS SO FAR BEHIND US IN HER WAY TO UNDERSTANDING WHAT THE AUDIENCE HAS FIGURED OUT IN THE FIRST MINUTES THAT EVERY STEP SHE MAKES ON THE PATH TO TRUTH BECOMES MORE AND MORE SURREALISTIC. WHEN SHE FINALLY REALIZES SOMETHING CRIMINALLY PECULIAR IS GOING ON, IT'S TOO LATE, SHE'S BEEN IN THE PLACE FOR EXACTLY TWO MONTHS AND IT'S DINNER TIME AGAIN!

DELPARD TOLD ME HOW HE MANAGED TO FIND HIS MARTINE: "SINCE THERE WAS NO DEAL WITH ITALY, DALILA DI LAZZARO WAS OUT OF OUR REACH, WE STARTED TO LOOK FOR OUR LEADING LADY AND WE SAW A LOT OF ACTRESSES, BUT NONE OF THEM WERE WHAT I HAD IN MIND. I FINALLY CHOSE ISABELLE GOGUEY, WHO USED TO ACT IN A FEW OF PIERSON'S EARLY MOVIES. SHE LOOKED YOUNG AND INNOCENT, JUST RIGHT FOR THE PART, AND ABOVE ALL SHE WAS IMMEDIATELY AVAILABLE."

ALTERNATELY FATUOUS, DUBIOUS OR JUST SCARED TO DEATH; THE YOUNG GINGER HEADED ACTRESS IMPERSONATES THE NAIVE MARTINE TO THE BEST OF HER ABILITIES, AND TRAVERSES THE WEIRD AND SHIVERING ATMOSPHERE WHICH IMPREGNATES THE MOVIE WITH SURPRISING EASE. I MET THE STILL SPARKLING ISABELLE IN 2014, LONG SINCE RETIRED FROM THE ACTING BUSINESS, WHO FONDLY RECALLED THE SHOOTING OF HER ONLY LEADING ROLE IN A FEATURE FILM. IT WAS THE FIRST INTERVIEW SHE'D DONE IN DECADES.

"I DON'T REALLY REMEMBER HOW I ARRIVED ON NIGHT OF DEATH", SHE EXPLAINED. "I HAD JUST DONE A SILLY COMEDY CALLED LES PHALLOCRATES, AND I GUESS RAPHAEL MUST HAVE SEEN ME IN IT.

176

AT THAT TIME, I HADN'T YET DECIDED IF I REALLY WANTED TO BE AN ACTRESS. I HAD HAD SOME VERY SMALL PARTS AS A CHILD, AND LATER AS A TEENAGER, IN A FEW MOVIES BY CLAUDE PIERSON, AND I STARTED WORKING IN THE CUTTING ROOM. THE STRANGE MOOD THAT COMES ACROSS IN THE MOVIE WAS ACTUALLY A DIRECT RESULT OF WHAT WAS HAPPENING ON THE SET. FIRST OF ALL, IT WAS VERY COLD, I WAS ONLY LIGHTLY CLOTHED IN MY NURSES' UNIFORM, AND I WAS HAVING SOME DIFFICULTIES CONCENTRATING ON MY DIALOGUE FOR SOME SCENES.''

"ALSO IT WAS A VERY FAST SHOOT, SOMETHING LIKE THREE WEEKS WITH VERY LONG HOURS, SO WE DIDN'T REALLY HAVE TIME TO GET OUT OF CHARACTER. THAT'S FUNNY BECAUSE I MOSTLY REMEMBER THE OTHER ACTORS AS THEIR CHARACTERS. THE GUY WHO PLAYED THE ROLE OF FLAVIEN INTIMIDATED ME AS MUCH AS HIS CHARACTER INTIMIDATED MARTINE IN THE MOVIE. I WAS PART OF THE PIERSON TEAM, BUT FOR NIGHT OF DEATH, RAPHAEL RECRUITED HIS OWN CAST AND CREW AND I COULDN'T ENJOY THE FAMILY ATMOSPHERE I WAS USED TO WHILE I WAS WORKING FOR CLAUDE. I DON'T EVEN REMEMBER SEEING HIM ON THE SET. "

INDEED PIERSON WAS PRESENT ON LOCATION WITH HIS USUAL CREW, BUT NEVER AT THE SAME TIME AS THE DELPARD CREW. THE RESIDENCE IN WHICH THE ACTION TAKES PLACE WAS AN OLD MANSION HE HAD RENTED FOR THE SHOOT. A SMART PRODUCER, HE DECIDED TO PROFIT ON THIS INVESTMENT BY SHOOTING PORN MOVIES AS SOON AS THE PLACE WAS AVAILABLE.

EVEN THOUGH DELPARD HAD AGREED TO SHOOT SEX MOVIES IN ORDER TO LAUNCH HIS CAREER, HE WAS NOT REALLY INTO NUDITY AND THUSLY NIGHT OF DEATH OFFERS A POOR HELPING IN LIVING FLESH (ALTHOUGH MANAGES SOME FULL FRONTAL NUDITY AND A FLASH OF BOOBS) BUT IS GENEROUS WHEN IT COMES TO SPLATTER TIME IN SPITE OF AN OBVIOUS LACK OF BUDGET. FOR INSTANCE, NICOLE'S VERY EFFECTIVE HALF-EATEN BODY SUSPENDED ON A HOOK IS AN FX PIECE DE RESISTANCE AND ONE OF THE MOST UNFORGETTABLE IMAGES OF THE MOVIE. FROM THE DISEMBOWELMENT SCENE AT THE START OF THE FILM TO THE RAVENOUS MADNESS OF THE LAST REEL (WHICH FEATURES PIERCED EYES, A HAND CUT OFF BY AN AXE AND AN EPISODE WITH A KNITTING NEEDLE, AND A NOT VERY SUBTLE POLITICAL SUBTEXT ABOUT THE RICH EATING THE WORKING CLASS) NIGHT OF DEATH IS A CHEAP, SINCERE AND WONDERFUL TRIP INTO THE OBSCURE SIDE OF FRENCH CINEMA.

ACCORDING TO RAPHAEL DELPARD, THE MOVIE WAS POORLY RECEIVED IN FRANCE BECAUSE PEOPLE DIDN'T REALLY KNOW HOW TO CATEGORIZE IT. "THE U.S. RECEPTION WAS MUCH BETTER" HE TOLD ME. "I EVEN GOT A LETTER FROM TOBE HOOPER IN WHICH HE CONGRATULATED ME ON THE MOVIE, IT WAS SOLD WORLDWIDE, MADE US MONEY AND IS STILL A CULT FILM OVERSEAS.''

REVIEW WRITTEN BY:	ILLUSTRATIONS BY:
ERIC PERETTI	ADAM "BEAN" WILSON

TEACHER FIRED FOR BEING IN PORN

MAN O MAN

THIS STUFF REALLY STEAMS MY CLAMS.

ANOTHER RANT BY THE BOUG, COMIN' UP!

IN 2005 A 25-YEAR-OLD WOMAN NAMED STACIE HALAS SUFFERED SOME SERIOUS FINANCIAL PROBLEMS AFTER HER BOYFRIEND LEFT HER, AND SHE WASN'T MAKING ENOUGH TO PAY HER RENT AND BILLS. $82,000 IN STUDENT-LOANS AND CREDIT-CARD DEBT WAS SLUNG ON TOP OF THE FACT THAT SHE WAS HELPING HER PARENTS OUT OF A FINANCIAL JAM. WITH HER BACK AGAINST THE WALL AND NO ONE ELSE TO TURN TO, STACIE BIT THE BULLET AND ANSWERED AN AD TO BE IN A PORN MOVIE.

DURING AN EIGHT-MONTH PERIOD FROM 2005 TO 2006 STACIE PERFORMED IN 20 PORNOS UNDER THE NAME TIFFANY SIX. SHE STARRED IN RELEASES LIKE: ANAL CONSUMPTION 5, BOOBAHOLICS ANONYMOUS 2, EAT MY BLACK MEAT 4, SEMEN SIPPERS, THIS BUTT'S 4 U, AND CHEEK SPLITTERS.

SHE MADE ABOUT $1,500 PER SCENE, AND EARNED EVERY PENNY OF THAT MONEY. THIS 5' 10 BLONDE WITH SIZE 36 TITS (REAL ONES) DID BUKAKKES. SHE DID ASS-TO-MOUTH. SHE DID DOUBLE PENETRATIONS. SHE DID GANG BANGS WITH AS MANY AS 6 MEN AT A TIME. SHE HANDLED GIANT 10-INCH BLACK PISS-PIPES LIKE A CHAMPION BUTT-SLUT. SHE FARTED COPIOUS AMOUNTS OF SEMEN FROM HER BLOWN-OPEN ANUS INTO A CUP, AND THEN DRANK IT. NEED I REALLY SAY MORE? YOU ALL KNOW HOW MODERN XXX WORKS. YOU GET IT.

IT WOULD ALL COME AT A PRICE, THOUGH. THOSE STUDENT LOANS WERE FOR HER SCHOOLING TO BECOME A TEACHER, AND SHE HAD BEEN DOING PART-TIME SUBSTITUTE JUNIOR HIGH SCHOOL TEACHING IN BETWEEN SOME OF HER PORN JOBS. HALAS MOVED ON FROM HER JOB AT THE SIMI VALLEY UNIFIED SCHOOL DISTRICT AND WAS ASKED TO NO LONGER REPORT FOR DUTY AT THE CONEJO VALLEY UNIFIED SCHOOL DISTRICT AS WELL. IN BOTH CASES, IT WAS AFTER ADMINISTRATORS WERE TOLD BY SPORTS COACHES WORKING AT THE SCHOOL THAT THEY RECOGNIZED HALAS FROM PORN THEY HAD BEEN WATCHING.

STUDENT LOANS MADE HER INTO A:

AAAAA

SQUIRT

SRUIRT

CUM-KWAT

TIFFANY

XXX

SIX

THE MALE TEACHERS THAT HAD BEEN JERKING OFF TO HER MOVIES GOT TO KEEP THEIR JOBS WITHOUT REPRIMAND, BUT SHE WAS TOLD TO FIND SUBSTITUTE TEACHER WORK ELSEWHERE. DESPITE THESE HICCUPS, IT ALL SEEMED TO BE WORTH IT WHEN SHE FINALLY LANDED A FULL TIME JOB AS A JUNIOR HIGH SCIENCE TEACHER AT HAYDOCK INTERMEDIATE SCHOOL IN OXNARD, CALIFORNIA. SHE'D FINALLY BE MAKING A RESPECTABLE WAGE TEACHING 7TH AND 8TH GRADE STUDENTS, AT LEAST ENOUGH SO THAT SHE WOULDN'T HAVE TO GO BACK TO DOING PORN IN ORDER TO SURVIVE.

AT THE AGE OF 32, HALAS WAS FIRED IN APRIL 2012 FROM HER JOB AFTER FOOTAGE OF HER STARRING IN PORN WAS DISCOVERED ONLINE BY HER STUDENTS AND FELLOW TEACHERS. IT WAS THREE STRIKES, AND YOU'RE OUT. HER CAREER IN TEACHING WAS NOW RUINED. MY MOM USED TO BE A HIGH SCHOOL TEACHER IN OXNARD AND SANTA PAULA. I KNOW THAT SCHOOL DISTRICT WELL. THIS NEWS WASN'T THAT SHOCKING...BUT IT WAS FRUSTRATING.

"ALTHOUGH HER PORNOGRAPHY CAREER HAS CONCLUDED, THE ONGOING AVAILABILITY OF HER PORNOGRAPHIC MATERIALS ON THE INTERNET WILL CONTINUE TO IMPEDE HER FROM BEING AN EFFECTIVE TEACHER AND RESPECTED COLLEAGUE," JUDGE JULIE CABOS-OWEN SAID IN THE 46-PAGE DECISION, WHERE AN APPEAL TO OVERTURN THE RULING WAS FLATLY DENIED.

"WE WERE HOPING WE COULD SHOW YOU COULD OVERCOME YOUR PAST," HALAS'S LAWYER, RICHARD SCHWAB SAID. "I THINK SHE'S REPRESENTATIVE OF A LOT OF PEOPLE WHO MAY HAVE A PAST THAT MAY NOT INVOLVE ANYTHING ILLEGAL, OR ANYTHING THAT HURTS ANYBODY."

DISTRICT SUPERINTENDENT JEFF CHANCER APPLAUDED THE COMMISSION'S RULING, AND STATED THAT HALAS' DECISION TO "ENGAGE IN PORNOGRAPHY WAS INCOMPATIBLE WITH HER RESPONSIBILITIES AS A ROLE MODEL FOR STUDENTS".

"SERVES HER RIGHT" WROTE A TYPICAL COMMENTER ON A HUFFINGTON POST ONLINE ARTICLE ABOUT THE STORY. "I WOULD NOT WANT MY CHILDREN ANYWHERE NEAR A PORN STAR, AND IN A SCHOOL OF ALL PLACES, ARE YOU KIDDING ME? THIS 'WOMAN' HAS ABSOLUTELY NO SYMPATHY FROM ME, SHE CHOSE TO BE A LEGALIZED PROSTITUTE AND NOW HER PAST HAS COME BACK TO HAUNT HER."

"I HAVE LITTLE EMPATHY FOR HER. SHE KNEW THE RISK AND TOOK IT." WROTE CINEMA SEWER READER SHANE BROWN. "AND EVERYONE WANTS TO SAY IT'S A CONSERVATIVE OR LIBERAL THING. I DON'T KNOW TOO MANY PEOPLE THAT WOULD SAY 'I JUST WOULD LOVE TO SEE MY KID GROW UP AND BE IN FUCK FLICKS.'"

PEOPLE DON'T SAY "I'D LOVE TO SEE MY KID GROW UP AND WORK IN A 7-11 HIS WHOLE LIFE" EITHER, BUT GUESS WHAT? THAT IS REALITY, MAN. THAT IS HOW A LARGE MAJORITY OF THE WORKFORCE IN OUR SOCIETY OPERATES: IN JOBS NO ONE ELSE PARTICULARLY WANTS. MAYBE IF THEY ACTUALLY PAID TEACHERS A FAIR SALARY, THEY WOULDN'T HAVE TO GET OTHER JOBS ON THE SIDE.

OVER AND ABOVE MY ISSUES WITH THE WAY OUR SOCIETY TREATS TEACHERS, I JUST CAN'T ABIDE SLUT-SHAMING. IT'S PURITANICAL GARBAGE. YOU MAY AS WELL DISREGARD SOMEONE FOR THE SIN OF BREATHING WHILE YOU'RE AT IT. IF YOU'RE GOING TO FIRE HER, FIRE HER FOR BEING A LOUSY TEACHER. AND YEAH, IF THERE WAS A BREACH OF CONTRACT THEN SHE DESERVES TO BE FIRED. BUT IT'S THESE "MORALITY" CONTRACTS AND EXPECTATIONS OF TEACHERS TO BE INHUMAN THAT IRKS ME. HUMANS ARE SEXUAL BEINGS, AND THAT SEXUALITY DOESN'T MAKE THEM BAD ROLE MODELS, NOR DOES IT MAKE THEM UNWORTHY OF RESPECT. IT MAKES THEM JUST LIKE THE REST OF US.

IN AN INTERVIEW SEGMENT FOR NO CUM DODGING ALLOWED 7, STACIE STATES IT'S "VERY RISKY" TO BE DOING WHAT SHE'S DOING "BECAUSE I AM A TEACHER", AND LATER SHE POINTS OUT "AT LEAST I DON'T DO THE STUDENTS". THIS EXCHANGE GOT CITED A LOT BY PEOPLE ONLINE WHO CLAIMED IT WAS RIGHT SHE WAS FIRED.

QUITE FRANKLY IT WAS DUMB FOR HER TO EVER LET THE PORNOGRAPHERS KNOW SHE WAS A TEACHER IN REAL LIFE -- BECAUSE OF COURSE THEY ARE GONNA BRING THAT UP AND TRY TO GET HER TO SAY SOMETHING FILTHY ABOUT IT. SHE COULD HAVE MADE UP ANY VOCATION, AND THEY WOULD HAVE GONE WITH IT. 90% OF THE STUFF IN THOSE INTERVIEWS IS FABRICATED, ANYWAY. YOU'RE SELLING FANTASY. YOU'RE SELLING FETISH.

TO ME THIS STORY WAS JUST YET ANOTHER PERFECT EXAMPLE OF HOW SEX-NEGATIVE OUR CULTURE IS. IF SHE HASN'T DONE ANYTHING ILLEGAL, WHAT IS IT THAT THEY'RE FIRING HER FOR? BECAUSE PARENTS DON'T WANT SOMEONE TEACHING THEIR KIDS WHO HAS HAD SEX? BECAUSE HER CO-WORKERS CAN'T WORK WITH SOMEONE WHO HAS HAD SEX? WHY DO WE EXPECT OUR COMMUNITY LEADERS TO BE SEXLESS? WHAT MAKES SOMEONE WHO MADE PORN UNABLE TO TEACH? BECAUSE SHE MIGHT TEACH HER STUDENTS TO FUCK FOR MONEY?! LUDICROUS. DOES THAT MEAN THAT IF YOU ONCE WORKED AT MCDONALDS YOU'RE NOW UNSUITABLE TO TEACH BECAUSE YOU MIGHT INSTRUCT YOUR STUDENTS TO FLIP BURGERS FOR A LIVING?

THE HYPOCRISY IN THIS CASE WAS STOMACH-CHURNING. MOST OF THE PEOPLE WHO SUPPORTED THE FIRING OF THIS WOMAN HAVE VIEWED PORN FOR THEIR OWN ENJOYMENT. IT'S LIKE CONDEMNING THE KILLING OF COWS, BUT ENJOYING STEAKS AND HAMBURGERS EVERY NIGHT. THE CONSERVATIVE MORALISTS LOOKING DOWN ON HALAS WERE THE SAME PEOPLE THAT HARP ON AND ON ABOUT A WELFARE STATE, AND CLAIM THAT POOR PEOPLE SHOULD BETTER THEMSELVES BY GETTING A JOB AND A CAREER THEN THEY TURN AROUND AND MAKE IMPROVING YOURSELF NEXT-TO-IMPOSSIBLE.

HOW ABOUT PARENTS MONITORING THEIR CHILDREN BETTER, SO THEY WON'T BE FINDING THEIR TEACHER'S PORNO ONLINE? HOW ABOUT A LESSON TO CHILDREN THAT A PERSON CAN RECOVER FROM CHOICES THEY MAY FIND REGRETTABLE AND SUCCESSFULLY MOVE ON? IS THAT NOT A MORE VALUABLE LESSON THAN WHAT HAS BEEN TAUGHT BY FIRING THIS WOMAN? (WHICH IS NOT TO IMPLY THAT PORN IS INHERENTLY A "REGRETTABLE CHOICE", AS IF SEX WORKERS CAN ONLY EARN THE RIGHT TO BE LEFT ALONE BY DENOUNCING THEIR SINFUL WAYS.)

GOOD GRIEF

NICE HYPOCRISY. YOU ALL LOOK AT PORN, AND I'M THE PERV?

THE ARGUMENT AGAINST HER RETAINING HER JOB THAT I HEARD OVER AND OVER WHEN DISCUSSING THIS STORY IN ONLINE FORUMS AND SOCIAL MEDIA WAS THAT IT WOULD BE IMPOSSIBLE FOR HER TO DO HER JOB NOW THAT EVERYONE KNOWS SHE WAS IN PORN. THAT NO LEARNING COULD TAKE PLACE NOW THAT THE ONLY THING ANYONE IN THE CLASSROOM WOULD THINK OF WAS HER GETTING A BIG COCK UP HER ASS.

"THAT'S RIDICULOUS", REMARKED A CARTOONIST FRIEND OF MINE, JEN MILLER. "WE HAD A TEACHER WHEN I WAS IN 7TH GRADE WHO WAS ALSO IN PORNO. ASIDE FROM SOME KID ALWAYS MANAGING TO DIG UP THE MAGAZINES SHE WAS IN EVERY YEAR, IT WASN'T A BIG DEAL."

I AGREE, AND THAT ARGUMENT JUST DOESN'T MAKE A LICK OF SENSE TO ME. I DON'T UNDERSTAND HOW IT IS ANYONE ELSE'S GODDAMN BUSINESS. WHAT A TEACHER DOES IN THEIR LEGAL AND CONSENSUAL SEX LIFE HAS NO BEARING ON HER DAY JOB WHATSOEVER. THE IDEA THAT A WOMAN -- TEACHER OR NOT -- IS SOMEHOW UNDESERVING OF A PROFESSIONAL CAREER SIMPLY BECAUSE SHE HAS HAD SEX -- FILMED OR NOT -- IS FUCKING MORONIC. CLEARLY EACH OF THOSE TEACHERS IN THAT OXNARD SCHOOL DISTRICT SUCKS AND FUCKS AND DOES WHATEVER OTHER KINKY SHIT THEY DO FOR THRILLS AS WELL. WHY DIDN'T THEY ALSO FIRE ALL HER CO-WORKERS THAT AREN'T VIRGINS JUST TO MAKE IT FAIR? IT'S REALLY THE ONLY THING TO DO IF YOU'RE GOING TO DISCRIMINATE AGAINST AN EMPLOYEE FOR HAVING SEX.

—BOUGIE 2013

DON'T PUT HER DOWN FOR PULLIN' EM **OFF** OR PULLIN' 'EM **UP!**

SONDRA CURRIE
TONY YOUNG
PHIL HOOVER
ELIZABETH STUART
CHUCK DANIEL
JEANIE BELL
LAURIE ROSE
EILEEN SAKI

¡DULCES MUJERES...!

DIRECTOR: LEE FROST · COLOR · A CROWN INTERNATIONAL PICTURES RELEASE

I'M NOT GOING TO REVIEW THE MOVIE BECAUSE I ALREADY DID BACK ON PAGE 175 OF CINEMA SEWER BOOK 2, BUT LEE FROST'S 1974 ODE TO LADY COPS, POLICEWOMEN, IS GETTING ANOTHER MENTION. WHY? BECAUSE OF THIS AWESOME SPANISH AD ART FROM THE COLLECTION OF STEVE FENTON! HIiiiiiiiii-YA!!

COOL!

BOUGIE 13

RANDOM TRIVIA

☆ DAN AYKROYD'S ORIGINAL SCRIPT FOR GHOSTBUSTERS (1984) ACTUALLY TOOK PLACE IN AN ODD FUTUREWORLD WHERE BEING A GHOSTBUSTER WAS AS EVERYDAY AS BEING A PLUMBER.

☆ JOHN CUSACK, TOM CRUISE, JOHNNY DEPP AND JIM CARREY WERE ALL SERIOUSLY CONSIDERED FOR THE PART OF FERRIS BUELLER, WHICH WENT TO A 24-YEAR-OLD MATTHEW BRODERICK.

REVIEW BY: MIKE "NEON" SULLIVAN
ART BY: BEN "MANIAC" NEWMAN

NEON MANIACS WAS NOT A HIT. IT WASN'T THE KIND OF MOVIE THAT EVENTUALLY FOUND A CULT AUDIENCE ON HOME VIDEO. IT'S A BARELY REMEMBERED, LITTLE-LOVED ALSO-RAN THAT TYPICALLY GARNERS ONE SENTENCE REVIEWS IN MOVIE GUIDES THAT BRUTALLY CRITICIZE THE FILM FOR LACKING BOTH NEON AND MANIACS.

THIS NEGATIVE PERCEPTION IS WHY I AVOIDED THIS FILM FOR MOST OF MY ADULT LIFE AND IT'S A DECISION I REGRET. PLEASE DON'T MAKE THE SAME MISTAKE I DID. NEON MANIACS IS FAR MORE ENTERTAINING THAN ITS LUKEWARM REPUTATION WOULD IMPLY. STOP IGNORING NEON MANIACS. OPEN YOUR HEART TO THE FILM. TAKE OUT WHATEVER DISC IS CURRENTLY IN YOUR DVD OR BLU-RAY PLAYER, BREAK IT IN HALF, VIOLENTLY SHAKE IT AS IF IT WERE A BABY THAT WON'T STOP CRYING, THROW IT INTO THE STREET AND PUT NEON MANIACS ON IN ITS STEAD. WHATEVER IT WAS YOU WERE CURRENTLY WATCHING WILL NO LONGER DESERVE YOUR ATTENTION EVER AGAIN (UNLESS YOU WERE MASTURBATING TO IT. IN WHICH CASE HOLD ONTO IT BECAUSE YOU'LL NEED IT AGAIN IN A FEW MINUTES) NEON MANIACS HAS ARRIVED AND IT IS TIME YOU STARTED APPRECIATING IT.

OF COURSE, YOU MAY ASK, WHY SHOULD I TOSS MY BROKEN DVD INTO THE STREET OR STOP MASTURBATING JUST TO ACCOMMODATE SOME UNFAMILIAR FILM FROM 1986? HERE'S WHY: IN NEON MANIACS THE STORYLINE DOESN'T PROGRESS IN A COHERENT OR LOGICAL MANNER. THINGS HAPPEN FOR APPARENTLY NO REASON. NOTHING IS EVER EXPLAINED AND NOTHING MAKES SENSE. IT'S BEAUTIFUL. LIKE A SOOTHING FORM OF SCHIZOPHRENIA, NEON MANIACS RETAINS ALL OF THE BENEFITS OF MENTAL ILLNESS BUT NONE OF THE NASTY SIDE EFFECTS.

AFTER A DISEMBODIED VOICE SOLEMNLY WARNS AGAINST THE DANGERS OF VIOLENCE, THE FADING OF MANKIND'S SOUL AND THE DARKENING OF CHILDREN'S PATHWAYS, NEON MANIACS OPENS WITH A CRUSTY OLD FISHERMAN FINDING A COW SKULL THAT CONTAINS FLASH CARDS DEPICTING THE TITULAR MANIACS (SORT OF PROTO-CENOBITES RESEMBLING AN INDIAN CHIEF, A SAMURAI, A LEATHER DADDY, A FERAL, MUSCLE-Y SANTA CLAUS, AN ELECTRIFIED GIMP, ETC.) UNNERVED TO FIND THIS SALTY DOG RIFLING THROUGH THEIR PERSONAL COW SKULLS, ONE OF THE MANIACS BURIES AN AXE IN THE BACK OF HIS HEAD. FROM THERE THE CREDITS UNFURL TO A SONG THAT EITHER SOUNDS LIKE A BUNGLED MIDI COVER OF GEORGE MICHAEL'S 'I'M NEVER GONNA DANCE AGAIN' OR SOMETHING THAT WOULD PLAY OVER A NES CUT-SCENE OF MEGAMAN RIDING IN AN ELEVATOR.

AFTER THAT: HIJINKS! TEEN HIJINKS! A JOCK HURLS ABUSE AT SOME PUNK KIDS FROM HIS VAN! A YOUNG TOUGH BELCHES MENACINGLY AT PASSERSBY! ALL KINDS OF LAYINGS, BLOWINGS AND FUCKINGS ARE OCCURRING AND A HAPPENING! IT'S TEEN TIME! AND MAN, OH, MAN THESE TEENS ARE _QUITE_ THE TEENS BECAUSE EVERYTHING THEY SAY AND DO IS VERY BELIEVABLE, VERY REAL AND VERY, VERY TRUE. ONE TEEN (HURTFULLY DUBBED THE BALLOONY MAN) IS ACCUSED OF HAVING "PASTA BREATH" WHEN HE TELLS ANOTHER TEEN THAT HIS "GROCER NEEDS A BOUNCER IN THE FRUIT SECTION". HOOHOO! YOU BETTER CALL THE FIRE DEPARTMENT BECAUSE SOMEBODY _JUST GOT_ BURNED! AT ANY RATE, AS THESE KIDS SHOUT AND MAKE LOVE AT EACH OTHER IN A PUBLIC PARK, THE MANIACS TRUNDLE ALONG SLASHING PEOPLE WITH SAMURAI SWORDS, FILLING FOOTBALLS FULL OF ARROWS AND GENERALLY SPOILING ALL KINDS OF BLOWJOBS. NOTHING CAN STOP THEM, NOT EVEN FIREWORKS OR HUMAN FISTS.

SURPRISINGLY, ONE TEEN NAMED NATALIE (LEILANI SARELLE, WHO MAY BE BETTER KNOWN FOR PLAYING ONE OF SHARON STONE'S LOVERS IN **BASIC INSTINCT**) MANAGES TO SURVIVE THIS MASSACRE. SHE IS SO TRAUMATIZED BY THE TRAGIC DEATHS OF HER FRIENDS THAT SHE'S ALMOST TOO DISTRAUGHT TO HOP ABOARD AN INNER TUBE AND BOB AROUND IN HER PARENT'S POOL (MY MOM USED TO CALL IT A SORROW SPRITZ). AT SCHOOL, TOUGH TALKING GIRLS PICK FIGHTS WITH NATALIE, PROMPTING BALLOONY MAN TO STEP IN AND AWKWARDLY PUSH THEM AWAY (IT SHOULD BE NOTED THAT AS BALLOONY MAN RESCUES NATALIE, BALLOONY MAN'S DONNY MOST-ISH LOOKING FRIEND PUMPS HIS FIST, LOUDLY YELPS AND ACTS AS IF BALLOONY MAN TOOK OUT THAT CRUEL, HULKING BLONDE KID WHO

KEEPS TIPPING OVER THE NERDY KIDS' TABLE AT LUNCH TIME WITH ONE PUNCH INSTEAD OF GENTLY SHOOING AWAY A TINY, LITTLE WOMAN WITH CRISPY BANGS THAT NATALIE PROBABLY COULD HAVE EASILY DEALT WITH HERSELF).

MEANWHILE, A TWENTY-YEAR-OLD WOMAN PRETENDS TO BE A TWELVE YEAR OLD GIRL AND STARTS INVESTIGATING THE NEON MANIACS AND THEIR MIDNIGHT CREEPS. UNFORTUNATELY HER EFFORTS ARE MOSTLY BLOCKED BY MEAN POLICE OFFICERS WHO NOT ONLY STEAL HER BICYCLE BUT ALSO MAKE "VROOM, VROOM" NOISES WITH THEIR MOUTHS AS THEY DO IT. WHEN DID IT STOP BEING AMERICA? EVENTUALLY SHE DISCOVERS THAT THE MANIACS MELT AWAY WHEN THEY'RE EXPOSED TO WATER, WHICH IS A LITTLE SURPRISING CONSIDERING THAT THEY LIVE UNDER THE GOLDEN GATE BRIDGE. IF WATER CAN KILL YOU, WOULDN'T YOU WANT TO LIVE AS FAR AWAY FROM IT AS YOU POSSIBLY COULD? BUT, NONETHELESS, THE DISCOVERY COULDN'T HAVE COME AT A BETTER TIME BECAUSE THE MANIACS HAVE BEEN GETTING OUT OF CONTROL. THEY'VE BEEN STALKING NATALIE, USING THEIR MAGICAL NEON MANIAC LASER BEAMS TO GET ON THE SUBWAY FOR FREE AND HANG PEOPLE WHO ONLY WANT TO LIVE THEIR LIVES AND UNNATURALLY TOSS KENNEDY HALF DOLLARS IN THE PITCH BLACK NIGHT AIR.

LUCKILY, THE WOMAN CHILD, BALLOONY MAN AND NATALIE COME UP WITH A PLAN TO STOP THE MANIACS ONCE AND FOR ALL. THEY'LL LURE THESE NEON NE'ER-DO-WELLS TO THIS EVENING'S BATTLE OF THE BANDS CONCERT AT THE LOCAL HIGH SCHOOL AND GIVE ALL OF THE ATTENDEES THEIR OWN SQUIRT-GUNS. BUT THIS PLAN IMMEDIATELY FALLS APART BECAUSE THE BATTLE OF THE BANDS IS ALSO, INEXPLICABLY, A COSTUME PARTY AND NO ONE IS TOLD WHY EXACTLY THEY HAVE SQUIRT GUNS. SO NOT ONLY DO THE MANIACS BLEND IN AMONGST THE CROWD AND REMAIN RELATIVELY UNNOTICED AS THEY HARVEST THE ORGANS OF A SLUMBERING JANITOR BUT WHEN THEIR PRESENCE IS FINALLY REVEALED BY ALL OF THEIR LOUD MOTORCYCLE, CROSSBOW AND GUN-BASED MURDERS, EVERYBODY QUITE NATURALLY LOSES THEIR SHIT, TOSSES THE SQUIRT-GUNS ON THE FLOOR AND RUNS HEADLONG TO THEIR DEATHS. AS THIS IS HAPPENING, BALLOONY MAN AND NATALIE KIND OF JUST SHRUG THEIR SHOULDERS AND FIND A PRIVATE OUT OF THE WAY CHEMISTRY ROOM TO FUCK THE FEAR AWAY.

TO GIVE CREDIT WHERE CREDIT IS DUE, NEON MANIACS SOLDIERED ON THROUGH THE KIND OF SEVERE PRODUCTION PROBLEMS THAT WOULD HAVE DESTROYED BIGGER, MORE RESPECTABLE FILMS. THE FILM WAS ORIGINALLY SCHEDULED FOR A MERE SIX-WEEK SHOOT BUT FINANCIAL PROBLEMS AND "CREATIVE DIFFERENCES" WITH THE PRODUCER CAUSED NEON MANIACS TO SHUT DOWN FOR THREE MONTHS. DURING THE HIATUS THE FILM'S ORIGINAL DP OLIVER WOOD DROPPED OUT OF THE FILM, AS DID MOST OF THE ORIGINAL MANIACS. ADDITIONALLY, THE SCRIPT'S AMBITIOUS SCOPE HAD TO BE SCALED BACK SIGNIFICANTLY AND ELABORATE SCENES INVOLVING MANIACS LIKE DECAPITATOR (ORIGINALLY HE WAS SUPPOSED TO HAVE TWIN CLEAVERS FOR HANDS) AND AXE HAD TO BE ELIMINATED.

BUT WITH ALL OF THAT SAID, AT NO POINT AMONGST ALL OF THESE PRODUCTION PROBLEMS DID ANYONE PULL SCREENWRITER MARK PATRICK CARDUCCI ASIDE, GENTLY KISS HIM ON THE FOREHEAD AND WHISPER SOFTLY IN HIS EAR, 'WHY DID YOU NEVER BOTHER TO EXPLAIN WHY THE MANIACS' MAIN WEAKNESS IS WATER? WHY, AFTER WATCHING HER FRIENDS GET MURDERED BY AN INDIAN CHIEF WHO LOOKS LIKE HE HAD A VERY SEVERE ALLERGIC REACTION TO A BEE STING, DID NATALIE MINDLESSLY FLOAT AROUND IN HER PARENTS POOL? WHY DO ALL OF THE TEENAGERS SOUND LIKE A 5-YEAR-OLD'S IDEA OF HOW A TEENAGER SPEAKS? AND, WHAT THE FUCK IS A NEON MANIAC? SERIOUSLY, WHAT THE FUCK IS IT? YOU REALIZE THAT THE CRITICS ARE GOING TO LAZILY USE THAT STUPID TITLE AGAINST THIS FILM UNTIL THE DAY LORD JESUS PERSONALLY DAMNS EVERY CRITIC TO THE SMELLIEST REACHES OF LUCIFER'S OTHERWORLDLY UNDER-BALLS, RIGHT?'

BUT I'M GLAD NOBODY SPOKE UP OR QUESTIONED THE FILM BECAUSE THESE DUMB IDEAS AND BIZARRE INCONSISTENCIES MAKE NEON MANIACS THE LOVABLY SILLY LITTLE FILM THAT IT IS. IT'S UNCONSCIOUSLY SURREAL AND DREAMLIKE. I DON'T WANT TO OVERRATE IT, BUT THIS IS THE KIND OF FILM THAT SALVADOR DALI WOULD HAVE MADE IF HE SUFFERED FROM SEVERE DEMENTIA AND SUDDENLY DECIDED HE WAS GOING TO MAKE A LOW BUDGET SLASHER FLICK. IT'S REWARDING AND PUNISHING AT THE SAME TIME. I LOVED THIS LIKE I WOULD LOVE AN UNCLE OR A DOG. IT'S NOT TRUE LOVE BUT IT'S UP THERE.

STILL, I SHOULD POINT OUT THERE IS NO NEON AND EVEN LESS MANIACS IN THIS FILM, SO TREAD LIGHTLY AND WATCH AT YOUR OWN RISK.

Bound by Sex: The Destiny of Max Pécas

A SPECTACLE OF UNRELENTING PASSION!

BOLD! SHOCKING!

FIVE WILD GIRLS

☆ ARTICLE BY ERIC PERETTI ☆

FRENCH DIRECTOR MAX PÉCAS HAD A CAREER THAT COULD EASILY BE DIVIDED INTO THREE DIFFERENT PARTS: THRILLERS, SOFT AND HARDCORE SEX FILMS, AND COMEDIES. THE ONE THING THEY ALL HAD IN COMMON, HOWEVER, WAS A SPECIFIC AND OVERT THEME OF SEX.

IN THE EARLY '60S, WHEN LEADERS OF THE FRENCH NEW WAVE WERE SHOOTING MOVIES ABOUT EVERYDAY LIFE, PÉCAS CHOSE A DIFFERENT PATH TO BREAK INTO THE BUSINESS. HE STARTED WITH A THRILLER. THE FILM WAS LE CERCLE VICIEUX (1960), AND THE PLOT REVOLVES AROUND A YOUNG UNFAITHFUL ARTIST WHO ACCIDENTALLY KILLS HIS JEALOUS, OLDER WIFE IN ORDER TO INHERIT HER MONEY. BUT THINGS AREN'T SO EASY AND THE ARRIVAL OF A BEAUTIFUL UNKNOWN STEPDAUGHTER WITH WHOM THE CRIMINAL FALLS IN LOVE MAKES THE SITUATION TRICKIER.

THE FOLLOWING YEAR, PÉCAS BROUGHT A GORGEOUS BLONDE GAL BACK FROM GERMANY, THE LOVELY ELKE SOMMER. AFTER GIVING HER THE LEADING ROLE IN HIS SECOND FEATURE FILM, DANIELLA BY NIGHT (AKA DE QUOI TU TE MÊLES, DANIELA!, 1961) A SPY WHODUNNIT THAT INCLUDED A BRIEF SCENE IN A CABARET (WITH A GLIMPSE OF NUDITY), HE CAST THE TEUTONIC BOMB AGAIN IN HIS NEXT FILM, THE RATHER BORING SWEET ECSTASY (AKA DOUCE VIOLENCE, 1962). IN AN ATTEMPT TO CREATE HIS OWN BRIGITTE BARDOT, PÉCAS SHOT A VERY SENSUAL SCENE IN THE FILM IN WHICH ELKE DANCES TANTALIZINGLY TO THE RHYTHM OF AFRICAN DRUMS. EVEN THOUGH THE MOVIE (MAINLY DEPICTING THE DULL LIFE OF THE GOLDEN YOUTH) IS SILLY, INCLUDING AN ESPECIALLY MORALISTIC ENDING, THE DANCE OF MISS SOMMER WAS UNFORGETTABLE.

FROM THAT POINT ON, THE DIE WAS CAST ON PÉCAS'S CAREER AND THE WORD "SEXY" WOULD FOREVER BE GLUED TO HIS MOVIES.

"IF I AM SHOOTING MOVIES, IT'S BECAUSE I LOVE THIS BUSINESS," PÉCAS SAID IN AN INTERVIEW WITH BRITT NINI FOR SEX STAR SYSTEM (ISSUE #5, 1975). "BUT IF I'M STILL DOING THIS KIND OF SEXY MOVIE, WHICH I DON'T REGRET AT ALL, IT'S NOT BY VOCATION OR BECAUSE I'M REALLY FOND OF THEM. MY FIRST THREE MOVIES WERE DIFFERENT FROM THOSE I'M DOING NOW. THEY WERE NOT ART HOUSE MOVIES, JUST GOOD OLD FASHIONED THRILLERS. I WANTED TO DO MORE OF THEM, BUT AFTER I FINISHED THE THIRD ONE, I DIDN'T WORK FOR A YEAR. SOMEONE SAID TO ME: 'IN SWEET ECSTASY THERE WAS A VERY WELL-EXECUTED EROTIC SEQUENCE. LOW-BUDGET SEXY MOVIES SEEM TO DO WELL NOW, I'LL PUT SOME MONEY INTO ONE FOR YOU. ARE YOU INTERESTED?' AND I SAID TO MYSELF,'WHY NOT?' AFTER ALL, I HAD ALREADY HAD THE OPPORTUNITY TO SERVE AS A TECHNICAL ADVISER ON LE CRI DE LA CHAIR (SIN ON THE BEACH, 1963), THE FIRST JOSÉ BÉNAZÉRAF SEX MOVIE, AND I RECALLED THINKING THAT I COULD DO THAT TOO. SO I ACCEPTED TO SHOOT ONE, THEN TWO, THEN THREE--THEN AFTER A WHILE I WAS TRAPPED AND I COULD NOT ESCAPE FROM THE GENRE. I WAS MARKED."

BETWEEN 1962 AND 1974 PÉCAS WAS VERY BUSY DIRECTING SOFTCORE FILMS WHICH BECAME MORE AND MORE SEXUALLY ORIENTED. HE MAY HAVE FELT TRAPPED AND LIMITED BY THE GENRE, BUT HIS SUCCESS AND SKILL AT MAKING SEXPLOITATION MOVIES LIKE THE SLAVE (1962), FIVE WILD GIRLS (1966), HEAT OF MIDNIGHT (1966), AND

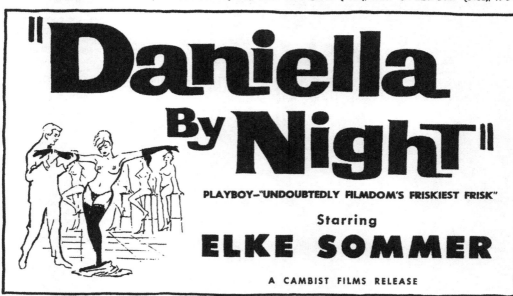

"Daniella By Night"

PLAYBOY—"UNDOUBTEDLY FILMDOM'S FRISKIEST FRISK"

Starring

ELKE SOMMER

A CAMBIST FILMS RELEASE

LOVE + FEAR = TORMENT (1967) MEANT THAT HE COULD ALWAYS FIND FUNDING FOR HIS NEXT SEX FILM SCRIPT, AND KEEP WORKING IN THE FILM INDUSTRY. EVENTUALLY HE ABANDONED THRILLERS AND INTENSE DRAMAS IN FAVOUR OF THE MORE DARING (ALTHOUGH SUPERFICIAL) SUBJECTS SUCH AS NYMPHOMANIA, SWINGERS AND FRIGIDITY. THE LACK OF SOLID NARRATIVE SUBSTANCE WAS OFTEN OFFSET BY SIMPLISTIC PSYCHOLOGY.

"I WAS ALWAYS BLAMED FOR MY HAPPY ENDINGS," COMPLAINED PÉCAS TO NINI. "BUT I HATE SLEAZE AND VULGARITY. THEY ALSO MADE FUN OF ME, SAYING MY MOVIES WERE MORALISTIC."

IN 1974, CENSORSHIP WAS ABANDONED IN FRANCE AND HARDCORE FEATURES WERE ALLOWED TO SHINE ON THE SILVER SCREEN. "IF LAWS OR CENSORSHIP ALLOW US TO DEPICT CERTAIN THINGS CLEARLY, I'LL SHOW THEM OF COURSE", HE CONCEDED IN THE SEX STAR SYSTEM INTERVIEW. "BUT I WON'T LIMIT MYSELF TO THAT. WHEN WE SPEND 10 MINUTES ON THE SAME SHOT, THE SCENE BEGINS TO GET BORING. IT CAN'T GENERATE EMOTIONS. BEFORE, IN MOVIES WE SPENT AT LEAST 15 MINUTES ELABORATING AN APPROACH FOR SHOWING SEX -- OR RATHER AN EROTIC SITUATION. NOW IT ONLY TAKES A POOR 2 MINUTES AND WE HAVE 15 MINUTES OF SEX. THAT'S WHAT I BEMOAN, THE WAVE OF MOVIES THAT IS KILLING THE GOOSE THAT LAYS THE GOLDEN EGG. PEOPLE REMAIN ROMANTIC AT HEART."

un film de MAX PÉCAS

DEUX ENFOIRÉS à St TROPEZ

THE ERA OF SOFTCORE WAS OVER AND PÉCAS, LIKE HIS AMERICAN COUNTERPART RADLEY METZGER, HAD NO OTHER CHOICE BUT TO GO WITH THE FLOW OF EXPLICITNESS. BUT THE OVERWHELMING SENTIMENTALITY THAT HAD SOMETIMES BEEN A HANDICAP IN HIS PREVIOUS FILMS SUDDENLY BECAME AN ASSET WHEN HE HOPPED, BRIEFLY, INTO REAL PORNOGRAPHY AT THE AGE OF 50 — WITHOUT EVEN USING A MONIKER. HIS FIRST VENTURE IN THE GENRE WAS FELICIA (LES 1001 PERVERSIONS DE FÉLICIA, 1975), SHOT IN TWO VERSIONS, SOFT AND EXPLICIT, WITH THE IRRESISTIBLE REBECCA BROOKE (ALIAS MARY MENDUM), WHO WAS AT THE SAME TIME INDUCING HARD-ONS IN THE AFOREMENTIONED RADLEY METZGER'S THE IMAGE, A MOVIE PRODUCED BY PÉCAS'S COMPANY, LES FILMS DU GRIFFON. IN THE EXPLICIT VERSION OF FÉLICIA INSIPID SENTIMENTAL TALK IMMEDIATELY FOUND A VIVID ECHO IN ITS CARNAL REPRESENTATION AND PÉCAS SUCCEEDED WHERE ALMOST EVERYBODY ELSE FAILED: HE PUT FEELING IN THE FLESH.

THE slave

MAX WAS EVEN MORE AMBITIOUS WITH HIS NEXT RELEASE, SWEET TASTE OF HONEY (LUXURE, 1976), AND WITH THIS ONE HE WRAPPED THE STORY OF A SUICIDAL BLONDE IN A DREAMY ATMOSPHERE, PUSHING THE BOUNDARIES OF CINEMATIC FANTASY. BUT AFTER ONLY TWO MOVIES, MAX PÉCAS DROPPED OFF. HE FELT CONFINED IN A GENRE THAT HAD ALREADY STARTED TO GO ROUND IN CIRCLES, ESPECIALLY SINCE THE X LAW WAS ADOPTED BY THE FRENCH GOVERNMENT, INCREASING TAXES ON PORN FILMS.

SO HE OPTED FOR ANOTHER WAY, HEAVY SEXY COMEDIES. IT WAS LIKE A EUROPEAN DISEASE: ITALY WAS SWALLOWING EDWIGE FENECH'S PUBIC COMEDIES, GERMANY WAS ENDURING BAVARIAN PIGTAILED MOUNTAINEERING COMEDIES AND FRANCE WAS SUFFERING THROUGH DULL SUNNY SUMMER HOLIDAY CAMP COMEDIES. THE BEACHES OF SAINT-TROPEZ BECAME PÉCAS' LAST BATTLEFIELD: INDECENT YOUNG CO-EDS WERE HIS TROOPERS, TITS AND ASSES WERE THE WEAPONS, AND FATAL FULL FRONTAL FINISHED OFF THE AUDIENCE. SUBTLETY WAS MISSING IN ACTION AND AMONGST CRITICS MAX PÉCAS'S NAME BECAME SYNONYMOUS WITH LOUSY MOVIES. THE RELEASE IN JANUARY 1985 OF THE DISTURBING HARDBOILED THRILLER BRIGADE OF DEATH (BRIGADES DE MOEURS) SEEMED TO ANNOUNCE A RETURN TO BASICS, BUT THE MOVIE REMAINS THE LAST GASP OF A VITAL FILMMAKER.

THE DARK JEWEL OF THE PÉCAS FILMOGRAPHY, BRIGADE OF DEATH IS WORTH TAKING SOME TIME TO DISSECT. CONTENT TO FILM DULL COMEDIES THROUGH THE LATE '70S, MAX PÉCAS SANG A DIFFERENT TUNE WITH THIS INFAMOUS RELEASE. HE LEAVES BEHIND LIGHTHEARTED BURLESQUE AND THE SUNNY LANDSCAPES OF SAINT

TRAPPED IN A WEB OF...

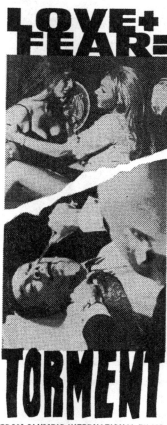

LOVE+FEAR=

TORMENT

FROM OLYMPIC INTERNATIONAL FILMS
PROHIBITED TO MINORS

TROPEZ IN ORDER TO SET THE MOVIE IN THE NEON-LIT UNDERWORLD OF A DARK AND GRIMY PARIS, A SORDID PLACE FILLED WITH PROSTITUTES AND SMALL TIME CROOKS. ALREADY RATHER DISTURBING AT THE TIME OF ITS RELEASE, BRIGADE OF DEATH REMAINS, 30 YEARS LATER, A JAW DROPPING PIECE DE RÉSISTANCE IN BAD TASTE, AND AN EMBARRASSING PUBIC HAIR IN THE SOUP OF FRENCH CULTURE.

"THIS MOVIE IS A KIND OF A COMEBACK TO THE THRILLER GENRE", PÉCAS TOLD INTERVIEWERS PIERRE CHARLES AND NORBERT MOUTIER FOR THEIR MARCH 1984 INTERVIEW IN CINÉ CHOC MAGAZINE. "BUT I HAD NEVER DONE SOMETHING AS VIOLENT AND TOUGH AS THIS ONE. IT CONTAINS EXTREME VIOLENCE AND I THINK IT'S A VERY REALISTIC MOVIE WHICH REFLECTS TODAY'S SOCIETY PRETTY WELL."

BEFORE THE OPENING CREDITS HAVE EVEN FINISHED, THE AUDIENCE HAS ALREADY HAD THE LIMP WANG OF A TRANSSEXUAL HOOKER AIMED AT THEM, BUT IT'S A SHOW THAT ENDS QUICKLY WHEN BIKERS START BLOWING EVERYBODY UP WITH SHOTGUNS. WITHOUT TRANSITION WE FIND OURSELVES IN A MORGUE WHERE BODIES ARE LAID OUT ON AUTOPSY TABLES, GUTS AND DICKS ALL OVER THE PLACE. ENTER INSPECTOR GERARD FROM THE VICE SQUAD, WHO COMES TO ENQUIRE ABOUT ONE OF THE VICTIMS WHO WAS HIS INFORMANT. AFTER A QUICK CHAT IT IS DECIDED THAT THE MASSACRE IS A RESULT OF A SETTLING OF ACCOUNTS. GERARD CONCLUDES BY SAYING "AND BESIDES THAT, WHAT'S UP GUYS?"

AND THAT'S JUST THE FIRST 5 MINUTES. THERE ARE NINETY MORE TO GO!

WRITTEN BY A FORMER CHIEF OF A POLICE DIVISION TURNED NOVELIST AFTER HIS RETIREMENT, ROGER LE TAILLANTER, AND REAL LIFE COP MARC PÉCAS (SON OF YOU-KNOW-WHO), THE SCRIPT OF BRIGADE OF DEATH DEALS WITH A SMUGGLER NICKNAMED "THE GREEK" WHO IS AT THE HEAD OF A PROSTITUTION RING. WHEN HIS WIFE SPLATTERS THE PAVEMENT AFTER JUMPING TO HER DEATH FROM A WINDOW IN AN ATTEMPT TO ESCAPE INTERROGATION FROM THE JUDGE IN CHARGE OF THE CASE, THE GREEK RETALIATES BY ORDERING THE DEATH OF THE MAGISTRATE'S WIFE, GERARD'S LITTLE SISTER. FROM NOW ON, GERARD TRACKS DOWN EVERY PERSON INVOLVED IN THIS ASSASSINATION IN ORDER TO TEACH THEM HIS OWN BRAND OF VIOLENT JUSTICE.

BRIGADE OF DEATH WAS NOT THE ONLY ONE OF ITS KIND IN FRENCH CINEMA. AS IN AMERICAN MOVIES IN THE MID '80S, HARDBOILED COPS WERE ALL OVER THE SCREEN, AND HUGE STARS LIKE ALAIN DELON AND JEAN-PAUL BELMONDO USED EXPEDITIOUS METHODS TO ENFORCE THEIR OWN LAWS TO THE GREAT PLEASURE OF THE AUDIENCE. BUT WHAT MAKES BRIGADE OF DEATH DIFFERENT FROM THE OTHER COP VIGILANTE MOVIES IS ITS CHOICE TO PUT AN EMPHASIS ON PARTICULARLY NASTY VIOLENCE. SOMEWHERE BETWEEN LUCIO FULCI'S CONTRABAND AND NEW YORK RIPPER, THE FILM CONTAINS SUCH GRATUITOUS NUDITY AND EPIC GORE AND VIOLENCE MOMENTS, SUCH AS: A HAND GETTING CHOPPED OFF, A MACHETE CHOP RIGHT IN THE FACE, FLICK-KNIFE SLASHES, A PIERCED EYEBALL, THE VERY GRAPHIC PROMISE TO USE A BROKEN BOTTLE AS A SPECULUM, AND

IT AIN'T EASY BEING A WOMAN IN THE ULTRA VIOLENT **BRIGADE OF DEATH** (1985)

THE THREAT OF AN ACID BURN ON A PAIR OF NICE BREASTS.

THERE IS NO EASY WAY TO DIE IN THIS FILM, BUT PÉCAS DEFENDED HIMSELF ON THE SUBJECT OF VIOLENCE IN HIS MOVIE IN THE CINÉ CHOC MAGAZINE INTERVIEW. "I DON'T AGREE WHEN PEOPLE SAY THAT VIOLENT CINEMA LEADS TO VIOLENCE," PÉCAS EXPLAINED. "IT'S NOT TRUE, AND WE ARE NOT GETTING OUR INSPIRATION FROM OUR IMAGINATION, BUT IN THE NEWSPAPERS, IN WHAT HAPPENS IN EVERYDAY LIFE."

"WE CAN ALSO, WITH A MOVIE LIKE BRIGADE OF DEATH, MAKE PEOPLE REALIZE THEIR DREAMS IN ANOTHER WAY, IN THE SENSE THAT THE EXTERMINATION OF VERMIN SATISFIES PEOPLE..... THESE ANIMALS, THOSE BEASTS YOU SEE IN THE MOVIE, SUCH AS THE PARANOID KILLER, HAVE NO BUSINESS LIVING ON THIS EARTH. ... FOR THE SEQUENCE WITH THE GRENADE AT THE END EVERYBODY APPLAUDS, EVERYBODY IS HAPPY TO SEE THE KILLER EXTERMINATED."

WITH NO STAR IN ITS CAST, BRIGADE OF DEATH MANAGES TO MAINTAIN ITS AURA OF DARK REALISM AND STANDS BY ITS STORY RATHER THAN RELYING ON AN ICONIC CHARACTER TO MAINTAIN THE AUDIENCE'S ATTENTION. NEVERTHELESS, THE ENLIGHTENED FAN WILL RECOGNIZE FORMER PORN STAR BRIGITTE LAHAIE AND JESS FRANCO'S REGULAR MURIEL MONTOSSÉ AKA VICKY ADAMS. POLITICALLY INCORRECT, IRREVERENT, AND MOSTLY FAR TOO SHOCKING AND CRUDE, BRIGADE OF DEATH WAS BRIEFLY X-RATED FOR VIOLENCE AND THUS BANNED, BEFORE BEING RATED 'R' AFTER SOME MINOR CUTS. IT HAS NEVER BEEN RELEASED IN AN ENGLISH LANGUAGE VERSION, AND AS OF THIS WRITING REMAINS UNKNOWN TO NORTH AMERICAN CULT FILM FANS.

SADLY, BRIGADE OF DEATH DID NOT DO VERY WELL AT THE BOX OFFICE AND THAT FAILURE PUT MAX PÉCAS BACK IN THE SANDBOX FOR TWO MORE COMEDIES BEFORE HE RETIRED FROM THE BUSINESS IN 1987. SINCE THE 1990S, THANKS TO CABLE TV AND THE INTERNET, PÉCAS HAS GRADUALLY BECAME A CULT FIGURE OF THE EUROPEAN EXPLOITATION MOVEMENT AND WITNESSED A REVIVAL OF HIS CAREER ORCHESTRATED BY A NEW GENERATION OF FILM FANS. WHEN HE DIED OF CANCER IN PARIS IN 2003, THERE WERE VERY FEW GOOD OBITUARIES. JOURNALISTS HARDLY SEEMED TO REMEMBER HIM AND WHEN THEY DID, THEY FOCUSED ON THE LATTER AND LESS INTERESTING PART OF HIS FILMOGRAPHY, REDUCING HIM TO AN INCOMPETENT CLOWN.

TRUE FANS, HOWEVER, CRIED AT THE LOSS OF A REAL ARTISAN, A GENEROUS AND UNPRETENTIOUS GUY WHO FOREVER BEQUEATHED TO THEM CHILLS, HARD-ONS AND LAUGHTER. MAY WE BE FOREVER GRATEFUL.

SANDRA JULLIEN
JANINE REYNAUD
YVES VINCENT

Je suis une NYMPHOMANE
IK BEN MANZIEK
FILM DE MAX PECAS

"I DON'T UNDERSTAND YOU, BUT I NEED YOU"   —BOUGIE '16

BOUG: MOVIE ZINE CREATOR
HA HA!   'ATS ME!

SUCH A POSEUR! WHAT AN EGO! NO ONE CARES! GET OVER YOURSELF

I JUST WANT TO SHARE MY LOVE OF MOVIES, YOU JUDGEMENTAL SUMBITCHES!!

WAAAIT! DON'T GO AWAY! I NEED SOMEONE TO READ THIS DUMB BULLSHIT!

CINEMA SEWER

'AINT THAT JUST THE WAY?

index

(Note: Entries in bold refer exclusively to illustrations.)

index

index

index

More FAB Press Cult Movie Books Written By Robin Bougie

CINEMA SEWER
The Adults Only Guide to History's
Sickest and Sexiest Movies!

ISBN: 978-1-903254-45-5
Pages: 192
UK Price: £14.99
US Price: $19.95

"What sets Cinema Sewer apart is that even
though the coverage is of the most insane,
repellent smut around, Robin's writing never
seems to pander... it's a refreshing approach."
Neon Madness magazine

CINEMA SEWER VOLUME 2
The Adults Only Guide to History's
Sickest and Sexiest Movies!

ISBN: 978-1-903254-56-1
Pages: 192
UK Price: £14.99
US Price: $19.95

"Prepare to veer wildly between curiosity,
arousal, disgust, laughter, embarrassment,
disbelief, confusion and uncontrollable glee.
Such is the power of Cinema Sewer."
The Nerve magazine

CINEMA SEWER VOLUME 3
The Adults Only Guide to History's
Sickest and Sexiest Movies!

ISBN: 978-1-903254-64-6
Pages: 192
UK Price: £14.99
US Price: $19.95

"Overwhelmingly positive in outlook. Intelligent,
relaxed and unpretentious, the book has a DIY
aesthetic that screams punk chic while the
text offers an unrelenting renegade attitude."
Sex Gore Mutants website

CINEMA SEWER VOLUME 4
The Adults Only Guide to History's
Sickest and Sexiest Movies!

ISBN: 978-1-903254-74-5
Pages: 192
UK Price: £14.99
US Price: $19.95

"Cinema Sewer is the direct heir and foremost
survivor of decades of mayhem-trash-film
fanzines, and Bougie has proven there's still
meatballs to be pulled out of the gravy."
www.quimbys.com

CINEMA SEWER VOLUME 5
The Adults Only Guide to History's
Sickest and Sexiest Movies!

ISBN: 978-1-903254-83-7
Pages: 192
UK Price: £14.99
US Price: $19.95

"Bougie and his contributors really know their
stuff, possessing a dizzying array of cinematic
knowledge, the likes of which should impress
even the most jaded and diehard film fan."
George Pacheco, Examiner.com

CINEMA SEWER VOLUME 7
The Adults Only Guide to History's
Sickest and Sexiest Movies!

ISBN: 978-1-913051-04-4
Pages: 192
UK Price: £14.99
US Price: $19.95

"I thought I had waded through the depth
of sleaze cinema, but Cinema Sewer
makes me realize I have only touched
the tip of the iceberg."
Kat Ellinger, thegoresplatteredcorner.com

For further information about these books and others in the acclaimed FAB Press line, visit our online store, where we also
have a fine selection of excellent cult movie magazines and other items of interest from all over the world!

www.fabpress.com